Communications
in Computer and Infor... 251

Azizah Abd Manaf   Akram Zeki
Mazdak Zamani   Suriayati Chuprat
Eyas El-Qawasmeh (Eds.)

Informatics Engineering and Information Science

International Conference, ICIEIS 2011
Kuala Lumpur, Malaysia, November 14-16, 2011
Proceedings, Part I

 Springer

Volume Editors

Azizah Abd Manaf
Advanced Informatics School (UTM AIS)
UTM International Campus
Kuala Lumpur, 54100, Malaysia
E-mail: azizah07@ic.utm.my

Akram Zeki
Kulliyah of Information and Communication Technology
International Islamic University
Kuala Lumpur, 54100, Malaysia
E-mail: akramzeki@yahoo.com

Mazdak Zamani
Advanced Informatics School (UTM AIS)
UTM International Campus
Kuala Lumpur, 54100, Malaysia
E-mail: mazdak@utm.my

Suriayati Chuprat
Advanced Informatics School (UTM AIS)
UTM International Campus
Kuala Lumpur, 54100, Malaysia
E-mail: suria@ic.utm.my

Eyas El-Qawasmeh
King Saud University, Information Systems Department
Riyadh, Saudi Arabia
E-mail: eyasa@usa.net

ISSN 1865-0929   e-ISSN 1865-0937
ISBN 978-3-642-25326-3   e-ISBN 978-3-642-25327-0
DOI 10.1007/978-3-642-25327-0
Springer Heidelberg Dordrecht London New York

Library of Congress Control Number: 2011941089

CR Subject Classification (1998): C.2, H.4, I.2, H.3, D.2, H.5

Typesetting: Camera-ready by author, data conversion by Scientific Publishing Services, Chennai, India

Printed on acid-free paper

Springer is part of Springer Science+Business Media (www.springer.com)

Message from the Chair

The International Conference on Informatics Engineering and Information Science (ICIEIS 2011)—co-sponsored by Springer—was organized and hosted by Universiti Teknologi Malaysia in Kuala Lumpur, Malaysia, during November 14–16, 2011 in association with the Society of Digital Information and Wireless Communications. ICIEIS 2011 was planned as a major event in the computer and information sciences and served as a forum for scientists and engineers to meet and present their latest research results, ideas, and papers in the diverse areas of digital information processing, digital communications, information security, information ethics, and data management, and other related topics.

This scientific conference comprised guest lectures and 210 research papers for presentation over many parallel sessions. This number was selected from more than 600 papers. For each presented paper, a minimum of two reviewers went through each paper and filled a reviewing form. The system involves assigning grades to each paper based on the reviewers' comments. The system that is used is open conference. It assigns grades for each paper that range from 6 to 1. After that, the Scientific Committee re-evaluates the paper and its reviewing and decides on either acceptance or rejection.

This meeting provided a great opportunity to exchange knowledge and experiences for all the participants who joined us from all over the world to discuss new ideas in the areas of data and information management and its applications. We are grateful to Universiti Teknologi Malaysia in Kuala Lumpur for hosting this conference. We use this occasion to express thanks to the Technical Committee and to all the external reviewers. We are grateful to Springer for co-sponsoring the event. Finally, we would like to thank all the participants and sponsors.

Azizah Abd Manaf

Preface

On behalf of the ICIEIS 2011 conference, the Program Committee and Universiti Teknologi Malaysia in Kuala Lumpur, I have the pleasure to present the proceedings of the International Conference on Informatics Engineering and Information Science' (ICIEIS 2011).

The ICIEIS 2011 conference explored new advances in digital information and data communications technologies. It brought together researchers from various areas of computer science, information sciences, and data communications to address both theoretical and applied aspects of digital communications and wireless technology. We hope that the discussions and exchange of ideas will contribute to advancements in the technology in the near future.

The conference received more than 600 papers of which 530 papers were considered for evaluation. The number of accepted papers 210. The accepted papers were authored by researchers from 39 countries covering many significant areas of digital information and data communications. Each paper was evaluated by a minimum of two reviewers.

Organization

General Chair

Azizah Abd Manaf   Universiti Teknologi Malaysia, Malaysia

Program Chair

Ezendu Ariwa   London Metropolitan University, UK
Mazdak Zamani   Universiti Teknologi Malaysia, Malaysia

Program Co-chairs

Yoshiro Imai   Kagawa University, Japan
Jacek Stando   Technical University of Lodz, Poland

Proceedings Chair

Jan Platos   VSB-Technical University of Ostrava,
  Czech Republic

Publicity Chair

Maitham Safar   Kuwait University, Kuwait
Zuqing Zhu   University of Science and Technology of China,
  China

International Program Committee

Abdullah Almansur   King Saud University, Saudi Arabia
Akram Zeki   International Islamic University Malaysia,
  Malaysia
Ali Dehghan Tanha   Asia Pacific University, Malaysia
Ali Sher   American University of Ras Al Khaimah, UAE
Altaf Mukati   Bahria University, Pakistan
Andre Leon S. Gradvohl   State University of Campinas, Brazil
Arash Habibi Lashkari   University Technology Malaysia (UTM),
  Malaysia
Asadollah Shahbahrami   Delft University of Technology,
  The Netherlands
Chantal Cherifi   Université de Corse, France
Craig Standing   Edith Cowan University, Australia

Radhamani Govindaraju   Damodaran College of Science, India
Ram Palanisamy   St. Francis Xavier University, Canada
Riaza Mohd Rias   University of Technology MARA, Malaysia
Salwani Mohd Daud   Universiti Teknologi Malaysia, Malaysia
Sami Alyazidi   King Saud University, Saudi Arabia
Shamsul Mohd Shahibudin   Universiti Teknologi Malaysia, Malaysia
Talib Mohammad   University of Botswana, Botswana
Valentina Dagiene   Institute of Mathematics and Informatics,
                             Lithuania
Viacheslav Wolfengagen   JurInfoR-MSU Institute, Russia
Waralak V. Sricharoen   University of the Thai Chamber of Commerce,
                             Thailand
Wojciech Mazurczyk   Warsaw University of Technology, Poland
Wojciech Zabierowski   Technical University of Lodz, Poland
Yi Pan   Georgia State University, USA
Zanifa Omary   Dublin Institute of Technology, Ireland
Zuqing Zhu   The University of Science and Technology
                             of China, China
Zuqing Zhu   University of Science and Technology of China,
                             China
Zurami Ismail   Universiti Teknologi Malaysia, Malaysia

Reviewers

Morteza Gholipour Geshnyani   University of Tehran, Iran
Asadollah Shahbahrami   University of Guilan, Iran
Mohd Faiz Hilmi   Universiti Sains Malaysia, Malaysia
Brij Gupta   Indian Institute of Technology, India
Naeem Shah   Xavor Corporation, Pakistan
Shanmugasundaram Hariharan B.S. Abdur Rahman University, India
Rajibul Islam   University Technology Malaysia, Malaysia
Luca Mazzola   Università della Svizzera Italiana, Italy
K.P. Yadav   Acme College of Engineering, India
Jesuk Ko   Gwangju University, Korea
Mohd Wahab   Universiti Tun Hussein Onn Malaysia, Malaysia
Luca Mazzola   Università della Svizzera Italiana, Italy
Anirban Kundu   West Bengal University of Technology, India
Hamouid Khaled   Batna University, Algeria
Muhammad Naveed   Iqra University, Pakistan
Yana Hassim   Universiti Tun Hussein Onn Malaysia, Malaysia
Reza Moradi Rad   University of Guilan, Iran
Rahman Attar   University of Guilan, Iran
Zulkefli Bin Mansor   Universiti Teknologi MARA, Malaysia
Mourad Amad   Bejaia University, Algeria
Reza Ebrahimi Atani   University of Guilan, Iran
Vishal Bharti   Dronacharya College of Engineering, India

Mohd Nazri Ismail	University of Kuala Lumpur, Malaysia
Nazanin Kazazi	University Technology Malaysia, Malaysia
Amir Danesh	University of Malaya, Malaysia
Tawfig Eltaif	Photronix Technologies, Malaysia
Ali Azim	COMSATS Institute of Information Technology, Pakistan
Iftikhar Ahmad	King Saud University, Saudi Arabia
Arash Lashkari	University Technology Malaysia, Malaysia
Zeeshan Qamar	COMSATS Institute of Information Technology, Pakistan
N. Mohankumar	Amrita Vishwa Vidyapeetham, India
Irfan Syamsuddin	State Polytechnic of Ujung Pandang, Indonesia
Yongyuth Permpoontanalarp	King Mongkut's University of Technology, Thailand
Jorge Coelho	Polytechnic Institute of Porto, Portugal
Zeeshan Qamar	COMSATS Institute of Information Technology, Pakistan
Aurobindo Ogra	University of Johannesburg, South Africa
Angkoon Phinyomark	Prince of Songkla University, Thailand
Subarmaniam Kannan	Multimedia University, Malaysia
Babak Bashari Rad	University Technology of MalaysiaMalaysia
Ng Hu	Multimedia University, Malaysia
Timothy Yap Tzen Vun	Multimedia University, Malaysia
Sophia Alim	University of Bradford, UK
Ali Hussein Maamar	Faculty of Electronic Technology, Libya
Tong Hau Lee	Multimedia University, Malaysia
Rachit Mohan	Jaypee University of Information Technology, India
Hamma Tadjine	IAV GmbH, Germany
Ahmad Nadali	Islamic Azad University, Iran
Kamaruazhar Bin Daud	Universiti Teknologi MARA, Malaysia
Mohd Dilshad Ansari	Jaypee University of Information Technology, India
Pramod Gaur	Wipro Technologies, India
Ashwani Kumar	Jaypee University of Information Technology, India
Velayutham Pavanasam	Adhiparasakthi Engineering College, India
Mazdak Zamani	Universiti Teknologi Malaysia, Malaysia
Azrina Kamaruddin	UiTM Shah Alam, Malaysia
Mazdak Zamani	Universiti Teknologi Malaysia, Malaysia
Rajendra Hegadi	Pragati College of Engineering and Management, India
Javad Rezazadeh	Universiti Teknologi Malaysia (UTM), Iran
A.K.M. Muzahidul Islam	Universiti Teknologi Malaysia, Malaysia
Asghar Shahrzad Khashandarag	Islamic Azad University, Iran

Thaweesak Yingthawornsuk	University of Technology Thonburi, Thailand
Chusak Thanawattano	Thailand
Ali AL-Mazari	AlFaisal University, Kingdom of Saudi Arabia
Amirtharajan Rengarajan	SASTRA University, India
Nur'Aini Abdul Rashid	Universiti Sains Malaysia, Malaysia
Mohammad Hossein Anisi	Universiti Teknologi Malaysia (UTM), Malaysia
Mohammad Nazir	University Technology of Malaysia, Malaysia
Desmond Lobo	Burapha University International College, Chonburi, Thailand
Salah Al-Mously	Koya University, Iraq
Gaurav Kumar	Chitkara University, India
Salah Eldin Abdelrahman	Menoufia University, Egypt
Vikram Mangla	Chitkara University, India
Deveshkumar Jinwala	S V National Institute of Technology, India
Nashwa El-Bendary	Arab Academy for Science, Technology & Maritime Transport, Egypt
Ashish Rastogi	Guru Ghasidas Central University, India
Vivek Kumar Singh	Banaras Hindu University, India
Sude Tavassoli	Islamic Azad University, Iran
Behnam Dezfouli	University Technology Malaysia (UTM), Malaysia
Marjan Radi	University Technology Malaysia (UTM), Malaysia
Chekra Ali Allani	Arab Open University, Kuwait
Jianfei Wu	North Dakota State University, USA
Ashish Sitaram	Guru Ghasidas University, India
Aissa Boudjella	Jalan Universiti Bandar Barat, Malaysia
Gouri Prakash	HSBC Bank, USA
Ka Ching Chan	La Trobe University, Australia
Azlan Mohd Zain	Universiti Teknologi Malaysia, Malaysia
Arshad Mansoor	SZABIST, Pakistan
Haw Su Cheng	Multimedia University (MMU), Malaysia
Deris Stiawan	Sriwijaya University, Indonesia
Akhilesh Dwivedi	Ambedkar Institute of Technology, India
Thiagarajan Balasubramanian	RVS College of Arts and Science, India
Simon Ewedafe	Universiti Tun Abdul Rahman, Malaysia
Roheet Bhatnagar	Sikkim Manipal Institute of Technology, India
Chekra Allani	The Arab Open University, Kuwait
Eduardo Ahumada-Tello	Universidad Autonoma de Baja California, Mexico
Jia Uddin	International Islamic University Chittagong, Bangladesh
Gulshan Shrivastava	Ambedkar Institute of Technology, India
Mohamad Forouzanfar	University of Ottawa, Canada

Kalum P. Udagepola	BBCG, Australia
Muhammad Javed	Dublin City University, Ireland
Partha Sarati Das	Dhaka University of Engineering, Bangladesh
Ainita Ban	Universiti Putra Malaysia, Malaysia
Noridayu Manshor	Universiti Putra Malaysia, Malaysia
Syed Muhammad Noman	Sir Syed University of Engineering and Technology, Pakistan
Zhefu Shi	University of Missouri, USA
Noraini Ibrahim	Universiti Teknologi Malaysia (UTM), Malaysia
Przemyslaw Pawluk	York University, Canada
Kumudha Raimond	Addis Ababa University, Ethiopia
Gurvan Le Guernic	KTH- Royal Institute of Technology, Sweden
Sarma A.D.N	Nagarjuna University, India
Utku Kose	Afyon Kocatepe University, Turkey
Kamal Srivastava	SRMCEM, India
Marzanah A. Jabar	Universiti Putra Malaysia, Malaysia
Eyas ElQawasmeh	King Saud University, Saudi Arabia
Adelina Tang	Sunway University, Malaysia
Samarjeet Borah	Sikkim Manipal Institute of Technology, India
Ayyoub Akbari	Universiti Putra Malaysia, Malaysia
Abbas Mehdizadeh	Universiti Putra Malaysia (UPM), Malaysia
Looi Qin En	Institute for Infocomm Research, Singapore
Krishna Prasad Miyapuram	Università degli Studi di Trento, Italy
M.Hemalatha	Karpagam University, India
Azizi Nabiha	Annaba University of Algeria, Algeria
Mallikarjun Hangarge	Science and Commerce College, India
J. Satheesh Kumar	Bharathiar University, India
Abbas Hanon AlAsadi	Basra University, Iraq
Maythem Abbas	Universiti Teknologi PETRONAS, Malaysia
Mohammad Reza Noruzi	Tarbiat Modarres University, Iran
Santoso Wibowo	CQ University Melbourne, Australia
Ramez Alkhatib	AlBaath University, Syrian Arab Republic
Ashraf Mohammed Iqbal	Dalhousie University, Canada
Hari Shanker Hota	GGV Central University, India
Tamer Beitelmal	Carleton University, Canada
Azlan Iqbal	Universiti Tenaga Nasional, Malaysia
Alias Balamurugan	Thiagarajar College of Engineering, India
Muhammad Sarfraz	Kuwait University, Kuwait
Vuong M. Ngo	HCMC University of Technology, Vietnam
Asad Malik	College of Electrical and Mechincal Engineering, Pakistan
Anju Sharma	Thapar University, India
Mohammad Ali Orumiehchiha	Macquarie University, Australia
Khalid Hussain	University Technology Malaysia, Malaysia

Parvinder Singh	Deenbandhu Chhotu Ram University of Science and Technology, India
Amir Hossein Azadnia	University Technology Malaysia (UTM), Malaysia
Zulkhar Nain	American University, United Arab Emirates
Shashirekha H.L.	Mangalore University, India
Dinesh Hanchate	Vidypratishthan's College Of Engineering, India
Mueen Uddin	Universiti Teknologi Malaysia (UTM), Malaysia
Muhammad Fahim	Kyung Hee University, Korea
Sharifah Mastura Syed Mohamad	Universiti Sains Malaysia, Malaysia
Baisa Gunjal	Amrutvahini College of Engineering, India
Ali Ahmad Alawneh	Philadelphia University, Jordan
Nabhan Hamadneh	Murdoch University, Australia
Vaitheeshwar Ramachandran	Tata Consultancy Services, India
Ahmad Shoara	Farabi Higher Education Institute, Iran
Murtaza Ali Khan	Royal University for Women, Bahrain
Norshidah Katiran	Universiti Teknologi Malaysia, Malaysia
Haniyeh Kazemitabar	Universiti Teknologi PETRONAS, Malaysia
Sharifah Mastura Syed Mohamad	Universiti Sains Malaysia, Malaysia
Somnuk Phon-Amnuaisuk	Universiti Tunku Abdul Rahman, Malaysia
Prasanalakshmi Balaji	Bharathiar University, India
Mueen Uddin	Universiti Teknologi Malaysia, Malaysia
Bhumika Patel	CKPithawalla College of Engineering and Technology, India
Sachin Thanekar	University of Pune, India
Nuzhat Shaikh	MES College of Engineering, India
Safiye Ghasemi	Islamic Azad University, Iran
Nor Laily Hashim	Universiti Utara Malaysia, Malaysia
Joao Pedro Costa	University of Coimbra, Portugal
S. Parthasarathy	Thiagarajar College of Engineering, India
Omar Kareem Jasim	Maaref College University, Iraq
Balasubramanian Thangavelu	SVM Arts and Science College, India
Lee Chai Har	Multimedia University (MMU), Malaysia
Md Asikur Rahman	Memorial University of Newfoundland, Canada
Renatus Michael	The Institute of Finance Management, Tanzania
Shin-ya Nishizaki	Tokyo Institute of Technology, Japan
Sahadeo Padhye	Motilal Nehru National Institute of Technology, India
Faith Shimba	The Institute of Finance Management, Tanzania
Subashini Selvarajan	Annamalai University, India

Valentina Emilia Balas	University of Arad, Romania
Muhammad Imran Khan	Universiti Teknologi PETRONAS, Malaysia
Daniel Koloseni	The Institute of Finance Management, Tanzania
Jacek Stando	Technical University of Lodz, Poland
Yang-Sae Moon	Kangwon National University, Korea
Mohammad Islam	University of Chittagong, Bangladesh
Joseph Ng	University Tunku Abdul Rahman, Malaysia
Umang Singh	ITS Group of Institutions, India
Sim-Hui Tee	Multimedia University, Malaysia
Ahmad Husni Mohd Shapri	Universiti Malaysia Perlis, Malaysia
Syaripah Ruzaini Syed Aris	Universiti Teknologi MARA, Malaysia
Ahmad Pahlavan	Islamic Azad University, Iran
Aaradhana Deshmukh	Pune University, India
Sanjay Singh	Manipal University, India
Subhashini Radhakrishnan	Sathyabama University, India
Binod Kumar	Lakshmi Narain College of Technology, India
Farah Jahan	University of Chittagong, Bangladesh
Masoumeh Bourjandi	Islamic Azad University, Iran
Rainer Schick	University of Siegen, Germany
Zaid Mujaiyid Putra Ahmad	Universiti Teknologi MARA, Malaysia
Abdul Syukor Mohamad Jaya	Universiti Teknikal Malaysia Melaka, Malaysia
Yasir Mahmood	NUST SEECS, Pakistan
Razulaimi Razali	Universiti Teknologi MARA, Malaysia
Anand Sharma	MITS, LAkshmangarh, India
Seung Ho Choi	Seoul National University of Science and Technology, Korea
Safoura Janosepah	Islamic Azad University, Iran
Rosiline Jeetha B	RVS College of Arts and Science, India
Mustafa Man	University Malaysia Terengganu, Malaysia
Intan Najua Kamal Nasir	Universiti Teknologi PETRONAS, Malaysia
Ali Tufail	Ajou University, Korea
Bowen Zhang	Beijing University of Posts and Telecommunications, China
Rekha Labade	Amrutvahini College of Engineering, India
Ariffin Abdul Mutalib	Universiti Utara Malaysia, Malaysia
Mohamed Saleem Haja Nazmudeen	Universiti Tunku Abdul Rahman, Malaysia
Norjihan Abdul Ghani	University of Malaya, Malaysia
Micheal Arockiaraj	Loyola College, India
A. Kannan	K.L.N.College of Engineering, India
Nursalasawati Rusli	Universiti Malaysia Perlis, Malaysia
Ali Dehghantanha	Asia-Pacific University, Malaysia
Kathiresan V.	RVS College of Arts and Science, India
Saeed Ahmed	CIIT,Islamabad, Pakistan
Muhammad Bilal	UET Peshawar, Pakistan

Ahmed Al-Haiqi	UKM, Malaysia
Dia AbuZeina	KFUPM, Saudi Arabia
Nikzad Manteghi	Islamic Azad University, Iran
Amin Kianpisheh	Universiti Sains Malaysia, Malaysia
Wattana Viriyasitavat	University of Oxford, UK
Sabeen Tahir	UTP Malaysia, Malaysia
Fauziah Redzuan	UiTM, Malaysia
Mazni Omar	UUM, Malaysia
Quazi Mahera Jabeen	Saitama University, Japan
A.V. Senthil Kumar	Hindusthan College of Arts and Science, India
Ruki Harwahyu	Universitas Indonesia, Indonesia
Sahel Alouneh	German Jordanian University, Jordan
Murad Taher	Hodieda University, Yemen
Yasaman Alioon	Sharif University of Technology, Iran
Muhammad Zaini Ahmad	Universiti Malaysia Perlis, Malaysia
Vasanthi Beulah	Queen Mary's College, India
Shanthi A.S.	Loyola College, Chennai, India
Siti Marwangi Mohamad Maharum	Universiti Teknologi Malaysia, Malaysia
Younes Elahi	UTM, Malaysia
Izzah Amani Tarmizi	Universiti Sains Malaysia, Malaysia
Yousef Farhang	Universiti Teknologi Malaysia, Malaysia
Mohammad M. Dehshibi	IACSIT, Iran
Ahmad Kueh Beng Hong	Universiti Teknologi Malaysia, Malaysia
Seyed Buhari	Universiti Brunei Darussalam, Brunei Darussalam
D. Christopher	RVS College of Arts and Science, India
NagaNandiniSujatha S	K.L.N. College of Engineering, India
Jasvir Singh	Guru Nanak Dev University, India
Omar Kareem	Alma'arif University College, Iraq
Faiz Asraf Saparudin	Universiti Teknologi Malaysia, Malaysia
Ilango M.R.	K.L.N. College of Engineering, India
Rajesh R.	Bharathiar University, India
Vijaykumar S.D.	RVS College of Arts and Science, India
Cyrus F. Nourani	AkdmkR&D, USA
Faiz Maazouzi	LabGED Laboratory, Algeria
Aimi Syamimi Ab Ghafar	Universiti Teknologi Malaysia, Malaysia
Md. Rezaul Karim	Kyung Hee University, Korea
Indrajit Das	VIT University, India
Muthukkaruppan Annamalai	Universiti Teknologi MARA, Malaysia
Prabhu S.	Loyola College, India
Sundara Rajan R.	Loyola College, India
Jacey-Lynn Minoi	Universiti Malaysia Sarawak, Malaysia
Nazrul Muhaimin Ahmad	Multimedia University, Malaysia
Anita Kanavalli	M.S. Ramaiah Institute of Technology, India
Tauseef Ali	University of Twente, The Netherlands

Hanumanthappa J.	University of Mangalore, India
Tomasz Kajdanowicz	Wroclaw University of Technology, Poland
Rehmat Ullah	University of Engineering and Technology, Peshawar, Pakistan
Nur Zuraifah Syazrah Othman	Universiti Teknologi Malaysia, Malaysia
Mourad Daoudi	University of Sciences and Technologies Houari Boumediene, Algeria
Mingyu Lee	Sugnkyunkwan University, Korea
Cyriac Grigorious	Loyola College, India
Sudeep Stephen	Loyola College, India
Amit K. Awasthi	Gautam Buddha University, India
Zaiton Abdul Mutalip	Universiti Teknikal Malaysia Melaka, Malaysia
Abdu Gumaei	King Saud University, Saudi Arabia
E. Martin	University of California, Berkeley, USA
Mareike Dornhöfer	University of Siegen, Germany
Arash Salehpour	University of Nabi Akram, Iran
Mojtaba Seyedzadegan	UPM, Malaysia
Raphael Jackson	Kentucky State University, USA
Abdul Mateen	Federal Urdu University of Science and Technology, Pakistan
Subhashini Ramakrishnan	Dr G.R. Damodaran College of Science, India
Randall Duran	Singapore Management University, Singapore
Yoshiro Imai	Kagawa University, Japan
Syaril Nizam	University Technology Malaysia, Malaysia
Pantea Keikhosrokiani	Universiti Sains Malaysia, Malaysia
Kok Chin Khor	Multimedia University, Malaysia
Salah Bindahman	Universiti Sains Malaysia, Malaysia
Sami Miniaoui	University of Dubai, United Arab Emirates
Intisar A.M. Al Sayed	Al Isra University, Jordan
Teddy Mantoro	International Islamic University Malaysia, Malaysia
Kitsiri Chochiang	PSU University, Thailand
Khadoudja Ghanem	University Mentouri Constantine, Algeria
Rozeha A. Rashid	Universiti Teknologi Malaysia, Malaysia
Redhwan Qasem Shaddad	Taiz University, Yemen
MuhammadAwais Khan	COMSATS Institute of Information and Technology, Pakistan
Noreen Kausar	Universiti Teknologi PETRONAS, Malaysia
Hala Jubara	UTM, Malaysia
Alsaidi Altaher	Universiti Sains Malaysia, Malaysia
Syed Abdul Rahman Al-Haddad	Universiti Putra Malaysia, Malaysia
Norma Alias	Universiti Teknologi Malaysia, Malaysia
Adib M. Monzer Habbal	University Utara Malaysia, Malaysia
Heri Kuswanto	Institut Teknologi Sepuluh Nopember, Indonesia

Table of Contents – Part I

E- Learning

Information Security

Software Engineering

Knowledge Mobilization for e-Living: Horizontal and Vertical Networks for Development

Ken Stevens

Faculty of Education
Memorial University of Newfoundland
St John's, NL,
Canada, A1B3X8
ken.stevens@vuw.ac.nz, stevensk@mun.ca

Abstract. The objective of this paper is to outline the development of knowledge mobilization in terms of inter-school and school to home collaboration to extend learning opportunities, particularly for students and their families who live in rural communities. The application of internet-based technologies has enabled networks to be established for the development of small schools located beyond major centres of population in ways that have expanded their learning capacities and, potentially, sustained the communities that host them. The creation of internet-based networks has, furthermore, enabled knowledge to be mobilized between schools and their communities, thereby promoting new e-living possibilities.

Keywords: Collaboration, cybercells, e-learning, intranet, rural, virtual.

1   Introduction

Many countries face the policy issue of providing learning opportunities for students who attend small schools in rural communities that are comparable to those expected by their urban peers. It is often difficult for governments to justify the expense of providing specialized teaching and other resources for small numbers of students in senior rural classrooms. Until the advent of the internet and its facilitation of virtual classes, senior students in rural communities were encouraged to enrol in boarding schools, most of which are located in urban areas. Another rural education policy in developed societies has been to transport senior students from small and isolated communities on a daily basis to larger centres to enable them to take advantage of more extensive curriculum options. The advent of the internet and its expanding role in the provision of education has enabled a new policy response that allows senior students in small rural schools to remain in their home communities while joining classes in schools in other places in both real (synchronous) and delayed (asynchronous) time. For parents and senior students in many rural communities in Canada and other societies there are now expectations that a full range of secondary school curriculum options will be provided in local schools [10].

A. Abd Manaf et al. (Eds.): ICIEIS 2011, Part I, CCIS 251, pp. 1–12, 2011.
© Springer-Verlag Berlin Heidelberg 2011

In the Canadian province of Newfoundland and Labrador most schools are located in small, geographically isolated, coastal communities. Many rural Newfoundland and Labrador communities are declining in size as people leave traditional occupations based on fishing to seek work in other parts of the country. Small schools are therefore becoming smaller and over the last two decades many have closed permanently. During this period of rural community school decline the Internet became available for educational use and in this part of Canada it has been the basis for the creation of new structures (intranets) and processes (e-learning). Internet-based structures and processes have provided ways of enhancing the provision of education in small rural communities by extending learning opportunities within and between them through the development of collaborative virtual classes [14].

Newfoundland and Labrador is Atlantic Canada's most eastern province. It has a population of approximately 500,000 people, of whom less than 28,000 live in Labrador. The province has a distinct culture, lifestyle and history and became part of Canada as recently as 1949. Beyond the capital city, St John's, the provincial population is located mostly in coastal settlements known as "outports" across a large geographic area (156,185 square miles) thereby presenting challenges for the delivery of education, particularly at senior high school level. Approximately two out of three schools in the province are located in rural communities and require special consideration in the development of collaborative, internet-based structures and processes.

2   Horizontal Networks: The Development of Digital Educational Structures and Processes

The search for appropriate new educational structures for the delivery of education to students in rural Newfoundland and Labrador led to the development of School District Intranets, within which virtual classes, based on e-learning, have been organized [5].

In the last decade there has been considerable re-organization of the school system in Newfoundland and Labrador, largely because of rural to urban migration together with a net outflow of people from the province. In 1996 ten Anglophone school district boards were created in the province together with one province-wide Francophone board, a reduction from 26 school boards. In this re-organization of school boards, the Vista School District was created. When it was established, the Vista School District contained 18 schools ranging in student enrolment from 650 down to 40 and covered a large area of about 7000 square kilometres. The region had a population of about 35,000 people and an economy supported by a diverse infrastructure including fishing, forestry, farming, mining, aquaculture and tourism. There were 5165 students enrolled in 18 schools in the district, taught by 366 teachers. The Vista School District was approximately two hours by road from the capital city, St Johns. With continued reduction in school size in many rural Newfoundland and Labrador communities, the provincial administration of schools was further reorganized in 2003 to create four Anglophone and one Francophone school boards.

Electronic collaboration between schools began almost two decades ago and the Canadian development outlined above was influenced by changes that were implemented in Iceland, [13, 20] Finland [8] and New Zealand [9]). The Icelandic Education Network was created in 1989 that linked all schools around this island nation, which, like Newfoundland, has an almost exclusively coastal population and one larger centre of population that is the capital city. Electronic collaboration between schools in Finnish Lapland and the capital, Helsinki, provided information on synchronous video instruction between diverse and distant sites [8] while audio-graphic collaboration between small schools in rural New Zealand, prior to the adoption of the internet, provided a model for implementation in Atlantic Canada [19].

The initial electronic linking of eight sites (or small rural schools) within a school district intranet in the Canadian province of Newfoundland and Labrador to support the teaching of selected Advanced Placement subjects created a series of classes that were administratively and academically open to each other. This was part of a broader pan-Canadian initiative over the last decade to prepare people in Canada for the information age [7]. By participating in open classes in real (synchronous) time, combined with a measure of independent (asynchronous) learning, senior students in some Newfoundland and Labrador schools were, a decade ago, able to interact with one another through audio, video and electronic whiteboards. More recently the internet has provided a vehicle for increased interaction in real time.

In eight schools within a rural school district of Newfoundland and Labrador, 55 students were enrolled in AP Biology, Chemistry, Mathematics and Physics courses. While AP courses are a well-established feature of senior secondary education in the United States and Canada, it was unusual for students to be able to enroll for instruction at this level in small schools in remote communities. The major change for the students in the first intranet in Newfoundland and Labrador however was the opportunity they were given to study advanced science subjects and mathematics as members of open classes from their small, remote communities. Without the electronic collaboration and organizational synergy of the initial intranet this educational opportunity would not have been available to them.

The intranet provided students with access to multiple sites simultaneously, as well as the opportunity to work independently of a teacher for part of the school day. The advent of the intranet had implications for students who began to interact with teachers and their peers in a variety of new ways. Many students experienced difficulty expressing themselves and, in particular, asking questions in open electronic classes when they did not know their peers from other small communities. As students became more comfortable with one another, inhibitions such as asking questions on-line were overcome. Today, interaction in intranets can be both synchronous and asynchronous [14].

The educational significance of the linking of schools in Iceland, Finland, New Zealand and the Canadian province of Newfoundland and Labrador was in the collaborative structures and processes that emerged. Schools that had been academically and administratively closed to one another were encouraged to become open collaborative learning environments. As classes in schools linked to teachers and learners in other classes, initially within schools districts, schools began to integrate academically and administratively [18,19]. Timetabling between sites became important, as did technological integration. More significantly however, was the advent of open virtual classes taking place in structures that were designed to provide face-to-face instruction in real time as closed, traditional classrooms. The advent of open, virtual classes led to collaborative teaching and collaborative learning. Students could have a teacher who was physically present as well as an online teacher who provided instruction from a distant site. Students were encouraged to share learning experiences and to collaborate in solving mathematical and scientific problems and later, to work together in other areas of the curriculum [14].

Advanced Placement (AP) courses are common throughout the United States and Canada. They enable senior students to begin undergraduate degrees with part of their program completed from high school if their AP courses are passed at grade levels specified by the university of their choice. Accordingly, advanced placement courses are demanding and only undertaken by academically-superior students.

At the time the first intranet was established in Newfoundland and Labrador, there were no AP subjects on line and, as far as could be ascertained, it was unlikely instruction was provided in other than large urban schools throughout the United States and Canada. The challenge was therefore two-fold: to put four science courses on line and to deliver them to dispersed rural students in the new electronic structure, the school district intranet. The development of AP web-based courses in Biology, Chemistry, Mathematics and Physics took place within a team in each subject area. A lead science teacher in each discipline was paired with a recent graduate in each of the disciplines of Biology, Chemistry, Mathematics and Physics who possessed advanced computer skills including web page design, Java and HTML. The lead teacher and the graduate assistant were advised from time to time by Faculty of Education specialists at Memorial University of Newfoundland in each curriculum area and, where possible, scientists from the Faculty of Science. The extent to which each web-based course was developed by a team of four people varied. Most course development took place through interaction between lead teachers and the recent graduates. Although at times professors had different opinions as to the most appropriate approach to the design of the courses, this model enabled the four courses to be developed over a sixteen-week summer recess period in time for the 1998 -1999 school year.

Minimum specifications were adopted for computer hardware and network connectivity. All schools involved in the project had DirecPC satellite dishes installed to provide a high- speed down-link. In most rural communities in this part of Canada, digital telecommunications infrastructures do not enable schools to have a high-speed up-link to the Internet. Appropriate software had to be identified and evaluated for both the development of the resources and the delivery of instruction within the Intranet. Front Page 98 was selected as the software package. Additional software was used for the development of images, animated gifs and other dimensions of course development. These included Snagit32, Gif Construction Set, Real Video, and similar packages. Many software packages were evaluated and finally WebCT was selected. This package enabled the instructor to track student progress, it contained online testing and evaluation, private E-mail, a calendar feature, public bulletin board for use by both instructor and student, a link to lessons and chat rooms for communication between teacher and student. For real - time instruction, Meeting Point and Microsoft NetMeeting were selected. This combination of software enabled a teacher to present real-time interactive instruction to multiple sites. An orientation session was provided for students in June 1998, prior to the implementation of this project in September. Students had to learn how to communicate with each other and with their instructor using these new technologies before classes could begin.

In the process of developing e-teaching and e-learning within intranets in rural Newfoundland and Labrador, teachers, learners and administrators had to adapt to a new, electronic educational structure. In the open teaching and learning environment of an intranet, participating institutions academically and administratively interface for that part of the school day during which classes are being taught. This is a different educational structure from the traditional and, by comparison, closed educational environment of the autonomous school with its own teachers and its own students. There is a potential conflict between a school as an autonomous educational institution serving a designated district and schools which become, in effect, sites within electronic teaching and learning networks. Principals and teachers appointed to the closed, autonomous learning environments of traditional schools frequently discovered that the administration of knowledge requires the development of open structures within which they were increasingly expected to collaborate with their peers located on a range of distant sites. Many now find that the positions to which they were appointed in traditional (closed) schools have become, in effect, locations within new (open) electronic schools in which a high degree of organizational synergy is necessary. After the inception of the first School District Intranet, a ministerial inquiry [6] into "distance learning in classrooms" was held involving extensive interviewing of students, teachers, administrators, technology providers and parents. The outcome of the ministerial inquiry was positive in that the Department of Education of Newfoundland and Labrador proceeded to develop a new entity known as the Centre for Distance Learning and Innovation (CDLI) that provides centralization in the provision of e-learning to all school districts in the province. The centre has the task of expanding the initial school district intranet model for rural schools in the province and also the range of subjects taught on line [1]. The Centre for Distance Learning and Innovation (http://www.cdli.ca/) has extended the provision of education in Newfoundland and Labrador. Most of the work of CDLI involves new program development to extend the curriculum in schools throughout the province. The centre also explores and assesses new technologies and evaluates their potential for teaching and learning in schools throughout Newfoundland and Labrador. The Centre for Distance Learning and Innovation is a federated structure that oversees and extends inter-school collaboration, particularly in rural Newfoundland and Labrador. Instruction can be provided directly from CDLI's e-teachers both synchronously and asynchronously. In small schools located in rural communities throughout the province, CDLI provides students with learning opportunities that would otherwise not be available to them. CDLI manages e-learning in communities throughout Newfoundland and Labrador thereby enhancing traditional on-site face to face teaching with virtual instruction. Perhaps the most significant contribution of the Centre for Distance Learning and Innovation has been the integration of traditional and virtual teaching and learning environments [21].

New teaching positions have been created by CDLI including e-teachers and, to assist them within the expanding range of sites (or rural schools that were becoming part of the digital network), mediating teachers, known as "m-teachers." Coffin [3] argued that in the expanding e-learning environment of Newfoundland and Labrador it was more appropriate to appoint m-teams than m-teachers. M-teams, he argued, could be established to replace m-teachers in rural schools in the province:

> "The report *Supporting Learning* [6] envisioned a teaching role to provide school-based support for students who were instructed by an off-site e-teacher…. A team concept is perhaps better suited to fulfilling CDLI's vision of small schools as 'beacons of technological innovation' with respect to distance learning. Conceptually, then, e-learning needs the support of a team of people providing four sets of skills: technical, coaching, administrative and resource advisor. … The idea of a team doesn't have to imply people getting together periodically to plan strategy or solve problems. The team represents more of a bank of resources easily accessible to on-line students which can be used to facilitate their learning."

An m-teaching scenario, outlined by Coffin [3] in a moderate-size rural high school with 100-250 students may have at least six teachers, a resource centre with at least a part-time resource teacher, some secretarial assistance, technical expertise (which may be located beyond the school in the local community) and a toll-free helpline for technical advice. Coffin argued that in a school "the technology teacher and coach would have some time in their schedules for discharging their responsibilities to on-line students. "

In small schools located in geographically remote communities e-students as well as their off-site e-teachers have to be supported to ensure the provision of education on a daily basis. The concept of an m-team includes many people within a small school as well as in the local community. Each person on the m-team according to the Coffin model would be responsible for specific support services. The technology teacher, the technician, the help-line desk and students would handle technical problems according to an agreed set of protocols. The coach would provide the nurturing, encouragement and advice that students need to persist in their studies. The technology teacher could also be the coach. The coach would also be the school-based contact for the e-teacher when that became necessary. These two professionals together would handle most of the pedagogical functions associated with on-line learning. Coaches were to be assigned to students, rather than courses because the services they provide were client-oriented rather than content-oriented. The school secretary would take responsibility for conveying hard-copy correspondence between the e-teacher and students and other clerical functions.

The resource teacher would provide services similar to those made available to students who were instructed face-to-face in traditional classes. The resource teacher would also catalogue, store and control the distribution of the learning resources for on-line courses. The administrator would provide the administrative support services that ensure the smooth and efficient operation of on-line learning (including supervision of instruction).

In the Coffin model the m-team may, in reality, be the whole staff of a small school, consisting of teachers, support staff, and administration. This approach to supporting e-learning in rural schools was subsequently adopted in Newfoundland and Labrador by the Centre for Distance Learning and Innovation and m-teams replaced m-teachers.

Today schools in each of the educational districts of Newfoundland and Labrador are digitally linked to a growing range of other schools. There has been considerable expansion of the number of subjects taught by e-teachers, supported by m-teams, to complement traditional on-site instruction. Networks of schools in each of the districts in the province are now part of a federated structure administered by the Centre for Distance Learning and Innovation within the Department of Education.

E-learning in Newfoundland and Labrador emerged through the development of reciprocal relationships between rural schools, information technologies and an acute awareness of a need for change if small schools in this part of Canada were to survive. The educational adoption of the Internet and, through it, e-learning, coincided with a period of declining enrolments in small schools and, indeed, the possibility of the end of local, on-site provision of education in rural communities. The adoption of the internet and e-learning enabled schools that were physically small in terms of the number of students who attend, in person, on a daily basis, to become large educational institutions in terms of the subjects that could be accessed and made available to students. New structures such as school district intranets and later, CDLI, initiated the possibilities of inter-institutional collaboration and the possibilities of schools being academically and administratively open rather than closed to one another. Co-operation, sharing and collaboration have become possible through the adoption of computers, the internet and membership of electronic learning organizations at both district and province-wide levels. Schools in rural Newfoundland and Labrador have changed because of demographic necessity, assisted by emerging educational technologies.

The development of virtual structures to support traditional small schools in rural communities has been accompanied by the creation of new teaching and learning processes. As schools have become increasingly open to one another within integrative frameworks, teaching and learning have become increasingly collaborative. E-teachers within CDLI supported by m-teams within schools are forging pedagogy within which actual (face to face) and virtual (online) teaching and learning are integrated. This model of educational provision in Newfoundland and Labrador differs from traditional distance education that is usually considered to be a separate, sometimes alternative, way of delivering education.

3   Vertical Integration: The Extension of e-Learning Networks from Schools to Communities

The horizontal linking of schools from rural Canadian and other communities has increased curriculum options, particularly for senior high school students and sustained these institutions by academically and administratively integrating them across dispersed sites. However, each rural school that has become, in effect, a site within a teaching and learning network, serves a local community. While senior rural students have been provided with increased learning opportunities through the horizontal integration of their classes with schools in other places, some members of their communities have not been as well served. Parents have seen their student sons and daughters provided with increased learning opportunities, particularly through the local and online provision of AP subjects, providing pathways for them from small and geographically-isolated communities to universities and employment in urban Canada. It is possible that the horizontal integration of rural schools contributes to the depopulation of small, isolated communities.

Many schools in rural Canada are now local beacons of advanced learning technologies that have the potential to serve their communities in other ways by reaching out not only horizontally to other schools, but to homes, businesses, adult groups and many aspects of local infrastructures. By reaching out to local homes, businesses and adult groups vertical integration becomes possible, thereby extending e-learning to e-living [15].

Two issues face rural schools when extending e-learning (that underpins horizontal integration) to vertical integration that promotes community e-living. First e-learning and the horizontal linking of small schools has to become more extensive so that rural adult learners and, in particular, those who seek a second chance to complete their schooling, are included. The second issue is the promotion by technologically enhanced rural schools of a Singapore model in their local communities. As a city-state, Singapore has grown rich by using its main resource, the talent and entrepreneurial drive of its citizens, to develop one of the highest standards of living in the world. Singaporeans, have applied their knowledge, skills and ingenuity to overcome problems of size and isolation including enhancing their education system with e-learning. The potential of technologically advanced small schools in rural communities for enabling and promoting local social, cultural and economic development has only recently been considered [15].

4   Cybercells and the Mobilization of Knowledge for e-Living

Acquisition of the skill of teaching within collaborative structures (intranets) is fundamental to the success of rural e-learning. Teachers have to learn to teach collaboratively with colleagues from multiple sites and have to judge when it is appropriate to teach on-line and when it is appropriate to teach students in traditional face-to-face ways. These judgements have to be defended on the basis of sound pedagogy [4,11]. It is becoming increasingly likely that new pedagogical issues will face rural e-teachers in the mobilization of knowledge within local communities.

A new pedagogical consideration has recently emerged in the integration of virtual and actual classes called cybercells [21] in which face to face groups extend their discussions to include virtual visitors. Cybercells have been made possible by the development of collaborative structures such as those outlined above. By linking groups in physical spaces, such as small rural schools, with emerging information technologies, cybercells enable virtual visitors to take part in discussions. Virtual visitors to small schools in rural communities could include parents, local businesses and service groups, some of which may have the potential to contribute to teaching and learning in local classrooms. The nature and the extent of community-based cybercells would, of course, be both determined by the school and managed by classroom teachers.

By extending existing physical (or actual) educational structures though the integration of virtual visitors, cybercells facilitate collaboration [16] and, thereby, the development of shared meaning [12]. Cybercells can be added to the range of activities and settings in regular classrooms to enable teachers and students to link with other individuals and groups at distant locations, to extend both teaching and learning. By joining a cybercell from a distance, physically isolated people such as those in rural communities, can become part of actual groups in real time, able to be seen and heard and, thereby, contribute to discussions. There are spatial, cultural, social, technological and pedagogical dimensions in the emergence of cybercells [14].

Spatially, cybercells make physical spaces larger by including within them, virtual visitors on demand. Virtual visitors could enter a rural classroom horizontally, through existing intranets, or vertically, from within local communities. For example, a classroom in a rural school in a geographically-isolated community consisting of a teacher and a small number of students (relative to large, urban institutions) supported by an m-team, can become a cybercell by linking with students or teachers who live beyond the community who become virtual visitors. Cybercells challenge small rural schools by extending their physical space to include non-physically present members (such as other students, specialist teachers and visiting experts). They further challenge these institutions by opening themselves digitally to knowledge and expertise at local community level. The significance of the location of teachers and the learners in relation to one another is reduced as virtual and actual teaching and learning spaces interact and merge in pursuit of common interests such as learning. It becomes difficult to define a school as "small" when, in teaching and learning terms they engage with people well beyond their actual (or physical) locations.

Culturally, cybercells can change classrooms and other physical spaces by facilitating new understandings between groups that are both actually and virtually present. Contact through the introduction of virtual visitors – both locally and from other places - to physical or actual spaces, in synchronous or asynchronous time, has the potential to alter perceptions groups have of one another and to make cultural differences and similarities real through interaction. The culture of a classroom has the potential to be changed through reality-sharing in a cybercell between those who have an actual presence and those who enter a physical space virtually. For example, the interaction of different ethnic or class cultures in a cybercell can challenge existing perceptions and facilitate new cultural awareness of both one's own and other cultures through interaction.

Socially, collaborative teaching and collaborative learning are facilitated by the linking of learning spaces. One of the possible outcomes of the advent of cybercells in teaching and learning is the breakdown of the concept of education as something that happens only in schools and in school time. The introduction of virtual visitors to small, geographically isolated classrooms who can talk about non-rural life in personal terms has potential to extend understanding of life in other places [17]. The introduction of selected virtual visitors from local communities to schools has the potential to expand existing intranets from horizontal relationships with people in other places, to vertical ones based on narratives with local people.

Cybercells make use of new learning technologies including the interactive nature of Web 2.0 within environments that extend well beyond the physical confines of classrooms. New technologies that support the integration of actual and virtual spaces enabling networking between teachers and students to occur include blogs (internet based journals), podcasts (home-made or organization made sound recordings available through the internet), forums (written asynchronous discussions) and wikis (web pages developed collaboratively). In the web 2.0 environment edubloggers (an international group of self-selected educationalists who use web 2.0 tools) can engage with one another.   Students and teachers can read what others have written, listen to podcasts of discussions, make their own blogs or wikis and join in live chats or webcasts [14].

An important pedagogical dimension of cybercells is their facilitation of collaboration between both teachers and students as well as between schools. Cybercells enable teachers, students and schools to engage virtual visitors in actual learning spaces using contemporary digital technologies at both distant and local levels. As students network, connect and interact through the use of web 2.0 technologies, their experiences may mediate their transition into the future world of learning beyond school.

5   Conclusion

Cybercells have the potential to expand traditional classrooms in terms of time, space and, above all, in terms of teaching and learning capacities. The integration of actual and virtual spaces in classrooms challenges traditional teaching and learning practices and provides opportunities for lessons to be both extended and enriched. Inter-class and inter-school integration of teaching and learning through cybercells has the potential to create new synergies [22] based on teamwork [2]. By integrating actual and virtual spaces horizontally and vertically, cybercells provide teachers with opportunities to fuse spatial, social and cultural dimensions of classrooms to promote collaboration and mutual construction of knowledge and understanding between learners on dispersed sites.

In rural Newfoundland and Labrador the open, collaborative model of teaching and learning within intranets has challenged the closed model of schooling. School district intranets provide horizontal integration between participating sites and new academic pathways for rural students as they access an expanding range of subjects of online, taught by e-teachers. A question now faces rural teachers and principals: can the successful horizontal integration of schools across rural Canada be complemented by vertical integration whereby community schools bring increased learning opportunities to local homes and businesses? When the horizontal integration of learning is accompanied by vertical integration, local and non-local learning will complement one another and provide a new synergy. Rural homes will be invited to become part of enriched learning environments, joining local schools that are already academically and administratively part of federated, electronic educational structures.

The educational, technological, pedagogical and policy problems that had to be overcome in the development of e-learning in small communities in rural Newfoundland and Labrador led to the development of collaborative structures within which virtual classes could be supported. It is possible that initiatives undertaken in this part of Canada, in which traditional schools have accepted virtual classes, could have application for rural schools in other parts of the world and, possibly, for the provision of education in urban areas.

References

1. Barbour, M.K.: Delivering Distance Education: The Ministerial Panel Report and the New Centre for Distance Learning and Innovation. Small Schools Newsletter, St. John's, Newfoundland, Faculty of Education, Memorial University of Newfoundland (2001)
2. Campbell, A., Guisinger, M.-L.: Redefining Teamwork: Collaboration Within Virtual Walls. The Online Educator 10(6) (2003),
    http://www.infotoday.com/MMSchools/nov03/
    campbell_guisinger.shtml
3. Coffin, G.: Mediating E-learning: M-teacher or M-team? Centre for Distance Learning and Innovation, Department of Education of Newfoundland and Labrador, St John's, Newfoundland (2002)
4. Dorniden, A.: K-12 Schools and Online Learning. In: Howard, C., Boettcher, J.V., Justice, L., Schenk, K., Rogers, P.L., Berg, G.A. (eds.) Encyclopedia of Distance Learning, pp. 1182–1188. Idea Group Reference, Hershey (2005)
5. Galway, G.: E-Learning as a means of promoting educational equity in rural and remote communities: A Canadian case study. Paper Presented at the 2003 OECD Workshop: Promoting Equity Through ICT in Education, Budapest, pp. 70–77 (2004)
6. Government of Newfoundland and Labrador: Supporting Learning: Report on the Ministerial Panel on Educational Delivery in the Classroom, St John's, NL, Department of Education (2000)
7. Information Highway Advisory Council: Preparing Canada for a Digital World, Ottawa, Industry Canada (1997)
8. Kynaslahti, H., Salminen, J., Stevens, K.J.: Alustavia Tuloksia Koulujen Verkottumisesta Suomessa Ja Uudessa Seelannissa (Some Preliminary Outcomes From Networked Classes in Finland and New Zealand). Julkaistavaksi Suomen Kasvatustieteelliessa Aikakauskirjassa 'Kasvatuksessa' Kasvatus - The Finnish Journal of Education 27(2), 196–205 (1996)
9. Lai, K-W.: e-Learning Communities: Teaching and Learning With the Web. University of Otago Press, Dunedin (2005)
10. Mathiasen, H.: Expectations of Technology: When the Intensive Application of IT in Teaching Becomes a Possibility. Journal of Research on Technology in Education 36(3), 273–294 (2004)
11. Pendergast, D., Kapitzke, C.: Virtual Vignettes and Pedagogical Potentials: Insights into a Virtual Schooling Service. In: Cavanaugh, C. (ed.) Development and Management of Virtual Schools: Issues and Trends, pp. 192–215. Information Science Publishing, Hershey (2004)

12. Scardamalia, M., Bereiter, C.: Knowledge-building: Theory, Pedagogy and Technology. In: Sawyer, R.K. (ed.) The Cambridge Handbook of the Learning Sciences. Cambridge University Press, New York (2006)
13. Stefansdottir, L.: The Icelandic Educational Network – Ismennt. In: Davies, G., Samways, B. (eds.) Teleteaching – Proceedings of the IFIP TC3 Third Teleteaching Conference, pp. 829–835. Elsevier Science Publishers, Amsterdam (1993)
14. Stevens, K.J.: The Development of Collaborative Structures to Support Virtual Classes in Small Schools. In: Salmons, J., Wilson, L. (eds.) Handbook of Research on Electronic Collaboration and Organizational Synergy, pp. 43–53. IGI Global, Hershey (2008)
15. Stevens, K.J.: From e-Learning to e-Living. Newfoundland Quarterly 100(4), 31–33 (2008)
16. Stevens, K.J.: Cybercells and the Development of Collaborative Teaching in Actual and Virtual Classes. In: Vasiu, R., Kimari, R., Andone, D. (eds.) The Future of E: Advanced Educational Technologies for a Future e-Europe, pp. 222–225. Editura Orizonturi Universitare, Timisoara (2006)
17. Stevens, K.J.: The Integration of Virtual and Actual Classes in Sparsely Populated Regions. In: Kinshuk, Sampson, D.G., Isaias, P. (eds.) Cognition and Exploratory Learning in the Digital Age, pp. 517–520. IADIS Press, Lisbon (2005)
18. Stevens, K.J.: Open Learning to Sustain Rural Schools: The Replication of a Three-Stage Model. New Zealand Annual Review of Education - Te Arotake a Tau o te ao o te Matauranga i Aotearoa (12), 173–186 (2003)
19. Stevens, K.J.: E-Learning and the Development of Open Classes for Rural Students in Atlantic Canada. In: Bradley, J. (ed.) The Open Classroom – Distance Learning In and Out of Schools, pp. 149–157. Kogan Page, London (2003)
20. Stevens, K.J.: Minnkandi heimur -Rafrænt net smárra skóla- Óvænt tengsl Íslenska menntanetsins við Nýja Sjáland og Kanada (Making the World Smaller -The Electronic Networking of Small Schools - Some Unseen Connections of the Icelandic Educational Network in New Zealand and Canada). Skólavarðan - Málgagn Kennarasambands Íslands 2(2), 22–24 (2002); (Introduction and translation into Icelandic by Karl Erlendsson)
21. Stevens, K.J., Stewart, D.: Cybercells – Learning in Actual and Virtual Groups. Thomson-Dunmore, Melbourne (2005)
22. Thompson, J., Bakken, L., Clark, F.L.: Creating Synergy: Collaborative Research Within a Professional Development School Partnership. The Teacher Educator 37(1), 49–57 (2001)

Towards Using Social Networks and Internet-Enabled Mobile Devices for Learning: Students' Preparedness

Daniel Koloseni[1] and Zanifa Omary[2]

[1] Department of Information Technology
Faculty of Computing, Information System and Mathematics
The Institute of Finance Management
Shabaan Robert Street, Dar es Salaam, Tanzania
koloseni@ifm.ac.tz
[2] School of Computing
Dublin Institute of Technology
Kevin Street, Dublin 8, Dublin, Ireland
Zanifa.Omary@dit.ie

Abstract. In this paper we investigate students' preparedness towards using Social Networks and Internet-enabled mobile devices for learning and propose requirements that need to be met before higher learning institutions can embrace these two technologies for learning. To achieve this we conducted a survey in higher learning institutions in Tanzania. We looked at students' possession of Internet-enabled mobile devices, affordability of the Internet, level of competency and experience in operating mobile devices and using Social Networks. We also assessed time that students spend on social networking sites. In conclusion, the survey reveals that students in higher learning institutions are almost ready in terms of infrastructure, experience, and competence needed for operating mobile devices for learning, hence making these tools appropriate to be used as supplementary pedagogical tools for learning.

Keywords: Learning, Social Networks, Mobile Devices, Internet-enabled, Student preparedness.

1 Introduction

The inception of Web 2.0 and advancement in mobile technology capabilities has revolutionized the way information is generated and disseminated. Additionally, the ability to send and retrieve information anywhere, anytime has changed the way we work and live[1]. These capabilities are the key drivers for growth of social networking sites around the globe attracting millions of users across all age groups and professions. Accessibility of information and data over the Internet-enabled mobile devices has encouraged many people, mostly the young, to join social networking sites hence making these sites to be among the largest community of people sharing information almost in real time [2].

A. Abd Manaf et al. (Eds.): ICIEIS 2011, Part I, CCIS 251, pp. 13–21, 2011.
© Springer-Verlag Berlin Heidelberg 2011

With increased utilization of mobile devices, improved Information and Communication Technologies (ICTs) infrastructure and decrease in Internet access costs, higher learning Institutions in Tanzania are in the right position to harness the power of social networking sites and mobile devices for learning and education delivery. This will help to define and transform new literacies in teaching and learning which will eventually offer students extra ICT skills and at the same time serving as a means for improving learning and education delivery [3].

Additionally, many institutions have realized that the learning environment extends beyond classroom settings and are thus exploiting a variety of technological options[4]. It is, therefore, the intention of this paper to gauge the readiness of students and examine the possibilities of using Social Networks and Internet-enabled mobile devices as a supplementary pedagogical tool for learning.

The rest of this paper is organized as follows. Section 2 provides definitions of key concepts and technologies that have been used throughout this paper. Section 3 discusses various applications of mobile devices for learning while section 4 provides a review on applications of Social Networks for learning. Research approach and results of the survey conducted are presented in section 5 and 6 respectively. Discussion of the findings is presented in section 7 and conclusion in section 8.

2   Definitions of Terms

In this section we provide definitions of key concepts and terminologies that have been used throughout this paper.

Social Networks (SN): Boyd and Ellison define Social Network as a web-based service that allows individuals to 1. Construct a public or semi-public profile within a bounded system 2. Articulate a list of other users with whom they share a connection, and 3. View and traverse their list of connections and those made by others within the system [5]. There are various Social Networking Sites (SNSs) available to date including Facebook, MySpace and Bebo. Since their introduction, these sites have attracted millions of users.

Mobile Devices: These are pocket-sized computing devices that consist of a screen, for displaying outputs, touch input and miniature keyboard. These devices range from cell phones, Smart phones, Personal Digital Assistants (PDAs) to Wireless-enabled portable media [6].

Learning: In literature there is no single-agreed definition of the term learning since it means different things to different people [7]. Oxford English Dictionary defines the term "as the process which leads to the modification of behaviour or the acquisition of new abilities or responses, and which is additional to natural development by growth or maturation"[8].

3   Applications of Mobile Devices for Learning

The ubiquitous nature of mobile devices and in-built capability of Social Networks to allow people to publish contents as opposed to Websites make these two the perfect tools for interactive learning. Due to massive use of Social Networks and Internet-enabled mobile devices, it is incumbent to think of integrating these tools as an alternative for education and learning.

The use of mobile phones for learning is not a new phenomenon. In 2000, Colella studied the use of PDA to stimulate the spread of computer virus [9]. In 2003 Riordan and Traxler investigated on supporting computing and Information Technology (IT) students identified as to be at risk due to poor literacy skills through Short Message Service (SMS)[10]. Furthermore, Attewell and Savill-Smith investigated on the application of mobile technologies for learning for young adults who are not in full-time education environment[11].Thorn and Houser, in 2005, researched on the use of mobile PDAs for English language learning in Japanese Universities [12]. And Levy and Kennedy reported on the use of mobile SMS for learning Italian[13].

Generally speaking, throughout these studies, the application of mobile devices has proved successful in motivating learning, improving interactivity and self-learning practice. Vogel et al state that, mobile devices such as PDAs and smart phones are increasingly pervasive, especially in students' populations making it easier to adapt them for learning in formal education[4].

Learning through mobile devices is made possible through numerous inbuilt capabilities. These capabilities include ability to host social software such as forums, blogs, Wikis, Moodle, RSS, Instant Messaging (IM), chats and podcasts. These capabilities when appropriately used can help create a virtual classroom that enables students to interact without appearing in a physical classroom.

Despite all the benefits offered by mobile devices in learning, these devices have some limitations that may affect learning and education delivery[13], [14]. Some of the issues include the presence of small screens that may cause some difficulties in learning, low image resolutions, input limitations, and memory as well as storage capacity.

4   Applications of Social Networks for Learning

Application of social networks as a pedagogical tool for learning is powered by its ability to allow sharing of information through user profiles, connecting to other users who are termed as contacts or friends, uploads, tagging, link other users to web-accessible contents and joining subsets of user groups based on common interests [14].

Social Networks Sites (SNS) provide teachers/ lecturers with new opportunities to reach students and improve their learning[15]. In order to take full advantage of Social Networks, educators in several universities and higher learning institutions in developing countries have already started harnessing the power of Social Networks as a new learning platform [16],[17].

In distance learning, for example, the presence of Social Networks is an important ingredient influencing education delivery[18]. Distance learning practitioners believe that interaction is a necessary component for a successfully learning experience. In this case, interactivity offered by Social Networks will definitely serve this purpose in fully. Throughout the transformational stage, subject lecturers are the key players in taking students from traditional classroom settings into virtual classroom by opening course groups, encouraging students to participate in electronic forums etc.

The application of Social Networks for learning is witnessed in works of Lockyer and Patterson who conducted an investigation on integrating social networking technologies in education delivery [14]. McLaughlin and Lee investigated the affordability of Web 2.0 and social software and the choices and constraints they offer to tertiary teachers and learners[19]. Bryant on the other hand ,discussed his experience in utilization of social software tools in supporting student collaboration at Dickinson college[16].

5   Research Approach

As previously discussed, this paper intends to provide the result of the survey conducted in higher learning institution in Tanzania to identify student's preparedness in using Internet-enabled mobile devices and social networks for learning.

Table 1. Subsets of population from where proportionate sample was drawn

Programme	Number of Students	Selected Students
Bachelors		
Accountancy	1275	47
Banking	1043	37
Computer Science	524	19
Information Technology	718	27
Insurance and Risk Management	523	19
Social Protection	276	10
Tax Administration	453	17
Postgraduate Diploma		
Accountancy	28	1
Insurance	48	2
Tax	55	2
Financial Management	150	6
Business Administration	91	3
Human Resource	30	1
Masters		
MSc. (IT and Management)	87	3
MBA (International Business)	100	4
Total	5401	198

The sampling frame used in the study was a list of currently full-time and part-time registered students of the Institute of Finance Management (IFM) studying different courses. A sample comprising 198 students was randomly selected using stratified sampling technique out of 5401 students. Sampling was necessary in order to establish a representative sample appropriate to the number drawn from homogenous subsets of student's population. Table 1 shows the subsets of population from where proportionate sample was drawn.

The questionnaires, for the study, were administered through a web link posted on a social networking site that is, Facebook while other questionnaires were hand-delivered to students in classes by subject lecturers. The total number of questionnaires completed and collected was 151 representing an effective respond rate of 76.2%.

6   Results

For the demographics of respondents, 48.3% of the respondents were between ages of 18-24 years and 51.7% were between ages of 25- 49 years of whom 44.6% were female and 53.4% were males. Education level of respondents ranged from certificate level to Masters Degree level covering seven areas of specializations, which are Information Technology, Computer Science, Accounting, Banking, Insurance and Risk Management, Human Resources and Tax Management. In this study it is assumed that students are computer literate as most of their studies depend on the use of computers and the Internet.

The study found that, 94.0% of respondents' own mobile phones with Internet capability, 58.0% own laptops, and 15.3% own Smart Phones while 1.3% own iPad PDAs. Possession of more than one mobile device with Internet capability increases the options for students during learning process. Ownership of these devices is one of the key steps in assessing student's readiness in using social networks for learning. Further, the study found that 86.4% of respondents surveyed have access to Internet at home using wireless modems or subscription from mobile telecommunication companies. With these figures in place then, higher learning institutions with wireless points will give students an affordable and convenient learning environment using the devices which they own.

Furthermore, 97.3% of respondents are able to operate mobile phones without difficult. Again, mastery in using mobile phones is key aspect in harnessing these devices for learning.

Experience in using computers and mobile phones is also crucial in assessing student's readiness in using social networks and Internet enabled devices for learning. Therefore, in order to assess this, students were asked to rate their experience in using computers and mobile Internet devices. As indicated in figure 1, the study found that, 64.2 % have been using mobile phones for more than 5 years, 24.5% between 3 to 5 years, 7.3% between 2 to 3 years, 3.3% for 1 year and 0.7% less than 1 year.

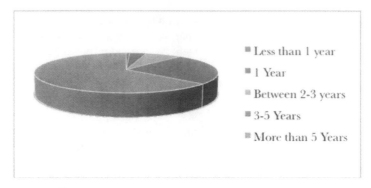

Fig. 1. Students experience in using Mobile Phones

As for experience in using computers, 41.7% have been using computers for more than 5 years, 21.9% between 3 to 5 years, 21.9% between 2 to 3 years, 8.6% for 1 year and 6% for less than 1 year. The comparison between usage of mobile phone and laptops indicates that students are more experienced in using the former due to high cost of the laptops in developing countries.

When the respondents were asked if they belong to any social networks, the study found that, 61.5% are members of social networks with 56.1% of respondents are members of more than one social network and the remaining 38.5% are not the members of social networks. It was further found out that, 76% of respondents who are members of social networks are regular users who access social networks 2 to 4 times a day while 54.4% of respondents spend less than 1 hour on social networks. 35% of respondents spend 2 to 4 hours and 10.7% of respondents use 5 hours a day.

Lastly, the survey found that, only 15.2% of respondents who are members in social networks have joined an education group in social networks and only 12.8% of respondents who owns smart phones have education program installed in their devices. We believe this is probably due to fact that most of education programs for smart phones are being sold and it requires a person to posses a credit card which most of the students, in developing countries, do not have. Regarding membership on social networks, this is due to the fact that most of students are using social networks for chatting and exchanging non-education information with their peers as pointed out by [20] and [21].

7   Discussion

The chance of using Social Networks and Internet-enabled mobile devices for learning in Higher learning Institutions in Tanzania in the future is promising. The study findings indicate that majority of the students in higher learning institutions own Internet-enabled hand held mobile devices. Most of these devices are capable of recording voice and video, sending and receiving files through Bluetooth or infrared and other capabilities that can be used to facilitate learning to students. This finding is closely related to a study conducted by Cochrane and Bateman in New Zealand[22].

Currently, the primary use of these devices is for calling friends and relatives. With 94% and 58% of respondents owning mobile phones and laptops respectively it is encouraging situation that these devices can be utilized in higher learning Institutions as a supplementary pedagogical tool for learning.

This approach is considered cost saving since the costs of acquisition of the tools (in this case handheld devices) have already been covered by students themselves. Since experience in operating Internet hand held devices is not a problem to students with 97.4% citing that they are able to operate mobile phones without difficulty and 64.2% have been using mobile phone for more than 5 years and 41.7% have more than 5 years experience in using computers the task to use these devices for learning is quite simplified. The only thing that is needed is to change the behavior of students from traditional use of these devices to include a new arena for learning.

The overall motivation for students to join education groups is low as only 15.2% of respondents are the members. This is due to the fact that Social Networks are primarily used for social interaction. If we have to use Social Networks for learning, higher learning institutions need to motivate students to create and join educational groups first. This can be done by subject lecturer to create education groups and invite students to join. These education groups will be acting as an arena for sharing views, information and spot for accessing lecture notes and other materials related to education.

Regarding low availability of education programs, we believe this is probably due to fact that most of education programs for smart phones are being sold and it requires a person to posses a credit card which most of the students, in developing countries especially Tanzania, do not have. Using free and open source technology to develop education programs will significantly reduce this problem as most of free and open source program will be accessed free of charge.

8   Conclusion

The primary objective of this study was to assess the readiness of students from higher learning institutions in Tanzania towards using Social Networks and Internet-enabled mobile devices towards learning. In particular we have analysed the possession of Internet-enabled mobile devices, affordability of the Internet, level of competency and the overall experience in operating devices. We have also assessed students' experience in using social networks, and time spent on social networks.

Based on the results from the survey we conclude that, students in higher learning institutions are almost ready in terms of infrastructure needed for learning such as Internet hand-held devices, willingness to join Social Networks, experience and ability to operate mobile devices without difficulty to use Social Networks for learning. However, in order to make this a success, higher learning institutions need to deploy reliable wireless networks to enable students to access Internet all the time, work in collaboration with government, non-governmental organizations, other stakeholders and software industry to develop tailor-made social software and education programs to facilitate learning using Social Networks and Internet-enabled mobile devices respectively. It should be noted that using private Social Networks for a formal learning is not a good idea since the owner of the Social Network is not accountable to higher learning Institution[23]. Instead higher learning institutions should develop their own social networks for learning using open source social software[16]. Lastly, higher learning institutions should lay down policies and regulations to ensure proper usage of Social Networks and Internet-enabled mobile devices for learning.

References

1. O'Murchu, I., Breslin, J.G., Decker, S.: Online social and business networking communities, p. 7 (2004)
2. Milrad, M., Spikol, D.: Anytime, anywhere learning supported by smart phones: experiences and results from the MUSIS Project. Subscription Prices and Ordering Information, 62 (2007)
3. Lankshear, C., Knobel, M.: New literacies: Everyday practices and classroom learning. Open Univ. Pr. (2006)
4. Vogel, D., Kennedy, D.M., Kuan, K., Kwok, R., Lai, J.: Do mobile device applications affect learning? In: Editor (Ed.)^(Eds.) Book Do mobile device applications affect learning?, p. 4. IEEE (2007)
5. Boyd, D.M., Ellison, N.B.: Social network sites: Definition, history, and scholarship. Journal of Computer Mediated Communication 13(1), 210–230 (2008)
6. Cochrane, T.: Learning with wireless mobile devices and social software. In: Who's Learning? Whose Technology? Proceedings Ascilite Sydney 2006 (2006)
7. Simonson, L.A.S.a.M.R.: Distance Education: Definition and Glossary of Terms. IAP (2006)
8. In: Editor (Ed.)^(Eds.) Book. Oxford University Press (2001)
9. Colella, V.: Participatory simulations: Building collaborative understanding through immersive dynamic modeling. Journal of the Learning Sciences, 471–500 (2000)
10. Riordan, B., Traxler, J.: Supporting computing students at risk using blended technologies. In: Editor (Ed.)^(Eds.) Book Supporting Computing Students at Risk Using Blended Technologies, pp. 26–28 (2003)
11. Attewell, J., Savill-Smith, C.: Mobile learning and social inclusion: focusing on learners and learning. Learning with Mobiledevices, 3 (2004)
12. Thornton, P., Houser, C.: Using mobile phones in English education in Japan. Journal of Computer Assisted Learning 21(3), 217–228 (2005)
13. Levy, M., Kennedy, C.: Learning Italian via mobile SMS. In: Mobile Learning: A Handbook for Educators and Trainers, pp. 76–83 (2005)
14. Lockyer, L., Patterson, J.: Integrating Social Networking Technologies in Education:? A Case Study of a Formal Learning Environment. In: Editor (Ed.)^(Eds.) Book Integrating Social Networking Technologies in Education:? A Case Study of a Formal Learning Environment, pp. 529–533. IEEE (2008)
15. Teclehaimanot, B., Hickman, T.: Student-Teacher Interaction on Facebook: What Students Find Appropriate. In: Proc. World Conference on E-Learning in Corporate, Government, Healthcare, and Higher Education, Vancouver, Canada (2009)
16. Bryant, T.: Social software in academia. Educause Quarterly 29(2), 61 (2006)
17. Minocha, S.: A study of the effective use of social software to support student learning and engagement (2009)

18. Gunawardena, C.N., McIsaac, M.S.: Distance education. In: Handbook of Research for Educational Communications and Technology, vol. 2, pp. 355–395 (2004)
19. McLoughlin, C., Lee, M.J.W.: Social software and participatory learning: Pedagogical choices with technology affordances in the Web 2.0 era. In: Editor (Ed.)^(Eds.) Book Social Software and Participatory Learning: Pedagogical Choices with Technology Affordances in the Web 2.0 Era (2007)
20. Boyd: Identity production in a networked culture: Why youth heart MySpace. MédiaMorphoses (21), 69–80 (2007)
21. Ellison, N.B., Steinfield, C., Lampe, C.: The benefits of Facebook "friends:" Social capital and college students use of online social network sites. Journal of Computer Mediated Communication 12(4), 1143–1168 (2007)
22. Cochrane, T., Bateman, R.: Smartphones give you wings: Pedagogical affordances of mobile Web 2.0. Australasian Journal of Educational Technology 26(1), 1–14
23. Ellison, N.: Facebook use on campus: A social capital perspective on social network sites. In: Editor (Ed.)^(Eds.) Book Facebook Use on Campus: A Social Capital Perspective on Social Network Sites (2007)

Enhanced Authentication on Targeted Online Surveys: A Case of Online Course Evaluation System

Kosmas Kapis[1] and Sijali Petro Korojelo[2]

[1] Computer Science and Engineering Department, University of Dar es Salaam, Tanzania
Kapis@udsm.ac.tz, KKapis@gmail.com
[2] Ruaha University College, Iringa, Tanzania
sijalipeter@yahoo.com

Abstract. Online survey offers cheapest data collection and processing cost, efficient service, easy data processing and wide coverage over traditional paper-and-pencil surveys; due to this its adoption recently has been inevitable. However, despite the number of advantages an online questionnaire can offer, there are still a number of problems and challenges related to authentication that need to be closely addressed. Multiple submissions, respondent authenticity/validity, and respondent's anonymity are among the issues that hinder the proliferation of online surveys.

This paper addresses the aforementioned challenges and fills the left gap by improving previous works and later presents an online survey system which behaves well. The system considers also the problem of identity theft.

Keywords: Security, Identity theft, Authentication, Confidentiality, Multiple Responses, and Online Surveys.

1   Introduction

Online surveys offers cheapest data collection and processing cost, efficient service, easy processing, and wide coverage over the traditional paper-and-pencil surveys according to [4], [3], [7], in this manner the its adoption has been inevitable in recent years.

Thomas in [10] defines an on-line survey as the collection of data through a self-administered electronic set of questions by e-mail, the web, or a combination of both. Online surveys falls under two major categories which are Email-based survey and web-based survey.

Email-based survey is the one in which the respondents are invited to participate in an online surveys through their email addresses. Usually the respondent of the survey receives an invitation email from the online survey administrator; the invitation email may contain a link address or URL which directs the respondent to the survey form. The other type of online survey is the web-based survey in which the survey form is made available online and accessible by anyone. This type of online survey is normally intended to the generic respondents where the user authentication is hardly given priority.

Some surveys may be specifically targeted to a certain defined sample. In developing such a system several issues must be well addressed such as: i) How will the person administering the questionnaire guarantee that this survey response comes

A. Abd Manaf et al. (Eds.): ICIEIS 2011, Part I, CCIS 251, pp. 22–32, 2011.

from the particular intended respondent and not someone un-intended?, ii) how will the person administering the survey make sure that all necessary survey questions are attempted by the respondent?, iii) How will multiple submissions from the same respondent be controlled so as not to cause biasness and "spoilage" of the reality of the survey results, iv) Lastly how to make sure that the submission of the survey form by the respondent is safe and that there is no easy tracking or identity theft by the third part (Hacker)? All of the above are the challenges and problems related to authentication which face the design and use of online surveys. Two people attempted to study and resolve some of the above named problems.

First, [11] presented the Web-based online survey system depicted in figure 1 which was used to collect data about the Library Information System (LIS). The system was used to research how the use of Internet has eased the work of researchers. The system was running in a Unix HP server. The web pages have been built using HTML, and the CGI program has been used to generate the case IDs. The system worked by inviting each respondent using the respondents' email addresses, to participate in the survey by receiving an email from the system administrator. Using a CGI program in the server side, a 10 digit random case ID was produced and printed on the cover letter. Each intended respondent receives, through email which contains a hyperlink to the survey page, a cover letter with a case ID printed on it.

The system used the 10 digit case ID produced by the CGI server as the means of identifying the intended respondent. After receiving an email with the case ID in the cover letter, a respondent follows the hyperlink to the survey page. He/she is then prompted to provide his/her case ID. The system then compares the given case ID with the list of those stored in a database. If the case ID is found in a database, then he/she is the legitimate user and thus authorized to access the survey page. The system used a database to store the case IDs, and other useful data about e-sources. Furthermore, it contains the "survey data" component which is used to record the submitted survey data so that respondents could review them later.

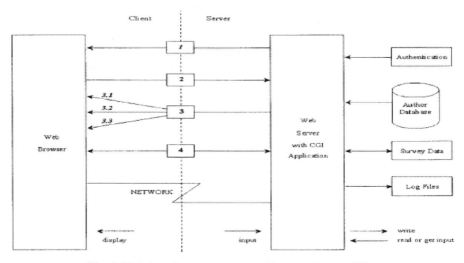

Fig. 1. Web-based survey system architecture (source: [9])

Second, [6] on the other hand studied the work of Zhang he came with an alternative system better than the Zhang's system. In his system, he used email based survey. The system is presented in figure 2.

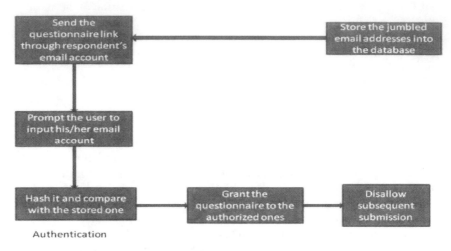

Fig. 2. Overview of Online Survey System (source: [7])

His system worked by the system administrator inviting the respondents to participate in an online survey by emailing them. The respondents are then linked to the survey home page where they are prompted to provide their email addresses. Using the one-way MD5 hash function the system compares the entered email address with that in the database. If the two hash codes match, then the respondent is an intended one and is thus privileged to access the questionnaire page. Otherwise the respondent is an un-intended one and thus he/she is denied the access to the questionnaire. After the first submission, the respondent is then prevented from any further subsequent responses.

Zhang's system did well in the area of tackling the problems of multiple responses of which he managed to control it but not for the cases of identity theft and respondent validity/authentication. His system failed in the case the survey invitation email is accidentally delivered to an un-intended respondent where that un-intended responded was able to access and fill the survey page since the case ID was printed on the invitation email. [6], on the other hand improved the work done by Zhang by tackling additional problem of respondent anonymity. He did it by hashing of respondent details before transmitting them hence someone could not tell the real identity of the person since the respondent details were hashed and could not be decrypted. However Hussein's work failed to do well in the case of respondent validity. It was seen that when the intended respondent received the survey link page from the system administrator and forwarded that link to another person who is not meant to receive the survey link before that particular intended respondent responds to the survey page, in that case this person receiving the survey link page could still access, fill and submit the survey page without any problems using the email address of its sender usually printed on the "from" field of the email.

This work reviews previous works of other people as far as the issue of authentication in online surveys is concerned, see what further authentication challenges, problems and weaknesses they face, proposes suitable alternatives for combating the problems and lastly presents the prototype of an advanced system which tackles the issues mentioned by combating the observed weaknesses. The authors of this work hypothesize that all the addressed problems above are associated by the use of poor authentication methods/techniques of which this work seek to find solution to them.

2   Approach

In order to resolve the prior named problems the authors used password authentication techniques/method. Deb [5] argues that most of people are familiar with password authentication, to log onto a computer or network, you enter a user account name and the password assigned to your account of which this password is checked against a database that contains all authorized users and their passwords. Password authentication method is usually considered weak, but in this work MD5 hash function was used to strengthen its performance. Using this function respondent details containing both email addresses and passwords were hashed before being stored or transmitted, this helps to tackle problems of respondent anonymity and respondent tracking by a third party user or hacker. The approach used to solve the problems is depicted in figure 3.

The use of both the email address and password eliminated the respondent validity problem which was unresolved by [6]. In the problem, when the intended respondent received the survey link page from the system administrator and forwarded that link to another person who is not meant to receive the survey link before that particular intended respondent responds to the survey page, it was seen that this person receiving the survey link page could still access, fill and submit the survey page without any problems using the email address of its sender usually printed on the "from" field of the email.

In this new system it is difficulty for any un-intended respondent to fill and submit the survey page unless he knows both email address and password of its sender (intended respondent) who has sent him/her the questionnaire, so even if he gets the email from the "from" field of the email received from the intended respondent he can't know the password of that particular respondent unless the intended respondent decides to give that person the password.

Other methods such as smartcard and biometrics are available but they are expensive and sometimes they require specialized hardware and software which are expensive, this makes them uneconomic for a person to use for the reason of collecting online data. The system is also built such that multiple submissions are rejected after first submission is successful.

In case of the authentication protocol, this work used CHAP (Challenge Handshake Authentication Protocol). Dax Networks [4], Argues that CHAP is a type of authentication in which the authentication agent (typically a network server) sends the client program a key to be used to encrypt the username and password. This enables the username and password to be transmitted in an encrypted form to protect them against eavesdroppers. [4] Further argues that Challenge Handshake Authentication

Protocol (CHAP) is used to periodically verify the identity of the peer using a 3-way handshake (challenge, response, failure or success message). CHAP is the best option for the work for several reasons, First CHAP verifies that the two devices have the same "shared secret" but doesn't require that the secret be sent over the link which is not good as far as security is concerned, second CHAP provides protection against replay attacks, where an unauthorized user captures a message and tries to send it again later on. This is done by changing an identifier in each message and varying the challenge text. Third using CHAP, the server controls the authentication process, not the client that is initiating the link. Lastly, [8] argues that CHAP is an only internet standard that uses MD5 (Message Digest (5th version)) hashing algorithm of which was also used in this work.

In this work a new system controlled by the system administrator, first stores respondent information including email accounts and passwords to access the survey page into the database, he/she then invites the respondents to participate in an online survey by emailing them and sending them the questionnaire link (see figure 4). The respondents are then linked to the survey home page where they are prompted to provide their identities which are the emails addresses and password known to them prior (either sent to them by a separate mail or by phone). Then using the one-way MD5 hash function the system compares the entered email address and password with that in the database by applying CHAP authentication protocol. If the two hash codes match, then the respondent is an intended one and is thus privileged to access. She or he then fills and submits the questionnaire page. Otherwise the respondent is an un-intended one and thus he/she is denied the access to the questionnaire. Multiple submissions are rejected after first submission is successful.

On its completion, the new system was tested in all challenging cases addressed prior. First in the case of respondent validity (either the respondent is intended or un-intended, see figure 5), second in the case of restricting multiple submission, and third for the case of avoiding respondent tracking/ tracing by the third part user also known as the system hacker and ensuring that respondent anonymity is preserved.

Twenty three users were involved in the system testing. Out of them, ten were asked to act as un-intended respondents, eleven as intended respondents, and two as system hackers who were asked to track/trace the system. The email was adopted as the means of communication between the survey users and the system administrator. It was used by both the system to invite the survey respondents to participate in the system testing and by the respondents to send back the findings to the administrator. All respondents whether intended or un-intended were emailed and asked to try logging into the system and access the survey page and provide the feedback of the findings to the system administrator.

On the other hand during the system evaluation against multiple responses, the intended respondents were emailed asked to attempt submitting the questionnaire several times as well as trying to forward the invitation email to someone else to respond on their behalf and finally they were asked to give the findings back to the system administrator. Lastly 2 users were emailed to act as the hacker and asked to try if they could trace the respondents by knowing which questionnaire has been submitted by whom.

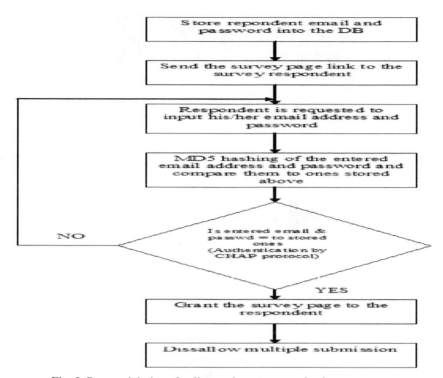

Fig. 3. Proposed design of online student course evaluation survey system

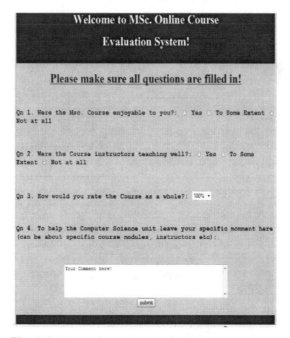

Fig. 4. Online student course evaluation survey page

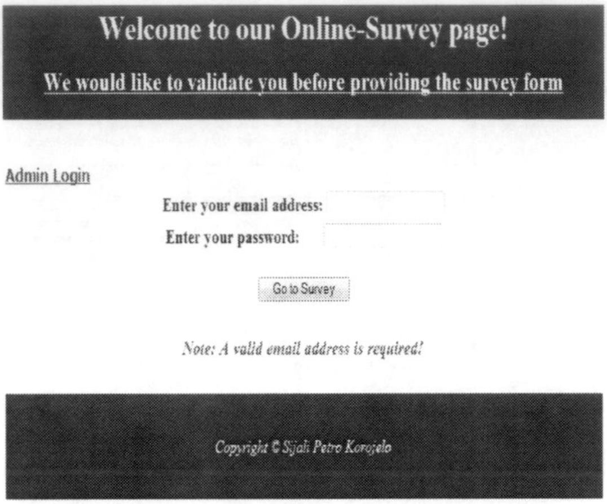

Fig. 5. Respondents Login page

3   Results

In this work, the online course evaluation survey system was implemented with 23 respondents being involved during system testing. The cases that the system was tested to see its performance are: the case of respondent validity (either the respondent is intended or un-intended), the case of multiple submission to see if the system could restrict that and the case of respondent tracking/ tracing by the third part user also known as the system hacker and the case of preserving respondent anonymity. Below are the results obtained during that system testing.

3.1   Respondent Validity/Authentication

Ten un-intended respondents were forwarded a survey invitation email, among ten un-intended respondents invited only 5 responded by attempting to access the questionnaire page. Each time they tried to login into the system they were not able access the survey page, their logging in details (email addresses and passwords) were captured and stored in the "non_respondents" table so that it can be used as evidence during the system evaluation. As shown in the figure 6 below five out of five un-intended respondents who tried to log into the system were blocked.

Furthermore, eleven intended respondents were forwarded a survey invitation email, among them, only seven filled and submitted the questionnaire successful, two respondents among ten did not attempt the survey but they were asked to try to forward the invitation email to someone else so that he/she can access the questionnaire page, results showed that those people forwarded the survey invitation email did not succeed to access and fill the survey and their details were blocked too.

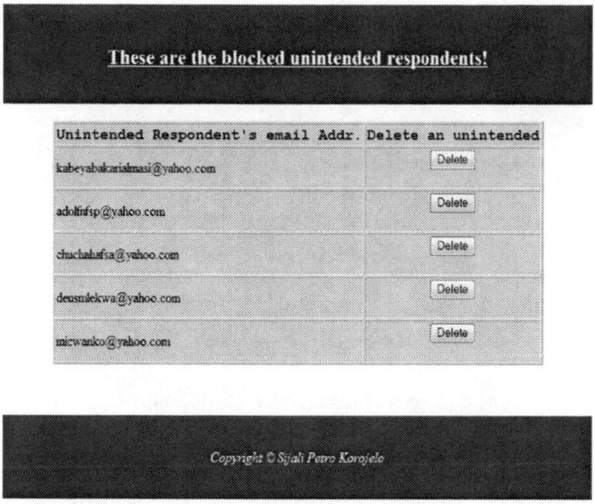

Fig. 6. List of un-intended respondent

3.2   Anonymity/Confidentiality and Respondent Tracking

Among the two users acting as system hackers who were asked to trace the system, only one tried to access the system's database where he was asked to trace which questionnaire has been submitted by whom. The hacker then reported that he couldn't do that because the submitted questionnaires and respondents' identities are stored in the separate tables within the database, see figure 7 and 8. Furthermore, even though he was privileged to access the system database such as "respondents' table which contains the respondents' hashed email addresses and passwords, stealing or identifying them was not possible at all and hence the anonymity of the respondents was preserved. This is due to the fact that the stored email-addresses and passwords were hashed using an MD5 hash function in which the encrypted values couldn't be decrypted back to their original format.

3.3   Multiple Submissions/Responses

Results showed that the submitted questionnaires were 7 even though each intended respondent was asked to attempt submitting them several times. This shows that after the respondent has responded once, then the rest of the subsequent responses were denied. However the system was tested by instructing one of the intended respondent who already filled and submitted the survey form to try to re-submit a new filled form once again. He argued that the attempt was denied by giving the error message "Sorry you have automatically restricted from submitting more than one questionnaire".

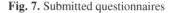

The submitted Questionnaires!

Module Enjoyed	Intructor's Competency	Module Rating	Comments	Delete Questionnaire
No	Moderately	75	I recommend lectures teachers to be commited more and more to their work than engaging in their own activities (Mikukuta).	Delete
Moderately	Yes	75	There should be optional courses...	Delete
Moderately	Yes	75	- there are no optional courses specified for the Msc. of computer science course. i think it is very important to include the optional courses in the Msc curriculum	Delete
Moderately	Moderately	50	Review of the caliculum is required	Delete
Yes	Moderately	75	Your Comment here!	Delete
Yes	Yes	75	course is fine	Delete
Yes	Yes	75	course is fine!!! congrats..	Delete

Fig. 7. Submitted questionnaires

	hashed_email	hashed_passwd
☐ ✎ ✗	00e23f264b82e9cc8b44ce4c4e2168d9	ed569bca88a52981de2a01ca79a47c14
☐ ✎ ✗	02416de9dcfa4c0cbe172453acbd9d74	496961fb0f873a7b2495de286b69c987
☐ ✎ ✗	0b9f22674a2e417151098699eeea1006	9648cf5cbd611d8e2fb6a5c039dc0b0e
☐ ✎ ✗	3ec59d67887e5b2e851979603dfd3a7a	3f4b8d3ecc38d6d864bad590b7044e48
☐ ✎ ✗	4ef506b7f10c07e76ea097d9556ebd64	811091ce83f26f727480301696c13515
☐ ✎ ✗	78e1fcb918dd58dae04f5f83fc55e25f	1b9154d5b5a75002116455c84ff37d4d
☐ ✎ ✗	7e2659ba09b2500e8f9f1983f1794aa3	f750a486d1474b703ccf073a1304fc77

Fig. 8. The database table of hashed respondent identities

4   Discussion

Respondent validity, anonymity, identity theft, tracking, and multiple responses are some of the critical problems that an online survey suffers from. Some of the suggested approaches such as that of [11] and [6] are still not sophisticated enough to provide complete solution to all the named problems.

The online course evaluation survey system that has been implemented in this work behaves well all of the challenging situations, first in the situation where the invitation email is accidentally sent to un-intended recipient by the administrator. In this case having received an invitation email, that particular un-intended respondent has to be authenticated using the valid email address and password of which he/she will not have because his/her details are not stored into the system database, second in the situation where the invitation email gets forwarded accidentally to un-intended respondent by the intended respondent having received the invitation email from the system administrator and before that particular intended respondents fills and submits the survey. The one who receives has to be authenticated like in the previous case, in this case even if the unintended respondent knows the sender email address from the "from" field of an email, he/she has to know also the sender's password (used to access the survey page) so to access the survey page, hence that particular un-intended respondent can't access the survey unless his/her sender decides to tell him/her the password of which this will be a purposive forwarding of the invitation email.

Based on the results obtained and discussed in the results section, the system proves to be more stable against the submission of multiple responses from the same respondent. The system accepted one and only one response from each respondent.

The system also offers the reasonable solution against both identity theft and respondent tracking, the results show the submitted questionnaires and the hashed respondent's identities are stored in the separate database tables. This indicates that even though someone accesses the system database, he/she can hardly tell who submitted a particular questionnaire. Storing the hashed identities indicates that even if one gets into the database and steals information, decrypting them will be difficulty since the encryption schemes used was only one way, i.e. you can only encrypt data but decryption isn't possible. Also hashing during authentication plays an important role against identity theft on transit.

Despite all of the above achievement of this work, there are still a number of challenges that particularly need to be dealt with. First low response rate is the issues which need much effort in order to establish a suitable online survey system. During the system test, out of 23 respondents invited to participate in the online questionnaire, only 13 responded (7 intended respondents, 5 un-intended respondents, 1 hacker). Second results show that only two respondent sent feedback during the system testing. This is because there wasn't a log file in which users could type the comments and send back to the system administrator instead of emailing him. This finding agrees with the "feedback" limitation as reported by other researchers.

References

1. Abdullah, A.: Protecting your good name: Identity Theft and its Prevention. In: On the Proceedings of the 1st Annual Conference on Information Security Curriculum. Kennesaw State University, Georgia (2004)
2. Anita, K.: Password Authentication with Insecure Communication. Department of Computer Science. University of Waterloo, Waterloo (1981)
3. Articlesbase. Advantages and Disadvantages of Using Online Surveys (2009),
   http://www.articlesbase.com/business-articles/
   advantages-and-disadvantages-of-using-online-surveys-
   1377003.html
4. Dax Networks. CHAP (Challenge Handshake Authentication Protocol),
   http://www.daxnetworks.com/Technology/TechDost/TD-061406.pdf
5. Deb, S.: Understanding and selecting authentication methods (2001),
   http://articles.techrepublic.com.com/
   5100-10878_11-1060518.html
6. Hussein, A.: Authentication in Online Surveys. University of Southampton, UK (2008)
7. Peter, M.: Advantages & Limitations of Forms in Web Pages (2010),
   http://www.ehow.com/list_6331726_advantages-limitations-
   forms-pages.html

8. Shinder, D.: Understanding and selecting authentication methods (2008),
   http://articles.techrepublic.com.com/
   5100-10878_11-1060518.html
9. ScienceDaily. Online Access With a Fingerprint (2010),
   http://www.sciencedaily.com/releases/2010/12/
   101215082942.htm
10. Thomas, M.: Points for Consideration On-Line Surveys. Ohio State University, USA (2003)
11. Zhang, Y.: Using the internet for Survey Research: A case Study. Journal of the American
   Society for Information Science, 57–68 (2000),
   http://www3.interscience.wiley.com/
   cgi-bin/fulltext/69500919/PDFSTART

E-mature – Report of an Electronic Mathematics Exam

Jacek Stańdo

Technical University of Lodz , Center of Mathematics, ul. Al. Politechniki 11 Łódź, Poland
jacek.stando@p.lodz.pl

Abstract. Internet applications have been revolutionary in our daily life since the moment that they were first implemented several years ago. An increasing number of institutions is changing traditional methods for the 'e' ones. It also affects the educational field. The beginnings were mainly about the external teaching. For a few years now extensive research, regarding the e-exams has been done [6],[7],[8], that is the system which enables checking pupils' knowledge and skills in the real time instead of doing written exams. This paper shows the report based on the first mock e-mature in mathematics in Poland.

Keywords: electronic examination, evaluation systems.

1   Introduction

At the beginning of January 2009 I presented the rector of the Technical University of Lodz with an idea of conducting the first mock e-mature in mathematics in Poland. A month later the rector and I went to the director of the Central Examination Board and the Minister of National Education in order to show the Project of 'E-mature'. The project was warmly received by the educational authorities, so we started working intensively. The first problem which we stumbled upon was the lack of proper computer equipment. Luckily, the IBM company was of much help as a sponsor and equipped our Institute with computers worth more than 60,000 euros. It took almost a year to prepare the first online mock exam in mathematics in the real time in Poland at such a big scale in Europe. On 29th October more than 3,500 mature students from 150 secondary schools (see, figure 1) sat at the computers connected with the Internet. The e-exam started at 9 a.m. sharp for everybody and lasted for 170 minutes. A few minutes after finishing the exam all the students learned about their results.

The main aim of the project was:

- To popularize the idea of supporting education in conducting examinations and evaluation by means of IT technology.

Detailed aims:

- To work on good methods of conducting examinations by means of technology
- To present the potential of multimedia and IT techniques in examinations
- To check the e-exam and evaluation system
- To do educational research in the form of an e-survey

A. Abd Manaf et al. (Eds.): ICIEIS 2011, Part I, CCIS 251, pp. 33–41, 2011.

Fig. 1. Map of Poland with the schools participating in the 'E-mature'

2   The System of External Evaluation in Poland

The new system of external evaluation in Poland, which has been brought in gradually since 2002, makes it possible to diagnose the achievements as well as shortcomings of students' education in order to evaluate the efficiency of teaching and to compare objectively current certificates and diplomas irrespective of the place where they have been issued.

The parts of the external examination system are:

- The Competence Test in the sixth class of primary school
- Lower Secondary School (Gymnasium) The examination conducted in the third class of lower secondary school
- The Mature Exam for graduates of comprehensive secondary schools, specialized secondary schools, technical secondary schools, supplementary secondary schools or post-secondary schools
- The Examination confirming Vocational Qualifications (vocational examination) for graduates of: vocational schools, technical schools and supplementary technical schools

The rules of external evaluation are described in detail in The Ordinance of the Minister of National Education. The external evaluation is conducted at the end of a particular stage of education given all the requirements to realize the educational assignments described in the Core Curriculum. The methods and results of implementing these assignments may vary owing to the autonomous character of each school. Accordingly, only the final effects of education and results achieved from a completed stage of education can be compared. The achievement standards signed by the Minister of National Education are the basis for conducting the tests and examinations. They have resulted from extensive consultations with teachers and the academic community, and are based on the educational objectives defined in the Core Curriculum. The establishment of uniform and clearly stated attainment standards has a direct influence on the fairness and standardization of the external evaluation. Furthermore, those standards are relevant to move the main interest of the assessment from knowledge to skills and abilities obtained at a particular stage of education. The Central Examination Board is a public education institution based in Warsaw. It was established on 1st January 1999 by the Minister of National Education on the strength of the Act on the System of Education, whose aim was to evaluate the educational achievements students, to monitor the quality of the educational influence of school and to make all the certificates comparable regardless of the place where they were issued. The responsibilities of the Central Examination Board are as follows:

- Preparing questions, tasks and exam sets for conducting the tests and examinations
- Preparing and presenting syllabuses containing a description of the scope of the tests and examinations, sample questions, tasks, tests, and criteria for evaluation
- Analyzing the results of the tests and examinations and reporting them to the Minister of Education in the form of an annual report of students' chievements at a given educational stage
- Stimulating research and innovation in the area of assessment and examination

The Mature Exam
The Mature Exam is an external examination, uniform throughout the country. It was brought in to ensure the uniformity of exam sets and criteria of assessment, comparability of results and objectivity of assessment (the coded answer sheets are marked by external examiners). The Mature Exam is also the basis of getting admitted to universities and colleges to continue further education. Only in special cases are additional entrance exams permitted (e.g. art colleges and some specialized faculties). The Mature Exam is not obligatory, so it is possible to opt out. The detailed information about the examination in each subject and sample papers are included in the Syllabus for each subject, published by the Central Examination Board in cooperation with the Regional Examination Boards.

After 25 years the Mature Exam in mathematics has returned as an obligatory subject for the students who want to pass the Mature Exam [3][4]. The Mature Exam in mathematics consists of two parts: Basic and extended. The basic part is taken by all the students. The extender part is only for the chosen students who want to continue their education at technical faculties (e.g. mathematics, physics, information technology, electronics, building etc…)

The traditional mature in mathematics from the basic part, which is taken by all the students consists of 25 closed tasks and of about 6-8 open-ended tasks. The total score for the tasks is 50. The closed tasks consist of four answers, one of which is correct. Students can receive 1 point for each task whereas for the open-ended tasks 2-5 points, depending on the evaluated skills.

Each student taking the exam receives a set of tasks on paper along with an answer sheet. The exam begins promptly at the appointed hour in Poland. Part one lasts 170 minutes. Specially prepared and trained examiners review and score the students' examinations. The answer sheets on which the answers are given to closed tasks (marked by students) and the results obtained by carrying out open tasks (written by examiners), are finally fed into electronic readers.

Since the introduction of a new examination system in Poland the extensive research related to the exams has been done. In the past ten years, over 20,000 students have participated in the mock exams organized. After the test, students completed the questionnaire prepared [5]. The results have been reported in many publications.

3   Closed and Open-ended Questions in "E-mature"

In the traditional mature in mathematics the tasks are marked by the examiners. In the 'E-mature' the examiner was the computer system. Each open task had an extra element of the instruction, such as: drag, mark, type in, draw, fill in. There are multimedia elements, in open as well as closed tasks, which were in many cases parts of the task content.

Sample open-ended tasks of 'E-mature'
Task 17 (see, figure 2). Point C moved along the straight shown in the figure. The student was to answer the question how the values of the surface areas of the triangles changed.

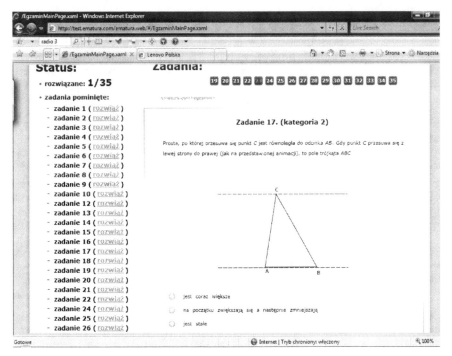

Fig. 2. Closed question „e-mature"

In task 12 the student watched the changing graphs of the square functions. His task was to answer the question: how the squared ratio changed.

Sample open-ended task of 'E-mature' Task 19, (see fig. 4) The student was to solve the square inequation. They marked the proper solution set on the numerical axis by means of a mouse. Evaluation system: 1 point – for defining the roots of the square equation, 1 point for marking the numerical bracket.

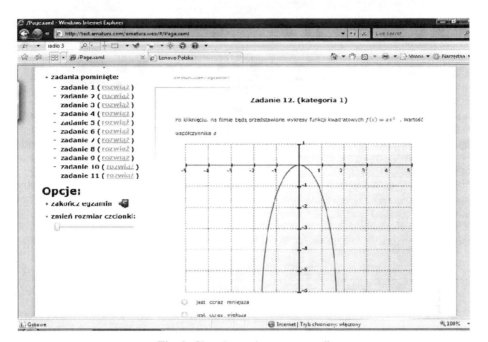

Fig. 3. Closed question „e-mature"

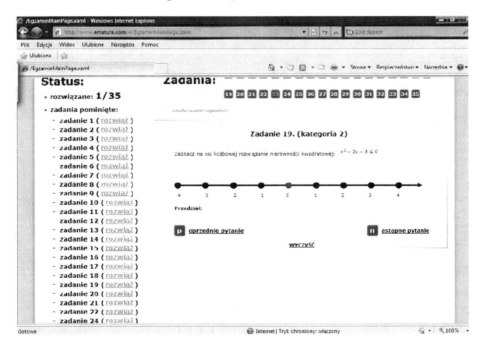

Fig. 4. Open-ended question „e-mature"

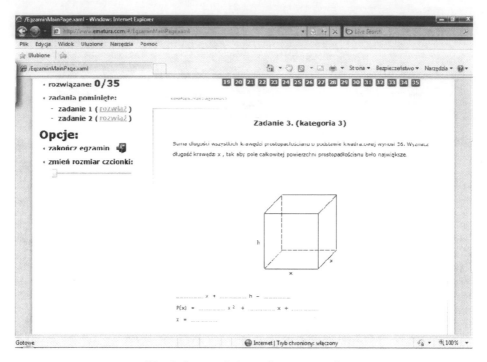

Fig. 5. Open-ended question „e-mature"

Fig. 6. Open-ended question „e-mature"

Task 3, (see fig. 5) referred to optimization. There was a cuboid with the square base and there was the sum of the length of all the edges. The students had to choose the dimensions of the edges to make the surface area of the cuboid the biggest. The students received 3 points for this task.

Evaluation system : 1 point – for writing the relation between the lengths of the edges, 1 point -for making a function of the surface area, depending on the base edges, 1 point – for defining the lengths of the edges for which the surface area is the biggest.

Task 4 (see fig. 6) The students were to analyze the problem and put forward a hypothesis. They had a sum of the squares of the subsequent two, three, four, six odd numbers. They analyzed the situation on the basis of the data.

Evaluation system: 1 point – for defining the sum of 5 subsequent squared odd numbers. 1 point – for defining the sum of 99 subsequent squared even numbers. 1 point – for putting forward a hypothesis of the formula for the sum of the subsequent squared odd numbers.

4   Conclusions

It is advisable to pose a question about the advantages and disadvantages of conducting the 'E-mature' online. To my mind, this topic is so broad that they should be tackled in a separate publication. Therefore, I will not bring up that issue at this point. The more significant question appears to be the conformity of examination standards and automatic evaluation system. Unfortunately it is impossible to mark 15-20% of the examination by means of the computer system. These tasks include e.g. proving. What is the solution to the problem then? In the future, students could do the tasks by means of a table and the processed picture could be passed on to the examiner, i.e. a man. Another part solution could be done by using artificial neuron nets [3] to process the picture in order to mark the open-ended questions. I began first such studies over a year ago [1]. The results are quite promising.

The 'E-mature' project was warmly received by students, teachers, educational authorities as well as the media. It was possible to hear about it in all the news programmes in public and private TV stations, on the biggest web news portals in Poland and also read about it in country-wide newspapers. At the same time, while the students were taking the e-mature they were holding a press conference with the educational authorities, the media, many guests and scientists. During the conference we contacted the students from schools all over Poland (by means of Skype) to attain the first-hand information from the course of the exam. (fig. 7). The possibility of tracking the results achieved by the students from particular tasks in the real time made the greatest impression on the conference participants. It all happened in the real time. A few minutes after finishing the examination we knew all the results.

Fig. 7. Dr Jacek Stańdo talking to a student during the 'E-mature'

In an interview Niven to the media, Minister of National Education Katarzyna Hall answered the question about the idea of the 'E-mature' and its future and said that: "Certainly, we will not have this kind of mature examination in the nearest future, however, it is a very serious enterprise to make sure that this kind of operation will be well-secured in the whole country" (fig. 8).

Fig. 8. The Minister of National Education while giving an interview for the TV

The 'E-mature' is still being worked on. The Technical University of Lodz has received over 1 mln euros, within the EU projects, from the Ministry of National Education to continue working on the project.

Acknowledgments. The author thanks the Ministry of Education and the Central Examination Board for the help and commitment to hold the first e-exam.

References

1. Bieniecki, W., Stoliński, S., Stańdo, J.: Automatic Evaluation of Examination Tasks in the Form of Function Plot. In: Proceedings of the 6th International IEEE Conference MEMSTECH 2010, Lviv-Polyana, Ukraine, pp. 140–143 (2010)

2. Krawczyk-Stańdo, D., Stańdo, J.: Supporting didactic processes with Mathematical E-emergency Services, Poland. Education (2(110)) (2010)
3. Krawczyk-Stańdo, D., Rudnicki, M., Stańdo, J.: Radial neural network learning using U-curve approach. Pol. Journal Environ. Stud. 17(2A), s.42–s.46 (2008)
4. Stańdo, J., Bieniecki, W.: Ways of application of different information technologies in education on the example of mathematical emergency e-services. In: Jałowiecki, P., Orłowski, A. (eds.) Distant Learning and Web Solutions for Education and Business, Warsaw (2010)
5. Stańdo, J.: The influence of economic factors on the trial exam results. Scientifict Bulletion of Chelm, Section of Mathematics and Computer Science (2007)
6. Thomas, P.G.: Evaluation of Electronic Marking of Examinations. In: Proceedings of the 8th Annual Conference on Innovation and Technology in Computer Science Education (ITiCSE 2003), Thesaloniki, Greece, pp. 50–54 (2003)
7. Thomas, P.G.: Grading Diagrams Automatically, Technical Report of the Computing Department, Open University, UK, TR2004/01 (2003)
8. Thomas, P.G., Paine, C.: Evaluation of experiments with electronic marking of examinations. Submitted to ETS (2002)
9. Thomas, P., Price, B., Paine, C., Richards, M.: Remote electronic examinations: student experiences. British Journal of Educational Technology 33(5), 537–549 (2002)

A Flexible Speech Recognition System for Cerebral Palsy Disabled

Mohd Hafidz Mohamad Jamil, S.A.R. Al-Haddad, and Chee Kyun Ng

Department of Computer and Communication Systems Engineering,
Faculty of Engineering, University Putra Malaysia,
UPM Serdang, 43400 Selangor, Malaysia
hafidzjamil@gmail.com, {sar,mpnck}@eng.upm.edu.my

Abstract. Cerebral palsy (CP) is a disability with condition where children have problem controlling their movement coordination as a result of damage in the part of the brain - cerebrum. It may also cause the speech fails to function properly which resulting CP disabled often communicate by using sign or body language. Speech impairment in CP disabled is common because of the connection error between the cortex and other parts of the brain such as the cerebellum. Therefore, most of the time CP disabled need to repeat their words or sentences in their conversations to make other people more understand. In this paper, the development of a flexible speech to text recognition system for CP disabled is presented. It is a system where the stored speech references in the database can be adapted flexibility according to speech of CP disabled. The development algorithms are including speech detection triggering, zero crossing rate (ZCR) for the endpoint detection, Mel-Frequency Cepstral Coefficients (MFCC) for the feature extraction, and dynamic time warping (DTW) for the pattern classification. In other words, this flexible system is based on the speech training of CP disabled and then recognizing their speech inputs. The results show the credibility of the developed recognition system by giving high accuracy of speech detection approximately which is ranged from 78% to 97% accuracy. This performance shows that the developed flexible speech recognition system is ready to give positive impacts to the CP disabled in terms of daily conversation with normal human.

Keywords: Cerebral palsy (CP), speech recognition, zcr, mfcc, dtw.

1 Introduction

A disability in humans may be physical, cognitive, sensory, emotional and developmental or some combination of it. A disability is an umbrella term, covering impairments, activity limitations and participation restrictions. Impairment is a problem in body function or structure which has a difficulty encountered by an individual in executing a task or action [1]. Speech articulatory disability or dysarthria can be arisen from a number of conditions including cerebral palsy (CP), multiple sclerosis, Parkinson's disease and others [2]. Any of the speech subsystems like resonance, prosody, respiration, phonation and articulation can be affected. CP is

A. Abd Manaf et al. (Eds.): ICIEIS 2011, Part I, CCIS 251, pp. 42–55, 2011.
© Springer-Verlag Berlin Heidelberg 2011

described as a group of chronic disorders that affecting muscle coordination and body movement which is "Cerebral" means brain and "Palsy" refers to problem in muscle movement [3]. The affected area of the brain most likely involves connection errors between the cortex and other parts of the brain such as the cerebellum, which can cause physical and speech disabilities in human development. CP disabled is often accompanied by secondary musculoskeletal problems that are arisen as a result of the underlying etiology [4].

Speech Recognition system is a great technology system that basically convert the spoken words to text that the user can read easily. It processes the spoken input and translates it into text as shown in Fig. 1. Sometimes, the speech recognition term is used with refer to the recognition system that must be trained from a particular speaker in the recognition software. Hence, there is an aspect of the speaker who is identified as the person to speak for better recognition than other persons. However, the speech recognition system is generally become more difficult when the speech is not spoken perfect or stable as usual and also has many similar sounded words. When the speech is produced in sequence of words, the language models or artificial grammars are used to restrict the combination of words. Hence, when CP disabled gives a speech, they sometime speak something that is really hard to be understood by this speech recognition system due to their oral articulation disorders. Therefore, a flexible speech recognition system should be developed to suit their disability and to make people easy to understand their speech.

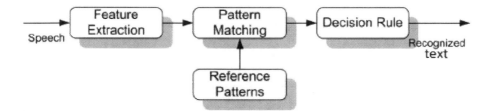

Fig. 1. The process of speech recognition system

In this paper, the development of a flexible speech recognition system is presented. It is a system where the stored speech references in the database can be adapted flexibility according to speech of CP disabled. This means that the stored speech references can be altered by flexibility recording the new version of speeches to update the speech database accordingly. The development algorithms are including speech detection triggering, zero crossing rate (ZCR) for the endpoint detection, Mel-Frequency Cepstral Coefficients (MFCC) for the feature extraction, and dynamic time warping (DTW) for the pattern classification. The developed flexible Speech recognition can help CP disabled in their conversation. The recognized words or sentences can be the final results for the application such as command and control, document preparation and data entry. It can also serve as the input for further linguistic processing in order to achieve better speech understanding. The developed sysem can also be one of the greatest solutions for normal human to understand the speech of CP disabled.

The rest of this paper is organized as follows: Section 2 presents the types of CP disability which include spastic, athetoid, ataxia and combination of them. Section 3 discusses the speech of CP disabled as dysarthria. The development of the flexible speech recognition system is described in Section 4. The performance evaluations of the developed system are discussed in Section 5. Finally, this paper is concluded in Section 6.

2   Cerebral Palsy (CP)

There are many types of CP disability nowadays and are divided into some classes like spastic, athetoid, ataxia and combination of them.

2.1   Spastic

Spastic CP disabled are accounted for 70% to 80% of all CP cases. It results in muscular stiffness and as such the affected parts of the body are difficult to control. Spastic is divided into three small groups which is spastic quadriplegia, spastic diplegia and spastic hemiplegia [5]. Spastic quadriplegia is a type of spastic which affects all four limbs involves both arms and legs with equal severity. Spastic diplegia is also same as spastic quadriplegia which affects all four limbs involved both arms and legs but the legs are more seriously affected compared to arms. Spastic hemiplegia is a type of spastic which affects only one side of the body which involves only one leg and one arm.

2.2   Athetoid

Athetoid CP disabled is characterized by involuntary and uncontrolled movement of the arms, hands, legs or feet. Athetoid CP is marked by writhing involuntary muscle movement and also slow movements. A mixed muscle tone where some are too high and others too low also characterize in it. It damages to the basal ganglia in the midbrain will cause athetoid CP. Approximately 25% of CP disabled are affected by athetoid CP [6].

2.3   Ataxia

Ataxia is another type of CP disabled. Those with this ataxic type have problem of starting and carrying out movements such as standing or walking. Such CP disabled are often labeled 'clumsy' because they walk with a staggering gait. Ataxic CP affects 5% to 10% of individuals with CP. IT is caused by damage of cerebellum at the base of the brain. The cerebellum is the main control center for coordinates the actions for different groups of muscles and also for balance and coordination for body [7].

2.4   Combination

There are roughly 10% of CP disabled suffer from a combination of two or more types of CP in the same time. This type combines the spastic elements and weak limbs, athetoid and/or ataxia. It is caused by injury to both the pyramidal and extra pyramidal areas in brain. This individual rottenly interferes with reaching, speaking, feeding, grasping, and other skills that required for coordinated movements [8].

3   Speech of CP Disabled

Speech articulatory disability or dysarthria can appear from a number of conditions such as CP, The dysarthric speech problem is resulted from a disruption of some muscular control due to lesions of either the peripheral or centre nervous systems. Any of the speech subsystems like resonance, prosody, respiration, phonation and articulation can be affected. Parts of people with dysarthric speech like CP individuals also face severely motor-impaired. They face it with the limited or cannot control of their local environment [9]. In general, CP individuals have less articulatory precision for mostly during childhood. Simple "steady-state" phonemes like vowels are physically which is the easiest way to produce since they do not require dynamic movement of the articulatory structures. In contrast, phonetic transitions such as consonants are the most difficult problem to produce since they require fine motor control. Fine motor control is used to precisely move the articulators. Usually, the mildly speech impaired differs in degree of disability rather than the quality [9].

There are many types of CP disabled's speech. They can be separated in several different classes by describing the types of utterances which have the ability to recognize it [10]. Based on the fact that these classes have the difficulty to recognize the ability of determine the start and finish of an utterance when a speaker speaks. Most of the packages can fit into one or more than one class. It is depends on which mode they are fitting in. There are many modes such as isolated utterance, continuous speech, speaker dependent and speaker independent. Nevertheless, the degree of speech impairment of CP disabled has been evaluated by authors in [11]. The utility of computer speech recognition that uses a statistical causal model is exploited. A case study of a dysarthric speaker compared against the normal speaker by serving as a control has been presented as well [11]. Other than that, an application of technology to severely dysarthric speakers has been investigated by examining prosodic parameters such as intensity contours and frequency [12].

4   Development of Flexible Speech Recognition System

The development of flexible speech recognition system is an important task because it can give guidelines to achieve the objectives and visions as well as solving the background problems of the speech of CP disabled. This section will discuss about the methodology of the system development as shown in Fig. 2.

The processes of the developed system are included speech sample database, input voice triggering and endpoint detection, feature extraction of the sampled voice data, and pattern matching and classification. These processes will be repeated for each input of the recorded speech from CP disabled which flexible to their ability.

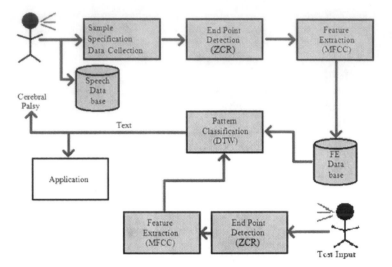

Fig. 2. The process of the developed flexible speech recognition system

4.1   Speech Sample Database

In the developed flexible speech recognition system, the speech of CP disabled is usually sampled at a rate between 6.6 kHz and 20 kHz. It is then processed as a sequence of vectors to produce a new representation of speech sample. It contains values that are called parameters. The vectors are usually comprised in range of 10 to 20 parameters. They are computed in every 10 or 20 ms. These parameter values are then used in the succeeding stages in estimation of the probability where the portion of the analyzed speech waveform which corresponds to a particular phonetic event occurs in the whole word reference unit. In the reality, the probability estimation is interacted together as part of the representation. Some may consider as part of the probability estimation process. Most speech recognition systems can be applying the criterion that if a process is applied to all speech it is part of the representation. But if its application is contingent on the phonetic hypothesis that being tested then it is part of the later matching stage. Table 1 shows the usual speech specification in term of parameters and range that are used nowadays.

Table 1. Speech specification for the developed system

Parameters	Range
Speaking mode	Isolated words to continuous speech
Speaking style	Read speech to spontaneous speech
Enrollment	Speaker-dependent to Speaker-independent
Vocabulary	Small (< 20 words) to large (> 20,000 words)
Language model	Finite-state to context-sensitive
Perplexity	Small (< 10) to large (> 100)
Signal to noise ratio (SNR)	High (> 30 dB) to low (< 10 dB)
Transducer	Voice-cancelling microphone to telephone

The collected data contains all important information about the CP disabled. This information is including name, address, gender, age, race, date of birthday, nationality and others. Then the type of speech can be classified into several categories. The data collection can be obtained by doing a randomly survey in the CP disabled centre. This data is collected as many as possible in order to increase the accuracy of the developed system.

4.2   Input Voice Triggering and Endpoint Detection

The sampled data is the input voice of CP disabled. The Input voice is an important part in speech recognition system. Hence, a input voice detection technique is designed by using voice triggering algorithm. This designed voice triggering algorithm is also developed such that the next input voice will be automatically triggered after the previous input voice is over for a period. There are many types of triggering technique such as activated by key from keyboard, activated from voice input and others. The used input voice triggering technique in this developed system is activated by the input voice. When a sample input voice is captured in the system the voice will activate the triggering part of recording.

After the input voice is triggered the recording of the voice sample will be continue until the endpoint of input voice is detected. This process is called endpoint detection. The combination of input voice triggering and endpoint detection techniques will generate two types of voice regions; sound and unsound regions. As compared to other endpoint detection approaches, ZCR technique requires less computation and fewer sets of parameters. Parameters such as average ZCR, density of ZCR within frames, excess threshold duration, standard deviation of the ZCR within frames, mean ZCR within frames, and energy estimates for each frame have all been used. The ZCR is the rate of sign-changes along a signal where the number of times that the signal crosses the zero level reference is determined. Hence, the ZCR should be directly related to the number of times the waveform repeats itself per unit time, which is given by

$$z(n) = \frac{1}{2} \sum_{m=1}^{N} \left| \mathrm{sgn}\left[x(m+1)\right] - \mathrm{sgn}\left[x(m)\right] \right| \tag{1}$$

where

$$\mathrm{sgn}\left[x(m)\right] = \begin{cases} +1 & x(m) \geq 0 \\ -1 & x(m) < 0 \end{cases} \tag{2}$$

The ZCR algorithm that is implemented in this system is based on two simple measurements, energy and zero-crossings. Both these parameters are fast and easy to calculate a fairly accurate indication of the presence or absence of speech to generate both sound and unsound regions.

4.3   Feature Extraction of the Sampled Speech Data

Feature extraction that involve of speech signal is used to reduce the data size before pattern classification. Feature extraction techniques are classified as temporal and spectral analysis techniques. In temporal analysis, the speech waveform itself is used for the analysis. In spectral analysis, spectral representation of speech signal is used for the analysis. Hence, the appropriate technique for both analyses is MFCC algorithm. The cepstral coefficient of MFCC is a set of features that is reported as robustness in some different pattern recognition tasks concerning human voice. Figure 3 shows the process block diagram of MFCC algorithm. MFCC has been widely used for the speech recognition.

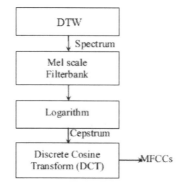

Fig. 3. The process of MFCC algorithm

A filter bank which is spaced uniformly on Mel-scale is used to simulate the subjective spectrum. The psychophysical study have shown that human perception of the physical content of sounds follow subjectively defined nonlinear scale which is known as Mel-scale. Mel-scale is defined as a logarithmic scale of frequency based on human speech pitch perception. The Mel-frequency scale is a linear frequency spaced below 1 kHz. The mapping from linear frequency to Mel-frequency is derived by

$$Mel(f) = 2595 \log_{10}\left(1 + \frac{f}{700}\right) \tag{3}$$

Finally, the Mel spectrum is converted to time. The output of this algorithm is called as MFCC and the coefficients are real numbers that can be converted into time domain using Discrete Cosine Transform (DCT). The MFCCs are used to discriminate the repetitions and prolongations in the stuttered speech.

4.4   Pattern Matching and Classification

The chosen algorithm for the pattern matching and classification in the developed system is DTW algorithm. DTW algorithm used to accommodate the differences in timing between sample words and templates used. The basic principle this algorithm is to allow a range of steps in the space of time frames in sample and time frames in template. It is also used to find the path through the space that maximizes the local match between the aligned time frames and the subject to the constraints implicit in the allowable steps. The total similarity cost found by this algorithm is a good indication of how well the sample and template to be matched, which can be used to choose the best-matching template.

The simplest way to recognize an isolated speech sample is to compare it against a number of stored word templates. It then determines which is the "best match" from the word templates. However, this goal is complicated by a number of factors. One of them is the different samples of a given speech have different durations. Nevertheless, DTW algorithm can be an efficient method for finding the optimal nonlinear alignment which uses dynamic programming as shown in Fig. 4. Its time and space complexity are merely linear in the duration of the speech sample and the vocabulary size.

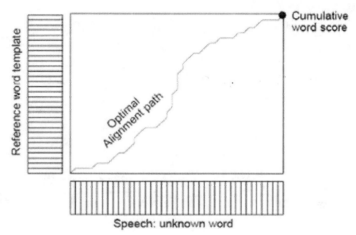

Fig. 4. The optimal alignment of DTW algorithm

For example, if D(x,y) is the Euclidean distance between frame x of the speech sample and frame y of the reference template, and if C(x,y) is the cumulative score along an optimal alignment path that leads to (x,y) as shown in Fig. 4, then if C(x,y) can be determined as

$$C(x, y) = \min\big(C(x - 1, y), C(x - 1, y - 1), C(x, y - 1)\big) + D(x, y) \qquad (4)$$

The resulting alignment path may be visualized as a low valley of Euclidean distance scores, meandering through the hilly landscape of the matrix, beginning at (0, 0) and ending at the final point (X,Y). By keeping track of back pointers, the full alignment path can be recovered by tracing backwards from (X,Y). An optimal alignment path is computed for each reference word template, and the one with the lowest cumulative score is considered to be the best match for the unknown speech sample.

5   Performance Analysis of the Developed System

The flexible speech recognition system for CP disabled has been developed and it is divided into two parts which are digits recording and words recording as shown in Fig. 5 but the design architecture of both parts are same. In the digits recording part, there are ten digits which are from 0 to 9, while in the words recoding part, there are eight daily words which are "Makan, Minum, Penat, Saya, Sakit Keluar, Kawan and Tandas" for the Malaysia national language. In the developed system, it contains of recording voice section which is using input voice triggering technique, playback voice section and lastly recognition section. The system provides the graphical user interface (GUI) which is developed from Matlab.

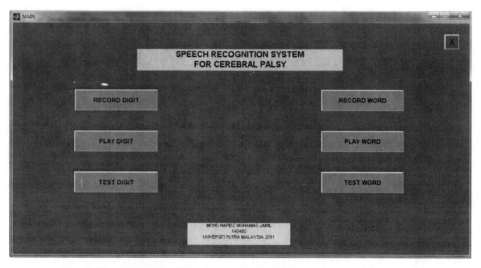

Fig. 5. The main page of the developed flexible speech recognition system

The speech of CP disabled will be first recorded to generate the reference template for the recognition system by using input voice triggering technique. When the input voice is captured, the triggering and endpoint detection algorithms will activate the recording automatically. For example in the recording page, the CP disabled want to record the speech of word "Makan" in the system as shown in Fig. 6. When the word is spoken through microphone, the captured speech of word "Makan" will generate its recorded waveform through the triggering and endpoint detection algorithms as shown in Fig. 7.

The recorded speech waveform spectrum will then undergo the feature extraction process to reduce the data size before pattern matching and classification. Feature extraction process is classified as temporal analysis and spectral analysis techniques which involve MFCC process. The MFCC filters the spectrum of recorded speech linearly at low frequencies and logarithmically at high frequencies in order to capture the phonetically important characteristics of the speech. Figure 8 shows the steps of MFCC process. In beginning, the framing process is applied to the recorded speech signal in frame block. Then, the signal spectrum is blocked into frames. After that, the windowing process is used to minimize the signal discontinuities between start and end of each frame. The Fast Fourier Transform (FFT) is used to convert each frame of speech samples into the frequency domain. The next process is Mel Frequency which is wrapped from obtained FFT spectrum. The process is to convert spectrum to the Mel spectrum. Finally, the log Mel spectrum is then converted back to time domain. The result is then recorded called MFCC output. The entire MFCC output will be stored in Matfile for the pattern matching and classification process in order to classify the recognition. Figure 9 shows the MFCC data in Matfile for the future extraction of the speech.

Fig. 6. The system recording page

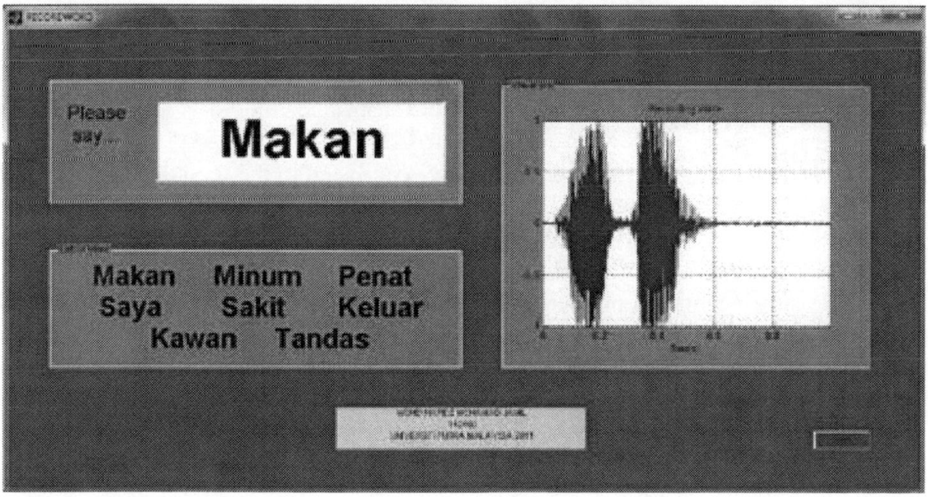

Fig. 7. The signal waveform of the captured speech

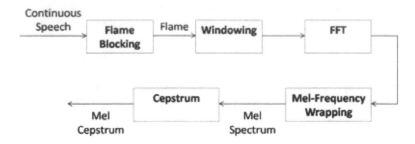

Fig. 8. The steps of MFCC for the developed speech recognition system

	1	2	3	4	5	6	7	8	9
1	-2.7543	-2.6841	-2.4521	-0.1064	0.4143	-1.2206	-0.5505	7.8134	7.6098
2	4.2158	3.5829	7.2214	1.7548	-8.8152	-7.6427	-4.1175	-4.5519	-8.0039
3	6.3141	2.6789	5.1255	-2.5740	-9.2576	-5.2016	0.3253	-5.8239	-7.8708
4	2.9059	4.2464	1.6075	-5.6579	1.4303	9.3429	1.4732	-7.7303	-8.5104
5	-1.0064	-3.3646	-9.4387	-5.5165	7.1792	8.8609	1.6544	-4.9888	-4.4130
6	2.9461	5.0514	-2.2042	0.5387	0.4143	-1.6498	-3.7263	-13.8189	-3.4455
7	0.3929	4.8322	-2.2202	-1.0304	3.0505	1.5721	1.8166	-10.1537	-11.8650
8	4.1194	0.7918	4.4915	-6.9839	1.5758	4.3648	3.1106	1.9085	5.2202
9	0.7276	3.6500	1.9859	-4.2922	4.4760	2.5136	3.8329	-2.5448	-3.5888
10	-0.5132	-1.2583	-2.9483	-1.5799	-2.0865	-6.3448	-5.4149	-10.0726	-2.6012
11	4.2534	-3.0138	5.9000	-2.4466	-4.7432	-9.5133	-2.6047	2.1610	3.8042
12	3.9252	13.2227	1.8055	4.4297	5.4776	-1.9679	-3.6517	2.2975	-10.1012
13	-0.1999	-0.1029	-0.1176	-0.0743	-0.0131	-0.0438	-0.0934	0.1738	0.2738
14	0.0399	0.5322	0.8639	0.5517	0.2413	1.4599	2.3149	2.2248	0.7484
15	0.6036	-0.1259	-2.7232	-3.7830	-3.1418	-0.7258	0.5371	-0.7524	-1.3784
16	-0.5878	-1.8830	-3.6261	-3.0009	-1.2093	0.3218	0.2286	-1.5845	-1.2597
17	-0.1160	-1.8330	-1.2759	1.0112	1.4829	-0.4006	-3.6858	-5.4692	-3.1050
18	-1.9497	-1.7726	1.3946	4.0795	3.6290	-0.4743	-3.7308	-3.3963	-1.5176
19	-0.8124	-0.9894	-0.9505	-1.0713	-0.5161	-3.2785	-1.9817	0.1104	1.2408
20	-0.0629	-0.5302	-0.0389	-0.1092	1.0834	-1.9323	-4.1399	-4.3088	-1.8493
21	-0.2769	-2.2020	-1.3048	0.4045	0.8402	1.9134	0.4647	-0.2127	-0.6737
22	0.4793	-0.9427	-0.1092	-0.0429	0.9854	0.2206	-2.1834	-1.4314	-0.7546
23	-0.6903	-0.5857	-0.4756	-1.0599	-1.0986	-2.1602	-0.6045	0.7506	1.9712

Fig. 9. The generated MFCC data in Matfile

After the recording process is done, the user can listen to the recorded speech from the playback page as shown in Fig. 10. In this page, the signal waveform of the recorded speech will be displayed as well in order for the user to see their speech waveform spectrum.

For recognizing the given speech the pattern matching and classification step is necessary. The given unknown speech will go through the pattern extraction comparison process. In this process, the result from the feature extraction of given unknown speech will be compared with the reference template in the stored database. This database is voice extraction stored in Matfile which is created from the training processes. It may be varied in term of speed or time. In order to complete the recognition process the DTW algorithm is used.

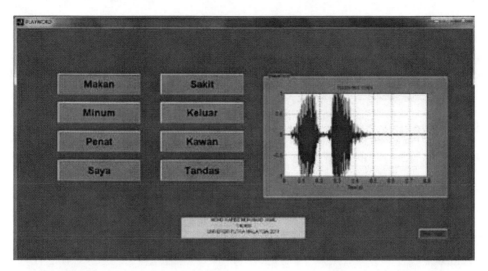

Fig. 10. The signal waveform spectrum of the captured speech in the playback page

The simplest way to recognize an unknown speech is to compare it against a number of stored word templates to determine which is the "best match". The developed system is based on the flexibility of CP disabled where all the subjects are needed to be trained first before the recognition process. The trained voice is stored as the reference template, When CP disabled want to recognize their spoken speech it will compare with reference speech template by using DTW algorithm to get the result. The recognition result will be generated in term of text that normal human can easily to read and understand. The voice recognition part of the developed system is shown in Fig. 11 when a CP disabled speaks the "MAKAN" word for recognition.

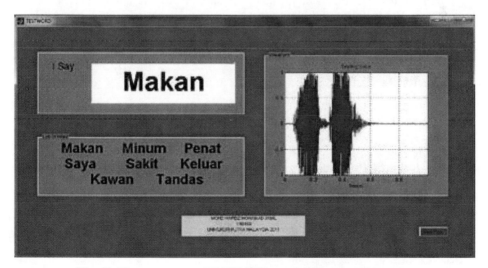

Fig. 11. The output text of "MAKAN" speech in the recognition page

The performance of the developed flexible speech recognition system has been evaluated. The detection accuracy result is obtained from the test of the speech CP disabled has spoken. They are 20 CP disabled are trained in the developed system and tested for one hundred times to obtain the accuracy performance. Tables 1 and 2 show the accuracy performance results for digit and word verification respectively.

Table 2. The accuracy of digit recognition

Digit	0	1	2	3	4	5	6	7	8	9
Accuracy (%)	97	89	93	95	87	79	85	92	85	96

Table 3. The accuracy of word recognition

Word	Makan	Minum	Penat	Saya	Sakit	Keluar	Kawan	Tandas
Accuracy (%)	95	89	87	88	78	89	78	97

From the results shown in Table 1, it clearly shows that the accuracy of detection digit from 0 to 9 is high on the average but different in the percentages among them. The digit "5" gave the lowest percentage compared to other digits because the pronunciation of "lima" is short than others digit. The digit "5" also may confuse the recognition of digit "1", "4", "6" and "8" due to some similarities in pronunciation during the training session. The digit "0", "2", "3", "7" and "9" gave the highest accuracy which is about above 90% due to the different in pronunciation and have their own unique sound. The word accuracy performance results in Table 2 show that the word "Makan" and 'Tandas" gives the highest accuracy because of the DTW algorithm for matching the incoming unknown speech with the stored reference words in database. The template with the lowest distance measure from the input pattern is the recognized word. The word "Sakit" gave the lowest accuracy percentage due to similarities to other words in term of pronunciation such as "Saya".

6   Conclusion

In this paper, the developed flexible speech recognition system for CP disabled has been presented. This system is developed based on the ZCR, MFCC and DTW techniques. The ZCR algorithm is used to detect the sound and unsound input signals, while the MFCC algorithm is used to extract the important data from the main part of the input inputs, and finally, the DTW algorithm is used to calculate the distance between the tested input signal and the stored templates inside the database in order to obtain correct recognition. The recognition results show that the system is work properly with high accuracy in range of 78% to 97%.

References

1. World Health Organization Page (2010),
   http://www.who.int/topics/disabilities/en/

2. Menendez-Pidal, X., Polikoff, J.B., Peters, S.M., Leonzio, J.E., Bunnell, H.T.: The Nemours Database of Dysarthric Speech. In: Fourth International Conference on Spoken Language Proceedings (ICSLP 1996), vol. 3, pp. 1962–1965 (1996)
3. Baram, Y., Lenger, R.: Gait Improvement in Patients with Cerebral Palsy by Visual and Auditory Feedback. In: Virtual Rehabilitation International Conference, pp. 146–149 (2009)
4. Pokhariya, H., Kulkarni, P., Kantroo, V., Jindal, T.: Navigo–Accessibility Solutions for Cerebral Palsy Affected. In: Proceedings of the International Conference on Computational Intelligence for Modeling Control and Automation and International Conference on Intelligent Agents Web Technologies and International Commerce (CIMCA 2006), p. 143 (2006)
5. Viloria, N., Bravo, R., Bueno, A., Quiroz, A., Diaz, M., Salazar, A., Robles, M.: Dynamic Electromyography Evaluation of Spastic Hemiplegia using a Linear Discriminator. In: Proceedings of the 25th Annual International Conference of the IEEE Engineering in Medicine and Biology Society, vol. 2, pp. 1866–1869 (2004)
6. Roy, D.M., Panayi, M.: Computer Recognition of Athetoid Cerebral Palsy Movement using Neural Networks. In: Proceedings of the 16th Annual International Conference of the IEEE Engineering in Medicine and Biology Society, Engineering Advances: New Opportunities for Biomedical Engineers, vol. 1, pp. 458–459 (1994)
7. Lopez, J.J.V., Sibenaller, S., Ding, D., Riviere, C.N.: Toward Filtering of Athetoid Motion with Neural Networks. In: 29th Annual International Conference of the IEEE Engineering in Medicine and Biology Society (EMBS 2007), pp. 1434–1436 (2007)
8. Pierce, S., Johnston, T.E., Smith, B.T., Orlin, M., McCarthy, J.J.: Effect of Percutaneous Electrical Stimulation on Ankle Kinematics in Children with Cerebral Palsy. In: Proceedings of the IEEE 28th Annual Northeast Bioengineering Conference, pp. 81–82 (2002)
9. Gold, J.C.: Cerebral Palsy. Enslow Publishers Inc., Berkeley Heights (2001)
10. Shore, J., Burton, D.: Discrete Utterance Speech Recognition without Time Alignment. IEEE Transactions on Information Theory 29(4), 473–491 (1983)
11. Sy, B.K., Horowitz, D.M.: A Statistical Causal Model for the Assessment of Dysarthric Speech and the Utility of Computer-Based Speech Recognition. IEEE Transactions on Biomedical Engineering 40(12), 1282–1298 (1993)
12. Patel, R.: Identifying Information Bearing Prosodic Parameters in Severely Dysarthric Speech. Doctoral Dissertation, University of Toronto, Canada (2000)

Online ICT-Courses Integrated for the Hearing-Impaired Individuals' Education:
A Preliminary Study from the Students' Perception

Rozniza Zaharudin, Norazah Nordin, and Mohd Hanafi Mohd Yasin

Faculty of Education, Universiti Kebangsaan Malaysia, Bangi, Selangor, Malaysia
rozniza.zaharudin@gmail.com, drnmn@ukm.my, mhmy6365@yahoo.com

Abstract. Computers and Internet have become necessities of life, mostly because they provide a gateway into the World Wide Web. The web-growth as a platform for online-learning makes the Web an essential technology; hence the accessibility issues in Web applications are vital, this includes the Hearing-Impaired Individuals. The objective of this research is to investigate the Hearing-Impaired Individuals' level of interests in the various ICT courses, hence to identify the most-demanded chosen ICT course, to offer via E-Learning. The Methodology of this research were designed in such a way where the questionnaires for the students acts as the research instrument involved in this research. A total of 24 schools executing the Hearing-Impaired Education Program from the whole of Malaysia is the research location. This brings a total of 245 Hearing-Impaired Students from Form 4 and Form 5 of the Secondary Level as the research sample. In evaluating the results of the questionnaires, among all the ICT courses, the Computer Graphics course has the majority chosen by the Hearing-Impaired Individuals, mainly for reasons like enhances deaf-creativity in drawing images, web-design, 3D-animation and multimedia purposes.

Keywords: E-Learning, ICT-Education, the Hearing-Impaired Individuals, Computer Courses.

1   Introduction

Computers and Internet have become a necessity of life, mostly because they provide a gateway into the World Wide Web. The web-growth as a platform for online-learning makes the Web an essential technology; hence the accessibility issues in Web applications are vital. In this research, the same goes for the Hearing Impaired Individuals too. The rapid Web evolutions given by legislation on Web accessibility have also motivated educators to include this theme in online Internet courses. It is very important for everyone in society to have the ability and right to use any software, hardware or any assistive technologies to understand and fully interact with the website content, regardless disability, geographical location, language barriers, or other impairing factor [1].

A. Abd Manaf et al. (Eds.): ICIEIS 2011, Part I, CCIS 251, pp. 56–63, 2011.
© Springer-Verlag Berlin Heidelberg 2011

Learning online also known as E-Learning; can be defined as the Learning Education conducted through the computer technology medium [2]. In other words, no face-to-face interaction exists here, since learning by electronic means are held in advance online learning in virtual learning spaces. It is very crucial that these virtual learning environments (VLE), learning management systems (LMS), web-based trainings (WBT) and other e-learning applications and educational technologies to be accessible to all type of individuals, mainly regarding to this study, the Hearing-Impaired Individuals. In this research, this study explored the interests of Hearing-Impaired Students towards the various ICT-Education courses (Information Communication Technology) via online-learning.

2   Background

In Malaysia, the higher education for the Hearing-Impaired Individuals is an important part of development for a country's nation. These higher educations will enable the Hearing-Impaired Individuals to obtain the requisite knowledge and skills for social survival and employment, just as same as the Normal-Hearing Individuals. An individual with disabilities is integrated in as natural an environment as possible, as defined in Education in a fully inclusive model [3]. However, for The Hearing-Impaired Individuals, the disability to detect frequencies or low-amplitude sounds exists, where they could not perceive sound due to their loss in the sense of hearing [4]. When this happens, the hearing loss affects the ability to both receive and produce spoken language, hence it is rather common for a Hearing-Impaired Individual to struggle with spoken and written language, as their understanding of speech acquisitions are poor [5]. Therefore, the language that they used in order to communicate with one another is the Sign Language. Sign Language is the most important social behavior to a Hearing-Impaired human being, and it is the most convenient and efficient communication tool. It is often true that in higher education like universities, numerous faculties support students and staff including interpreters who are fluent in both signing and speech.

ICT Education in Malaysia has increasingly become a popular major in higher education, not only for the normal individuals, but for the disabled individuals too; mainly courses like Computer Graphics, Multimedia, Web-Design and 3D-Animation. Academic Educators teaching computer courses must make efforts to ensure the disable individuals have full access to computer applications and programming tools, moreover with the current trend towards teaching Graphical User Interfaces (GUI). This is of course, taught, learnt and shown with the help of the Sign Language too. The continuous computer technology development has made ICT and educational technology becomes progressively more vital in education. However, although Academic educators play a primary role in the use of online learning environment by students, these students can only utilize those that the educators make available to them, in a specific learning context [6].

The field of Computing Education offers challenging, high-paying careers which are more accessible than other careers. Computing careers are potentially open to individuals with disabilities because of advancements in assistive technology that provide access to computers [7]. Furthermore in Malaysia, ICT has opened up many opportunities for the Hearing-Impaired Individuals, because many jobs were opened through the ICT industry. The goals surrounding the aspects of the Hearing-Impaired Individuals career development, research in this process and professionals training to work with these Individuals; and significant progress towards these goals were achieved [8]. ICT improves productivity, as it increases activity for the Hearing-Impaired Individuals. In other words, ICT too empowers these Hearing-Impaired Individuals. With computer, many career opportunities are open for the Hearing-Impaired Individuals, in areas like Data Entry, Graphics animation, Computer Operations, Computer Programming, Computer Technician, Software testing and development, Web Design Development and IT entrepreneur. There is a broad recognition that innovation in computing requires a diverse workforce of qualified systems designers, computer scientists, information professionals, software developers, information systems analysts, technology teachers, computing faculty, and other computing professionals.

ICT Education is essential for the Hearing-Impaired Individuals. While voice is used in a normal-teaching physical class lecture, sign language is used to teach the Hearing-Impaired Individuals. In some cases, interpreters are available in the classroom too. Supported visual media aids like graphs, charts and tables are frequently used for computer education, as these individuals have to depend more on vision, due to their defect of hearing [9]. Even in operating software, the visual display plan an important role for the Hearing-Impaired Individuals, as only the visual displays can help them understand a task. Computer education does fit for the Hearing-Impaired Individuals, because computers are very much adaptable to them, mainly for reasons like minimal supervision, enhances deaf-creativity, and computers being Deaf-Friendly. Due to their visual concentration, huge majority of the Hearing-Impaired Individuals are highly skilled in drawing and designing, therefore they excel well in fields like Web Design, Visual Arts and Graphics Animation. This perspective is suitable for the Hearing-Impaired Individuals to learn about computer, as it studies how they interact with the learning materials online.

3   Research Methodology

This study is descriptive where it explains the current status of a phenomenon, in other words, it interprets the existing scenario that is being studied. This method emphasized on the current practice that exists in a situation, the criteria in the situation, and the process involved forming the situation.

Based on the descriptive method, this study uses a questionnaire to collect data from a huge number of students, whereby the aim is to explore the current scenarios in a particular school (towards ICT courses), to understand the relationship among the students with the computers usage and most importantly, to explore the level of interest of these students in ICT courses, mainly courses like Computer Graphics, Multimedia, Web-Design, Animation, and 3D. By doing this questionnaire, we seek to achieve the most demanded ICT course by the Hearing-Impaired Individuals, in order to offer the desired course via e-learning.

This study was carried out throughout the whole of Peninsular Malaysia, Sabah and Sarawak. The location background chosen was the secondary schools consisting Hearing Impaired Individuals of Form 4 and Form 5, for the whole of Malaysia, including Sabah and Sarawak. Altogether, there were 24 schools involved being the research location, which consists of 20 schools from the Peninsular of Malaysia, and 4 schools from the East Malaysia; that executes the Hearing-Impaired Education Program. This means that there were 24 schools that became the location of data collection.

3.1   Research Sample, Data Collection and Data Analysis

The research sample of students involve in this study are the Hearing-Impaired Students in Form 4 and Form 5. These students are from the schools all throughout Malaysia, including Sabah and Sarawak, who suffers from Hearing-Impairment. The respondents of this study are divided into two groups of students, which are from schools that offer Computer Classes, and schools that do not offer Computer classes.

For the Data Collection Method, 20 schools were from Peninsular Malaysia, and 4 schools were from East Malaysia, that was involved in the execution of the Hearing-Impaired Education Program. Researcher had started the research from North, including Penang, Kedah, Kelantan, and goes down to Perak, and Kuala Terengganu. Then, researcher started at Central, which are Selangor, Kuala Lumpur, and goes south to Negeri Sembilan, Malacca and Johore. The last destinations were the East Malaysia which are Sabah, and ended with Sarawak schools. All studies were done weekdays, and it took several days for the students to complete the questionnaires. Researcher does not wish to disturb the PnP (Teaching and Learning) in each school, therefore each completed questionnaires are submitted based on the teachers' convenience.

In the process of Data Analysis; the data collection techniques used were the quantitative data; therefore the *Statistical Software package for the Social science module (SPSS)* program were used to obtain answers to the research questions. In this study, the data analysis procedures were analyzed using descriptive statistics, for the respondents' demographics. Each variable are analyzed by the use of means and percentages, which are presented in tables and graphs. In summary, the data of this study were analyzed using the Statistic Package of Social Science (SPSS) version 11. This technique simplifies researcher to code and score the respondents' answers. Overall, questionnaires has prepared several awareness towards the context, counting the answers given, that is later known as data, organize the data and interprets the data into its own context.

3.2   Research Instrument

For this study, the instrument of Questionnaires was conducted. Questionnaires are a popular research instrument among researchers and respondents because it gives information fast and simple. The importance of questionnaires can be appreciated anywhere although the respondents are geographically dispersed. For the used of Data Analysis, this technique simplifies researcher to code and score the respondents' answers. Overall, questionnaires has prepared several awareness towards the context, counting the answers given, that is later known as data, organize the data and interprets the data into its own context.

The researcher had used two techniques for the questionnaires. One was with a fixed scaling response set by the researcher based on the study reading, and two was the open-ended questions, which gives the respondents (students) a wider space to answer the questions freely. This way, the students can justify their opinion appropriately. The aspects of this study were analyzed in accordance with the aspects of the problem stated in this study. All the questions in the questionnaires are simple questions that do not involve many words other than necessary explanation needed.

This questionnaire mainly seeks to explore on the levels of knowledge, use, satisfaction, and most importantly the interests of students (who suffers from hearing-impairment), towards the ICT Education of computer courses, mainly courses like Computer Graphics, Multimedia, Web-Design, Animation, and 3D. Simultaneously it also focused on the existing Computer Education Program that was already exist in some selected schools for the Hearing-Impaired Education Program.

The questionnaire provided consists of 8 parts, (part I): Background information on the students, (part II) General information on Computers, (part III) Level of Interests on Computers, (part IV) Computers Usage, (part V) Computers Equipments, (part VI) Infrastructure/Facilities of Computer Lab/Equipments, (part VII) Levels of Interests on various Computer Courses, and the last (part VIII) is the Opinions/Suggestions.

For the Part I, the demographic respondents must answer the questions related to their demographic data like sex, age, race, form, state, name of school, and favorite subject in school. For Part II until Part VII, the questions are in statements forms, based on the Likert Scaling Scores Values, whereby respondents circle any one number from 1-5 as their choice, in each item given. The statement items presented in the questionnaires are all in positive form, so that it eases the researcher to code and analyze the data. These answers are based on knowledge, feelings, and experiences in the context of Hearing-Impaired Education Program as follows:

> 1 - if respondents strongly disagree
> 2 - if respondents disagree
> 3 - if respondents are not sure
> 4 - if respondents agree
> 5 - if respondents strongly agree

Only at the last part, which is Part VIII, is the open-ended questions whereby respondents can state their own answers freely.

4   Findings

A total of 245 students of Hearing-Impaired Education participated in this study. From that total, 126 are male students (51.4%), while 119 were female students (48.6%). The number of students in this study was from Form 4 which are 126 (51.4%), and Form 5 which are 119 (48.6%) respectively.

For the race category, 145 students (59.2%) were Malay respondents, 57 students (23.3%) were Chinese respondents, 17 students (6.9%) were Indian respondents, and another 26 students (10.6%) were from other ethnic races, like Kadazan, Iban, Bidayuh, Melanau, etc.

For the state category, 38 students (15.5%) were respondents from Johore, 34 students (13.9%) were respondents from Penang, 29 students (11.8%) were respondents from Kuala Lumpur, 24 students (9.8%) were respondents from Sabah, 23 students (9.4%) were respondents from Sarawak, 22 students (9.0%) were respondents from Terengganu, 21 students (8.6%) were respondents from Selangor, also 21 students (8.6%) were respondents from Kedah, 15 students (6.1%) were respondents from Negeri Sembilan, 8 students (3.3%) were respondents from Malacca, 4 students (1.6%) were respondents from Pahang, 3 students (1.2%) were respondents from Perak, 2 students (15.5%) were respondents from Labuan, and only 1 student (0.4%) was a respondent from Kelantan.

Based on the 245 respondents throughout Malaysia who are involved answering this questionnaire, 171 respondents answered Yes (69.8%), and another 74 respondents answered No (30.2%), on the question of learning Computer Graphics course via e-learning. This shows that almost 70% of the students agree on learning computer graphics online, compared to the other 30% who disagrees.

In Table 1 and Table 2 below, for the questionnaires on various ICT computer courses, majority of the questions were answered as 'Strongly Agree and Agree' on courses like 3D Animation, Multimedia, Web-Design, and Computer Graphics, as shown in Table 1; compared to other non-graphic courses like Database Organization, Programming, and Networking, as shown in Table 2. The summary of these differences of Computer Courses chosen can be seen clearly in Table 1 and Table 2:

Table 1. Distribution of various ICT Courses on Graphic-related courses

COURSES / RANKING	Computer Graphics		3D-Animation		Multimedia		Web-Design	
	Freq	%	Freq	%	Freq	%	Freq	%
Strongly Disagree	9	3.7	12	4.9	13	5.3	9	3.7
Disagree	13	13.5	27	11.0	26	10.6	35	14.3
Unsure	52	25.3	39	15.9	86	35.1	71	29.0
Agree	93	33.9	69	28.2	79	32.2	85	34.7
Strongly Agree	78	23.7	98	40.0	41	16.7	45	18.4
Total	245	100.0	245	100.0	245	100.0	245	100.0

Table 2. Distribution of various ICT Courses on Non-Graphic-related courses

COURSES / RANKING	Database Organisation		Programming		Networking	
	Freq	%	Freq	%	Freq	%
Strongly Disagree	26	10.6	22	9.0	13	5.3
Disagree	35	14.3	36	14.7	36	14.7
Unsure	107	43.7	104	42.4	98	40.0
Agree	56	22.9	60	24.5	66	26.9
Strongly Agree	21	8.6	23	9.4	32	13.1
Total	245	100.0	245	100.0	245	100.0

In Table 1, more students had chosen ICT courses like computer graphics (171 students), 3D-animation (167 students), multimedia (120 students) and Web-Design (130 students). This is mainly because courses that contain attractive graphics, multimedia-supported content, and attractive animation and designs catch the attention of the Hearing-Impaired individuals' vision. In contrast shown in Table 2, less students had chosen non-graphical ICT courses such as Database Organization (77 students), Programming (83 students), and Networking (98 students). This is mainly because these courses are in plain black and while graphic-less form, hence it doesn't really attract the vision of the Hearing-Impaired Individuals.

5   Discussion

From the results above, proved that the Hearing-Impaired Individuals are strongly interested in ICT Courses like Computer Graphics, 3D-Animation, Multimedia and Web-Design compared to other ICT courses like Database Organisation, Programming and Networking. Hence, the connection between the results of their interest in chosen ICT-Courses, and the Hearing-Impaired Individuals' vision and interest, clearly motivate an approach of method to develop a medium for them to learn these ICT Courses online. Hence, an E-Learning Portal of ICT-Education is suggested, to help these students learn ICT Courses online.

In specific, for the open-ended questions, when being asked whether the respective schools offer any computer subjects, 66 respondents answered Yes, and the average responses were courses like Adobe Photoshop, Computer Graphics (only for 3 schools), Basic Computer Literature, and Desktop Publishing. While, the remaining respondents answered No. Some of the respondents gave explanation that they are very much interested in learning computer courses, however due to the inadequate equipments, and the time-table, computer courses were not offered for them. This problem do not only affect the students' comfort as the number of interested respondents are many, but even the availability of the classrooms and computer equipments also need to be increased.

To breakdown according to schools, a total of 3 schools do offer Computer Graphics Course in their school, a total of 4 schools offer basic Computer Literature courses, and the remaining 17 schools do not have any computer courses at all offered in their schools. The schools offering Computer Graphics are one in Negeri Sembilan, one in Johore, and another in Terengganu. However when being asked to learn them online, the demands were high to have this course available online (via E-Learning), to help them with tutorials, etc. The schools offering basic Computer Literature are two in Kuala Lumpur, and two in Johore; and when being asked on their interests on Computer Graphics course online (via E-Learning), they were very positively determined to learn them virtually.

Besides learning computer courses online, when being asked the content that should be included in a portal, various answers were given by respondents. Among the answers were to have attractive visual graphics with animation and 3D; information on the Deafs, Bahasa Melayu Hand Code (Kod Tangan Bahasa Melayu), Videos showing Sign Language alongside with captions and subtitles, References/Tips for Final exams, Job Opportunities, Education Institution to Further Studies, Blogging, Chatting System, Download/Upload Files, and a membership profile to sign-up for the students, teachers and parents; and a score record of students' performance.

6   Conclusion

Overall, the results showed that most students had chosen Computer Graphics as their desired choice, online; among all other computer courses stated. Although some of the schools that do not have computer courses offered to them at all, do wish to have these courses taught in their schools. Some do claim that the courses are being taught for the Normal-Hearing students, however not for the hearing-impaired individuals. An equal teaching and learning should exist between the normal students and the hearing-impaired students. This will give opportunities for the hearing-impaired students to enable them master the computer proficiency too; and simultaneously develop each potentials. The computer classes should not be divided unfairly to only for the normal students, and neglecting the hearing-impaired students. This will only affect the confidence and faith of the hearing-impaired students.

From the questionnaires conducted, many opinions were raised individually from the respondents. With regards to the ICT Education, computer courses were infact a demanding major and learning them online was resulted in a positive form.

References

[1] Sierkowski, B.: Achieving Web Accessibility. In: On SIGUCCS 2002: Proceedings of 30th ACM SIGUCCS Conference on User Services, pp. 288–291. ACM Press (2002)

[2] Boettcher, J., Conrad, R.M.: Faculty Guide for Moving Teaching and Learning to the Web. In: League for Innovation in the Community College, Laguna Hills, CA (2004)

[3] Morrison, G.S.: The Early Childhood Education Today. Pearson, NJ (2004)

[4] Vanderheiden, G.C.: Design for people with functional limitations resulting from disability, aging, or circumstance. In: Salvendy, G. (ed.) Handbook of Human Factors and Ergonomics, 2nd edn. Purdue University, John Wiley and Sons, New York (1997)

[5] Mahshie, J.J., Vari-Alquist, D., Waddy-Smith, B., Bernstein, L.E.: Speech Training aids for hearingimpaired individuals: III. Preliminary Observations in the Clinic and Children's Homes, Journal of Rehabilitation Research and Development 25(4), 69–82 (1988)

[6] Bolliger, D.U., Wasilik, O.: Factors influencing faculty satisfaction with online teaching and learning in higher education. Distance Education 30(1), 103–116 (2009)

[7] Burgstahler, S., Ladner, R.: An alliance to increase the participation of individuals with disabilities in computing careers. SIGACCESS Access. Comput. 85, 3–9 (2006)

[8] Beil, D.H., Panko, J.W.: Educational Opportunities For The Deaf in Data Processing at Rochester Institute Of Technology (1997)

[9] Murakami, H., Minagawa, H., Nishioka, T., Shimizu, Y.: Computer education and assistive equipment for hearing impaired people. TCT Education of Disabilities 1(1) (2002)

Kansei Design Model for Engagement in Online Learning: A Proposed Model

Fauziah Redzuan[1,2], Anitawati Mohd. Lokman[1], Zulaiha Ali Othman[2], and Salha Abdullah[2]

[1] Faculty of Computer and Mathematical Sciences, Universiti Teknologi MARA (UiTM), 40450 Shah Alam, Selangor, Malaysia
[2] Faculty of Information Science and Technology, Universiti Kebangsaan Malaysia (UKM), 43600 Bangi, Selangor, Malaysia
fauziahr@tmsk.uitm.edu.my
zao@ftsm.ukm.edu.my

Abstract. Positive user experience is associated with positive emotion which is important to engage students in online learning. Most of the previous studies focused only in one element when studying the user experience for example elements in the interface design only or in the interaction design only. This research proposed a model with the combination of design elements in the interface, content and interaction design to understand the experience specifically the students' engagement with the online learning material. The proposed model of students' engagement is based on the principles of Aptum model and interaction design. As the dimensions in the model is general, therefore to extract the details of the design elements, the Kansei Engineering technique is adopted as it has been proven able to extract the design elements in many areas of studies. This paper described the proposed model and explained the main design elements in interface, content and interaction design dimensions. Discussions on user experience, emotion and engagement in learning, a brief explanation about Kansei Engineering technique and some conclusion about the research are also presented.

Keywords: User Experience, Kansei Engineering, Emotion, Engagement, E-Learning Material, Aptum Model, Online Learning.

1 Introduction

There are some concerning issues for higher levels of learning. For example [1] stated that there is a need to quickly identify and support the at risk students. In addition, [2] stated that there is a need "to study the qualitative nature of online interaction in terms of teaching and learning approaches". [2] also suggested that there is a need to further investigate in order to understand the nature of online learning especially for higher levels of learning. A good online learning system might be helpful to not only of the at risk students but also to other students as a way to enhance their learning capabilities.

A. Abd Manaf et al. (Eds.): ICIEIS 2011, Part I, CCIS 251, pp. 64–78, 2011.
© Springer-Verlag Berlin Heidelberg 2011

How to tailor towards the need of having a good online learning experience especially for higher levels of learning?

User experience is one of the important elements in learning. Reference [3] emphasized that "users' experience of their interaction with computers and interactive systems is becoming increasingly important". In addition, according to Zaharias and Poylymenakou, affective and emotional aspects of interaction are important components in order to understand better the user experience [4]. Furthermore, [5] also stressed on the emotional aspect of the learners and the learning experience they are going through. According to them a good e-learning system "would facilitate an experience with the learner that creates emotional tags, thus enhancing the ability to learn from that experience" [5].   [6] also emphasized that there is not yet any tool to measure emotional experience in the interaction with websites.

References [7] and [8] argued that "user's emotional responses to an interface performance, ways of interaction and content can be modeled, evaluated and supported". Therefore how to measure the user experience or emotional experience especially in learning? Usability metrics alone might not able to accurately measure the user experience [9, 10]. In their study they have demonstrated that the usability metrics of time on task and number of errors alone would not sufficiently measure the overall user experience of the product or interfaces. According to their research emotional responses could also play significant role to measure the user experience as well as to judge the usability of the product or interfaces. This is further supported by [8]   stated that there are more usability issues in human-computer interaction (HCI) and the role of emotions in interaction is "simplified or ignored". In addition [10] stated that there are many researchers stated the importance of emotion in user performance as well as user experience.

[11] also noted that some people stay longer in front of one painting but only in a short while in front of the others even though the two paintings are alike. The question posed is what makes "one experience so compelling and the other barely noticeable" [11]. In the same direction in online learning, what makes one learner engaged in an online learning material and be able to absorb and learn efficiently in the online learning material as compared to the others? What are the elements that contributed to the students' experience and engagement in the online learning material?

Some problems in online learning are related to the online learning material as have been highlighted by previous researchers. Fredskild (2008) (as cited in [12]) highlighted the fact that "some of the e-learning courses are poorly designed with little attention to pedagogical aspect, less user interaction and low quality course material design". In addition, Schaik and Ling also emphasized that poorly designed pages could rapidly turn users away [13].

Furthermore according to [14], currently there is a discrepancy between the designs of e-learning and the learners' need or preferences resulting poor learning among students. This is further supported by [15] that the designers should employed the principles of user or learner centered design. Even though there are many e-learning material which employed multimedia elements as well as interactivity but still this does not meet the expectation of the user (Greitzer, 2002) as cited in [15]. The root might be because of the poor design, organization of the content as well as usability. Accordingly, previous researcher also noted the difficulty to design the online learning interfaces as compared to the design of web pages as stated by Kreijins et al (2002) as cited in [16].

Reference [17] also added some argument to the poor design problem such as "a Web interface that is boring, a multimedia presentation that does not captivate users' attention ....are quickly dismissed with a simple mouse click". O'Brien and Tom also highlighted that it is important to engage users in a web site as failing to do so might lead to information not being transferred. Further they emphasized that in order for technologies to be successful they must not only usable but they should engage users as well.

From previous researches it is evidenced that a good design is important in online learning. Furthermore, a good design might influence the experience of the learners thus promotes engagement of the learners in learning the online material.

This paper is organized in the following order; it starts off with an introduction, followed by some discussions on users' experience, emotion and engagement, then followed by the proposal of the model with some discussions of each of the dimensions, and lastly the conclusion of the research.

2   User Experience, Emotion and Engagement

According to [3] the principle of "what is beautiful is usable" is still not confirmed and they suggested that more research should be conducted relating to the principles and factors behind in other products. Accordingly, these authors also noted that user experience is increasingly known in the HCI field and one important aspects of research in this area is the process where users formed aesthetic and other judgment of the interactive products. To attract the users' attention, the attractiveness of the first page of the web site plays an important role as highlighted by [18]. Within 50 ms the attractiveness of the website will be judged by the users. In addition, [3] also noted that, [19] proposed that by following the "immediate positive judgment" of the first page, users would further make "positive initial deliberate judgment" usually within 10 seconds. However [3] argued on three important things mentioned in previous studies. The studies did not present a context of use, did not include a test of users' use of web sites and did not examine their perceptions after use. The studies carried out by [18] and [19] also linked to a wide range of unrelated domains. The issue is as to whether the statement will be the same if the domains are related.

2.1 User Experience

Reference [20] defined user experience as "the experience the product creates for the people who use it in the real world". He also added that in term of product design most people only think about the "aesthetic appeal" and "functional terms". The aesthetic appeal is "a well-designed product that looks good to the eye and feels good to the touch". Meanwhile the functional terms is "a well designed product that does what it promises to do". He further argued that these elements would "certainly be failures of design". When aiming to design a product for users' experience, Garrett claimed that the designer should be looking beyond the functional or aesthetic terms.

On the other hand [21] argued that user experience compound of three basic elements. The elements are perception of instrumental qualities, perception of non-instrumental qualities and user emotional responses to system behavior. The study also supported the notion of user experience as a compound of emotions and perceptions of instrumental and non-instrumental qualities in the proposed Component of User Experience Model (CUE-Model). The perception of instrumental qualities is related to usability and usefulness of a system. The perception of non-instrumental qualities is related to appeal or attractiveness. The perception of instrumental qualities and perception of non-instrumental qualities might affect the emotional reaction of user, be it happy, sad, surprise or others.

In the same direction, Lokman (2011) also observed that affective qualities are also an important component in user experience which comprises the functional and non-functional qualities. The functional qualities are for example usability, usefulness and accessibility while non-functional qualities are aesthetic, symbolic, motivational and others [22]. In addition, she also stressed on the aspect of affective qualities which comprise of subjective feelings, physiological reaction, cognitive appraisal and behavior tendency from users. The affective qualities include both of the components of functional and non-functional qualities.

In another definition of user experience, [23] stated "the degree of positive or negative emotions that can be experienced by a specific user in a specific context during and after product use and that motivates for further usage". From this definition it is evidenced that user experience also involves the emotions of the users and thus emotions plays important role in user experience. However, in this definition one could argue that, if it is positive emotion experienced by the users then it could motivate the users for further usage of the product or services they experiencing. If it is of a negative emotion, then consequently, it will demotivate the users from further using the product or services.

From these previous studies, it is obvious that user experience has always includes the effect on emotion or affect, visual appealing, and usability. Thus the importance of this study lies on the affect or emotion particularly in this research it is focusing on the emotional experience of the learners in online learning.

2.2 Emotion in Learning

Reference [5] emphasized on the importance of emotion in association with learning or online learning. They stated that:

"Understanding and harnessing the power of emotion can improve an individual's ability to learn.... A passion to learn or a deep passion related to the content of learning embeds strong emotional tags with what is being learned ... When positive emotions create this impact, learning becomes exciting and the memory of what is learned stays with us. Memory is further enhanced when learning includes meaning and understanding of the material." page 210.

According to [24], positive emotion can be associated with positive in learning. Reference [24] emphasized that "positive emotion can pave the way for memory and higher order thought". Recent brain research also indicates that emotions is essential in learning [25]. In order for learning to take place the attention of the learners must be engaged first and emotional responses could "trigger" the learners' attention [25]. In addition, Jensen (1998), as cited in [26] also revealed that "emotions drive attention, meaning and memory and critical to patterning in the brain".

Reference [27] also emphasized that students will not learn very well if they have negative emotions. In addition, they also affirmed that emotion also plays important role to motivate student.

Emotional issues cannot be ignored and should be included in all types of learning and more research is needed in this area [25]. In addition, [28] also highlighted the importance of studying emotions especially in the context of student's engagement and learning.

From previous researches, it can be concluded that emotion plays an important role to attract the attention of the learner as being emphasized by [26] and [25]. When the attention of the learner is captured then engagement will take place and learning will be much easier.

2.3 Engagement in Learning

Reference [29] study in detail the engagement based on four main application areas; in online shopping, educational web-casting, web searching and video games. They also highlighted that "poor web site design and usability maybe useful for predicting potential barriers to engagement" page 941. Furthermore, it would be benefit to further research in order to better understand on how to design for system engagement based on distinct motivations especially in interactive searching, browsing and learning systems [30]. Engagement is defined as "a quality of user experience" which have six factors such as focused attention, perceived usability, endurability, novelty, aesthetics and felt involvement [30].

[31] stated that one could believed that to enhance student's learning experience learner-centered and collaborative activities should be employed rather than lecture-based or instructor-based pedagogy. It was also highlighted that Corno and Mandinach (1983) who were the first to define and examine student cognitive engagement, have proposed that student engagement can be observed when "students' demonstrated prolonged attention to a mentally challenging task, resulting in authentic learning and increased levels of higher order thinking" [31].

Previous studies showed that computers and information technology plays a positive role to support student engagement [32]. Based on previous research, "online learning can stimulate students to use higher order skills such as problem solving, collaboration, and stimulation" but it is still "unclear if the students learn more in online courses" [32]. This therefore, demanded more research on how learning is related to the design of the online learning material to promote engagement and later resulted in positive learning experiences.

On the other hand, [33] stated that there is a recent research in order to understand the effect of emotions towards student engagement and achievement. The research focused on the study of the engagement of students in science based on factors such as positive emotion of enjoyment in combination with other variables such as interest, embedded interest, science knowledge, personal value of science and others. The students' interest in learning science mediated the effect of enjoyment of science on embedded interest ("student's expression of their desire to engage further with topics they had been working on"). Therefore it can be concluded that positive emotion is important to engage the learners.

In addition, while many researches has been conducted in the area of multiuser environment to estimate user attention, less research try to estimates the user attention or engagement in HCI environment [34].

In terms of defining the type of engagement based on previous research, [35] have defined engagement in three ways based on the work of Fredricks, Blumenfeld and Paris (2004) namely the behavioral engagement, emotional engagement and cognitive engagement. Behavioral engagement is based on students' participation which "includes involvement in academic and on task behavior". While emotional engagement relates to "student attitudes, interest and values", the cognitive engagement is more towards "motivational goals and self–regulated learning". It was also highlighted that "positive engagement in learning is therefore a cognitive-affective condition in which students want to learn". Previous researches have demonstrated that students' engagement strongly influenced academic achievement [35]. Other types of engagement as defined by previous researchers are depicted in Table 1 below.

Table 1. The type of engagement discussed by previous researchers

Engagement Type	[35]	[36]	[37]
Behavioral	√	√	√
Psychological (Emotional)	√	√	√
Cognitive	√	√	√
Social-behavioral		√	
Academic			√

There is less research in the emotional engagement and cognitive engagement as it is quite abstract and therefore difficult to measure [37]. In another domain, such as in online consumer experience, [38] defined online engagement as "a cognitive and affective commitment to an active relationship with the brand as personified by the website or other computer-mediated entities designed to communicate brand value". Online engagement "must incorporate the satisfying of instrumental value (utility and relevance) and experiential value (emotional congruence)" [38].

[39] stated that engagement is one of the "indicators of students' motivation". Attractive design according to them plays important role to motivate the student as well adding the multimedia features and game activities. On the other hand [35] stated that engagement is a bigger concept than motivation to learn. They also noted that engagement and motivation might overlap with each other.

While most studies relate engagement to the student physical behavioral, there is less research in understanding the effect of the design of learning material to students' engagement especially in higher education. Therefore, this study tries to argue that a good design of online learning material will have a positive influence on the students' engagement.

3 Proposed Model

In this section, the researchers described the model that is proposed for this research. The aim of the research is to elicit the design elements that are related to emotional engagement in online learning. There are two important questions posed. The first one is what are the dimensions or constructs or design elements that evoke the learners' emotion? Secondly, do the dimensions or constructs or design elements able to engage the learners in online learning environment and stimulate the learning experience?

A few models and theories were evaluated. The theories and model that has been evaluated are the Flow theory by Csikszentmihalyi [40], Engagement theory by Kearsley and Schneiderman [41], OCC (Ortony, Clore & Collins, 1988) model [42, 43, 44], and Aptum model [47]. Based on these theories, it is understood that the engagement is related more towards the user action or behavior, and there are no possible dimensions or construct to identify what makes the elements induced emotion or engagement. On the other hand, even though the OCC model is related to emotion, the importance of the model is on the ability to deduce emotions from action, and not to identify the elements or dimension that evoke the emotions.

After evaluating relevant theories and models, the selected model is based on the principles of Aptum model. Aptum model was being considered as it consists of the elements that are strongly proposed for effective communication and more importantly, it is also associated with emotion. The Aptum model lay out the important elements for an effective communication to take place such as interface, content and others as this paper argues that instructors communicate knowledge to their students via good communication to make sure the student understand the concept behind it. Not only that, Aptum model also identifies emotion as one of the important elements in persuasive communication. Other models and theories do not give any hints to the elements of effective communication.

Aptum model is a general model. In order to get to the specific design elements, the Kansei Engineering (KE) technique is being employed so as to extract the combination of the elements that show the effect on emotional experience in the learning of the material in online environment. KE has been around for 40 years since 1970. The founder of KE is Professor Mitsuo Nagamachi. From previous researches, KE is a proven technique to extract the design elements in many areas such as manufacturing, entertainment and others. The application of KE in education, however, is still at its infancy [12]. In this paper, KE technique would not be explained in detail. For further reading please refer to [45, 46].

Therefore, based on the principles of Aptum model, this paper argues that there is not only one element affecting the positive emotional experience in online learning, but is the combination of many elements that affecting the positive emotional experience in online learning.

Aptum model, according to Hasle (2006), was based on the concepts found in Aristotle's Rhetoric and further developed by Cicero. Even though the Aptum model is for persuasive effect it is however related to emotion. "The idea that a communication is there not just to inform and to achieve a goal but also to create as much pleasure, or joy, as possible is very characteristic of Rhetoric" [47]. Thus, this model also involved emotional value. In addition, according to Garrett (2011), "effective communication is a key factor in the success of your product" when referring to the communication in the web site [20].

There are five elements in the Aptum model. It is the Orator (the speaker or sender), the Scena (the audience or hearer or receiver), the Res (the subject matter or the content), the Verba (the style, choice and deployment or the form of presentation) and the Situatio (the circumstances surrounding the presentation or the context). The model stresses on the importance of the balance among the elements to achieve the apt. The more the balance is, the better the apt.

The strength of Aptum model is also similar to the work by Morville and Rosenfeld's Information Architecture Iceberg [47]. In comparing the model with the architecture, [47] stressed on the importance of the users, content, context and interface which is similar to the Aptum model such as *scena, res, situatio,* and *verba* respectively.

[3] in their study on the role of context (the *Situato*) or define as mode of use, in perceptions of the aesthetics of web pages over time indicated that the following factors are important elements in studying the user perception of web sites, namely context (the mode of use), aesthetic design, and experience of using a product. Among of the three elements, the context is a very critical factor which could influence the user's perceptions and must then be "explicitly addressed" in the study of users' experience [3]. In accordance to this, this research tries to identify whether this is true in the online learning with a specified course.

Even though other researchers have highlighted many different ways to deal with emotions and online learning, to the best of the authors' knowledge, research that combines the elements of balance among interface design, interaction design and content design with KE technique is still lacking. Fig. 1 depicts the proposed model.

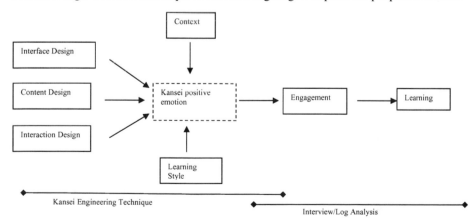

Fig. 1. The proposed model: Kansei Design Model for Engagement in Online Learning (KDM-EOL)

The interaction design is added since the literature has proven it as to be an important element in learning whereby interaction happens between the material and the learner. There are more discussions on the interface, content and interaction design in the following sections.

3.1 Interface Design (The *Verba*)

Reference [11] described aesthetics as "something to do with pleasure and harmony which human beings are capable of experiencing". In addition [11] also highlighted pleasant experience with emotion by stating; "to the extent that aesthetics is a pleasant experience or an experience that leads to pleasure, it implies a relationship to emotion". It is important to include visual appeals that usually demonstrate aesthetic value. The visual appeal for learning material is related to the interface of online learning. Does the visual appeal also important in online learning?

In addition, while emphasis is being put on the importance of the aesthetics of the web page design, [13] stressed that this area still need further investigation especially in the empirical investigation. Citing Hoffman and Krauss (2004), [13] emphasized on the visual impact of a web page which may have a significant role in user experience as well as for effective communications.

In order to understand better the important design elements in the interface, the design elements that are being studied by other researchers is being evaluated. As there is a limited space for discussion therefore the authors only provide the summary of some of the design elements for interface discussed by previous researchers.

In short, most of the interface design elements from past studies are the quality of visual aesthetic, graphic, text, text color, background color, color combination and immersion of the interface, layout, column width, image placement, empty spaces, sound, animation, headings, body text, contrast, background, hyperlinks, banners, navigation, multimedia, toolbars and icons ([48], [49], [50], [51], [52], [53],[13],[16] [54], [55]).

3.2 Content Design (The *Res)*

Kushnir (2004) and Hiltz and Turoff (1985) as cited in [56] gave similar opinion that "overly busy e-learning environments that contain irrelevant information, are over-stimulating, distracting and can "clog up" valuable (cognitive) processing resources" and "when e-learning environments contain unorganized information, students find it difficult to decipher the relevance of information, and thus feel overloaded". This shows the importance of organization of information in online learning environment so as to improve the student learning ability.

Other researchers have also stressed on the importance of content such as Rachel Lovinger as cited in [57] who said: "The main goal of content strategy is to use words and data to create unambiguous content that supports meaningful, interactive, experiences".

Garrett also highlighted the importance of content: "If the sites consists mainly content or information, the main goal is to communicate that information as effectively as possible. It is not enough just to put it out there. It has to be presented in a way that helps people absorb it and understand it" [20]. It was also noted that "Content is the king" on the Web. The most important thing most website can offer is content that users find valuable. Garrett further argued that users usually do not visit websites just because of "the joy of navigation". Instead the content also has important roles to attract the user.

The summary of the content design elements from the past literature includes problem and exercise, animations, story based instruction, interactivity, text based, figures, games, sound based, situated game-based and combinations of different content form such as text only, text and picture, animation only, picture and text and animation, and animation and text, game based learning, real case study, example first and then concept, quiz and exercise with automatic feedback, picture, graph, diagram, animation, video clips, 3D demo, interactive visual tools, visual material in test or exercises, self assessment in exercise, real case analysis, forum newsgroup, easy to difficult material, audio format, outline or summarize materials and take notes using online tools ([58], [59], [60], [14]). In addition, some of the researchers also form different combinations of the elements in order to identify the best combination to understand the content.

3.3 Interaction Design

Reference [61] stated that from previous literature there is little agreement among the researchers between the meaning of "interaction" and "interactive". [61] defined interaction as "a process in which the "actions" executed by learners and their learning environment are mutually dependent on each other". They further emphasized that even though the interactivity involved "overt" action, most of the researchers agreed that it is not the action that cultivate learning but actually the "cognitive process" that resulted from the interactivity.

Bransford et al (1999) as cited in [62] suggested that "Interactivity makes it easy for students to revisit specific parts of the environments to explore them more fully, to test ideas and to receive feedback". They also added that non-interactive environment is less effective for students' learning in terms of the ability to "explore and reexamine" the materials.

The effect of interactivity on students learning still yields different result. According to [62] there is still some who claimed there is the advantages of interactivity, while others claimed mixed results of interactivity. Others also claimed there is some drawbacks of interactivity [61, 62]. Therefore it can be argued that there is still room for more research in this area. Especially in order to recognize which element of interactivity helps in student learning, and which is not.

Other than that Renkl and Atkinson (2007) as cited in [62] commented that "Interactive learning environments are viewed as a promising option not merely for presenting information but for allowing the learner to engage actively in the learning process". According to [62] the meaning of interactivity could be very different from one researcher to another researcher. [63] also stressed the importance of interactivity in online learning experience as from previous researches it is one of the most crucial factors in contributing to the quality and success of online learning.

Williams et al, 1988 as cited in [63] claimed that, interactivity is one of the important factors for successful online learning experiences. There are a few definitions of interactivity highlighted in their study. Based on other researchers' definitions, they also concluded that "interactivity refers to those functions or operations that are available to the users and that enable them to work with content presented in a computer-mediated environment and receive feedback".

According to [63], there are five interaction types in a learner-centered Course Management System (CMS), namely learner-learner interaction, learner-instructor interaction, learner-interface interaction, learner-self interaction, learner-content interaction. For the purpose of this research, the focus would only be on the of learner-content interaction types. Based on the findings, they indicated that the adoption rate of the learner-learner was the highest, and the last one was learner-content type. The result of poor adoption rates in the learner-content interaction might indicate that less learner-content interactive functions were being incorporated in the CMSs.

The summary of the elements of interaction discussed by previous researchers include games-based learning [64]; dialoging, controlling, manipulating, searching, navigating with multiple presentation mode; sequencing, controlling contents and representation format in hypermedia environment; pacing of a video-based model; predicting, reacting to reflection or self explanation prompts in example-based environments, problem solving with intelligent tutorial assistance [61]; links to related educational systems, links to related learning materials, multimedia presentation, push media, online quiz, online exam, study guide, FAQ, online help, content-difficulty detection, individualized learning record, individualized instruction, individualized test/quiz, materials-viewed tracking, note-taking, learner contribution to learning materials, sweeptakes, educational games, jokes [63]; multimedia learning, video, CBI [62].

Other related interaction design elements that have been recently researched on engaging learners or capturing the learners' attention are related to virtual human ([65], [67], [27]), agents and avatar ([66], [69]) and animation and visual cueing [70]. Even though there are many studies conducted using the virtual human, avatar and agent, still there are mixed results on the effectiveness towards students' learning. Some stated positive results [27, 68] and others, despite of some positive outcomes, still reported some drawbacks [65-67, 70]

4 Conclusion

Based on the review of the literature and the review of some related models and theories, a proposed model was developed to promote students' engagement in the online learning through the learning material. The proposed model was based on the principles of Aptum model, which combined the elements of interface, content and context. Additionally, the element of interaction is also added as it is perceived important in the learning environment. In order to extract the design elements, Kansei Engineering technique is adopted, giving the name to the proposed model - Kansei Design Model for Engagement in Online Learning (KDM-EOL). The proposed model is hoped to act as a guideline for the designer to design an emotionally engaged online learning material to help in promoting positive learning experience in order to foster learning.

Future research will be conducted to confirm the proposed model by extracting the design elements using the Kansei Engineering technique, performing some analysis using the log records as well as conducting interview with the students.

References

1. Macfadyen, L.P., Dawson, S.: Mining LMS Data to Develop an 'Early Warning System' for Educators: A Proof of Concept. Computers and Education 54, 588–599 (2010)
2. Garrison, D.R., Cleveland-Innes, M.: Facilitating Cognitive Presence in Online Learning: Interaction Is Not Enough. The American Journal of Distance Education 19, 133–148 (2005)
3. Schaik, P.v., Ling, J.: The Role of Context in Perceptions of the Aesthetics of Web Pages over Time. International Journal of Human - Computer Studies 67, 79–89 (2009)
4. Zaharias, P., Poylymenakou, A.: Developing a Usability Evaluation Method for E-Learning Applications: Beyond Functional Usability. International Journal of Human - Computer Interaction 25, 75–98 (2009)
5. Bennet, A., Bennet, D.: E-Learning as Energetic Learning. VINE: The Journal of Information and Knowledge Management Systems 38, 206–220 (2008)
6. Capota, K., Hout, M.v., Geest, T.v.d.: Measuring the Emotional Impact of Websites: A Study on Combining a Dimensional and Discrete Emotion Approach in Measuring Visual Appeal of University Websites. In: International Conference on Designing Pleasurable Products and Interfaces, pp. 135–147. ACM, Helsinki (2007)
7. Tzvetanova, S.: Emotional Interface Methodology. In: International Association of Societies of Design Research (IASDR 2007). The Hong Kong Polytechnic University (2007)
8. Yung, S.T., Tang, M.-X., Justice, L.: Modelling and Evaluation of Emotional Interfaces. In: Maurtua, I. (ed.) Human-Computer Interaction, pp. 279–296. INTECH (2009)
9. Agarwal, A., Meyer, A.: Beyond Usability: Evaluating Emotional Response as an Integral Part of the User Experience. In: The 27th International Conference on Human Factors in Computing Systems (CHI 2009), pp. 2919–2930. ACM, Boston (2009)
10. Agarwal, A., Prabaker, M.: Building on the Usability Study: Two Explorations on How to Better Understand an Interface. In: Jacko, J.A. (ed.) HCI International 2009. LNCS, vol. 5610, pp. 385–394. Springer, Heidelberg (2009)
11. Lindgaard, G.: Aesthetics, Visual Appeal, Usability and User Satisfaction: What Do the User's Eyes Tell the User's Brain? Australian Journal of Emerging Technologies and Society 5, 1–14 (2007)
12. Sandanayake, T.C., Madurapperuma, A.P.: Conceptual Model for E-Learning Systems Using Kansei Engineering Techniques. In: International Conference on Biometrics and Kansei Engineering, pp. 148–152. IEEE (2009)
13. Schaik, P.v., Ling, J.: Modelling User Experience with Web Sites: Usability, Hedonic Value, Beauty and Goodness. Interacting with Computers 20, 419–432 (2008)
14. Liu, F.: Personalized Learning Using Adapted Content Modality Design for Science Students. In: ECCE Conference, London, UK, pp. 293–296 (2007)
15. Stephenson, J., Morris, W., Tempest, H., Griffin, D., Mileham, A., Payne, A.: The Use of an E-Learning Constructivist Solution in Workplace Learning. In: ECCE Conference, London, UK, pp. 133–138 (2007)
16. Fadel, L.M., Dyson, M.C.: Enhancing Interactivity in an Online Learning Environment. In: Baranauskas, C., Abascal, J., Barbosa, S.D.J. (eds.) INTERACT 2007, Part II. LNCS, vol. 4663, pp. 332–344. Springer, Heidelberg (2007)
17. O'Brien, H.L., Toms, E.G.: What Is User Engagement? A Conceptual Framework for Defining User Engagement with Technology. Journal of the American Society for Information Science and Technology 59, 938–955 (2008)

18. Lindgaard, G., Fernandes, G., Dudek, C., Brown, J.: Attention Web Designers: You Have 50 Milliseconds to Make a Good First Impression! Behaviour & Information Technology 25, 115–126 (2006)
19. Tractinsky, N., Cokhavi, A., Kirschenbaum, M., Sharfi, T.: Evaluating the Consistency of Immediate Aesthetic Perceptions of Web Pages. International Journal of Human - Computer Studies 64, 1071–1083 (2006)
20. Garrett, J.J.: The Elements of User Experience: User-Centered Design for the Web and Beyond. New Riders, Berkeley (2011)
21. Thuring, M., Mahlke, S.: Usability, Aesthetics and Emotions in Human-Technology Interaction. International Journal of Psychology 42, 253–264 (2007)
22. Lokman, A.M.: Kansei/Affective Engineering and Web Design. In: Nagamachi, M. (ed.) Kansei/Affective Engineering, pp. 227–251. CRC Press, Taylor & Francis Group, Boca Raton, Florida (2011)
23. Schulze, K., Kromker, H.: A Framework to Measure User Experience of Interactive Online Products. In: Spink, A.J., Grieco, F., Krips, O.E., Loijens, L.W.S., Nodus, L.P.J.J., Zimmerman, P.H. (eds.) Measuring Behavior, Eindhoven, The Netherlands (2010)
24. Clapper, T.C.: Beyond Knowles: What Those Conducting Simulation Need to Know About Adult Learning Theory. Clinical Simulation in Nursing 6, e7–e14 (2010)
25. Rager, K.B.: I Feel, Therefore I Learn: The Role of Emotion in Self-Directed Learning. New Horizons in Adult Education and Human Resource Development 23, 22–33 (2009)
26. MacFadden, R.J.: Souls on Ice: Incorporating Emotion in Web-Based Education. Journal of Technology in Human Services 23, 79–98 (2005)
27. Wang, C.-Y., Ke, S.-Y., Chuang, H.-C., Tseng, H.-Y., Chen, G.-D.: E-Learning System Design with Humor and Empathy Interaction by Virtual Human to Improve Students' Learning. In: Wong, S.L. (ed.) The 18th International Conference on Computers in Education, Asia-Pacific Society for Computers in Education, Putrajaya, Malaysia, pp. 615–622 (2010)
28. Linnenbrink-Garcia, L., Pekrun, R.: Students' Emotions and Academic Engagement: Introduction to the Special Issue. Contemporary Educational Psychology 36, 1–3 (2011)
29. O'Brien, H.L., Toms, E.G.: The Development and Evaluation of a Survey to Measure User Engagement. Journal of the American Society for Information Science and Technology 61, 50–69 (2010)
30. O'Brien, H.L.: The Influence of Hedonic and Utilitarian Motivations on User Engagement: The Case of Online Shopping Experiences. Interacting with Computers 22, 344–352 (2010)
31. Floyd, K.S., Harrington, S.J., Santiago, J.: The Effect of Engagement and Perceived Course Value on Deep and Surface Learning Strategies. Informing Science: The International Journal of an Emerging Transdiscipline 12, 181–190 (2009)
32. Chen, P.-S.D., Lambert, A.D., Guidry, K.R.: Engaging Online Learners: The Impact of Web-Based Learning Technology on College Student Engagement. Computers & Education 54, 1222–1232 (2010)
33. Ainley, M., Ainley, J.: Student Engagement with Science in Early Adolescence: The Contribution of Enjoyment to Students' Continuing Interest in Learning About Science. Contemporary Educational Psychology 36, 4–12 (2011)
34. Asteriadis, S., Karpouzis, K., Kollias, S.: Feature Extraction and Selection for Inferring User Engagement in an HCI Environment. In: Jacko, J.A. (ed.) HCI International 2009, Part I. LNCS, vol. 5610, pp. 22–29. Springer, Heidelberg (2009)

35. Sharan, S., Tan, I.G.C.: Student Engagement in Learning. In: Organizing Schools for Productive Learning, pp. 41–45. Springer Science + Business Media B. V, Heidelberg (2008)
36. Linnenbrink-Garcia, L., Rogat, T.K., Koskey, K.L.K.: Affect and Engagement During Small Group Instruction. Contemporary Educational Psychology 36, 13–24 (2011)
37. Harris, L.: Secondary Teachers' Conceptions of Student Engagement: Engagement in Learning or in Schooling? Teaching and Teacher Education 27, 376–386 (2011)
38. Mollen, A., Wilson, H.: Engagement, Telepresence and Interactivity in Online Consumer Experience: Reconciling Scholastic and Managerial Perspectives. Journal of Business Research 63, 919–925 (2010)
39. Cocea, M., Weibelzahl, S.: Cross-System Validation of Engagement Prediction from Log Files. In: Duval, E., Klamma, R., Wolpers, M. (eds.) EC-TEL 2007. LNCS, vol. 4753, pp. 14–25. Springer, Heidelberg (2007)
40. Shin, N.: Online Learner's 'Flow' Experience: An Empirical Study. British Journal of Educational Technology 37, 705–720 (2006)
41. Kearsley, G., Shneiderman, B.: Engagement Theory: A Framework for Techology-Based Teaching and Learning, p. 6 (1999)
42. Bartneck, C.: Integrating the OCC Model of Emotions in Embodied Characters. In: Workshop on Virtual Conversational Characters: Applications, Methods and Research Challenges, Melbourne (2002)
43. Steunebrink, B.R., Dastani, M., Meyer, J.-J.C.: The OCC Model Revisited. In: Reichardt, D. (ed.) The 4th Workshop on Emotion and Computing (2009)
44. Jaques, P.A., Vicari, R.M.: A BDI Approach to Infer Student's Emotions in an Intelligent Learning Environment. Computers and Education 49, 360–384 (2007)
45. Nagamachi, M.: Kansei/Affective Engineering and History of Kansei/Affective Engineering in the World. In: Nagamachi, M. (ed.) Kansei/Affective Engineering, pp. 1–12. CRC Press, Taylor & Francis Group, Boca Raton, Florida (2011)
46. Nagamachi, M., Lokman, A.M.: Innovations of Kansei Engineering. CRC Press, Taylor & Francis Group, Boca Raton, Florida (2011)
47. Hasle, P.F.V.: The Persuasive Expansion - Rhetoric, Information Architecture, and Conceptual Structure. In: Schärfe, H., Hitzler, P., Øhrstrøm, P. (eds.) ICCS 2006. LNCS (LNAI), vol. 4068, pp. 2–21. Springer, Heidelberg (2006)
48. Hedberg, J.G., Metros, S.: Engaging Learners through Intuitive Interfaces. In: Hung, D., Khine, M.S. (eds.) Engaged Learning with Emerging Technologies, pp. 107–125. Springer, Netherlands (2006)
49. Park, S., Lim, J.: Promoting Positive Emotion in Multimedia Learning Using Visual Illustrations. Journal of Educational Multimedia and Hypermedia 16, 141–162 (2007)
50. Um, E.R., Song, H., Plass, J.: The Effect of Positive Emotions on Multimedia Learning. In: Montgomerie, C., Seale, J. (eds.) World Conference on Educational Multimedia, Hypermedia and Telecommunications (EDMEDIA) 2007, pp. 4176–4185. AACE, Vancouver (2007)
51. Zufic, J., Kalpic, D.: More Efficient E-Learning through Design: Color of Text and Background. In: World Conference on E-Learning in Corporate, Government, Healthcare and Higher Education, E-LEARN (2009)
52. Cyr, D., Head, M., Larios, H.: Colour Appeal in Website Design within and across Cultures: A Multi-Method Evaluation. International Journal of Human-Computer Studies 68, 1–21 (2010)
53. Karlsson, M.: Expressions, Emotions and Website Design. CoDesign 3, 75–89 (2007)

54. Rivera-Nivar, M., Pomales-Garcia, C.: E-Training: Can Young and Older Users Be Accommodated with the Same Interface? Computers & Education 55, 949–960 (2010)
55. Laborda, J.G.: Interface Architecture for Testing in Foreign Language Education. Procedia Social and Behavioral Sciences 1, 2754–2757 (2009)
56. Kushnir, L.P.: When Knowing More Means Knowing Less: Understanding the Impact of Computer Experience on E-Learning and E-Learning Outcomes. Electronic Journal of e-Learning 7, 289–300 (2009)
57. Halvorson, K.: Content Strategy for the Web. New Riders, Berkeley (2010)
58. Cagiltay, N.E., Aydin, E., Aydin, C.C., Kara, A., Alexandru, M.: Seven Principles of Instructional Content Design for a Remote Laboratory: A Case Study on ERRL. IEEE Transactions on Education (2010)
59. Chen, H.-R., Lin, Y.-S., Huang, S.-Y., Shiau, S.-Y.: Content Design for Situated Game-Based Learning: An Exploration of Chinese Language Poetry Learning. In: International Conference on Computational Intelligence and Software Engineering, pp. 1–4. IEEE (2009)
60. Cinar, M., Torenli, N.: Redesign Online Courses with Student Expectations: A Case Study with a New Infrastructure. Procedia Social and Behavioral Sciences 9, 2013–2016 (2010)
61. Renkl, A., Atkinson, R.K.: Interactive Learning Environments: Contemporary Issues and Trends. An Introduction to the Special Issue. Educational Psychology Review 19, 235–238 (2007)
62. Domagk, S., Schwartz, R.N., Plass, J.L.: Interactivity in Multimedia Learning: An Integrated Model. Computers in Human Behavior 26, 1024–1033 (2010)
63. Chou, C., Peng, H., Chang, C.-Y.: The Technical Framework of Interactive Functions for Course-Management Systems: Students' Perceptions, Uses and Evaluations. Computers & Education 55, 1004–1017 (2010)
64. Connolly, T.M., Stansfield, M., McLellan, E.: Using an Online Games-Based Learning Approach to Teach Database Design Concepts. The Electronic Journal of e-Learning 4, 103–110 (2006)
65. Huang, C.-Y., Wang, C.-Y., Chen, G.-D.: Building a Humorous Virtual Human to Enhance Student's Motivation and Performance in E-Learning Environment. In: Kong, S.C., Ogata, H., Arnseth, H.C., Chan, C.K.K. (eds.) 17th International Conference on Computers in Education, pp. 900–904. Asia-Pacific Society for Computers in Education, Hong Kong (2009)
66. Jaques, P.A., Lehmann, M., Pesty, S.: Evaluating the Affective Tactics of an Emotional Pedagogical Agent. In: The ACM Symposium on Applied Computing, pp. 104–109. ACM, Honolulu (2009)
67. Wang, C.-Y., Chen, G.-D., Liu, C.-C., Liu, B.-J.: Design an Empathic Virtual Human to Encourage and Persuade Learners in E-Learning System. In: ACM International Workshop on Multimedia Technologies for Distance Learning (MTDL), pp. 27–32. ACM, Beijing (2009)
68. Kim, G., Yang, H.-R., Kang, K.-K., Kim, D.: Entertaining Education: User Friendly Cutting Interface for Digital Textbooks. In: Yang, H.S., Malaka, R., Hoshino, J., Han, J.H. (eds.) ICEC 2010. LNCS, vol. 6243, pp. 405–412. Springer, Heidelberg (2010)
69. Baylor, A.L.: The Design of Motivational Agents and Avatars. Education Technology Research Development 59, 291–300 (2011)
70. Lin, L., Atkinson, R.K.: Using Animations and Visual Cueing to Support Learning of Scientific Concepts and Processes. Computers & Education 56, 650–658 (2011)

Integrating Perception into *V-Hajj*: 3D Tawaf Training Simulation Application

Nur Zuraifah Syazrah Othman, Mohd Shafry Mohd Rahim, and Masitah Ghazali

Fakulti Sains Komputer & Sistem Maklumat, Universiti Teknologi Malaysia, UTM Skudai,
81310 Johor, Malaysia
{zuraifah,shafry,masitah}@utm.my

Abstract. To achieve realism in computer graphics traditionally requires increasingly complex algorithms, along with greater computer power and hardware resources. However, the recent growing integration of perception research into computer graphics offers a more economical solution. Psychophysical experiments are now conducted to find out areas that can be manipulated to transform complex computations to "computation cuts". This perception based approach provides better resource consumption to elements that matters most to humans, so the output is still perceived as visually correct. This paper explores the opportunity to apply perceptual concepts in the development of *V-Hajj*; a 3D simulation application for Tawaf (a Hajj ritual) training. Recent findings from related psychophysical experiments are discussed to identify at which prospect perception can be applied in *V-Hajj*. It is ultimately believed that integrating perceptual concepts would help in developing a more efficient and less consumptive real-time rendering techniques that further improve user immersion and interactivity.

Keywords: Perception, Hajj, Virtual Reality, Psychophysical Experiments.

1 Introduction

Achieving realism has always been one of the top goals in computer graphics application development. To achieve this goal, researchers have continued producing increasingly complex algorithm, greatly facilitated by the advances in hardware resources and computer power. However, it has recently come to light that extreme realism might not be worth the excessive resources used due to these sophisticated algorithms. Rather, researchers are now questioning themselves "when is 'real' realistic enough?" and "how do we know when to stop?" and start excluding elements deemed as "unnecessary" [1]. But how can we be sure what is unnecessary? These questions arise as a result of the emerging integration of human perception and computer graphics research.

In computer graphics application development, taking into account human perception is vital because applications are designed for humans to process, to see, to

A. Abd Manaf et al. (Eds.): ICIEIS 2011, Part I, CCIS 251, pp. 79–92, 2011.

feel, and to understand. It is for humans to use, and thus it is practical to study how human see and percept things in their environment. A large part of perception process involves the visual system. It is important for developers to keep in mind that their application is ultimately seen by the human visual system (HVS). In cognitive psychology it is known that when HVS is processing a scene it will be mainly in either *bottom-up* or *top-down* visual attention process. This process determines where the visual attention will be located. The bottom-up process is automatic and driven by stimulus. This means that the human eyes could be attracted to different objects in a scene driven by stimulus like motion, color, shape, or orientation. The top-down process, on the other hand, is somewhat a bit more controlled. This happens when a person process a scene with a task in mind, and the HVS will focus on only those parts of a scene which are necessary for the current task. Often the concentration will lead to perceptual/inattentional blindness [3], where he or she fails to perceive other objects in his surroundings. In conclusion, human visual attention is thus generally directed to 1.) objects that have high saliency or 2.) objects that we are interested in. These two factors can be exploited in computer graphics application to reduce overall computation time without a loss in perceptual quality, as largely investigated in previous research, see [1].

2   Interactive Hajj Training

The Hajj is the fifth pillar of Islam, a pilgrimage to Mecca performed at least once in a lifetime by Muslims around the world. In some countries like Malaysia, training of the hajj pilgrims are conducted yearly, through conventional teaching method of talks and seminars, and walk-through practices using scaled models of the Kaaba (the epicentre structure of the pilgrimage ritual). Unsurprisingly these methods are generally considered dull, laborious and even tedious. Figure 1 shows an example of this conventional training.

Recently there have been initiatives to make hajj training more entertaining and engaging, and certainly much more comprehensive. This is particularly true when users can have direct interaction in an immersive training environment, such offered by a virtual reality environment system. For example, [4] proposed the use of situated learning (SL) via 3D virtual reality environment in which avatar is used to represent the hajj pilgrims. In this paper we proposed *V-Hajj*; a 3D simulation application for Tawaf (Hajj ritual) that aims to offer a much more immersive experience through the use of virtual reality devices. A prototype version of *V-Hajj* (with very basic rendering) has been developed (see Figure 2), which can be attached to a head mounted device (HMD) and a haptic device, that can transport the user straight into the virtual environment itself to interact with the virtual objects and feel sensations of the environment going through their senses. However, for the commercial development of the *V-Hajj* the amount of resources needed to translate the complex Hajj scene into immersive 3D environment can be daunting. Hence this paper

Fig. 1. The conventional method of hajj training, using scaled model of the Kaaba

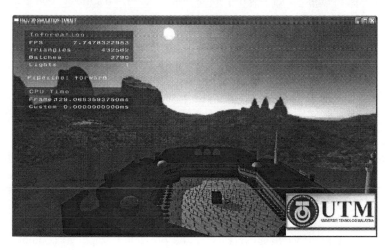

Fig. 2. Rendering the al-Haram Mosque with crowd simulation

investigates the opportunity to rely on perception to see whether it can assists the development towards a more resource efficient system, and to further improve and elevate the hajj candidate experience and acceptance of the 3D virtual reality training of the hajj pilgrimage.

2.1   The Tawaf Ritual

The Hajj comprises several pillars or rituals that must be executed. The focus ritual in this study is the Tawaf ritual, one of the most challenging to represent in 3D virtual environment as it involves many computational aspects. During Tawaf, a hajj pilgrim is to move, in harmony, with millions of other pilgrims circling the Kaaba, which is situated at the center of the al-Haram Mosque. The circling is to be done 7 times, in a counterclockwise direction. A hajj pilgrim begins the circling from the corner of the Kaaba where a black stone named Hajar Aswad is placed, and if possible, touch the stone or kiss it. Often though, this is not possible due to large crowds, so it is acceptable to simply point at the stone at each lap. Also, it is recommended for men to make the first three laps at a hurried pace, followed by four times at a leisurely pace.

From this brief description of the Tawaf ritual, several challenges are already apparent. Modelling the main 3D object, the al-Haram Mosque would require a substantial number of polygons. Nine minarets surround the current structure that covers an area of 356,800 square metres (88.2 acres) including outdoor and indoor praying spaces. At the centre of the mosque, the Kaaba is a square building covered with a black curtain with gold embroidered Qur'anic text, with the Hajar Aswad placed at the eastern corner. Paying attention to the details of the Qur'anic text is essential, while keeping in mind that the texture of the Kaaba is of fabric origin. The mosque can accommodate up to four million worshippers during the Hajj period, one of the largest annual gatherings of people in the world. This means that aside from the environment, it would also require a substantial amount of resources to model such mass of human characters. The circumambulation that includes the touching or the pointing at the stone and the different paces of the Tawaf laps would also require a good crowd collision algorithm and user interaction modality. These challenges are important to be addressed in order to make the Tawaf simulation as realistic as possible.

3   Methodology

Hajj training through this 3D environment setting aim to let users have an immersive and interactive experience through the use of advanced modes of projections and interaction devices. This in turn can enhance the user's understanding and comprehension of what they need to do during the actual pilgrimage. When emphasizing on immersiveness, improving the real-time rendering techniques is essential, including the visual quality of the projected graphical content. Instead of relying on the traditional trend of using sophisticated programmable graphics pipelines, perceptual concepts can help transform complex computations to "computation cuts" that resulted in outputs that are still perceived as visually correct by human observers. The perception-based development of *V-Hajj* is guided with the goal of making it efficient in resource and effective in training. In order to do so, a systematic methodology is needed, and is outlined as below.

3.1   Determining Target Users

The demographics for the Hajj users are enormous, making it a challenging task to carefully analyze the needs of the individual users. For *V-Hajj*, the user age is expected to start from 12 to 60, in which 5 age groups are identified consisting of single teens, single young adults, single working adults, married working adults, and retirees. In addition of each users coming from very vastly different backgrounds, each of these age groups has different needs, commitments and constraints that have to be put into consideration.

3.2   Data Collection

To ensure the validity of this study, a comprehensive collection of data involving the users is required.   Most data regarding the Hajj were acquired from the official organization that conducts the Malaysian hajj training each year. The data includes complete demographics of the pilgrims dating from year 2000. The current targeted users will be interviewed and be given a set of survey questions relating to the need of the Hajj. Targeted users will also test out the prototype system of *V-Hajj* where their initial reaction and feedback will be recorded.

3.3   System Architecture and 3D Modeling

The *V-Hajj* prototype is divided into three main elements: input, main process and output. Haptic devices are used for controlling the movement of camera inside the al-Haram Mosque environment. The main process of the system is 3D model design, loading and rendering by using *horde 3D* game engine. Output of the system is displayed using head-mounted display (HMD). This prototype version will proceed to simulate a mass of human crowd performing the Tawaf ritual with the Kaaba as the epicenter. Using these interactive devices, users will be able to join the crowd, and walk around the Kaaba performing the Tawaf ritual.

3.4   Integrating Perception Concepts - Psychophysical Experiments

Based on the findings from data collection stage, the prototype will be upgraded, guided by the finding from perception experiments. Often referred to as psychophysical experiments, it is formulated on the basis that human behavior is influenced with what they perceive. By studying these behaviors under appropriate conditions; we can deduce how the mechanism of perception works [1]. There are several aspects of a perceptual experiment, with the basics include the following, what gets shown (stimulus generation), who gets to see it (participant selection), how they get to see it (stimulus presentation), what they do with it (task design), and how we analyse the responses (data analysis) [1]. Through these experiments researchers now are able to pinpoint which areas that can be exploited, and in the case of *V-Hajj*, two main areas have been identified, design and interaction. The overall methodology/architecture of the *V-Hajj* system is illustrated in the figure below.

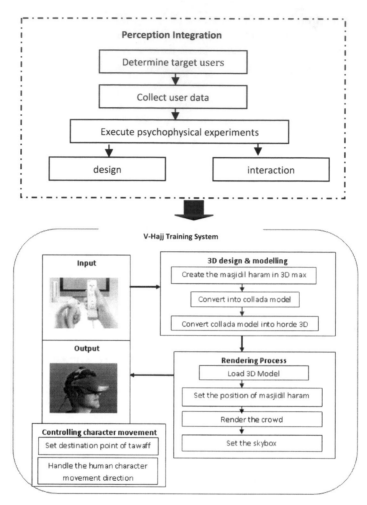

Fig. 3. The architecture of *V-Hajj*

4   Making *V-Hajj* Perceptually Adaptive

This paper will firstly focus on the design aspects where several initial elements important in a Tawaf scene; lighting, texture, image, distance, horizon, human characters, and crowd are identified. Recent findings from psychophysical experiments related to these elements are discussed to observe the suitability and the necessity of integrating the perception findings in *V-Hajj*.

4.1   3D Environment

In a 3D environment, visual cues such as lighting, texture, image, distance and horizon which can enhance the fidelity of a Tawaf scene can be constructed based on the process of perception in the human visual system (HVS). The basic insights from perception experiments suggest that the HVS extracts data deemed as significant while disregarding unnecessary information. This means that we can avoid several complex computations, leading to enormous resource saving solutions.

The first of these visual cues, lighting or illumination, is arguably the life of computer graphics rendering. When applied correctly, it can make a scene come to life, and therefore is essential in the environment scene of a Tawaf ritual. Ideally, illumination algorithms should take into account not only light which comes directly from a light source, but also light rays from the same source that are reflected by other surfaces in the scene. The location for the Tawaf ritual is Mecca, Saudi Arabia, where sunlight is abundant all year round, and summer temperatures can break the 40 degrees mark. This means that if a Tawaf is performed on a sunny afternoon, the light source from the sun not only directly illuminate the al-Haram Mosque, but can be reflected by the building's vastly different angle surfaces. The material of the grand mosque surface, which is marble is also incredibly different from the surface of the Kaaba, which is fabric. This contributes to the complexity in rendering the Tawaf scene, where illumination must be aesthetically consistent with the multiple light sources and material properties.

However, (in)consistencies just might be a factor that can be put to our advantage, as shown in the recent study of [5]. They have explored the ability of human to detect inconsistencies in the illumination of objects in images. Psychophysical experiments of four different tests had been done using synthetic objects and digitally manipulated real images, and determine which variations in the direction vector of the lights will not be noticed by a human observer. Figure 4 shows an example. In conducting the experiments, they analyze several factors involved in the general light detection process, while measuring their degree of influence. The relevant factors include object material, texture frequency, the presence of visual cues, light positions and the level of user training. The result provides quantifiable data which in turn suggest approximate perceptual thresholds. These thresholds can provide valid error limits that can greatly assists in the complexity reduction of illumination algorithm. Additionally, they have shown that threshold seems to be even larger for real-world scenes; richer visual cues (texture, shading, highlights..) in real world scenes might make inconsistencies harder to detect.

Applying this finding in the development of *V-Hajj*, although the environment of the *V-Hajj* scenes is based on real world scenes, it is still undeniably human generated CG scene. Consequently the challenge lies in finding the right balance of generating rich visual cues to prevent the detection of lighting inconsistencies without having to use too much resource as it would defeat the original purpose of integrating perception concepts.

Although illumination helps with the realistic perception of a 3D object, evidence also suggested that a viewer's perception of the 3D shape of a polygonally-defined object can be significantly affected (either masked or enhanced) by the presence of a surface texture pattern. In a Tawaf environment, the al-Haram Mosque is best described as large, spacious but with numerous different structures. The structures include two storey floors, nine surrounding minarets, domes, stone arcades, columns,

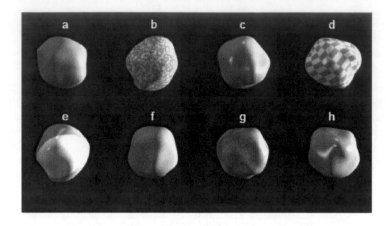

Fig. 4. Example image from one of the experiments; all of the objects are lit from the same angle, except for one, which is lit with a varying degree of divergence with respect to the rest. [5].

and praying halls with intricate designs. The structures contribute to the different shapes and sizes of the mosque, and to create the 3D model of the mosque, one must pay attention that these details are not lost. However, it can be deemed as impossible to ensure that all the objects shapes are perceived as how it should be. The texture element though can help alleviate the task load by manipulating human visual system into thinking that an object's shape is how as it appears to be.

Fig. 5. Example image depicting the complex structures of the al-Haram Mosque

Fig. 6. Sample of close-up images in an experiment examining the effect on shape perception of differently oriented anisotropic texture patterns. The underlying surface shape is identical in all three cases [6].

One such experiment on textures had been done by [6], where they investigated into the specific mechanisms of texture's effect on shape perception and also provide an automatic algorithm for seamlessly synthesizing a sample 2D pattern, into a high resolution fitted surface texture that best facilitate and enhance the shape perception. One important note they have found is that the orientation of how we lay out the texture significantly affect shape perception, Figure 6 shows this example and this knowledge can help in designing and applying the complex Tawaf environment textures that facilitate the accurate and intuitive perception of a surface's 3D shape.

The textures used for the 3D models will usually be extracted from photos or images with the desired pattern. Often the textures will appear tiled, resulting from the repeating patterns applied on the models. In a Tawaf scene for example, the fabric that covers the Kaaba also consists of tiled pattern textures (see Figure 7). There are instances where the image of the pattern texture needs to be stretched or resized to accommodate to the different angles of the 3D models. In a series of psychophysical experiments, [7] have shown that the perception of stretching is a complex phenomenon depending on a myriad of factors including the amount of distortion, the image content, the viewer's cultural background, and the observation time. The researchers have also provide a methodology for creating images that avoid unfair cues to stretching, as they had shown that even small stretches can be detected in some cases. The original goal for this experiment was to determine the threshold for detection of stretching, that is the amount of stretch required to expect a viewer's performance to be better than chance. The study shows that people's perception of image stretch depends on a variety of factors, such as stretch scale, image content, and subjects. The data show that people's sensitivity to image stretch increases with the stretch scale. They also found that people are more sensitive to stretch in images with humans, animals and man-made objects than those with natural scenes. This revelation can have conflicting effect in a 3D Tawaf environment where man-made objects such as the al-Haram Mosque and the Kaaba are the objects likely to use tiled images as textures.

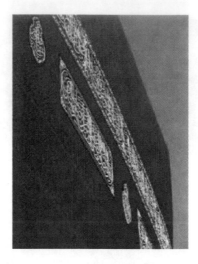

Fig. 7. A close up image of the Kaaba depicting the gold writings and black-colored tiled texture pattern of the fabric

The grand scale of the al-Haram Mosque presents a challenge in representing it in the virtual world. The mosque is recognized as the largest in the world, and to convey this in a virtual world would certainly help in achieving realism. However, many studies also show that virtual worlds still appear to be smaller to the user than they are intended. As a result, a long standing problem with virtual environment application is users often have a hard time estimating the distance between themselves and the virtual objects. It will lead to users walking awkwardly and almost hesitantly in the environment, which greatly hampers the 3D virtual experience. The weight of the head-mounted display (HMD) and the quality of the computer graphics had been suggested as possible causes of this problem [8, 9, and 10].

Recently [11] had conducted a series of psychophysical experiment to further investigate whether distances are also underestimated in a semispherical large screen display immersive virtual environment (LSDI VE). For *V-Hajj*, we would also like to give the users more interaction options to enhance their experience. Hence in addition of using HMD, we are also interested in the possibility of using LSDI VE; and this study provides us the insights of such application and issues arising from it. The experiment was conducted in both the real world using a real room, and the large screen display immersive virtual environment using a 3D model room. Subjects were asked to make egocentric judgments of distances where several important perception factors are noted in this experiment. To make a fair comparison, a real room and a 3D model of that real room were used for the experiment. To make the 3D room more believable, same room dimensions are used and the materials in the scene are as realistic as possible. To give familiar size cues, the content of the real room were also modeled. The textures used in the scene were extracted from photos of the real room. For better real-time performance the objects had textures with repeating patterns. Since, no repeating patterns exist in the real room, the textures were done in a way that the user cannot notice any tiling of the carpet, the ceiling, etc. of the 3D model.

This was done to prevent the participants from using the tiled textures to make relative judgments between the different trials. Figure 8 below illustrate the rooms that were used in the experiment.

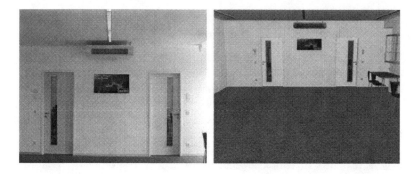

Fig. 8. Left: the real room. Right: 3D model of the room [11].

As response measure, the researchers used both verbal reports and blind walking for the real world condition, and verbal reports only for the VE condition. For verbal reports, subjects have to call out how far from them the targeted object was located, and in blind walking, subjects have to close their eyes and walk to where they thought the targeted object was located. The results showed a significant underestimation of verbal reports of egocentric distances in the large screen display immersive virtual environment, while the distance judgments of the real world were closer to veridical (the actual distance value). Moreover, they observed that in the real world closer distances were slightly underestimated, while further distances were slightly overestimated. In contrast to the real world, in the virtual environment subjects overestimated closer distances and underestimated further distances. The researchers suggested that possible reason for this effect of distances in the virtual environment may be that subjects perceived stereo cues differently when the target was projected on the floor versus on the front of the large screen.

It has also been suggested that horizon is a relating factor to distance estimation. The horizon position and orientation in an environment is an important cue in a scene layout that will help in inferring viewer orientation and scene structure in general. Hence, when users are able to judge the horizon position and orientation accurately, they will have better estimation of distances as well. Through psychophysical experiment [12] had investigated the ability of humans to estimate the position of the horizon in briefly shown images. Contrary to the experiment done by [11] where participants were encouraged to take time in getting familiar with the experiment surroundings (of the real room and the VR room), the participants in this experiment had only milliseconds of image presentation. This is to see how well people can estimate the horizon in an image if they see it very briefly. From the experiment, the researchers have shown that humans can estimate the horizon position given an image presentation of only 150 milliseconds. Also, the images were shown in upright, blurred, inverted, and cropped conditions to investigate the influence of different information types on the perceptual decision. The results found that despite individual variations, horizon estimates were fairly consistent across participants and conformed well to annotated data. In addition, inversion resulted in significant differences in performance, whereas blurring did not yield any different results, highlighting the importance of global, low-frequency information for making judgments about horizon position.

4.2   Human Characters – The Pilgrims

Discussion so far involved experiments relating to rendering a perceptually adaptive Tawaf scene environment; emphasis should also be on the human characters of the Tawaf scene. Up to millions of pilgrims from around the world attend hajj each year. It has been touted as the largest gathering of humans in the world, where arguably in the Tawaf ritual a single hajj pilgrim will encounter the most number of people from different races he has ever met in his life. To achieve a sense of realism in a 3D Tawaf application, human characters from all these different races are best included to portray the actual mix of people in the Tawaf scene. Therefore to create a realistic Tawaf scene, the face characteristics of the human avatars should also be vastly varied. The question is how to create perceptually real human characters? Is there a way where we can create these varied characteristics of faces to promote a sense of realism, but still somehow reduce the complexity of it? Interestingly, psychological research indicates that humans recognize faces of their own race more accurately than faces of other races. It has been found that rather than social prejudice, perception plays a larger part in this phenomenon which begins in early infancy; the amount and quality of experience an infant has with faces of different races will apparently impact the future ability of face recognition [13]. Based on this argument, it is interesting that there is a justified reason to sidestep altogether the need to model vastly different facial characteristics of the pilgrim characters.

The existence of pilgrim characters lead to formation of crowds. Simulating the Tawaf crowd is another highly challenging task. A simulated crowd has to be plausible enough to promote a sense of realism. With the advancement in animation and modelling, the characteristics of human characters in 3D environment are becoming more and more life-like. However, what is always overlooked is that how the crowd forms and moves also has to be perceptually real. In the work done by [14], the researchers noted that to simulate a perceptually real crowd, it has to be generated according to context, and by context, they refer to each individual's relationship with respect to both its environment and neighbours. For example, a pedestrian will usually be seen walking on paths, are often directed towards exit or goal positions when mobile, and do not walk into obstacles or other individuals, while people walking in groups are usually walking close in proximity and may have other properties in common. Hence, to simulate these examples, it has to be appropriate and consistent with common experience. In order to test this, the researchers compare scenes where individuals' positions and orientations have been generated according to contextual rules with those directly derived from real scenes, and those that have been randomly generated. The study aimed to generate formations of pedestrians in a way that is perceptually real to the viewer by considering the context of the scene. Based on their psychophysical experiment, they have found that by applying rules based on the contextual information of the scene, the perceived realism of the crowd formations is improved compared to random formations. The idea can be applied in the creation of the Tawaf virtual crowd. The Tawaf crowd moves in unison circling the Kaaba.

Thus, to create a virtual Tawaf crowd, the formation must be based on the contextual information of this scene.

5   Summary

The motivation of this study stems from the need to upgrade the current training system of the hajj pilgrims in Malaysia. In Malaysia, thousands register for hajj training each year and there has been requests by the organizers to replace the conventional method as interests among the participants to experience a more comprehensive, interactive and immersive system through 3D application increases. However, interpreting a Tawaf scene in a 3D environment can be a daunting task as it involves incredible amount of rendering due to the massive human crowd and complex 3D model structures. It is believed that by making *V-Hajj* perceptually adaptive, we can maximize efficiency in resource while still ensuring the effectiveness in training of the pilgrims.

Reiterating the point mentioned earlier in this paper, the human visual attention is generally directed to 1.) objects that have high saliency or 2.) objects that we are interested in. As the Tawaf is a task-based ritual, whenever a user wants to complete a certain task, his attention will only focus on objects that can help him accomplish the task, causing inattentional blindness. This situation can be exploited by reducing the rendering quality of other objects that is not of interest. For example, a user would be so fixated on completing the tasks required in a Tawaf lap that he probably would not pay attention on the reduced expression details of other pilgrim characters. On the other hand, we can highlight and put more emphasis on objects that is of interest to the user that can help him accomplish the task. This is one of the basic foundations on making the *V-Hajj* perceptually adaptive.

Therefore this paper had presented the initial finding of the review study; investigating what elements are important in a Tawaf 3D scene, finding out how the elements relate to the users and to the system, and based on the findings from recent perception experiments on these elements we had discussed how far perception can help the development of *V-Hajj* to be more resource efficient. Although the literature review done is not yet exhaustive, it has so far assured us the necessity of integrating perception concepts into *V-Hajj*. Subsequently, psychophysical experiments are expected to be done on a large scale on each and every different aspects of a Tawaf ritual and reviews on past psychophysical experiments will continue to be examined and explored in the hopes of devising the most suitable framework/model of a perceptually adaptive 3D Tawaf training simulation.

References

1. Bartz, D., Cunningham, D., Fisher, J., Wallraven, C.: State-of-the-Art of the Role of Perception for Computer Graphics. In: 29th Annual Conference Eurographics, pp. 65–86. Blackwell, Oxford (2008)
2. Ramskov, C.B.: Psychology Notes. Kendall Hunt Publishing (2008)

3. Mack, A., Rock, I.: Inattentional Blindness. MIT Press (1998)
4. Yasin, A.M., Yusoff, F.H., Isa, M.A.M., Zain, N.H.M.: Avatar Implementation in Virtual Reality Environment Using Situated Learning For "Sa'i" (Muslim Hajj Ritual). In: International Conference on Educational and Information Technology (ICEIT 2010), vol. 2, pp. 286–290. IEEE (2010)
5. Moreno, J.L., Sundstedt, V., Sangorrin, F., Gutierrez, D.: Measuring the Perception of Light Inconsistencies. In: APGV 2010 Proceedings of the 7th Symposium on Applied Perception in Graphics and Visualization, pp. 25–32. ACM (2010)
6. Gorla, G., Sapiro, G.: Texture Synthesis for 3D Shape Representation. IEEE Transactions on Visualization and Computer Graphics 9(4) (2003)
7. Niu, Y., Liu, F., Li, X., Bao, H., Gelicher, M.: Detection of Image Stretching Environment. In: APGV 2010 Proceedings of the 7th Symposium on Applied Perception in Graphics and Visualization, pp. 93–100. ACM (2010)
8. Willemsen, P., Gooch, A.A., Thompson, W.B., Creem-Regehr, S.H.: Effects of stereo viewing conditions on distance perception in virtual environments. Presence: Teleoperators & Virtual Environments 17(1), 91–101 (2008)
9. Thompson, B., Willemsen, P., Gooch, A.A., Creem-Regehr, S.H., Loomis, J.M., Beall, A.C.: Does the quality of the computer graphics matter when judging distances in visually immersive environments? Presence: Teleoperators & Virtual Environments 13(5), 560–571 (2004)
10. Kunz, B.R., Wouters, L., Smith, D., Thompson, W.B., Creem-Regehr, S.H.: Revisiting the effect of quality of graphics on distance judgments in virtual environments: A comparison of verbal reports and blind walking. Attention, Perception, & Psychophysics 71(6), 1284–1293 (2009)
11. Alexandrova, I.V., Teneva, P.T., De la Rosa, S., Kloos, U., Bulthoff, H.H., Mohler, B.J.: Egocentric Distance Judgements in a Large Screen Display Immersive Virtual Environment. In: APGV 2010 Proceedings of the 7th Symposium on Applied Perception in Graphics and Visualization, pp. 57–60. ACM (2010)
12. Herdtweck, C., Wallraven, C.: Horizon Estimation: perceptual and computational experiments. In: APGV 2010 Proceedings of the 7th Symposium on Applied Perception in Graphics and Visualization, pp. 49–56. ACM (2010)
13. Kelly, D.J., Quinn, P.C., Slater, A., Lee, K., Ge, L., Pascalis, O.: The other-race effect develops during infancy: Evidence of perceptual narrowing. Psychological Science 18(12), 1084–1089 (2007)
14. Ennis, C., Peters, C., O'Sullivan, C.: Perceptual Effects of Scene and Viewpoint for Virtual Pedestrian Crowds. ACM Transactions on Applied Perception 8(2), Article No.:10 (2011)

Possibilities of Modelling Web-Based Education Using IF-THEN Rules and Fuzzy Petri Nets in LMS

Zoltán Balogh and Milan Turčáni

Department of Informatics, Faculty of Natural Sciences,
Constantine the Philosopher University in Nitra
Tr. A. Hlinku 1,
949 74 Nitra, Slovakia
{zbalogh,mturcani}@ukf.sk

Abstract. Basic requirements, which are imposed on LMS (Learning Management System) from the point of view of the needs of a teacher, are to present the contents of instruction, manage the instruction, communicate with students, motivate them to study, observe their progress and evaluate them. The article deals with an opportunity to implement fuzzy logic into web-based education using the created IF-THEN rules and modelling in Petri nets. By an application of fuzzy logic into Petri nets there arises a strong tool for modelling teaching processes, mainly thanks to the easy understandability and sophisticated mathematical setup, supporting a rather simple design of educational activities managed by LMS, for the compendious modularity of solution and robustness of the design.

Keywords: Learning Management System (LMS), Fuzzy logic, Petri nets, IF-THEN rules, Model, Web Based Education, E-learning.

1   Introduction

Static structure of information on the web, the task of which is to provide information, has long been overcome. More and more web software systems, which are more complex than ever before, originate. From the point of view of application of these systems, there is a more and more frequent necessity to enrich the information space of heterogenous sources, managed by the mentioned systems, with elements of adaptation to the user and/or the environment, in which the user operates. The aim is to present the user personalized information, if possible only such that are relevant for the user, and in such a way, which suits the given user most [1].

Education was always the most popular application area for adaptive hypermedia systems. A number of interesting methods and techniques of adaptive hypermedia were originally developed for in various adaptive educational hypermedia systems. In turn, most of the early research on adaptive educational hypermedia were inspired by the area of intelligent tutoring systems [2],[3] and were born in a trial to combine an intelligent tutoring system (ITS) and educational hypermedia.

With the rapid advance of the Internet, e-learning systems have become more and more popular [4],[5]. An e-learning system provides the following functions: (1)

A. Abd Manaf et al. (Eds.): ICIEIS 2011, Part I, CCIS 251, pp. 93–106, 2011.

delivery of learning content for students via the Internet; (2) record of learning progress and portfolio; (3) management of learning content, assessment and course; and so on [6].

The Internet and related web technologies do offer great solutions for presenting, publishing and sharing learning content and information, as is the case in many other areas. Special software called Learning Management System (LMS) (Fig.1.) is generally used in most institutions providing web-based learning [7]. The most of universities combine form of learning using one of a number of commercial or free LMS. They decided to use products such as Claroline, Fle3, ILIAS, MS Class Server, WebCT, Eden, Enterprise Knowledge Platform, LearningSpace, eAmos, eDoceo, Uniforms, uLern, Aspen, Oracle iLearnin, NETOPIL School and Moodle [8].

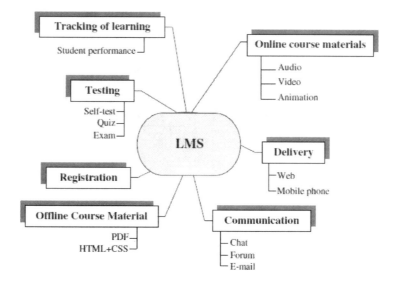

Fig. 1. Structure of the Learning Management System (LMS) [7]

Now that the Internet is recognized as the main platform for education, web-based applications are preferred when it comes to educational activities, channels for communications and systems to access knowledge. LMS are often viewed as the starting point of any web-based learning program [9]. Many pedagogues were introducing their models of electronic education in the early 20th century, but they had no sufficient tools to their effective implementation at that time [10]. Nowadays electronic learning systems provide possibility to save all information about student's activities in one place. Teacher could monitor student's activities after his login into system. Systems offer submitting the file, testing manage the communication and cooperation too. LMSs facilitates teacher to keep his methodical portfolio dynamic and offer electronic students´ portfolio in every moment [11]. An LMS provides the platform for the web-based learning environment.

Because of the huge number of e-learning systems, and the availability of a large number of LMSs, one needs a systematic way, or a tool to evaluate the quality, efficiency, and the performance of LMSs and make a choice that will satisfy most or all of the requirements [12]. LMS systems usually have large number of features and it becomes a tedious task to make a manual selection. One possibility is to automate this evaluation process using computer aided techniques [7].

The target function of LMS managing the instruction is the direction of communication as to the student´s knowledge and abilities, thus changing the amount and demandingness of the materials submitted to the student. In the theory of management there is an obvious transition from combination procedures to sequence chains and optimized processes (the strategy of continuous assessment of the student instruction reflection, and based on that, adaptation of the following instruction, is comparable with the dual principle of identification and adaptive management). For the description of the communication of a man with a computer it is suitable to use graphic tools [13], allowing for suitably describing and expressing the interaction. The teaching interaction between a student and an information system managing the instruction is a complex process, for which Petri nets should be applied. Another attitude to the description of true and real teaching procedures is an application of fuzzy modelling [14]. Most frequently, the personalization of e-learning courses is realized based on extracted knowledge of usage data by means of the web log mining techniques [15], [16], [17], however, we focus on the personalization using fuzzy Petri nets.

2   Modelling Teaching Processes in Fuzzy Petri Nets

For the description of the behaviour of teaching processes the so called serial machines, which, however, have several limitations, e.g. in the number of statuses when modelling complex processes, are suitably used. That is why Petri nets are used for the given purposes, which have originated just on the ground of expanding modelling possibilities of serial machines.

One of the advantages of modelling teaching processes using Petri nets is their formal description, which is complemented by visual graphic depiction. This allows for a precise and exact specification of the teaching process being designed and removal of ambiguity, vagueness and contradiction upon designing. Besides the visual graphic manifestation, Petri nets have also square defined mathematical bases, which can be suitably used in various software tools for the specification and analysis of computer-solved teaching processes [18], [19].

Fuzzy logic allows for using vague requirements either directly, or can simply represent them [20].

Incorporating the fuzzy logic into the classical Petri nets can be realized in this way: We draw from the definition of the fuzzy logic Petri nets.

$FLPN = (P,T,F,M_0,D,h,a,\theta,l)$ where

$P = \{p_1, ..., p_n\}$ is the finite set of places,

$T = \{t_1, ..., t_m\}$ is the finite set of transitions,

$F \subseteq (P \times T) \cup (T \times P)$ is the flow relation, where

$\forall t \in T \; \exists p,q \in P : (p,t) \vee (t,q) \in F$,

$M_0: P \rightarrow \{0,1\}$ is the initial marking,

D is the finite set of statements – $P \cap D = T \cap D = \varnothing, |P| = |D|$,

h: $P \to D$ is the associated function, representing the bijection from the place to the statement,

a: $P \to [0,1]$ is the associated function representing the value in the place out of the set of real numbers 0 through 1,

$\theta, l: T \to [0,1]$ is the associated function representing the transition through the value out of the set 0 through 1.

For $\forall p \in P$, the following marking applies:

$M'(p) = M(p) + 1$, if $p \in t^{\bullet} - {}^{\bullet}t$;

$M'(p) = M(p) - 1$, if $p \in {}^{\bullet}t - t^{\bullet}$;

$M'(p) = M(p)$, otherwise,

$\alpha(p) = \lambda_i \alpha(p')$ if $\alpha_i \geq \theta_i \wedge p \in t^{\bullet} \wedge p' \in {}^{\bullet}t$.

For $t \in T^{AND}$ $\alpha(p) = \lambda_i \min_{\forall p' \in {}^{\bullet}t} \alpha(p')$ applies, if $\min_{\forall p' \in {}^{\bullet}t}\{\alpha(p')\} \geq \theta_i \wedge p \in t^{\bullet}$

and for $t \in T^{OR}$ $\alpha(p) = \lambda_i \max_{\forall p' \in {}^{\bullet}t} \alpha(p')$ applies, if $\max_{\forall p' \in {}^{\bullet}t}\{\alpha(p')\} \geq \theta_i \wedge p \in t^{\bullet}$.

Now, let us express, by means of Petri nets, the rules of the IF-THEN type and their transformation into the fuzzy logic:

The rule IF P1 THEN P2 will be expressed as

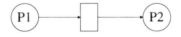

and in the fuzzy logic $\alpha_2 = \lambda_i \alpha_1$ if $\alpha_1 \geq \theta_i$.
The rule IF P1 AND P2 THEN P3 will be expressed as

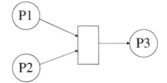

and in the fuzzy logic $\alpha_3 = \lambda_i \min_{\alpha_i \geq \theta_{i,AND}} \{\alpha_1 \alpha_2\}$ for i=1 $\wedge$ 2.

The rule IF P1 OR P2 THEN P3 will be expressed using inhibition edges as

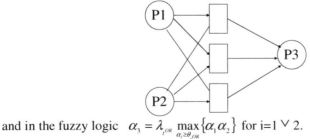

and in the fuzzy logic $\alpha_3 = \lambda_{i OR} \max_{\alpha_i \geq \theta_{i OR}} \{\alpha_1 \alpha_2\}$ for i=1 $\vee$ 2.

The rule IF P1 XOR P2 THEN P3 will be expressed using inhibition edges as

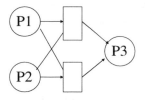

and in the fuzzy logic $\alpha_3 = \lambda_{t\,XOR}\,\alpha_1$ if $\alpha_1 \geq \theta_{t\,XOR} \wedge \alpha_2 = 0$,

$\alpha_3 = \lambda_{t\,XOR}\,\alpha_2$ if $\alpha_2 \geq \theta_{t\,XOR} \wedge \alpha_1 = 0$.

Such definition of FPN comes out of the definitions of the transfer of the classical logic into the fuzzy logic.

In the following table the survey of basic functions will be described.

Table 1. An outline of basic functions of logical rules of Petri nets [21]

No.	Rules	Logical Petri Nets	Fuzzy Computing
1.	IF d_1 THEN d_2	P1 —t— P2	$\alpha_2 = \lambda_t \alpha_1$ if $\alpha_1 \geq \theta_t$
2.	IF d_1 AND d_2 THEN d_3	P1, P2, t^{AND} — P3	$\alpha_3 = \lambda_{t\,OR} \min_{\substack{\alpha_i \succ \theta_{t\,OR} \\ i=1 \wedge 2}}\{\alpha_1, \alpha_2\}$
3.	IF d_1 OR d_2 THEN d_3	P1, P2, t^{OR} — P3	$\alpha_3 = \lambda_{t\,OR} \max_{\substack{\alpha_i \succ \theta_{t\,OR} \\ i=1 \vee 2}}\{\alpha_1, \alpha_2\}$
4.	IF d_1 XOR d_2 THEN d_3	P1, P2, t^{XOR} — P3	$\alpha_3 = \begin{cases} \lambda_{t\,XOR}\,\alpha_1\,if\,\alpha_1 \geq \theta_{t\,XOR} \\ \wedge\,\alpha_2 = 0 \\ \lambda_{t\,XOR}\,\alpha_2\,if\,\alpha_2 \geq \theta_{t\,XOR} \\ \wedge\,\alpha_1 = 0 \end{cases}$

3   Model of Adaptation of Teaching Using IF - THEN Rules

For the specification of a concrete model of adaptation of teaching we have to define model inputs first. Let us assume that we are able to name these input information:

Motivation to teaching

Motivation to teaching is defined by the answers to four basic questions: if I want to teach and how much I care, if I show interest in teaching, if I like the way I am successful.

motivation = {low, average, high}

Concentration

Concentration means focusing on the contents and not taking a note of external or internal perturbing influences, which reduce efficiency of teaching/learning. Among the internal influences belong visualization and thoughts, or recollections of what does not belong to the given object. Among the outer negative influences belong for example noise, music or speech, overheating or cold, etc.

concentration = {low, average, high}

Memory

Memory is a capability to receive, process, store and find where necessary various contents in the memory.

memory = {very good, good, average, poor}

Time of learning

It is necessary to find suitable time for studying. There exist people, who prefer early morning hours, while others belong among „night students"- owls. The time of studying should correspond to the biorhythms of human organism.

Time of learning = {improper, proper}

Length of learning

The length of learning depends on age, experience and habits. In the course of learning there are periods of attenuation caused by fatigue. It is inevitable to arrange short breaks (5 minutes) for the recovery of attention and concentration.

Length of learning = {very short, adequate, very long}

Time

The overall time spent by studying.

time = {very short, short, adequate, long, very long}

Access/entry

The number of accesses of the student to the educational activity (e-course).

Access/entry = {low, average, high}
Number of entries = {low, average, high}

Environment

Learning process is influenced by the environment – light, size and colour of the bench, shape and firmness of the chair, room temperature, ventilation, surroundings of the work table.

Educational environment
- external – surroundings (of the school, family, workplace) with economical, social and cultural, demographic, ethnical characteristics,
- internal
  - physical – ergonomic parameters (lighting, spatial arrangement, application of colours, furniture structure, etc.),
  - psycho-social
    - static – more permanent relationships among the participants of the educational process (among parents and children, teachers and pupils) – teaching atmosphere
    - changeable – short-term influences having an impact on the contents and character of communication among the participants of educational processes

environment = { very bad, bad, good, very good}

Way of living
Proper way of living can be defined as regular sleep, proper nutrition and physical and mental hygiene.
Way of living = { very good, good, wrong}

Studying the text – effective reading
The process of reading includes deliberate bearing on the text to be decoded, transfer of graphic codes into the brain, their decoding, arrangement into words, storing in a short-term memory, assigning the meaning and allocating it within the relationships, including deeper comprehension or forecasting.

From the point of view of an average reader we can differentiate roughly five types of speed [22]:
- easy reading – 250 words/min, e.g. unpretentious middle article, simple newspaper article, advertising,
- normal reading – 180 words/min, long newspaper articles, business correspondence, majority of working papers,
- thorough reading – 135 words/min, texts from less known scientific branches or topics, we are not acquainted with,
- difficult reading – 75 words/min, texts from data, numbers, formulas, technical text, foreign-language texts,
- extraordinary reading – texts with formulas, difficult foreign texts
  reading = { simple, normal, thorough, difficult, extraordinary}

Teaching materials - theory
Theory – amount of theory contained in the e-learning course.
theory = { very little, little, adequately, much, very much}

Teaching materials - examples
Examples – amount of specimen and examples contained in the e-learning course.
    examples = {very few, few, adequately, many, great many}

If we were able to define also other inputs, we would certainly improve the adaptation process quality. Other inputs include:

Intelligence
Intelligent people have retentive memory, which is, however, very often only selective one (i.e. the ability to remember only some area). Besides that, they use a better style of learning and acquire new knowledge much faster than people of lower rational level. There exist several types of intelligence. The speed of acquisition of the knowledge from the given area studied depends on the type of intelligence.

Emotional intelligence
Emotional intelligence includes the ability to perceive one´s own emotions, to allow for manipulating with these emotions, to use them in favour of a certain thing, to be able to find motivation, or the ability to empathize (empathy).
    Emotional intelligence is defined as part of social intelligence, which includes the ability to follow one´s or outside emotions and feelings, to differentiate them and use these pieces of information in one´s own thinking and behaviour.

Specific learning disorders
Specific disorders of learning are often light brain dysfunction (LMD). It is often related to children with almost average, average or above average general intelligence with certain disorders or behavioural disturbances, which are connected with deviations of the CNS system.
The following rating represents the output of adaptation:
    Knowledge – it is an ability to recollect or remember facts
    knowledge = {perfect, very good, good, poor, very poor}

    Comprehension – it is an ability to comprehend and interpreted the acquired information.
    comprehension = {perfect, very good, good, poor, very poor}

    Applicability – it is an ability to use the acquired material in new situations, i.e. to implement thoughts and principles into the problem being solved.
    applicability = {perfect, very good, good, poor, very poor}

3.1   Definition of the Model of Adaptation

Inputs
    environs = {very bad, bad, good, very good}
    motivation = {low, average, high}
    memory = {very good, good, average, bad}

concentration = {low, average, high}
regime = {very good, good, bad}
time of teaching = {improper, suitable}
length of learning = {very short, adequate, very long}
time = {very short, short, average, long, very long}
reading = {easy, normal, thorough, difficult, extraordinary}
attitude = {low, average, high}
theory = {very little, little, average, a lot of, very much}
examples = {very few, few, average, a lot of, very many}

Outputs
knowledge = {excellent, very good, good, poor, very poor}
understanding = {excellent, very good, good, poor, very poor}
application = {excellent, very good, good, poor, very poor}

Rules
IF (environs = very bad AND concentration = low) THEN knowledge = very poor
IF (motivation = low AND time of teaching = improper) THEN understanding = very poor
IF (memory = bad AND regime = bad) THEN application = very poor
IF (environs = bad AND length of learning = very long) THEN knowledge = poor
IF (environs = good AND reading = extraordinary AND attitude = low) THEN knowledge = poor
IF (motivation = average AND time = very short) THEN understanding = poor
IF (memory = average AND theory = very little) THEN application = very poor
IF (concentration = average AND examples = very few AND) THEN comprehension = bad
IF (regime = good AND time of learning = suitable AND reading = extraordinary) THEN understanding = bad
IF (time of teaching = suitable AND reading = thorough AND theory = very much) THEN knowledge = good
IF (memory = very good AND length of learning = adequate AND examples = very few) THEN understanding = poor
IF (reading = difficult AND theory= a lot of AND attitude = average) THEN knowledge = poor
IF (regime = very good AND time of teaching = suitable AND examples = few) THEN understanding = poor
IF (memory = bad AND time of teaching = improper AND attitude = low) THEN application = very poor
IF (memory = good AND length of learning = adequate AND theory = adequate) THEN knowledge = good
IF (reading = normal AND time = average AND examples = adequate) THEN understanding = good
IF (environs = very good AND theory = adequate AND examples = adequate) THEN application = good

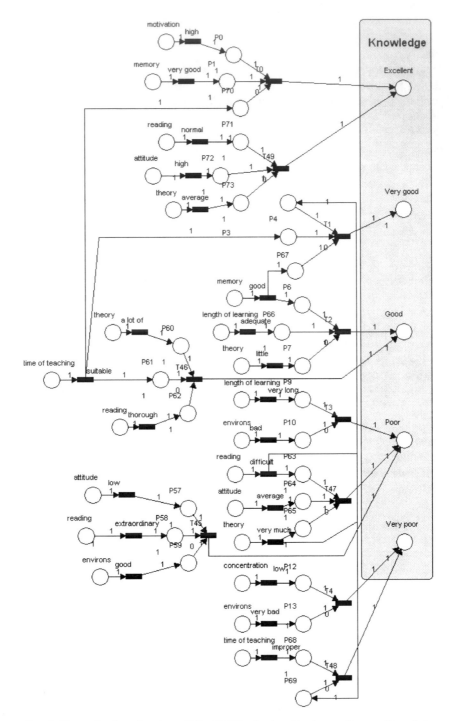

Fig. 2. Example of application of IF - THEN rules into Petri nets. Output: Knowledge.

IF (time of teaching = suitable AND memory = good AND theory = adequate) THEN knowledge = very good

IF (memory = very good AND reading = easy AND examples = adequate) THEN understanding = very good

IF (motivation = high AND time = long AND examples = many) THEN application = very good

IF (time of teaching = very short AND reading = difficult) THEN knowledge = very poor

IF (time = short AND attitude = high) THEN application = very poor

IF (time = very long AND reading = difficult AND examples = few) THEN understanding = poor

IF (concentration = high AND examples = a lot of AND time of teaching = suitable) THEN understanding = excellent

IF (environs = very good AND memory = very good AND theory = adequate) THEN understanding = excellent

IF (motivation = high AND memory = very good AND time of teaching = suitable) THEN knowledge = excellent

IF (reading = thorough AND attitude = adequate AND theory = adequate) THEN knowledge = excellent

IF (concentration = high AND time of teaching = suitable AND examples = a lot of) THEN application = excellent

IF (reading = normal AND regimen = fair AND concentration = high) THEN application = excellent

3.2   Application of IF - THEN Rules Using Petri Nets

By an application of IF - THEN rules into Petri nets there originates a strong tool for modelling teaching processes, and mainly for their easy comprehensibility and sophisticated mathematical setup, a rather simple design, for the comprendious modularity of solution (it is possible to add or remove individual modules without any necessity to fully rework the whole system) and for the robustness of the design (the system need not be modified in case of a change in parameters of solution of the task within a certain environment). In fig. 2 we can see the draft of the model of adaptation of teaching process created by means of Petri nets for one of the outputs – knowledge.

4   Discussion

If we want to describe all teaching processes in details, it would lead to an enormous number of detailed information, which nobody could be able to read. If so, then a natural language would be needed in order to understand the essence of what is described in them; however, it will result in an inaccurate characteristics. If it be to the contrary, it would inescapably be lost in exact details, since human psychic has only limited possibilities. It turns out that accuracy is only an illusion, since, on principle, it is unreachable. All these facts stand in the background of considerations of the founders of fuzzy logic [23]. Nevertheless, fuzzy logic arises from the theory of fuzzy aggregates and is focused on vagueness, which it mathematically describes. In this context, fuzzy aggregate is a set, which, besides a full or null membership, allows also for a partial membership. The function, which assigns the degree of adherence to each element of the universe, is called adherence function. Fuzzy theory tries to cover reality in its inaccurateness and vagueness, and during its almost 40-year-long existence it has earned a good reputation in terms of solving several technical problems, which could not have been handled in the practice by means of other means. It is possible to gradually assign each element the so-called degree of adherence, which expresses the rate of adherence of the given element to the fuzzy aggregate. In classical determination, in this case, it is rather difficult to define the limit of what is still allowed and what is already not allowed. It can be done by allocation of a number from the <0,1> interval, which expresses the measure of our confidence. The task of the fuzzy theory is to catch the vaguely specified requirements in the query and adequately calculate the degree of adherence to it.

Let us solve the following task: to create an educational activity using the know LMS and use for the draft the above mentioned modelling setup, which will allow us to realize the personalization of education using Web Based systems. What and how do we intend to model using Petri nets? A student, who will require study materials necessary for learning a certain sphere, enters the teaching process managed by a suitable LMS. The entering student will enter input information according to the requirements of LMS on his knowledge, time for learning, etc. – it is not possible to exactly define whether he has/or has not any knowledge and how much time he should devote to learning. The following input information will arise: I have little knowledge, I have sound knowledge, I am busy, I have a lot of time, etc. Based on this input information LMS defines the process of learning of the student. For a faster definition of the learning process we can use a Petri net prepared in advance, which will describe individual statuses, which could occur in the student. We shall implement certain IF – THEN rules, according to which the net will be built. E.g.: IF he has little knowledge AND much time THEN all chapters of the study material will be used. Having setup this net we have to define in a certain way importance of individual transitions from one status into another. This significance will be set in Petri nets using the value from Fuzzy aggregate (0,1) upon transitions.

At the moment we set up such Fuzzy Petri net, we enter tokens into initial statuses, which will take the values of the Fuzzy aggregate (0,1) again. These tokens will define with their values just the sound, small, medium knowledge, etc. After the simulation of the Fuzzy Petri net using the rules to be written out, LMS will receive the learning procedure. Before we start to enter the initial tokens, it is suitable to define terminology of input data and assign the particular values. For example: small = 0.3, a little = 0.4, much = 0.8 etc.

By the application of fuzzy logic into Petri nets originates a strong tool for the modelling of educational processes, mainly thanks to:

- understandability and sophisticated mathematical mechanism,
- rather simple design,
- modularity of solution,
- it is possible to ad and remove individual module without the necessary complete re-working of the whole system.

5   Conclusion

A common feature of various adaptive Web systems is the application of user models (also known as profiles) to adapt the systems' behaviour to individual users. User models represent the information about users that is essential to support the adaptation functionality of the systems. Adaptive Web systems have investigated a range of approaches to user modelling, exploring how to organize the storage for user information, how to populate it with user data, and how to maintain the current state of the user. The majority of modern adaptive Web systems use feature-based approach to represent and model information about the users. The competing stereotype-based approach, once popular in the pre-Web area of adaptive interfaces, has lost dominance but is still applied, especially in combination with the feature-based approaches [24].

One of the main advantages of using a formal method for student modelling is its robustness. Once this model behaves in a stable and theoretically-correct fashion, the evaluation of a system can be focused on other components (such as quality of the learning material, learning strategies used, or adaptation capabilities). The future adaptation learning algorithm would then be able to process each user's interactive behaviour information and simultaneously update the structure of the model [24].

Basic requirements, which are imposed on LMS from the point of view of the needs of a teacher, are to present the contents of instruction, manage the instruction, communicate with students, motivate them to study, observe their progress and evaluate them. The bottleneck of the description of all these processes realized within LMS is the formalization of the description of obligation of individual operations and management of individual activities. Therefore, for the provision of a good quality management of e-learning education it is suitable to integrate the classical LMS with the process system. This integration will allow for changing the way through the study of teaching materials and other compulsory activities of a student. Individual parts of teaching materials are automatically activated by means of the process system, i.e. that LMS provides for the advancement of functions for students, thus passing messages to the process system, which assesses it and makes advancement in the process map [19].

Acknowledgments. This publication is published thanks to the financial support of the project KEGA 368-043UKF-4/2010 named: Implementation of elements of interactivity in the contentual transformation of professional informatics subjects.

References

1. Bieliková, M., Návrat, P.: Modelovanie adaptívnych webových systémov. In: Štúdie Vybraných tém Softvérového Inžinierstva, STU, Bratislava, pp. 207–232 (2006)
2. Brusilovsky, P., Schwarz, E., Weber, G.: ELM-ART: An Intelligent Tutoring System on World Wide Web. In: Lesgold, A.M., Frasson, C., Gauthier, G. (eds.) ITS 1996. LNCS, vol. 1086, pp. 261–269. Springer, Heidelberg (1996)
3. Brusilovsky, P.: Adaptive Hypermedia: From Intelligent Tutoring Systems to Web-Based Education. In: Gauthier, G., VanLehn, K., Frasson, C. (eds.) ITS 2000. LNCS, vol. 1839, pp. 1–7. Springer, Heidelberg (2000)

4. Gomez-Albarran, M.: The teaching and learning of programming. A Survey of Supporting Software Tools, The Computer Journal 48(2), 130–144 (2005)
5. Jun-Ming, S. et al.: Constructing SCORM compliant course based on High-Level Petri Nets. Computer Standards and Interfaces 28(3), 336–355 (2006)
6. Scorm, Sharable content object reference model, 4th edn. Version 1.1. Advanced distributed learning,
   http://www.adlnet.gov/Technologies/scorm/SCORMSDocuments/2004%204th%20Edition/Documentation.aspx
7. Cavus, N.: Education technologies of the information age: course management systems. Extend 28(2) (2008)
8. Cápay, M., Tomanová, J.: E-learning support for computer graphics teaching and testing. In: 9th WSEAS International Conference on Telecommunications and Informatics, TELE-INFO 2010, pp. 117–121 (2010)
9. Cavus, N., Uzunboylu, D.H.I.: Assessing the success of students using a learning management system and together with a collaborative tool in webbased teaching of programming languages. J. Educ. Comput. Res. 36(3), 301–321 (2007)
10. Skalka, J., Drlík, M.: Avoiding Plagiarism in Computer Science E-learning Courses. Information & Communicaton Technology in Natural Science Education 16 (2009)
11. Cápay, M., Tomanová, J.: Enhancing the quality of administration, teaching and testing of computer science using learning management system. WSEAS Transactions on Information Science and Applications 7(9), 1126–1136 (2010)
12. Cavus, N., Momani, A.M.: Computer aided evaluation of learning management systems. Procedia.-Soc. Behav. Sci. (2009)
13. Markl, J.: HPSim 1.1 – uživatelská příručka,
    http://www.cs.vsb.cz/markl/pn/hpsim
14. Novák, V.: Základy fuzzy modelovania. BEN press, Praha (2000)
15. Munk, M., Kapusta, J., Švec, P.: Data preprocessing evaluation for web log mining: reconstruction of activities of a web visitor. Procedia Computer Science 1(1), 2273–2280 (2010)
16. Munk, M., Vrábelová, M., Kapusta, J.: Probability modeling of accesses to the web parts of portal. Procedia Computer Science 3, 677–683 (2011)
17. Munk, M., Kapusta, J., Švec, P., Turčáni, M.: Data advance preparation factors affecting results of sequence rule analysis in web log mining. E&M Ekonomie a Management 13(4), 143–160 (2010)
18. Balogh, Z., Turčáni, M., Burianová, M.: Modelling web-based educational activities within the combined forms of education with the support of applied informatics with an e-learning support. In: Proceeding of the 7th International Conference Efficiency and Responsibility in Education (ERIE 2010), pp. 14–23. Czech University of Life Sciences (2010)
19. Balogh, Z., Klimeš, C., Turčáni, M.: Instruction Adaptation Modelling Using Fuzzy Petrinets. In: Distance Learning, Simulation and Communication 2011, pp. 22–29. University of Defence (2011)
20. Strak, M.: Fuzzy Petri Net Based Reasoning for the Diagnosis of Bus Condition. In: SYM-OP-IS (2001)
21. Changjun, J.: Fuzzy Reasoning Based On Petri Nets,
    http://sic.ici.ro/sic2000_3/art04.html
22. Zielke, W.: Jak číst rychleji a lépe, Praha, Svoboda (1988)
23. Zadeh, L.A.: Fuzzy sets. Information and Control 8, 338–353 (1965)
24. Brusilovsky, P., Millán, E.: User Models for Adaptive Hypermedia and Adaptive Educational Systems. In: Brusilovsky, P., Kobsa, A., Nejdl, W. (eds.) Adaptive Web 2007. LNCS, vol. 4321, pp. 3–53. Springer, Heidelberg (2007)

Enhanced Alert Correlation Framework
for Heterogeneous Log

Robiah Yusof, Siti Rahayu Selamat, Shahrin Sahib, Mohd Zaki Mas'ud,
and Mohd Faizal Abdollah

Faculty of Information and Communication Technology,
Universiti Teknikal Malaysia Melaka,
Durian Tunggal, Melaka,
Malaysia
{robiah,sitirahayu,shahrinsahib,zaki.masud,
faizalabdollah}@utem.edu.my

Abstract. Management of intrusion alarms particularly in identifying malware attack is becoming more demanding due to large amount of alert produced by low-level detectors. Alert correlation can provide high-level view of intrusion alerts but incapable of handling large amount of alarm. This paper proposes an enhanced Alert Correlation Framework for sensors and heterogeneous log. It can reduce the large amount of false alarm and identify the perspective of the attack. This framework is mainly focusing on the alert correlation module which consists of Alarm Thread Reconstruction, Log Thread Reconstruction, Attack Session Reconstruction, Alarm Merging and Attack Pattern Identification module. It is evaluated using metric for effectiveness that shows high correlation rate, reduction rate, identification rate and low misclassification rate. Meanwhile in statistical validation it has highly significance result with p < 0.05. This enhanced Alert Correlation Framework can be extended into research areas in alert correlation and computer forensic investigation.

Keywords: alert correlation, alert correlation framework, heterogeneous log.

1 Introduction

Internet is considered as one of the important communication services. Thus, companies have increasingly put critical resources online for effective business management. This has given rise to activities of cyber criminals which are related to malicious software (malware) as mentioned by [1] and [2]. A very large volumes of malware can also be found with extreme variety and sophisticated features as reported by [3].

Virtually, all organizations face increase threats to their networks and the services that they provide and this will lead to network security issues. This statement has been proven by the increasing number of computer security incidents related to vulnerabilities from 171 in 1995 to 7,236 in 2007 and 6,058 in Q3, 2008 as reported by Computer Emergency Response Team [4]. Meanwhile, CyberSecurity Malaysia [5] has also reported that the malicious code incident has the third highest percentage

A. Abd Manaf et al. (Eds.): ICIEIS 2011, Part I, CCIS 251, pp. 107–122, 2011.

of incidents which is at 11%. Hence, this kind of activity can be captured by the wide deployment of IDSs and it can also process large amount of traffic which can generate a huge amount of data as stated by [6 - 12]. However, this huge amount of data can exhaust the network administrator's time and implicate cost as mentioned by [13] and [14]. The data can be used to find the intruder if new outbreak attack happens, especially involving malware attack. Meanwhile, reducing false alarms is a serious problem in ensuring IDS efficiency and usability as mentioned by [15]. In order to increase the detection rate, the use of multiple IDSs can be used to correlate the alert, but in return, it increases the number of alerts to process [16]. Therefore, certain mechanisms need to be integrated with IDS alert in order to guarantee the malware is detected in the IDS alert log. Hence, this research will focus on the correlation of alert in heterogeneous logs instead of correlation of alert in sensors log. The aim of this research is to reduce the large false alarm and at the same time identifying the attack's perspective (attacker, victim, victim/attacker).

Alert correlation is defined as a multi-step process that includes several modules which can enable the administrator to analyze alerts and providing high-level view [17] of the network under surveillance. This several modules are consolidated in a framework called Alert Correlation Framework (ACF). Alert Correlation goals are to reduce the total number of alerts by elimination, fusion, aggregation and synthesis. It is also expected to improve diagnostic by identifying the type of activity, relevance and verification. The final goal of alert correlation is to track the activity regarding the information leaked by the attacker. In order to achieve these goals, the researchers have done few researches on various alert correlation frameworks done by other researchers in identifying the appropriate modules that should be included in the enhanced ACF. Later on this enhanced framework shall be integrated with the new formulated alert correlation rule set.

The rest of the paper is structured as follows. Section 2 discusses the related work on the ACF. Section 3 presents the new enhanced ACF. Section 4 discusses the result of the evaluation and validation of the ACF. Finally, Section 5 concludes and summarizes future directions of this work.

2   Related Work

There are five researchers implementing various kinds of correlation framework that have motivated the researchers to further analyze the frameworks. [18] have proposed a log correlation framework to assist analyst in the evidence search process and [19] have demonstrated alarm reduction via static and adaptive filtering, normalization, aggregation and correlation. Meanwhile, [20] have proposed cooperative module for IDS (CRIM) architecture for MIRADOR project and [21] have focused on Security Information Management (SIM) systems and claim that consolidation, aggregation and correlation module play a key role in analyzing of IDS logs. Finally, [22] have proposed a general framework for correlation that includes a comprehensive set of modules.

The researchers have found thirteen different terminologies used to describe the modules in the framework which are *event filtering, normalization, pre-processing, alert fusion, alert verification, alert clustering, alert merging, alert aggregation, alert* correlation, intention recognition, impact analysis, prioritization and reaction. Various terminologies are used to describe similar modules and it can cause confusion in understanding the whole activity involves in the alert correlation framework. Thus, it is important to understand each module's activities so that the researcher can develop enhanced ACF with the appropriate module. The researchers have analyzed these terminologies and it is summarized in Table 1.

Table 1. General Terminology to Describe the Module in Alert Correlation Framework

No	Component	Description
1	Event Filtering	To reduce the multiple occurrence of the same event (cluster) To substitute similar alarms into a unique alarm (merging) To delete low priority events (prioritization) To classify events into classes (prioritization)
2	Normalization	To standardized the information of log into one common format which is similar to consolidation function.
3	Pre-processing	All attributes are assigned with meaningful value.
4	Alert Fusion	To combine alerts that has the same attributes except for timestamp. It will combine duplicate alert into a group.
5	Alert Verification	To verify either the single alert attack is a true attack where alert report can be produced, a non-contextual or a false positive attack.
6	Alert Clustering	Attempts to cluster the alerts that respond to the same occurrence of attack
7	Alert Merging	Its input is from alert clustering process. It will create new alert that represent the information contained in the various alerts in the cluster.
8	Alert Aggregation	It will group similar events and give simple answer on how many times an attack can happen over certain period of time according to certain criteria.
9	Alert Correlation	Multi-step process that receives alerts from one or more intrusion as an input and produces a high-level description of the malicious activity on the network.
10	Intention Recognition	This function will extrapolate the candidate past, present and future plans.
11	Impact Analysis	It will contextualize the alerts with respect to a specific target in the network and determine the impact of the attack to asset
12	Prioritization	To assign priority to every alert and the properties of the network resources in asset database.
13	Reaction	The action taken after an alert is confirmed as a true attack. It can either be active or passive reaction.

In this analysis, the researchers have identified that some of the modules such as *alert fusion* and *alert merging* have similar functions due to the same objective to achieve which is to combine alerts and represent it into new information. It is similar to *alert clustering* and *alert aggregation* which tends to cluster or group the same alert that refers to the same occurrence. Both examples can be referred to Table 2 where each researcher will choose to implement only either one of this module. For example *Log Correlation Framework* and *CRIM Framework* have chosen the combination of *alert clustering* and *alert merging* activity; thus *alert aggregation* and *alert fusion* is not chosen.

Further analysis is carrying out to verify the selections of the modules to be integrated in the enhanced ACF. Referring to Table 2, the researcher will focus on the total number of occurrence which has the value of 2 and above. This is due to the facts that this module is implemented by all of the researchers and it is needed to enable the researcher to implement the alert correlation process.

Table 2. Analysis of Modules Involved in Alert Correlation Framework (Module Found=√, Module Not Found=X)

No	Researchers/Modules	Filtering	Normalization	Pre-processing	Alert Fusion	Alert Verification	Alert Clustering	Alert Merging	Alert Aggregation	Alert Correlation	Intention Recognition	Impact Analysis	Prioritization	Reaction
1	Log Correlation Framework [18]	x	√	x	x	x	√	√	x	√	x	√	√	x
2	Alarm Reduction Framework [19]	√	√	x	x	x	x	x	√	√	x	x	x	x
3	CRIM Framework [20]	x	√	x	x	x	√	√	x	√	√	x	x	√
4	SIM Framework [21]	x	√	x	x	x	x	x	√	√	x	√	x	x
5	Comprehensive ID Framework [22]	x	√	√	√	√	x	x	x	√	x	√	√	√
	Total No. of occurrence (√)	1	5	1	1	1	2	2	2	5	1	3	2	2

Hence, the modules involved in alert correlation framework shall mainly consist of *normalization* or *consolidation process, alert clustering, alert merging* or *alert aggregation, alert correlation, impact analysis, prioritization* and *reaction*. Therefore, these seven main modules are selected and further discussed in the next section.

3   Proposed Enhanced Alert Correlation Framework

This section shall discuss the proposed enhance Alert Correlation Framework (ACF), dataset preparation and general procedure involve in validating the framework.

Based on the related work and analysis done in previous section, the researchers have formed enhanced ACF which consists of three main stages: *Data Preparation, Data Analysis* and *Data Reporting*. Each of this stage shall consist of proposed modules as listed in Table 3.

Table 3. Proposed Modules in Alert Correlation Framework

Main Stages	Analyzed Modules in Table 2	Proposed Modules
Data Preparation	• Normalization or Consolidation process. • Alert Clustering	• Data Consolidation and Pre-Process • Alarm Reduction

Data Analysis (Attack Pattern Analysis)	• Alert Correlation
	 • Alert Merging
		• Alert Correlation Process
		   - Alarm Thread Reconstruction
		   - Log Thread Reconstruction
		   - Attack Session Reconstruction
		   - Alert Merging

Data Reporting	• Impact Analysis • Prioritization • Reaction	• Attack Pattern Identification • Intrusion Reporting

Referring to Table 3, there are two modules involves in **Data Preparation**: *Data Consolidation and Pre-Process* which is similar to *normalization or consolidation process* module; and *Alarm Reduction* is the same as *alert clustering* module. Meanwhile, in **Data Analysis** or **Attack Pattern Analysis** stage, the *Alert Correlation Process* consists of four main modules: *Alarm Thread Reconstruction, Log Thread Reconstruction, Attack Session Reconstruction* and *Alert Merging* module. In this research, the focus is mainly on these four critical modules and this stage cover the main objective of this research which is to reduce the alarm. Hence in **Data Reporting** stage, the researchers will do research up to the identification of the intruder in *Attack Pattern Identification* and then come up with the report in *Intrusion Reporting*. All of the proposed modules discuss above are consolidated in one framework call enhanced ACF. This framework is as illustrated in Fig 1.

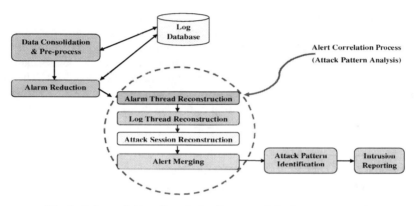

Fig. 1. Enhanced Alert Correlation Framework for heterogeneous logs

In Fig 1, the *Data Consolidation and Pre-Process* data are performed on all alerts. During *Data Consolidation and Pre-Process*, every alert is translated into a standardized format that can be understood by all alert correlation modules and all logs are assigned with IP address respectively. This is necessary because alerts from different sensors and workstations can be encoded in different format. The alert is then assigned with meaningful values.

In *Alarm Reduction (ALR)*, the alarm is compared and clustered for the same occurrence of attack; to reduce the multiple occurrence of the same event. Then, the reduced alarm is processed in the alert correlation module which consists of four main modules: *Alarm Thread Reconstruction (ATR), Log Thread Reconstruction (LTR), Attack Session Reconstruction (ASR)* and *Alert Merging (AM)*.

The main goal of the *ATR* is to associate series of alarm within host's or sensor's log. Meanwhile, the *LTR* is responsible to link the alarm in a host environment; *Personal firewall log, System log, Security log* and *Application log*. This correlation is needed in order to minimize the alarm generated in host level. Next, *ASR* will link series of related alarm in the host and sensor. This correlation is required to represent the attack scenario in the network environment. Later on, *AM* will merge the duplicate alarms from the same host and thus, reducing the multiple alarms. This module is the final stage of alert correlation process. The major purpose of the *Alert Correlation Process* is to produce the high-level of security-related activity on the network and; its objectives are to reduce the total number of alerts, to improve diagnostic and to trace the activity done by the attacker.

Finally, *API* is used to identify the perspectives of the attack: TRUE attacker, TRUE victim and victim/attacker. The output of this process will transform the alert generated by various logs into intrusion reports. These modules are further evaluated and validated in Section 4.

In order to evaluate and validate the enhanced ACF, a few considerations are taken so that the collected data can be evaluated effectively and the main objective of proposing this framework which are to reduce the large amount of alarm and identifying the attack perspective (either it is attacker, victim or victim/attacker) can be achieved. Listed below are the needed criteria for this dataset preparation:

1. The datasets used in this evaluations need to be generated in a controlled environment so that the rules can be evaluated on the targeted malware. Moreover, it is much secure as the researcher is using the real-binary malware code. In non-controlled environment, the possibility to access the victim's logs is minimal as the logs are secure and confidential; hence the modules cannot be tested due to lack of data from victim's and victim/attacker's logs. Therefore, using the controlled environment the researcher is able to access the administrative logs and then evaluate the modules. Due to the controlled environment, the network environment setup for these datasets is similar to the setup in [23].
2. The datasets are generated until the multi-step activity is detected. This is to enable the researcher to test the capability of the rules set to identify the multi-step attacker (victim/attacker) as well as the attacker and the victim.

Using these criteria, this research has generate twelve sets of datasets which consists of heterogeneous logs such as network sensor's log using *Snort* and host's logs which are *Personal firewall log, System log, Security log* and *Application log*. This host logs is selected based on the proposed general malware's attack pattern proposed in [24]. Heterogeneous log sources can contribute useful information regarding the intrusion attempts [25] and it can also improve detection rate and coverage within the system as mentioned by [17]. There are four types of malware variants used in these datasets. The total alarms generated by these heterogeneous logs ranges from 6,326 to 492,065 and the duration of the datasets are generated at the range of 2 minutes and 1 second to 3 hours, 5 minutes and 51 seconds. As mention previously, the duration of the data generation depends on the activation of multi-step attack activity. Once the multi-step attack is activated the experiment is terminated. These datasets will become an input to the enhanced ACF during evaluation and validation in terms of its functionality to identify the attack's perspective and reduce the false alarms.

A general procedure for testing and validation is proposed as in Fig. 2. The objective of this procedure is to validate the effectiveness of the modules in the enhanced ACF in terms of its alarm reduction rate, correlation rate, misclassification rate and identification rate. The higher percentage of alarm reduction rate and correlation rate and lower misclassification rate will determine the effectiveness of the correlation method [29]. The indicator of higher and lower percentage for certain metric has not been mentioned specifically in any research. Hence, the rule of thumb of indicating higher or lower percentage is to ensure that the rate percentage of *correlation rate (CR)* and *alarm reduction rate (ARR)* must be greater than the rate percentage of *misclassification rate (MR)* and the formula can be referred to [29].

Fig. 2. General procedure for testing and validation

In general, as depicted in Fig. 2, this proposed procedure will gather result from each module; and then the result will be evaluated by specific metrics which are *CR*, *MR*, *ARR* and *identification rate (IDR)*. Consequently, the calculated data are further analyzed, evaluated and later on validated using statistical method to verify the effectiveness of the enhanced ACF. This general procedure is further elaborated in the results and validation sections.

4   Results and Validation

In this section, the result of evaluation using metric for effectiveness, validation using statistical method and summary of both evaluation and validation are discussed. However, for the purpose of this research paper, the result of evaluation using metric for effectiveness is summarized to enable the researcher to further elaborate the results and validation of the enhanced ACF using statistical method.

In view of the module functionality using **metric for effectiveness**, Table 4 shows the summary of the evaluation. All of the modules; *ATR, LTR, ASR* and *AM* have high rate percentage of *CR* in the range of 78.20% to 100% and *ARR* in the range of 51.75% up to 93.50% and low rate percentage of *MR in the range of 21.80% down to 0.00%*. Meanwhile, *ALR* module has high rate percentage of *ARR* in the range of 76.02% to 99.22% and *API* module has high rate percentage of *IDR* of *100%*.

Table 4. Summary of Evaluation Using Metric for Effectiveness (high rate= High, low rate= Low, not applicable=*NA*)

Component	%CR	%MR	%ARR	%IDR
ALR	*NA*	*NA*	High	*NA*
ATR	High	Low	High	*NA*
LTR	High	Low	High	*NA*
ASR	High	Low	High	*NA*
AM	High	Low	High	*NA*
API	*NA*	*NA*	*NA*	High

This module has achieved its aim to effectively reduce the false alarm by obtaining high rate of *CR, ARR* and low rate of *MR* and capable to identify the perspective of the attack by gaining high rate of *IDR*.

In view of **statistical method validation**, this research involves a quantitative analysis and it has been identified that the data involved in this research is a continuous type. An inference statistic is implemented in this research and [26], [27] and [28] have stated that it is as a suitable analysis method to describe the relationship between variable, to describe the sample characteristics selected from a population and also to generalize the sample characteristics about its population. The example of test related to this inference statistic is *T Test, ANOVA test, Chi-square test, Pearson Correlation* and so on. The researcher has deployed *ANOVA test and T Test* due to its suitability with the data available in this research in terms of its analysis method and data type.

According to [26 - 28], *one-way analysis of variance* or *one-way ANOVA* is a test to determine whether a relationship exists between three or more group means. This method is suitable with this research and it can be applied to cases where the groups are independent and random, the distributions are normal and the populations have similar variances. Another inference statistic's test applied in this research is *t-test*. According to [26], there are four types of t-test: *Independent-Samples T Test, Paired-Samples T Test, Matched-Samples T Test* and *One-Sample T Test. Paired-Samples T Test* is chosen as it can compares the means of two variables and computes the difference between the two variables for each case, and tests to see if the average difference is significantly different from zero. Hence, the functionality of each module in the enhanced ACF will be validated using the statistical method; *one-way ANOVA* and *Paired-Samples T Test* related to the three issue listed below.

i.   Module functionality related to correlation alarm in each module.
ii.   Module functionality related to alarm reduction in each module.
iii.   Module functionality related to identification of the alarm in the perspective of the attack.

These three issues are created to fulfill the main objectives to be achieved in this research which are to reduce the false alarm and identify the perspective of the attack using the alert correlation technique. The details of the issues are further elaborated in the next sub-sections.

i.   Correlation Alarm Analysis

A test is conducted to compare the effect of the module type on number of alarm correlated in *ATR, LTR, ASR* and *AM*. The hypothesis statement for this analysis is as shown below.

H_1: There is a relationship between module type and number of alarm correlated. ($p < 0.05$)

H_0: There is no relationship between module type and number of alarm correlated.($p >= 0.05$)

The critical value or p-value for this test is 0.05. This p-value is chosen based on typical setting for significant test as mentioned by [26], [27] and [28]. Based on hypothesis given above, a *one-way ANOVA* is performed and Table 5 shows the result of the analysis of variance on number of alarm correlated in these four modules.

Table 5. Result of ANOVA on Correlated Alarm

	Sum of Squares	df	Mean Square	F	Sig.
Between groups	2.404E8	3	80141620.250	4.849	.005
Within Groups	7.272E8	44	16527042.799		
Total	9.676E8	47			

In Table 5, a *one-way ANOVA* shows that the module type has a statistically significant effect on the number of alarm correlated, $F(3,44) = 4.849$, p = 0.005. Post hoc comparison is initiated using Paired-samples T test at critical value of 0.05. Six pair's samples t-tests are used to make post hoc comparisons between conditions. The result of the comparison is depicted in Table 6.

Table 6. Paired Samples Test for Correlation Alarm Analysis

		Paired Differences		
		Mean	Std. Deviation	Sig. (2-tailed)
Pair 1	Correlated Alarm in ATR - Correlated Alarm in LTR	4664.250	7695.183	.060
Pair 2	Correlated Alarm in ATR - Correlated Alarm in ASR	5351.000	8120.747	.043
Pair 3	Correlated Alarm in ATR - Correlated Alarm in AM	5365.583	8124.101	.043
Pair 4	Correlated Alarm in LTR - Correlated Alarm in ASR	686.750	434.519	.000
Pair 5	Correlated Alarm in LTR - Correlated Alarm in AM	701.333	437.706	.000
Pair 6	Correlated Alarm in ASR - Correlated Alarm in AM	14.583	5.265	.000

A first and second paired samples t-test indicated that there is no significant difference in the number of alarm correlated using *ATR* (*M* = 5381.92, *SD* = 8119.106) and *LTR* (*M* = 717.67, *SD* =433.732); and *ATR* (*M* = 5381.92, *SD* = 8119.106) and *ASR* (*M* = 30.92, *SD* = 8.218) respectively. Similarly goes to the third paired samples t-test which indicated that there is no significant difference in the number of alarm correlated using *ATR* (*M* = 5381.92, *SD* = 8119.106) and *AM* (*M* = 16.33, *SD* = 9.829).

A fourth and fifth paired samples t-test indicated that there is a significant difference in the number of alarm correlated using *LTR* (*M* = 717.67, *SD* = 433.732) and *ASR* (*M* = 30.92, *SD* = 8.218); and *LTR* (*M* = 717.67, *SD* = 433.732) and *AM* (*M* = 16.33, *SD* = 9.829) respectively. A sixth paired samples t-test indicated that there is a significant difference in the number of alarm correlated using *ASR* (*M* = 30.92, *SD* = 8.218) and *AM* (*M* = 16.33, *SD* = 9.829).

Since the p-value using the *one-way ANOVA* and *Paired-samples T test* is less than 0.05, H_0 or null hypothesis is rejected. These results suggest that module types which are LTR, ASR and AM really do have a relationship or effect on number of alarm correlated.

However, there is no real difference in number of alarm correlated when comparing *ATR* with *LTR*, *ASR* and *AM* as these results suggest that *ATR* is the first correlation module, hence it has no statistically significant effect if it is compared with other module since it has to be implemented in the first order in a sequence of *ATR, LTR, ASR* and *AM* as suggested in the enhanced ACF. Therefore based on this significance result, it is prove that *ATR, LTR, ASR* and *AM* module are valid for correlating the alarm.

ii.   Alarm Reduction Analysis

A *one-way ANOVA* is performed to compare the effect of the alarm type on number of alarm reduce in *Duplicate Alarm, False Alarm* and *True Alarm*. The data of Duplicate Alarm are taken from the *ALR* module since this module is focusing on the reduction of duplicate data, while the data of *False Alarm* is taken from the *ATR, LTR, ASR* and *AM* module. Finally, the data of the *True Alarm* are collected from *API* module. Hence, the analysis of the alarm reduction is indirectly related to all modules in the enhanced ACF. The hypothesis statement for this analysis is as shown below.

H_1: There is a relationship between alarm type and number of alarm reduces.
   $(p < 0.05)$
H_0: There is no relationship between alarm type and number of alarm reduces.
   $(p >= 0.05)$

The critical value or p-value for this test is 0.05. Based on hypothesis given above, a *one-way ANOVA* is performed and Table 7 shows the result of the analysis of variance on number of alarm reduces according to this alarm type.

Table 7. Result of ANOVA on Alarm Reduction Analysis

	Sum of Squares	df	Mean Square	F	Sig.
Between groups	1.524E11	2	7.619E10	7.684	.002
Within Groups	3.272E11	33	9.916E9		
Total	4.796E11	35			

In Table 7, a *one-way ANOVA* shows that the alarm type has a statistically significant effect on the number of alarm reduce, $F(2,33) = 7.684$, p = 0.002. *Paired-samples T test* which consists of three pair's samples t-tests are used to make post hoc comparisons between conditions at critical value of 0.05. The result of the comparison is illustrated in Table 8. A first paired samples t-test indicated that there is a significant difference in the number of alarm reduce in *Duplicate Alarm* ($M = 138031.75$, $SD = 172472.764$) and *False Alarm* ($M = 23.58$, $SD = 12.139$). A second paired samples t-test indicated that there is also a significant difference in the number of alarm reduce in *Duplicate Alarm* ($M = 138031.75$, $SD = 172472.764$) and *True Alarm* ($M = 6.42$, $SD = 1.832$).

Table 8. Paired Samples Test for Alarm Reduction Analysis

		Paired Differences		
		Mean	Std. Deviation	Sig. (2-tailed)
Pair 1	Duplicate Alarm - False Alarm	138008.167	172476.839	.018
Pair 2	Duplicate Alarm - True Alarm	138025.333	172474.083	.018
Pair 3	False Alarm - True Alarm	17.167	11.352	.000

Finally, a third paired samples t-test indicated that there is a significant difference in the number of alarm reduce in *False Alarm* ($M = 23.58$, $SD = 12.139$) and *True Alarm* ($M = 6.42$, $SD = 1.832$). Since the p-value using the *one-way ANOVA* and *Paired-samples T test* is less than 0.05, H_0 or null hypothesis is rejected. These results suggest that alarm type really does have a relationship or an effect on number of alarm reduce specifically, when comparing *Duplicate Alarm* with *False Alarm*; and comparing *Duplicate Alarm* with *True Alarm*; and *False Alarm* with *True Alarm*. Therefore, once again it is prove that the modules involved in each alarm type which is *ALR, ATR, LTR, ASR* and *AM module* are valid for reducing the alarm.

iii. Identification Perspective Analysis

A *one-way ANOVA* is executed to compare the effect of log type on number of alarm identified in *personal firewall log, security log, system log, application log* and *IDS log*. The hypothesis statement for this analysis is as shown below.

H_1: There is a relationship between log type and number of alarm identified.
   ($p < 0.05$)
H_0: There is no relationship between log type and number of alarm identified.
   ($p \geq 0.05$)

Again, the critical value or p-value for this test is 0.05. Based on hypothesis given above, a *one-way ANOVA* is performed and Table 9 shows the result of the analysis of variance on number of alarm identified according to this log type.

Table 9. Result of ANOVA on Identification Perspective Analysis

	Sum of Squares	df	Mean Square	F	Sig.
Between Groups	170300.767	4	42575.192	70.835	.000
Within Groups	33057.417	55	601.044		
Total	203358.183	59			

In Table 9, a *one-way ANOVA* test shows that the log type has a significant effect on the number of alarm identified, $F(4,55) = 70.835$, $p < 0.05$. Paired-samples T test which consists of ten pair's samples t-tests are used to make post hoc comparisons between conditions at critical value of 0.05. The result of the comparison is illustrated in Table 10. A first paired samples t-test indicated that there is a significant difference in the number of alarm identified in *personal firewall log* ($M = 50.50$, $SD = 16.600$) and *security log* ($M = 157.25$, $SD = 41.591$). A second paired samples t-test indicated that there is no significant difference in the number of alarm identified in *personal firewall log* ($M = 50.50$, $SD = 16.600$) and *system log* ($M = 35.75$, $SD = 28.614$). A third paired samples t-test indicated that there is a significant difference in the number of alarm identified in *personal firewall log* ($M = 50.50$, $SD = 16.600$) and *IDS log* ($M = 28.50$, $SD = 11.666$).

A fourth paired samples t-test indicated that there is a significant difference in the number of alarm identified in *personal firewall log* ($M = 50.50$, $SD = 16.600$) and *application log* ($M = 3.58$, $SD = 6.708$). A fifth paired samples t-test indicated that there is a significant difference in the number of alarm identified in *security log* ($M = 157.25$, $SD = 41.591$) and *system log* ($M = 35.75$, $SD = 28.614$). A sixth paired samples t-test indicated that there is a significant difference in the number of alarm identified in *security log* ($M = 157.25$, $SD = 41.591$) and *IDS log* ($M = 28.50$, $SD = 11.666$).

A seventh paired samples t-test indicated that there is a significant difference in the number of alarm identified in *security log* ($M = 157.25$, $SD = 41.591$) and *application log* ($M = 3.58$, $SD = 6.708$). An eight paired samples t-test indicated that there is no significant difference in the number of alarm identified in *System log* ($M = 35.75$, $SD = 28.614$) and *IDS log* ($M = 28.50$, $SD = 11.666$). A nine paired samples t-test indicated that there is a significant difference in the number of alarm identified in *system log* ($M = 35.75$, $SD = 28.614$) and *application log* ($M = 3.58$, $SD = 6.708$). A ten paired samples t-test indicated that there is a significant difference in the number of alarm identified in *IDS log* ($M = 28.50$, $SD = 11.666$) and *application log* ($M = 3.58$, $SD = 6.708$).

Table 10. Paired Samples Test for Identification Perspectives Analysis

		Paired Differences		
		Mean	Std. Deviation	Sig. (2-tailed)
Pair 1	Attribute in PFW log - Attribute in Security log	-106.750	35.798	.000
Pair 2	Attribute in PFW log - Attribute in System log	14.750	39.568	.223
Pair 3	Attribute in PFW log - Attribute in IDS log	22.000	13.705	.000
Pair 4	Attribute in PFW log - Attribute in Appl log	46.917	17.916	.000
Pair 5	Attribute in Security log - Attribute in System log	121.500	66.952	.000
Pair 6	Attribute in Security log - Attribute in IDS log	128.750	42.883	.000
Pair 7	Attribute in Security log - Attribute in Appl log	153.667	44.830	.000
Pair 8	Attribute in System log - Attribute in IDS log	7.250	34.594	.483
Pair 9	Attribute in System log - Attribute in Appl log	32.167	28.232	.002
Pair 10	Attribute in IDS log - Attribute in Appl log	24.917	9.931	.000

Since the p-value using the *one-way ANOVA* and *Paired-samples T test* is less than 0.05, H_0 or null hypothesis is rejected. These results suggest that log type really does have an effect on number of alarm identified specifically, when using *personal firewall log, security log, system log, application log* and *IDS log*. However, there is no real difference in the number of alarm identified when comparing *personal firewall log* to *system log*; and comparing *system log* to *IDS log*.

Therefore, again based on this significance result, it is prove that all of the logs selected to be verified using *API* module are valid for identifying the perspective of the attack. In other words, *API* module is capable to identify the perspective with the assistance of well selected logs. The summary of the validation using statistical method is shown in Table 11.

Refer to Table 11, all of the three issues: *Correlation Alarm analysis, Alarm Reduction analysis* and *Identification Perspective analysis* have shown a significant result using *one-way ANOVA*. These results explain that there are relationship between correlation alarm, reduction alarm and identification of perspective with the module proposed in the enhanced ACF.

As for *Paired-Samples T Test*, in *Correlation Alarm analysis*, the *LTR, ASR and AM module* have a significance relationship with each other. This is to show that these three modules depend on each other to ensure the correlation process is effective. Nevertheless, the *ATR module* has no significance relationship with *LTR, ASR* and *AM module* since this module does not depend on *LTR, ASR* and *AM* module to link series of alarm within host's or sensor's log. It is independent of any other modules in correlating the alarm.

Table 11. Summary of Validation using Statistical Method

Issue Analyse	One-way ANOVA (Highly significance)	Paired-Samples T test (Significance)	Paired-Samples T test (Not Significance)
Correlation Alarm	p = 0.005;	LTR and ASR ; p < 0.05 LTR and AM ; p < 0.05 ASR and AM ; p < 0.05	ATR and LTR ATR and ASR ATR and AM
Alarm Reduction	p = 0.002;	FA and TA ; p < 0.05 DA and FA ; p = 0.018 DA and TA ; p = 0.018	
Identification of Perspective	P < 0.05;	PFW and Sec ; p < 0.05 PFW and IDS ; p < 0.05 PFW and Appl ; p < 0.05 Sec and IDS ; p < 0.05 Sec and Appl ; p < 0.05 Sys and Appl ; p = 0.002 IDS and Appl ; p < 0.05 Sec and Sys ; p < 0.05	PFW and Sys Sys and IDS

Note:

PFW is Personal firewall log   DA is the Duplicate Alarm
Sec is Security log   FA is the False Alarm
Sys is System log   TA is the True Alarm
Appl is Application log   IDS is the IDS log or sensor log

In *Alarm Reduction analysis*, the *Duplicate Alarm, False Alarm* and *True Alarm* have a significance relationship with each other. This is to shows that the modules involved *in Duplicate Alarm* which is *ALR, False Alarm* which is *ATR, LTR, ASR, AM* and *True Alarm* which is *API* is closely related. This is proven by *Paired-samples T test*, which shows that there is significance relationship between *Duplicate Alarm, False Alarm* and *True Alarm*.

In *Identification of Perspective analysis*, all of the logs have significance relationship except for *system log* and *Personal Firewall log*; and *system log* and *IDS log*. This is to show that the selected logs attributes have significance relationship with identifying the attack perspective. The reason of system log has no significance relationship with *Personal Firewall log* and *IDS log* is due to the fact that the data gathered in *system log* act as a secondary log and not as primary log. The analysis of this validation using statistical method on the enhanced ACF has shown significance result which is p is less than 0.05.

In summary, this evaluation and validation is purposely done to evaluate and validate the effectiveness of the module functionality of the enhanced ACF. The effectiveness is determined based on rate percentage of *CR, MR, ARR* and *IDR*. The higher percentage of *Correlation Rate, Alarm Reduction Rate* and *Identification Rate;* and lower percentage of *Misclassification Rate* will reflect the effectiveness of the enhanced ACF in reducing the alarms related to malware's attack. The enhanced ACF has achieved its aim to obtain high rate of *CR, ARR* and *IDR*, low rate of *MR* and highly significant result of *Correlation Alarm Analysis, Alarm Reduction Analysis* and *Identification Perspective Analysis*. Thus, the significant result gained from both evaluations has validated that the enhanced ACF is effective in identifying the true alarm and reducing the false alarm.

5   Conclusion and Future Work

In this paper, the researchers have introduced the enhanced Alert Correlation Framework (ACF) which consists of four main correlation modules: *Alarm Thread Reconstruction (ATR), Log Thread Reconstruction (LTR), Attack Session Reconstruction (ASR), Alert Merging (AM)* and one module for identifying perspective namely *Attack Pattern Identification (API)* and one module for handling duplication known as *Alarm Reduction (ALR)*. This framework is later on evaluated using metric for effectiveness with high rate of alarm correlation, high rate of alarm reduction, high rate of identification alarm and low rate of misclassification alarm. It is then validated using the statistical method which shows significance result where p-value is less than 0.05. The output of the analysis are the enhanced Alert Correlation Framework for heterogeneous log. This proposed framework is then extended to be further used in correlating alarm for heterogeneous log in various scenarios. The finding is essential for further research in alert correlation and computer forensic investigation.

Acknowledgement. This research was kindly supported by Universiti Teknikal Malaysia Melaka.

References

1. Lee, D., Seo, J., Ryou, J.: Alerts Correlation System to Enhance the Performance of the Network-Based Intrusion Detection System. In: Third International Conference on Grid and Cooperative Computing, pp. 333–340 (2004)
2. Andreas, M., Christopher, K., Engin, K.: Limits of Static Analysis for Malware Detection. In: 23rd Annual Computer Security Applications Conference, pp. 421–430 (2007)
3. Georgia Tech Information Security Center: Emerging Cyber Threats Report 2011. Technical report, GTISC (2011)
4. CERT Statistics (2009), http://www.cert.org/stats/

5. MyCERT Quarterly Summary, Q4 (2009),
   http://www.mycert.org.my/en/services/advisories/mycert/2009/
   main/detail/723/index.html
6. Alharby, A., Imai, H.: IDS False Alarm Reduction Using Continuous and Discontinuous Patterns. In: Ioannidis, J., Keromytis, A.D., Yung, M. (eds.) ACNS 2005. LNCS, vol. 3531, pp. 192–205. Springer, Heidelberg (2005)
7. Peng, J., Feng, C., Rozenblit, J.W.: A Hybrid Intrusion Detection and Visualization System. In: 13th Annual IEEE International Symposium and Workshop on Engineering of Computer Based Systems, pp. 505–506 (2006)
8. Barford, P., Jha, S., Yegneswaran, V.: Fusion and Filtering in Distributed Intrusion Detection Systems. In: 42nd Annual Allerton Conference on Communication, Control and Computing, pp. 1546–1551 (2004)
9. Peyman, K., Ali, A.G.: A Rule-Based Temporal Alert Correlation System. International Journal of Network Security 5(1), 66–72 (2007)
10. Benjamin, M., Ludovic, M., Herve, D., Mireille, D.: M4D4: a Logical Framework to Support Alert Correlation in Intrusion Detection. Journal of Information Fusion 10(4), 285–299 (2009)
11. Massimo, F., Luigi, R.: A Correlation Approach to Intrusion Detection. In: Mobile Lightweight Wireless Systems Conference, pp. 203–215 (2010)
12. Tjhai, G.C., Papadaki, M., Furnell, S.M., Clarke, N.L.: Investigating the Problem of IDS False Alarms: An Experimental Study Using Snort. In: 23rd International Information Security Conference, pp. 253–267 (2008)
13. Thonnarda, O., Dacier, M.: A Framework for Attack Patterns' Discovery in Honeynet Data. Journal of Digital Investigation 8, 128–139 (2008)
14. Sadoddin, R., Ghorbani, A.: An Incremental Frequent Structure Mining Framework for Real-Time Alert Correlation. Journal Computer & Security 28, 153–173 (2009)
15. Tjhai, G.C., Papadaki, M., Furnell, S.M., Clarke, N.L.: The Problem of False Alarms: Evaluation with Snort and DARPA 1999 Dataset. In: 5th International Conference of Trust, Privacy and Security in Digital Business, pp. 139–150 (2008)
16. Autrel, F., Cuppens, F.: Using an Intrusion Detection Alert Similarity Operator to Aggregate and Fuse Alerts. In: 4th Conference on Security and Network Architectures, pp. 312–322 (2005)
17. Siraj, A., Vaughn, R.B.: A Cognitive Model for Alert Correlation in a Distributed Environment. In: Kantor, P., Muresan, G., Roberts, F., Zeng, D.D., Wang, F.-Y., Chen, H., Merkle, R.C. (eds.) ISI 2005. LNCS, vol. 3495, pp. 218–230. Springer, Heidelberg (2005)
18. Herrerias, J., Gomez, R.: A Log correlation model to support the Evidence Search Process in a Forensic Investigation. In: 2nd International Workshop on Systematic Approach to Digital Forensic Engineering, pp. 31–42 (2007)
19. Chyssler, T., Burschka, S., Semling, M., Lingvall, T., Burbeck, K.: Alarm Reduction and Correlation in IDS. In: Proceeding of the DIMVA 2004, pp. 9–24 (2004)
20. Cuppens, F., Miege, A.: Alert Correlation in a Cooperative Intrusion Detection Framework. In: IEEE Symposium on Security and Privacy 2002, pp. 202–215 (2002)
21. Beckers, J., Paul Ballerini, J.: Advanced Analysis of Intrusion Detection Logs. Journal Computer Fraud & Security 2003, 9–12 (2003)
22. Valeur, F., Vigna, G., Kruegel, C., Kemerrer, R.A.: A Comprehensive Approach to Intrusion Detection Alert Correlation. IEEE Transaction on Dependable and Secure Computing 1(3), 146–169 (2004)
23. Robiah, Y., Siti Rahayu, S., Shahrin, S., Mohd Faizal, A., Mohd Zaki, M., Marliza, R.: New Multi-step Worm Attack Model. Journal of Computing 2(1), 1–7 (2010)

24. Robiah, Y., Siti Rahayu, S., Shahrin, S., Mohd Faizal, A., Mohd Zaki, M., Marliza, R.: An Improved Traditional Worm Attack Pattern. In: 4th International Symposium on Information Technology 2010, pp. 1067–1072 (2010)
25. Barse, E.L., Jonsson, E.: Extracting Attack Manifestations to Determine Log Data Requirements for Intrusion Detection. In: 20th Annual Computer Security Applications Conference, pp. 158–167. IEEE Computer Society (2004)
26. Piaw, C.Y.: Asas Statistik Penyelidikan Buku 2. McGraw-Hill, Malaysia (2006)
27. Myatt, G.J.: Making Sense of Data. A Practical Guide to Exploratory Data Analysis and Data Mining. A John Wiley & Sons, Inc., Publications, New Jersey (2007)
28. Field, A.: Discovering Statistics Using SPSS, 2nd edn. Sage Publications Ltd., London (2005)
29. Valeur, F.: Real-Time Intrusion Detection Alert Correlation. PhD Dissertation, University of California, Santa Barbara, CA (2006)

Morphed Virus Family Classification Based on Opcodes Statistical Feature Using Decision Tree

Babak Bashari Rad[1], Maslin Masrom[2], Suhaimi Ibrahim[3], and Subariah Ibrahim[4]

[1,4] Faculty of Computer Science and Information Systems, [2]Razak School of Engineering and Advanced Technology, [3]Advanced Informatics School
University Technology of Malaysia, Malaysia
babak.basharirad@hotmail.com, maslin@ic.utm.my,
{suhaimiibrahim,subariah}@utm.my

Abstract. Use of morphing engine in metamorphic and polymorphic malware, and virus creation kits aid malware authors to produce a plenty number of variants for a virus. These variants belong to a family and have common behavioral and some statistical characteristics. However, these variants are not detectable via a single common string signature. Some statistical analyses have been tested in recent years to fight against these types of multi-variants family malware. In this research, we introduce and examine an opcodes statistical-based classifier using decision tree. This method is very simple in implementation. Our experimental outcome shows that different malware family executable files are classifiable using their opcodes statistical feature, with a high degree of reliability.

Keywords: morphed virus, metamorphic malware, virus family classification, malware classification, opcodes statistical feature, decision tree.

1 Introduction

The most common and popular method is being used by antivirus software is string signature scanning [1]. Generally, string signature is a sequence of byte string, which is unique for a known virus and extracted by an antivirus expert during the analysis process of the virus. It is used as a feature to identify a virus or a family of virus. The most important problem with this method is that the antivirus database of signatures must be updated regularly in order for the software to be trusted. Even though it is the most reliable method with a low false positive and false negative, but it is not practically effective for detection of self-mutation malware [2]. Because the metamorphic virus employ various mutation engines [3], usually finding a constant byte string, which is common among the different variants of a metamorphic virus, is not possible [4]. For this reason, string signature-based detection is not a suitable method for this type of malware. Although using the wildcards may be able to detect simple mutated ones, but it is not adequately successful for highly obfuscated virus.

Other methodologies such as behavior analysis or, static and dynamic heuristic detection methods are also being used by the antivirus software for detection of obfuscated viruses. However, these methods are not perfectly working in a high level

A. Abd Manaf et al. (Eds.): ICIEIS 2011, Part I, CCIS 251, pp. 123–131, 2011.
© Springer-Verlag Berlin Heidelberg 2011

of accuracy or speed. This leads the antivirus technology researchers to find other methodologies to improve the antivirus products in terms of performance, both accuracy and complexity. Using statistical features of the malware for detection of self-mutated viruses is a relatively new approach, which has been developed in recent years [5].

In this paper, we aim to introduce a method to utilize the statistical feature of the malware code as a tool in order to classify self-mutated engines and family viruses. In the next section, we survey the previous related works, briefly. In section 3, we introduce our proposed methodology. Then, we present the implementation of the method, experiments and results in section 4, and finally, in last part, we give the conclusion and some suggestion for future trends.

2   Related Works

Since the early appearance of the metamorphic malware, various methodologies have been studied and developed to detect the morphed malicious code family. Many of these methods are based on the statistical properties of the morphing-code engine.

In [6], Chouchane *et al.* suggested that statistical properties obtained from analyzing the code of various instances of a virus family can be exploited as a signature. They introduced a method to build a classifier for deciding whether a suspicious program is a variant of a virus family or not. They use a model of the probabilistic engine to foresee the anticipated distribution of morphed formats of instructions in different instances of the virus. Then they exploit these anticipated distributions to define the statistical feature of the engine. In this manner, a classifier can rapidly classify the input as a virus member or non-member based on distance between observed and anticipated distributions.

Govindaraju [5] proposed a statistic-based metamorphic virus detection technique. He showed that detection based on statistics properties is a useful approach in detecting self-mutated malwares. He chose six statistic features that include of percentage of NOP instruction at the end of subroutines, percentage of NOP instruction in random, JMP instruction profile, short jump instruction profile, all subroutine profile, and subroutines without a CALL instruction, which interact with some particular forms of code mutation techniques, as junk code insertion, subroutine permutation and code reordering. His proposed technique is able to detect four family viruses in the test data set containing of NGVCK, VCL, G2 and MPCGEN variants.

In [7], Milgo recommended and evaluated two methods to link the variants of malware generated by automatic engines to their related engines. Their methods utilized the NFV of the opcodes as a feature vector. Their second approach, which was an extension of the former, exploits optimized 2-gram frequency vectors as feature and classifies variants according to their closeness to the average value of the NFVs of known instances.

Rad *et al.* [8] utilized a statistical technique to compare the dissimilarity between two executable files suspected to be infected by different morphed variants of metamorphic virus. Their proposed technique is based on the comparison of opcodes frequency histograms. They shows that the frequency histogram of opcodes can be exploited as a feature to recognize the obfuscated versions of metamorphic viruses.

3   Proposed Approach

Our proposed approach is based on this concept that each morphing engine or virus creation tool has some common characteristics in terms of generated instructions statistical feature. We believe that though a morphing engine attempts to produce different shapes of viral family, but the created viruses by the same engine or generator tool have similar statistical attributes. Anyhow, different obfuscation techniques create various types of metamorphic viruses with different level of mutation complexity, but some of obfuscation techniques have no significant impact on the statistical properties of their produced variants. Moreover, the code generated by a morphing engine of the malware or by a virus construction kit is not well optimized as much as benign normal programs generated with advanced compiler and there are some major differences between them [9]. As a result, by analyzing a morphing engine or a creation kit, it is possible to extract the engine statistical feature. Based on this statistical feature, different types of statistical models can be trained and later be used to classify and detect the variants belonging to a virus family.

The proposed methodology to create and train a statistical classifier based on decision tree consists of three consecutive phases. First, we disassemble the executable files to obtain assembly source program. This phase is performed for each set of different class of programs. Then, from the assembly source program, statistics of the instruction opcodes can be extracted for the members of each family group. After the statistics are extracted, it is possible to derive a decision tree for classification. Fig. 1 illustrates the process phases, briefly.

There are numerous Intel x86 instructions, so instead of considering all these instructions, which most of them are not very frequent in executable files, it is logical to examine only the most frequently occurred instructions. Based on the research done by Bilar in [10], only 14 instructions in total set of Intel instructions are most frequently occurred. As it is shown in the Fig. 2 [10] , these instructions are MOV, PUSH, CALL, POP, CMP, JZ, LEA, TEST, JMP, ADD, JNZ, RETN, XOR, and AND.

In this approach, in addition to these 14 most frequently occurred opcodes, we involve all 32 different forms of conditional and unconditional jump instruction opcodes, because morphing engines utilize conditional jumps to transpose the code and change the code execution flow.

4   Experiments and Findings

With a collection of 4 classes of different types of executable programs, include of a set of benign programs, a set of metamorphic variants of NGVCK virus family, a set of VCL virus family, and a set of Win32.Evul family viruses, we examine the proposed methodology.

4.1   Data Set

To create a classifier, firstly, we need to setup a valid data collection. With the data set built, it is possible to make and train a decision tree based on the statistics extracted from each class, such is able to understand and recognize different classes of programs.

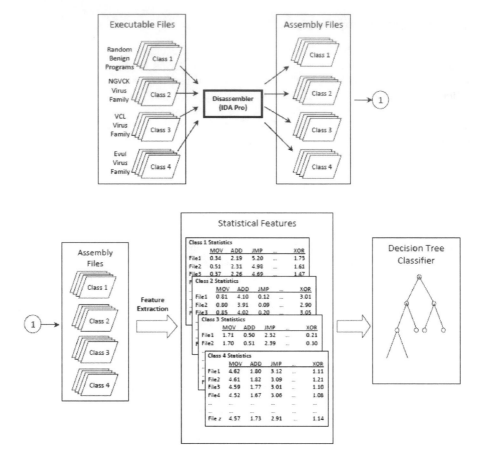

Fig. 1. Proposed methodology consists of disassembly phase, statistical feature extraction, and creating a decision tree classifier

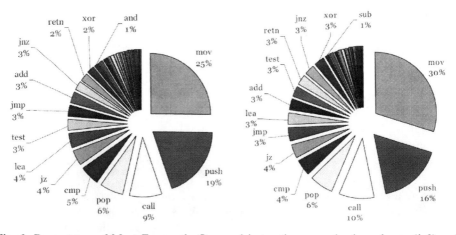

Fig. 2. Percentages of Most Frequently Occurred instructions opcodes in malware (*left*) and benign (*right*) programs [10]

Our training data set is contained of four different classes of executable programs. We train the decision tree to classify these four classes. The first class is contained of normal benign executable programs. To form this class, 122 executable files are randomly chosen from the normal windows 7 operating system directory and some third party applications. The next class is included of 40 virus created by Next Generation Virus Creation Kit (NGVCK). It is one of the most famous metamorphic virus creation tools, introduced by SnakeByte [11]. To form the third class, we used Virus Creation Lab (VCL). VCL is a program to produce virus, automatically. The virus created by this tool have common characteristics and known as a family. We create 10 different variants of VCL, using different options provided in the software graphical interface. The last selected category of executables is contained of eight different variants of Win32.Evul.8192. Table 1 summarized our data set.

All these virus creation kits and variants of Win32.Evul are accessible and downloadable from VXHeavens website [12].

Table 1. Training data set containing of four classes

Class No.	Description	Number of Files
Class 1	Normal Benign Programs	122
Class 2	NGVCK Metamorphic Family	40
Class 3	VCL Virus Family	10
Class 4	Evul.8192 Metamorphic Family	8

4.2   Disassembly

In disassembly phase, all executable files are disassembled and converted to assembly source program. To keep the uniformity, we implement this process using a specific disassembler program. We use IDA Pro Advanced (Interactive Disassembler) Version 5.5.0.925t (32-bit) of HexRays SA [13]. All programs of four classes, include of 122 benign programs, 40 NGVCK viruses, 10 VCL virus family members and 8 variants of Win32.Evul are disassembled and converted into the form of assembly source code.

4.3   Feature Extraction

Once the executable files of four classes are converted to assembly source codes, instructions statistics can be elicited by analyzing the assembly files. We developed some codes in MATLAB 7.6.0 (R2008a) [14] to automatically analyze and extract the frequency of targeted opcodes in all files of each class. Table 2 shows the minimum, maximum, and average values of opcodes statistics for each class. The statistical values in Table 2 are computed as the following equation:

$$\text{Statistic for Opcode } X = \frac{\text{Count of Opcode } X}{\text{Total number of all Opcodes in the file}} \times 100 \qquad (1)$$

Table 2. Opcodes Statistics for each class of our data set

		jmps	mov	add	xor	sub	cmp	call	push	pop	lea	test	retn
	min	0.67	0.82	0.06	0.13	0.04	0.28	0.28	0.75	0.21	0.00	0.00	0.09
C1	max	11.21	20.98	4.41	5.47	2.10	4.92	9.24	24.76	5.89	5.01	3.55	2.41
	avg	4.87	8.24	0.85	1.19	0.40	2.21	3.59	8.38	1.93	1.42	1.30	0.89
	min	5.32	13.96	8.27	1.77	2.53	1.93	3.85	7.21	3.31	1.19	0.33	0.00
C2	max	4.54	10.43	6.26	0.83	1.04	1.32	3.26	5.91	2.26	0.74	0.00	0.00
	avg	6.18	17.18	11.47	3.44	4.12	2.62	4.28	8.15	4.33	2.05	0.81	0.00
	min	14.01	12.25	2.35	1.05	1.07	2.37	8.14	5.08	1.03	1.01	0.81	1.01
C3	max	13.59	12.08	1.90	0.92	0.99	2.28	7.91	4.34	0.91	0.95	0.64	0.95
	avg	14.36	12.48	3.14	1.19	1.18	2.44	8.37	6.46	1.21	1.12	0.91	1.07
	min	4.84	5.93	1.02	0.00	0.20	3.38	8.01	12.06	0.13	0.13	0.00	0.32
C4	max	0.59	3.38	0.27	0.00	0.02	0.42	1.08	2.07	0.00	0.00	0.00	0.15
	avg	6.72	7.04	1.33	0.00	0.27	4.73	10.80	16.00	0.25	0.25	0.00	0.50

4.4   Decision Tree

After the statistical features are extracted for our categorized data set, it is possible to derive a decision tree based on these statistics. The plenty of training data collection results more accurate decision tree. As we classified our training data set to four different classes, the decision tree is able to find statistical features of each class, so it can classify any test input into one class.

We implement the decision tree using MATLAB Statistics Toolbox. The following functions are used to create a decision tree and display it:

```
t = treefit(Opcodes_Statistics,Categories)
treedisp(t,'names',List_of_Opcodes)
```

The following code is the decision tree resulted from the above function `treefit` function with constructed data set:

```
Decision tree for classification
  1   if x3<5.33222 then node 2 else node 3
  2   if x1<12.3983 then node 4 else node 5
  3   class = NGVCK
  4   if x4<0.0625782 then node 6 else node 7
  5   class = VCL
  6   class = Evul
  7   class = Normal
```

Fig. 3 display the decision tree obtained for our data set, graphically. As it can be seen in the figure, all NGVCK variants have ADD opcodes more than 5.33222, all members of VCL family have a rate of ADD opcodes less than 5.33222 and JUMP instructions more than 12.3983, and so on. By this decision tree, it is possible to classify the variants of each family based on their opcodes statistics.

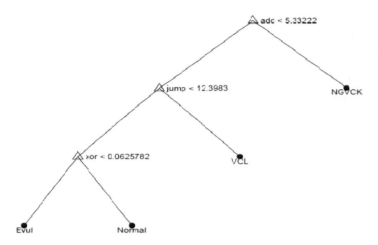

Fig. 3. Decision tree derived for out data set

4.5   Classification Test and Results

To examine the proposed methodology, we made a collection of different types of executables, include of 36 normal benign programs, 10 variants of NGVCK, and 5 variants of VCL family viruses. We use the trained decision tree obtained from training data set to classify the test data collection. As it is shown in Table 3, our decision tree is able to classify all 51 different executable files, correctly. It means we have no false positives and false negative, in our experiment.

Table 3. Classification results

Real Class of Input Executables	Total Number of Files in test data collection	True Positive	False Positive	Precision (%)	Total Accuracy (%)
C1	36	36	0	100	100
C2	10	10	0	100	100
C3	5	5	0	100	100

The Precision and Total Accuracy are calculated via the equations 2 and 3 [15]:

$$Precision = \frac{TP}{TP + FP} \cdot \qquad (2)$$

$$Total\ Accuracy = \frac{TP + TN}{TP + TN + FP + FN} \cdot \qquad (3)$$

5   Conclusion and Future Recommendations

We presented and examined a classification method based on the opcodes statistical feature of the morphing engine code. In this simple method, a decision tree is produced and trained with the statistical feature of different classes of codes. Later, this decision tree can be used to classify the input codes into each training classes. In our experiment to evaluate the efficiency of the proposed method, we built a training data set of four different classes of codes.

The result of our experiment shows that this method can be used as a trustable method for classification problem of malicious family codes. Although in our test, the results present a very high quality classifier, but the output may be different with a larger data training set. As a more thoroughly evaluating the method, it is useful to examine the method on a larger set of training codes and test collection. In addition, it is a good evaluation if the method would be tested for more number of classes.

A major drawback with this method is that it needs a disassembly pre-process, which is a very time-consuming procedure. A future attempt to improve this approach is to train and obtain a decision tree directly on binary codes of executable files.

Acknowledgement. The financial support of research grant from Ministry of Higher Education, Malaysia (Fundamental Research Grant Scheme; Vote: 4F057) is gratefully acknowledged.

References

1. Sathyanarayan, V.S., Kohli, P., Bruhadeshwar, B.: Signature Generation and Detection of Malware Families. In: Mu, Y., Susilo, W., Seberry, J. (eds.) ACISP 2008. LNCS, vol. 5107, pp. 336–349. Springer, Heidelberg (2008)
2. Rad, B.B., Masrom, M., Ibrahim, S.: Evolution of Computer Virus Concealment and Anti-Virus Techniques: A Short Survey. International Journal of Computer Science Issues (IJCSI) 8, 113–121 (2011)
3. Desai, P., Stamp, M.: A highly metamorphic virus generator. International Journal of Multimedia Intelligence and Security 1, 402–427 (2010)
4. Leder, F., Steinbock, B., Martini, P.: Classification and detection of metamorphic malware using value set analysis. In: 4th International Conference on Malicious and Unwanted Software (MALWARE), pp. 39–46 (2009)
5. Govindaraju, A.: Exhaustive Statistical Analysis for Detection of Metamorphic Malware. Faculty of the Department of Computer Science, Master Thesis. San Jose State University, San Jose, CA (2010)
6. Chouchane, M.R., Walenstein, A., Lakhotia, A.: Statistical Signatures for Fast Filtering of Instruction-substituting Metamorphic Malware. In: Worm 2007: Proceedings of the 2007 ACM Workshop on Recurring Malcode, pp. 31–37 (2007)
7. Milgo, E.C.: Statistical Tools for Linking Engine-generated Malware to Its Engine. In: College of Business and Computer Science, Master, p. 47. Columbus State University (2009)
8. Rad, B.B., Masrom, M.: Metamorphic Virus Variants Classification Using Opcode Frequency Histogram. In: 14th WSEAS International Conference on COMPUTERS, pp. 147–155. WSEAS Press (2010)
9. Merkel, R., Hoppe, T., Kraetzer, C., Dittmann, J.: Statistical Detection of Malicious PE-Executables for Fast Offline Analysis. In: De Decker, B., Schaumüller-Bichl, I. (eds.) CMS 2010. LNCS, vol. 6109, pp. 93–105. Springer, Heidelberg (2010)

10. Bilar, D.: Statistical Structures: Fingerprinting malicious code through statistical opcode analysis. In: 3rd International Conference on Global E-Security, ICGeS 2007 (2007)
11. Szor, P.: The Art of Computer Virus Research and Defense. Addison-Wesley Professional (2005)
12. VXHeavens, http://vx.netlux.org/vl.php
13. IDA Pro Disassembler and Debugger, http://www.hex-rays.com
14. MathWorks, MATLAB - The Language Of Technical Computing, http://www.mathworks.com/
15. Ronghua, T., Batten, L., Islam, R., Versteeg, S.: An automated classification system based on the strings of trojan and virus families. In: 4th International Conference on Malicious and Unwanted Software (MALWARE), pp. 23–30 (2009)

Development of Code-Theoretic Scheme on Generalized Cascade Codes

Tamara Zhukabayeva, Meruert Akzhigitova, and Khu Ven –Tsen

South-Kazakhstan State University, Shymkent, Kazakhstan
{tamara_kokenovna,meruert_diana}@mail.ru, qbcba@bk.ru

Abstract. The questions of construction of generalized cascade codes with algebraic codes on the external level are investigated in the article. The procedure of encoding and decoding with algebraic codes on the external level of generalized cascade code. Cryptosystems of theoretical resistance, construction of which is based on using algebraic block codes (code-theoretic schemes) are considered. Resistance of cascade code-theoretic schemes to hacking by an opponent with the help of the method of permutable decoding is researched.

Keywords: information security, cryptosystem, cascade codes, nonalgebraic decoding.

1 Introduction

Issue raising in general form and literature analysis. Development and research of code-theoretic schemes are perspective trend in development of theory of secret systems – secret systems of being proved resistance, hacking problem of which is amounted to solving theoretically complexity problem of decoding of random code [1-4]. Well-known methods of constructing code-theoretic schemes possess a range of disadvantages: great volume of key data and high complexity of realization in comparison with block-symmetric cryptoalgorithms [3-6]. Working out code-theoretic scheme on cascade code constructions is perspective trend of their development. Their employment, as shown in this work, allows to construct secret system, free from defects.

2 Code-Theoretic Scheme Construction

By definition [1-4], code-theoretic scheme is a secret system, constructed using intractable problem of decoding of random code (n, k, d) over $GF(q)$. Formally it is fixed by aggregate of following sets:

- set of clear texts

$$M = \{M1, M2, \ldots, Mqk\}, \text{ where } Mi = \{I1, I2, \ldots, Ik\}, \forall Ij \in GF(q);$$

- set of cryptograms

A. Abd Manaf et al. (Eds.): ICIEIS 2011, Part I, CCIS 251, pp. 132–140, 2011.

$$E = \{E1, E2, \ldots, Eqk\}, \text{ where } Ei = \{C1, C2, \ldots, Cn\}, \forall Cj \in GF(q);$$

set of direct mappings

$$\phi = \{\phi1, \phi2, \ldots, \phi s\}, \text{where } \phi i: M \rightarrow E, i = 1, 2, \ldots, s;$$

- set of inverse mappings

$$\phi\text{-}1^{-1} = \{\phi1\text{-}^{-1}, \phi2^{-1}, \ldots, \phi s^{-1}\}, \text{where } \phi i^{-1}: E \rightarrow M, i = 1, 2, \ldots, s;$$

- set of keys, parametrizing direct mappings

$$K = \{K_1, K_2, \ldots, Ks\} == \{G_X^1, G_X^2, \ldots, G_X^s\}, \phi_i : M \xrightarrow{K_i} E$$

- set of keys, parametrizing inverse mappings

$$K^* = \{K_1^*, K_2^*, \ldots, Ks^*\} = \{\{X, P, D\}_1,$$

$$\{X, P, D\}_2, \ldots, \{X, P, D\}_s\}, \phi_i^{-1} =: E \xrightarrow{K_i^*} M$$

so, that complexity of realization of inverse mapping φ^{-1} without knowing the key $K_i^* \in K^*$ is conjugated to solving theoretically intricate problem of decoding random code (code of general position).

Thus, algebraic (n, k, d) code with quick algorithm of decoding is dissimulated under random (n, k, d) code by means of multiplying generating matrix G^i, i=1…s, on dissimulating matrices X^i, P^i and D^i kept under wraps: $G_X^i = X^i\ G^i\ P^i\ D^i$

Without knowing rules of dissimulating, an opponent has to use intricate algorithm of decoding random code [3]. On the contrary, authorized user, knowing the rule of dissimulating, can use quick algorithm of decoding algebraic code. Direct mapping (encrypting) $\phi_i : M \xrightarrow{K_i} E$ in classical code-theoretic schemes is understood as a procedure of coding by dissimulated algebraic code and adding random error vector to it (with weight of error less or equal to correcting ability of the code): $C_x^j = M_j \cdot G_x^i + e$, where $e = \{e_1, e_2, \ldots, e_n\}$, $w(e) \le t = (d-1)/2$.

Construction of cascade code-theoretic schemes. To construct cascade code-theoretic scheme, we will fix generalized cascade code of m order. By definition [5] algebraically fixed generalized cascade code of m order is univalently defined by n_2 square binary matrices $H_0^j, j = \overline{1, n_2}$ orde n_1 (fixing (n_1, k_i, d_{1i}) of codes of first level) and m+1 group ones over $GF(2^{ai})$, i= $\overline{1, m+1}$ codes of second level with parameters (n_2 b_i, d_{2i}). Values ai > 0 and bi ≥ 0 ,, defining inner structure of generalized cascade (n, k, d) code, are chosen in an arbitrary way, at that (n, k, d) parameters meet the following correlations:

$$n = n_1 n_2; \quad k = \sum_{i=1}^{m+1} a_i b_i;$$

$$d \ge \begin{cases} min\{d_{1i}d_{2i}: i = \overline{1, m}\}, b_{m+1} = 0 \\ min\{d_{2m+1}, d_{1i}d_{2i}: i = \overline{1, m}\}, b_{m+1} \ne 0 \end{cases}$$

According to made conclusions in the work [5], dissimulating all codes of the second level is the most efficient (from the point of view of key data volumes) variant of code-theoretic scheme construction on generalized cascade codes. In this case we will understand the procedure of coding generalized cascade code with dissimulated codes of external level and adding random error vector to it (with weight of error less or equal to correcting ability of the code) as direct mapping (encrypting)

$\phi_i : M \xrightarrow{K_i} E$. We will understand the decoding process of code word with errors of generalized cascade code with dissimulated code of external level as inverse mapping (decrypting) $\phi_i^{-1} =: E \xrightarrow{K^*_i} M$. The direct mapping will be parametrized by the key $K_i \in K$, univalently fixing dissimulating code (e.g. as a aggregate of generating and/or correcting matrices of generalized code). The inverse mapping will be parametrized by the key $K_i^* \in K^*$, allowing to reestablish the rule of quick decoding (e.g. with the help of dissimulation matrices). We will introduce abstract definition of cascade code-theoretic scheme, constructed in generalized cascade (n, k, d) code of m order as an aggregate of following sets:

-     set of clear texts

$M = \{M_1, M_2, ..., M_qk\}$,where each M_i represents information block of the form

$$M_i = \{(I_{1,1}, I_{1,2}, ..., I_{1,a1}), (I_{2,1}, I_{2,2}, ..., I_{2,a1}),..., (I_{b1,1}, I_{b1,2}, ..., I_{b1,a1}),$$

$$(I_{1,1}, I_{1,2}, ..., I_{1,a2}), (I_{2,1}, I_{2,2}, ..., I_{2,a2}),..., (I_{b2,1}, I_{b2,2}, ..., I_{b2,a2}),...,$$

$$(I_{1,1}, I_{1,2}, ..., I_{1,}a_{m+1}), (I_{2,1}, I_{2,2}, ..., I_{2, am+1}),..., (I_{bm+1,1}, I_{bm+1,2}, ..., I_{bm+1, am+1}) \};$$

-     set of cryptograms

$$E = \{E_1, E_2, ..., E_qk\},$$

where each E_i represents a code word of the form $E_i = C_i + e_i$ that is the sum of the code word of generalized cascade code with random error vector e_i, besides

$$C_i = \{(C_{1,1}, C_{1,2}, ..., C_{1,a1}), (C_{2,1}, C_{2,2}, ..., C_{2,a1}),..., (C_{n2,1}, C_{n2,2}, ..., C_{n2,a1}), (C_{1,1},$$
$$C_{1,2}, ..., C_{1,a2}), (C_{2,1}, C_{2,2}, ..., C_{2,a2}),..., (C_{n2,1}, C_{n2,2}, ..., C_{n2,a2}),$$

$$...$$

$$(C_{1,1}, C_{1,2}, ..., C_{1,}a_{m+1}), (C_{2,1}, C_{2,2}, ..., C_{2, am+1}),..., (C_{n2,1}, C_{n2,2}, ..., C_{n2, am+1}), \};$$

$$\text{Or } C_i = \{(\gamma_{1,1}, \gamma_{1,2}, ..., \gamma_{1,n2}), (\gamma_{2,1}, \gamma_{2,2}, ..., \gamma_{2,n2}),...,$$

$$(\gamma_{m+1,1}, \gamma_{m+1,2}, ..., \gamma_{m+1, n2});$$

$$\text{where } \gamma_{1,j} =(C_{i,1}, C_{i,2}, ..., C_{i,aj}).$$

Thus, the codogram is a vector $E_i = \{(\gamma^*_{1,1}, \gamma^*_{1,2}, ..., \gamma^*_{1,n2}), (\gamma^*_{2,1}, \gamma^*_{2,2}, ..., \gamma^*_{2,n2}),..., (\gamma^*_{m+1,1}, \gamma^*_{m+1,2}, ..., \gamma^*_{m+1, n2})$,where, $\gamma^*_{ij} = \gamma_{ij} + e_{ij}$ – a binary vector of the a_i length,

$$\sum_{i=1}^{m+1} a_i = n_1$$

e_{ij} -elements of random error vector of ai length (session key);

-     set of direct mappings

$$\phi = \left\{\phi_1, \phi_2, ..., \phi_s\right\}$$ where $\phi_i : M \rightarrow E$, i=1,2,...,s

-   set of inverse mappings

$$\phi^{-1} = \left\{\phi_1^{-1}, \phi_2^{-1}, ..., \phi_s^{-1}\right\}$$ where $\phi_i^{-1} : E \rightarrow M$, i=1,2,...,s

-   set of keys, parametrizing direct mappings

where Ki = $\{G_X^1, G_X^2, ..., G_X^{m+1}\}$ – a set of generating matrices, which give m+1 of dissimulated codes of external level;

-   set of keys, parametrizing inverse mappings

$$K^* = \{K_1^*, K_2^*, ..., Ks^*\}, \phi_i : E \xrightarrow{K_i} M$$

where $K_i^* = \{\{X^1, P^1, D^1\}, \{X^2, P^2, D^2\}, ..., \{X^{m+1}, P^{m+1}, D^{m+1}\}\}$ – set of matrices, dissimulating m+1 of codes of external level.

To evaluate parameters of cascade code-theoretic scheme we will formulate and prove the following theorem.

Theorem 1. Let us assume that cascade code-theoretic scheme in generalized cascade code of m order is set by dissimulating all its codes of the second level. Then the volume of the key (in bytes) of direct mapping is set by the expression:

$$1_k = n_2 \sum_{j=1}^{m+1} b_j \cdot a_j \tag{1}$$

key volume (in bits) of inverse mapping is set by the formula

$$1_{k^*} = n_2^2 \sum_{i=1}^{m+1} b_i^2 \cdot a_j, \tag{2}$$

the length of information block of data and length of codogram (in bits) are set, correspondingly, by expressions:

$$1_m = \sum_{j=1}^{m+1} b_j \cdot a_j ; \quad 1_E = n1 \cdot n2 \tag{3}$$

and relative speed of data transfer is set

$$R = \frac{1}{n_1 \cdot n_2} \sum_{j=1}^{m+1} b_j \cdot a_j \tag{4}$$

Proof 1. To dissimulate all codes of the second level of generalized cascade code of m order the procedure of multiplication of corresponding generating matrices $G^1, G^2, \ldots, G^{m+1}$, by dissimulation matrice

$$\{X^1, P^1, D^1\}, \{X^2, P^2, D^2\}, \ldots, \{X^{m+1}, P^{m+1}, D^{m+1}\} : G_X^{-1} = X^1 \cdot G^1 \cdot P^1 \cdot D^1$$

$$\ldots\ldots$$

$$G_X^{m+1} = X^{m+1} \cdot G^{m+1} \cdot P^{m+1} \cdot D^{m+1}.$$

Consequently, to conserve the key of direct mapping it is necessary to save m+ matrices, size of each of which is set by parameters of corresponding code of external level of generalized cascade code. So, for example, G_X^j matrix sets dissimulated (n_2, b_j, d_{2j}) code of external level, that is has dimensionality of $n_2 \times b_j$ symbols from $GF(2^a_j)$. Practically it means that to conserve elements of G_X^j matrices $n_2, b_j, a_j)$ bit is needed. In all to conserve a key of direct mapping

$$L_k = \sum_{j=1}^{m+1} n_2 \cdot b_j \cdot a_j = n_2 \sum_{j=1}^{m+1} b_j \cdot a_j \text{ bit.}$$

To conserve corresponding key of inverse mapping it is necessary to save matrices $\{X^j, P^j, D^j\}$, $j=1, \ldots, m+1$. Matrix X^j has dimensionality of $b_j \times b_j$ symbols from $GF(2^a_j)$ and matrix $\Delta^j = P^j \cdot D^j$ has dimensionality of $n_2 \times n_2$ symbols from $GF(2^a_j)$. Practically it means that to conserve the key of inverse mapping as an aggregate of dissimulating matrices

$$\{X^1, P^1, D^1\}, \{X^2, P^2, D^2\}, \ldots, \{X^{m+1}, P^{m+1}, D^{m+1}\}$$

it is necessary to save

$$L_k^* = \sum_{j=0}^{m+1} (b_j \cdot b_j \cdot a_j + n_2 \cdot n_2 \cdot a_j) = n_2 \sum_{j=1}^{m+1} b_j^2 \cdot a_j \text{ bit.}$$

The length of information block l_M, length of codogram l_E and relative speed of information transfer $R = l_M / l_E$ are defined by corresponding parameters of generalized cascade code:

$$l_m = k = \sum_{j=1}^{m+1} b_j \cdot a_j, l_E = n = n1 \cdot n_2,$$

$$R = \frac{l_M}{l_E} = R = \frac{1}{n_1 \cdot n_2} \sum_{j=1}^{m+1} b_j \cdot a_j$$

this completes the proof.

The formulated theorem establishes important interaction between parameters of generalized cascade code and main indexes of cascade code-theoretic scheme. Expressions (1)-(5) disclose analytical dependence between code characteristics of codes of external level of generalized cascade code and characteristics of cryptosystem constructed on their basis.

The analysis of received correlations shows that employment of generalized cascade codes allows to build code schemes of information security with small sizes of key data. The complexity of operation realization of encrypting and decrypting is defined by the intricacy of operation of coding and decoding of generalized cascade code.

3   Attacks, Based on Nonalgebraic Methods of Decoding

Decoding of certain linear code (code of general position) is a considerably intricate computational task, the intricacy of its decision rises exponentially. So, for correlation decoding of certain (n, k, d) code over GF(q) it is necessary, in the general case, to compare accepted consequence with all q^k code words and choose the nearest one (in Hamming distance). Even for small n, k, d and q task of correlation decoding is considerably cumbersome. This position is the basis for all non-symmetrical code-theoretic schemes. Dissimulating the code with rapid algorithm of decoding (polynomial intricacy) in certain (random) linear code, decoding task for outside observer (possible intruder) can be presented as a computationally intricate task (exponential intricacy). For an authorized user (having a secret key) decoding is a polynomially solvable task.

One of the most efficient methods of decoding of linear code is use of a permutable decoder. The main idea of such decoding consists in the fact that unit of information sets is used to form corresponding choice of candidates in code words. Further, according to algorithm, among these candidates the nearest one is chosen. If whereby there is no error in one of the information components in the accepted consequence, transferred code word will be in the list of candidates. Thus, if factual combination of errors can be corrected by the decoder of maximum likelihood, the code word will have the lowest distance to the accepted consequence and be chosen by permutable decoder. While considering resettable decoding errors combination will be found, if finding such information set, fully containing this combination turns out well. Such set, roofing combination of errors, and unit of control sets, covering all units of errors of the given type, are called overlapping. The task of the decoder is to find a control set, covering unknown combination of errors. Let's consider bounds for quantity of roofing sets. Let's suppose that all combinations out of t or smaller quantity of errors are corrected with the help of the code (n, k, d). Let's consider the combination only out of t-multiple errors, as all errors of less multiplicity will be covered. The general quantity of errors in all n positions is equal to C_n^t. By virtue of the fact that the volume of roofing set is equal to n-k, maximum quantity of errors combinations, which can be covered by the given set, equals to C_{n-k}^t. The least quantity of sets, which can correct all combinations out of t errors, is restricted to the expression [9]:

$$\delta \geq \frac{C_n^t}{C_{n-k}^t} \tag{5}$$

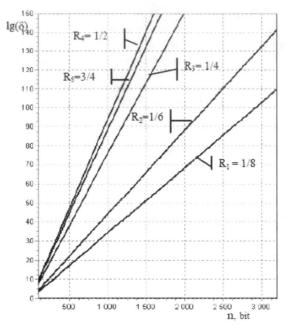

Fig. 1. The intricacy of the hacking task of code-theoretic scheme as decoding task decision of a elliptical code by permutable decoder

In Fig.1 as an example dependences of hacking intricacy of code-theoretic scheme by an opponent, constructed by elliptical code with relative rate of coding R are given [7]. As it is seen from the presented dependences, permutable decoder becomes inefficient even at values n>500. Consequently, hacking of code-theoretic schemes at corresponding choice of parameters of random code is computationally unavailable. Thus, carried out researches have shown that code-theoretic schemes allow to provide required resistance to cryptanalytic attacks of an opponent at appropriate choosing parameters of dissimulated code. Correlation (1) determines an analytical dependence between parameters of code-theoretic scheme and its stability to corresponding attacks.

4   Results

Expression (5) while using generalized cascade codes is transformed as:

$$\delta \geq v \cdot \sum_{i=0}^{m+1} \frac{C_{n2}^{ti}}{C_{n2-bi}^{ti}} \qquad (6)$$

where t_i – correcting ability of i code of external level, $d_{2i}=2t_i+1$; v – number of construction variants of generalized cascade code, at unknown order of generalized cascade code – $v=2^{nl-1}$, at known order – $v= C_{nl-1}^{m+1}$.

It should be noted that construction of code-theoretic schemes is based on dissimulating error-control (n, k, d) block code with rapid algorithm of decoding in random code. At this random vector of errors e, weight of which is less or equal to correcting ability of the code w(e)≤t, where t= ⌊d-1/2⌋ is introduced into code word (n, k, d) of block code. Let's denote the weight deal of errors vector of vector e, arriving for artificial entry of code-theoretic scheme, with the symbol ρ: ρ=w(e)/t. Then potential resistance of code-theoretic scheme will be defined by magnitude ρ·t, and error-control of transferred codograms is defined by magnitude (1-ρ)·t. At this expression (6) will be rewritten as:

$$\delta \geq v \cdot \sum_{i=0}^{m+1} \frac{C_{n2}^{\rho_i t_i}}{C_{n2-bi}^{\rho_i t_i}} \qquad (7)$$

where ρ_1 – deal of correcting ability of i code of external level, arriving for artificial entry of errors.

In fig.2 dependences of hacking intricacy of cascade code-theoretic scheme by the opponent, constructed by generalized cascade code with relative rate of coding R are given.

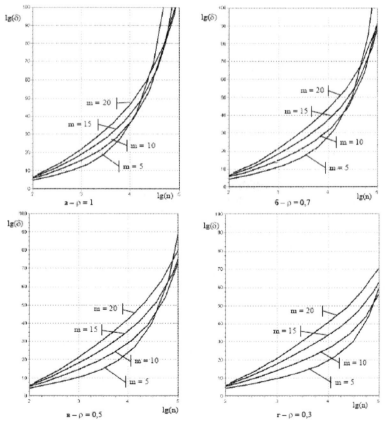

Fig. 2. Intricacy of hacking task of cascade code scheme as a decoding task decision of generalized cascade code by permutable decoder, R=1/2

The analysis of dependences shows that the number of searches, necessary for opponent to decode a code word, considerably rises with increasing m group ones over $GF(2^{ai})$, $i = \overline{1, m+1}$, codes of external levels of generalized cascade code, deal of correcting ability of the code of external level, arriving for artificial entry of errors – ρ, and also with increasing of the number of n_1 number decomposing variants, extending finite Galois field $GF(2^{ai})$, over which corresponding codes of external level are constructed.

Hence, attack realization intricacy by permutable decoder rises according to exponential dependence and at values:

$$\rho > 0.5\text{-}0.7;$$

$$m = 10\text{-}20;$$

$$n > 2000$$

high resistance of suggested constructions to hacking by an opponent with the help of the method of permutable decoding (from 10^{25} and more group operations) is achieved.

5 Conclusions

As a result of carried out researches cascade code-theoretic schemes, based on codes dissimilating operation of external level of generalized cascade code have been developed. Main apalytic correlations in evaluation of their parameters have been received. It is shown that employment of cascade construction lifts main practical restrictions in volume of key and realization complexity.

References

1. McEliece, R.J.: A Public-Key Criptosystem Based on Algebraic Theory DGN Progres Report42-44, Jet Propulsi on Lab. Pasadena, CA, pp. 114–116 (January-February 1978)
2. Rao, T.R.N., Nam, K.-H.: Private-Key Algebraic-Coded Cryptosystems. In: Odlyzko, A.M. (ed.) CRYPTO 1986. LNCS, vol. 263, pp. 35–48. Springer, Heidelberg (1987)
3. Sidelnikov, V.M.: Cryptography and coding theory NTK materials 'MSU and cryptography development in Russia'
4. Kuznetsov, A.A., Stasev, Y.V.: Non-symmetric code-theoretic schemes using algebro-geometric codes. Cybernetics and System Analysis
5. Blokh, E.L., Zyablov, V.V.: Generalized cascade codes (Algebraic theory and realization intricacy)
6. Clark, D.-m., Kane J.: Encoding linier corrected errors in digital communications: Trans. from English. In: Tsybakova, B.S. (ed.) Radio and Communications (1987)
7. Kuznetsov, A.A., Lysenko, V.N., Evseev, S.P.: The study of the properties of asymmetric code-theoretic schemes with elliptic codes. System Information. - H.: HVU 9(37) (2004)

Generalization of Weger's Attack

Navaneet Ojha and Sahadeo Padhye

Department of Mathematics
Motilal Nehru National Institute of Technology
Allahabad-211004, India
navaneet15@gmail.com, sahadeo_mathrsu@yahoo.com

Abstract. In 2002, De Weger show that choosing an RSA modulus with a small difference of its prime factors yields improvements on the small private exponent attacks of Wiener and Boneh-Durfee. In this paper, we extend the Weger's bound of the Boneh-Durfee attack for the RSA modulus $N = pq$, when $\frac{p}{q}$ being close to $\frac{b}{a}$ with small integers a and b. We improve the bound of de Weger for the weaker and stronger results of Boneh-Durfee attack.

Keywords: RSA, Cryptanalysis, Lattices, Wiener's attack, Boneh-Durfee Attack.

1 Introduction

The RSA cryptosystem [10] invented by Rivest, Shamir and Adleman in 1978 is one of the most practical and popular public key cryptosystem in the history of the cryptology. Since then, the RSA system has been the most widely accepted public key cryptosystem in the world. In the RSA cryptosystem, let $N = pq$ be an RSA modulus, where p and q are primes of equal bit size. Let e be the public exponent and d be the secret exponent satisfying $ed \equiv 1 mod(\phi(N))$, where $\phi(N)$, is the Euler totient function.

To speed up the RSA encryption or decryption one may try to use small public or secret exponent. The choice of small e or d is especially interesting when there is a large difference in computing power between two communication devices, e.g; in communication between a smart card and a larger computer. In this situation, it would be desirable for the smart card to have a small secret exponent, and for the larger computer to have a small public exponent in order to reduce the processing required in the smart card. Unfortunately, in 1990, Wiener [12] showed that if the private key $d < \frac{1}{3}N^{\frac{1}{4}}$ then N can be factored in polynomial time. Wiener's attack is based on approximations using the continued fraction[6] expansion of $\frac{e}{N}$. In 1999, Boneh and Durfee [2] described an improvement of Wiener's bound by showing that RSA is insecure if $d < N^{0.284}$ using lattice reduction technique [3,7]. They further improved their result $d < N^{0.284}$ to $d < N^{0.292}$ by using the notions of *geometrically progressive* matrices.

A. Abd Manaf et al. (Eds.): ICIEIS 2011, Part I, CCIS 251, pp. 141–150, 2011.

This two bounds are called weaker and stronger results of Booneh-Durfee attack respectively. In 2002, Weger [11] improved Wiener's bound to $d < N^\delta$, where $\delta < \frac{3}{4} - \beta$ and Boneh-Durfee's weaker and stronger bound to $d < N^\delta$, where $\delta < \frac{1}{6}(4\beta + 5) - \frac{1}{3}\sqrt{(4\beta + 5)(4\beta - 1)}$ and $2 - 4\beta < \delta < 1 - \sqrt{2\beta - \frac{1}{2}}$ respectively by assuming that $\phi(N) > \frac{3}{4}N$ and N with a small difference between its prime factors $p - q = N^\beta, \frac{1}{4} \leq \beta \leq \frac{1}{2}$.

In [11], de Weger suggested for further work to investigate the effects on small private exponent attacks when $\frac{p}{q}$ being close to some rational number $\frac{b}{a}$ (other than 1) with small numerator and denominator. On the other hand, in $X9.31 - 1997$ standard for public key cryptography, Section 4.1.2, there are a number of recommendations for the generation of the primes of an RSA modulus. Among them is the ratio of the primes shall not be closed to the ratio of the small integers.

1.1   Our Contribution

In this paper, we extend the Weger's bound of the Boneh-Durfee attack for the RSA modulus $N = pq$, when $\frac{p}{q}$ being close to $\frac{b}{a}$ with small integers a and b. Also a and b can be generated by Stern Brocot Tree [5]. Let

$$|ap - bq| = N^\beta$$

where

$$\frac{1}{4} \leq \beta \leq \frac{1}{2}$$

We improve the bound of de Weger [11] for the weaker result of Boneh-Durfee [2] attack by

$$\delta < \frac{1}{6}(4\beta + 2\gamma + 5) - \frac{1}{3}\sqrt{(4\beta + 2\gamma + 5)(4\beta + 2\gamma - 1)}$$

and for the stronger result of Boneh-Durfee attack by

$$2 - 4\beta + 2\gamma < \delta < 1 - \sqrt{2\beta + \gamma - \frac{1}{2}}$$

Here γ depends only on a and b. Our method combines LLL algorithm [7], Coppersmith [3] method and the method discussed in [4]. We have shown that the result given by B. de Weger can be obtained by our result as a particular case.

1.2   Roadmap

The rest of the paper is organized as follows. In the Section 2 we give a brief introduction to lattices. In the Section 3 we present our main work. The Section 4 concludes the paper.

2   Preliminaries

In this section, we briefly discuss about the lattices.

2.1   Lattices

Let $u_1, ..., u_w \epsilon Z^n$ be linearly independent vectors with $w \leq n$. A lattice L spanned by $\langle u_1, ..., u_w \rangle$ is the set of all integer linear combinations of $u_1, ..., u_w$. We say that the lattice is full rank if $w = n$. We state a few basic results about lattices and lattice basis reduction and refer to [2] and L. Lovasz [8] for an introduction.

Let L be a lattice spanned by $\langle u_1, ..., u_w \rangle$. We denote by $u_1^*, ..., u_w^*$ the vectors obtained by applying the Gram-Schmidt process to the vectors $u_1, ..., u_w$. We define the determinant of the lattice L as

$$det(L) = \prod_{i=1}^{w} ||u_i^*||$$

where $||.||$ denotes the Euclidean norm on vectors.

2.2   (LLL)

Fact 1 [2]. Let L be a lattice spanned by $\langle u_1, ..., u_w \rangle$. The LLL algorithm, given $\langle u_1, ..., u_w \rangle$, runs in polynomial time and produces a new basis $\langle b_1, ..., b_w \rangle$ of L satisfying

   1.$||b_i^*||^2 \leq ||b_{i+1}^*||$,for all $1 \leq i < w$.

   2. For all i, if $b_i = b_i^* + \sum_{j=1}^{i-1} \mu_j b_j^*$, then $|\mu_j| \leq \frac{1}{2}$ for all j.

Fact 2 [2]. Let L be a lattice and $b_1, ..., b_w$ be an LLL reduced basis of L. Then

$$||b_1|| \leq 2^{\frac{w}{2}} det(L)^{\frac{1}{w}}$$

Fact 3 [2]. Let L be a lattice spanned by $u_1, ..., u_w$ and $b_1, ..., b_w$ be the result of applying LLL to the given basis. Suppose $u_{min}^* \geq 1$. Then

$$||b_2|| \leq 2^{\frac{w}{2}} dt(L)^{\frac{1}{w-1}}$$

2.3   Geometrically Progressive Matrices [2]

Let u, v be positive integers and let M be an $(u + 1)v \times (u + 1)v$ matrix. We index the columns by the pairs i,j, with $i = 0, ..., u$ and $j = 1, ..., v$, so that the pair (i,j) corresponds to the $(vi + j)^{th}$ column of M. Similarly, we use the pair (k,l) to index the $(vk + l)^{th}$ row of M, for $k = 0, .., u$ and $l = 1, ...v$. The entry in the $(i,j)^{th}$ column of the $(k,l)^{th}$ row is denoted by $M(i,j,k,l)$. Note that the diagonal entries of M are precisely those of the form $M(k,l,k,l)$.

2.4   Definition 1 [2]

Let $C, D, c_0, c_1, c_2, c_3, c_4, \lambda$ be a real numbers with $C, D, \lambda \geq 1$. A matrix M is said to be geometrically progressive with parameters $(C, D, c_0, c_1, c_2, c_3, c_4, \lambda)$ if the following conditions hold for all $i, k = 0, \ldots, u$ and $j, l = 1, \ldots v$:

1. $|M(i,j,k,l)| \leq C.D^{c_0+c_1 i+c_2 j+c_3 k+c_4 l}$.
2. $M(k,l,k,l) = D^{c_0+c_1 i+c_2 j+c_3 k+c_4 l}$.
3. $M(i,j,k,l) = 0$, whenever $i > k$ or $j > l$.
4. $\lambda c_1 + c_3 \geq 0$ and $\lambda c_2 + c_4 \geq 0$.

When the parameters $C, D, c_0, c_1, c_2, c_3, c_4, \lambda$ are understood we say simply that M is geometrically progressive.

2.5   Proposition [4]

Let p and q be two RSA primes satisfying $p < q < 2p$. If $\frac{p}{q}$ is close to $\frac{b}{a}$ s.t.

$$(b(a^2 + 1)p - a(b^2 + 1)q)(ap - bq) > 0$$

then

$$\frac{a+b}{\sqrt{ab}}\sqrt{N} - p - q < \frac{(ap - bq)^2}{(\frac{a+b}{\sqrt{ab}} + 2)\sqrt{N}}$$

3   Main Result

In the paper [11] Benne de Weger extended the weaker and stronger result of Boneh-Durfee attack [2] for the RSA modulus with small prime difference. In this section we investigate the effects on Boneh-Durfee attacks of the RSA prime fraction $\frac{p}{q}$ being close to some rational number with small numerator and denominator.

3.1   Extending the Boneh-Durfee Attack I

In this section we will show how to extend the weaker result of [2] to the case of the ratio of two RSA primes $\frac{p}{q}$ is close to $\frac{b}{a}$ with small integers a and b. In the next section we will do the same for the stronger result of [2].

Assuming that e is of the same order of magnitude as N, i.e.; if $e = N^\alpha$ for some α close to 1.
Let $d = N^\delta$, assume $e \approx N$ as for $e < N$ one can get better bound on δ [2].
Since

$$\begin{aligned} ed &= 1 + k\phi(N) \\ &= 1 + k(N + 1 - p - q) \\ &= 1 + k(N + 1 - (\frac{a+b}{\sqrt{ab}})\sqrt{N} - (p + q - (\frac{a+b}{\sqrt{ab}})\sqrt{N})) \\ &= 1 + x(A + y) \end{aligned}$$

where $x = k < d = N^\delta, A = N + 1 - \frac{a+b}{\sqrt{ab}}\sqrt{N}$ and $y = (\frac{a+b}{\sqrt{ab}})\sqrt{N}) - (p+q)$,

or,

$$y < \frac{(ap-bq)^2}{(\frac{a+b}{\sqrt{ab}}+2)\sqrt{N}}, \qquad (1)$$

by Proposition (above) [4].

Using $e \approx N$, we have, $x < e^\delta$.
Let $\frac{1}{\frac{a+b}{\sqrt{ab}}+2} = N^\gamma$, then from (1) we have

$$|y| < \frac{|ap-bq|^2}{(\frac{a+b}{\sqrt{ab}}+2)\sqrt{N}}$$
$$\le N^{2\beta}N^\gamma N^{-\frac{1}{2}}$$
$$= e^{2\beta+\gamma-\frac{1}{2}}$$

we have to find x, y s.t.

$$1 \mid x(\Lambda \mid y) \equiv 0 \bmod e$$

where

$$|x| < N^\delta \approx e^\delta$$

and

$$|y| < e^{2\beta+\gamma-\frac{1}{2}}$$

Following the idea of [2], let $X_1 = e^\delta$, $Y_1 = e^{2\beta+\gamma-\frac{1}{2}}$.

In order to the guarantee the existence of short enough vectors in the lattice, a condition on the determinant and the dimension has to be fulfilled. For the determinant of the lattice with only x-shifts, which has dimension $w = \frac{1}{2}m^2 + o(m^2)$, we have

$$det_x = e^{\frac{m(m+1)(m+2)}{3}} X_1^{\frac{m(m+1)(m+2)}{3}} Y_1^{\frac{m(m+1)(m+2)}{6}} \qquad (2)$$

so similar the idea of Weger [11], when we take no y-shifts at all, the condition

$$det_x < e^{mw} \qquad (3)$$

to be fulfilled (up to the negligible constant)

$$det_x = e^{\frac{m(m+1)(m+2)}{3}} e^{\frac{\delta m(m+1)(m+2)}{3}} e^{\frac{(2\beta+\gamma-\frac{1}{2})m(m+1)(m+2)}{6}}$$
$$= e^{m^3[\frac{1}{4}+\frac{\delta}{3}+\frac{\beta}{3}+\frac{\gamma}{6}]+0(m^3)} < e^{mw} \qquad (4)$$

Now from (4), we have

$$\frac{1}{4} + \frac{\delta}{3} + \frac{\beta}{3} + \frac{\gamma}{6} < \frac{1}{2}$$

thus

$$\delta < \frac{3}{4} - (\beta + \frac{\gamma}{2}) \tag{5}$$

This is similar to

$$\delta < \frac{3}{4} - \beta$$

as in Wiener's extended attack given in [11], if $\gamma = 0$.

Similarly including the y-shifts, given in Boneh [2], we find for the contribution of the y-shifts to the determinant that

$$det_y = e^{\frac{tm(m+1)}{2}} X_1^{\frac{tm(m+1)}{2}} Y_1^{\frac{t(m+1)(m+t+1)}{2}} \tag{6}$$

Putting the values of X_1 & Y_1 in (6), we have

$$det_y = e^{\frac{tm(m+1)}{2}} e^{\frac{t\delta m(m+1)}{2}} e^{\frac{(2\beta+\gamma-\frac{1}{2})t(m+1)(m+t+1)}{2}}$$

$$= e^{tm^2[\frac{1}{4}+\frac{\delta}{2}+\beta+\frac{\gamma}{2}]+t^2m(\beta+\frac{\gamma}{2}-\frac{1}{4})+0(tm^2)}$$

Now the determinant of the entire matrix is

$$det(L) = det_x det_y$$

Since we know from [2] that,

$$det(L) < e^{mw}$$

where dimension

$$w = \frac{(m+1)(m+2)}{2} + t(m+1) = \frac{m^2}{2} + tm + 0(m^2)$$

So,

$$det_x det_y < e^{mw}$$

or,

$$m^2[-\frac{1}{4} + \frac{\delta}{3} + \frac{\beta}{3} + \frac{\gamma}{6}] + tm[-\frac{3}{4} + \frac{\delta}{2} + \beta + \frac{\gamma}{2}] + t^2[\beta + \frac{\gamma}{2} - \frac{1}{4}] < 0 \tag{7}$$

After fixing an m, the left hand side is minimized at

$$t = (\frac{\frac{3}{4} - \frac{\delta}{2} - \beta - \frac{\gamma}{2}}{2\beta + \gamma - \frac{1}{2}})m$$

Putting this value of t in (7), we have

$$[-\tfrac{1}{4}+\tfrac{\delta}{3}+\tfrac{\beta}{3}+\tfrac{\gamma}{6}]+(\tfrac{\frac{3}{4}-\frac{\delta}{2}-\beta-\frac{\gamma}{2}}{2\beta+\gamma-\frac{1}{2}})(-\tfrac{3}{4}+\tfrac{\delta}{2}+\beta+\tfrac{\gamma}{2})+(\tfrac{\frac{3}{4}-\frac{\delta}{2}-\beta-\frac{\gamma}{2}}{2\beta+\gamma-\frac{1}{2}})^2(\beta+\tfrac{\gamma}{2}-\tfrac{1}{4})<0$$

On simplifying above, we get the result

$$\delta < \tfrac{1}{6}(4\beta+2\gamma+5)-\tfrac{1}{3}\sqrt{(4\beta+2\gamma+5)(4\beta+2\gamma-1)}.$$

Similar to the idea given in [2], if the first two elements (polynomials $g_1(x,y)$, $g_2(x,y)$) of the reduced basis out of the L^3 algorithm are algebraically independent(i.e.; non-zero resultant $res(g_1,g_2)$) which is a polynomial of y, say), then we get y by solving $res(g_1,g_2)=0$, allowing us to find the factorization of N. Note that if $\gamma=0$, we recover the result of de Weger [11]. For $\gamma=0, \beta=\tfrac{1}{2}$, we recover Boneh and Durfee's result

$$\delta < \tfrac{7}{6}-\tfrac{1}{3}\sqrt{7}.$$

3.2   Extending the Boneh-Durfee Attack II

In [2], Boneh gave an idea to improve the result

$$\delta < \tfrac{7}{6}-\tfrac{1}{3}\sqrt{7} \text{ to } \delta < 1-\tfrac{1}{2}\sqrt{2}.$$

In this section we will follow their argument with the conditions $Y_1 = e^{2\beta+\gamma-\frac{1}{2}}$ instead of $Y_1 = e^{\frac{1}{2}}$. Lemma 5.2 from [2] can be improved to M_y (It is the $(m+1)t \times (m+1)t$ lower right- hand submatrix of the matrix M) being geometrically progressive with the obvious parameter choice $(m^{2m}, e, m, \delta+2\beta+\gamma-\tfrac{1}{2}, 2\beta+\gamma-\tfrac{3}{2}, -1, 1, \lambda)$ for some λ. Here we can check easily the conditions of $1, 2, 3$ of definition 1(see above). The condition 4 causes some trouble. Namely λ should satisfy

$$\lambda(\delta+2\beta+\gamma-\tfrac{1}{2})-1 \geq 0$$

and

$$\lambda(2\beta+\gamma-\frac{3}{2})+1 \geq 0 \tag{8}$$

and these conditions are contradictory when

$$\delta < 2-4\beta+2\gamma.$$

So we must assume

$$\delta > 2-4\beta+2\gamma.$$

So, we can take from (8),

$$\lambda = \frac{2}{3 - 4\beta + 2\gamma}.$$

The optimal choice for t is

$$t = \left(\frac{\frac{3}{2} - \delta - 2\beta - \gamma}{2\beta + \gamma - \frac{1}{2}}\right)m.$$

Now,

$$M_y(k,l,k,l) = e^{m + (\delta + 2\beta + \gamma - \frac{1}{2})k + (2\beta + \gamma - \frac{3}{2})l + (-1)k + 1.l}$$

$$= e^{m + (\delta + 2\beta + \gamma - \frac{3}{2})k + (2\beta + \gamma - \frac{1}{2})l}$$

We begin by computing w'. Let $S \subseteq \{0, ..., m\} \times \{1...., t\}$ be the subset of indices s.t.

$$M_y(k,l,k,l) \leq e^m \text{ for } (k,l)\epsilon S,$$

so that

$$w' = |S|.$$

Since

$$(k,l)\epsilon S$$

only if

$$e^{m + (\delta + 2\beta + \gamma - \frac{3}{2})k + (2\beta + \gamma - \frac{1}{2})l} < e^m,$$

then

$$l = \left(\frac{\frac{3}{2} - \delta - 2\beta - \gamma}{2\beta + \gamma - \frac{1}{2}}\right)k.$$

Since we have taken

$$t = \left(\frac{\frac{3}{2} - \delta - 2\beta - \gamma}{2\beta + \gamma - \frac{1}{2}}\right)m,$$

we know every pair satisfies

$$l \leq \left(\frac{\frac{3}{2} - \delta - 2\beta - \gamma}{2\beta + \gamma - \frac{1}{2}}\right)k \leq t,$$

so

$$l \leq \left(\frac{\frac{3}{2} - \delta - 2\beta - \gamma}{2\beta + \gamma - \frac{1}{2}}\right)k$$

iff

$$(k,l)\epsilon S.$$

Thus

$$w' = |S|$$

$$= \Sigma_{k=0}^{m} \lfloor(\frac{\frac{3}{2} - \delta - 2\beta - \gamma}{2\beta + \gamma - \frac{1}{2}})k\rfloor$$

$$\geq \Sigma_{k=0}^{m} [(\frac{\frac{3}{2} - \delta - 2\beta - \gamma}{2\beta + \gamma - \frac{1}{2}})k - 1]$$

$$= (\frac{\frac{3}{2} - \delta - 2\beta - \gamma}{4\beta + 2\gamma - 1})k + 0(m^2)$$

Now,

$$w' + \frac{(m + 1)(m + 2)}{2} = (\frac{\frac{3}{2} - \delta - 2\beta - \gamma}{4\beta + 2\gamma - 1})m^2 + \frac{1}{2}m^2 + 0(m^2)$$

$$= (\frac{1 - \delta}{4\beta + 2\gamma - 1})m^2 + 0(m^2)$$

Now, we have to find $det(L'_y)$. Since this lattice is defined by the rows $(k,l)\epsilon S$ of M_y, by Theorem (5.1) from [2], we have

$$det(L'_y) = e^{m^3(\frac{9 - 4(\delta + 2\beta + \gamma)^2}{12(4\beta + 2\gamma - 1)}) + 0(m^3)} \tag{9}$$

Actually (9) is very tedious and complicated calculation and it is closely following the idea given by [2].

Finally, from the previous section

$$det(\Delta) = det_x = e^{m^3[\frac{1}{4} + \frac{\delta}{3} + \frac{\beta}{3} + \frac{\gamma}{6}] + 0(m^3)}$$

Thus,

$$det(L_1) = det(\Delta)det(L'_y)$$

$$\leq e^{m^3[\frac{1}{4} + \frac{\delta}{3} + \frac{\beta}{3} + \frac{\gamma}{6}] + 0(m^3)} e^{m^3(\frac{9 - 4(\delta + 2\beta + \gamma)^2}{12(4\beta + 2\gamma - 1)}) + 0(m^3)}$$

$$< e^{mw}$$

$$= e^{m^3(\frac{1 - \delta}{4\beta + 2\gamma - 1}) + 0(m^3)}$$

this implies that

$$\delta < 1 - \sqrt{2\beta + \gamma - \frac{1}{2}}$$

Hence following the idea given by [2], the factorization of N can be possible. Here, $\gamma = 0$ and $\beta = \frac{1}{2}$, we recover the Boneh result $\delta < 1 - \frac{\sqrt{2}}{2}$. Here also we can say that the de weger result is a particular case of our result.

4   Conclusion

In this paper we extend the weaker and stronger result of Boneh-Durfee attacks of the RSA prime fraction $\frac{p}{q}$ being close to some rational number with small numerator and denominator. We have shown that the result given by B. de Weger can be obtained by our result as a particular case. Our method also generalize the method given by Maitra & Sarkar [9].

References

1. Blömer, J., May, A.: A Generalized Wiener Attack on RSA. In: Bao, F., Deng, R., Zhou, J. (eds.) PKC 2004. LNCS, vol. 2947, pp. 1–13. Springer, Heidelberg (2004)
2. Boneh, D., Durfee, G.: Cryptanalysis RSA with private key $d < N^{0.292}$. In: Stern, J. (ed.) EUROCRYPT 1999. LNCS, vol. 1592, pp. 1–11. Springer, Heidelberg (1999)
3. Coppersmith, D.: Small solutions to polynomial equations and low exponent vulnerabilities. Journal of Cryptology 20(1), 39–50 (2007)
4. Chen, C.Y., Hsueh, C.C., Lin, Y.F.: A Generalization of de Weger's Method. In: Fifth International Conference on Information Assurance and Security (2009), doi:10(1109/IAS)
5. Graham, R.L., Knuth, D.E., Patashnik, O.: Concrete Mathematics-A foundation for computer science, 2nd edn. Addition-Wesley (1994)
6. Hardy, G.H., Wright, E.M.: An introduction to the Theory of Numbers. Oxford University Press, London (1965)
7. Lenstra, A., Lenstra, H., Lovasz, L.: Factoring polynomials with rational coefficients. Math. Annalen (261), 515–534 (1982)
8. Lovasz, L.: An algorithmic theory of numbers, graphs, and convexity. In: SIAM CBMS-NSF Regional Conf. Series in Applied Mathematics, vol. (50) (1986)
9. Maitra, S., Sarkar, S.: Revisiting Wiener's Attack – New Weak Keys in RSA. In: Wu, T.-C., Lei, C.-L., Rijmen, V., Lee, D.-T. (eds.) ISC 2008. LNCS, vol. 5222, pp. 228–243. Springer, Heidelberg (2008)
10. Rivest, R.L., Shamir, A., Adleman, L.M.: A method of obtaining digital signatures and public key cryptosystem. Comm. of the ACM 21(2), 120–126 (1978)
11. de Weger, B.: Cryptanalysis of RSA with small prime difference. In: Applicable Algebra in Engineering, Communication and Computing, AAECC, vol. (13), pp. 17–28 (2002)
12. Wiener, M.J.: Cryptanalysis of short RSA secret exponents. IEEE Trans. on Information Theory, IT (36), 553–558 (1990)

Comparative Analysis and Implementation of Certificateless Based Authentication Scheme

Nazrul M. Ahmad, Asrul H. Yaacob, Alireza Khorram, JinFu Tan,
YiHao Ong, and YewMeng Leong

Faculty of Information Science & Technology (FIST)
Multimedia University (MMU)
Jalan Ayer Keroh Lama
75450 Melaka, Malaysia
{nazrul.muhaimin,asrulhadi.yaacob,alireza.khorram}@mmu.edu.my

Abstract. Certificateless Public Key Infrastructure (CL-PKI) combines
the merits of the trust management in Public Key Infrastructure (PKI)
and the absence of certificate management in identity-based cryptosystem. Inspired by the advantages of CL-PKI, this paper presents the implementation of certificateless based authentication scheme called CLS.
To prove the functionality and practicality of CLS authentication scheme,
this paper presents a comprehensive performance analysis of various security levels of CLS in terms of public key size, signature block size and
the execution time spent on signing and verification operations. The results show that various security levels of the CLS have direct influence
on the length of public key and more importantly, the efficiency of the
scheme in terms of bandwidth usage and run time.

Keywords: certificateless public key infrastructure, bilinear pairing,
authentication scheme, performance.

1 Introduction

In Public Key Infrastructure (PKI), the ownership of the public key depends on
the digital certificate which binds the key to the identity of a person or an organization [1,2]. The core component of a PKI is the Certificate Authority (CA),
a Trusted Third Party (TTP) who is responsible for issuing the certificates. It is
critical that trust environment is presented on a large scale infrastructure and
this can be achieved by the mutual recognition of each digital certificate issued
by the multiple CAs. However, there are several technical issues that slacken the
growth of PKI, one of which is the compatibility of the digital certificates issued
by various CAs resulting in PKI as a costly technology to be maintained.

An Identity-based Cryptosystem (IBC) is a cryptographic scheme proposed
by Shamir in the year 1984 [3]. In IBC, the public key of a user is created
by applying a public hash function to the user's publicly known identifier such
as e-mail address, username or the IP address. This scheme allows two users
to interact or communicate securely and verify each other's signatures without

A. Abd Manaf et al. (Eds.): ICIEIS 2011, Part I, CCIS 251, pp. 151–162, 2011.
© Springer-Verlag Berlin Heidelberg 2011

exchanging their own public keys. Then, a trusted third party known as Private Key Generator (PKG) can generate the corresponding private key to the user after the verification of the user's identity. This verification is essentially the same as that required for issuing a certificate in a typical PKI. In such a scheme there are four algorithms: (1) **setup** generates global system parameters and a master-key, (2) **extract** uses the master-key to generate the private key corresponding to an arbitrary public key string (3) **encrypt** encrypts messages using the public key ID, and (4) **decrypt** decrypts messages using the corresponding private key.

Certificateless Public Key Infrastructure (CL-PKI) was proposed in the hope of resolving the complexity of certificate management in PKI and the key escrow problem in IBC [4]. CL-PKI is the combination of PKI and IBC as it contains the trust environment of PKI and the absence of certificates in verifying the identities between nodes. Certification distribution causes additional overhead and some security issues. For example, an attacker may forge a valid certificate which may appear to be coming from the valid CA. In CL-PKI, the public key used is no longer an arbitrary string. In fact, it is similar to the public key generated in conventional PKI. As it will become apparent, CL-PKI offers an interesting alternative to PKI and IBC. Due to its lightweight infrastructure, we propose various security strengths of authentication scheme based on CL-PKI.

This paper is organized as follows. Section 2 gives a summary of the mathematical concepts of bilinear pairing and certificateless signature scheme. Section 3 presents the details of an authentication scheme by using certificateless signature. Then, Section 4 discusses the general performance analysis of the implementation of various security strengths of the authentication scheme. Finally, Section 5 concludes this paper.

2   Certificateless Public Key Infrastructure

In CL-PKI, the authenticity of a public key is ensured by the Key Generator Center (KGC). In this paper, we focus on the Certificateless Signature (CLS) scheme as only the authentication service is needed. In this section, we describe the concepts of bilinear pairing and related mathematical problems. We then present the models and algorithms used in CLS. The security and efficiency of the CLS can be referred to the original paper [5].

2.1   Bilinear Pairing

In CL-PKI, a pairing function will give a mapping from a cyclic group to another cyclic group. Particularly in our case, we have a mapping from a subgroup of additive group of elliptic curve points to a subgroup of multiplicative group of the finite field. Let $E(\mathbb{F}_q)$ be an elliptic curve over finite field $\mathbb{F}_q$, with q a large prime element.

$$y^2 \equiv x^3 + ax + b \pmod{q} \tag{1}$$

Let $(\mathbb{G}_1, +)$, $(\mathbb{G}_2, +)$ and $(\mathbb{G}_T, \times)$ be cyclic groups of prime order r. The pairing function is an admissible map $e : \mathbb{G}_1 \times \mathbb{G}_2 \longrightarrow \mathbb{G}_T$ if satisfies the following properties [5]:

- Bilinearity: $e(aP, bQ) = e(P, Q)^{ab}$ for all $P \in \mathbb{G}_1$, $Q \in \mathbb{G}_2$ and $a, b \in \mathbb{Z}_r^*$.
- Non-degeneracy: $e(P, Q) = 1_{G_T}$ for all $Q \in \mathbb{G}_2$ if and only if $P = 1_{G_1}$, and similarly $e(P, Q) = 1_{G_T}$ for all $P \in \mathbb{G}_1$ if and only if $Q = 1_{G_2}$.
- Computability: For any $P \in \mathbb{G}_1$, $Q \in \mathbb{G}_2$, there is an efficient algorithm to compute $e(P, Q)$.

2.2   Certificateless Signature

A formal CLS structure is a 7-tuple polynomial time algorithms: **Setup,
Partial-Secret-Key-Extract, Set-Secret, Set-Secret-Key, Set-Public-
Key, Sign** and **Verify**. The KGC will execute **Setup** and **Partial-Secret-
Key-Extract** whereas the node will execute **Set-Secret, Set-Secret-Key**, and
Set-Public-Key. The algorithms are based on the proposed CLS scheme by [5]
which provides a better performance compared to [6,7]. We recall the details
of the algorithm here. The discussion on the security and performance can be
found in the original papers [5,6,7].

Setup. This algorithm calculates the parameters of CLS *params* and master
secret key *msk*. This algorithm runs as follows:

- Run a generator to output cyclic groups $\mathbb{G}_1$, $\mathbb{G}_2$ (where $\mathbb{G}_1 \neq \mathbb{G}_2$) and $\mathbb{G}_T$
of prime order r and a bilinear pairing

$$e : \mathbb{G}_1 \times \mathbb{G}_2 \longrightarrow \mathbb{G}_T \tag{2}$$

- Choose two arbitrary generators $G \in \mathbb{G}_1$, $H \in \mathbb{G}_2$ and generate

$$g = e(G, H) \in \mathbb{G}_T \tag{3}$$

- Select a random $s \in \mathbb{Z}_r^*$ and set master public key

$$K_{KGC} = sH \tag{4}$$

- Choose hash function

$$\text{Hash} : \{0, 1\}^* \rightarrow \mathbb{Z}_r^* \tag{5}$$

The outputs of this algorithm are:

- the domain parameter which is public

$$params = \{G, H, g, K_{KGC}, e, Hash\} \tag{6}$$

- master private key which is private to KGC

$$msk = s \in \mathbb{Z}_r^* \tag{7}$$

Partial-Secret-Key-Extract. This algorithm is executed by KGC when a node requests its partial secret key. The input of this algorithm are *params*, *msk* and the node identity ID. Prior to the release of the partial secret key, the node must be authenticated by the system. The algorithm returns

$$partial\_key = (\text{Hash}\,(ID) + msk)^{-1}\,G \in \mathbb{G}_1 \tag{8}$$

The key is transmitted over a secure channel to the node.

Set-Secret. This algorithm computes the secret value used in CLS. The node chooses a random $s_{ID} \in \mathbb{Z}_r^*$. This secret value will be used in the next algorithm to create the node's secret key.

Set-Secret-Key. This algorithm creates the node's secret key. This key is kept safely by the node and it will be used in the signing process.

$$nsk = (partial\_key, s_{ID}) \in \mathbb{G}_1 \times \mathbb{Z}_r^* \tag{9}$$

Set-Public-Key. This algorithm takes as input the *params* and s_{ID} to compute the node's public key. This public key will be used to verify the signature. The public key corresponding to the node is

$$npk = g^{s_{ID}} \in \mathbb{G}_T \tag{10}$$

Signing Process. Given a message $M \in \mathcal{M} = \{0,1\}^*$, this algorithm uses the *params*, and ID as well as its npk and s_{ID} to compute the signature, σ. The steps are as follows:

- Choose randomly $x \in \mathbb{Z}_r^*$
- Compute $t = g^x \in \mathbb{G}_T$
- Calculate the hash

$$h = Hash\,(M||ID||npk||t) \in \mathbb{Z}_r^* \tag{11}$$

- Compute S

$$S = (x + h \cdot s_{ID}) \cdot partial\_key \in \mathbb{G}_1 \tag{12}$$

- The signature on M is

$$\sigma = (S, h) \in \mathbb{G}_1 \times \mathbb{Z}_r^* \tag{13}$$

Verification Process. To verify the authenticity of a message M with the signature $\sigma = (S, h)$, the other node computes

$$t' = e\,(S, Hash\,(ID)\,H + K_{KGC})\,(npk)^{-h} \tag{14}$$

$$h' = Hash\,(M||ID||npk||t') \tag{15}$$

The message is authentic if and only if $h' = h$.

3   Certificateless Signature Authentication Scheme

In this paper, we propose an authentication scheme based on certificateless signature. We develop three algorithms namely CLS160, CLS224, and CLS256 based on the instantiation of the CLS algorithm using supersingular curve (type A), MNT curve (type D), and Barreto-Naehrig (BN) curve (type F), respectively as defined in Pairing Based Cryptography (PBC) [8]. CLS160 is characterized by having symmetric bilinear pairing ($G_1 = G_2$) whereas CLS224 and CLS256 are characterized by having asymmetric bilinear pairing ($G_1 \neq G_2$). A specification for different security strengths of the authentication scheme is depicted in Table 1.

To provide fast pairing computation, normally elliptic curves from symmetric bilinear groups with small embedding degrees are chosen. On the other hand, elliptic curves from asymmetric bilinear groups with high embedding degree offer a good option for short group element size. Even though CLS224 and CLS256 provide high level of security, the schemes suffer from performance degradation especially in terms of pairing computation.

Table 1. Curve Parameters, Corresponding Embedding Degree and Level of Security of CLS Authentication Schemes

	CLS160	CLS224	CLS256
Security Parameter, k	1024	1344	3072
Bits of Security	80	112	128
Size of q (bits)	512	224	256
Size of r (bits)	160	224	256
Curve	$y^2 = x^3 + x$	$y^2 = x^3 + ax + b$	$y^2 = x^3 + b$
Embedding Degree, l	2	6	12

3.1   KGC Setup

KGC is the main entity in CL-PKI based authentication scheme. A KGC is involved in generating the public parameters and deriving a partial secret key from the user's identity whose is assumed to be unique in a trust domain. KGC executes **Setup** algorithm to generate a list of public parameters *params* and master secret key *msk*. This algorithm is executed only when a new set of *params* needs to be generated or in case of KGC is compromised (in practice very seldom). Moreover, the request from the server to increase or decrease its security level may also cause KGC to run **Setup**. It should be noted that the strength of the authentication scheme depends on the security parameter k as required by the server in trust domain (i.e., moon.testbed.com as shown in Figure 1).

The CL-PKI *params* contain all the information that the user requires to generate public/secret key pair, and to sign and verify the message. The domain *params* consist of $\{G, H, g, K_{KGC}, Hash, e\}$. Apart from these *params*, two additional parameters are listed. KGC_{ADDR} and KGC_{PORT} are IP address of hostname of the KGC and port on which the KGC is listening, respectively. These two parameters are used by the user to request *partial_key* from the KGC.

3.2 Distribution of Public Parameters

To facilitate the authentication operation between two users, the KGC is required to distribute the *params* to the participating users. The most feasible solution to distribute the KGC's *params* is to use the existing network infrastructure such as DNS server. Once KGC executes **Setup**, KGC is then responsible to publish the *params* to the DNS server. To provide secure and authenticated update to the DNS server, KGC deploys Transaction Signature (TSIG) [9], a cryptographically means of identifying each endpoint of a connection that involves in making or responding to a DNS update. Due to the unavailability of current DNS Resource Record (RR) to support *params*, there is a necessity to introduce a new RR namely PARAMS.

The structure of PARAMS RR utilizes the same format as that of KEY RR [10], but with different functionality. PARAMS RR comprises of flags, protocols, algorithms, one additional field known as serial, and data. Serial is introduced to support the implementation of various security strengths in CLS algorithms. A 16-bit serial field consists of two parts, type and version. From the user's perspective, the serial is interpreted as a 4-digit hexadecimal value. The most significant hexadecimal value determines the security strength of the algorithm. It is used to indicate the CLS160, CLS224, or CLS256 algorithm. The remaining 12 bits of serial denote the version of *params* which determine the latest *params* updated by KGC. The version is incremented by the KGC whenever the KGC runs **Setup**. Final field of PARAMS RR represents a base64 encoding of the *params*.

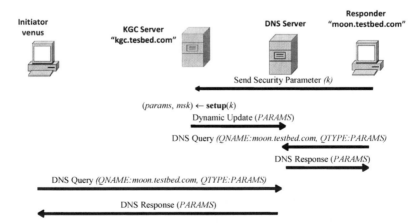

Fig. 1. CLS Public Parameters Update and Query

As shown in Figure 1, to authenticate the user to the server, the initiator (i.e. venus) sends DNS query to DNS server by setting the QNAME of the query to Fully Qualified Domain Name (FQDN) of the responder and QTYPE of the query to PARAMS RR in order to obtain the domain's *params*. For the responder or server (i.e. moon.testbed.com), the DNS query is performed by specifying the QNAME to its FQDN. The query can be conducted soon after the server has forced the KGC to regenerate the *params* in case of the server is compromised or there is a requirement for the server to change its security level. A user should refetch the *params* at pre-determined interval to ensure that he has the most current version of *params*. In this matter, Time to Live (TTL) of PARAMS RR can be used to force the user to refetch *params* from DNS server. Presumably the KGC is in a closely-monitored and well-protected entity, frequent dynamic updates can be avoided for a reasonably long period of time. Therefore, the TTL can be specified in the order of days.

3.3   Public/Secret Key Pair Generation

Once the *params* are obtained from the DNS server, Venus can easily find KGC information in PARAMS RR to query KGC for its *partial_key* which is needed to generate the secret key. To obtain *partial_key*, Venus uses KGC_{ADDR} and KGC_{PORT} in conjunction with its identity *ID* such as email address or IP address to query KGC. Once the KGC has received partial key query from Venus, it runs **Partial-Secret-Key-Extract** algorithm using Venus's ID, *params* and its *msk* to generate a *partial_key* and then sends it to Venus via secure channel. Upon receiving *partial_key*, Venus uses the *params* to generate a random S_{ID} and runs **Set-Public-Key** and **Set-Secret-Key** algorithms using *params* and S_{ID} to make its *npk* and *nsk*, respectively. Generation of public/secret key pair is depicted in Figure 2.

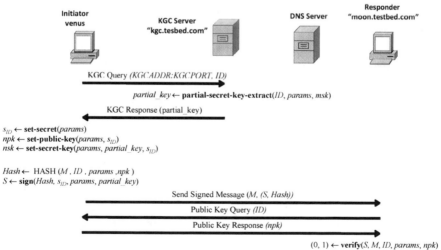

Fig. 2. Keys Generation and Authentication Operation

3.4   Authentication Mechanism

In our scenario, let's assume moon.testbed.com wants to authenticate Venus. Once Venus possesses all the required parameters (i.e. key pair and *params*), she generates a message digest using pre-determined hashing algorithm. The selection of hashing algorithm is based on the size of r (from Table 1). In this work, the size of r influences the selection of either SHA1, SHA224, or SHA256. Then, the message digest is signed by using Venus's secret key. She then sends the signed message to moon.testbed.com. The signed message includes the message, the signature of the message and the message digest. Once the server received the signed message, it requests Venus's public key to verify her signature. This can be done through a public channel. The server generates the value t' by using Venus's public key, the signed message that Venus sent, and *params*. Based on the generated value t', the server recalculates the message digest. If message digests of Venus and server are same, the message integrity has not been compromised.

4   Performance Analysis

In this work, we built a testbed on Linux platform. We implement the CLS authentication scheme in C using PBC library (version 0.5.8) [8]. To proof the validity of the CLS algorithm, we have implemented and tested the Internet Key Exchange (IKE) authentication by using the CLS160 algorithm [11]. Moreover, a comparison of CLS160 against a well-known RSA scheme can be referred to the original paper [12]. To store and update the DNS record, we deploy BIND 9.8.0-P2, the most commonly used DNS server application on the Internet [13]. It supports TSIG which is used in our implementation to maintain secure transaction between KGC and DNS. In this section, we analyze the performance of three CL-PKI based authentication schemes in terms of the public key size, the size of signature block, and the speed for generating or verifying the signature.

4.1   Public Key Size

The public key of authentication scheme is represented as an element in the finite field F_{q^l} where F_{q^l} is a generator of extension group G_T and it is implemented as $F_q[X]/f(X)$, where l is the embedding degree and $f(X)$ is the irreducible polynomial. The element in F_{q^l} is represented by using polynomial basis $(1, X, X^2, ..., X^{l-1})$ of degree at most l - 1, where X is a root of the irreducible polynomial over F_{q^l}.

For instance, CLS160 has an element $A(X)$ in F_{q^2} which is represented as $a_1 X + a_0$ (a_1, $a_0 \in F_q$). However, in this implementation, $A(X)$ is encoded as (a_1, a_0). Since the size of an element in F_q is 512 bits and the embedding degree is 2, the CLS160 public key is formed by two 512-bit elements, giving a total key size of 1024 bits or 128 bytes. Alternatively, the public key sizes for CLS224 with embedding degree of 6 and CLS256 with embedding degree of 12 are constructed by six of 224-bit elements and 12 of 256-bit elements, respectively. The public key sizes of different CLS authentication schemes are tabulated in Table 2.

Table 2. Public Key Size of CLS Authentication Schemes

Authentication Scheme	CLS160	CLS224	CLS256
Public Key Size (bytes)	128	168	384

In this implementation, we also indicate the cryptographic strength or system security parameter of CLS160, CLS224, and CLS256 based on the bit size of G_T, $k = l \times log_2\ q$. It corresponds to the modulus bit-size of comparable security in Diffie-Hellman or RSA public-key cryptosystems. In short, the length of the public key linearly grows with the security level of the authentication schemes. Table 3 shows the samples of public keys for CLS160, CLS224, and CLS256 that are generated by **Set-Public-Key** algorithm.

Table 3. CL-PKI Public Key, npk

CLS160	44DBCBE1	89CB0A02	088551F2	CDF31A21	E1904DF7	59810937	A5521278	486AD623
	02B82F51	F6D38991	3DD72474	9013D5B7	13C436CE	FEBCFCD8	FADFB86A	DFAC405A,
	61F0E0BF	98A42498	DD92F09C	27B347E1	8292F9CB	F49D3F23	DB14544E	95FF1184
	B31117DE	1DDDF0FB	659DFF22	0D5ECAAB	1FA677B3	77B086B2	EB260140	18BBFF58
CLS224	08867C9C	719FC7DF	E5606265	9CFF250D	06C07718	1FB4DAE9	8EA74571,	
	07C288CA	DBE076A2	0E2AA6B2	DF18546E	674E0641	B8B96A65	1A18F424,	
	77DGFE06	F1E0DEEA	0F0FAC1F	E8F4A732	E60E1D09	44ACF199	15414C05,	
	043BDA9C	4963521D	8BEABBB1	B92B304A	8FBD4931	1ED3ED61	458247DE,	
	8703163C	16081DE5	1B7E4B7D	43A5FBD8	3934B0EB	5F96992A	47FF5CFC,	
	22CFC46D	A60B679D	BEABFC37	370343CD	DB8D806A	FDC13FCD	BC58273F	
CLS256	0ADD74C3	9D12DG0G	20D5102G	79F2CEFD	C5A9302A	0D68F02F	0B4F63DC	1AE2EEB3,
	0C107079	6CEAC2E6	AC1BB4EC	A56CE396	D1B928EA	5A85208A	EA66AC38	3017E89B,
	11DA12D7	052D74E9	0F6B2BF0	3D957CAD	7384ECD7	C49E4655	9402C56F	9E9EBF16,
	204B1452	28D660D7	92226918	9F8C6B33	C8637879	AD700437	86777BF3	7DBE11D1,
	1D26690F	3484E171	B771A650	DE3E209D	47CF4256	F632ECC5	53956682	8D278CBE,
	1B4DE17F	3CB98D2C	C93E8B3B	1957B530	F00E3BEB	FF2F03ED	74D493D5	D633A612,
	08E04FAD	9A88F3ED	78BCF357	C5D07534	EF5237A0	0078758B	F8EAF8B7	0B118E92,
	091AD382	ADBB3CF9	9D1B2FB2	3115C277	7CD1E561	C2DD642D	B6E19F1D	F9CBB58A,
	189664B0	433EBBBC	D5B4E5DE	C7E34604	4CEAE824	5D92FED9	60D734B2	2347FDF2,
	23E2ABBC	74F2DDE8	15A0DC7F	ABC32190	0B6B4B1D	B80FA613	BFC9F3E7	2EA56E46,
	021FC27A	01D64655	D4FFE43D	11F98BF8	56FC2797	2339D957	6E24741F	2B295280,
	0E841238	8B176E5B	5B533D41	EF53935D	BF89A03D	CC359D2B	4CF45716	1E283694

4.2   Signature Block Size

Signature block consists of (S, h), where S is a signature of the authentication scheme and it is represented as a point on the elliptic curve $(S \in G_1)$. On the other hand, h is an output of a pseudorandom function based on the hashing algorithm for each scheme. Therefore, the signature block size is computed based on the combination of size of r and twice the size of q. However, to achieve bandwidth-efficient authentication, there is a standard compression technique that can be used to reduce the elliptic curve point size by a factor of 2. Elliptic curve point compression allows the y-coordinate of the point to be represented compactly using a single additional bit [14].

In CLS160 scheme with the size of q of 512-bit and size of SHA1, the S is represented by two 64-byte elements and h is represented by 160 bits. Therefore, the length of the signature block for CLS160 is $128 + 20 = 148$ bytes. CLS224

Table 4. Signature Block Size of CLS Authentication Schemes

Authentication Scheme	CLS160	CLS224	CLS256
Signature Size (bytes)	85	57	65

uses 224-bit element with SHA224 has a total block size of 84 bytes, whereas CLS256 uses 256-bit with SHA256 has a block size of 96 bytes. In our authentication scheme, we deploy the point compression, this would then require $64 + 1 = 65$ bytes, giving a total signature size of 85 bytes for CLS160, 57 bytes for CLS224 and 65 bytes for CLS256. The summarized results are tabulated in Table 4. Overall, there is a reduction in block size ranging from 32.14% to 42.57% for CLS160, CLS224 and CLS256 after we deployed elliptic curve point compression technique. The simulated uncompress signature block of the various schemes is illustrated in the Table 5.

Table 5. CL-PKI Signature Block,$[S, h]$

CLS160	[[1C477124 2B520B5F AA730D65 9E15AF49 A43F61DE 49D32CD1 81A16DF6 7622918E FC97A5F7 4C1D913B 7942A39A CB829C8A B8C26159 6A9C5D11 B2D3D7F0 3512C3EF, 2ED79A9A FDC61879 07B48D43 EBD8D052 FA13E014 460CBD36 F7EA4C89 1C40D51D 74829511 438EB223 C50C99DF D508024D 0E368F77 5A0B7094 1206F95B E04FFF3B], 942AB762 C3AC5905 009F1AB7 AB2FDCC1 195D3D69]
CLS224	[[09135186 511AB6BC 35126EB6 0F5168C1 ED04B19F 988FCB76 16DF0D9B, 48B41F44 FA3FF92D 042FB4E6 8A5994EC F9DD60EE 03B4570C 60A8961B], 6986F6C9 89A6425A 8DF8EE13 77974235 751B0203 806986F6 C989A642]
CLS256	[[18CCFE2E E2539EA7 3C80C0E7 E60B00ED 24D7EB78 072C2A5D AF904062 473D5F2D, 1DE96E32 8CCA2AA9 46542EF8 1DC72FED 3AFA7775 5BC35937 467BEBA8 C8B71D60], 22511D80 D27F3A75 3EFF152E D2AF407D D016D454 0D0E9F14 50A4A8FC 38F3373E]

Authentication scheme with high level of security such as CLS224 and CLS256 is implemented from elliptic curve with high embedding degree. Hence, it is more suitable for shorter group G_1 element. Since the size of S directly corresponds to the base field size of G_1, this results in smaller signature block.

4.3 Signing and Verification Execution Time

This section presents the analysis on the signing and verification execution times for CL-PKI based authentication schemes. The experiments were conducted on a 2.93 GHz Core i5 Linux PC. Table 6 shows the experimental results for an average of 100 execution times of both operations.

There are two expensive computations underlying the CL-PKI based authentication scheme namely modular exponentiation and pairing. Both signing and verification operations require one modular exponentiation and one pairing computation. However, in signing operation, the pairing $e(G, H) = g$ can be precomputed and published as the public parameter *params*. Thus, it eliminates the pairing computation and the operation can be greatly accelerated. Based on Table 6, due to unavoidable pairing computation in the verification operation, the signing operation is more faster than the verification operation for all schemes.

Table 6. Signing and Verification Execution Time (in milliseconds) of CLS Authentication Schemes

Authentication Scheme	CLS160	CLS224	CLS256
Signing	2.975	11.155	12.865
Verification	4.112	53.601	60.414

Pairing generally maps problems over elliptic curves to the problems over finite fields and vice-versa, and it is the most expensive computation in elliptic curve cryptosystem. The decisive factor to measure the complexity of pairing is the embedding degree l which determines the field extension G_T over the groups G_1 and G_2 that are involved in pairing computation. Therefore, to achieve faster extension field operations, it requires efficient pairing computation and the necessity to have elliptic curve with small embedding degree. However, this results in the reduction of security strength of the scheme.

For instance, at 80 bits of security, CLS160 uses a supersingular elliptic curve with embedding degree of 2. In contrast, to achieve 128 bits of security or higher, embedding degrees of 12 and larger are optimal. In this work, CLS256 has the highest security strength by using BN curves with embedding degree of 12. It takes about 60.414 msec to execute pairing and modular exponentiation in the verification operation, while CLS160 takes about 4.112 msec.

Generally, in order to guarantee the reliable security of a pairing-based cryptosystem, the discrete logarithm problems in the extension group of G_T must be computationally infeasible. However, embedding degree of the elliptic curves directly influences the size of G_T and the security level of the cryptosystem. Hence, it increases the complexity of pairing computation. In this work, our authentication scheme offers different types of CLS algorithms that can be chosen based on the trade-off between speed and necessary security according to the requirement of different applications.

5 Conclusion

Due to its lightweight infrastructure, CL-PKI offers a promising solution to address the complexity of certificate management as in PKI and the inherent key escrow as in IBC. This paper discussed a CL-PKI based authentication scheme and described three different security strengths of the scheme namely CLS160, CLS224, and CLS256. Each of the CL-PKI schemes is evaluated and compared with respect to their performance and security levels. Undeniably, the implementation of CL-PKI based authentication scheme provides flexibility and security. However, there is an increase of performance overhead and the complexity in signing and verification processes due to the inclusion of a computationally expensive pairing operation.

Acknowledgments. The research is funded by Ministry of Science, Technology, and Innovation (MOSTI), Government of Malaysia, under e-ScienceFund grant No. 01-02-01-SF0170.

References

1. Jancic, A., Warren, M.J.: PKI - Advantages and Obstacles. In: 2nd Australian Information Security Management Conference (2004)
2. Peyravian, M., Roginsky, A., Zunic, N.: Non-PKI Methods for Public Key Distribution. Computers & Security 23, 97–103 (2004)
3. Shamir, A.: Identity-Based Cryptosystems and Signature Schemes. In: Blakely, G.R., Chaum, D. (eds.) CRYPTO 1984. LNCS, vol. 196, pp. 47–53. Springer, Heidelberg (1985)
4. Al-Riyami, S.S., Paterson, K.G.: Certificateless Public Key Cryptography. In: Laih, C.-S. (ed.) ASIACRYPT 2003. LNCS, vol. 2894, pp. 452–473. Springer, Heidelberg (2003)
5. Terada, R., Denise, H.G.: A Certificateless Signature Scheme based in Bilinear Pairing Functions. In: Symposium on Cryptography and Information Security (2007)
6. Lifeng, G., Lei, H., Yong, L.: A Practical Certificateless Signature Scheme. In: International Symposium on Data, Privacy, and E-Commerce, pp. 248–253 (2007)
7. Wang, C., Huang, H., Tang, Y.: An Efficient Certificateless Signature from Pairings. In: International Symposium on Data, Privacy, and E-Commerce, pp. 236–238 (2007)
8. The Pairing-Based Cryptography (PBC) Library, http://crypto.stanford.edu/pbc/
9. Vixie, P., Gudmundsson, O., Eastlake, D., Wellington, B.: Secret Key Transaction Authentication for DNS (TSIG). RFC 2845 (2000)
10. Eastlake, D.: Domain Name System Security Extensions. RFC 2535 (1999)
11. Yaacob, A.H., Ahmad, N.M., Fauzi, R.: IKE Authentication using Certificateless Signature. In: IEEE Proceedings of the 25th International Conference on Information Networking, ICOIN (2011)
12. Ahmad, N.M., Yaacob, A.H., Fauzi, R., Khorram, A.: Performance Analysis of Certificateless Signature for IKE Authentication. World Academy Science, Engineering and Technology 74, 358–365 (2011)
13. BIND - Internet Systems Consortium, http://www.isc.org/software/bind
14. Certicom Research: SEC1: Elliptic Curve Cryptography. In: Standards for Efficient Cryptography (2000)

Data Leakage Tracking –
Non-Repudiation of Forwarding

Rainer Schick and Christoph Ruland

University of Siegen, Chair for Data Communications Systems,
Hoelderlinstr. 3, 57076 Siegen, Germany
{rainer.schick,christoph.ruland}@uni-siegen.de

Abstract. Current security systems dealing with sensitive private data do not
provide sufficient options to find data leaks. An approach to find the last
authorized receiver of a protected copy is proposed in this paper. Existing
security concepts are extended by a new security service based on reliable
tracking data embedding. Additionally, a new mechanism to protect the new
tracking data is shown. Digital watermarking techniques are used to provide
tracking abilities for forwarded copies of the protected data. This paper briefly
describes approaches to improve security for both the owner of protected data
and its recipients.

Keywords: information security, security services, data hiding, digital forensic,
digital watermark, fingerprinting.

1 Introduction

Nowadays most sensitive and private data are generated, processed and stored
digitally. This circumstance causes many efforts to protect these data from access by
unauthorized attackers. Fortunately, modern security services provide confidentiality,
authenticity and integrity for data worth protecting. But these services only provide
security against attacks by unauthorized external attackers. The even worse attacks
conducted by employees and authorized receivers of such data are often neglected.
The main problem is that control over confidentiality ends with decryption. The
sender does not know what the receiver does with the data. This is even worse for a
data owner. If he shares information with trusted users and one of them misbehaves,
the owner cannot prove who has been the "mole".

Figure 1 illustrates the problem for a data owner in a decentralized information
distribution system. The approaches described in this paper solve two different goals:
First, a reliable data tracking system is provided. Each receiver is able to track the
way protected data have taken so far. Additionally, only authorized receivers are able
to decrypt the received data. The goal is a new security service which provides non-
repudiation of forwarding for recipients. A receiver of such protected data cannot
repudiate that he had access to it. Second, a mechanism to prove forwarding of such
protected data is provided for the owner. If he or she finds a copy of these data, he is
able to track the last authorized receiver of it. Then the owner can check if it is an
authorized or unauthorized copy.

A. Abd Manaf et al. (Eds.): ICIEIS 2011, Part I, CCIS 251, pp. 163–173, 2011.
© Springer-Verlag Berlin Heidelberg 2011

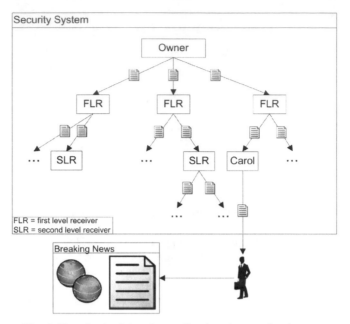

Fig. 1. Unauthorized data forwarding in a decentralized system

Finally, the approaches shown in this paper should lead to a new security service. This service extends recent non-repudiation services described in ISO/IEC 13888. The fields of application of the data tracking service are those depending on provable authentic information. Examples are the protection of company secrets and warrants or the realization of notary authorities. The service does not prevent unauthorized forwarding, it provides data leakage tracking. It is not meant to replace copyright protections in the sense of preventing or detecting illegal file sharing applications.

2   Related Work

There are several approaches which provide control over digital data. For example, companies often install so-called "Data Leakage Prevention" on their systems [11]. This is also called "Endpoint Security", because it is often a software extension installed on client computers. These software solutions limit the user rights on these systems, such that an employee cannot copy data on a private USB device or use a private e-mail account for conversations.

Another approach is Digital Rights Management. DRM provides access control for copyright holders to limit the use of digital content. It is often stated as a copy protection mechanism, but it is not. Copying cannot be prevented by this technique. Instead, the copies contain digital watermarks. These watermarks support the copyright owners to track the leak if an unauthorized copy is found [2], [5], [6], [7], [10]. Digital watermarking has to cope with different problems. One is the limited embedding capacity in relation to the size of its carrier [8]. Another is the collusion attack, where attackers combine their copies to withdraw their fingerprints. This attack is tried to be solved by frameproof codes [1], [9].

Unfortunately, there is no feasible possibility to prevent unauthorized information forwarding under all circumstances. If a user is able to view the plaintext information (and authorized receivers should be able to do so), he or she has several possibilities to create copies. The recipient may print it, photograph the screen or at least rewrite it (if the confidential information is a text). This fact makes a rethink in using digital data inevitable. Users should not believe in digital data instead its authenticity and the authenticity of its source can be proven. At least if sensitive and confidential information are shared.

Nevertheless, usually attackers do not care for the existence of a valid digital signature. They forward data they have stolen or received by misbehaving authorized personnel. It is not part of this work to find the one who published the data. Instead, the last authorized receiver should be traceable, such that the source of the data leak can be found. In contrast to the approaches mentioned above, each authorized receiver of the data is trusted. If he or she is not in possession of a needed security module, the receiver is not able to obtain a plaintext copy of the protected information.

3   Notations

The following terms and notations apply for this paper:

- m: Data/Information that must be protected by the document tracking service.
- CD: Specific configuration data added by the data owner. This may contain an expiry date, specific receiver identifier or group policies.
- $x//y$: The result of the concatenation of x and y in that order. An appropriate encoding must be used so that the data items can be recovered from the concatenated string.
- $\sigma_O(m')$: The source signature calculated by the data owner. As long as this signature accompanies m and can be verified successfully, the data is valid. The signature is calculated over the concatenation of data $m' = m//CD$.
- m_O: The concatenated data $m'//\sigma_O(m')$.
- PID_n: The unique personal identifier of user n.
- FID: The unique file identifier of data m.
- TID_n: The unique transaction identifier for the transmission of data m from user n to user $n+1$.
- TS_n: Timestamp of TID_n.
- TD_n: The tracking data of user n. These data are defined as the concatenation of $PID_0...PID_{n+1}//FID//TID_0...TID_n//TS_0...TS_n$
- $\sigma_n(TD_n)$: The signature calculated by user n signing the current tracking data TD_n.
- $SSTK_n$: Secret Storage Key.
- DEK_n: Secret Data Encryption Key.
- SWK_n: Secret Watermarking Key.
- SCK: Secret Confusion Key.
- $TDEK$: Secret Tracking Data Encryption Key.

4   System Design

The system aims at two different goals, so that the approach consists of two main parts: one is the data tracking part and the other is the displaying or watermarking part. Before these parts are described in detail, the basic idea of the data flow is explained. The data tracking part secures the sensitive information during storage, transmission and processing. The embedded tracking data provide non-repudiation of forwarding for an authorized receiver n. With the use of the embedded tracking data a receiver n can prove the chain of receivers for all users $0...n-1$.

The figuring part embeds a digital watermark into the visible content on the receiver's side. If such a watermarked copy is found and not manipulated, the data owner can prove the forwarding of the last authorized receiver. Figure 2 sketches the flow of such protected data. It shows the functionality for sending and receiving data using the data tracking service. It also shows the branch of the visible data. These data are watermarked using a watermarking key SWK_n. The watermarked copy is for viewing only and should not be forwarded to anybody by the authorized receiver. The encrypted data contains the tracking data of all previous recipients of the confidential information.

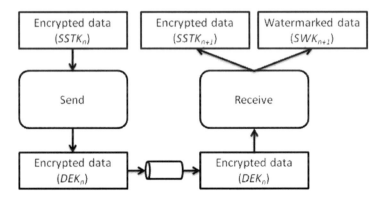

Fig. 2. Data flow of the data tracking scheme

5   Data Tracking

The approach of data tracking can basically be conceived as a "smart" letter: The receiver of the data gets a letter in an envelope. The envelope contains a field for the signature consisting of carbon paper. If the user has signed the receipt on the closed envelope, the letter internally checks the signature and reveals the secret content only if that signature is valid. That is, the signature and the confirmation of the recipient of the receiver are already added to the letter once he can view it and cannot be removed anymore. When this letter is published, he cannot repudiate that he was the last authorized recipient of it. For each receiver, the personal signature and confirmation of recipient is added to the tracking information of the letter, such that it contains all information of the previous receivers. When the letter is sent to the next authorized receiver, it is put into a smart envelope again and the letter is now accompanied by the tracking data.

The data tracking part is figured as the path of the encrypted data shown in figure 2. Regarding the layer architecture, the new service is applied in the application layer. Summarized, each receiver of the protected data signs the receipt before he or she is able to process the data. This measurement improves security for all authorized users of the security system. A receiver of such protected information can verify the way the data have taken up to him. The owner of the data protects them by access control: only users with an appropriate security module can decrypt the data. Additionally, the owner can proof if a suspicious plaintext copy of his document is authorized or not. This idea of non-repudiation of forwarding is explained in the following.

6   Tracking Data Protection

In order to protect the tracking data from targeted manipulations, two solutions are proposed in this paper. One is based on a known block cipher mode of operation with infinite error propagation. The other is a new mechanism called data confusion. This mechanism confuses data of arbitrary size, such that data in one block is not only permuted within that block. The following requirements must be fulfilled by the approaches:

- If an attacker manipulates any of the protected data, the source signature must be destroyed with very high probability. Thus, the confidential information is not authentic anymore.
- The tracking data of a receiver must be added before he or she is able to access the plaintext.

$PID_0...PID_n$	FID	$TID_0...TID_{n-1}$	$TS_0...TS_{n-1}$	$\sigma(TD_{n-1})$	m_O

Fig. 3. Structure of the data

6.1   Security Module

The previously mentioned requirements make the use of a security module inevitable. This module must provide different functionalities:

- A secure storage for different private keys. The owner of the security module must not be able to read them out.
- Generation and validation of digital signatures.
- Support SSL/TLS. The key agreement is done using a public key that corresponds to a securely stored private key within the module. The negotiated data encryption key is DEK_n.
- Three different functions must be provided for data processing. These functions are described in the following.

The "prepare"-function works as follows:

1. The sensitive data m which must be protected by the data tracking service are input into the security module.
2. The user adds configuration data CD, such as expiry dates for the data, valid receiver PID's or a maximum number of allowed forwarding.
3. The source signature $\sigma_O(m')$ is calculated. Thus, m_O is generated.
4. Finally, m_O is encrypted using a secret storage key $SSTK_0$. The encrypted copy is stored locally stored until it is processed again.

The "receive"-function works as follows:

1. Data encrypted using DEK_n are received and decrypted. The structure of such data is shown in figure 3. The tracking data within this output are protected using either the PCBC data encryption or the data confusion mechanism as described later in this chapter.
2. The tracking data signature $\sigma(TD_{n-1})$ is verified. If the validation fails, the module stops processing.
3. The previous tracking data are displayed. The receiver can check the chain of receivers of the protected information.
4. If the receiver applies the receipt, the source signature $\sigma_O(m')$ is verified to check integrity and authenticity of m'.
5. A digital watermark is added to m (as defined in chapter 3) using SWK_n. The watermarked copy m_ψ is output to the receiver. The idea of adding a digital watermark to the document is shown in chapter 7.
6. For local storage, the tracking data are protected again and the data are encrypted using a secret storage key $SSTK_n$.

The "send"-function works as follows:

1. The locally stored data encrypted by $SSTK_n$ are decrypted again. If the sender is not the data owner (e.g. no tracking data are available yet), continue with step 3.
2. The PID_0 of the data owner and the unique FID are added. The owner proceeds with step 4.
3. Both signatures $\sigma_O(m')$ and $\sigma(TD_{n-1})$ are verified again in order to detect manipulations during storage. If an error occurs, the module stops processing.
4. The security module adds the PID_{n+1} of the next receiver, a unique TID_n for the transmission and the current timestamp TS_n.
5. The signature $\sigma(TD_{n-1})$ is discarded and replaced by the new tracking data signature $\sigma(TD_n)$. The new signature authenticates all tracking data including those of previous receivers.
6. The resulting data are encrypted using DEK_{n+1} and transmitted to the next receiver.

The three security module functions work as a black box. The data are input into the module, and certain data are output (if no error occurs). Figure 4 illustrates the functions from the users' view. The "receive"-function additionally outputs a watermarked plaintext copy of the protected data. This output will be explained in the watermarking chapter and is not shown in figure 4.

6.2   PCBC Data Encryption

The propagating cipher-block chaining (PCBC) mode is used if small changes in a ciphertext should cause infinite error propagation when the data are decrypted. This mode of operation is chosen such that every data following the manipulated is also manipulated. For logical reasons, an attacker will try to manipulate or remove his personal tracking data. It is one requirement to make sure that such an attack is not successful. Therefore the tracking data have to be added ahead the existing data as shown in figure 3. If these data are encrypted using the PCBC mode, the manipulation of any of the tracking data leads to a useless plaintext. Neither the source signature $\sigma_O(m')$ nor the original message m can be recovered. The tracking data signature $\sigma(TD_n)$ is also destroyed if any preceding data is manipulated. For that reason, a receiver of such manipulated data recognizes the attack before he gets access to the message and before his tracks are added. Unfortunately, the PCBC mode deals with different problems and it is claimed to be insecure. If two adjacent ciphertext blocks are exchanged, it does not affect the decryption of subsequent blocks [12]. For this reason, an alternative mechanism is presented: the data confusion.

6.3   Tracking Data Confusion

The data confusion mechanism confuses the structure of certain data [13]. It is an approach to protect tracking data embedded by the security module from manipulations by authorized receivers. Nobody can remove or change certain information in the data unless he or she is in possession of the required private key. Unlike other mixing schemes or encryption functions, the permutations in this approach do not shuffle data block by block [3], [4]. Instead, it considers the protected data as a single block of arbitrary size. This is for a good reason: If an attacker knows that the exact position of his own tracking data, he or she also knows which block must be manipulated. Targeted obliteration of traces must be prevented by the data tracking scheme.

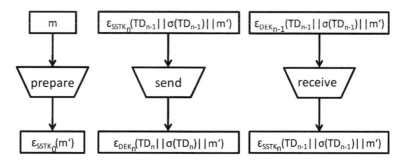

Fig. 4. The three functions of the security module

Figure 5 sketches the flow of the protected data from the data owner to the n-th receiver. The tracking data including configuration data CD and the source signature $\sigma_O(m')$ are first mixed using the data confusion mechanism. This mechanism uses a pseudorandom generator with a minimum period of v (with v as the length of the data

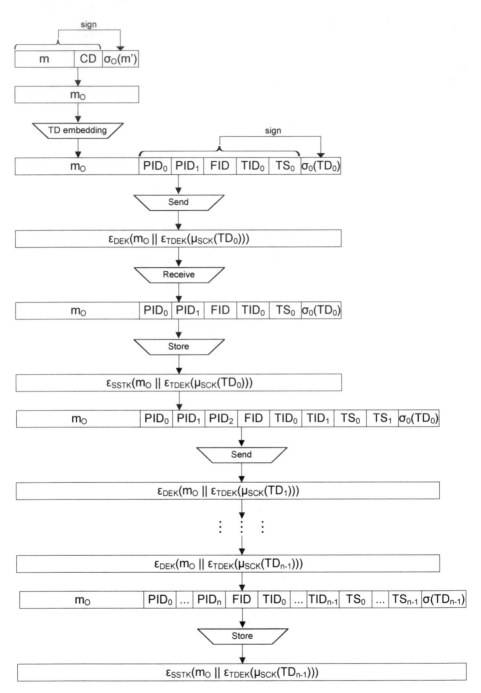

Fig. 5. Data flow using the data confusion mechanism

in bytes). This function must be initialized using a private key *SCK*. The PRNG calculates the new positions of the confused data block. Under these circumstances it can be guaranteed that each byte might have changed its positions to any new position. Only users who know the start value *SCK* are able to reverse the confusion process. The confused data are additionally encrypted using a common symmetric cipher like AES. As a side effect, the cipher behaves as a block by block mixing function. It follows that each bit of the confused data are additionally permuted within the block. Symmetric key algorithms are key-controlled and therefore another private key *TDEK* is needed. Again, this key must only be known to the security module.

The proposal of the data confusion mechanism is an approach to randomize data of arbitrary size. If such data are encrypted only, the manipulation of certain tracking data might lead to an invalid tracking data block while the source signature still remains valid. In comparison with other protection mechanisms, the data confusion mechanism should be faster and less memory-consuming. This is an important fact concerning the required resource-constrained security module. The new data confusion mechanism ensures that the source signature $\sigma_O(m')$ and the tracking data signature $\sigma(TD_n)$ become invalid if an attacker manipulates any of the confused data. A precise description of the data confusion mechanism and an implementation of it is part of future work. Finally, it must be compared with existing approaches.

7   Digital Watermarking

As already stated in the introduction, the unauthorized forwarding of confidential data cannot be prevented under all circumstances. The services mentioned before focus on protecting data from attacks by authorized users during storage and transmission. The system proposed in this paper should also provide traceability for plaintext copies of these data. Digital watermarks are chosen to meet this requirement. The plaintext document output by the receive function is declared as m_Ψ. The watermark Ψ contains the unique identifier PID_n of the last authorized receiver. Additionally, the timestamp of watermark generation TS_{Ψ_n} is added. Finally, these data are signed, thus $\sigma_n(PID_n//TS_{\Psi_n})$ is generated and added to Ψ. If a copy of m_Ψ is found by the data owner, the signature $\sigma_n(PID_n//TS_{\Psi_n})$ is used to prove the authenticity of the watermark.

If Ψ was extracted and the signature was verified successfully, the user with identifier PID_n as extracted from Ψ cannot repudiate that he or she was the last authorized recipient of it. This feature of the proposed watermarking process is called the non-repudiation of forwarding. The data owner (or another administrative instance) decides if this data forwarding was authorized or not. Unauthorized information distribution must not be intentional. It is also possible that the security module of the user was stolen or broken. Or the watermarked plaintext data as output by the security module might have been stolen. These scenarios lead to digital forensic aspects. This research field will be considered more detailed in future work. The investigation or punishment of a proven forwarding is not part of this paper.

The watermark embedding process is key-controlled using securely stored watermarking key SWK_n. This key initializes a pseudorandom generator to choose the embedding positions within the carrier in the frequency domain. Due to the nature of digital watermarks, the carrier must provide enough embedding capacity for invisible and robust data embedding. It is desirable that protected data are destroyed if someone tries to manipulate the protected information or the embedded tracking data. A trade-off between robustness, imperceptibility and embedding capacity must be found.

8   Conclusions

This paper proposes a security service which provides data tracking abilities. A suitable security module is needed to decrypt the protected data. A receiver is able to track the way the data have taken and prove the forwarding of the sensitive information by previous receivers. If a suspicious watermarked copy appears, the data owner can associate the copy to the last authorized receiver. Thus, two new security services are introduced in this paper: the non-repudiation of forwarding for both the data owner and for all receivers of protected data.

Two suggestions to protect the new tracking data are made: The PCBC encryption protects the data with infinite error propagation if an attacker manipulates his tracking data. The new data confusion mechanism shuffles certain data and encrypts them. If an attacker manipulates any of these confused data, every confused data are also manipulated with very high probability. With the current approach, the data tracking part can handle any kind of data. The watermarking part is subject to the restrictions of digital watermarking and is currently limited to image data.

This paper describes the approaches in a superficial way and shows the big picture of the ideas. More detailed descriptions will be published in future work, including precise descriptions of the used mechanisms. It is also planned to describe another way to protect the tracking data using authenticated encryption.

Acknowledgment. This work is funded by the German Research Foundation (DFG) as part of the research training group GRK 1564 "Imaging New Modalities".

References

1. Lin, Y.T., Wu, J.L.: Traceable multimedia fingerprinting based on the multilevel user grouping. In: Proceedings of Multimedia and Expo., pp. 345–348 (2008), doi:10.1109/ICME.2008.4607442
2. Liu, K.J., Trappe, W., Wang, Z.J., Wu, M., Zhao, H.: Multimedia fingerprinting forensics for traitor tracing. In: EURASIP Book Series on Signal Processing and Communications. Hindawi Publishing Corporation (2005) ISBN 977-5945-18-6
3. Matyas, M., Peyravian, M., Roginsky, A., Zunic, N.: Reversible data mixing procedure for efficient public-key encryption. Computers & Security 17(3), 265–272 (1998)
4. Jakobsson, M., Stern, J.P., Yung, M.: Scramble All, Encrypt Small. In: Knudsen, L.R. (ed.) FSE 1999. LNCS, vol. 1636, pp. 95–111. Springer, Heidelberg (1999)
5. Chae, J.J., Manjunath, B.S.: A robust embedded data from Wavelet coefficients. In: Proceedings of Storage and Retrieval for Image and Video Databases (SPIE), pp. 308–319 (1998)

6. Wang, Y., Doherty, J.F., van Dyck, R.E.: A watermarking algorithm for fingerprinting intelligence images. In: Proceedings of Conference on Information Sciences and Systems, pp. 21–24 (2001)
7. Celik, M.U., Sharma, G., Tekalp, A.M., Saber, E.: Lossless generalized-LSB data embedding. IEEE Transactions on Image Processing 14(2), 253–266 (2005)
8. Barg, A., Blakley, G.R., Kabatiansky, G.A.: Digital fingerprinting codes: problem statements, constructions, identification of traitors. IEEE Transactions on Information Theory, 852–865 (2003)
9. Boneh, D., Shaw, J.: Collusion-Secure Fingerprinting for Digital Data. In: Coppersmith, D. (ed.) CRYPTO 1995. LNCS, vol. 963, pp. 452–465. Springer, Heidelberg (1995)
10. Dittmann, J., Behr, A., Stabenau, M., Schmitt, P., Schwenk, J., Ueberberg, J.: Combining digital watermarks and collusion secure fingerprints for digital images. In: JEI, pp. 456–467 (2000)
11. Scheidemann, V.: Endpoint Security: Data Loss Prevention. Security Advisor ePublication (2008)
12. Kohl, J.T.: The Use of Encryption in Kerberos for Network Authentication. In: Brassard, G. (ed.) CRYPTO 1989. LNCS, vol. 435, pp. 35–43. Springer, Heidelberg (1990)
13. Schick, R., Ruland, C.: Document Tracking – One the Way to a New Security Service. In: Proc. Conf. on Network Architectures and Information Systems Security (2011)

New ID-Based Proxy Multi-signature from Pairings

Rajeev Anand Sahu and Sahadeo Padhye

Department of Mathematics
Motilal Nehru National Institute of Technology
Allahabad-211004, India
{rajeevs.crypto,sahadeomathrsu}@gmail.com

Abstract. A proxy signature scheme permits a proxy signer to sign messages on behalf of an original signer. Proxy multi-signature is one of the proxy signature primitives, where a group of original signers delegate their signing rights to the same proxy signer. However, as yet, to our knowledge, an ID-based proxy multi-signature scheme from bilinear pairings based on inverse computational Diffie-Hellman problem (INV-CDHP) has not been proposed. In this paper, we present the above scheme using advantage of the 'k-plus' problem and give a detailed analysis of the same. Due to a single pairing computation in verification phase, the new scheme is more efficient in computational and timing sense than other available schemes. Moreover, the proposed scheme fulfills all the security requirements of a safe proxy signature.

Keywords: ID-based cryptography, Digital signature, Bilinear pairings, Proxy multi-signature.

1 Introduction

The basic infrastructure of traditional PKC prevents its applications in ad-hoc and distributed systems. Also, it is much costly in complexity point of view due to the large overhead of certificate maintenance and transformation. The proposal of ID-based cryptosystem (IBC) by Shamir [16] in 1984, removed the need of traditional PKC. The main essence of IBC is to construct public keys directly from identities of users for example, IP address, e-mail, phone no. etc. Signature algorithms are mainly applicable for source authentication and data integrity purpose in cryptography. Many classical key agreement protocols, signcryptions and signature schemes [2,5,17] have been proposed following the ID-based setting of Shamir. Various signature schemes along with the ID-based settings provide a lot of new extensions, such as ID-based blind signature scheme, ID-based ring signature scheme, ID-based proxy signature scheme, etc. [23,24]. The property of linearity in both components make bilinear pairings very effective in terms of both efficiency and functionality. After the work of Boneh and Franklin [1], the bilinear pairings are highly applicable for constructing efficient ID-based signatures [3,7,14,21].

A. Abd Manaf et al. (Eds.): ICIEIS 2011, Part I, CCIS 251, pp. 174–184, 2011.

In many events, the signer may not be available at the desired time to sign any document(s). Proxy signature is one of the solutions for such a situation. In a proxy signature scheme, an original signer can delegate its signing capability to a proxy signer and then the proxy signer can generate a valid signature on the document(s) on behalf of the original signer. The concept of proxy signature was first introduced by Mambo et al. [12] in 1996. Proxy signature schemes are very much applicable in grid computing, distributed systems etc. where the delegation of right is quite common. Proxy signatures can be combined with other signatures to obtain new extensions as multi-proxy signature, proxy multi-signature, multi-proxy multi-signature, threshold proxy signature etc. In some situations, a group of original signers may require to delegate their signing rights to a single proxy signer as for example, the president of any company may be authorized to sign any document(s) in the absence of heads of different departments. The proxy signature scheme that achieves such a purpose is called the proxy multi-signature scheme. The notion of proxy multi-signature was first introduced by Yi et al. [22] in 2000. Li and Chen [9] constructed the first proxy multi-signature in ID-based setting using bilinear pairings, but their scheme is much expensive in complexity point of view due to large pairing computations and hence it is not suitable for economic implementations.

Most of the ID-based proxy multi-signature schemes proposed recently [4,9,15,19] are constructed using Hess's signature scheme [7] as a standard signature and hence their security depends on computational Diffie-Hellman problem (CDHP). Previously Du and Wen [6] have proposed an ID-based signature scheme and Zhang et al. [25] proposed a proxy signature scheme using the k-CAA problem [11], which is based on the hardness of INV-CDHP. But up to the best of our knowledge, no ID-based proxy multi-signature scheme from bilinear pairings is designed using the inverse CDHP till now. So, taking advantage of the 'k-plus' problem [13] similar to the 'k-CAA' problem [11], we propose here an ID-based proxy multi-signature scheme from bilinear pairings. Unforgeability of the proposed scheme depends on the hardness of the INV-CDHP. We note that in pairing based cryptosystems, computation of bilinear pairing is a time-consuming exercise. The additional beauty of our new scheme is that it uses less pairing operations than previously proposed schemes [4,9,15,19] and hence, is significantly more efficient than previous schemes in computational and timing sense. Our scheme do not require a clerk in the original group. Moreover, the proposed scheme fulfills all the security requirements of a safe proxy signature.

The rest of this paper is organized as follows. In Section 2, some related preliminaries are described. In Section 3, we firstly define a formal model for ID-based proxy multi-signature schemes and then review the security requirements of a safe proxy signature given by Li et al. [10]. Our new scheme is presented in Section 4. Section 5 investigates the correctness, security and efficiency analysis of the proposed scheme and finally Section 6 gives a brief conclusion of the proposed work.

2   Preliminaries

In this section, we briefly describe the concept of bilinear pairings over the elliptic curve, and some related mathematical problems.

2.1   Bilinear Pairing

Let G_1 be an additive cyclic group with generator P and G_2 be a multiplicative group with generator g. Let the both groups are of the same prime order q. Then a map $e : G_1 \times G_1 \rightarrow G_2$ satisfying the following properties, is called bilinear pairing, also known as bilinear map:

(a)Bilinearity: $e(aP, bQ) = e(P, Q)^{ab} \forall a, b \in Z_q^*$ and $P, Q \in G_1$. In other way $e(P + Q, R) = e(P, R)e(Q, R)$ and $e(P, Q + R) = e(P, Q)e(P, R) \ \forall P, Q, R \in G_1$.
(b)Non-Degeneracy: There exists $P, Q \in G_1$ such that $e(P, Q) \neq 1$.
(c)Computability: There exists an efficient algorithm to compute $e(P, Q) \in G_2$, for any $P, Q \in G_1$.

The Weil pairing and Tate pairing over supersingular elliptic curves are examples of cryptographic bilinear pairings/maps.

2.2   CDHP

For given $P, aP, bP \in G_1$, to compute $abP \in G_1$. Where $a, b \in Z_q^*$.

2.3   Inverse CDHP (INV-CDHP)

To compute $a^{-1}P$ for given $P, aP \in G_1$, where $a \in Z_q^*$.

2.4   INV-CDH Assumption

If G_1 is a group of prime order q with a generator P, then a (t, ϵ)INV-CDH assumption holds in G_1 if there is no algorithm which takes at most t running time and can solve INV-CDHP with at least ϵ probability.

2.5   The k-CAA Problem   [11]

To compute $\frac{1}{s+e_0}P$, for some $e_0 \in Z_q^*$ when given $P, sP \in G_1, e_1, e_2, .., e_k \in Z_q^*$ and $\frac{1}{s+e_1}P, \frac{1}{s+e_2}P, .., \frac{1}{s+e_k}P \in G_1$.

2.6   k-Plus Problem   [13]

For given $P, P_{pub} = sP \in G_1, V = g^e \in G_2, e_1, e_2....e_k \in Z_q$, $\{\frac{e+e_1}{s}P, \frac{e+e_2}{s}P, ...\frac{e+e_k}{s}P\} \in G_1$, To find a pair $\{e', \frac{e+e'}{s}P\}$, where $e', e, s \in Z_q$, $e' \notin \{e_1, e_2....e_k\}$ and k is a constant number.

3   ID-Based Proxy Multi-signature Scheme and Its Security

Here we give the formal definition of an ID-based proxy multi-signature scheme, based on the work of Wang and Cao [18], Wang et al. [20] and Cao and Cao [4]. Then we review the security requirements of a safe proxy signature scheme.

3.1   Definition of ID-Based Proxy Multi-signature Scheme

In ID-based proxy multi-signature scheme, a group of original signers is authorized to delegate their signing rights to a proxy signer to make a signature on their behalf, where public and private keys of original signers and proxy signer are generated by a private key generator (PKG), using their corresponding identities. Let A_i for $1 \leq i \leq n$, be the n original signers with corresponding identities ID_{A_i} and B be the proxy signer with identity ID_B. Precisely, an ID-based proxy multi-signature scheme is consists of the following phases:

Setup: For a security parameter k, the PKG runs this algorithm and generates the public parameters *params* of the system and a master secret. The PKG publishes *params* and keeps the master secret to itself.

Extract: This is an algorithm run by PKG for private key generation. For a given identity ID, public parameter *params* and master secret, this algorithm generates private key S_{ID} of the user with identity ID. Finally the PKG provides private keys through a secure channel to all the users participating in the protocol.

Proxy del: This is a protocol, where a group of original signers interacts with the proxy signer for the delegation of signing rights. This algorithm takes the public parameters *params*, message warrant w, signers identity ID and its corresponding private key S_{ID} as an input and outputs a signed warrant say W.

Proxy veri: On input of public parameters *params*, identities of the original signers say ID_{A_i} for $1 \leq i \leq n$, warrant w and signed warrant W, the algorithm outputs 1 if W is a valid delegation for identities ID_{A_i} and outputs 0 otherwise.

Proxy-key gen: This algorithm takes input the identity of proxy signer ID_B, its corresponding private key S_{ID_B} and delegation warrant W. Finally as a result of above interaction, proxy signer outputs its proxy signing key say P_{sk}.

Proxy multi-sign: This algorithm takes proxy signing key P_{sk} of the proxy signer, the warrant w, message m and outputs the proxy multi-signature σ_P.

Proxy multi-veri: It takes input as public parameters *params*, identities of all the users $ID_{A_1}, ID_{A_2}, ..ID_{A_n}, ID_B$, the warrant w, the message m and proxy multi-signature σ_P. The algorithm outputs 1 if the signature σ_P is a valid proxy multi-signature on m by the proxy signer on behalf of the group of original signers, and outputs 0 otherwise.

3.2   Security Requirements for a Proxy Signature

In 2001, Lee et. al. proposed some extensions on security requirements of a proxy signature scheme proposed by Mambo et. al. [12] in 1996. According to [10], a secure proxy signature scheme should satisfy the following security properties [10]:

Strong unforgeability: No one other than the legal proxy signer can generate a valid proxy signature on behalf of original signer. Even the original signer cannot make proxy signature.

Verifiability: The signature can be verified by anyone, and the signed message should confirm to the delegation warrant. That means, any verifier can be convinced of the original signer's agreement on the signed message.

Strong identifiability: Identity of corresponding proxy signer can be determined by anyone.

Strong undeniability: The proxy signer cannot deny his signature, which he generates ever.

Prevention of misuse: The proxy signer cannot sign any message, which has not been authorized by the original signer. Or alternatively, It should be confident that proxy key cannot be used for other purposes. In the case of misuse, the responsibility of proxy signer should be determined explicitly.

4 Proposed Scheme

In this section, we describe our proposed ID-based proxy multi-signature scheme. Our scheme is simply divided into seven phases: System setup phase, Key extraction phase, Delegation generation phase, Delegation verification phase, Proxy key generation phase, Proxy multi-signature generation phase and Proxy multi-signature verification phase.

4.1 System Setup

For a security parameter k, the PKG generates system's public parameters $params = (k, G_1, G_2, q, e, H_1, H_2, P, g, P_{pub})$, where G_1 is a cyclic additive group and G_2 is a cyclic multiplicative group, a prime number q is order of both the groups. The setup uses above defined bilinear pairing $e : G_1 \times G_1 \rightarrow G_2$. Two cryptographic hash functions $H_1 : \{0,1\}^* \rightarrow Z_q^*$ and $H_2 : \{0,1\}^* \times G_2 \rightarrow Z_q^*$ are defined for the security purpose. P is a generator of G_1, and $g = e(P, P)$ is generator of G_2. System's public key is $P_{pub} = sP \in G_1$, and $s \in Z_q^*$ is system's master key. PKG publishes the $params$ and keeps the master-key s secret.

4.2 Extraction

For given identity ID, the PKG computes public key and private key as follows
Public key: $Q_{ID} = H_1(ID)$
Private Key: $S_{ID} = \frac{Q_{ID}}{s}P$, where $P \in G_1$ is generator of G_1.
Thus all the original signers ($say A_i$), have their public keys as $Q_{ID_{A_i}}$, and consequent private keys as $S_{ID_{A_i}}$, for $1 \leq i \leq n$. Similarly, the proxy signer's public key is Q_{ID_B} and consequent private key is S_{ID_B} .

4.3   Delegation Gen

In this phase, the group of original signers delegate their signing capability to the proxy signer through a signed warrant. The warrant w includes the time of delegation, identity of proxy and original signers, period of validity etc. To delegate the signing rights to the proxy signer, the group of original signers perform the following:

For $1 \leq i \leq n$, each original signer A_i randomly
chooses $t_i \in Z_q^*$ and computes
$V_{t_i} = g^{t_i} \in G_2$, and make V_{t_i} publicly available.
they further computes $h = H_2(w, V_T) \in Z_q^*$, where $V_T = \prod_{i=1}^n V_{t_i}$.
and $D_i = (t_i + h)S_{ID_{A_i}}$
finally each original signer sends (w, D_i) to the proxy signer as their partial delegation value.

4.4   Delegation Veri

Receiving (w, D_i) from each original signer A_i, the proxy signer
computes $h = H_2(w, V_T) \in Z_q^*$
then checks the validity of each partial delegation by the following:
$e(P_{pub}, D_i) = (V_{t_i} g^h)^{Q_{ID_{A_i}}}$.
If the above equality holds for $1 \leq i \leq n$, the proxy signer agree on the delegation value otherwise he requests for a new one, or terminate the protocol.

4.5   Proxy Key Generation

In this phase, the proxy signer generates a proxy key by delegation value, to sign message on behalf of the group of original signers. For this he does the following:
selects a random integer $x \in Z_q^*$
computes $V_x = g^x \in G_2$, and makes it public.
finally he computes the proxy signing key $S_{pk} = D + xS_{ID_B}$, where $D = \sum_{i=1}^n D_i$
and S_{ID_B} is his private key.

4.6   Proxy Multi-signature

To sign a message m, on behalf of the group of original signers, the proxy signer does the following: computes $h' = H_2(m, V_T) \in Z_q^*$
and $\sigma_p = h'S_{pk}$
(σ_p, w) is the proxy multi-signature on message m by the proxy signer on behalf of the group of original signers.

4.7   Verification

Receiving the proxy multi-signature (σ_p, w) and message m, any verifier proceeds on following steps to validate it:

(1) Checks the validity of message m with respect to the warrant w. Continue, if its valid one. Rejects otherwise.

(2) Checks whether the proxy signer B is authorized or not in warrant w, by the group of n original signers. If not, then stop. Continue otherwise.

(3) Agrees on the proxy multi-signature on message m, if and only if the following equality holds:

$$e(P_{pub}, \sigma_p) = \prod_{i=1}^{n}[(V_{t_i}^{h'} g^{hh'})^{Q_{ID_{A_i}}}](V_x^{h'})^{Q_{ID_B}}.$$

5 Analysis of Proposed Scheme

In this section, we first give the correctness of verification phase and then analyze the security of our scheme and will show that the proposed scheme satisfies all the security requirements of a safe proxy signature. Finally we compare the computational efficiency of our scheme with other similar schemes [4,9,15,19] and will show that our scheme is significantly more efficient than other schemes.

5.1 Correctness

Correctness of our scheme is satisfied as follows:

$$
\begin{aligned}
e(P_{pub}, \sigma_p) &= e(sP, h'(D + xS_{ID_B})) \\
&= e(sP, h'(\sum_{i=1}^{n} D_i + xS_{ID_B})) \\
&= e(sP, h'(\sum_{i}^{n}[(t_i + h)S_{ID_{A_i}}] + xS_{ID_B})) \\
&= e(sP, h'(\sum_{i}^{n}[(t_i + h)\frac{Q_{ID_{A_i}}}{s}P] + x\frac{Q_{ID_B}}{s}P)) \\
&= e(P, h'\sum_{i=1}^{n}(t_i + h)Q_{ID_{A_i}}P)e(P, h'xQ_{ID_B}P) \text{ (Bilinearity).} \\
&= \prod_{i=1}^{n} e(h'P, (t_i + h)Q_{ID_{A_i}}P)e(P, h'xQ_{ID_B}P) \\
&= \prod_{i=1}^{n} e(P, P)^{h'(t_i+h)Q_{ID_{A_i}}} e(P, P)^{h'xQ_{ID_B}} \text{ (Bilinearity).} \\
&= \prod_{i=1}^{n}[\{(g^{t_i})^{h'} g^{hh'}\}^{Q_{ID_{A_i}}}][\{(g^x)^{h'}\}^{Q_{ID_B}}] \\
&= \prod_{i=1}^{n}[(V_{t_i}^{h'} g^{hh'})^{Q_{ID_{A_i}}}](V_x^{h'})^{Q_{ID_B}}.
\end{aligned}
$$

5.2 Security Analysis

In this section, we analyze the security of our scheme. We will show that our scheme satisfies all the security requirements of a safe proxy signature mentioned in section 3.

(i)*Strong unforgeability*: The attempt of forgery to the signature can be made by either of any original signers, the proxy signer or by any third party who do not participate in the protocol. We'll show that no one from the above, can forge the proposed signature.

Claim : The proposed ID-based proxy multi-signature scheme is strongly unforgeable if the INV-CHP problem is hard in G_1.

For this, we see firstly, anyone from the group of original signers can not generate a valid proxy multi-signature, because it involves the private key of the proxy signer $S_{ID_B} = \frac{Q_{ID_B}}{s}P$, getting of which for the known Q_{ID_B} and P and sP, is equivalent to forging the 'k-plus' problem in G_1, and reduced in INV-CDHP in G_1 which is assumed to be hard.

Secondly, the proxy signer B can not forge the proxy multi-signature. For this, suppose if he wants to sign a false message m', for this, he will have to use the delegation value D to generate his proxy secret key and for being a legitimate proxy signer authorized by the original group. But using D to sign a different message m' will not validate the message and message warrant in verification phase. Also, if the proxy signer plans to construct a false delegation value D' satisfying its new message and corresponding warrant, he will be needed the private keys $S_{ID_{A_i}}$ for $1 \leq i \leq n$ of all the original signers, getting of which is equivalent to forging the 'k-plus' problem in G_1, and reduced in INV-CDHP in G_1, which is assumed to be hard.

Lastly, any third party who do not participate in the protocol can not forge the signature even having signatures of all the original signers, since for that, he will be needed the private keys of all the original signers, getting of which is again equivalent to forging the INV-CDHP in G_1, which is assumed to be hard.

Finally, since forgery to the proposed scheme from any party depends on the hardness of the INV-CDHP in G_1. Hence the proposed ID-based proxy multi-signature scheme is strongly unforgeable if the INV-CHP is hard in G_1.

(ii) *Verifiability:* Any verifier can easily verify the proposed proxy multi-signature and can check whether the signed message confirms to the delegation warrant or not. Correctness of the verification is described above.

(iii)*Strong identifiability:* By warrant anyone can determine the identity of proxy signer.

(iv)*Strong undeniability:* The proxy signer can not deny his involvement in signature protocol, since the message verifies using the public key of the proxy signer.

(v)*Prevention of misuse:* Since the message warrant is attached specifying the delegation period, nature of message, identities of original signers etc., the proxy signer can not sign any message which does not confirms to the warrant and has not been authorized by the group of original signers.

Hence by the above analysis it is clear that the proposed ID-based proxy multi-signature scheme is secure according to [10].

5.3   Efficiency Comparison

In this subsection, we compare the efficiency of our scheme with other ID-based proxy multi-signature schemes [4,9,15,19]. We note that the operation time for one pairing computation is 20.04 miliseconds, that of one exponentiation computation is 5.31 miliseconds and for one hash function, it is 3.04 miliseconds [8]. On the basis of these timing of computations, one can easily verify from following tables that the proposed scheme is computationally more efficient than others.

Proxy generation phase: This phase includes delegation generation, delegation verification and proxy key generation.

Scheme	Bilinear map	Hashing	Exponent	Operation time
Li & Chen's scheme (2005) [9]	3	2	1	71.51 ms
Wang & Cao (2007) [19]	3	4	0	72.28 ms
Z. Shao scheme (2009) [15]	3	2	0	66.20 ms
Cao & Cao's scheme (2009) [4]	3	3	0	69.24 ms
Our scheme	**1**	**2**	**1**	**31.43 ms**

Proxy multi-signature generation phase:

Scheme	Bilinear map	Hashing	Exponent	Operation time
Li & Chen's scheme (2005) [9]	1	1	1	28.39 ms
Wang & Cao (2007) [19]	0	1	0	3.04 ms
Z. Shao scheme (2009) [15]	0	1	0	3.04 ms
Cao & Cao's scheme (2009) [4]	0	1	0	3.04 ms
Our scheme	**0**	**1**	**0**	**3.04 ms**

Verification phase:

Scheme	Bilinear map	Hashing	Exponent	Operation time
Li & Chen's scheme (2005) [9]	3	2	2	76.82 ms
Wang & Cao (2007) [19]	3	3	0	69.24 ms
Z. Shao scheme (2009) [15]	3	2	0	66.20 ms
Cao & Cao's scheme (2009) [4]	4	3	0	89.28 ms
Our scheme	**1**	**2**	**5**	**51.167 ms**

From the above comparison tables, it is clear that our scheme is computationally more efficient and takes less operation time than schemes given in [4,9,15,19].

6   Conclusion

Up to the best knowledge, the authors believe that no ID-based proxy multi-signature scheme from bilinear pairings has been proposed based on INV-CDHP till now. So, taking advantage of the 'k-plus' problem, in this paper, we have proposed an ID-based proxy multi-signature scheme using bilinear pairings. Security of our scheme is based on the INV-CDHP. The major benefit of presented scheme is that it is very much efficient in computational senses due to less pairing operations. Moreover, the proposed scheme satisfies all the security requirements of a safe proxy signature.

References

1. Boneh, D., Franklin, M.: Identity-Based Encryption from the Weil Pairing. In: Kilian, J. (ed.) CRYPTO 2001. LNCS, vol. 2139, pp. 213–229. Springer, Heidelberg (2001)

2. Barreto, P.S.L.M., Libert, B., McCullagh, N., Quisquater, J.-J.: Efficient and Provably-Secure Identity-Based Signatures and Signcryption from Bilinear Maps. In: Roy, B. (ed.) ASIACRYPT 2005. LNCS, vol. 3788, pp. 515–532. Springer, Heidelberg (2005)
3. Cha, J.C., Cheon, J.H.: An Identity-Based Signature from Gap Diffie-Hellman Groups. In: Desmedt, Y.G. (ed.) PKC 2003. LNCS, vol. 2567, pp. 18–30. Springer, Heidelberg (2002)
4. Cao, F., Cao, Z.: A secure identity-based proxy multi-signature scheme. Information Sciences 179, 292–302 (2009)
5. Delos, O., Quisquater, J.-J.: An Identity-Based Signature Scheme with Bounded Life-Span. In: Desmedt, Y.G. (ed.) CRYPTO 1994. LNCS, vol. 839, pp. 83–94. Springer, Heidelberg (1994)
6. Du, H., Wen, Q.: An efficient Identity-based short signature scheme from bilinear pairings. In: International Conference on Computer Inteligency and Security (ICCIS 2007), pp. 725–729 (2007)
7. Hesss, F.: Efficient Identity Based Signature Schemes Based on Pairings. In: Nyberg, K., Heys, H.M. (eds.) SAC 2002. LNCS, vol. 2595, pp. 310–324. Springer, Heidelberg (2003)
8. He, D., Chen, J., Hu, J.H.: An ID-based proxy signature scheme without bilinear pairings. Annlas of Telecommunications (February 2011), doi:10.1007/s12243-011-0244-0
9. Li, X., Chen, K.: ID-based multi-proxy signature, proxy multi-signature and multi-proxy multi-signature schemes from bilinear pairings. Applied Mathematics and Computation 169, 437–450 (2005)
10. Lee, B., Kim, H., Kim, K.: Strong proxy signature and its applications. In: Proceedings of The 2001 Symposium on Cryptography and Information Security (SCIS), pp. 603–608 (2001)
11. Mitsunari, S., Sakai, R., Kasahara, M.: A new traitor tracing. IEICE Transictions E85-A(2), 481–484 (2002)
12. Mambo, M., Usuda, K., Okmamoto, E.: Proxy signatures: delegation of the power to sign message. IEICE Transaction Functional E79-A(9), 1338–1354 (1996)
13. Okamoto, T., Inomata, A., Okamoto, E.: A proposal of short proxy signature using pairing. In: Proceedings of International Conference on Information Technology Coding and Computing (ITCC 2005), pp. 631–635 (2005)
14. Paterson, K.G.: Id-based signatures from pairings on elliptic curves. Cryptology ePrint Archive, Report 2002/004 (2002), http://eprint.iacr.org/2002/004
15. Shao, Z.: Improvement of identity-based proxy multi-signature scheme. The Journal of Systems and Software 82, 794–800 (2009)
16. Shamir, A.: Identity-Based Cryptosystems and Signature Schemes. In: Blakely, G.R., Chaum, D. (eds.) CRYPTO 1984. LNCS, vol. 196, pp. 47–53. Springer, Heidelberg (1985)
17. Smart, N.P.: An identity based authenticated key agreement protocol based on the weil pairing. Electronic Letters 38(13), 630–632 (2002)
18. Wang, Q., Cao, Z.: Security arguments for partial delegation with warrant proxy signature schemes. Cryptology ePrint Archive, Report 2004/315 (2002), http://eprint.iacr.org/2004/315
19. Wang, Q., Cao, Z.: Identity based proxy multi-signature. The Journal of Systems and Software 80, 1023–1029 (2007)
20. Wang, Q., Cao, Z., Wang, S.: Formalized security model of multi-proxy signature schemes. In: Proceedings of The fifth International Conference on Computers and Information Technology (CIT 2005), pp. 668–672. IEEE Computer Society (2005)

21. Yi, X.: An identity-based signature scheme from the Weil pairing. IEEE Communication Letters 7(2), 76–78 (2003)
22. Yi, L., Bai, G., Xiao, G.: Proxy multi-signature scheme: a new type of proxy signature scheme. Electronics Letters 36(6), 527–528 (2000)
23. Zhang, F., Kim, K.: ID-Based Blind Signature and Ring Signature from Pairings. In: Zheng, Y. (ed.) ASIACRYPT 2002. LNCS, vol. 2501, pp. 533–547. Springer, Heidelberg (2002)
24. Zhang, F., Kim, K.: Efficient ID-Based Blind Signature and Proxy Signature from Bilinear Pairings. In: Safavi-Naini, R., Seberry, J. (eds.) ACISP 2003. LNCS, vol. 2727, pp. 312–323. Springer, Heidelberg (2003)
25. Zhang, F., Safavi-Naini, R., Susilo, W.: An Efficient Signature Scheme from Bilinear Pairings and Its Applications. In: Bao, F., Robert, H., Deng, R.H., Zhou, J. (eds.) PKC 2004. LNCS, vol. 2947, pp. 277–290. Springer, Heidelberg (2004)

On the Affine Ciphers in Cryptography

Manocheher Kazemi, Hassan Naraghi, and Hmid Mottaghi Golshan

Department of Mathematics, Ashtian Branch, Islamic Azad University, Iran
{kazemi,naraghi,mottaghi}@mail.aiau.ac.ir

Abstract. Before letter frequency analysis and the formation of the black chambers, the basic monoalphabetic substitution ciphers were practically unbreakable and sufficient for common use. But as encryption became used more widely, the need to break these cryptosystems became inevitable. With the development of letter frequency analysis and advancement of black chambers, each message encrypted with a type of monoalphabetic substitution was easily broken. As soon as a commonly used monoalphabetic substitution cipher was broken, the word spread and that particular cryptosystem was useless. The affine cipher is simply a special case of the more general monoalphabetic substitution cipher. In this paper, we study the affine cipher and generalized affine cipher.

Keywords: Affine cipher, Encryption, Cryptography, Decryption, Monoalphabetic.

1 Introduction

Cryptography is the study of mathematical techniques for all aspects of information security. Cryptanalysis is the complementary science concerned with the methods to defeat these techniques. Cryptology is the study of cryptography and cryptanalysis. The security of information encompasses the following aspects:

- confidentiality or privacy,
- data integrity,
- authentication,
- nonrepudiation.

Each of these aspects of message security can addressed by standard methods in cryptography. Besides exchange of messages, tools from cryptography can be applied to sharing an access key between multiple parties so that no one person can gain access to a vault by any two of them can. Another role is in the design of electronic forms of cash.

As we have seen, shift ciphers offer very little security. The problem is that the letter substitutions, or shifts, are not mixed up enough. The idea of an affine cipher is to use multiplication combined with addition, modulo m, where m is an integer, to create a more mixed-up substitution[1]. The affine cipher is simply a special case of the more general monoalphabetic substitution cipher. The key for the affine cipher consists of an ordered pair, say (a, b). In selecting the key, it

A. Abd Manaf et al. (Eds.): ICIEIS 2011, Part I, CCIS 251, pp. 185–199, 2011.
© Springer-Verlag Berlin Heidelberg 2011

is important to note the following restrictions; $a \neq 0$ and b must be chosen from among the integers $0, 1, 2, 3, \cdots, m - 1$ and $a \neq 0$ must be relatively prime to m (i.e. a should have no factors in common with m). For example, assuming we use a 26 character alphabet (i.e. $m = 26$), 15 and 26 have no factors in common and therefore 15 is an acceptable value for a. On the other hand, if we chose 12 for the value of a, it is obvious that 12 would be an unacceptable value since 12 and 26 have common factors, specifically 2. In General, an affine cipher is a cipher system in which plaintext letters are enciphered mathematically by the function, $y = ax + b \mod m$, and using function notation, we have, $\epsilon(x) = ax + b \mod m$, where x is the numerical equivalent of the plaintext letter and m is the number of letters in the alphabet.

2   Preliminaries

Whenever possible we follow the notation, terminology and examples of [1,2,4] and subjects of history of cryptology selected of [3,5,6].

Encryption = the process of disguising a message so as to hide the information it contains; this process can include both encoding and enciphering (see definitions below).

Protocol = an algorithm, defined by a sequence of steps, precisely specifying the actions of multiple parties in order to achieve an objective.

Plaintext = the message to be transmitted or stored.

Ciphertext = the disguised message.

Alphabet = a collection of symbols, also referred to as characters.

Character = an element of an alphabet.

Bit = a character 0 or 1 of the binary alphabet.

String = a finite sequence of characters in some alphabet.

Example 1. The following are some standard alphabets.

$A, \cdots, Z$	26 symbols	MSDOS(less punctuation)
$ASCII$	$7 - bitwords(128symbols)$	American standard
$extended$	8-bit words(256 symbols)	
$ISO - 8859 - 1$	8-bit words(256 symbols)	European standard
$Binary$	$\{0, 1\}$	Numerical alphabet base 2
$Octal$	$\{0, \cdots, 7\}$	Numerical alphabet base 8
$Decimal$	$\{0, \cdots, 9\}$	Numerical alphabet base 10
$Hexadecimal$	$\{0, \cdots, 9, a, b, c, d, e, f\}$	Numerical alphabet base 16

Encode = to convert a message into a representation in a standard alphabet, such as to the alphabet $\{A, \cdots, Z\}$ or to numerical alphabet.

Decode = to convert the encoded message back to its original alphabet and original form the term plaintext will apply to either the original or the encoded form. The process of encoding a message is not an obscure process, and the result that we get can be considered equivalent to the plaintext message.

Cipher = a map from a space of plaintext to a space of ciphertext.

Encipher = to convert plaintext into ciphertext.

Decipher = to convert ciphertext back to plaintext.

Stream cipher = a cipher which acts on the plaintext one symbol at a time.

Block cipher = a cipher which acts on the plaintext in blocks of symbols.

Substitution cipher = a stream cipher which acts on the plaintext by making a substitution of the characters with elements of a new alphabet or by a permutation of the characters in the plaintext alphabet.

Transposition cipher = a block cipher which acts on the plaintext by permuting the positions of the characters in the plaintext.

Example 2. The following is an example of a substitution cipher:

$$A\ B\ C\ D\ E\ F\ G\ H\ \cdots\ Z\ -$$
$$\downarrow\ \downarrow\ \downarrow\ \downarrow\ \downarrow\ \downarrow\ \downarrow\ \downarrow\ \cdots\ \downarrow\ \downarrow$$
$$P\ C\ -\ O\ N\ A\ W\ Y\ \cdots\ L\ S$$

which takes the plaintext BAD CAFE BED to the ciphertext CPOS ANSNO.

2.1   Cryptosystems

Given an alphabet $\mathcal{A}$ we define $\mathcal{A}^*$ to be the set of all strings over $\mathcal{A}$. In order to define a cryptosystem, we require a collection of sets:

$$\mathcal{A} =\text{plaintext alphabet}\quad \mathcal{A}' -\text{ciphertext alphabet}$$
$$\mathcal{M} =\text{plaintext space}\quad \mathcal{C} =\text{ciphertext space}$$
$$\mathcal{K} =\text{(plaintext) keyspace}\ \mathcal{K}' =\text{(ciphertext) keyspace}$$

where $\mathcal{M}$ is a subset of $\mathcal{A}^*$, $\mathcal{C}$ is a subset of $\mathcal{A}'^*$, and $\mathcal{K}$ and $\mathcal{K}'$ are sets which are generally strings of fixed finite length over some alphabets (e.g. $\mathcal{A}^n$ or $\mathcal{A}'^n$). A cryptosystem or encryption scheme is a pair (E, D) of maps

$$E : \mathcal{K} \times \mathcal{M} \to \mathcal{C}, \quad D : \mathcal{K}' \times \mathcal{C} \to \mathcal{M}$$

such that for each K in $\mathcal{K}$ there exists a K' in $\mathcal{K}'$ such that

$$D(K', E(K, M)) = M$$

for all M in $\mathcal{M}$. We write E_K for the map $E(K, .) : \mathcal{M} \to \mathcal{C}$ and similarly write $D_{K'}$ for $D(K', .) : \mathcal{C} \to \mathcal{M}$. With this notation the condition on E, D, K and K' is that $D_{K'} o E_K$ is the identity map on $\mathcal{M}$. We will refer to E_K as a cipher, and note that a cipher is necessarily injective. For many cryptosystems, there will exist a unique inverse ciphertext key K' associated to each plaintext key K. A cryptosystem for which the inverse key K' is K itself (hence $K = K'$) is said to be symmetric. If the inverse key K' associated to K is neither K itself nor easily computable function of K, then we say that the cryptosystem is asymmetric or a public key cryptosystem. A fundamental principle of cryptography is that the security of a cipher E_K (i.e. the difficulty in finding $D_{K'}$) does not rest on the lack of knowledge of the cryptosystem (E, D). Instead, security should be based on the secrecy of K'. Recall that a (cryptographic) protocol is an algorithm, defined by a sequence of steps, precisely specifying the actions of multiple parties in order to achieve a (security) objective. An example of a cryptographic protocol, we describe the steps for message exchange using a symmetric key cryptosystem.

1. Alice and Bob publicly agree on a cryptosystem (E, D).
2. For each message M Alice$\to$ Bob:

a) Alice and Bob agree on a secret key K.
b) Alice computes $C = E_K(M)$ and sends it to Bob.
c) Bob computes $M = D_K(C)$ to obtain the plaintext.

The difficulty of step 2.a was one of the fundamental obstructions to cryptography before the advent of public key cryptography. Asymmetric cryptography provides an elegant solution to the problem of distribution of private keys.

3   Affine Cipher

Another type of substitution cipher is the affine cipher (or linear cipher). Even though affine ciphers are examples of substitution ciphers, and are thus far from secure, they can be easily altered to make a system which is, in fact, secure. To set up an affine cipher, you pick two values a and b, and then set $\epsilon(m) = am + b$ mod 26. For example, if we take $a = 3$ and $b = 8$, then the encryption function is $\epsilon(m) = 3m + 8$ mod 26. To encrypt the letter C, we first note that C corresponds to the number 02. Plugging this in for m, we get $\epsilon(02) = 3(02) + 8 = 14$, and so C is encrypted as O. To find our decryption function, we set $s = \epsilon(m)$ and solve for m in terms of s. We have $s \equiv 3m + 8$ mod 26 therefore $s - 8 \equiv 3m$ mod 26, so $3m \equiv s - 8$ mod 26.

Definition 1. *[1]. A multiplicative inverse of an integer a modulo m is an integer b, in the range 1 to $m - 1$, such that $ab \equiv 1$ mod m. When a and m are relatively prime, such ab will exist and we call b the multiplicative inverse of a and label it a^{-1}.*

Since $\gcd(3, 26) = 1$, we know that there will be an x with $3x \equiv 1$ mod 26. We could use the Extended Euclidean Algorithm to find x, or we can simply notice that $(3)(9) = 27 \equiv 1$ mod 26 and so $x = 9$ works. Now we multiply both sides by 9: $27m \equiv 9(s - 8) \equiv 9s - 72 \equiv 9s + 6$ mod 26, which tells us that $m = \delta(s) = 9s + 6$ mod 26. In general, to construct an affine cipher, we begin by choosing a and b with $\gcd(a, 26) = 1$. Then $\epsilon(m) = am + b$ mod 26 and $\delta(s) = x(s - b)$ mod 26, where x satisfies $ax \equiv 1$ mod 26.

Exercise 1. This exercise has two parts. Working in teams of 2,

1. you and your partner will create an affine cipher by choosing a and b with $\gcd(a, 26) = 1$. Using your cipher, $\epsilon(m) = am + b$ mod 26, encode a message that is between 8 and 12 letters long. Give this encoded message, along with your values of a and b, to another team to decipher.

2. you and your partner will decipher the message that the other team gave you. Using their values of a and b, decode their message using $\delta(s) = x(s-b)$ mod 26, where x satisfies $ax \equiv 1$ mod 26.

As we mentioned earlier, affine ciphers are not secure because they're really just special examples of substitution ciphers and so one may use "frequency analysis" to crack them. However, we can tweak the idea a bit and consider affine block ciphers instead. The mathematics is the same, only now instead of encrypting one letter at a time, we encrypt a block of letters together. As an example, suppose we want to take our block-length to be 4. This means that we divide our message into blocks of 4 letters and encrypt each block separately. The largest number we could end up with is 456,975 (corresponding to the highly unlikely 4-letter block "ZZZZ"), and so we need to be sure that our modulus is greater than 456,975. We could use 456,976 but it's just as easy (if not easier) to use 1,000,000. Now we proceed just as before. We choose a and b and set $\epsilon(m) = am+b$ mod $1,000,000$. As long as we've chosen a so that $\gcd(a, 1,000,000) = 1$, we can find an integer x such that $ax \equiv 1$ mod $1,000,000$. In this case, our decryption function is $\delta(s) = x(s - b)$ mod $1,000,000$. Because we're now encrypting blocks of letters rather than single letters, frequency analysis will not work here. In other words, affine block ciphers are reasonably secure as long as the block size is large enough (blocks of size four will most likely be big enough). Even though affine block ciphers are secure, there's still a problem with them. The problem is that they're symmetric. This means that anyone who knows the encryption function $\epsilon(m)$ also knows (or can easily figure out) the decryption function $\delta(s)$. For example, all one needs to do to figure out the formula for $\delta(s)$ given that $\epsilon(m) = am + b$ mod $1,000,000$ is use the Extended Euclidean Algorithm to find x such that $ax \equiv 1$ mod $1,000,000$. This is easy to do either by hand or with the help of a computer.

Example 3. Suppose we want to set up correspondence where a message is encrypted with the key $(7, 11)$ and using a twenty-six letter alphabet. Substituting our given key and modulus into the Affine Cipher encryption function, we have $\epsilon(x) = 7x + 11$ mod 26. Then, using table1, the message, ATTACK, has numerical equivalent $0, 19, 19, 0, 2, 10$, and to encrypt the plaintext we substitute the integer values into the Affine Cipher encryption function as follows

$$7 \times 0 + 11 \mod 26 = 11 \mod 26 = 11$$

$$7 \times 19 + 11 \mod 26 = 144 \mod 26 = 14$$

Table 1. The integers corresponding to the twenty-six letter

A	B	C	D	E	F	G	H	I	J	K	L	M
0	1	2	3	4	5	6	7	8	9	10	11	12
N	O	P	Q	R	S	T	U	V	W	X	Y	Z
13	14	15	16	17	18	19	20	21	22	23	24	25

$$7 \times 19 + 11 \quad \mod 26 = 144 \quad \mod 26 = 14$$

$$7 \times 0 + 11 \quad \mod 26 = 11 \quad \mod 26 = 11$$

$$7 \times 2 + 11 \quad \mod 26 = 25 \quad \mod 26 = 25$$

$$7 \times 10 + 11 \quad \mod 26 = 81 \quad \mod 26 = 3,$$

Hence, the numerical equivalents of the ciphertext are $11, 14, 14, 11, 25, 3$. Finally, we translate the encrypted integers back into letters using table1 and get **LOOLZD**.

All of the examples presented thus far have been calculated modulo 26, with the numbers 0 thru 25 corresponding to letters A thru Z respectively. When we take into consideration using lower case, upper case, punctuation, and other symbols, more numbers are required. To help us define alphabets other than the standard twenty-six letter upper case alphabet, we will employ shifted ASCII codes, which are numerical values assigned to every character on a computer keyboard, to generate three additional alphabets, specifically, the Mod 29 alphabet, which is formed from the mod 26 alphabet by adding a space, period, and question mark, the Mod 89 alphabet, which are the ASCII codes of a certain 89 characters shifted left 34 units, and the Mod 95 alphabet, which are the ASCII codes shifted left 32 units.

Note 1. Each of these additional alphabets are located in Appendix[2, A].

Decryption of the ciphertext obtained by applying the Affine Cipher encryption function can be accomplished similar to the encryption process. However, as we seen with the Shift Cipher, we must first perform the steps, learned in algebra, to find the inverse function. As we previously stated, the Affine Cipher consists of both multiplication and addition and unlike the Shift Cipher, it is necessary to define the multiplicative inverse of an integer a modulo m.

Note 2. For the purposes of this project, the multiplicative inverses of invertible elements in the alphabets modulo $26, 29, 89$, and 95 will be supplied in Appendix[2, B]. However, there is a process that can be used to calculate the multiplicative inverse, generally seen in Discrete Mathematics and Number Theory, known as the Euclidean Algorithm.

Example 4. Using the derived decryption function for the Affine Cipher, let us decipher the ciphertext, LOOLZD, from the previous example to ensure we get the correct plaintext. Our plaintext was encrypted using a key of $(7, 11)$, where $a = 7$ and $b = 11$, and therefore we must first find 7^{-1} modulo 26. By table2,

Table 2. Multiplicative Inverses modulo 26

x	1	3	5	7	9	11	15	17	19	21	23	25
$x - 1 \mod 26$	1	9	21	15	3	19	7	23	11	5	17	25

$7^{-1} = 15$, so our decryption formula will be $\delta(x) = 15(x - 11)$ mod 26. The numerical equivalents of the encrypted message are

$$11, 14, 14, 11, 25, 3.$$

Substituting these values for x in the derived decryption function we get

$$15(11 - 11) \quad \text{mod } 26 = 0 \quad \text{mod } 26 = 0$$

$$15(14 - 11) \quad \text{mod } 26 = 45 \quad \text{mod } 26 = 19$$

$$15(14 - 11) \quad \text{mod } 26 = 45 \quad \text{mod } 26 = 19$$

$$15(11 - 11) \quad \text{mod } 26 = 0 \quad \text{mod } 26 = 0$$

$$15(25 - 11) \quad \text{mod } 26 = 210 \quad \text{mod } 26 = 2$$

$$15(3 - 11) \quad \text{mod } 26 = -120 \quad \text{mod } 26 = 10$$

Therefore, the numerical equivalents of our calculated plaintext are

$$0, 19, 19, 0, 2, 10.$$

Finally, the last step is to translate the decrypted integers back into letters using table1, and get ATTACK.

Now suppose we want to encrypt a message twice. Suppose we use the mod 95 alphabet in Appendix[2, A], we would then need to select two separate keys, say $(17, 62)$ and $(9, 24)$. Substituting our two keys and the selected modulus into the Affine Cipher encryption function, we get two functions g and h as follows

$$g(x) = 17x + 62 \quad \text{mod } 95, h(x) = 9x + 24 \quad \text{mod } 95.$$

Using the same process as the previous example, let us encrypt the message, Retreat NOW!, first using function g and then h. Do note, since we are using a 95 character alphabet, we must take into account using lower and upper case letters, punctuation, and empty spaces. Using Mod 95 Alphabet, in Appendix[2, A], the numerical equivalents of Retreat NOW! are

$$50, 69, 84, 82, 69, 65, 84, 0, 46, 47, 55, 1$$

and encrypting the message by first using g we get

$$17 \times 50 + 62 \quad \text{mod } 95 = 912 \quad \text{mod } 95 = 57$$

$$17 \times 69 + 62 \quad \text{mod } 95 = 1235 \quad \text{mod } 95 = 0$$

$$17 \times 84 + 62 \quad \text{mod } 95 = 1490 \quad \text{mod } 95 = 65$$

$$17 \times 82 + 62 \quad \text{mod } 95 = 1456 \quad \text{mod } 95 = 31$$

$$17 \times 69 + 62 \quad \text{mod } 95 = 1235 \quad \text{mod } 95 = 0$$

$$17 \times 65 + 62 \quad \mod 95 = 1167 \quad \mod 95 = 27$$

$$17 \times 84 + 62 \quad \mod 95 = 1490 \quad \mod 95 = 65$$

$$17 \times 0 + 62 \quad \mod 95 = 62 \quad \mod 95 = 62$$

$$17 \times 46 + 62 \quad \mod 95 = 844 \quad \mod 95 = 84$$

$$17 \times 47 + 62 \quad \mod 95 = 861 \quad \mod 95 = 6$$

$$17 \times 55 + 62 \quad \mod 95 = 997 \quad \mod 95 = 47$$

$$17 \times 1 + 62 \quad \mod 95 = 79 \quad \mod 95 = 79$$

Hence, the integer values of the encrypted plaintext using g are

$$57, 0, 65, 31, 0, 27, 65, 62, 84, 6, 47, 79.$$

For the second encryption, we will use the integer values found using g and plug them into h as follows

$$9 \times 57 + 24 \quad \mod 95 = 537 \quad \mod 95 = 62$$

$$9 \times 0 + 24 \quad \mod 95 = 24 \quad \mod 95 = 24$$

$$9 \times 65 + 24 \quad \mod 95 = 609 \quad \mod 95 = 39$$

$$9 \times 31 + 24 \quad \mod 95 = 303 \quad \mod 95 = 18$$

$$9 \times 0 + 24 \quad \mod 95 = 24 \quad \mod 95 = 24$$

$$9 \times 27 + 24 \quad \mod 95 = 267 \quad \mod 95 = 77$$

$$9 \times 65 + 24 \quad \mod 95 = 609 \quad \mod 95 = 39$$

$$9 \times 62 + 24 \quad \mod 95 = 582 \quad \mod 95 = 12$$

$$9 \times 84 + 24 \quad \mod 95 = 780 \quad \mod 95 = 20$$

$$9 \times 6 + 24 \quad \mod 95 = 78 \quad \mod 95 = 78$$

$$9 \times 47 + 24 \quad \mod 95 = 447 \quad \mod 95 = 67$$

$$9 \times 79 + 24 \quad \mod 95 = 735 \quad \mod 95 = 70$$

After twice encrypting the plaintext with a key of $(17, 62)$ and then with $(9, 24)$ we get the integers

$$62, 24, 39, 18, 24, 77, 39, 12, 20, 78, 67, 70.$$

Finally, we translate the encrypted integers back into letters using the Mod 95 Alphabet in Appendix[2, A] and get the following ciphertext

$$\wedge\, 8\, G\, 2\, 8\, m\, G, 4\, n\, c\, f.$$

The process of encrypting plaintext multiple times can be lengthy and time consuming. To shorten the process we can use function composition to create one function for encryption. However, before we begin it is important to note that $f(k(x)) \neq k(f(x))$, except for special cases, therefore, we must take caution when performing function composition. As a general rule, take the first encryption function and insert into the second encryption function. In our case take g and insert it into h, specifically $f(x) = h(g(x))$, as follows

$$9(17x + 62) + 24 \quad \text{mod } 95$$

$$153x + 558 + 24 \quad \text{mod } 95$$

$$153x + 582 \quad \text{mod } 95$$

Since we are calculating modulo 95, all integer values must be reduced modulo 95. Hence, our new function composition is $f(x) = 58x + 12 \mod 95$. Using our function composition, let us encrypt the same message, Retreat NOW!, to show we get the same ciphertext as the process of double encrypting. First, using Mod 95 Alphabet, in Appendix[2, A], the numerical equivalents of Retreat NOW! are $50, 69, 84, 82, 69, 65, 84, 0, 46, 47, 55, 1$ and encrypting using f we get

$$58 \times 50 + 12 \quad \text{mod } 95 = 2912 \quad \text{mod } 95 = 62$$

$$58 \times 69 + 12 \quad \text{mod } 95 = 4014 \quad \text{mod } 95 = 24$$

$$58 \times 84 + 12 \quad \text{mod } 95 = 4884 \quad \text{mod } 95 = 39$$

$$58 \times 82 + 12 \quad \text{mod } 95 = 4768 \quad \text{mod } 95 = 18$$

$$58 \times 69 + 12 \quad \text{mod } 95 = 4014 \quad \text{mod } 95 = 24$$

$$58 \times 65 + 12 \quad \text{mod } 95 = 3782 \quad \text{mod } 95 = 77$$

$$58 \times 84 + 12 \quad \text{mod } 95 = 4884 \quad \text{mod } 95 = 39$$

$$58 \times 0 + 12 \quad \text{mod } 95 = 12 \quad \text{mod } 95 = 12$$

$$58 \times 46 + 12 \quad \text{mod } 95 = 2680 \quad \text{mod } 95 = 20$$

$$58 \times 47 + 12 \quad \text{mod } 95 = 2738 \quad \text{mod } 95 = 78$$

$$58 \times 55 + 12 \quad \text{mod } 95 = 3202 \quad \text{mod } 95 = 67$$

$$58 \times 1 + 12 \quad \text{mod } 95 = 70 \quad \text{mod } 95 = 70$$

The resulting integers after applying our composition function are

$$62, 24, 39, 18, 24, 77, 39, 12, 20, 78, 67, 70,$$

and using Mod 95 Alphabet in Appendix[2, A] we can look up the ciphertext, which is

$$\wedge\, 8\, G\, 2\, 8\, m\, G, 4\, n\, c\, f$$

Finally, we can see that we can use function composition in place of using multiple encryption functions which will save time and tedious computations. Decrypting the previous example can be accomplished by finding and applying

$f^{-1}(x)$ to the ciphertext or by finding and applying $h^{-1}(x)$ then $g^{-1}(x)$ to the ciphertext. We will show both processes. First, we will apply $f^{-1}(x)$ to the ciphertext. Since our plaintext was encrypted using the key $(58, 12)$, where $a = 58$ and $b = 12$, we must find 58^{-1} modulo 95. Using the Multiplicative Inverses modulo 95 table in Appendix[2, B], $58^{-1} = 77$. Substituting 58^{-1} and $b = 12$ into the Affine Cipher decryption function, we get $f^{-1}(x) = 77(x-12) \mod 95$. Now, using the Mod 95 Alphabet in Appendix[2, A], the numerical equivalents of the encrypted message are

$$62, 24, 39, 18, 24, 77, 39, 12, 20, 78, 67, 70.$$

Substituting these values for x in the derived decryption function we get

$$77(62 - 12) \mod 95 = 3850 \mod 95 = 50$$

$$77(24 - 12) \mod 95 = 924 \mod 95 = 69$$

$$77(39 - 12) \mod 95 = 2079 \mod 95 = 84$$

$$77(18 - 12) \mod 95 = 462 \mod 95 = 82$$

$$77(24 - 12) \mod 95 = 924 \mod 95 = 69$$

$$77(77 - 12) \mod 95 = 5005 \mod 95 = 65$$

$$77(39 - 12) \mod 95 = 2079 \mod 95 = 84$$

$$77(12 - 12) \mod 95 = 0 \mod 95 = 0$$

$$77(20 - 12) \mod 95 = 616 \mod 95 = 46$$

$$77(78 - 12) \mod 95 = 5082 \mod 95 = 47$$

$$77(67 - 12) \mod 95 = 4235 \mod 95 = 55$$

$$77(70 - 12) \mod 95 = 4466 \mod 95 = 1$$

Therefore, the numerical equivalents of our calculated plaintext are

$$50, 69, 84, 82, 69, 65, 84, 0, 46, 47, 55, 1.$$

Finally, the last step is to translate the decrypted integers back into characters using the Mod 95 Alphabet in Appendix[2, A], and get Retreat NOW! For our second option, we need to find and apply $h^{-1}(x)$ then $g^{-1}(x)$. For h, our key was $(9, 24)$, where $a = 9$ and $b = 24$, and we must therefore find 9^{-1} modulo 95. Using the Multiplicative Inverses modulo 95 table in Appendix[2, B], $9^{-1} = 74$. Substituting 9^{-1} and $b = 24$ into the Affine Cipher decryption function we get $h^{-1}(x) = 74(x - 24) \mod 95$. For g, our key was $(17, 62)$, where $a = 17$ and $b = 62$, and we must therefore find 17^{-1} modulo 95. Using the Multiplicative Inverses modulo 95 table in Appendix[2, B], $17^{-1} = 28$. Substituting 17^{-1} and $b = 62$ into the Affine Cipher decryption function we get $g^{-1}(x) = 28(x - 62)$

mod 95. Now, using the Mod 95 Alphabet in Appendix[2, A], the numerical equivalents of the encrypted message,

$$\wedge\ 8\ G\ 2\ 8\ m\ G, 4\ n\ c\ f,$$

are $62, 24, 39, 18, 24, 77, 39, 12, 20, 78, 67, 70$. Substituting these values for x into h^{-1} first we get

$$74(62 - 24)\quad \mathrm{mod}\ 95 = 2812\quad \mathrm{mod}\ 95 = 57$$

$$74(24 - 24)\quad \mathrm{mod}\ 95 = 0\quad \mathrm{mod}\ 95 = 0$$

$$74(39 - 24)\quad \mathrm{mod}\ 95 = 1110\quad \mathrm{mod}\ 95 = 65$$

$$74(18 - 24)\quad \mathrm{mod}\ 95 = -444\quad \mathrm{mod}\ 95 = 31$$

$$74(24 - 24)\quad \mathrm{mod}\ 95 = 0\quad \mathrm{mod}\ 95 = 0$$

$$74(77 - 24)\quad \mathrm{mod}\ 95 = 3922\quad \mathrm{mod}\ 95 = 27$$

$$74(39 - 24)\quad \mathrm{mod}\ 95 = 1110\quad \mathrm{mod}\ 95 = 65$$

$$74(12 - 24)\quad \mathrm{mod}\ 95 = -888\quad \mathrm{mod}\ 95 = 62$$

$$74(20 - 24)\quad \mathrm{mod}\ 95 = -296\quad \mathrm{mod}\ 95 = 84$$

$$74(78 - 24)\quad \mathrm{mod}\ 95 = 3996\quad \mathrm{mod}\ 95 = 6$$

$$74(67 - 24)\quad \mathrm{mod}\ 95 - 3182\quad \mathrm{mod}\ 95 - 47$$

$$74(70 - 24)\quad \mathrm{mod}\ 95 = 3404\quad \mathrm{mod}\ 95 = 79$$

hence, the integer values from first applying h^{-1} to the ciphertext are

$$57, 0, 65, 31, 0, 2765, 62, 84, 6, 47, 79.$$

Next, we will use the integer values found using h^{-1} and substitute them into g^{-1} as follows

$$28(57 - 62)\quad \mathrm{mod}\ 95 = -140\quad \mathrm{mod}\ 95 = 50$$

$$28(0 - 62)\quad \mathrm{mod}\ 95 = -1736\quad \mathrm{mod}\ 95 = 69$$

$$28(65 - 62)\quad \mathrm{mod}\ 95 = 84\quad \mathrm{mod}\ 95 = 84$$

$$28(31 - 62)\quad \mathrm{mod}\ 95 = -868\quad \mathrm{mod}\ 95 = 82$$

$$28(0 - 62)\quad \mathrm{mod}\ 95 = -1736\quad \mathrm{mod}\ 95 = 69$$

$$28(27 - 62)\quad \mathrm{mod}\ 95 = -980\quad \mathrm{mod}\ 95 = 65$$

$$28(65 - 62)\quad \mathrm{mod}\ 95 = 84\quad \mathrm{mod}\ 95 = 84$$

$$28(62 - 62)\quad \mathrm{mod}\ 95 = 0\quad \mathrm{mod}\ 95 = 0$$

$$28(84 - 62)\quad \mathrm{mod}\ 95 = 616\quad \mathrm{mod}\ 95 = 46$$

$$28(6 - 62)\quad \mathrm{mod}\ 95 = -1568\quad \mathrm{mod}\ 95 = 47$$

$$28(47 - 62) \quad \text{mod } 95 = -420 \quad \text{mod } 95 = 55$$

$$28(79 - 62) \quad \text{mod } 95 = 476 \quad \text{mod } 95 = 1$$

Therefore, the numerical equivalents, after apply h^{-1} and g^{-1}, of our calculated plaintext are $50, 69, 84, 82, 69, 65, 84, 0, 46, 47, 55, 1$. Finally, the last step is to translate the decrypted integers back into characters using the Mod 95 Alphabet in Appendix[2, A], and get

RetreatNOW!

We have shown that text encrypted by the composition, $f = hog$, can be decrypted in two ways: first, by finding f^{-1} and applying it to the ciphertext or second, by applying h^{-1} to the ciphertext and then applying g^{-1} to the result. Thus illustrating

$$f^{-1} = (hog)^{-1} = (g^{-1}oh^{-1}).$$

4   Hill Cipher

In this section, whenever possible we follow the notation, terminology and examples of [2, chapter 4].

Introduced in 1929 by Lester Hill, the Hill cipher is a poly-alphabetic cipher that uses matrices to encode plaintext messages. The key for this cipher system consist of an $n \times n$ square invertible matrix A, where the larger the dimensions the more secure the encryption will be. To ensure the key matrix A is invertible it is important to note that the determinant of A, $\det(A)$, must be relatively prime to the modulus m. The basic idea of the Hill cipher is to put the letters of the plaintext into blocks of length n, assuming an $n \times n$ key matrix, and then each block of plaintext letters is then converted into a column matrix of integers according to the alphabet chosen and then pre-multiplied by the $n \times n$ key matrix. The results are then converted back to letters and the ciphertext message is produced. Due to the complexity of working with large matrices, we will stick with using a 2×2 matrix $\begin{bmatrix} a & b \\ c & d \end{bmatrix}$ that is invertible modulo 26 and where $\det(A) = (ad - bc) \mod 26$.

Example 5. Suppose we want to encrypt the message $TROJAN$ using the key matrix $\begin{bmatrix} 3 & 7 \\ 9 & 10 \end{bmatrix}$ modulo 26. The first step is to assign each letter of the plaintext its numerical equivalent, using table1, which are $19, 17, 14, 9, 0, 13$. In the event that the length of the plaintext is not a multiple of the size of the key matrix, random letters can be added to the end of the plaintext. We then perform matrix multiplication as follows

$$\begin{bmatrix} 3 & 7 \\ 9 & 10 \end{bmatrix} \begin{bmatrix} 19 \\ 17 \end{bmatrix} = \begin{bmatrix} 176 \\ 341 \end{bmatrix} = \begin{bmatrix} 20 \\ 30 \end{bmatrix} \quad \text{mod } 26$$

$$\begin{bmatrix} 3 & 7 \\ 9 & 10 \end{bmatrix} \begin{bmatrix} 14 \\ 9 \end{bmatrix} = \begin{bmatrix} 105 \\ 216 \end{bmatrix} = \begin{bmatrix} 1 \\ 8 \end{bmatrix} \quad \text{mod } 26$$

$$\begin{bmatrix} 3 & 7 \\ 9 & 10 \end{bmatrix} \begin{bmatrix} 0 \\ 13 \end{bmatrix} = \begin{bmatrix} 91 \\ 130 \end{bmatrix} = \begin{bmatrix} 13 \\ 0 \end{bmatrix} \quad \text{mod } 26$$

So the numerical equivalents of the ciphertext are $20, 3, 1, 8, 13, 0$. This corresponds to the letter sequence

$$UDBINA.$$

As previously stated, when selecting a key matrix A it is imperative that it be invertible. To determine if the key matrix A is invertible, the $\det(A)$ must be relatively prime to the modulus m. By definition of an inverse matrix, the inverse of a matrix must be a matrix such that when multiplied by the original matrix, or key matrix in our case, the product yields the identity matrix $\begin{bmatrix} 1 & 0 \\ 0 & 1 \end{bmatrix}$. There are at least a couple techniques for finding the inverse of an invertible matrix, whose entries come from a ring $< \mathbb{Z}, +, \cdot >$, where $+$ denotes addition modulo m and $\cdot$ denotes multiplication modulo m. It is possible to use a modified Gauss-Jordan method for finding inverses of 2×2 invertible matrices. For a 2×2 invertible matrix, $\begin{bmatrix} a & b \\ c & d \end{bmatrix}$, we will use the following rule $A^{-1} = [\det(A)]^{-1} \begin{bmatrix} d & -b \\ -c & c \end{bmatrix}$ mod m , where $[det(A)]^{-1}$ is the multiplicative inverse of $\det(A)$ modulo m, provided it exists. To decipher the previous encrypted message, $UDBINA$, which was encrypted with the key matrix , we need to find A^{-1}. First, since the $\det(A) = 30 - 63 = -33 = 19 \mod 26$, we have $A^{-1} - 19^{-1} \begin{bmatrix} 10 & -7 \\ -9 & 3 \end{bmatrix}$ mod 26. Using the multiplicative inverse modulo 26 table in Appendix[2, B], $19^{-1} - 11$. Hence we have $A^{-1} = 11 \begin{bmatrix} 10 & -7 \\ -9 & 3 \end{bmatrix} = \begin{bmatrix} 110 & -77 \\ -99 & 33 \end{bmatrix} = \begin{bmatrix} 6 & 1 \\ 5 & 7 \end{bmatrix}$ mod 26. Now, the numerical equivalents of the ciphertext are

$$20, 3, 1, 8, 13, 0,$$

and we calculate

$$\begin{bmatrix} 6 & 1 \\ 5 & 7 \end{bmatrix} \begin{bmatrix} 20 \\ 3 \end{bmatrix} = \begin{bmatrix} 123 \\ 121 \end{bmatrix} = \begin{bmatrix} 19 \\ 17 \end{bmatrix} \quad \text{mod } 26$$

$$\begin{bmatrix} 6 & 1 \\ 5 & 7 \end{bmatrix} \begin{bmatrix} 1 \\ 8 \end{bmatrix} = \begin{bmatrix} 14 \\ 61 \end{bmatrix} = \begin{bmatrix} 14 \\ 9 \end{bmatrix} \quad \text{mod } 26$$

$$\begin{bmatrix} 6 & 1 \\ 5 & 7 \end{bmatrix} \begin{bmatrix} 13 \\ 0 \end{bmatrix} = \begin{bmatrix} 78 \\ 65 \end{bmatrix} = \begin{bmatrix} 0 \\ 13 \end{bmatrix} \quad \text{mod } 26$$

The numerical equivalents of the calculated plaintext is

$$19, 17, 14, 9, 0, 13,$$

and converting each calculated integer to its respective letter using table1 we obtain

$$TROJAN.$$

The Hill cipher is an excellent application that enables students to practice matrix operations in an interesting and exciting way. As with the previous examples of classical ciphers, it is assumed that the student is familiar with each classical cipher's respective mathematical process.

5   Generalized Affine Cipher

An extension of affine cipher is a cipher system in which plaintext letters are enciphered mathematically by the function,

$$f(X) = AX + B \quad \mod m$$

where X is a column matrix of integers according to the alphabet chosen and then pre-multiplied by a $n \times n$ key matrix A such that A is an $n \times n$ square invertible matrix, the $\det(A)$ must be relatively prime to the modulus m and B is a column matrix and m is the number of letters in the alphabet.

Example 6. Suppose we want to encrypt the message $ATTACK$ using the key matrix $A = \begin{bmatrix} 3 & 7 & 0 \\ 9 & 10 & 0 \\ 0 & 0 & 1 \end{bmatrix}$ modulo 26. The first step is to assign each letter of the plaintext its numerical equivalent, using table1, which are

$$0, 19, 19, 0, 2, 10.$$

In the event that the length of the plaintext is not a multiple of the size of the key matrix, random letters can be added to the end of the plaintext. Let $X_1 = \begin{bmatrix} 0 \\ 19 \\ 19 \end{bmatrix}$ and $X_2 = \begin{bmatrix} 0 \\ 2 \\ 10 \end{bmatrix}$, then perform matrix multiplication as follows

$$\begin{bmatrix} 3 & 7 & 0 \\ 9 & 10 & 0 \\ 0 & 0 & 1 \end{bmatrix} \begin{bmatrix} 0 \\ 19 \\ 19 \end{bmatrix} = \begin{bmatrix} 133 \\ 190 \\ 19 \end{bmatrix} = \begin{bmatrix} 3 \\ 8 \\ 19 \end{bmatrix} \quad \mod 26$$

$$\begin{bmatrix} 3 & 7 & 0 \\ 9 & 10 & 0 \\ 0 & 0 & 1 \end{bmatrix} \begin{bmatrix} 0 \\ 2 \\ 10 \end{bmatrix} = \begin{bmatrix} 14 \\ 20 \\ 10 \end{bmatrix} \quad \mod 26$$

Let $B = \begin{bmatrix} 1 \\ 2 \\ 3 \end{bmatrix}$, then $AX_1 + B = \begin{bmatrix} 4 \\ 10 \\ 22 \end{bmatrix}$, $AX_2 + B = \begin{bmatrix} 15 \\ 22 \\ 13 \end{bmatrix}$. So the numerical equivalents of the ciphertext are

$$4, 10, 22, 15, 22, 13.$$

This corresponds to the letter sequence

$$EKWPWN.$$

It is possible to use a modified Gauss-Jordan method, $A^{-1} = \begin{bmatrix} 6 & 1 & 0 \\ 5 & 7 & 0 \\ 0 & 0 & 1 \end{bmatrix}$. Now, the numerical equivalents of the ciphertext are

$$4, 10, 22, 15, 22, 13,$$

and we calculate

$$A^{-1}(\begin{bmatrix} 4 \\ 10 \\ 22 \end{bmatrix} - B) = \begin{bmatrix} 0 \\ 19 \\ 19 \end{bmatrix} \mod 26, A^{-1}(\begin{bmatrix} 15 \\ 22 \\ 13 \end{bmatrix} - B) = \begin{bmatrix} 0 \\ 2 \\ 10 \end{bmatrix} \mod 26.$$

The numerical equivalents of the calculated plaintext is

$$0, 19, 19, 0, 2, 10,$$

and converting each calculated integer to its respective letter using table1 we obtain

$$ATTACK.$$

6   Conclusion and Further Research

All our previous results show that the concept of affine cipher in this paper can constitute a significant aspect of computer and information science. It is clear that its study started here can successfully be extended to cipher systems in which plaintext letters are enciphered mathematically by a liner function. This will surely be subject of some further research.

Finally, we mention an open problems concerning to this topic.

Problem 1. For the affine cipher, how can be enciphered plaintext letters mathematically by a multilinear function?

Acknowledgments. The authors are grateful to the reviewers for their remarks which improve the previous version of the paper. Authors are deeply grateful to the Islamic Azad University, Ashtian Branch for the financial support for the proposal entitled "Analysis and Design of Affine Ciphers in Cryptography".

References

1. Barr, T.H.: Invitation to Cryptology. Prentice Hall, Inc., Upper Saddle River (2002)
2. Castaneda, R.G.: Using Classical Ciphers in Secondary Mathematics, THESIS, Presented to the Honors Committee of McMurry University (2009)
3. Flannery, S., Flannery, D.: In Code: A Mathematical Journey. Algonquin Books of Chapel Hill, Chapel Hill (2001)
4. Shannon, C.E.: Communication Theory of Secrecy Systems. Bell System Technical Journal 28, 657–715 (1949)
5. Singh, S.: The Code Book. Anchor Books, New York (1999)
6. Wrixon, F.B.: Codes, Ciphers, Secrets and Cryptic Communication. Black Dog and Leventhal Publishers, Inc., New York (1998)

A Secure Protocol for Ultralightweight Radio Frequency Identification (RFID) Tags

Aras Eghdamian and Azman Samsudin

School of Computer Sciences, Universiti Sains Malaysia, 11800 Pulau Pinang, Malaysia
ae11_com109@student.usm.my, azman@cs.usm.my

Abstract. Recently, an ultra light weight protocol for RFID tags has been published. The advantage of this protocol was its low computation cost, but it fails in its security objectives, being vulnerable to several important attacks such as traceability, full disclosure, cloning and desynchronization. In this research, that protocol was enhanced and a new Ultralightweight RFID authentication protocol with mutual authentication was proposed, while keeping the computation cost low. The proposed protocol requires only simple bit-wise operations and can resist various attacks which the previous one could not.

Keywords: RFID, Security, Ultralightweight RFID, Mutual Authentication Protocol.

1 Introduction

RFID as a significant and simultaneously growing technology has revolutionized the automatic identification of objects. RFID is used in many different areas ranging from automobile manufacturing, microchip fabrication industries, credit cards, e-passports, and many more. The advantages in this unique technology are numerous but the most notable is contactless, so that the *Tag* can be read from a distance.

The challenge that most of the Ultralightweight RFID systems face is the issue of authentication, in which the inadequate secure authentication mechanism, in most of the RFID systems, is currently being debated. Researchers have been directed toward making a mutual authentication in which the security is in its maximum. If security measures are not taken, a *Tag* or a *Reader* may lose its information easily. Protecting the privacy is a vital requirement for *Tag* holders; in which most of the RFID systems are lacking.

Peris et al. in their investigation in 2006 [1,2,3] initiated the design of Ultralightweight RFID protocols which includes only simple bitwise logical or arithmetic operations such as bitwise *XOR*, *OR*, *AND*, and addition. This combination of operations was discovered later to be inadequate for security. In 2007, Chien et al. proposed the SASI protocol [4] in order to offer a better security and they added the bitwise rotation to the set of supported operations. Although certain attacks have been published against the SASI protocol, this scheme reflected as a turning point in the design of Ultralightweight RFID protocols [5,6,7]. In 2008, a new protocol, named

A. Abd Manaf et al. (Eds.): ICIEIS 2011, Part I, CCIS 251, pp. 200–213, 2011.

"Gossamer" [8], was proposed that can be considered as a further development of both the UMAP [1,2,3] family and SASI [4].

Lee et al. in 2009 [9] has published a RFID scheme that resemblance SASI. Although the computation cost of Lee's protocol in comparison with other existing protocols is low, it fails in its security objectives, being vulnerable to several important attacks like traceability, full disclosure, cloning and desynchronization [10]. This research propose an Ultralightweight RFID authentication protocol with mutual authentication based on Lee's protocol but without its security short comings, and at the same time, keep the computation cost low.

2   Lee et al.'s Protocol

There are three entities in the Lee et al.'s protocol [9]: *Tag*, *Reader*, and *Server* on the backend. Suppose that the channel between the *Reader* and the backend *Server* is secure, but the communication channel between the *Reader* and the *Tag* is susceptible to all the possible attacks due to its open nature. Let *ID* be a static identification for a *Tag*. *Tag* shares a dynamic temporary identification (*IDT*) and secret key (*K*) with the backend *Server*. The length of each *ID*, *IDT* or *K* is 128 bits. To resist the possible desynchronization attack, each *Tag* keeps two entries of (*IDT*, *K*): one is for the old values and the other is for the potential next values. The protocol consists of two main stages: authentication phase and key updating phase. In authentication phase, the *Reader* first inquires the *Tag*, and then the *Reader* and the *Tag* authenticate each other. In the following key updating phase, the *Reader* and the *Tag*, respectively, update their temporary identifications and secret keys.

In Lee et al.'s protocol, the random number generator is installed in the *Server* only, and calculations at the *Tags* involve only simple bitwise operations such as *XOR* ($\oplus$), *OR* ($\vee$), *AND* ($\wedge$), and left rotate Rot(*A*, *B*), where Rot(*A*, *B*) denotes left rotate the value of *A* with *n* bits, where *n* is the number of "1" in *B*.

Without loss of generality, suppose that the initial message in the *Tag* and *Server* are (IDT_0, K_0), and (*A* → *B*: *C*) denotes *A* sends message *C* to *B*. At the *i*-th session, both the *Tag* and *Server* store (IDT_i, K_i) and ($IDT_{i\,1}$, $K_{i\,1}$) in their memory. The authentication and key updating procedures are then described in the following subsections.

2.1   Authentication Phase

Step 1. (*Tag* → *Reader*: IDT_i): The *Tag* first transmits IDT_i to the *Reader* after the *Tag* receives a request message. Note that the temporary identification and secret key are updated on each session of the authentication.

Step 2. (*Reader* →*Tag*: *A*, *B*): After receiving IDT_i in Step 1, The *Reader* finds the *Tag*'s corresponding secret key K_i. Then the *Reader* generates a random number N_i and computes (*A*, *B*) as follows.

$$A = K_i \oplus N_i \,. \tag{1}$$

$$B = \mathrm{Rot}(K_i, K_i) \oplus \mathrm{Rot}(N_i, N_i) \,. \tag{2}$$

The *Reader* sends (A, B) to the *Tag*.

Step 3. (*Tag →Reader: C*): Upon receiving (*A, B*) in Step 2, *Tag* obtains $N_i{}'$ by calculating:

$$Ni' = A \oplus K_i \,. \tag{3}$$

Then the *Tag* computes *B′* with K_i and $N_i{}'$ by calculating:

$$B' = \mathrm{Rot}(K_i, K_i) \oplus \mathrm{Rot}(N_i', N_i') \,. \tag{4}$$

The *Reader* will be authenticated if *B′=B*. The *Tag* computes *C* as follows if *Reader* is authenticated:

$$C = (K_i \vee \mathrm{Rot}(N_i, N_i)) \oplus ((\mathrm{Rot}(K_i, K_i) \wedge N_i) \,. \tag{5}$$

Finally, *Tag* sends *C* to the *Reader*.

2.2   Key Updating Phase

Step 4. *Reader* authenticates *Tag*, and updates the temporary identification and the secret key: After receiving *C*, the *Reader* will authenticate the *Tag* by checking whether *C* is valid. If the *Tag* is authenticated, *Reader* and *Tag* will compute a new identification and a secret key by calculating:

$$IDT_{i+1} = K_i \oplus \mathrm{Rot}(N_i, N_i) \,. \tag{6}$$

$$K_{i+1} = \mathrm{Rot}(K_i, K_i) \oplus N_i \,. \tag{7}$$

Note that, the *Tag* and the *Server* keeps $\{(IDT_{i+1}, K_{i+1}), (IDT_i, K_i)\}$ in memory after the authentication. For illustration, the protocol is shown in Figure 1.

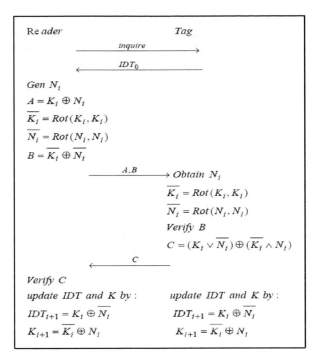

Fig. 1. Lee's protocol; (Data from [9])

3   Proposed Protocol

As a consequence of detailed analysis on the existing Ultralightweight RFID protocols, a new protocol has been derived. The initial inspiration was originated from the Lee's scheme [9] but without its weaknesses, as pointed out by Peris-Lopez et al. in [10]. The main aim of the current research is to define a protocol with adequate security level that can realistically be employed in Ultralightweight RFID *Tags*.

3.1   Model Assumptions

Each *Tag* stores *ID*, *IDS* and *K* in its memory;

- A static identifier (*ID*): The *ID* of a *Tag* is unique and it is the *Tag*'s identification.
- An index-pseudonym (*IDS*): The *IDS* is employed as a search index to allocate all the information related to each *Tag* in the database. To prevent traceability and tracking, the *IDS* updates after each successful authentication.

- A key (K): Each Tag has a secret key (K) which is used in data transfer to encrypt the data. Since each Tag has its own secret key, if the *Reader* encrypts a message using this key then just the specific *Tag* that has the same secret key can decrypt the message.

All the information mentioned above is stored at the back-end database. The length of these elements is 96 bits. Additionally, in order to avoid the desynchronization attacks, the *Tags* are given the added requirement of storing the old and potential new values of the tuple (*IDS, K*). In a desynchronization attack, after the successful mutual authentication (when the *Tag* updates its (*IDS, K*)), the *Reader* should update the (*IDS, K*) of the back-end database as well. Note that an adversary can block the message C from being reached by the *Reader* and as the consequence the *Reader* will not recognize subsequence communication request; that is, the *Tag* has updated its data and the *Reader* will not update the data on database.

When a desynchronization attack happened, the *Tag* has new tuple of (*IDS, K*) but the *Reader* will still has the old tuple. That is why the *Tag* should save the old tuple in memory; therefore if the *Tag* and the *Reader* could not authenticate each other with the recent *IDS* then they will use the old tuple of (*IDS, K*) instead.

For the implementation of the proposed protocol, only simple operations are available on the *Tags*:

- Simple bitwise XOR ($\oplus$)
- Bitwise AND ($\wedge$)
- Bitwise OR ($\vee$)
- Addition mod 2^m (+)
- Left rotating x according to y's bits, ($Rot(x,y)$).

Random number generation is a costly operation which is required in the protocol to supply freshness to the dynamic data. Therefore, in the proposed protocol such operation is performed by the *Reader* and not the *Tag*.

Since *Tags* are passive, communications have to be initiated by *Readers*. It is taken for granted that the communication channel between the *Reader* and the database is generally secure, however, the channel between the *Reader* and the *Tag* can be eavesdropped. Attacks involving modification of the exchanged messages such as the insertion of fraudulent new messages and/or message blocking (active attacks) can be discounted.

3.2   The Protocol

The proposed protocol comprises three stages. These stages are classified based on their sequence of operation that is *Tag* identification phase, mutual authentication phase, and updating phase. Figure 2 shows these three phases.

Tag Identification. When a communication between a *Tag* and a *Reader* is about to start, the *Reader* needs to identify the *Tag*. After this identification, the *Reader* can use the correct key to encrypt data and sends them to *Tag*. This identification should be done by using *IDS* because using the *ID* for identification means to publish the *ID* and it will cause traceability problem. However, by using the *IDS* and updating it after each successful mutual authentication the *Tag* will not easily be traceable.

- The *Reader* first sends a "Hello" message to the *Tag*.
- *Tag* answers with its potential next *IDS*.
- With the *IDS*, the *Reader* tries to find an identical entry in the database. If this search succeeds, the mutual authentication phase starts. Otherwise, the identification is retried but not with the same *IDS* (IDS_{next}) rather with the old one which is backscattered by the *Tag* upon request.

Mutual Authentication. A *Tag* or a *Reader* might give away its information too easily if security measures are not taken. Many different items are tagged all throughout the world and it may lead to loss of privacy. In mutual authentication, the identity of a *Reader* and a *Tag* is not revealed if some criteria have not been met. Typically this type of authentication is proven through the knowledge of secret information shared between two entities. Besides sharing a secret, an affordable way to encrypt the data must be devised; and appropriate measures must be taken to prevent other types of attack (such as message replay).

- After *Tag* identification phase succeeds, the mutual authentication phase will start.
- With *IDS*, the *Reader* acquires the private information linked to the *Tag* that is identified from the database (*Tag*'s secret key (K)).
- Then the *Reader* generates random number N and builds A and B and sends them to the *Tag* (see Figure 2).

$$A = K \oplus N . \tag{8}$$

$$B = Rot(K, N) \wedge Rot(N, K) \wedge Rot(N, N) . \tag{9}$$

- From message A, the *Tag* extracts random number N. The *Tag* XOR the message A with its secret key (K) and the result will be the random number (N).

$$A \oplus K = K \oplus N \oplus K = N . \tag{10}$$

- Then the *Tag* generates a local version of message B which is compared with the received value. If the comparison is verified, the *Reader* is authenticated.
- On the final phase, the *Tag* creates and sends message C to the *Reader*.

$$C = Rot((K + Rot(N, N)), (Rot(K, K) \lor N)) . \tag{11}$$

- When the message C is received, the *Reader* compares this value with a computed local version. If the comparison is successful, the *Tag* is authenticated; otherwise the protocol is abandoned.

Index-Pseudonym and Key Updating. Tracking and traceability are two important side effects of RFID *Tags* that may faced by the *Tag* holders. If the *Tag* uses its unique *ID* to identify itself to *Readers* then it will be easy for an adversary to find where the *Tag* is and trace where it was.

To avoid these kinds of information leak, the *Tags* use *IDS* instead of *ID* (because *ID* is unique and can't be updated), and update the *IDS* and the key after each successful mutual authentication. As a result, tracing and tracking will be more difficult because the *Tag* and the *Reader* use a dynamic secret random number to update the *IDS* and the key. With such mechanism in place, no adversary will know what will be the next *IDS* and the next key.

As represented in Figure 2, when the mutual authentication phase between the *Reader* and the *Tag* is successfully completed, they will locally update and synchronize the *IDS* and the key (K) separately.

$$IDS_{next} = K \land Rot(N, (K \lor N)) . \tag{12}$$

$$K_{next} = Rot((N + Rot(K, K)), (Rot(N, N) \land K)) . \tag{13}$$

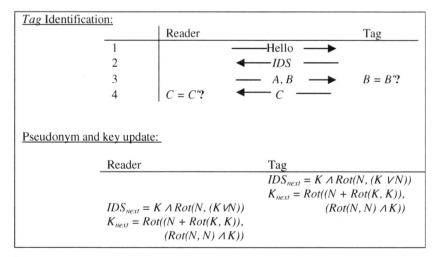

Fig. 2. Mutual Identification – Pseudonym and key update of the proposed protocol

4   Security Analysis

4.1   Data Privacy

All public messages are composed of at least two secret values shared only by the legitimate *Reader*s and genuine *Tags*. Note that we consider private information (*ID*, *K*), random number (*N*), and internal values as secret values (Internal values mean any combination of *N* or *K* which has been rotated with Rot procedure). The static identifier and the secret keys cannot, therefore, be easily obtained by an eavesdropper.

4.2   Anonymity of *Tag*

Each *Tag* updates *IDS* and private key (*K*) after each successful authentication, and this update process involves internal random numbers. A fresh *IDS* is backscattered, when the *Tag* is interrogated again. In addition, all public messages (*A*, *B* and *C*) are anonymized by the use of random numbers (*N* and internal random numbers). As a consequence, location privacy of the *Tag* owner is not compromise, and *Tag* anonymity is guaranteed.

4.3   Mutual Authentication

The proposed protocol provides mutual authentication. Only a genuine *Reader* possessing key (*K*), can build a valid messages *A* and *B*. In the same way, just a legitimate *Tag* can derive random number *N* from *A*, and then compute message *C*. Messages *B* and *C*, which involve the internal secret values and the random number (*N*), allow data integrity to be checked; and these values are used in the updating phase (next *IDS* and key).

4.4   Replay Attacks

All the messages exchanged by a protocol, could be eavesdropped and stored by an eavesdropper. He could replay message *C* to impersonate the *Tag*. Nevertheless, such attack would be invalid as different random numbers are used in each session (*N* and internal random numbers).

Moreover, the attacker could pretend that the *Reader* didn't do the updating phase in the last session. In this case, the *Tag* is identified by the old *IDS* and the attacker may forward the eavesdropped values of *A* and *B*. Still if this is successful, the attacker could not get any secret information and the internal state is unchanged in the legitimate *Tag*, so these kinds of attacks are unsuccessful as well.

4.5   Forward Security

If the *Tag* is compromised, the forward security feature prevent previous secrets from being obtained by adversary. It is possible that a *Tag* is exposed and therefore exposing its secret information (ID, K). In this scenario, the adversary will still not be able to find the previous secret message because random number N and internal secret values involved in the message creation (mutual authentication phase) are unknown to the adversary. In addition, these internal values are employed in the updating phase. As a result, past communications is not a risk.

4.6   Desynchronization Resistant

The current research assumes that *Tags* and *Readers* share certain secret values. As these values have been updated locally, synchronization is needed. Messages B and C provide confirmation of the internal secret values and the random number N. These values are employed in the updating stage. So the correct update of values IDS and key (K) is completely ensured by messages B and C.

Since a radio link is used, accidental transmission errors can happen in the received messages. This is very serious issue for message C, since it can result in a loss of synchronization. However, the tuple (IDS, K) is stored twice in the *Tag* memory (once with the old values, the other with the next values). With this mechanism, even if message C is incorrectly received, the *Reader* and the *Tag* can still authenticate each other with the old values. So the *Tag* and the *Reader* are able to recover their synchronized state.

On the other hand, if an adversary intends to release de-synchronization attack by sending fake message C, the *Reader* and *Tag* cannot obtain mutual authentication by using (IDS_i, K_i). However, the *Reader* and *Tag* still can use old value (IDS_{i-1}, K_{i-1}) for a successful communication. Therefore, the proposed protocol can withstand desynchronization attack.

5   Proposed Protocol vs. Lee's Protocol

Based on the investigations done by Peris-Lopez et al. [10] on Lee's protocol [9], some problems had been identified. Considering the proposed protocol, none of the mentioned problems exist in the proposed protocol.

5.1   Full Disclosure Attack

The *Tag* and the *Reader* share a secret key. The main purpose of this key is for authentication of both entities. The key is combined with a random number to hamper its acquisition by the attacker when passed over the non-secure channel. The above idea is well conceived but the Lee's protocol abuses the usage of $Rot(K_i, K_i)$ and $Rot(N_i, N_i)$. Indeed, this fact facilitates a sort of linear cryptanalysis of the scheme, despite the combination of triangular and non-triangular functions.

Problem 1 [10]: In Lee's protocol, a passive attacker, after eavesdropping two consecutive authentication sessions {n, n+1} between an authentic *Tag* (T) and a genuine *Reader* (R), can discover the secret key shared by these two entities by simply computing an *XOR* among some of the public messages transmitted over the radio channel:

$$K_{n+1} = A_n \oplus B_n \oplus IDT_{n+1} . \tag{14}$$

Comparison: In the proposed protocol the attacker cannot acquire the secret key by computing *XOR* between the public messages because of the different design approach. The main problem of Lee's protocol is using of the *XOR* operation in all messages and it makes these messages vulnerable. However, in the proposed protocol each message has different design and use different operations.

5.2   Cloning Attack

RFID *Tags* are usually not designed to be tamper resistant, because this will significantly increase their price. An active attacker may tamper with the *Tag* in order to read from or write to its memory in which secret values are stored. Low-cost RFID *Tags* cannot offer protection to this sort of attacks but should be resistant, at least, to the passive attacks. Following are steps for a passive attacker to clone a *Tag* after revealing the whole secrets stored from the *Tag*, but without requiring any physical manipulation of the *Tag*.

Problem 2 [10]: In Lee's protocol, a passive attacker, after eavesdropping two consecutive authentication sessions *{n, n+1}* between an authentic *Tag* (*T*) and a genuine *Reader* (*R*), can clone the *Tag* by computing:

$$IDT_{n+2} = K_{n+1} \oplus Rot(N_{n+1}, N_{n+1}) . \tag{15}$$

$$K_{n+2} = Rot(K_{n+1}, K_{n+1}) \oplus N_{n+1} . \tag{16}$$

Comparison: This attack is based on discovering the secret key and since the proposed protocol's secret key cannot be discovered, such an attack is naturally being eliminated.

5.3   Desynchronization Attack by Using the Key

Tags and *Readers* have to remain synchronized to run the protocol successfully. The authors take the extra precaution of storing the old and potential new values of the pair *(IDT, K)* to fight against desynchronization attacks. Despite this countermeasure, an attacker is able to desynchronize a *Tag* and a *Reader* by exploiting loop holes as stated in Problem 1.

Problem 3 [10]: In Lee's protocol, a passive attacker, after eavesdropping two consecutive authentication sessions $\{n, n+1\}$ and performing a man-in-the-middle attack between an authentic *Tag* (*T*) and a genuine *Reader* (*R*), can desynchronize these two entities by sending:

$$A_{n+1} = K_{n+1} \oplus N^{*}_{n+1} . \tag{17}$$

$$B_{n+1} = Rot(K_{n+1}, K_{n+1}) \oplus Rot(N^{*}_{n+1}, N^{*}_{n+1}) . \tag{18}$$

$$C_{n+1} = (K_{n+1} \vee Rot(N_{n+1}, N_{n+1})) \oplus (Rot(K_{n+1}, K_{n+1}) \wedge N_{n+1}) . \tag{19}$$

Comparison: Similar to the previous attack (cloning attack), the proposed protocol is resistant against this attack because the desynchronization attack depends on the secret key, which is secure in the proposed protocol.

5.4 Desynchronization Attack by Reusing Old Values

As an easy alternatively to the last attack, an adversary can desynchronize *Tags* and *Reader*s using the non-resistance of bitwise operations. The adversary can reuse old values, transmitted through the channel, to compute new valid authentication messages. Specifically, an *XOR* operation between the captured value and a constant value properly selected is enough to achieve this objective.

Problem 4 [10]: In Lee's protocol, a passive attacker, after eavesdropping an authentication session *n* between an authentic *Tag* (*T*) and a genuine *Reader* (*R*), can desynchronize these two entities by sending: $A_{n+1} = A_n \oplus C_1$, $B_{n+1} = B_n \oplus C_2$, where $\{C_i\}^2_{i=1}$ are any constant values whose Hamming weight is exactly 2.

Comparison: Because of using *XOR* in all messages the attacker can predict the number of bits that will be filliped after a change in the main message. That is the reason of using C_2 with Hamming weight of 2 in the attack. However, in the proposed protocol, the *AND* operation is used in message *B*, and the attacker will not be able to predict the exact number of bits that need to be flipped in message *B*.

6   Performance Analysis

The proposed protocol is now examined from the point of view of computational cost, storage requirements and communication cost.

6.1   Computational Cost

In the proposed protocol, the *Tag* uses simple bitwise *XOR* ($\oplus$), *AND* ($\wedge$), *OR* ($\vee$), modular addition (+), and rotate operations (Rot). These operations are simple operations and can be effectively implemented on Ultralightweight RFID *Tags* (See

Table 1). The pseudo random number generator is not a simple or computationally effective algorithm for a *Tag*. If a system pseudo random number generator is not properly adopted attackers can break it easily. In general, it is not easy for Ultralightweight RFID *Tag* to install and execute a secure pseudo random number generator, because of its limitation on memory and computational power. In current scheme, only the *Server* needs pseudo random number generator. With such scheme pseudo random number can be implemented easily and security is ensured.

6.2   Storage Requirement

Each *Tag* stores its static identifier (*ID*) and two records of the tuple (*IDS, K*) with old and new values. A 96-bit length is assumed for all elements in accordance with EPCGlobal. The *ID* is a static value, thus stored in ROM. As for the remaining values (96 × 4 = 384 bits), the values need to be updated and they are stored in a rewritable memory. So, if each identification or secret is 96 bits in length, only 480 bits of memory is required which is fewer than other existing schemes (See Table 1). In SASI [4] and Gossamer [8] protocols, two random numbers are linked to each session; but in this protocol one random number is used, therefore it makes this protocol cheaper and easier to implement.

Table 1. Security and Performance of Ultralightweight Authentication Protocols; (Data from [10])

	UMAP Family [1,2,3]	SASI [4]	Lee et al.'s Protocol [9]	Gossamer [8]	Proposed Protocol
Resistance to Desynchronization Attacks	No	No	No	Yes	Yes
Resistance to Disclosure Attacks	No	No	No	Yes	Yes
Privacy and Anonymity	No	No	No	Yes	Yes
Mutual Auth. and Forward Security	Yes	Yes	Yes	Yes	Yes
Total Messages for Mutual Auth.	4-5*L*	4L	3L	4L	3L
Memory Size on *Tag*	6L	7L	5L	7L	5L
Operation Types on *Tag*	$\oplus$, $\wedge$, V,+	$\oplus$, $\wedge$, V,+, Rot	$\oplus$, $\wedge$, V, Rot	$\oplus$, +, Rot, MixBits	$\oplus$, $\wedge$, V,+, Rot

The *L* designates the bit length of variables used.

6.3   Communication Cost

As it is showed on Table 1, the proposed protocol performs mutual authentication and integrity protection with only three messages, so in this sense it is less than the SASI [4] and the Gossamer [8] scheme. In the identification phase, a "Hello" and *IDS* message are sent over the channel. Messages *A*, *B* and *C* are transmitted in the authentication phase. So a total of 424 bits are sent over the channel (considering 5 bytes for the "Hello" message).

7   Conclusion

In this paper, a new Ultralightweight RFID protocol is proposed and analyzed. First, the resistance of the proposed protocol against important attacks was highlighted. Also being carried out is the comparison between the most up-to-date Ultralightweight RFID protocol and the proposed protocol. In this comparison it has been shown that the security flaws of the existing protocol are solved in the new proposed protocol. Finally the performance of the proposed protocol is analyzed. The storage requirement and the number of message passes during the communication phase of the proposed protocol were compared with previous existing Ultralightweight RFID protocols. The performance comparison showed that the proposed protocol is a highly efficient Ultralightweight RFID protocol when compared against its peers.

References

1. Peris-Lopez, P., Hernandez-Castro, J.C., Estevez-Tapiador, J.M., Ribagorda, A.: M2AP: A Minimalist Mutual-Authentication Protocol for Low-Cost RFID Tags. In: Ma, J., Jin, H., Yang, L.T., Tsai, J.J.-P. (eds.) UIC 2006. LNCS, vol. 4159, pp. 912–923. Springer, Heidelberg (2006)
2. Peris-Lopez, P., Hernandez-Castro, J.C., Estevez-Tapiador, J.M., Ribagorda, A.: LMAP: A Real Lightweight Mutual Authentication Protocol for Low-Cost RFID Tags. In: Hand. of Workshop on RFID and Lightweight Crypto (2006)
3. Peris-Lopez, P., Hernandez-Castro, J.C., Estevez-Tapiador, J.M., Ribagorda, A.: EMAP: An Efficient Mutual-Authentication Protocol for Low-Cost RFID Tags. In: Meersman, R., Tari, Z., Herrero, P. (eds.) OTM 2006 Workshops. LNCS, vol. 4277, pp. 352–361. Springer, Heidelberg (2006)
4. Chien, H.Y.: SASI: A New Ultralightweight RFID Authentication Protocol Providing Strong Authentication and Strong Integrity. IEEE Transactions on Dependable and Secure Computing 4(4), 337–340 (2007)
5. Sun, H.M., Ting, W.C., Wang, K.H.: On the Security of Chien's Ultralightweight RFID Authentication Protocol. Cryptology ePrint Archive (2008), http://eprint.iacr.org/2008/083
6. Cao, T., Bertino, E., Lei, H.: Security Analysis of the SASI Protocol. IEEE Transactions on Dependable and Secure Computing (2008)

7. D'Arco, P., De Santis, A.: From Weaknesses to Secret Disclosure in a Recent Ultra-Lightweight RFID Authentication Protocol. Cryptology ePrint Archive (2008), http://eprint.iacr.org/2008/470
8. Peris-Lopez, P., Hernandez-Castro, J.C., Tapiador, J.M.E., Ribagorda, A.: Advances in Ultralightweight Cryptography for Low-Cost RFID Tags: Gossamer Protocol. In: Chung, K.-I., Sohn, K., Yung, M. (eds.) WISA 2008. LNCS, vol. 5379, pp. 56–68. Springer, Heidelberg (2009)
9. Lee, Y.C., Hsieh, Y.C., You, P.S., Chen, T.C.: A New Ultralightweight RFID Protocol with Mutual Authentication. In: Proc. of WASE 2009, vol. 2, pp. 58–61 (2009)
10. Peris-Lopez, P., Hernandez-Castro, J.C., Estevez-Tapiador, J.M., Ribagorda, A.: Security Flaws in a Recent Ultralightweight RFID Protocol (2009), http://arxiv.org/abs/0910.2115

Authentication Tests Based on Distributed Temporal Protocol Logic for the Analysis of Security Protocols

Shahabuddin Muhammad

College of Computer Engineering and Science,
Prince Mohammad Bin Fahd University,
Al-Khobar 31952, Kingdom of Saudi Arabia
smuhammad@pmu.edu.sa

Abstract. Authentication protocols are used to ensure the identity of a participant in a distributed environment. Since designing authentication protocols is an error prone process, formal verification techniques are used to verify the correctness of authentication protocols. In this paper, we develop simple but rigorous logic-based tests for the analysis of authentication protocols. In particular, we extend the framework of Distributed Temporal Protocol Logic (DTPL), and provide authentication tests at a higher level of abstraction. These tests can be easily applied on a variety of authentication protocols, yet they are rigorous enough to capture full capabilities of a typical Dolev-Yao intruder.

Keywords: Authentication Protocols, Verification, Network Security, DTPL.

1 Introduction

Before sending any sensitive information in a distributed environment, it is imperative that the participants involved in communication are aware of the true identities of each other. Merely encrypting senstive information with strong keys and sending the encrypted message over distributed network is not sufficient to ensure that the sensitive information will eventually reach to the intended recepient. One needs to first make sure that the participant siting on the other side is actually the one that he claims to be. Authentication protocols are used for this purpose where participants authenticate each other before sending critical information on the network.

A security protocol (or authentication protocol) is a sequence of messages between two or more parties in which encryption is used to provide authentication or to distribute cryptographic keys for new conversations [1]. The network is assumed to be hostile as it contains intruders with the capabilities to encrypt, decrypt, copy, forward, delete, and so forth. Considering an active intruder with such powerful capabilities, it becomes extremely difficult to guarantee proper working of a security protocol. Several examples show how carefully designed

A. Abd Manaf et al. (Eds.): ICIEIS 2011, Part I, CCIS 251, pp. 214–228, 2011.

protocols were later found out to have security breaches. This situation led the researchers to formalize the verification of security protocols.

Over the past two decades, formal verification has been rigorously applied in the domain of security protocols. Researchers have developed numerous formal techniques and tools and successfully applied them either to verify a security property or to catch a flaw in a security protocol. The authors in [2] contributed the early work in the application of formal methods to verify cryptographic protocols. Since then, legions of new methods based on formal verification began to occupy the attention of researchers. We do not intend to provide an exhaustive survey of the field. The interested readers should see [3] for a good survey in this area. Generally speaking, most of the proposed schemes can be broadly categorized into logic-based techniques, process algebra, theorem proving, and model checking approaches [4]. The graph-theoretic approach of Strand Spaces has also been applied in this direction [5]. All of these techniques, with their own merits and demerits, have been successfully used to find flaws in many protocols.

In this paper, we confine ourself to the logic-based approaches. Logic-based verification is one of the widely used formal verification techniques in the domain of security protocols. This is due to both, the simplicity of the logic-based methods and the conciseness of the proof they generate [6]. The logic of belief of [7], known as BAN logic, provided the initial impetus in applying modal logic in a proof-based environment. With the emergence of BAN, several researchers have applied various logic-based techniques for the formal verification of security protocols. BAN logic has also been extended in many ways [8,9]. All of these logics have been used successfully to identify a number of flaws in many protocols.

A relatively new logic, called distributed temporal protocol logic (DTPL), has been proposed in [10] which provides an object-level tool to model distributed communication. DTPL's distinguishing characteristics is its capability to be used as a metalevel tool for comparative analysis of security protocol models and properties. Moreover, as an extension of temporal logic, DTPL enjoys a rich set of temporal operators that can capture various activities of an agent at different times. In this paper, we use distributed temporal protocol logic to analyze security protocol at a higher level of abstraction. In particular, we analyze a protocol by first representing the run of each participant of the protocol in terms of its corresponding life-cycle. Next, we try to achieve match in the parameters among the participants of a protocol. Authentication is achieved if critical parameters of a participant match with the parameters of the rest of the participants of a protocol. This is in accordance with the agreement properties of [11].

In an effort to find matching parameters, each participant investigates its own life-cycle and tries to find out the originators of each of its received messages. More specifically, each participant initiates a challenge and waits for the response of that challenge in order to ensure the identity of the originator of its received messages. We use this challenge-response criterion to develop simple tests like the one developed in the framework of Strand Space Formalism [12]. Given these tests, one can determine the identity of the originator of the response of a challenge generated by a participant. A protocol fails to achieve authentication either if we find a mismatch in the parameters among the participants, or if we find an unintended originator of a received message at any participant's local life-cycle.

The resulting verification strategy not only contains the expressibility of the existing DTPL model but it also provides a concise tool that can be used as a heuristic to investigate authentication protocols. Moreover, due to DTPL's rich interpretation structure of Winskel [13], analyzing a protocol becomes clearer as compared to other logic-based techniques. Because of the authentication tests of [12] , the verification process does not need to explicitly model an intruder, thereby obviating the need to apply all combinations of intruder behaviors for protocol analysis. This results in considerable simplicity in the way a protocol is analyzed.

We have organized the rest of the paper as follows. Section 2 summarizes the essential features of DTPL. In Section 3, we present how security protocols follow a challenge-response strategy and how DTPL can be used to find the originator of a received message. Using these concepts, Section 4 derives high-level authentication tests for the challenge-response types of protocols. We conclude in Section 5.

2   Distributed Temporal Protocol Logic

We briefly introduce distributed temporal protocol logic (DTPL) of [10], a version of distributed temporal logic DTL, to reason about protocols and their properties. In DTPL, a distributed system is viewed as a collection of communicating sequential objects (principals or agents) that interact by exchanging messages through an insecure channel Ch. We usually represent by $\mathbf{A}$ the set of messages that principals communicate where we refer to the elements of $\mathbf{A}$ as *terms* or *messages*. Moreover, we assume $\mathbf{A}$ is freely generated from two disjoint sets, T (for texts, e.g, nonces or principal ids) and K (for keys). Local alphabet of each participant A comprises of actions Act_A and state propositions $Prop_A$. Act_A includes operations such as $send(M, B')$, $rec(M)$, $spy(M)$, $nonce(N)$, and $key(K)$ whereas $Prop_A$ includes only $knows(M)$. Channel's actions Act_{Ch} include $in(M, A')$, $out(M, A')$, and $leak$ and there is no state proposition associated with the channel.

The *global language* and the *local language* of the logic are defined by the grammar

$$L ::= @_i[L_i]| \perp |L \Rightarrow L$$

$$L_i ::= Act_i|Prop_i| \perp |L_i \Rightarrow L_i|L_i \mathsf{U} L_i|L_i \mathsf{S} L_i|j : L_j$$

where

- $i, j \in Id$, a set of principal's ids.
- U and S are temporal operators *until* and *since*,
- $@_i[\phi]$ means that ϕ holds at the current local state of agent i, and

- $j : \phi$ appearing inside a formula in L_i is called a *communication formula*. It means that agent i has just communicated with agent j for whom ϕ held.

Due to the concurrent nature of the distributed system, event structures are used instead of Kripke structures as the interpretation structures in DTPL. In particular, the interpretation structure $\mu = \langle \lambda, \alpha, \pi \rangle$ of L are suitably labeled distributed life-cycles, built upon a simplified form of Winskel's *event structures* [13]. If Ev_i represents a discrete, linearly ordered, set of events for each agent $i \in Id$:

- λ: is a distributed life-cycle. That is, a prime event structure without conflict, built form Ev_i.
- $\alpha_i : Ev_i \rightarrow Act_i$ associates a local action to each local event.
- $\pi_i : \Xi_i \rightarrow \wp(Prop_i)$ associates a set of local state propositions to each *local configuration*.

Here, *local configuration* of an agent i means a collection of all the local events that have occurred up to a given point. In other words, local configuration of an agent i is a finite set $\xi_i \subseteq Ev_i$ closed under local causality. That is, if $\rightarrow_i$ represents the local successor relation between the events in Ev_i, $e \rightarrow_i^* e'$, and $e' \in \xi_i$ then also $e \in \xi_i$. Every non-empty local configuration ξ_i is reached by the occurrence of an event $last(\zeta_i)$ from the local configuration $\zeta_i \backslash last(\zeta_i)$. A *global configuration* is a finite set $\xi \subseteq Ev$ closed under global causality, that is, if $e \rightarrow^* e'$, and $e' \in \xi$ then also $e \in \xi$. Every global configuration ξ includes the local configuration $\xi|_i = \xi \cap Ev_i$ of each agent i. Moreover, given $e \in Ev$, $e \downarrow = \{e' \in Ev | e' \rightarrow^* e\}$ is always a global configuration. The distributed life-cycle of agents A, B, and C is shown in Fig. 1 where dotted vertical line represents communication point. The progress of agent A in shown in Fig. 2.

$$
\begin{array}{lccc}
A & e_1 \longrightarrow & e_4 \longrightarrow & e_7 \rightarrow \cdots\cdots \\
B & e_2 \longrightarrow\longrightarrow & e_6 \longrightarrow & \rightarrow \cdots\cdots \\
C & e_3 \longrightarrow & e_5 \longrightarrow & c_6 \longrightarrow \rightarrow \cdots\cdots
\end{array}
$$

Fig. 1. A distributed life-cycle for agents A, B, and C

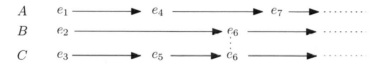

$$\pi_A(\emptyset) \xrightarrow{\alpha_A(e_1)} \pi_A(\{e_1\}) \xrightarrow{\alpha_A(e_4)} \pi_A(\{e_1, e_4\}) \xrightarrow{\alpha_A(e_7)} \pi_A(\{e_1, e_4, e_7\}) \quad \cdots\cdots$$

Fig. 2. The progress of agent A

Using the interpretation structure defined above, the global satisfaction relation at a global configuration ξ of μ can be defined as:

- $\mu, \xi \Vdash @_i[\phi]$ if $\mu, \xi|_i \Vdash_i \phi$,

- $\mu, \xi \not\Vdash \bot$,
- $\mu, \xi \Vdash \gamma \Rightarrow \delta$ if $\mu, \xi \not\Vdash \gamma$ or $\mu, \xi \Vdash \delta$,

where the local satisfaction relations $\Vdash_i$ at local configurations are defined as:

- $\mu, \xi_i \Vdash_i act$ if $\xi_i \neq \emptyset$ and $\alpha_i(last(\xi_i)) = act$,
- $\mu, \xi_i \Vdash_i p$ if $p \in \pi_i(\xi_i)$,
- $\mu, \xi_i \not\Vdash_i \bot$,
- $\mu, \xi_i \Vdash_i \varphi \Rightarrow \psi$ if $\mu, \xi_i \not\Vdash_i \varphi$ or $\mu, \xi_i \Vdash_i \psi$,
- $\mu, \xi_i \Vdash_i \varphi \cup \psi$ if there exists $\xi_i'' \in \Xi_i$ with $\xi_i \subsetneq \xi_i''$ such that $\mu, \xi_i'' \Vdash_i \psi$, and $\mu, \xi_i' \Vdash_i \phi$ for every $\xi_i' \in \Xi_i$ with $\xi_i \subsetneq \xi_i' \subsetneq \xi_i''$,
- $\mu, \xi_i \Vdash_i \varphi \, S \, \psi$ if there exists $\xi_i'' \in \Xi_i$ with $\xi_i'' \subsetneq \xi_i$ such that $\mu, \xi_i'' \Vdash_i \psi$, and $\mu, \xi_i' \Vdash_i \phi$ for every $\xi_i' \in \Xi_i$ with $\xi_i'' \subsetneq \xi_i' \subsetneq \xi_i$, and
- $\mu, \xi_i \Vdash_i j : \phi$ if $\xi_i \neq \emptyset$, $last(\xi_i) \in Ev_j$ and $\mu, (last(\xi_i) \downarrow)|_j \Vdash_j \varphi$.

The interpretation structure μ is called a *model* of $\Gamma \subseteq L$ if $\mu, \xi \Vdash \gamma$ for every global configuration ξ of μ and every $\gamma \in \Gamma$. Other standard operators are defined in Table 1.

Table 1. Temporal Operators

Operator	Meaning	Operator	Meaning
$X \varphi \equiv \bot \cup \varphi$	next	$\dagger \equiv \neg X \top$	in the end
$Y \varphi \equiv \bot S \varphi$	previous	$* \equiv \neg Y \top$	in the beginning
$F \varphi \equiv \top \cup \varphi$	sometime in the future	$F_o \varphi \equiv \varphi \vee F \varphi$	now or sometime in the future
$P \varphi \equiv \top S \varphi$	sometime in the past	$P_o \varphi \equiv \varphi \vee P \varphi$	now or sometime in the past
$G \varphi \equiv \neg F \neg \varphi$	always in the future	$G_o \varphi \equiv \varphi \wedge G \varphi$	now and always in the future
$H \varphi \equiv \neg P \neg \varphi$	always in the past	$H_o \varphi \equiv \varphi \wedge H \varphi$	now and always in the past

In [14], a number of axiom schemas are defined to represent the specifications of the communication network. These axiom schemas represent the notion of perfect cryptography. That is, knowledge of each participant only depends on his initial knowledge and on the actions that have occurred. The behavior of the channel and the way participants communicate with each other are also captured in terms of axiom schemas. Finally, the axiom schemas also capture the freshness and uniqueness of the nonces. In DTPL, the principals are also equipped with two functions *synth* and *analz* to compose (through concatenation and encryption) and decompose (through projection and decryption) messages respectively. We don't list the axioms here for the sake of brevity. Interested reader should refer to [14] for details.

3　Developing Authentication Tests

Using the DTPL framework described in the previous section, we present the motivation behind our work and extend the framework of DTPL in this section.

Authentication protocols often comprise of two or more participants sending or receiving messages to or from each other in a challenge response style. Protocol analysis comprises of identifying the parameter n used as a challenge by a participant. Generally either the challenge message M_c contains n in the encrypted form discernable to only legitimate participants, or the response message M_r is in a form that can only be constructed by a legitimate participant. Once the challenge and the response at a participant are identified, we investigate the originator of the response. In order to find the true originator of a response, following observations are made:

- In asymmetric-key cryptography, a signed message originates from the participant who has access to the private-key with which the message was signed. We assume the private-key of a participant to be its safe secret. Since participant's *ids* are unique and their mapping to the private-keys are injective in asymmetric cryptography, signing a message by a participant's private-key ensures the originator of the signed message.
- In symmetric-key cryptography, an encrypted message can originate only from the participants having access to the encryption key with which the message was encrypted. This is a direct consequence of the assumption of ideal cryptography. Since in symmetric-key cryptography, a key is assumed to be a participant's safe secret, encrypting a message under symmetric-key ensures the possession of the key, and hence the origination of the message by a participant having that key.
- If n is a fresh secret uniquely originated in an encrypted challenge message M_c at a participant such that only a participant P has the key to decrypt M_c and obtain n, and M_r is the correct response, then the reception of M_r ensures its origination at P.

Successful identification of the originator of the response message ensures the reception of the challenge message at the responder. This results into *agreement* in the parameters of the challenge message between the challenger and the responder. Based on the abovementioned categories of authentication protocols, the authors in [12] proposed three different tests. These tests perceive security protocols as an implementation of a generic challenge-response protocol. Depending upon the structure of the challenge and the response messages, an analyzer can choose any combination of these tests to either prove that the protocol achieves authentication or use them as a heuristic for finding attacks against incorrect protocols.

In order to derive authentication tests in DTPL, we need to modify the existing framework. In this section, we state some notions that are either defined in [12] or define the translation of it in the DTPL framework. Moreover, we define some concepts such as *life span*, a basic ingredient behind authentication tests, and give new characteristics to the distributed channel. In the next section, we will use these definitions to construct high-level authentication formulas. The overall idea behind authentication tests is to trace the originating point of a received message in order to investigate who could have originated the messages of certain forms.

3.1 Message Components

Informally speaking, either the atomic terms or encrypted terms are called components of a message. If an encrypted term contains another encrypted term inside, then the outermost encrypted term is called component. Let t be a component of a message M, then $t \sqsubset M^1$, which we represent by M_t, i.e. t is a subterm of M. Let $C_{M_t} = \{send(M_t, B'), rec(M_t), spy(M_t)\}$. At the local configuration ξ_i of a participant, a component t is *new* in a message M if $t \sqsubset M$, $last(\xi_i) = e$, $\alpha(e) \in C_{M_t}$, and $\forall e' \in \xi_i \backslash e$, $\alpha(e') \notin C_{M'_t}$. That is, the participant never communicated a message containing that component previously.

$$@_A[send(M_t, B') \vee rec(M_t) \vee spy(M_t) \Rightarrow \mathsf{H}(\neg send(M'_t, B') \wedge \neg rec(M'_t) \wedge \neg spy(M'_t))]$$

Note that a component t in a message $M_t = abtcd$ is new even though if a participant communicated a message $\{t\}_K$ before.

3.2 Message Origination

If a participant sends a term N inside a message M, $N \sqsubset M$, such that he never communicated that term inside any message M' in the past then he originates the term in its sending message. Let $Comm_N = \{send(M'_N, B'), rec(M'_N), spy(M'_N)\}$. At the local configuration ξ_i of a participant, a term N originates in a message M if $N \sqsubset M$, $last(\xi_i) = e$, $\alpha(e) = send(M_N, B')$, and $\forall e' \in \xi_i \backslash e$, $e' \notin Comm_N$. That is, the participant never communicated any message containing N previously. We say the term N originates in the message M at ξ_A if it satisfies the following condition. We call it (O1)

$$\mu, \xi_A \Vdash_A send(M_N, B') \wedge \mathsf{H}(\neg send(M'_N, C') \wedge \neg rec(M'_N) \wedge \neg spy(M'_N))$$

3.3 Life Span

A portion of the local life-cycle of a participant is called its life span represented by $\langle Ev', \rightarrow' \rangle$, $Ev' \subset Ev_i$, $\rightarrow' \subset \rightarrow_i$ such that Ev' is backward closed under local causality $\rightarrow'^+$ until we reach an event e. That is, if $e' = last(\xi_i)$, $e' \in Ev'$ and $e'' \rightarrow'^+ e'$, then $e'' \in Ev'$ until we encounter an event $e \in Ev'$. We also represent life span as $e \hookrightarrow e'$ where e and $e' \in Ev'$ are the first and the last events in the life span of a participant.

3.4 Path

Upon receiving a message, Strand Space Method (SSM) [12] identifies a unique participant sending that message whereas we find some amount of indetermination in the DTPL models. In the DTPL, many choices exist when tracing back the origin of a received message. Therefore, in order to derive the DTPL equivalent of the SSM's inter-strand communication construct $\rightarrow$, we need to modify the channel. We constrain the DTPL channel by modifying it as follows:

(C1') $@_{Ch}[in(M, A') \Rightarrow B : send(M, A')]$,[2]

---

[1] $\sqsubset$ represents the relation *subterm*. Interested readers can refer to [12] for the formal definition of *component* and *subterm*.

[2] Naming convention used in our axioms are coherent with the one mentioned in [14].

(P3') $@_A[rec(M) \Rightarrow Ch : out(M, A')]$,
(P4') $@_A[spy(M) \Rightarrow Ch : (leak \wedge \mathsf{P}\ in(M, B'))]$

That is, channel does not receive a message unless it is sent by an agent (C1').
Channel must send a message out in order for an agent to receive it (P3'). An
agent can spy a message only if the channel has received the message before and
leaked it (P4'). Now we prove the following communication formulas

(C4) $@_A[rec(M)] \Rightarrow @_B[\mathsf{P}\ send(M, A')]$

Proof. Its proof is a direct consequence of applying P3', C2[3] and C1'.   □

(C5) $@_A[spy(M)] \Rightarrow @_B[\mathsf{P}\ send(M, C')]$

Proof. Its proof is a direct consequence of applying P4' and C1'.   □

Notice that given a message is received by a participant, C4 and C5 essentially
provide a shortcut by not involving the details of the communication through
channel.

The life span of a participant in DTPL can emulate the arrow $\Rightarrow^+$ in SSM
(see $run2str(u)$ in [14], for example) except that for honest participants, the
local events corresponding to the actions $nonce(N)$ and $key(K)$ in DTPL have
no explicit role in SSM. Life span together with the communication formulas C4
and C5 define a path. A path p in a model μ and configuration ξ is any finite
sequence of events and edges $e_1 \mapsto e_2 \mapsto \cdots \mapsto e_k$ such that:

- $\bigcup_{x=1}^{k} e_x \subseteq \xi$
- $\alpha_i(e_1)$ is $send(M, A)$ and $\alpha_j(e_k)$ is $rec(M')$.
- $e \mapsto e'$ means
  - Either life span $e \hookrightarrow e'$ with $\alpha_i(e) = rec(M)$ or $spy(M)$ and $\alpha_i(e') = send(M', A)$, or else
  - $\alpha_i(e) = send(M, A)$ and $\alpha_j(e') = rec(M)$ (or $spy(M)$ if $e' \neq e_k$). The participants i and j are such that the messages in the rec and $send$ actions are compatible and $e' \downarrow \supset e \downarrow$.

That is, a path starts from a sending event and terminates at the receiving
event of an honest participant. Honesty is due to the assumption that $\alpha_j(e_k) \neq spy(M')$. It is worth mentioning that a participant is deemed honest if he plays
by the rules of the protocol since nobody knows the intruder beforehand. If a
message destined for participant B is received by B, it can terminate the *path*
even if B intends to use the message for illegitimate activity in the future. Since
some honest participant has sent the message to B, the latter will be considered
legitimate in that activity. However, even though a spy event can lie within the
path, it can not terminate the path. In general, only either the local sequence of
events of a participant, or the common communication event specified by C4 or
C5 constitutes a path. We use $|p|$ to represent the length and $l(p)$ to represent
the last event of a path. For example, in the above path p, $|p| = k$ and $l(p) = e_k$.

---

[3] From [14], (C2) $@_{Ch}[out(M, A') \Rightarrow \mathsf{P}\ in(M, A')]$.

3.5   Transformed Life

The life span $e \hookrightarrow e'$ of a participant i is called a transformed life for $a \in \mathbf{A}$ if

- $\alpha_i(e) = send(M, A)$ and $\alpha_i(e') = rec(M')$.
- $a \sqsubset M$.
- there is a new component t in M' such that $a \sqsubset t$.

We can formulate the above definition for a model μ and local configuration ξ_i as follows:

$$\mu, \xi_i \Vdash_i rec(M'_{t^{new}_a}) \wedge \mathsf{P}\ send(M_a, A)$$

where M_{t_n} represents a message M with t as its component such that a term n is a subterm of t. Moreover, t^{new} represents a new component. Since honest participants use the transformed life to authenticate other participants, no event corresponds to the $spy(M)$ action.

3.6   Transforming Life

The life span $e \hookrightarrow e'$ of a participant i is called a transforming life for $a \in \mathbf{A}$ if

- $\alpha_i(e) = rec(M)$ or $spy(M)$ and $\alpha_i(e') = send(M', A)$.
- $a \sqsubset M$.
- there is a new component t in M' such that $a \sqsubset t$.

For a model μ and local configuration ξ_i, transforming life satisfies the following:

$$\mu, \xi_i \Vdash_i send(M'_{t^{new}_a}, A) \wedge \mathsf{P}\ (rec(M_a) \vee spy(M_a))$$

Note that for honest participants, the transforming life can be easily recognized in DTPL as honest principals strictly follow the protocol rules. However, due to the absence of explicit intruder behavior in DTPL, an illegitimate participant takes part in transforming life only if it can construct an M'-producing S-bundle where S is the resource available to the intruder. In other words, $M' \in synth(analz(S))$ [14]. We will further elaborate this issue in the later part of this section. For the definition of an M-producing S-bundle, see [12].

3.7   Transformation Path

Let (e_i, t_i) be a pair where e_i is an event and t_i is the component of the message involved in $\alpha(e_i)$. Then the transformation path is a *path* in which if (e_i, t_i) then (e_{i+1}, t_i) unless a life span $e_i \hookrightarrow e_{i+1}$ occurs in the life-cycle of a participant X and t_{i+1} is new at ξ_X. Transformation path does not have to terminate at this point.

Note that in a transformation path if $t_i \neq t_{i+1}$, $a \sqsubset t_i$, and $a \sqsubset t_{i+1}$, then $e_i \hookrightarrow e_{i+1}$ is a transforming life for a.

3.8   Finding the Originator of a Message

Given a DTPL model μ and configuration ξ such that $e_1 \in \xi$ in (e_1, t_1), $\alpha(e_1) = rec(M_{t_1})$ and $a \sqsubset t_1$.

Then there is a transformation path p in μ, ξ such that a originates at p_1, $l(p) = e_1$, $t_{|p|} = t_1$, and $\forall i, a \sqsubset t_i$.

Proof. Let us consider the following transformation path p (indexed in reverse order):

$$e_{k+1} \mapsto e_k \mapsto \cdots \mapsto e_1$$

where each event e_i is paired with a component t_i in (e_i, t_i) such that $\forall j \in e_j, a \sqsubset t_j$. If a originates at t_{k+1} in (e_{k+1}, t_{k+1}) then p is complete. So suppose that a does not originate at t_{k+1}.

- If $\alpha_A(e_{k+1}) = rec(M)$, then using C4, $B : send(M, A)$. Extend p backward to (e_{k+2}, c_{k+2}).
- If $\alpha_A(e_{k+1}) = spy(M)$, then using C5, $B : send(M, C)$. Extend p backward to (e_{k+2}, c_{k+2}).
- If $\alpha_A(e_{k+1}) = send(M, B)$, then
  - If t_{k+1} is new, using the definition of origination, there exists $e_{k+2} \hookrightarrow e_{k+1}$ such that $a \sqsubset t_{k+2}$ and $\alpha_A(e_{k+2}) = rec(M')$ or $spy(M')$, since a does not originate at t_{k+1}. Extend p backward to contain such (e_{k+2}, t_{k+2}).
  - If t_{k+1} is not new, then there exists $e_{k+2} \hookrightarrow e_{k+1}$ such that $\alpha_A(e_{k+2}) = rec(M')$ or $spy(M')$ and M' has a component t_{k+1}. Extend p backward to contain such (e_{k+2}, t_{k+1}).

Since a distributed life-cycle $\rightarrow^*$ defines a partial order of global causality on the set $Ev = \bigcup_{i \in Id} Ev_i$ of all events, the set Ξ of all global configurations constitutes a lattice, under inclusion, and has $\emptyset$ as the minimal element [10]. Therefore, following the path in the reverse order as described above, we will reach a point (e_j, t_j) where a originates.   □

3.9   Honest Transformation

Since DTPL treats an intruder almost the same way as it treats an honest participant, the normal form for intruder strands in protocol bundles obtained in [12] does not have a DTPL counterpart [14]. Unlike DTPL, the SSM strictly specifies how an intruder constructs a message. The DTPL leaves the task up to the *analz* and *synth* functions. But we can benefit from the back-and-forth translation between the capabilities of an intruder in the DTPL model and that in the SSM model given in [14] as follows:

"If S be a set of messages. Then $M \in synth(analz(S))$ if and only if there exists an M-producing S-bundle.[4]"

If p is a transformation path in which p_i represents a pair (e_i, t_i) such that

---

[4] See [12] for the definition of M-producing S-bundle.

- $\forall i,\ a \sqsubset t_i$.
- p_1 and $p_{|p|}$ lie at honest participants.
- $t_1 \neq t_{|p|}$.
- t_1 is of the form $\{h_1\}_{K_1}$.
- t_1 is not a proper subterm of any honest component.
- $K_1^{-1} \notin K_P$.

If α is the smallest index such that $t_\alpha \neq t_{\alpha+1}$, then p_α lies at honest participant and $p_\alpha \hookrightarrow p_{\alpha+1}$ is a transforming life for a.

Proof. (Sketch) If p_α lies at an intruder then according to the above conditions, the intruder produces new component $t_{\alpha+1}$ in a message M from its available resources S using the functions *synth* and *analz*. Note that *synth* and *analz* precisely cover the intruder attacks caused by the strands **C**, **S**, **E**, and **D** in SSM. The only intruder strand that can produce a new component is either **E** or **D** because **C** and **S** simply use previous components and do not introduce new one. Given $K_1^{-1} \notin K_P$, we are left with only **E** strand to construct M-producing S-bundle. With the help of only **E** strand, suppose a penetrator constructs an M-producing S-bundle such that $t_{\alpha+1} \sqsubset M$. Now it is easy to see that no matter how many times the penetrator tries to construct an M-producing S-bundle, $t_\alpha \sqsubset t_{\alpha+1} \sqsubset t_{\alpha+2}$ and so on. So we reach a point where t_α is a proper subterm of $t_{|p|}$ resulting into contradiction. As mentioned above, the restricted class of intruder gets no benefit by using redundant operations like **E-D** or **C-S** which can always be eliminated as shown in [12]. In other words, after using redundancy elimination and applying the freeness assumption on message algebra, once a penetrator uses a **E** or **C** strand, it can not gain any benefit by using **D** or **S** strand afterwards. Therefore, a penetrator can not produce M and p_α can not lie at the intruder, but must lie at a legitimate participant.   □

Similarly, if p is a transformation path in which p_i represents a pair (e_i, t_i) such that

- $\forall i,\ a \sqsubset t_i$.
- p_1 and $p_{|p|}$ lie at honest participants.
- $t_1 \neq t_{|p|}$.
- $t_{|p|}$ is of the form $\{h_1\}_{K_1}$.
- $t_{|p|}$ is not a proper subterm of any honest component.
- $K_1^{-1} \notin K_P$.

If α is the largest index such that $t_\alpha \neq t_{\alpha-1}$, then p_α is honest and $p_{\alpha-1} \rightarrow^+ p_\alpha$ is a transforming life for a. Its proof is very similar to the previous proof.

4   Authentication Tests

So far, we have modified the DTPL framework for our purpose. In this section, we use the above-mentioned concepts to derive authentication tests in DTPL equivalent to the one established in [12] using SSM.

4.1   Outgoing Test for the DTPL Model Configurations

The life span $e_0 \hookrightarrow e_1$ of a participant is an outgoing test for $a \in \mathbf{A}$ in $t = \{h\}_K$, $a \sqsubset t$ if:

- $\alpha(e_0) = send(M, B)$ and $\alpha(e_1) = rec(M')$.
- t is a component of M.
- The term a uniquely originates at e_0 in M.
- a does not occur in any component of M other than t.
- The term t is not a proper subterm of a component of any message in the local life-cycle of an honest participant.
- There is a new component t' of M' such that $a \sqsubset t'$.
- $K^{-1} \notin K_P$.

Let μ be a DTPL model and ξ be a configuration with $e_1 \in \xi$, and let $e_0 \hookrightarrow e_1$ be an outgoing test for $a \in \mathbf{A}$ in t, then

- There exist an honest participant i with the life span $m \hookrightarrow m'$, $(m, m' \in \xi)$, such that $\alpha_i(m) = rec(M'')$ and $\alpha_i(m') = send(\mathsf{M}, C)$.
- $a \sqsubset M''$ and t is a component of M''.
- There is a new component t'' of M such that $a \sqsubset t''$.

Moreover, if:

- a occurs only in component $t'' = \{h'\}_{K'}$ of M.
- The term t'' is not a proper subterm of any honest component.
- $K'^{-1} \notin K_P$.

then, there is an event e in the local life-cycle of an honest participant such that $\alpha(e) = rec(M')$ and t'' is a component of M'.

Proof. (Sketch) Note that the life span $e_0 \hookrightarrow e_1$ represents a transformed life for a. We can benefit from finding the originator of a message presented in Section 3.8 in order to trace the transformation path p such that p in μ, ξ, a originates at p_1, $l(p) = e_1$, $t_{|p|} = t'$, and $\forall i, a \sqsubset t_i$. Since t' is new in e_1, $t \neq t'$. Moreover, since a does not occur in any component of M other than $t = \{h\}_K$, $t_1 = t$ and $t_1 \neq t_{|p|}$. Using the idea of honest transformation introduced in the previous section, the smallest index such that $t_\alpha \neq t_{\alpha+1}$ exists in which p_α is honest. Also note that according to the definition, $p_\alpha \hookrightarrow p_{\alpha+1}$ is a transforming life. Therefore, $t = t_1 = t_\alpha$ is a component of M'' and $m = p_\alpha$. Now we have $m' = p_{\alpha+1}$, $\alpha_i(m') = send(\mathsf{M}, C)$, t'' is a new component of M, $a \sqsubset t''$, and a occurs only in component $t'' = \{h'\}_{K'}$ of M. Therefore, $t_{\alpha+1} = t''$. Now either $t' = t''$ or use the concept of honest transformation again to reach the conclusion. $\square$

Now we represent the outgoing test in terms of a formula in DTPL.

$$@_A[rec(M'_{t'_a new}) \wedge \mathsf{P}\,(send(M_{t_a}, B'))] \Rightarrow \bigvee_B @_B[\mathsf{P}\,(send(\mathsf{M}_{t''_a new}, C') \wedge \mathsf{P}\,(rec(M''_{t_a})))]$$

where $B \in Princ\backslash\{A\}$ and m_{t_a} represents a message m with t as its component such that a term a is a subterm of t. Moreover, t^{new} represents a new component. In the above, $t_a = \{h\}_K$ in M_{t_a} such that $K^{-1} \notin K_P$ and a uniquely originates in M_{t_a}. Since a represents a term such as a nonce, the action $nonce(N)$ combined with the axioms N1 and N2 impose the condition of unique origination in DTPL. As the general requirements for the authentication test to hold, the term N does not occur in any component of M_{t_a} other than t and the term t is not a proper subterm of any honest component.

Finally, if a occurs only in the component $t_a''^{new}$ in M above, $t_a''^{new}$ is not a proper subterm of a component of any message of an honest participant, and $t_a''^{new} = \{h'\}_{K'}$ such that $K'^{-1} \notin K_P$, then there exists an honest event $rec(M'_{t''})$ with t'' as a component.

4.2   Incoming Test for the DTPL Model Configurations

The local life-cycle $e_0 \rightarrow^+ e_1$ is an incoming test for $a \in \mathbf{A}$ in $t = \{h\}_K$ if:

- The term a uniquely originates in M at e_0.
- $\alpha(e_0) = send(M, B)$ and $\alpha(e_1) = rec(M')$.
- The term t is not a proper subterm of a component of any message in the local life-cycle of an honest participant.
- t is a new component of M' such that $a \sqsubset t$.
- $K \notin K_P$.

Let μ be a DTPL model and ξ be a configuration with $e_1 \in \xi$, and let $e_0 \rightarrow^+ e_1$ be an incoming test for $a \in \mathbf{A}$ in t, then

- There exist an honest participant i with the life span $m \hookrightarrow m'$, $(m, m' \in \xi)$, such that $\alpha_i(m) = rec(M'')$ and $\alpha_i(m') = send(\mathsf{M}, C)$.
- $a \sqsubset M''$ and t is a new component of M in which $a \sqsubset t$.

Proof. (Sketch) We trace the transformation path p as we did in the outgoing test such that p in μ, ξ, a originates at $p_1 = e_0$, $l(p) = e_1$, $t_{|p|} = t$, and $\forall i, a \sqsubset t_i$. Since t is new in e_1, $t_1 \neq t_{|p|}$. Using the result of honest transformation, the largest index α such that $t_\alpha \neq t_{\alpha-1}$ has $t_{\alpha-1}$ honest and $p_{\alpha-1} \hookrightarrow p_\alpha$ is a transforming life. Therefore, $t_{|p|} = t = t_\alpha$ is a component of $p_\alpha = m'$ where $\alpha(m') = send(\mathsf{M}, C)$. □

Let μ is a DTPL model of a protocol such that ξ is a configuration of μ equivalent to the bundle C mentioned in the above incoming test. Then, the following DTPL formula expresses the incoming test.

$$@_A[rec(M'_{t_a^{new}}) \wedge \mathsf{P}\,(send(M_a, B'))] \Rightarrow \bigvee_B @_B[\mathsf{P}\,(send(\mathsf{M}_{t_a^{new}}, C') \wedge \mathsf{P}\,(rec(M''_a)))]$$

Here, $B \in Princ\backslash\{A\}$ and $t_a^{new} = \{h\}_K$ such that $K \notin K_P$ and a uniquely originates in M_a. Moreover, the term t is not a proper subterm of any honest component. As obvious, we can use the nonce N for the value of a.

4.3 Unsolicited Test for the DTPL Model Configurations

An event e such that $\alpha(e) = rec(M)$ is an unsolicited test for $t = \{h\}_K$ if for any a in M:

- $a \sqsubset t$ and t is a component of M.
- t is not a proper subterm of a component of any message in the local life-cycle of an honest participant.
- $K \notin K_P$.

Let μ be a DTPL model and ξ be a configuration with $e \in \xi$ such that e is an unsolicited test for $t = \{h\}_K$, then there exists an honest participant with event $m \in \xi$, $\alpha(m) = send(M', C')$ such that t is a component of M'.

Proof. (Sketch) In order to find the originator of message M, we trace the transformation path p in μ, ξ such that a originates at p_1, $l(p) = e$, $t_{|p|} = t$, and $\forall i, a \sqsubset t_i$ in (e_i, t_i). It is easy to see that the penetrator can originate a message only by using its $send(M, B')$ action in which the originating term $t \sqsubset M$ can be obtained only by using *nonce* or *key* actions or by applying *analz* and *synth* functions on the set of messages available to the penetrator. Obviously *nonce* or *key* actions can not produce an encrypted term t. So we are left with the *analz* and *synth* functions in which *analz* can not originate a message (see the definition of message origination) whereas *synth* can originate a message t only by encrypting a message m with any key available to the penetrator K_P. Since $K \notin K_P$, using the assumption of free message algebra, the penetrator can not produce $t = \{h\}_K$. Moreover, since t is not a proper subterm of any regular component, it is a component of M'. □

The following DTPL axiomatization captures the unsolicited test.

$$@_A[rec(M_{t_a})] \Rightarrow \bigvee_{B \in Princ \backslash \{A\}} @_B[\mathsf{P}\ send(M'_{t_a}, C')]$$

where, $t_a = \{h\}_K$, $K \notin K_P$, and t is not a proper subterm of any honest component.

We have used the authentication tests of strand spaces and have formulated the corresponding tests using distributed temporal protocol logic. Due to DTPL's rich set of operators, it can easily capture the detailed temporal activities of any participant in a protocol run. Moreover, each run of a protocol can be clearly represented as local and distributed life-cycle using event structures. Overall, our extended framework can be used to analyze auathentication property in a wide range of authentication protocols by treating them as a sequence of challenge-response messages. These tests have been successfully applied on many protocols in the strand space setting. Our future goal is to compare these DTPL based tests with other existing schemes.

5   Conclusion

We have developed logic-based authentication tests for the verification of authentication protocols. We used distributed temporal protocol logic and extended the DTPL framework to abstract out the intricate details of the process involved in authentication. Once an authentication protocols is perceived in terms of challenge-response messages, protocol analysis is simply a matter of investigating the true originator of a received message. Successful identification of the originator of a received message guarantees that the critical parameters of the participants match with each other. This results into an agreement between participants of a protocol that eventually leads to successful authentication. On the other hand, lack of parameter matching among the participants of a protocol can be used as a guide towards finding a successful attack on the protocol.

References

1. Needham, R.M., Schroeder, M.: Using encryption for authentication in large networks of computers. Communications of the ACM 21(12), 993–999 (1978)
2. Dolev, D., Yao, A.C.: On the security of public key protocols. IEEE Transactions on Information Theory 29, 198–208 (1983)
3. Meadows, C.: Formal methods for cryptographic protocol analysis: Emerging issues and trends. IEEE Journal on Selected Areas in Communications 21(1), 44–54 (2003)
4. Fidge, C.: A survey of verification techniques for security protocols. Tech. Rep. 01-22, Software Verification Research Centre, School of Information Technology, The University of Queensland (2001)
5. Thayer, F.J., Swarup, V., Guttman, J.D.: Metric Strand Spaces for Locale Authentication Protocols. In: Nishigaki, M., Jøsang, A., Murayama, Y., Marsh, S. (eds.) IFIPTM 2010. IFIP AICT, vol. 321, pp. 79–94. Springer, Heidelberg (2010)
6. Coffey, T., Dojen, R., Flanagan, T.: Formal verification: an imperative step in the design of security protocols. Computer Networks 43, 601–618 (2003)
7. Burrows, Abadi, Needham: A logic of authentication. ACM Transactions on Computer Systems, 18–36 (1990)
8. Syverson, P.F., Cervesato, I.: The Logic of Authentication Protocols. In: Focardi, R., Gorrieri, R. (eds.) FOSAD 2000. LNCS, vol. 2171, pp. 63–136. Springer, Heidelberg (2001)
9. Orgun, M.A., Governatori, G., Liu, C.: Modal tableaux for verifying stream authentication protocols. Journal of Autonomous Agents and Multi Agent Systems 19(1), 53–75 (2009)
10. Caleiro, Vigano, Basin: Metareasoning about security protocols using distributed temporal logic. Electronic Notes in Theoretical Computer Science 125, 67–89 (2005)
11. Lowe, G.: A hierarchy of authentication specification. In: Proceedings of the 1997 IEEE Computer Society Symposium on Research in Security and Privacy, pp. 31–43 (1997)
12. Guttman, J.D., Fabrega, F.J.T.: Authentication tests and the structure of bundles. Theoretical Computer Science 283, 333–380 (2003)
13. Winskel, G.: Event structures. In: Brauer, W., Reisig, W., Rozenberg, G. (eds.) APN 1986. LNCS, vol. 255, pp. 325–392. Springer, Heidelberg (1987)
14. Caleiro, C., Vigano, L., Basin, D.: Relating strand spaces and distributed temporal logic for security protocol analysis. Logic Journal of IGPL 13(6), 637–663 (2005)

User Profiling with Virtual Pet for Mobile Device Authentication

Shu Yun Lim[1] and Jason N.M. Kho[2]

[1] Faculty of Information Technology, University of Management and Technology, Malaysia
[2] M2O Solutions, Malaysia
lim_sy@umtech.edu.my,
jason@m2o-publishing.com

Abstract. Since mobile devices have become an inseparable part of peoples' lives, gathering user profiles from mobile devices can provide a better grasp of the device ownership. Mobile user profiling is done by focusing on information that can be used to authenticate the real owner of a device. A novel human-machine authentication mechanism is proposed. This objective is achieved via profiling of the user through his or her interaction with a virtual pet that resides on the mobile device to provide robust, intelligent, continuous and transparent authentication of the user. Virtual pets that reside in devices can turn phones into 'sentient beings' and are able to analyse the users' behaviour through constant interaction with them.

Keywords: mobile device, user profiling, virtual pet, human-machine authentication.

1 Introduction

We now have smart phones that offer many functions in our daily lives and many are heavily involved and immersed in the mobile device world. In this day and age, mobile devices are more a lifestyle statement than simply a communications tool. They are highly customised according to users' preferences and have been extended to perform day-to-day activities for instance mobile banking, net surfing, and instant messaging. Mobile devices let users work anywhere, anytime and have brought users an unprecedented level of convenience and flexibility. They are always small, lightweight and handy to carry around. However, due to their size and characteristics of their common usage environment, they are very vulnerable to theft and loss which is becoming a top security concern.

Along with the value of lost hardware, users are as well worried about the exposure of sensitive information carried in their mobile devices. People store vast amounts of personal data on their mobile devices and the loss of a device may lead to exposure of sensitive data. At present, password login has long been a solution for mobile device security. Nonetheless password-based authentication has proven to be ineffective and inconvenient on mobile devices. In fact, if password is required, most users would prefer to use the same password to unlock everything they touch. The simple password is weak, easily guessed and often defeated by brute-force guessing.

A. Abd Manaf et al. (Eds.): ICIEIS 2011, Part I, CCIS 251, pp. 229–237, 2011.

A password prompt during device power-on would not prevent whoever found or stolen a device from casually browsing content and racking up calls or emails but prompting for password too frequently can also be a problem.

Advanced biometric methods serve as an alternative. Biometric methods have gained favour on notebooks and smart phones. For example, some smart phones now include fingerprint readers that offer an alternative to power-on passwords. A few mobile security products can also process handwritten signatures [1] [2], (entered with a stylus) or voiceprints (entered by speaking a phrase into your smart phone), otoacoustic signal [3] (a microphone near the earpiece emits clicks into the user's ear and the speaker of the phone measures the response from the ear). Such methods can prevent devices from being used by anyone except the owner but unlocking a mobile is still relatively taxing. The application of biometrics in the fashion is somewhat ineffective if there is no physical or logical access control for the owner. Typically, the environment is intrusive in nature. Devices need to be monitored constantly, preferably without user's intervention.

In view of this, some mobile security products can defer auto-locking by detecting passive use or owner proximity. Transient authentication [4] has been proposed to lift the burden of authentication from the user by use of a wearable token that constantly attests to the user's presence. When the user departs, the token and device lose contact and the device secures itself. On the other hand, keystroke dynamics [5] has also been introduced for transparent authentication. This is to authenticate users successfully based on their interactions with a mobile device keypad. The method focuses upon the concept of keystroke analysis which can offer a cost-effective and continuous authentication solution for mobile devices.

To further improve the security, flexibility and universality, we propose a human-machine authentication scheme that is capable of profiling a mobile phone owner through interactions with a virtual pet on the mobile device to provide an intelligent user authentication mechanism. This scheme also takes into consideration the interactions between a virtual pet with other virtual pets on other phones in its proximity. There will be constant checking of the device ownership and secure itself when a user who is not its owner is sensed.

2   Previous Works

Device authentication research work can be traced back to [6]. Frank Stajano discussed about the balance between security and usability. Performing authentication by means other than password is to increase usability but biometrics and token is not the way out due to some inherent problems. In his discussion, a mobile device could benefit from having both public and private modes that would draw a security perimeter around private data. Some data need to be made private when users were compelled to hand their device to another person. Stajano theorise about the data and services that might be assigned to the public and privates modes, flow-of-control requirements in switching between modes, and the tradeoffs of alternative authentication methods and implementation models. Another significant work is the biometric daemon proposed by Pam Briggs et. al. [7]. It is a user-centred and adaptive authentication system. The daemon shares identity with its owner and requires nurturing. It takes inspiration from two sources, the imprinted biometric properties of its owner (owner commit identity information to the daemon) and also regularly updated with the fluid of biometric properties of its owner, by which the daemon comes to recognise the stable elements of its environment and is subsequently reassured by them.

Numerous application systems were developed and progressions have been made. These profiling systems are always done in different way to make systems more adaptive or to make their results more relevant. Nilton Bila et. at. [8] proposed a scheme for gathering profile information about mobile phone users so that the information can be used to enhance targeting of advertisement. The two-tier approach involves statistical learning from network observable data and involves explicit queries to the user. This serve as a basis for our framework whereby mobile user behaviour can be observed and their location and activity habits can provide useful information for authentication. User profiling was also proposed in [9] for context aware service provisioning. Profiled information was used to configure and manage mobile terminal and services for the personalized use according to the needs and preferences of a mobile user. The direction was to provide a customization framework that is able to support the users in the configuration and use of services.

Very frequently the success of a security scheme relies on an owner's willingness to use it. Research must target both the system-level implementation as well as user-guided approaches that match varying user preferences. Therefore, further research is needed to understand what constitutes a tractable, useful and usable set of usage profiles for smart phones.

3   Proposed Scheme

In our proposal, the virtual agent can take the form of any creature, such as a dog, cat, genie, etc. It is integrated into the phone operating system and built into the underlying security framework of the OS. This ensures that the agent is always running (even in the background) and has full control and access to all the security aspects of the mobile phone. The agent is not the only interface to the mobile phone operations. The user can still use the traditional methods to access phone functions. However, the agent will pop up on the screen at certain appropriate times in a random fashion, depending on its 'mood' or can be called up by the owner at any time whenever the owner wishes to interact with it.

Since the mobile phone is a very personal device, the pet interacts almost exclusively with the owner. The owner is able to perform a number of tasks on a regular basis with the pet, such as feeding, bathing and playing, to simulate caring treatments for the pet. Through such frequent and personal interactions, the pet grows and develops a distinct personality or behaviour that is known only to the owner. This creates a virtual bond between pet and owner which will later be used for authentication and verification.

3.1   Virtual Pet Life Stages

Like other existing virtual pets [10] [11], the virtual pet in this scheme goes through a series of growth stages throughout its lifespan. The pet starts off at stage zero in the form of an egg. This is the initial stage that comes with new mobile phones. The phone is still brand new and there is no profile of both pet and owner. The owner is required to preset an emergency number to call or send a text message to, when the pet determined that it has been stolen, sometime in the future. As soon as the owner goes through the set up with some kind of wizard to initialise growth, the egg will hatch and the pet begins the first growth stage. The first growth stage is the infant stage where the pet takes on a pre-adolescent form. At this stage, the pet has no bond with its owner yet; hence no authentication and verification can take place during the first growth stage. From here, the pet and the owner start to develop a bond.

Through caring treatments from the owner, the pet advances to the second stage. The second stage is the learning stage and represents the stage where the pet builds a model of its owner and their surroundings. In the second stage, the pet would exhibit physical characteristics to indicate growth and maturity. The pet would also develop language capability. The pet communicates with the owner via text sentences. The pet will randomly ask the owner personal questions from a precompiled list to mimic the pet's curiosity of its owner and their surroundings. The owner will have to reply the pet by selecting from a list of answers or by typing the answers. Answers from the owner represent the owner's preferences. Life pattern and character are stored in memory to build a profile of the owner's identity. The period for the second stage should not be too long relative to the average lifespan of a typical mobile phone. For this scheme, we assume that it take two weeks as the growth period for the second stage. Besides that, the pet also uses information from its surrounding to profile its owner. In a mobile ad-hoc network, it is able to communicate automatically with virtual pets in its vicinity. This process mimics virtual pets befriending virtual pets on other phones nearby. This starts right from the second stage. The information is used to profile the owner's surroundings so that it knows whenever it is in familiar territory. When the phone is stolen for instance, the pet will realise that it no longer senses familiar phones and this information is used by the pet to determine whether or not it has been stolen.

For the third and final stage, the pet reaches maturity. Its physical appearance onscreen will take on characteristics to indicate further maturity. The appearance change as well as the transition period from the second to the third stage depends on the caring treatments by the owner. The transition period should typically be the same as the second stage which is about two weeks. During the second stage of growth, the pet's profile of its owner and surroundings may not be complete but authentication and verification may take place.

At the third stage, the owner profiling is complete. The pet has built its owner's profile which includes personal preferences, patterns, intimate knowledge of the pet's own personality and familiar virtual pets in its vicinity. At this stage, the pet is already familiar with its owner and vice versa. It will continue to interact regularly with the owner and at random times it will use information stored in its profile of the owner to test the owner's authenticity. The pet will not reveal whether the answer provided is correct or otherwise. Correct answers reinforce owner's identity, while wrong answers trigger doubt and create insecurity in the pet. When the doubt level of the pet is non-zero (phone integrity level is low) it will test the owner's authenticity more frequently. Similarly, correct answers reinforce the owner's identity while wrong answers trigger more doubt. Through this process, the pet will realize that the answers given by the current user is markedly different from its profile of its original owner. It will also make use of information of the existence of other virtual pets in its vicinity to evaluate the integrity level. Once the integrity level drops below a certain threshold, the pet can infer that its current user is not its owner and this will trigger the emergency call or text message to the preset number. Authentication and alert will be further discussed in section 3.3.

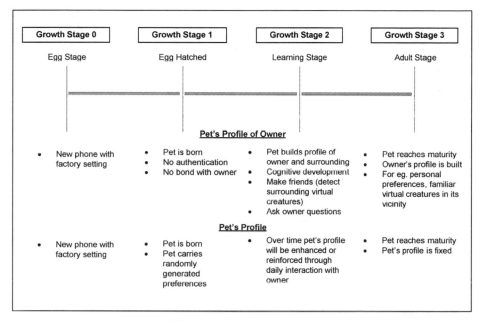

Fig. 1. Virtual pet life stages

3.2   Profile Aggregation

All the virtual pet starts from the egg stage. This is when the new phone has not been configured and comes only with factory setting. Soon after mobile user customises the phone based on their own preferences, the egg is hatched and a virtual pet is born. At this instant there is no authentication taking place and there is no bond between the pet and owner.

The pet grows, evolves individuality and perceived intelligence at learning stage. The virtual pet starts to learn about the owner and the interaction between owner and the pet will help to build the pet's characteristics. Two profiles will be built at the end of this stage, the profile of a pet and the pet's profile of its owner. In addition, it could use GPS and Wi-Fi to determine spatiotemporal context or perform a Bluetooth scan on devices in its vicinity. If Bluetooth devices were found, the virtual pet will then pop up a question to ask the owner about its location whether it is in office, at home, friend's house or some public place. Based on the owner's reply, it will add the device names and locations to the owner's profile. If any of the Bluetooth devices have a virtual pet living in it, the pets will exchange information (i.e. name, age, and owner's name) for the purpose of profiling user. All the information obtained are not accessible to the owner but can be used by the pet to authenticate the owner later on. Lastly when the pet enters adult stage, profile of the owner is sufficient for the pet to authenticate the mobile user. Virtual pet will be very familiar with owner's personal preferences and virtual pets reside on other phones in its surrounding area.

In conclusion, the user profile can be enriched by aggregating pet's profile and pet's profile of the owner. The resulting user profile will hold information regarding user behaviour, context and other preferences. The profile is transferable when user changes phone once the pet reaches its maturity.

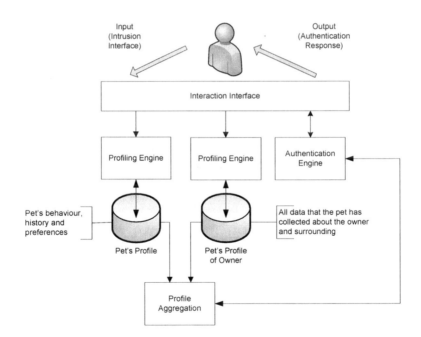

Fig. 2. Profile aggregation framework

3.3   Authentication and Alert

Authentication is carried out at the background to constantly check on the device ownership. Before the owner can expose this virtual pet to an environment or new activities, the identity of the mobile user will be verified with intrusive type of authentication via Q&A. Mobile phone user's profile can be built through learning the social interactions with virtual pet. Full authentication process takes place after the virtual pet reaches maturity. From this point, a virtual pet can perform authentication to obscurely check on the environment where the phone is presence. Virtual pet is aware of its location through scanning Wi-Fi access points or Bluetooth devices in its surrounding area. This is because in the pet's second growth stage, it is able to associate neighbouring devices with the location by asking owner questions about its location. So armed with this information, the pet can determine if it is located in either a familiar environment or a new, unfamiliar environment.

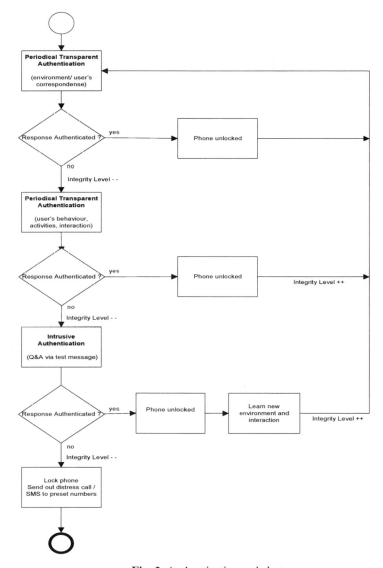

Fig. 3. Authentication and alert

If the authentication response is negative, it will go through another round of transparent authentication whereby owner's behaviour and interaction with the virtual pet is being monitored. Virtual pet is able to behave emotionally towards the treatment it receives from owner. Owner's action may stimulate either positive or negative emotions. At this phase, owner might be prompted to carry out some activities that are normally being done and the interaction is excerpted to match against the normal profile. For instance, owner could be monitored upon the food they feed or the game they play, whether it fits the virtual pet's liking.

When both transparent authentications failed, intrusive type of authentication will be carried out. From day to day activities, virtual pet is able to gather sufficient knowledge unique to the owner and generate questions based on the knowledge it holds. At this point, questions will be prompted to verify owner's identity via text messages and mobile phone user is required to give exact answers else authentication will fail. The questions can be generated using aggregated information from both profiles. When all three stages of authentication failed, the phone can be programmed to lock down all the access, send out distress call or SMS to the preset numbers during first growth stage. Besides, we can allow the pet to access to the front-facing camera and social networks such as Facebook and Twitter. Pictures can be taken and the location data can be posted together on owner's social network page whenever authentication failed. On the other hand, if the mobile user is successfully authenticated, virtual pet will need to learn up this new environment, owner's behaviour and the interaction between them.

4   Conclusion

Significant opportunities exist today to develop a strong market for mobile devices and data protection. The reality is that the evolution of mobile networking has increased the sensitivity of the information stored and access through them. The loss or access of devices without the owner even noticing it brings in a zone of discomfort. Certain interactivity should exist to bring back this comfort to the user. The proposed scheme tries to make an effort in that direction. The proposed scheme has increased security beyond secret-knowledge techniques, provide transparent authentication since it is done without inconveniencing the user and authenticate the user continuously to maintain confidence in the identity of the user and at the same time, secure the device and data. This easy to adopt, fun and interactive authentication mechanisms can be implemented in other devices associated with human beings, be it smart phones, mobile phone, laptops, since the virtual pet can be seen as a sentient being that can recognise its owner all the time.

References

1. Murase, T., Maeda, T., Matsunaga, S.: Computer readable medium recording handwritten signature authentication program, and handwritten signature authentication method apparatus. 7206436 US Patent (2007)
2. Gaines, M., Kardamilas, C., Livengood, S.: System and method of user authentication using handwritten signatures for an MFP. 20080005579 US Patent (2008)

3. Choyi, V., Marquet, B.: Mobile phone locking system using multiple biometric factors for owner authentication. 20080005575 US Patent (2008)
4. Nicholson, A.J., Corner, M.D., Noble, B.D.: Mobile Device Security Using Transient Authentication. IEEE Transactions on Mobile Computing 5(11), 1489–1502 (2006)
5. Clarke, N.L., Furnell, S.M.: Authenticating mobile phone users using keystroke analysis. Source International Journal of Information Security 6(1) (December 2006)
6. Stajano, F.: One User, Many Hats; and, Sometimes, No Hat: Towards a Secure Yet Usable PDA. In: Christianson, B., Crispo, B., Malcolm, J.A., Roe, M. (eds.) Security Protocols 2004. LNCS, vol. 3957, pp. 51–64. Springer, Heidelberg (2006)
7. Briggs, P., Olivier, P.L.: Biometric Daemons: Authentication via electronic pets. In: CHI 2008 Extended Abstracts on Human Factors in Computing Systems. ACM (2008)
8. Nilton, B., et al.: Mobile User Profile Acquisition Through Network Observables and Explicit User Queries. In: The Ninth International Conference on Mobile Data Management. IEEE CS (2008)
9. Bartolomeo, G., et al.: Handling User Profiles for the Secure and Convenient Configuration and Management of Mobile Terminal Services. In: Proceeding of The Sixteenth International Workshop on Database and Expert Systems Applications (2005)
10. Akihiro, Y.: Breeding, Simulation Apparatus for Virtual Creatures. 7104884 US Patent (2006)
11. Rosenberg, L.B.: Methods and Apparatus for Providing Haptic Feedback in Interacting with Virtual Pets. 0080987 US Patent (2003)
12. Zheng, Y., Xia, J., He, D.: Trusted User Authentication Scheme Combining Password with Fingerprint for Mobile Devices. In: International Symposium on Biometrics and Security Technologies (2008)

A Study of Attribute-Based Encryption
for Body Sensor Networks

Yar-Ling Tan, Bok-Min Goi, Ryoichi Komiya, and Syh-Yuan Tan

Faculty of Engineering and Science,
Universiti Tunku Abdul Rahman,
53300 Kuala Lumpur, Malaysia
tanyl@mail2.utar.edu.my

Abstract. Body sensor network (BSN) is a network with sensors attached on different parts of human body to collect various vital signs for the purpose of healthcare monitoring. In order to ensure the privacy and confidentiality of these data fused at BSN coordinator which is a low power and computing mobile device, i.e., smartphone, Attribute-Based Encryption (ABE) is promising. This is because ABE allows fine-grained sharing of encrypted data. ABE provides differential access rights arrangement for a set of users such as healthcare providers and allows flexibility in designating the access rights of individual users over the encrypted data. In this paper, we study and analyze the suitability of Key-Policy Attribute-Based Encryption scheme (KP-ABE) and Ciphertext-Policy Attribute-Based Encryption scheme (CP-ABE) on BSN. Then we conclude that Key-Policy Attribute-Based Encryption (KP-ABE) is preferable for designing a lightweight ABE for BSN to be implemented in low power and computing devices to fulfill all the security requirements.

Keywords: Attribute-base encryption, body sensor networks, cryptology.

1   Introduction

The advances of today's computing technologies as well as the wireless sensor networks have brought remarkable progress on current electronic healthcare. Electronic healthcare device such as the body sensor network (BSN) [1-3] is built on human body in order to collect vital signs. This set of sensors allows healthcare providers to monitor the health condition of remotely located patients via communication networks [4-7]. The collected vital signs will be stored and shared by any medical people at server sites. The servers should be robust enough to protect the privacy and confidentiality of patients' data. Therefore, these data need to be encrypted before sending and storing at any other server sites. There are two sections where the encryption can be applied as shown in Fig. 1. One (first section) is between each vital sign sensor and low computation mobile device and the other (second section) is between low computation mobile device and remote server site. However, data sent from each vital sign sensor to the low computation mobile device are simple raw data without any personal information so that no complicated encryption is

A. Abd Manaf et al. (Eds.): ICIEIS 2011, Part I, CCIS 251, pp. 238–247, 2011.
© Springer-Verlag Berlin Heidelberg 2011

required. However, at low computation mobile device, all data from vital signs are fused and relevant data to identify patient will be added. Therefore, fused vital signs encryption between the low computation mobile device and remote server is significantly important. In this paper we discuss the data encryption for the second section.

Sharing of encrypted data at fine-grained level allows authorized personnel to access certain pieces of data from the full encrypted data. For example, in a hospital or even ubiquitously, doctors should have the access right to view all his/her responsible patients' medical information but nurses can only have limited access right to the patients' general information such as name, address and etc. Thus, in this paper, Attribute-Based Encryption (ABE) is discussed for data encryption as it allows fine-grained encryption with future expandability for data. Our contributions in this paper are providing comprehensive study and analysis of suitability of KP-ABE and CP-ABE on BSN as well as making the comparisons between the 2 schemes.

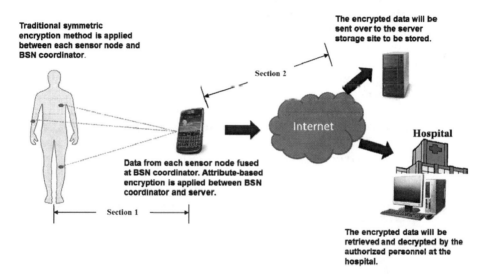

Fig. 1. Body Sensor Network (BSN)

2   Background

In 1984, Shamir proposed an idea of constructing a public encryption scheme where the public key can be an arbitrary string [8]. The use of Identity-Based Encryption scheme (IBE) was proposed in order to allow user to encrypt data and send the encrypted data to another user through an unsecure channel without the use of public key certificates as in the traditional public encryption scheme.

After the idea of IBE was proposed in 1984, Boneh and Franklin came up with the first secure and practical IBE in year 2001 [9]. In 2005, Sahai and Water [10] introduced the concept of Fuzzy-Identity Based Encryption (FIBE). In the IBE system, identities are viewed as a string of characters. As for FIBE, identities are viewed as a set of descriptive attributes. In an FIBE scheme, a user with the secret key corresponding to a set of identity, *ID* will only able to decrypt a ciphertext encrypted with the public key, *ID'* if and only if *ID* and *ID'* overlap each other by some metric, *d* which allows a certain amount of error tolerance in the identities. The work of Sahai and Water in FIBE also bring forth to the application of Attribute-Based Encryption (ABE).

In 2006, Goyal et al. introduced the Key-Policy Attribute Based Encryption (KP-ABE) for fine-grained sharing of encrypted data [11]. Fine-grained sharing of encrypted data allows different authorized users to remotely retrieve and decrypt different pieces of encrypted data from the server site based on the access policy. In KP-ABE cryptosystem, ciphertexts are labeled with sets of attributes and private keys are associated with access policy that controls for which ciphertexts a user is allowed to decrypt. This system facilitates granting different access rights to a set of users. It also allows flexibility in specifying the access rights of each user. Therefore, while the data is stored in the server in an encrypted form, different users can still manage to decrypt different pieces of data corresponding to the security policy.

Ciphertext-Policy Attribute-Based Encryption (CP-ABE) on the other hand is another type of ABE proposed by Bethencourt et al. [12]. In CP-ABE, the private keys are labeled with sets of attributes while the ciphertexts are associated with the access policy. A user can encrypt a data with a specific access policy, defining types of receivers who will be able to decrypt the ciphertext. Any users who possess sets of attributes may obtain their corresponding secret attribute keys from the third party, private key generator (PKG). In order for that user to decrypt the message, his/her particular user's attributes must satisfy the access policy associated to the ciphertext. Table 1 summarizes terminology definition in this section.

Table 1. Terminology List

Terminology	Definition
Attribute	Identities/characteristics of a person
Access Policy	Policy to define which ciphertext an authorized user is able to decrypt
Private Key Generator	A trusted third party who handles the issuance of private key

3 Algorithms

This section shows the algorithms of KP-ABE scheme [11] and CP-ABE scheme [12].

3.1 Definition of KP-ABE Scheme

The KP-ABE scheme consists of four algorithms.

- Setup (1^k): The setup algorithm takes as input a security parameter, 1^k and outputs the public parameters, *PK* and a master key, *msk* which is known only to the private key generator (PKG).

- Enc (m, PK, γ): The encryption algorithm takes as input a message, m, a set of attributes, γ and the public parameters, PK. It outputs the ciphertext, c.
- KeyGen $(PK, \text{msk}, \mathbb{A})$: The key generation algorithm takes as input the public parameters, PK, the master key, msk and an access policy, $\mathbb{A}$. It outputs the private key, $D_{\mathbb{A}}$.
- Dec $(c, PK, D_{\mathbb{A}})$: The decryption algorithm takes as input the ciphertext, c which was encrypted under the set of attributes, γ, the public key parameters, PK and the private key, $D_{\mathbb{A}}$ for access control structure, $\mathbb{A}$. It outputs the message m if $\gamma \in \mathbb{A}$.

3.2   Definition of CP-ABE Scheme

The CP-ABE scheme consists of four algorithms.

- Setup (1^k): The setup algorithm takes as input a security parameter, 1^k and outputs the public parameters, PK and a master key, msk which is known only to the private key generator (PKG).
- Enc $(m, PK, \mathbb{A})$: The encryption algorithm takes as input a message, m, an access policy, $\mathbb{A}$, and the public parameters, PK. It outputs the ciphertext, c.
- KeyGen (PK, msk, γ): The key generation algorithm takes as input the public parameters, PK, the master key, msk and a set of attributes, γ. It outputs the private key, D_{γ}.
- Dec (c, PK, D_{γ}): The decryption algorithm takes as input the ciphertext, c which was encrypted with an access policy, $\mathbb{A}$, the public key parameters, PK and the private key, D_{γ}. It outputs the message, m if the set of attributes, γ, satisfies the access policy, $\mathbb{A}$.

4   Comparison between KP-ABE and CP-ABE

In this section, we will discuss comparisons between KP-ABE and CP-ABE in terms of the encryption efficiency, access control, assignment of attribute and access policy and hardware implementation.

4.1   Encryption Efficiency

In order to secure the privacy of the patients' data, data have to be encrypted before sending over to the remote server sites to be stored. The vital sign in the encrypted form however, limits the sharing of data among different users (i.e. healthcare provider). Therefore, it is essential to design a selective sharing of the encrypted data at a fine-grained level.

Both KP-ABE and CP-ABE schemes are able to share encrypted data at fine-grained level. Therefore, authorized parties are able to retrieve and decrypt selected pieces of the encrypted vital sign based on the specified attributes and security policy. Users need to register themselves to a third party key generator (PKG) before they are able to request and retrieve any private key. The PKG then will have to manage the information of the registered users in order to issue the right private keys according to their authorities as shown in Fig. 2. PKG also needs to handle the management of the key issued.

In KP-ABE, attributes are being encrypted in the vital signs and access policy is embedded in the private key. Therefore, the PKG plays an important role in private key issuing with embedded access policy to the authorized user. In another words, patients need to fully trust the PKG in term of key issuance and management. If the PKG itself is compromised by non-authorized user, the confidentiality of the patients together with their vital signs could be exposed.

On the other hand, in CP-ABE, access policy is embedded in the ciphertext and attributes are embedded in the private key. In CP-ABE, the security and protection of the encrypted vital sign data is mainly based on the access policy which is embedded in the ciphertext. Private key is issued based on attributes of the authorized user. Therefore, patient may embed more specific access policy in the ciphertext in order to limit the number users who are allowed decryption of the vital sign data.

Table 2 shows the responsibility of different parties for the encryption and decryption of vital signs as well as the private key generation. Encryption is done at patient side, either by using attributes (KP-ABE) or access policy (CP-ABE). The encryption by using attributes/access policy is pre-set; we will design in such a way that data will be encrypted based on a standard set of attribute/access policy. Patients can change the attributes/access policy accordingly by the help of a medical agent specializing in this system (i.e. company who sell this product to the patient/healthcare provider). If the patients request to change any attribute/access policy, they will need to consult the medical agent. This is to confirm the change of any encryption attribute/access policy between the medical agent and healthcare provider. Then, the updated equipment will be sent to patient.

In our work, we are going to encrypt the vital signs by using a low computation mobile device. Therefore, it is important that the encryption scheme is lightweight and secure. Therefore, KP-ABE would be more suitable to be used. This is because encryption with attributes requires lower computing complexity and lower power consumption yet provides sufficient security.

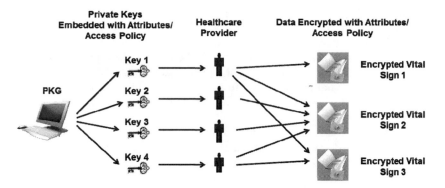

Fig. 2. Key Issuance and Access to Encrypted Data

Table 2. Responsible Parties for Data Encryption and Decryption and Key Generation

ABE	Encryption (Attributes)	Encryption (Access Policy)	Generation of Private Key (Attributes)	Generation of Private Key (Access Policy)	Decryption	Remark
KP-ABE	Patients	-	-	PKG	Healthcare Provider	Assumption made for PKG to be secured and reliable
CP-ABE	-	Patients	PKG	-	Healthcare Provider	It is power consuming and high computing complexity for patients to encrypt access policy in low power and computation device

4.2   Access Control of Data

Healthcare providers of different specialities and level may have different access rights towards the encrypted vital signs. Thus, the access control mechanism should be taken into consideration. KP-ABE as shown in Fig. 3, allows the access control of data to users by assigning the private keys with different access structure. CP-ABE as shown in Fig. 4, allows the access control of data to users by encrypting the vital signs with different access structure. Both schemes can express any monotonic and non-monotonic access structure of "AND", "OR" and "NOT" gate.

In both schemes, users are unable to collude whereby their attributes or access structure cannot be combined with another access data set which they are authorized to access. In order to allow an unauthorized user to access to a certain piece of encrypted data without collusion, delegation of private keys is a desirable feature. Individual users are able to use their private key to generate a more restrictive private key which then can be delegated to another user. This is essential in the area of body sensor network whereby private keys are able to be delegated to another doctor of the same field if the particular doctor is not able to attend to the patient for a period of time.

In KP-ABE, patient may not have full control of the authorized user having the access to his/her vital signs. This is because the private key is assigned to the authorized user by PKG. PKG will issue the private keys to any person who has the authority to have the vital signs access. In CP-ABE, patient can have full control of the authorized user having the access to his/her vital signs as the access policy is embedded in the ciphertext.

For BSN, KP-ABE access control would be sufficient as when the encrypted vital signs are able to be decrypted by any authorized user whose private key's access policy matched the specified attributes in the ciphertext. On the other hand, if the patient take full control of the authorization of the access rights, it could be dangerous if the patient falls into coma and is in a critical condition with the authorized user who is allowed the access of the encrypted vital signs is unable to be contacted. This is because no other party has the authorization to alter his/her access policy. Therefore, KP-ABE access control would be sufficient and secured with assumption that the PKG is secured. Table 3 shows the advantage and disadvantage of the access control between KP-ABE and CP-ABE.

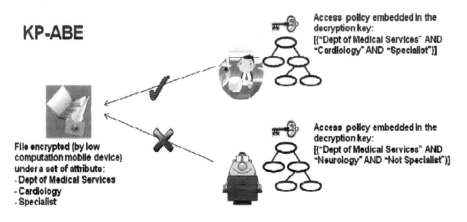

Fig. 3. Key-Policy Attribute-Based Encryption

4.3   Assignment of Attribute and Access Policy

Attributes are the identities or characteristics of a person. For example, "General Doctor", "Specialist", "Kuala Lumpur", "Cardiologist" and etc. Access policy on the other hand is the access structure. For example, {("General Doctor" AND "Specialist") AND ("Kuala Lumpur" OR "Penang") OR "Medical Experience>20years" OR "Name: Dr.Hosanna"}.

All private keys are being issued and managed by the PKG. Therefore, PKG is responsible for the assignment of attributes and access policy which are embedded in the private key. Meanwhile, for the assignment of attributes and access policy embedded in the ciphertext, it is the responsibility of the patients with the assistance from the medical agents.

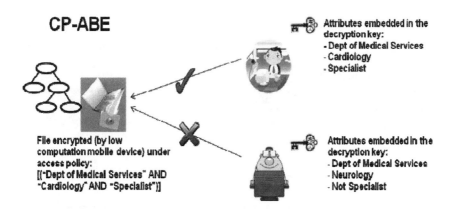

Fig. 4. Ciphertext-Policy Attribute-Based Encryption

Table 3. Advantage and Disadvantage of Access Control

ABE	Advantage	Disadvantage
KP-ABE	Less restriction and limitation place onto the authorized user allowed to decrypt the encrypted vital signs	Patient has no full control of who can access to the data that he/she encrypts, but only by the choice of descriptive attributes used to encrypt the data
CP-ABE	Patient can has full control of the authorized party allowed for data encryption by encrypting the data with the design of specific access policy	More restriction and limitation onto the authorized user allowed to decrypt the encrypted vital signs

Again, KP-ABE scheme would be preferred. This is because assigning attributes by patient with the assistance from medical agents are much simpler than assigning the access policy in the ciphertext. Patient may also be able to alter the attributes accordingly in a more efficient and faster manner than making changes onto the access policy. This is due to the reason that by making a slight mistake of alteration of the access policy may cause a complication in the entire encryption and decryption system.

4.4   Hardware Implementation

The low computation mobile device which is used to collect vital signs from different body sensor nodes has constraint resources (in terms of memory space, computing power, energy, real-time requirement, and etc.).

Thus, the encryption scheme has to be simple, secure and lightweight. In KP-ABE, during the encryption process, attributes are being embedded into the encrypted vital signs. As for CP-ABE, access policy is being embedded into the encrypted vital signs.

Table 4. Comparison of Encryption Efficiency between KP-ABE and CP-ABE

Efficiency	KP-ABE	CP-ABE
Encryption computation time	1 exponentiation for each attribute	2 exponentiations for each leaf in the ciphertext's access tree
Ciphertext size	1 group element for each attribute	2 group elements for each tree leaf

Table 4 shows the efficiency of encryption computation time and ciphertext size [11], [12]. As mentioned above that the hardware has resource constraint, it is essential that the encryption process should be fast and less complicated yet still able to provide sufficient security for the vital sign data. This is to reduce the computing power, thus extending the battery life of the low computation mobile device. It is also important that the ciphertext size should not be too large which would need much storage size and transferring time.

Therefore, KP-ABE scheme would be used as it would realize lightweight encryption and smaller ciphertext size which is suitable for resource constraint condition. For KP-ABE, the high complexity and processing work to embed the access policy in private keys will be done by the PKG. CP-ABE on the other hand, having the drawback of longer encryption computation time and larger ciphertext size. The encryption computation complexity is heavier than KP-ABE because much processing work of encryption is needed due to the embedded access policy in the ciphertext.

5   Conclusion and Future Work

In this paper, the comparison between KP-ABE and CP-ABE is conducted. From the viewpoints of encryption efficiency, access control, assignment of attributes and access control, and hardware implementation, KP-ABE is preferable for the body sensor network. KP-ABE is able to provide simple and secure encryption which grants differential access rights to each patient for data decryption purpose in BSN.

For future work, a new lightweight KP-ABE-based encryption will be designed and developed to confirm its performance of high security and usability by healthcare people.

Acknowledgments. The authors would acknowledge the Universiti Tunku Abdul Rahman Research Fund (UTARRF, Project No.: 6200/G03) and the Malaysia Exploratory Research Grant Scheme (ERGS, Project No.: 4409/G01).

References

1. Lo, B., Thiemjarus, S., King, R., Yang, G.Z.: Body Sensor Network - A Wireless Sensor Platform for Pervasive Healthcare Monitoring. In: Adjunct Proceedings of the 3rd International Conference on Pervasive Computing, pp. 77–80 (2005)
2. Lo, B., Yang, G.Z.: Architecture for Body Sensor Networks. In: IEEE Proceedings of the Perspective in Pervasive Computing, pp. 23–28 (2005)
3. Lo, B., Yang, G.Z.: Key Technical Challenges and Current Implementations of Body Sensor Networks. In: IEEE Proceedings of the 2nd International Workshop on Body Sensor Networks, pp. 1–5 (2005)
4. Istepanian, R.S.H., Jovanov, E., Zhang, Y.T.: Guest Editorial Introduction to the Special Section on M-Health: Beyond Seamless Mobility and Global Wireless Health-Care Connectivity. IEEE Transactions on Information Technology in Biomedicine 8(2) (2004)
5. Tan, C.C., Wang, H., Zhong, S., Li, Q.: IBE-Lite: A Lightweight Identity-Based Cryptography for Body Sensor Networks. IEEE Transactions on Information Technology in Biomedicine 13(6), 926–932 (2009)
6. Singh, K., Muthukkumarasamy, V.: Authenticated key establishment protocols for a home health care system. In: Proceedings of the Third International Conference on Intelligent Sensors, Sensor Networks and Information Processing (2007)
7. Laerhoven, K.V., Lo, B., Ng, J., Thiemjarus, S., King, R., Kwan, S., Gellersen, H.W., Sloman, M., Wells, O., Needham, P., Peters, N., Darzi, A., Toumazou, C., Yang, G.Z.: Medical Healthcare Monitoring with Wearable and Implantable Sensors. In: International Workshop on Ubiquitous Computing for Pervasive Healthcare Applications (2004)
8. Shamir, A.: Identity-Based Cryptosystems and Signature Schemes. In: Blakely, G.R., Chaum, D. (eds.) CRYPTO 1984. LNCS, vol. 196, pp. 47–53. Springer, Heidelberg (1985)
9. Boneh, D., Franklin, M.: Identity-Based Encryption from the Weil Pairing. In: Kilian, J. (ed.) CRYPTO 2001. LNCS, vol. 2139, pp. 213–229. Springer, Heidelberg (2001)
10. Sahai, A., Waters, B.: Fuzzy Identity-Based Encryption. In: Cramer, R. (ed.) EUROCRYPT 2005. LNCS, vol. 3494, pp. 457–473. Springer, Heidelberg (2005)
11. Goyal, V., Pandey, O., Sahai, A., Waters, B.: Attribute Based Encryption for Fine-Grained Access Control of Encrypted Data. In: ACM Conference on Computer and Communications Security, pp. 89–98 (2006)
12. Bethencourt, J., Sahai, A., Waters, B.: Ciphertext-policy attribute-based encryption. In: IEEE Symposium on Security & Privacy, pp. 321–334 (2007)

DNS Request for Normal Minima Length Distribution Based on Reference Matrix

S.N. Omar and M.A. Ngadi

Faculty of Computer Science and Information Systems,
Universiti Teknologi Malaysia, Skudai, Johor, Malaysia
Snizam36@live.utm.my, dr.asri@utm.my

Abstract. Packet length covert channels are the methods to indirect conceal a secret message in the packet. A consideration on the distribution of the packet length in the network is necessary to assure the normal distribution of the packet. An analysis on standard DNS queries within a campus network showed that the distribution range of the packet is between 24 to 63 bytes of length. Hitherto, previous packet length covert channel produce abnormal packet length when the range of the packet length is less than 40. Therefore, this problem motivated the study to propose a novel hidden method based on indirect reference to DNS query to conceal the secret message. The proposed method was experimented against three DNS query sample. The result showed the propose method was within the normal packet length distribution. The contribution of this study was a normal distribution of packet length within a constrain of minima length distribution.

Keywords: covert channels, DNS request, packet lengths.

1   Introduction

Encryption is a method where the readable messages are scrambled to unreadable messages based on a key to protect the information from readable by unauthorized party [1]. However, encryption alone could not protect the confidentiality of the messages because it will attract the attacker to attack the communication channel and decrypt the message [2]. Furthermore, in communication, the encryption itself raises suspicion and triggers further investigation action [3] and knowing there exist a communication between two parties is already valuable information to the attacker [4]. Therefore, this motivates the study to use covert channels to deliver a secret message.

Covert channels are a technique used to hide the message in packets [5]. Covert channels are the desirable's choices because it hidden the information in a stealth manner and did not leave a trail because the packets are a volatile medium [6]. Moreover, the quantity of data that could be moving through Covert Channel per annually could be as much as 26GB of data, although the data being moved one bit at a time [7].

A. Abd Manaf et al. (Eds.): ICIEIS 2011, Part I, CCIS 251, pp. 248–258, 2011.

In essence, the ways the data is hide in the packets have the strong correlations with the stealthiest of the covert channel [8]. Indirect technique substituted the symbols with the property of the packets whereas the direct technique directly embeds the data into the field of the packet [9]. The rest of study in this paper is based on indirect method refer to packet lengths.

Packet lengths are the covert channels based on indirect method. Packet lengths have been studies by Padlipsky [10], Girling [11], Yao [12] and Liping [8]. However, their method produced abnormal packet length when compare to normal packet length distribution. The previous method required a network with substantial minimum and max length different. In contrast, when the sample of DNS packet length was taken an on-campus network, the study found that, the different was very minima, around 39 different lengths. With 39 different lengths, it is not feasible for the previous message length covert channels to produce normal length distributions when the size of the message is larger than 64 bytes.

The contributions of this paper are a normal distribution of the length within the campus network with a long secret message that is difficult to be detected under length frequency analysis or statistical test.

2   Related Work

Padlipsky introduced packet lengths' covert channels in [10]. Padlipsky associated the lengths of link layer frames with a symbol to conceal the secret message. Shortly, Girling realized Padlipsky's idea in [11]. Girling represented the length of the link layer with 256 symbols. Which, the method required 256 different packet lengths, and each packet length represents a byte's of information. The experiment was done in an isolated network to eliminate the noise of other packets such as buffering, reblocking and spurious message insertion from a high-level protocol. In real networks, the controls of block size and packet length are actually being modulated and depend on the network conditions [13]. Conveniently, Padlipsky method could be very effective within the same network segment.

Later, Yao and Zhang in [12] used a secret matrix with 256 rows and randomly associated it with the length of packets. The arrangement of the length in the matrix will be transformed according to the agreement between the sender and receiver. The Yao and Zhang method has successfully improved the Girling. However, a study by Liping in [8] shown that, the randomly packet length will trigger the detection because it produced abnormal network traffic.

To overcome the abnormal network traffic, Liping in [8] proposed a method based on a reference of length. Liping's method required the sender and receiver to agree upon the length of the packets that the sender sent to the receiver. The agreeable length of several packets is set as a default reference. To send a secret message, the sender takes the byte of the message and adds it to the length of the reference. To get the byte of the message, the receiver will deduce the received length with the initial reference. However, as mention by Liping in [8], this method was not efficient when the size of the message is long because the method will update the default reference with every length it received.

Other noble works in covert channels such as IP were done in [14], [15] and [16], ICMP in [17], [2]and [18], DNS in [19] and [20], TCP in [14], [21]and [22] and VOIP in [23] and [24].

3   The Design of DNS Reference Covert Channel (DRCC)

The study subdivided the entire process into the method similar to OSI model for better understanding as follows:

- Level 0; Starting from Alice's side, Clear Message (M) is a readable message that Alice wished to send to Bob.
- Level 1; Alice's M is encrypted (Em) with a block cipher algorithm and stored the Em in the queue.
- Level 2; The indirect algorithm will associate the corresponding Em with standard URL name. It then generated the Stego-packet (Sp) and stored into a buffer.
- Level 3; The Sp will be injected into the network that will passes through the protection network as normal DNS query packets.
- Level 3; On the Bob side, all received packets will be picking up and stored in memory stack.
- Level 2; Indirect Detection module will determine the correct Sp. The correct Sp will be processed and the byte of the message will be stored until the end of the flow control is found.
- Level 1; Together with the Sk, the Decryption Decoder will decode Em recover M.
- Level 0 if the Em is successfully decoded, Bob will be able to read the M which sent by Alice.

3.1   Proposed Indirect Method

The DNS reference covert channel (DRCC) is based on URL name to represent the Base 16 values. The URL name could be any agreeable URL name that is normally used in the network where the senders reside. The preferable solutions are to choose the URL that normally requested by the clients in the network. Importantly, the DNS queried datagram should not exceed 300 bytes and 512 bytes as stated in [25]. Albeit, there are certain condition which allow the DNS query to specify the response datagram can exceed 512 bytes by using the OPT Resource Record [26]. However, as stated in [27] the length of the URL should not exceed 140 bytes.

The indirect module will process the Em in block size of 4 bits. For each block, the module will find the corresponding Base 16 values. The row of the corresponding Base 16 is the current number of block being processed. Notes that, the module determined the row of the reference based on the result of the number of the block mod with 16. Consequently, the value will be in between 0 to 15. This value is the row that the process will find the corresponding position of Based 16 value. Once the value of Base 16 is found in column[n] and row[n], the module will generate the DNS packets with corresponding URL name and store in stack. The process of covert the Em to corresponding URL name will end when all the byte in the Em has been processed.

4   Experiment

The proposed indirect algorithm was tested based on the URL name collected from campus network. The proposed schema was compared with five different sizes of a message.

4.1   Dataset

The DNS data set was collected on-campus network. The study used tcpdump to collect the packets. Table 1 shows the three samples that have been captured on three times. The group lengths are base on the UDP packet length analysis. The range of the packet length is in 4 bytes, based on the number of bytes in one row of the protocol header. The study found that, minimum packet length was 25, which appear in samples B and C. This is actually a minimum DNS query based on a character. However, there are a number of characters of the DNS query, which is not advisable to be exploits for covert channels unless as a command and control.

Table 1. The campus DNS packets in percentages of range of length

DNS Samples		A	B	C
Number of Packets		34607	398067	649962
Length Range (%)	24-27	0.000	0.002	0.001
	28-31	0.029	0.208	0.190
	32-35	0.220	1.421	1.632
	36-39	48.905	12.303	10.293
	40-43	11.218	23.879	25.117
	44-47	12.943	29.318	30.459
	48-51	5.788	14.209	17.789
	52-55	9.692	11.153	8.688
	56-59	10.414	5.800	4.195
	60-63	0.792	1.709	1.637

Sample A has about 34,607 thousand standard DNS query, which a large amount of the DNS query is in the range of 36-39, 40-43, 44-47,48-51,52-55 and 56-59. Sample B has 398,067 thousand standard DNS query packets with average packets query in the range 36-39, 40-43, 44-47,48-51,52-55 and 56-59. Sample C has about 649,962 thousand standard DNS query packets which most of the query in the range of 36-39, 40-43, 44-47, 48-51, 52-55 and 56-59.

The most important point with this data, the number of the standard length that could be used for covert channels is only 39 of different ranges. This means, the covert channels will have only about 39 different lengths to be manipulated and not to exceed 63 bytes lengths. Moreover, the majority of the DNS packets in each sample's are in the range of 36 to 51 bytes. With the range from 36 to 51, it only provides 15 different lengths to be manipulated for covert channels. Therefore, the propose covert channels should make sure the number of the URL names are according to the average packets size as in Table 1. Otherwise, its will show an abnormality in the networks. Albeit, it could be tolerated to say that, it should be normal for the covert channels with plus or minus 5 percent of the average packet length in between 36 to 59.

4.2   Experiment Setup

The implementation of the proposed covert channel was done using the winpcap library to send and capture the standard DNS query. To capture the packets for the purpose to be validated, evaluated and monitor, the study used Ethereal and Wireshark. There are five secret messages of different lengths for the experiment. The sizes of the secret messages before encryptions are 64, 128, 256, 512 and 1024 bytes. The message was encrypted using 256 block cipher algorithm with shared key. The size of the secret message after encrypted was 88, 172, 344, 684 and 1368 bytes. The Oracle Virtual Box was used to running the operating systems with 100Mbps internet speed

4.3   Experiment Results

The experiment results were discussed based on the percentages of packet lengths, graph of normal frequency distribution of the DNS packet lengths and T-test.

4.3.1   Comparison of Length Percentages in Group of Length Range

Table 2 shows the result of the different message size and the number of DNS query required by the covert channels to deliver the secret messages. To deliver 64 bytes of a message, proposes covert channels required 356 packets. The 356 packets are the formation of four packets for the mark of start and end of covert channels packet, and 352 packets for the cipher message which are the embedded of 4 bits in one packets and for each 4 bits, there is redundant DNS query packets to formulate the normal DNS query. The formations of the covert channels packets are same for all message length as shown in Table 2. The results in Table 2 shown that, for every message length, there are no packets being generated by the proposed covert channels' schema because the chosen of the URL names was based on the packet lengths from 36 to 63.

This is because, based on the analysis in Table 1, on samples A, there is less than 0.2% of packet length in the range from 24 to 35, which, if the URL name being chosen in the range of 24 to 35, could expose the covert channels because the number of the packets in that range is very small. However, this doesn't mean the proposed

Table 2. The campus DNS packets in percentages of range of length

Size of Message		64	128	256	512
Size of Cipher		88	345	689	1369
Number of Packets		356	692	1380	2740
	24-27	0.000	0.000	0.000	0.000
	28-31	0.000	0.000	0.000	0.000
	32-35	0.000	0.000	0.000	0.000
	36-39	14.045	12.428	10.145	10.292
Length Range (%)	40-43	25.281	26.879	29.710	30.803
	44-47	33.708	34.104	29.565	29.489
	48-51	14.607	15.896	18.696	17.810
	52-55	8.989	8.092	9.710	9.635
	56-59	1.124	1.156	0.870	0.876
	60-63	2.247	1.445	1.304	1.095

covert channels packets are abnormal than normal DNS query packets. The proposed covert channel actually was normal based on the result comparison of percentages of packet length as shown in Fig 1. It shows that, there were normal when compared to percentages of packet length in campus B and C. Albeit, the proposed covert channels could be abnormal when compare to sample A, the proposed covert channels still normal because the covert channels' packet lengths are within the packet length range.

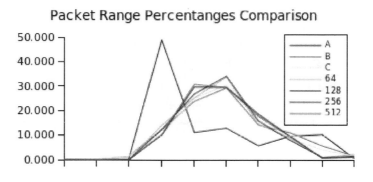

Fig. 1. Overall Packet Range Percentages Comparison

4.3.2 Comparison of Frequency Distribution

The study further analyzes the covert channels' packet lengths for different size of a message with normal campus packets for the purposes to evaluate the packet length on a different angle, to further see, whether the covert channels' packet lengths abnormal or normal when compare to sample packet length taken from campus network. The comparison was done by looking on the frequency of the packet starting from the minimum length to the max length. The same amounts of packets from the campus network were taken for comparison according to the exactly amount need by covert packets for each message size.

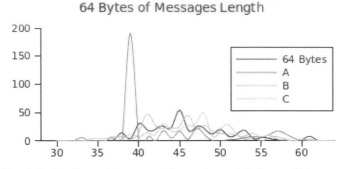

Fig. 2. Packet Range Percentages Comparison of 64 Bytes of Message

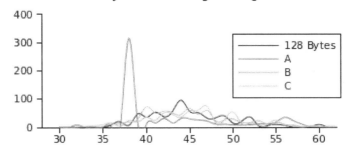

Fig. 3. Packet Range Percentages Comparison of 128 Bytes of Message

Fig 2, 3, 4, and 5 depict the frequency of proposes covert channels' packets for different message length to campus network with the length frequency starting from 28 to 64. The x-axis denoted the packet length while the y-axis denoted the occurrence of the packet in that particular length. The chart in Fig 2, 3, 4, and 5 shown clearly that the frequent length peak of the proposed covert channel was according to the percentages' length range as illustrated in Table 2, which is between 43to 47 for every message length.

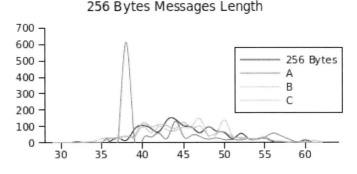

Fig. 4. Packet Range Percentages Comparison of 256 Bytes of Message

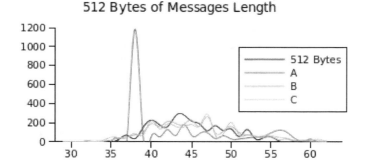

Fig. 5. Packet Range Percentages Comparison of 512 Bytes of Message

This peak was also according to the normal campus length of B and C as shown in Table 1. Moreover, the frequent length of each proposed covert messages in the range of 36 to 39, 48 to 51, 52 to 55, 56 to 59 and 60 to 63 as shown in Fig 2, 3, 4, and 5 are according to the normal percentages' campus ranges of B and C as shown in Table 1. Therefore, the result of the frequency comparison between proposed covert message are aligned with the result of percentage's comparison as depict in Fig 1 proof that the proposed covert channel a normal to the normal campus B and C. Albeit, there is slightly different when compare to samples A. However, this not affects the effectiveness of the proposed covert channel if the comparison is done on the range above 40.

4.3.3 Statistical T-test

T-test is used to measure the significant different in the distributions of the test data. The null hypothesis in this study is the proposed length result is same with the sample length result. The t-test calculations are performing on all the packets that the study captures on the particular message length. Example, to transfer 64 bytes of a message, the proposed covert channels required 365 packets. Thus, the length of every packet in 365 packets is stored read and store in excel. Then, the same amount of packets was also read from samples A, B and C. Then, the proposed covert channels' length was compared to samples A, B and C. The T-test results for each message length are presented in Table 3, 4, 5 and 6.

Table 3. The T-test on 64 bytes of messages

Comparison against P	T-stat	T-crit	P-value	Decision
A and P	4.64	1.96	0.000004	Do not accept H_o
B and P	1.15	1.96	0.25	Accept H_o
C and P	1.92	1.96	0.06	Accept H_o

The result in Table 3 shown that, there is no significant statistic that the proposed covert channels produce abnormal length when compare to samples B and C. Albeit, there is the weak significant statistic when compare to C. Based on the chart in Fig 2, this is probably come from the different frequency peak. The proposed covert channel was peak on 45 whereas the sample C was peaked at 47 to 48.

Table 4. The T-test on 128 bytes of messages

Comparison against P	T-stat	T-crit	P-value	Decision
A and P	4.95	1.96	0.000004	Do not accept H_o
B and P	1.57	1.96	0.12	Accept H_o
C and P	4.92	1.96	0.00000007	Do not accept H_o

The result shown in Table 4 is about the significant different of the proposed covert channel length distribution against sample the A, B and C in sending 128 bytes of a message. The results show that, there is no significant different between sample B and the proposed covert channel length distribution. However, there is a significant distribution of packet length when compare to sample A and C.

Table 5. The T-test on 256 bytes of messages

Comparison against P	T-stat	T-crit	P-value	Decision
A and P	8.32	1.96	1.4E-16	Do not accept H_o
B and P	0.66	1.96	0.51	Accept H_o
C and P	1.38	1.96	0.17	Accept H_o

The result shown in Table 5 is about the significant different of the proposed covert channel length distribution against the sample A, B and C in sending 256 bytes of a message. The result shows that there is no significant different between the normal packet length distribution of samples B and C when compare to the proposed covert channels' packet length distribution. However, there is a significant different of all samples when the comparison was done on 512 bytes of messages as shown in Table 6. Albeit, this weakness didn't effect if the message is not encrypted before sent, as shown in Table 2, for 256 bytes of messages, there is about 689 bytes of data has been successful sent with distribution normality achieve when compare to sample B and C. Therefore, supports by the T-test result on the different size of a message, the proposed covert channel has proven to be normal in the distribution of the packet length against the different sample taken from campus network.

Table 6. The T-test on 512 bytes of messages

Comparison against P	T-stat	T-crit	P-value	Decision
A and P	8.4	1.96	5.33E-17	Do not accept H_o
B and P	2.85	1.96	0.04	Do not accept H_o
C and P	4.81	1.96	7.76E-07	Do not accept H_o

4.3.4 Bandwidth

The bandwidth of the cover channels could be calculated based on the formula proposed by Girling [11] as follows:

$$T = S + 8 * B+N/V \tag{1}$$

C = H / T, Where
T = Time to transmit a message;
S = Time used in software; independent of message size;
B = Size of transmitted message;
N = Size of network protocol overhead;
V = Network Speed;
H = the number of bits hidden in each message.

In this study, the size of the average transmitted message is B = 37 bytes (DNS minus UDP header); the size of the network overhead N = 42 bytes (14 bytes of Ethernet header + 20 bytes of IP header + 8 bytes of UDP header); the network speed V = 100 Mbps. S = 8.76 msec based on the assumption make by Kamran in [16]. Therefore, the bandwidth of the covert channel is estimated to be 60 bps (C = 4 bits * T = 15.08).

5   Conclusion

In this research, the study had proposed a novel covert channel based on message length that is normal to packet length distribution within the minima distribution of length, that is lest than 40. The experiments show that the proposed covert channel was resistant to frequency length analysis and statistical test on a different sample taken from campus network.

References

1. Frikha, L., Trabelsi, Z.: A new covert channel in WIFI networks. In: Risks and Security of Internet and Systems (CRISIS 2008), pp. 255–260 (2008)
2. Trabelsi, Z., El-Hajj, W.: Implementation of an ICMP-based covert channel for file and message transfer. In: Proceedings of the 15th IEEE International Conference on Electronics, Circuits and Systems, ICECS 2008, pp. 894–897 (2008)
3. Armitage, G., Branch, P., Zander, S.: Covert channels in multiplayer first person shooter online games. In: 33rd IEEE Conference on Local Computer Networks, Montreal, Que, pp. 215–222 (2008)
4. El-Atawy, A., Al-Shaer, E.: Building covert channels over the packet reordering phenomenon. In: INFOCOM, pp. 2186–2194 (2009)
5. Desoky, A.: List-based steganography methodology. International Journal of Information Security 8, 247–261 (2009)
6. Lubacz, J., Mazurczyk, W., Szczypiorski, K.: Vice over IP. IEEE Spectrum 47, 42–47 (2010)

7. Fisk, G., Fisk, M., Papadopoulos, C., Neil, J.: Eliminating steganography in Internet traffic with active wardens. Information Hiding 22 (2002)
8. Ji, L., Jiang, W., Dai, B., Niu, X.: A novel covert channel based on length of messages. In: International Symposium on Information Engineering and Electronic Commerce, IEEC 2009, pp. 551–554 (2009)
9. Khan, H., Javed, M., Khayam, S.A., Mirza, F.: Designing a cluster-based covert channel to evade disk investigation and forensics. Computers and Security 30, 35–49 (2011)
10. Padlipsky, M.A., Snow, D.W., Karger, P.A.: Limitations of end-to-end encryption in secure computernNetworks. Tech. Rep. ESD-TR-78- (1978)
11. Girling, C.: Covert channels in LAN's. IEEE Transactions on Software Engineering, SE-13, 292–296 (1987)
12. Yao, Q., Zhang, P.: Coverting channel based on packet length. Computer Engineering 34 (2008)
13. Armitage, G., Branch, P., Zander, S.: An empirical evaluation of IP time to live covert channels. In: Proceedings of IEEE International Conference on Networks (ICON), pp. 42–47 (2007)
14. Rowland, C.: Covert channels in the TCP/IP protocol suite. Tech. rep., First Monday. ACM Transactions on Information and Systems Security 12, Article 22 (1997)
15. Mehta, Y.: Communication over the Internet using covert channels (2005), https://www.cs.drexel.edu/~vp/CS743/Papers/ypm23-hw2.pdf
16. Ahsan, K., Kundur, D.: Practical data hiding in TCP/IP. In: Proceedings of the Workshop on Multimedia Security at ACM Multimedia, pp. 63–70 (2002)
17. Ray, B., Mishra, S.: A protocol for building secure and reliable covert channel. In: Proceedings of the 2008 Sixth Annual Conference on Privacy, Security and Trust, pp. 246–253. IEEE Computer Society, Washington, DC, USA (2008)
18. Zelenchuk, I.: Skeeve - ICMP Bounce Tunnel (2004)
19. Gil, T.M.: IP-over-DNS using NSTX (2005)
20. Kaminsky, D.: IP-over-DNS using Ozyman (2004)
21. Rutkowska, J.: The implementation of passive covert channels in the Linux kernel. In: Proc. Chaos Communication Congress (December 2004)
22. Murdoch, S.J., Lewis, S.: Embedding covert channels into TCP/IP. In: The 7th Information Hiding Workshop, pp. 247–261 (2005)
23. Mazurczyk, W., Lubacz, J.: LACK—a VoIP steganographic method. Telecommunication Systems (2009)
24. Mazurczyk, W., Szczypiorski, K.: Steganography of VoIP Streams. In: Chung, S. (ed.) OTM 2008, Part II. LNCS, vol. 5332, pp. 1001–1018. Springer, Heidelberg (2008)
25. Hoeflin, D., Meier-Hellstern, K., Karasaridis, A.: NIS04-2: Detection of DNS anomalies using flow data analysis. In: Global Telecommunications Conference, pp. 1–6 (2006)
26. Vixie, P.: Extension mechanisms for DNS, EDNS0 (1999)
27. Neyron, P., Richard, O., Nussbaum, L.: On robust covert channels inside DNS. In: 24th IFIP International Security Conference, Pafos, Cyprus, pp. 51–62 (2009)

Realizing Proxy Re-encryption
in the Symmetric World

Amril Syalim, Takashi Nishide, and Kouichi Sakurai

Department of Informatics, Kyushu University, Fukuoka, Japan
amr@itslab.csce.kyushu-u.ac.jp, {nishide,sakurai}@inf.kyushu-u.ac.jp

Abstract. Proxy re-encryption is a useful concept and many proxy re-encryption schemes have been proposed in the asymmetric encryption setting. In the asymmetric encryption setting, proxy re-encryption can be beautifully implemented because many operations are available to directly transform a cipher to another cipher without the proxy needs to access the plaintexts. However, in many situations, for a better performance, the data is encrypted using symmetric ciphers. Most symmetric ciphers do not support proxy cryptography because of malleability (that is needed to implement the proxy re-encryption) is not a desired property in a secure encryption scheme. In this paper, we suggest an idea to implement a pure proxy re-encryption for the symmetric ciphers by first transforming the plaintext into a random sequence of blocks using an All or nothing transform (AONT). We show an example of the proxy re-encryption scheme using a weak encryption (i.e. simple permutation) that has a simple conversion function to convert a permutation to another. The encryption scheme exploits three characteristics of an AONT transformation: (1) the output of an AONT is a pseudorandom, (2) the output of an AONT cannot be transformed back if any parts is missing, and (3) the output of an AONT cannot be transformed back without having all blocks with correct position. We show security argument of the proposed scheme and its performance evaluation.

Keywords: Database Encryption, Symmetric Key Encryption, Proxy Re-encryption, All or Nothing Transform (AONT).

1   Introduction

Proxy cryptography is a useful concept that can be applied in many contexts. An example is when a data owner store his/her data in a server in the Internet so that the data can be accessed from anywhere at anytime. Although this model has many advantages, the data owner should consider the security of his/her confidential data, because without additional security mechanisms an attacker (who breaks the security of the server) and also the database administrator can do anything to the data: accessing, updating or removing the data.

The data owner can implement an access control mechanism to secure their data. The access control mechanism is normally implemented by a trusted reference monitor in the server that intercepts access to the data. In an untrusted

A. Abd Manaf et al. (Eds.): ICIEIS 2011, Part I, CCIS 251, pp. 259–274, 2011.
© Springer-Verlag Berlin Heidelberg 2011

server, this solution is not convenient and cost-heavy because the data owner needs to install a trusted hardware in the server securely.

The access control can also be implemented by using cryptography (encryption mechanism). This method is convenient because the data owner does not need to interact with the data service provider (to set up a trusted hardware). The data owner encrypts the sensitive data and stores the encrypted data in the server. The data owner can share the data (granting access) to other users accessing the database by providing the encryption keys.

However, there are some inflexibilities with the encryption solution and access granting by providing the encryption keys. A user who has the encryption key can always decrypt the data–although the user's access right has been revoked. To completely revoke the access of the user, the data owner needs to re-encrypt the data with a new key. Using a naive solution, re-encryption is a costly computation, because basically the data owner needs to download the data, decrypt the data and encrypt with the new key and then upload the data to the database.

A promising solution is by securely delegating re-encryption mechanism to a proxy in the database server. Before re-encryption, the owner only needs to send a re-encryption key to the proxy. The proxy re-encrypt the data without the need to decrypt any parts of the data. The proxy should be a semi-trusted party: it should execute the protocol correctly even though we do not trust the proxy accessing unencrypted data.

To implement the proxy re- encryption, we need to find a function that translates the ciphertext from one key to another key without having to access the plaintext. In a symmetric encryption setting, a solution is by encrypting the data using a two layers symmetric encryption [5]. Re-encryption is performed only in the second layer encryption, however, to re-encrypt the data, the proxy needs to execute two costly computations: decrypt and then encrypt.

There are many solutions for proxy re-encryption in the public-key world [1,4,8,11]. The problem with these schemes is the schemes cannot be applied directly to the database because, for performance reason, the database is normally encrypted using symmetric key encryption. The public-key proxy re-encryption can be efficiently used to re-encrypt the private key that is used to encrypt the data with the symmetric ciphers [1]. However, this scheme has a weakness, because re-encrypting the key does not update the actual key used to encrypt data (the key of the symmetric encryption), so the users who has the previous key can use the same key to decrypt the data. For example, the data is encrypted with a private key SK. To protect the SK, it is encrypted with the owner public key PK_O. The owner grants access to another user (for instance the user A) by re-encrypting SK using the user A's public key PK_A, so now user A can decrypt the private key SK using his/her private key. After somewhile, the owner revokes user A's access by re-encrypting the SK using another key that cannot be decrypted by the user A (i.e. the key is re-encrypted with the user B's public key).

As shown in the above example, the actual secret key SK remains the same. The public-key re-encryption scheme is only used to re-encrypt the key but not the data. In the above example, the user A can always access data because he has SK even though the SK has been re-encrypted for another user. To fully revoke the user A access we need to update SK with a new key not known by the user A.

Contributions of this paper: It is desirable to have the symmetric encryption scheme that can directly convert one cipher to another. However, to be able to re-encrypt one cipher directly to another, we need to have a one-way function which output can be transformed meaningfully (i.e. malleability [7])– the properties that are removed from currently wide used practical one-way function (i.e. SHA or AES)[1]. We suggest a feasible solution by first transforming the data using an All or Nothing Transform (AONT) and exploits some of its characteristics to implement efficient proxy re-encryptions schemes[2]. Those useful characteristics are [6,12]: (1) the output of an AONT is a pseudorandom (so that the probability to find the same output for two different blocks are small), (2) the output of an AONT can only be transformed back if we have all blocks with correct position, and (3) the output of an AONT cannot be transformed back if any parts is missing. By exploiting those characteristics, we can develop a symmetric cipher proxy re-encryption scheme that is weak if is used with general input plaintext, but it is strong if the input is transformed with an AONT.

2   Related Works

There are many solutions for proxy re-encryption in the asymmetric encryption world. A seminal paper by Blaze et al. [3] proposes a bidirectional proxy re-encryption based on El- Gamal's encryption. The scheme works for a generator g of a group prime order q, the private key $sk_a = a$ is a randomly selected element of $\mathbb{Z}_q^*$ and the public key pk_a is g^a. The ciphertext c_a for the message m is $(g^r.m, g^{ar})$ that can be decrypted back using the private key a to get the plaintext $m = \frac{g^r.m}{(g^{ar})^{1/a}}$. A proxy can directly convert c_a to ciphertext c_b (for the private key $sk_b = b \in \mathbb{Z}_q^*$ and public key $pk_b = g^b$) using a re-encryption key $rk_{a \to b} = b/a$. This re-encryption is possible because $c_b = (g^r.m, (g^{ar})^{b/a})$. This scheme is bidirectional, because the proxy can also compute $rk_{b \to a} = a/b$ and if the proxy colludes with one of the users, they can recover the private key of the other user (i.e. $(a/b) * b = a$).

Many schemes are proposed to improve the Blaze et al.'s scheme [1,4,8,11]. An example is the work of Atenise et al. [1] that uses pairing. The scheme works for bilinear map $e : \mathbb{G}_1 \times \mathbb{G}_1 \Rightarrow \mathbb{G}_2$ with system parameter the random

---

[1] We show the argument in the full version of the paper that can be accessed from
   http://itslab.csce.kyushu-u.ac.jp/~amr/index.html

[2] We can also implement more efficient proxy re-encryption using asymmetric ciphers by only encrypting a small part of AONT transforms. However, this scheme has a weakness because the previous users may store this small encrypted part and use it for decrypting the message even if the encryption key in the actual data has been changed.

generator $g \in \mathbb{G}_1$ and $Z = e(g,g) \in \mathbb{G}_2$. The public key of the first user is $pk_a = (Z^{a1}, g^{a2})$ and the private key is $sk_a = (a_1, a_2)$. The encrypted form of a message $m \in \mathbb{G}_2$ is $c_a = (g^r, m.Z^{ra_1})$ for random $r \in Z_q$. The proxy can convert c_a to another ciphertext using the pairing property $(e(g_1^a, g_2^b) = e(g_1, g_2)^{ab})$ by computing $c_b = (e(g^r, g^{a_1 b}), m.Z^{ra_1}) = (Z^{br'}, m.Z^{r'})$, for $r' = a_1 r$ so that it can be decrypted by a second user with public key $pk_b = g^b$ and the private key is $sk_a = b$ to get $m = \frac{(m.Z^{r'})}{(Z^{br'})1/b}$.

Cook et al. [5] showed that the symmetric ciphers that are closed under functional composition [10] (i.e. for encryption E and message m, there exists encryption keys k_1, k_2, k_3 so that $E_{k_3}(m) = E_{k_2}(E_{k_1}(m)))$ has a security weakness because it is vulnerable to known plaintext attack only requiring $2^{|k|/2}$ rather than $2^{|k|}$ for brute force key search. Cook et al. suggest a solution for proxy re-encryption for symmetric ciphers by using double encryption [5]. In this scheme, the owner encrypts the data m with a key k_1 and re-encrypt with another key k_2 to get, for example the ciphertext $c = E_{k_2}(E_{k_1}(m))$. To grant access to a user, the owner should provide both of keys k_1 and k_2 to the user. The re-encryption is done by the proxy for the second encryption by providing k_2 to the proxy. During re-encryption process, the proxy can not access the data m, because the data is protected by the first encryption layer. Using this method, the proxy needs to execute two costly computations: decrypting with the old key and encrypting with the new key.

Another related work in re-encryption for symmetric cipher is the work of Hirose [9]. The author develops a conversion method for cipher encrypted with Galois Counter Mode (GCM) mode. This method is not intended for proxy re-encryption but to find the conversion method that is faster than decrypt-then-encrypt. The author define GCTR as encryption function without producing authentication tag in the GCM. For the plaintext $P_1, .., P_{n-1}, P_n^*$ where P_n^* is the last bit string and a block cipher $H = E(K, 0^{128})$, the GCTR is defined as follows. For $Y_i = \text{incr}(Y_{i-1})$ where $i = 1, ..., n$, the ciphertext $C_i = P_i \oplus E(K, Y_i)$ for $i = 1, ..., n-1$, $C_n^* = P_n^* \oplus \text{MSB}_u(E(K, Y_n))$ where u is the number of bit of the last string. The ciphertext C is $C_1 || C_2 || ... || C_{n-1} || C_n^*$. The GCM mode encrypt by calling the function GCM-AE as folows. Let $Y_0 = IV || 0^{31}1$ if $\text{len}(IV) = 96$ and $\text{GHASH}(H, \{\}, IV)$ otherwise. The ciphertext $C = \text{GCTR}(K, Y_0, P)$ and the tag $T = \text{MSB}_t(\text{GHASH}(H, A, C) \oplus E(K, Y_0))$ where GHASH is the function to compute the tag using Galois field with input authenticated data A and the ciphertext C. The GCM-AE produces the ciphertext C and the tag T (with length t). To re-encrypt $(C^A, T^A) = \text{GCM-AE}(K^A, IV^A, P, A)$ to another ciphertext and tag $(C^B, T^B) = \text{GCM-AE}(K^B, IV^B, P, A)$, we use the following steps:

1. produce $(C^R, T^R) = \text{GCM-AE}(K^B, IV^B, C^A, A)$, and
   $S^A = \text{GCTR}(K^A, (Y_0)^A, 0^{|P|})$
2. compute $C^B = C^R \oplus S^A$ and $T^B = T^R \oplus \text{MSB}_t(\oplus_{i=1}^{n-1} S_i^R.H^{n+1-i})$

It is easy to see the correctness of this approach because

$$C_i^A = P_i \oplus E_{K^A}(Y_i^A)$$
$$C_i^R = C_i^A \oplus E_{K^B}(Y_i^B)$$
$$S^A = 0^{|P|} \oplus E_{K^A}(Y_i^A)$$
$$C^R \oplus S^A = (P_i \oplus E_{K^A}(Y_i^A) \oplus E_{K^B}(Y_i^B))$$
$$\oplus 0^{|P|} \oplus E_{K^A}(Y_i^A)$$
$$= P_i \oplus E_{K^B}(Y_i^B) = C_i^B$$

Because we need to execute two encryptions, the performance of this mechanism is not much better than decrypt-then-encrypt approach.

3   Security Requirements

In this section, we describe the security requirements of the proxy re-encryption scheme. The setting of the system is a data owner stores his/her data in a semi-trusted database server. To protect the data from malicious users and also the database administrator, the owner encrypts the data before storing them in the database. The share the data to other users, the data owner provides the decryption keys so that the other users can download and decrypt the data.

A semi-trusted proxy (i.e. it always executes the protocol correctly although it cannot be trusted with sensitive data) is contacted whenever the data owner needs to re-encrypt the data (to revoke user's access, or to update the keys because the previous keys are leaked/lost to an unauthorized/unknown parties). We cannot prevent a user who has access to the data downloads and stores the data in other place. The purposes of the re-encryption scheme are not only to protect the data but also to protect the current encryption key be inferred by the previous users who have access to parts or all parts of the data. We summarize security requirements for the proxy re-encryption as follows:

1. the proxy can convert the ciphertext encrypted with one key to another without the need to decrypt or access the plaintext
2. the proxy cannot access the unencrypted data (i.e. the plaintexts) directly or when executing the proxy re-encryption protocol
3. the proxy cannot re-encrypt the data without the owner's consent
4. a user who owns the previous decryption keys before re-encryption cannot infer/calculate the current key even if he know all plaintext, previous ciphertext and the current ciphertext
5. the encryption scheme is also secure in the standard senses (i.e. Chosen Plaintext Attack–CPA), any outside attackers cannot decrypt the data without having the correct decryption keys

4   Security Primitives

4.1   All or Nothing Transform (AONT)

All or nothing transformation (AONT) converts n blocks message $M = m_0, ..., m_{s-1}$ into a pseudo message $M' = m'_1, ..., m'_{n-1}$ for $n > s$ so that any blocks of the original message cannot be recovered if any block of the pseudo message is missing. Rivest [12] proposed an AONT that converts the message by encrypting each block with a random key and xor-ing the random key with the hash of all blocks, so that the encryption key cannot be recovered without having all part of the pseudo message. This scheme works for $n = s + 1$ where for each block message M and random key K' compute $m'_i = m_i \oplus E(K', i)$. Then, compute $m'_{n'-1} = K' \oplus h_1 \oplus h_2 \oplus \ldots \oplus h_n$ where $h_i = E(K_0, m'_i \oplus i)$ and K_0 is a fixed (and publicly known) key.

The Rivest scheme is a specific form of the Optimal Asymmetric Encryption Padding (OAEP) proposed by Bellare et.al [2]. OAEP is intended as a padding method before encrypting with RSA. The OAEP works for parameters n and k_0 where the OAEP transformation $\{0,1\}^n \times \{0,1\}^{k_0}] \rightarrow \{0,1\}^{n'}$, for $n' = n + k_0$ is defined as

$$OAEP^{G,H}(x, r) = x \oplus G(r)\|r \oplus H(x \oplus G(r)),$$

where $G : \{0,1\}^{k_0} \rightarrow \{0,1\}^n$ is a random generator, and $H : \{0,1\}^n \rightarrow \{0,1\}^{k_0}$ is a hash function. The Rivest scheme is an OAEP if we assume random r as the key K', $G(r)$ as $E(K', 1), E(K', 2), \ldots)$ and H as $h_1 \oplus h_2 \oplus \ldots \oplus h_n$.

4.2   *Perm, DePerm* and *FindCK*

A permutation *Perm* is a bijection function that takes input two sequences with the same size n. The first sequence is the permutation key $k_0, k_1, \ldots, k_{n-1}$ where $0 \leq k_i \leq n-1$ for $0 \leq i \leq n-1$ and $k_a \neq k_b$ for $a \neq b$. The second sequence is any sequence $s_0, s_1, \ldots, s_{n-1}$ for with each element has the same size b for $b \geq 1$. The permutation *Perm* transforms the second input sequence by changing the order of the sequence according to the first input sequence (permutation key). For example a permutation $Perm((3, 1, 2, 0), (a, b, c, d))$ transforms the the second input into (d, b, c, a). The permutation algorithm is shown in the Algorithm 1.

Inputs: sequence size n, permutation key KEP, input PIN
Outputs: permuted sequence $POUT$
for $i = 0$ to $n - 1$ **do**
    $POUT[i] \leftarrow PIN[KEP[i]]$
end for
return $POUT$

Algorithm 1. Permutation Algorithm

A de-permutation *DePerm* is a bijection function that takes two inputs as *Perm*. The difference is the *DePerm* converts back the second sequence that has been permuted using the *Perm*. An example is $DePerm((3, 1, 2, 0), (d, b, c, a)) = (a, b, c, d)$. The *DePerm* an algorithm is shown in the Algorithm 2.

An output of a permutation can be converted directly to an output of another permutation by finding a conversion key CK. The conversion key of a

Inputs: sequence size n, permutation key KEP, input $DPIN$
Outputs: de-permuted sequence $DPOUT$
for $i = 0$ to $n - 1$ **do**
   $DPOUT[KEP[i]] = DPIN[i]$
end for
return $DPOUT$

Algorithm 2. DePermutation Algorithm

Inputs: sequence size n, first permutation KP_A, and second permutation KP_B
Outputs: the conversion key CK
for $i = 0$ to $n - 1$ **do**
   for $j = 0$ to $n - 1$ **do**
      if $KP_A[i] == KP_B[j]$ **then**
         $CK[j] = i$
         break
      end if
   end for
end for
return CK

Algorithm 3. Find Conversion Key Algorithm

permutation key KP_A to permutation key KP_B is a permutation key so that for input sequence $InSeq$, $Perm(KP_B, InSeq) = Perm(CK, Perm(KP_A, InSeq))$. We can find the conversion key CK easily if we have the first permutation key KP_A and the second permutation key KP_B using algorithm shown in the Algorithm 3.

4.3   Permutation Key Generator ($PGen$)

The permutation key generator is used to generate permutation keys where each of them consists of a sequence of distinct numbers from 0 to $n-1$. A permutation key can be generated from a smaller size of key using a function that takes input a key k and the number of elements in the sequence (n). The function has a property that without knowing the key k, the output cannot be computed better than a random guess. We implement the function using a deterministic encryption function $E(k, p)$ that takes an input k and a plaintext p using the algorithm shown in the Algorithm 4.

5   Using All-or-Nothing Transformation to Develop a Symmetric Cipher Proxy Re-encryption Scheme

5.1   Preliminaries

Let $m_0, m_2, ..., m_{s-1}$ is a sequence of s blocks message where the size of each m_i is b. A proxy re-encryption algorithm $\mathcal{PR}$ is a quintiple algorithms $= (G, E, D, RG, RE)$ where:

Prepare $n \log n$ bits input and store in array A with n elements
Fill each element of the array with the number 0 to $n-1$
for $i = 0$ to $n-1$ **do**
   $tmp = E(k, i)$
   $tmp = \log n$ bits of the least significant bits of tmp
   swap $A[i]$ with $A[tmp]$
end for
return A

Algorithm 4. Permutation Key Generation Algorithm

- G is a key generation algorithm that regenerate random keys to be used by E
- E is the encryption algorithm that converts s blocks input $m_0, m_1, ..., m_{s-1}$ that outputs n blocks ciphertext $c_0, c_1, ..., c_{n-1}$ using keys generated by G
- D is the decryption algorithm that transforms the ciphertext $c_0, c_1, ..., c_{n-1}$ back into the plaintext $m_0, m_1, ..., m_{s-1}$
- RG is an algorithm to generate keys for re-encryption algorithm RE
- RE is the re-encryption algorithm that transforms the ciphertext $c_0^A, c_1^A, ..., c_{n-1}^A$ encrypted with private key K_A into ciphertext $c_0^B, c_1^B, ..., c_{n-1}^B$ encrypted with private key K_B

5.2 Symmetric Cipher Proxy Re-encryption algorithm

The proxy re-encryption algorithm $\mathcal{PR} = (G, E, D, RG, RE)$ works on $b \times s$ bits message $m = m_0, m_2, ..., m_{s-1}$ where the message is divided into s blocks with size b.

- **Key Generation** (G)
  - The data owner generates three random keys K_1, K_2, and K_3 with the size the same as k in the permutation generator algorithm in Section 4.3.
  - The data owner generates a random b bits XOR key K_X.
- **Encryption** (E). The data owner encrypts the message m using the keys K_1, K_2, K_3, and K_X.
  - Transform the message $m = m_0, m_2, ..., m_{s-1}$ using an AONT that outputs a $b \times n$ pseudo message $m' = m'_0, m'_1, ..., m'_{n-1}$
  - Generate three permutation keys P_1, P_2 and P_3 using the permutation generator algorithm (in Section 4.3) with inputs (K_1, b), (K_2, b) and (K_3, n) respectively.
  - Apply the permutation with key P_3 to all blocks (the size of each element in the sequence m' is b bits)

$$m' = Perm(P_3, m')$$

  - For $i = 0$ to $n-1$, apply the following transformation for each block m'_i (now the size of each element in the sequence m'_i is 1 bit):

$$c_0 = Perm(P_1, m'_0) \oplus Perm(P_2, K_X)$$
$$c_i = Perm(P_1, m'_i) \oplus Perm(P_2, c_{i-1})$$

– **Decryption** (D). To decrypt the ciphertext c, a user needs to have all keys K_1, K_2, K_3, and K_X.
  - Generate three permutation keys P_1, P_2 and P_3 using the permutation generator algorithm (in Section 4.3) with inputs (K_1, b), (K_2, b) and (K_3, n) respectively.
  - For $i = n - 1$ to 0 apply the following transformation for each block c_i to get m_i':

  $$m_i' = DePerm(P_1, c_i \oplus Perm(P_2, c_{i-1})$$
  $$m_0' = DePerm(P_1, c_0 \oplus Perm(P_2, K_X))$$

  - Apply the DePermutation with key P_3 to all blocks:

  $$m' = DePerm(P_3, m')$$

  - Transform the pseudo message $m' = m_0', m_1', ..., m_{n-1}'$ back using AONT to get the original message $m = m_0, m_2, ..., m_{s-1}$
– **Re-encryption Key Generation** (RG). The data owner generates the re-encryption keys that are sent to the proxy for re-encrypting the ciphertext with the new keys
  - Generate three new random keys $K_1', K_2',$ and K_3'
  - Generate a new random b bits XOR key K_X'
  - Find the conversion key from K_1 to K_1': $CK_1 = FindCK(PGen(K_1, b), PGen(K_1', b))$ that produces $b \log b$ bits conversion key CK_1
  - Find the conversion key from K_3 to K_3': $CK_3 = FindCK(PGen(K_3, n), PGen(K_3', n))$ that produces $n \log n$ bits conversion key CK_3
  - Re-encryption keys are $CK_1, CK_3, K_X, K_X', K_2$ and K_2'
– **Re-Encryption** (RE). The proxy re-encrypts the ciphertext c using the re-encryption keys $CK_1, CK_3, K_X, K_X', K_2$ and K_2':
  - Compute $P_2 = PGen(K_2)$ and $P_2' = PGen(K_2')$
  - For i from $n - 1$ to 0 apply the following transformation:

  $$c_i' = Perm(CK_1, c_i \oplus Perm(P_2, c_{i-1}))$$
  $$c_0' = Perm(CK_1, c_0 \oplus Perm(P_2, K_X))$$

  - Apply the permutation with key CK_3 to all blocks

  $$c' = Perm(CK_3, c')$$

  - For $i = 0$ to $n - 1$ apply the following transformation for each block c:

  $$c_0' = c_0' \oplus Perm(P_2', K_X')$$
  $$c_i' = c_i' \oplus Perm(P_2, c_{i-1}')$$

Correctness of the re-encryption algorithm The ciphertext of each block before re-encryption is as follows:

$$m' = Perm(P_3, m')$$
$$c_0 = Perm(P_1, m'_0) \oplus Perm(P_2, K_X)$$
$$c_i = Perm(P_1, m'_i) \oplus Perm(P_2, c_{i-1})$$

To re-encrypt, we use the following equalities:

$$Perm(P_1, m'_0) = c_0 \oplus Perm(P_2, K_X)$$
$$Perm(P_1, m'_i) = c_i \oplus Perm(P_2, c_{i-1}))$$
$$Perm(CK_1, Perm(P_1, c_i)) = Perm(P'_1, c_i), \text{ and}$$
$$Perm(CK_3, Perm(P_3, c')) = Perm(P'_3, c')$$

To re-encrypt, first the proxy transforms c' using the following transformation for i from $n-1$ to 0 to converts key K_1 to K'_1:

$$c'_i = Perm(CK_1, c_i \oplus Perm(P_2, c_{i-1})) = Perm(K'_1, m'_i)$$
$$c'_0 = Perm(CK_1, c_0 \oplus Perm(P_2, K_X)) = Perm(K'_1, m'_0)$$

Then permute the results using CK_3 to convert K_3 to K'_3:

$$c' = Perm(CK_3, c') = Perm(K'_3, c')$$

The last step is to apply the following transformation for $i = 0$ to $n-1$ that converts the P_2 to P'_2 and K_X to K'_X:

$$c'_0 = c'_0 \oplus Perm(P'_2, K'_X) = Perm(K'_1, m'_0) \oplus Perm(P'_2, K'_X)$$
$$c'_i = c'_i \oplus Perm(P_2, c'_{i-1}) = Perm(K'_1, m'_i) \oplus Perm(P_2, c'_{i-1})$$

All of these steps correctly convert the keys from K_1, K_2, K_3 and K_X to K'_1, K'_2, K'_3 and K'_X. $\square$

6   Security Analysis

Using this scheme, to encrypt the pseudomessage, we use the following formula:

$$m' = Perm(P_3, m') \tag{1}$$
$$c_0 = Perm(P_1, m'_0) \oplus Perm(P_2, K_X) \tag{2}$$
$$c_i = Perm(P_1, m'_i) \oplus Perm(P_2, c_{i-1}) \tag{3}$$

We classify three types of potential attackers. They are the previous users, the proxy and the outsiders.

6.1   The Previous Users

The previous users are the users who were previously granted access by providing the previous correct encryption keys. The previous users may store some parts or all of the pseudomessages (which has not been changed when updating the keys) and also the unencrypted data in their previous access sessions. The previous users may also store all or parts of the previous ciphertexts and they can access all of the current ciphertexts. The purpose of the previous user's attacks is to find the new encryption keys which are not authorized to have. (One motivation of the previous users to get the new keys eventhough he/she may store the unencrypted data locally is to easily share the data to other users by sharing the new encryption–it is more convenient to share the data by only sharing the keys rather than the large data). We analyze the security of this scheme against the previous users by playing a Known Plaintext Attack (KPA) game. The rationale of this game is that the output of an AONT is a pseudorandom, so that each pseudo-message is unique (there is no two exactly same blocks of pseudomessages). It should be noted that we assume the proxy does not collude with any previous users. It is easy to check that the previous user can recover the current encryption key if he/she get the re-encryption key. (However, as a comparison, even a costly double encryption method [5] is not resistant to the collusion attack).

Known Plaintext Attack (KPA) game ReEnc$_{\mathcal{UA},\Pi}^{kpa}$ for previous user $\mathcal{UA}$ and proxy re-encryption scheme Π:

1. The previous user has access to all pseudomessages (m') and the ciphertexts (c).
2. The previous user chooses two pseudomessage blocks m'_a and m'_b and sends the indexes a and b to an encryption oracle
3. The encryption oracle chooses one of the indexes $j = a$ or b and sends back $c_j = Perm(P_1, m'_j) \oplus Perm(P_2, c_{j-1})$ if $j > 0$ and $c_j = Perm(P_1, m'_0) \oplus Perm(P_2, K_X)$ for $j = 0$
4. The previous user chooses $k = a$ or b. The previous user wins if $k = j$. If the previous user wins ReEnc$_{\mathcal{UA},\Pi}^{kpa} = 1$ otherwise 0.

We should show that the advantage of the previous user is very small (represented by a small number ϵ).

$$\Pr[\mathsf{ReEnc}_{\mathcal{UA},\Pi}^{kpa} = 1] \leq \frac{1}{2} + \epsilon$$

Theorem 1. *If each of the outputs of AONT m' and the ciphertext c is unique and pseudorandom, and the output of permutation key generator (described in Section 4.3) is pseudorandom, the proxy re-encryption scheme shown in Section 5.2 is secure in the Known Plaintext Attack (KPA) game* ReEnc$_{\mathcal{UA},\Pi}^{kpa}$.

Proof. From the equation 1, to guess j, the previous user $\mathcal{UA}$ should guess the permutation key P_3. Because P_3 is pseudorandom it cannot be guessed better than the random guess (we can prove formally by showing that the problem to guess the bits of the permutation key is the same as the problem to guess the outputs of underlying encryption function $E(k, p)$ used in $PGen$ described in Section 4.3).

- The previous user tries to find the first $\log n$ bits of the key P_3 by comparing m'_a and m'_b with c_j
  - Because each c_j does not reveal either the number of 0s or 1s bits of the m'_a and m'_b, the previous user cannot guess the permutation key by checking the number of 0s or 1s bits
  - The previous users can guess the permutation with success probability $\frac{1}{2}$ (by assuming that the outputs of $E(k, p)$ are pseudorandom).
- To win the game, the previous user should solve the equation $c_0 = Perm(P_1, m'_0) \oplus Perm(P_2, K_X)$ and $c_i = Perm(P_1, m'_i) \oplus Perm(P_2, c_{i-1})$ (equations 2 and 3)
  - The previous users cannot reduce $c_i = Perm(P_1, m'_i) \oplus Perm(P_2, c_{i-1})$ into $c_a + c_b = Perm(P_1, m'_a + m'_b)$ or $c_a + c_b = Perm(P_1, c_{a-1} + m_{b-1})$ by xor-ing two equations because each m_i and c_{i-1} is unique.
  - The previous user should solve the $c_i = Perm(P_1, m'_i) \oplus Perm(P_2, c_{i-1})$ directly.
- Because P_1 and P_2 are also pseudorandom (by assuming that $E(k, p)$ is secure), the previous user do not have better advantage than random guessing. □

6.2   The Proxy

The proxy is the semi-trusted entity that converts the ciphertexts from one key to another key without decrypting the data. The proxy does not have access to the pseudo messages, the data, or any previous keys. However, the proxy has access to all re-encryption keys ($CK_1, CK_3, K_X, K'_X, K_2$ and K'_2), all previous ciphertexts and all current ciphertexts. Although the proxy correctly executes the re-encryption protocol he/she may try to decrypt some ciphertexts or to infer any current encryption/decryption keys. We analyze the security of this scheme againts the proxy in a Ciphertext Only Attack (COA) game.

Ciphertext Only Attack (COA) game $\mathsf{ReEnc}^{coa}_{\mathcal{PA}, \Pi}$ for the proxy $\mathcal{PA}$ and proxy re-encryption scheme Π:

1. The proxy has access to all the ciphertexts (c).
2. The proxy chooses two ciphertext blocks c'_a and c'_b and sends the indexes a and b to a decryption oracle
3. The encryption oracle chooses one of the indexes $j = a$ or b and sends back the plaintext m_j or m_0 where $m'_j = DePerm(P_1, c_i \oplus Perm(P_2, c_{i-1}))$ if $j > 0$ and $m'_0 = DePerm(P_1, c_0 \oplus Perm(P_2, K_X))$ for $j = 0$
4. The proxy chooses $k = a$ or b. The previous user wins if $k = j$. If the previous user wins, $\mathsf{ReEnc}^{coa}_{\mathcal{PA}, \Pi} = 1$, otherwise 0.

We should show that the advantage of the proxy is very small (ϵ).

$$\Pr[\mathsf{ReEnc}^{coa}_{\mathcal{P}\mathcal{A},\Pi} = 1] \leq \frac{1}{2} + \epsilon$$

Theorem 2. *If each of the outputs of AONT m' and the ciphertext c is unique and pseudorandom, and the output of permutation key generator (described in Section 4.3) is pseudorandom, the proxy re-encryption scheme shown in Section 5.2 is secure in the Ciphertext Only Attack (COA) game* $\mathsf{ReEnc}^{coa}_{\mathcal{P}\mathcal{A},\Pi}$.

Proof. To win the ciphertext only game, the proxy should guess a large number bits of the keys as shown below:

1. The proxy tries to guess the correct j. Because P_1 and P_2 are pseudorandom (by assuming that $E(k, p)$ is secure), eventhough the proxy knowns P_2, the proxy cannot guess P_1 better that random guessing, so guessing j is also no better than random guessing. To check the correctness of the guessing, the proxy should decrypt the ciphertext. However, to decrypt any blocks, the proxy should find all correct bits of the key for all blocks of the pseudo messages. So, before correctly decrypting all ciphertexts to get all blocks of the pseudo messages, the proxy cannot check the correctness of j.
2. The proxy tries to guess the current keys (P_1 and P_3) using the re-encryption keys. However without knowing the previous keys, the proxy cannot infer anything about the current keys (by assuming that encryption function $E(k, p)$ used in $PGen$ is secure).
3. What can be done by the proxy is to try to guess all possible keys (brute force attack) and decrypting all blocks for each guessing. This attack is impractical for a large number of blocks of the pseudo messages. $\square$

6.3   The Outsiders

The outsiders are the other attackers that cannot be classified into the previous users or the proxy. The outsiders do not have access to any of the previous keys, any re-encryption keys or any pseudomessage. However, we assume the outsiders have access to all ciphertexts (previous or current ciphertext). The purposes of the outsider's attack are to decrypt any parts of the ciphertext or finding any keys. The outsider's game is similar to the proxy game in Section 6.2 except that the outsider does not know the P_2. So the outsider has less security advantage than the proxy.

7   Performance Evaluation

We analyze the performance of the scheme by calculating the computation costs to execute the scheme. Table 1 shows the computation costs that are needed by the scheme for the key generation (KeyGen), encryption (Enc), decryption (Dec), re-encryption key generation (ReKeyGen), and re-encryption (ReEnc).

The computational costs are represented by the number of executions of the primitives for n number of blocks. The primitives are: AONT transform/de-transform (AONT), permutation ($Perm$), de-permutation ($DePerm$), finding conversion key ($FindCK$), permutation key generation ($PGen$), random bits generation (RandGen) and XOR operation ($\oplus$).

Table 1. The number of primitives execution

Primitives	KeyGen	Enc	Dec	ReKeyGen	ReEnc
AONT	-	1	1	-	-
$Perm$	-	$2n+1$	-	-	$3n+1$
$DePerm$	-	-	$2n+1$	-	-
$FindCK$	-	-	-	2	-
$PGen$	-	3	3	4	2
RandGen	4	-	-	4	-
XOR ($\oplus$)	-	n	n	-	$2n$

$Perm$, $DePerm$, $FindCK$, and XOR are cheap operations. The costs of AONT, $PGen$ and RandGen operations are linear to a symmetric cipher operation. For example, the AONT scheme proposed by Rivest needs $2n$ encryption operations [12]. As shown in Table 1, the costs of key generation and re-encryption key generation are linear to symmetric cipher operations because key generation needs 4 random bits generations (RandGen) while re-encryption keys generation needs 2 operations of find conversion key ($FindCK$), 4 permutation key generations ($PGen$) and 4 random bits generations (RandGen). The costs of encryption and decryption are also linear to symmetric cipher operations because encryption needs execution of an AONT transform, $2n+1$ permutations, 3 permutation key generations, and n times XOR, while decryption needs execution of an AONT transform, $2n+1$ de-permutations, 3 permutation key generations, and n times XOR. Re-encryption in this scheme is very efficient because it only needs 2 permutation key generations regardless of the number of blocks and a linear number of cheap $Perm$ and XOR operations ($3n+1$ $Perm$ and $2n$ XOR operations).

8   Discussion: Using CBC and CTR Modes as Alternatives to AONT

The security of the scheme in Section 5.2 relies on the difficulty to find the correct position of the AONT transformation. Other encryption modes (CBC and CTR) also have characteristics that the blocks cannot be decrypted correctly if we cannot find the correct position of the blocks. In CTR, we should know the correct position of a block for decrypting the block. In CBC mode, we should know a pair of consecutive blocks to decrypt a block. It is interesting to know whether it is possible to implement the scheme showed in Section 5.2 using CBC or CTR.

8.1   Using CBC Mode

Each block encrypted with CBC is defined as $c_i = E(k, p_i \oplus c_{i-1}), c_0 = IV$, where IV is an initialization vector. To decrypt a block c_i we use the following formula: $p_i = E(k, c_i) \oplus c_{i-1}, c_0 = IV$. If we substitute the AONT with a CBC mode there are some features of AONT that cannot be substituted by CBC:

1. In CBC, we only need to know two consecutive modes and decrypt a block to get a block of the plaintext, while in the AONT we need to know all blocks with correct position and decrypt all blocks to get any block of the plaintext.
2. In CBC, we do not need to have all of blocks, we can decrypt any blocks and get a block of plaintext by knowing two consecutive blocks.

Those characteristics of CBC affects the security of the re-encryption as follows:

- the previous user does not need to know all bits key P_3 to decrypt a part of the blocks. By using CBC, it is possible the previous user shares a part of the blocks without knowing all bits of the key (which is not possible in All-or-Nothing-Transform (AONT), because in AONT to leak a block, we need to have all correct bits of the key).
- for the proxy and the outsiders, by using CBC mode, attack to find the encryption key is easier, because the proxy and the outsider can check the correctness of a key for a block by only decrypting the block rather than decrypting all blocks of the message with correct keys for all blocks in AONT scheme to test the correctness of any bits of key in a block.

8.2   Using CTR Mode

In CTR, we use a nonce n and counter i to encrypt each block of the message. Each block encrypted with CTR is defined as $c_i = E(k, n \oplus i) \oplus p_i$. To decrypt a block c_i we use the following formula: $p_i = E(k, n \oplus i) \oplus c_i$. The CTR mode has the same weaknesses as the CBC so if we use CTR there are some advantages for the previous users, the proxy and the outsiders:

- the previous user does not need to know all bits key P_3 to decrypt a part of the blocks. By using CTR, it is possible the previous user shares a part of the blocks without knowing all bits of the key (which is not possible in scheme that uses AONT).
- attack to find the encryption key is easier for the proxy and the outsiders if we use CTR, because the proxy and the outsider are able to check the correctness of a key (for the block) by only decrypting a block of message rather than decrypting all blocks with the correct key in AONT scheme.

9   Conclusion

In this paper, we have described a proxy re-encryption scheme for the symmetric ciphers. The scheme exploits some characteristics of All-or-nothing (AONT) transformation to develop an efficient proxy re-encryption scheme. We showed security and performance evaluation of the scheme. We also discussed the possibility to use CBC and CTR modes as AONT's substitutes.

References

1. Ateniese, G., Fu, K., Green, M., Hohenberger, S.: Improved proxy re-encryption schemes with applications to secure distributed storage. ACM Trans. Inf. Syst. Secur. 9(1), 1–30 (2006)
2. Bellare, M., Rogaway, P.: Optimal Asymmetric Encryption. In: De Santis, A. (ed.) EUROCRYPT 1994. LNCS, vol. 950, pp. 92–111. Springer, Heidelberg (1995)
3. Blaze, M., Bleumer, G., Strauss, M.J.: Divertible Protocols and Atomic Proxy Cryptography. In: Nyberg, K. (ed.) EUROCRYPT 1998. LNCS, vol. 1403, pp. 127–144. Springer, Heidelberg (1998)
4. Canetti, R., Hohenberger, S.: Chosen-ciphertext secure proxy re-encryption. In: Proceedings of the 14th ACM Conference on Computer and Communications Security, pp. 185–194. ACM (2007)
5. Cook, D.L., Keromytis, A.D.: Conversion and proxy functions for symmetric key ciphers. In: ITCC, pp. 662–667 (2005)
6. Desai, A.: The Security of All-or-Nothing Encryption: Protecting Against Exhaustive Key Search. In: Bellare, M. (ed.) CRYPTO 2000. LNCS, vol. 1880, pp. 359–375. Springer, Heidelberg (2000)
7. Dolev, D., Dwork, C., Naor, M.: Nonmalleable cryptography. SIAM J. Comput. 30(2), 391–437 (2000)
8. Green, M., Ateniese, G.: Identity-Based Proxy Re-Encryption. In: Katz, J., Yung, M. (eds.) ACNS 2007. LNCS, vol. 4521, pp. 288–306. Springer, Heidelberg (2007)
9. Hirose, S.: On re-encryption for symmetric authenticated encryption. In: Computer Security Symposium, CSS 2010 (2010)
10. Kaliski Jr., B.S., Rivest, R.L., Sherman, A.T.: Is the data encryption standard a group? (results of cycling experiments on des). J. Cryptology 1(1), 3–36 (1988)
11. Libert, B., Vergnaud, D.: Unidirectional chosen-ciphertext secure proxy re-encryption. IEEE Transactions on Information Theory 57(3), 1786–1802 (2011)
12. Rivest, R.L.: All-or-Nothing Encryption and the Package Transform. In: Biham, E. (ed.) FSE 1997. LNCS, vol. 1267, pp. 210–218. Springer, Heidelberg (1997)

Protocol Share Based Traffic Rate Analysis (PSBTRA) for UDP Bandwidth Attack

Zohair Ihsan, Mohd. Yazid Idris[*], Khalid Hussain, Deris Stiawan,
and Khalid Mahmood Awan

Faculty of Computer Science and Information System, Universiti Teknologi Malaysia,
Skudai, 81310, Johor. Malaysia
{izohair2,hkhalid2,sderis2,makhalid2}@live.utm.my,
yazid@utm.my

Abstract. Internet is based on best effort and end to end design principles. Although they are the reasons for the Internet's high efficiency and popularity, they also resulted in many inherent security problems such as the Bandwidth Attacks. There are two main characteristics of bandwidth attack. First, during an attack the incoming traffic rate is much higher than the outgoing traffic rate. Second, the proportion of protocol exploited by the attacker is higher as compare to other protocols in the traffic. Based on these two characteristics, a UDP bandwidth attack detection system based on Protocol Share Based Traffic Rate Analysis (PSBTRA) is proposed. Experiments on real world network shows that this approach can effectively detect UDP bandwidth attacks.

Keywords: Distributed Denial of Service Attack, Bandwidth Attack, UDP Flooding Attack.

1 Introduction

Since the novel ideas of packet switching networks in mid of 1960's and the first packet switching network ARPANET in 1969 [1], computer networks have become highly important components of contemporary societies. At present, computer networks are use everywhere and this trend is not likely to change in the future. The ARPANET was created as a research network sponsored by the Advanced Research Projects Agency (ARPA) of Department of Defense (DoD) in the United States of America. The aim was to develop a communication network for researchers to share their research and that network is now commonly known as the Internet. The Internet's best effort and end to end design principles [2] along with the TCP/IP protocol suite [3] are major factors for the Internet's dominant success, but they also inherent security problems. Although the Internet has been proved extremely robust in cases of random failures, it has also been proven extremely sensitive to specifically targeted attacks [4]. This is due to the fact that Internet was not designed to be use in

---

[*] Corresponding author.

A. Abd Manaf et al. (Eds.): ICIEIS 2011, Part I, CCIS 251, pp. 275–289, 2011.

such a way it is being used nowadays, which leads to the poor security design. For instance, already in the late eighties [5], several security problems within TCP/IP protocol suite were pointed out.

One of the Internet's largest security concerns is its intrinsic inability to deal with denial of service attacks. The term denial of service referrers to a situation, where a legitimate requestor of a service cannot receive the requested service for one reason or the other. Denial of service (DoS) attacks are characterized by the attacker's primary intention to cause denial of service to the requestors of the service in question.

DoS attacks can very well be launched both locally and remotely and they range from software vulnerabilities to bandwidth consumption. A majority of DoS attacks can be countered relatively. For instance, attacks that target software can mostly be eliminated by patching the vulnerabilities but unfortunately, the number of vulnerabilities reported each year is increasing according to CERT statistics [6]. Hence, an attacker can control a large number of insecure systems by exploiting their vulnerabilities. Attacks that target network resources are more of a problem such as bandwidth attack. The bandwidth attacks are built within the principles of the Internet and thus it appears that any absolute solution would require a change in the principles themselves.

2   Denial of Service Attacks: The Concept

The Internet is based on best effort and end to end design principles and although they are the reasons for the Internet's high efficiency and popularity, they are also the sources of many inherent security problems as well. As discussed previously, DoS attacks exist due to this fact. The best effort principle accompanied with the end to end principle, means that the Internet's only concerned with the routing packets injected to it as fast as possible to the specified destinations, leaving everything else for the end hosts to handle [2]. This means that at the core level, the Internet is only concerned with what the IP portion of a packet embodies. The IP specifies the network level header according to which the users are ought to construct their packets in order to transfer data through the Internet [7]. In Internet this information is extracted from the packets, specifically from the IP portion and operations are performed on the bases of extracted information. Internet is not concerned with whom created the packets or from where they are coming and where they are heading. This means that everything else is left for the user to construct.

"Denial of service" and *"denial of service attack"* are two completely different concepts where the former refers to an event or a situation and the latter refers to an intention driven illegal act. [8] States, *"The most comprehensive perspective would be that regardless of the cause, if a service is supposed to be available and it is not, then service has been denied."* The definition of denial of service used in this paper was created on these bases. Denial of service is an event or a situation, in which a legitimate client cannot access the requested service to which the client is entitled to and which should be available to it.

According to [9], *"A denial of service attack is characterized by an explicit attempt by attackers to prevent legitimate users of a service from using that service."* [8] States the same in a slightly more verbose manner, *"A denial of service attack is considered to take place only when access to a computer or network resource is intentionally blocked or degraded as a result of malicious action taken by another user."* With a slight modification, the definition provided by [9] is the definition for DoS attack used in this paper.

"A denial of service attack is characterized by an exclusive function of the attack and an explicit attempt by one or more attackers to prevent one or more legitimate users of a service from using that service."

With these modifications, the stress is on two important points. First, the number of targets or attackers is irrelevant. Second, the single purpose of the attack must be to cause a denial of service, which means that if the attack has any other functions besides causing denial of service, the attack cannot be categorized as a denial of service attack.

As some other attacks may cause denial of service situations as a side effect. For instance, it is common for viruses and worms to consume much of both host and network resources while propagating and executing their primary functions, this has often leaded to severe denial of service situations. These attacks cannot be characterized as DoS attack, unless their primary objective it to cause denial of service, such a case was witnessed with the Morris Worm in 1989 [10].

Probably the most common definition of a Distributed Denial of Service (DDoS) attack follows the idea of having multiple machines each deploying a DoS attack towards one or more targets [11]. Such a definition is almost correct, however, it fails to include the aspect of coordination between the attackers, which is the most fundamental characteristic of a DDoS attack. For that reason a new definition is formulated as.

"Distributed denial of service attack is a denial of service attack, in which a multitude of attackers performs denial of service attacks in a coordinated manner to one or more targets."

This definition emphasizes three important aspects. First, DDoS attack is essentially a denial of service attack. More accurately, DDoS attacks are a subset of Denial of Service attacks. Second, there must be more than one source attacking. Third, there must be coordination between the attackers. In case either one of these conditions is not met, the attack cannot be characterized as a DDoS attack.

It is important to note that, there exists the concept of denial of service, but there is no such thing as Distributed Denial of Service in the same sense. The service can be denied, but the service cannot be denied distributed unless the service itself is distributed. Only Distributed Denial of Service attack can exist.

The bandwidth attack is any activity that aims to disable the services provided by the target by sending an excessive volume of useless traffic [12]. This is in contrast to the flash crowd which occurs when a large number of legitimate users access a server at the same time. So the bandwidth attack is defined as.

"Bandwidth attack is an attack that consumes a target's resources through a massive volume of useless traffic."

DDoS attacks are always about multiple DoS attacks targeted to one or more specific target. As it was argued in the previously, coordination is a crucial part of DDoS Attack. Coordination of multiple hosts in turn implies the existence of some sort of a network structure, which could be titled as distributed denial of service attack network and define as.

"Distributed denial of service attack network is a network of computers that are being controlled by same entity administrating the distributed denial of service attacks."

3   Distributed Denial of Service Attack

In Distributed Denial of Service attack, the attack traffic is launched from the multiple distributed sources. The attack power of a DDoS attack is based on the massive number of attack sources. A typical DDoS is executed in two stages. First stage is to compromise vulnerable systems over the Internet this is known as turning these computers into zombies. In the second stage, the attacker sends an attack command to these zombies through a secure channel to launch an attack against the victim [13]. Spoofed source IP address are used to hide the identity of the zombies and a possible risk of being trace back to the attacker via zombies.

3.1   Attacks That Target Software

Distributed Denial of Service attacks that target software rely on the attacker's ability to perform a function or an operation against the target software, which either immediately or eventually causes denial of service situation. In other words, the aim of DDoS attack targeting the software is either system or software crash or system resource consumption. The targeted software can be anything ranging from operating systems to lightweight applications.

3.2   Attacks That Target Protocols

Distributed Denial of Service attacks that target protocols rely to the attacker's ability to exploit specifications of the protocols in a way that will result in denial of service. Differentiating protocol attack traffic from normal traffic is more difficult as compared to attacks that target software. The individual packets of the attack traffic stream may not contain any kind of signature diverging from normal packets. The traffic streams, however, may contain distinguishable patterns, such as abnormally high percentage of TCP SYN packets, which could be a sign of an ongoing TCP SYN attack.

3.3   Attacks That Target Bandwidth

Attacks that target bandwidth may appear as the easiest in nature, but in fact they are the most flexible and configurable DDoS attacks. These attacks aim to overwhelm the target or the links on which the target's network relies, with such an amount of traffic that it causes either partial or complete denial of service. Hence it is not necessary for the attack traffic to reach the target. However, the attack traffic must be able to reach and congest the communication links. For instance, such links could be the routers of the target's Internet Service Provider that routes the target's traffic. Unlike other two classes of DDoS attacks, attacks that target bandwidth always succeeds, given that sufficient amount of attack traffic is able to reach the target.

Bandwidth attack sends an excessive volume of useless traffic. This is in contrast to the flash crowd where a large number of legitimate users access a server at the same time. The comparison between bandwidth attacks and flash crowds is shown in Table 1.

Table 1. Comparison between bandwidth attack and flash crowds [14]

	Bandwidth Attack	Flash Crowd
Network impact	Congested	Congested
Server impact	Overloaded	Overloaded
Traffic	Illegitimate	Genuine
Response to traffic	Unresponsive	Responsive
Traffic	Any	Mostly web
Number of flows	Any	Large number of flows
Predictability	Unpredictable	Mostly predictable

The bandwidth attack consumes the resources of a victim. Since the resources are limited (such as processing of NIC), high volume of traffic will result in dropping of incoming traffic by NIC. This traffic consist of both the legitimate traffic and attack traffic. As a result legitimate client will reduce their sending rate while the attackers will maintain or increase their sending rate. Eventually, the resources on the victim such as CPU and memory will be exhausted and the victim will not be able to provide the service. Bandwidth attack may also dominate the communication links of the network which is more threating then the resource consumption of victim. In this case the legitimate traffic to the server will be blocked, and if these links are the backbone links, any network or subnet which relies on these links will be effected.

4   UDP Flood Attack

The User Datagram Protocol (UDP) is a connectionless protocol that does not have flow control mechanisms, i.e., there is no built in mechanism for the sender and receiver to be synchronized or adapt to changing network conditions. The UDP flood is a type of bandwidth attack that uses UDP packets. Since UDP does not have flow control mechanisms, when traffic congestion happens, both legitimate and attack flows will not reduce their sending rates. Hence, the victim is unable to decide whether a source is an attack source or legitimate source by just checking the source's sending rate. Moreover, unlike TCP, UDP does not have a negotiation mechanism before setting up a connection. Therefore, it is easier to spoof UDP traffic without being detected by the victim. Fig. 1(a) shows a typical UDP Flooding attack while Fig. 1 (b) gives an illustration of how a single spoofed UDP packet can initiate a never ending attack stream. The attacker sends a UDP packet to victim 1, claiming to be from victim 2, requesting the echo service. Since victim 1 does not know this is a spoofed packet, it echoes a UDP packet to victim 2 at port 7 (echo service). Then victim 2 does exactly the same as victim 1 and the loop of sending echo requests will never end unless it is stopped by an external entity [15].

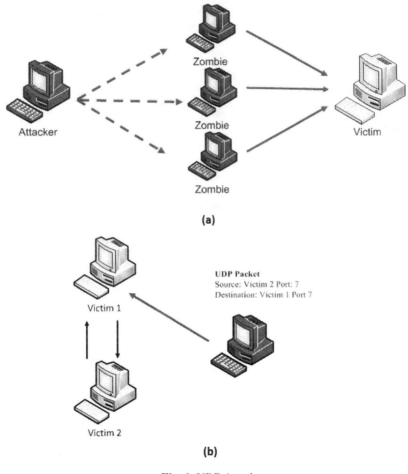

Fig. 1. UDP Attacks

5   Current Countermeasures

The DDoS attacks can be handled at three different levels. The majority of work has been done at the IP Layer. At this level, the defensive mechanism   attempts to detect attack by analyzing certain features such as the IP filtering, IP logging, IP trace back, TTL values, Packet marking, Route statistics, IP header information and Flow monitoring

[16,17,18,19,20,21]. The other place to defend from such attacks is the TCP Layer. TCP, ICMP, UDP, SIN, FIN and similar packets are analyze or match against different rules to distinguish the attack traffic from normal traffic [22,23,24,25,26,] The last place to handle such attacks is the application layer. Defense mechanism at this level includes the monitoring of user browsing behavior for anomalies [27,28,], HTTP session analysis and limiting session rates [29], using statistical techniques for constraint random request attacks [30], usage of K-means clusters [31], using probabilistic techniques such as CAPTCHAs, graphic puzzles [32].

DDoS attacks are most commonly about consuming bandwidth and these attacks are the most difficult to defend against. As it was already mentioned, there are no absolute defense solutions to bandwidth consumption attacks, however, certain defense methods might be effective when they are properly implemented. Still, the technical defense methods are only a part of well-constructed risk management. Detection mechanisms refer to the actions performed to identify one or more ongoing attacks. Detection is the process of determining is the target under an attack, an attack must first be detected in order to level an appropriate defensive response.

MULTOPS [18] monitors the packet rate of uplink and downlink of a router. It works on the principle that under normal conditions, there is a proportional traffic transfer rate between two hosts. As a DDoS attack is initiated, a significant disproportional difference occurs in uplink and downlink traffic. Statistical approach for detection of SYN flood attack is proposed by Wang et al. [22]. Ratio of SYN packets to FIN and RST is used to detect such attacks. A similar approach by Blazek et al. [23] detects the DDoS attack using TCP and UDP traffic volume. Both methodologies used the assumption that during a DDoS attack, there will be a statistical change in traffic which can be used for detection of attack. Cheng et al. [21] used spectral analysis of packet arrival in a fixed interval as a sign of DDoS attack. During DDoS attack, large number of similar malicious packets is send from different sources to the victim. However, in case of legitimate traffic there will be many different traffic types. On the bases of this Kulkarni et al. [19] proposed a Kolmogorov detection system which uses the randomness and correlation in traffic flow to detect DDoS attack.

Cabrera et al. [25] used the correlation of traffic behavior at attack source as well as at victim. In the first step key variables from victim are extracted and analyzed in statistical tools to match variable of potential attacks in the second step. In the third step, normal profile is built which is further used with the variable to detect the potential attacks. Statistical approach used by Manikopoulos and Papavassiliou [20] is based on anomaly detection. First a normal profile is build using statistical modeling and neural network. Similarity distance is use for detection of attack. If the distance between monitor traffic and normal profile is greater than the threshold, it is assumed that a DDoS attack is in progress.

6   Proposed Solution (PSBTRA)

We proposed a solution for real time UDP flood attack detection. After evaluating the number of time in connectionless environment the proposed solution seems to be computationally fast and effective. When a server is under bandwidth attack, it cannot reply to any requested service after maximum waiting time or due to unavailability of bandwidth. So it is assumed that a server under bandwidth attack will have higher incoming traffic and lower outgoing traffic and with a higher variation between them. It is further assumed that even if the server is still able to provide the requested service, the Quality of Service (QoS) will be degraded due to the limited bandwidth available to the legitimate users. Based on these assumptions we defined the traffic ratio *Traffic(T)* as:

$$Traffic(T) = Traffic(IN) / Traffic(OUT) \tag{1}$$

In eq (1), the *Traffic(IN)* is Number of incoming packets per second and *Traffic(OUT)* is Number of outgoing packets per second.

6.1   *Traffic(T)* Ratio

In order to confirm it, a study has been during which network traffic of a proxy server was captured through wireshark [33] and stored in libpcap format for further analysis. The capture traffic contains both the normal traffic and UDP flood attacks.

The analysis shows that during normal time period, the incoming and outgoing traffic is 62% and 38% respectively, while during the attack time period, it changed to 88% and 12% as shown in Fig. 2. The network traffic directed toward victim with a higher load of incoming over outgoing traffic is most likely intrusive and the value of *Traffic(T)* will be higher with a possibility of bandwidth attack. The traffic ratio *Traffic(T)* was also calculated for normal traffic eq (2) and for attack traffic eq (3).

$$Traffic(T_{Normal}) = 178953 / 108121 = 1.655118 \tag{2}$$

$$Traffic(T_{Attack}) = 768502 / 103093 = 7.454454 \tag{3}$$

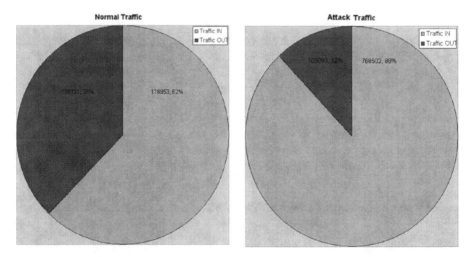

Fig. 2. Incoming and outing traffic under normal condition and during attack

It is clear that during the bandwidth attack the value of *Traffic(T)* is higher as compare to normal traffic. It was also reported by the users that they faced degradation in the Quality of Service (QoS) of Proxy Server during the attack time period, so this confirms the assumptions that during a bandwidth attack, system under bandwidth attack will have higher incoming traffic and low outgoing traffic and with a higher variation between them along with low QoS.Although, the *Traffic(T)* can detect bandwidth attacks, it has a short come. This ratio fails to distinguish between the bandwidth attack and flash crowd. The flash crowd which occurs when a large number of legitimate users access a server at the same time. A better approach is to use protocol composition with traffic ratio.

6.2   Protocol Proportion

When a specific attack is commenced, the proportion of the specific exploited protocol increases abruptly. Since the proportion of each protocol in traffic is related to each other, the increase in the proportion of exploit protocol makes the proportion of other protocols to decease. Therefore a detection technique can be design by monitoring the variation of the incoming and outgoing traffic by each protocol. As stated in Table 1 during flash crowd, the traffic is mostly web traffic. So a more better approach is to use *Traffic(T)* ratio along with the proportion of different protocols in network traffic. It was also observed that during the UDP flood attack, the proportion of UDP was considerably more than the other protocol.

Fig. 3 shows the proportion of incoming and outgoing TCP(96.47%), ICMP(0.71%) and UDP(3.82%) under normal traffic, while fig. 4 shows the proportion of incoming and outgoing TCP(4.43%), ICMP(10.12%) and UDP(85.36%) during attack.

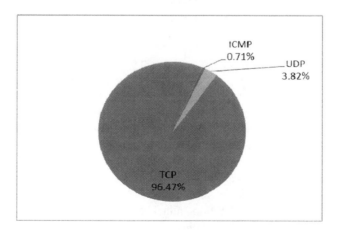

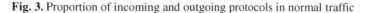

Fig. 3. Proportion of incoming and outgoing protocols in normal traffic

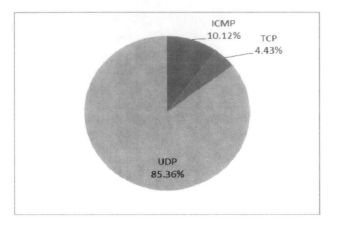

Fig. 4. Proportion of incoming and outgoing protocols during attack

6.3   Detection of UDP Flood Attack

The UDP Flood attack can be detected using the Equation (4).

$$IN_p(UDP) > (IN_p(ICMP) + IN_p(TCP)) \text{ and} (OUT_p(ICMP) > OUT_p(TCP)) \text{and}$$
$$OUT_P(ICMP_{type}) == 3 \tag{4}$$

In Equation (4), the

$IN_p\ (IUDP)$	Proportion of incoming UDP traffic.
$IN_p\ (ICMP)$	Proportion of incoming ICMP traffic.
$IN_p\ (TCP)$	Proportion of incoming TCP traffic.
$OUT_p\ (ICMP)$	Proportion of outgoing ICMP traffic.
$OUT_p\ (TCP)$	Proportion of outgoing TCP traffic.
$OUT_P(ICMP_{type})$	Outgoing ICMP type 3(ICMP Destination Unreachable)

When an UDP packet is received, the PSBTRA becomes active. PSBTRA first compare the current proportion of incoming UDP traffic with current aggregated proportion of incoming ICMP and TCP traffic. Then it compares the current proportion of outgoing ICMP with the current proportion of outgoing TCP. PSBTRA also checks type of outgoing ICMP traffic. If the incoming proportion of UDP is greater than incoming ICMP and TCP and outgoing proportion of ICMP greater then out proportion of TCP and the ICMP type is equal to 3. The detection system alerts an UDP flooding attack. The reason to compare the current proportion of outing ICMP traffic with the current proportion of outgoing TCP and checking it type equal to 3 is that, when a system is under UDP flood attack, an outgoing ICMP traffic is generated. This outgoing traffic is ICMP Destination Unreachable (type code 3) messages informing the client that the destination cannot be reached.

7   Simulations and Results

In order to validate the PSBTRA, experiments were perform on real network having more than 500 clients. Since our research objective was to develop a real work solution, we didn't use any simulation tool or dataset like KDD[34] or DARPA[35]. During experiments an active proxy server was attack using Tribe Flood Network 2000(TFN2K) [36]. PSBTRA was implemented as Linux based application written in C on the proxy server during experiment to generate the traffic statistics and to detect UDP flood attack. Libpcap APIs [37] were use in the application for live packet capturing. The UDP flood attack using TFN2K was generated from 20 clients having 100 Mbps using packet starting with 20 packets per second and was gradually increased. We assumed these 20 clients as zombies. The source addresses of the UDP packets were spoofed. Fig. 5 shows the network layout of the experiment.

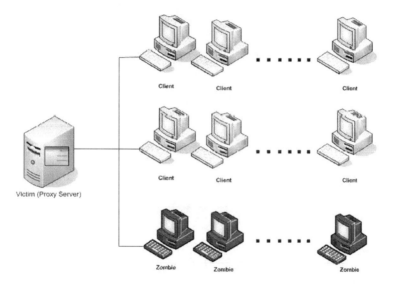

Fig. 5. Network layout of experiment

Fig. 6, 7 and 8 shows the incoming and outgoing TCP, UDP and ICMP traffic. Y axis shows the number of packets per second while X axis shows the time in seconds. A total of 19 minutes traffic was captured and processed. This traffic also includes the UDP flooding attack. As the attack occurs, the incoming UDP traffic rate is increased, at the same time the outgoing ICMP (Destination Unreachable) traffic rate also increases while both the incoming and outgoing TCP rates decreases. Fig. 9 shows the detection of attack by the PSBTRA. As the attack occurs, the PSBTRA immediately detects it and attack alert is generated. Once the attack is finished, the traffic rate of TCP, UDP and ICMP becomes normal.

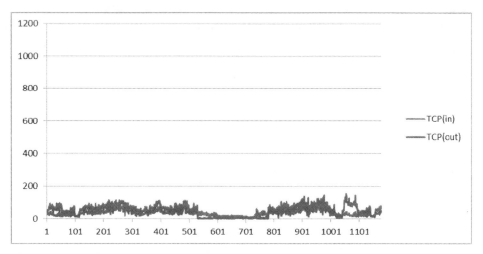

Fig. 6. Number of incoming and outgoing TCP packet. Y axis shows the number of packets per second while X axis shows the time in seconds.

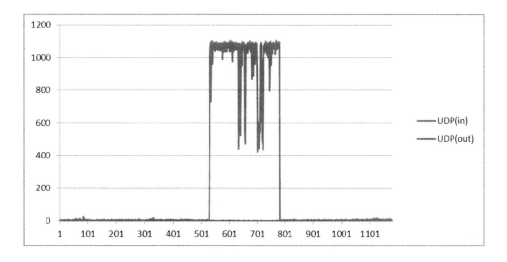

Fig. 7. Number of incoming and outgoing UDP packet. Y axis shows the number of packets per second while X axis shows the time in seconds.

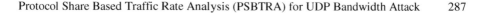

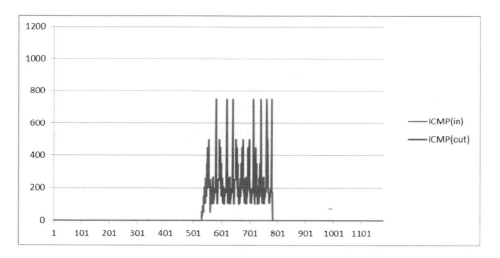

Fig. 8. Number of incoming and outgoing ICMP packet. Y axis shows the number of packets per second while X axis shows the time in seconds.

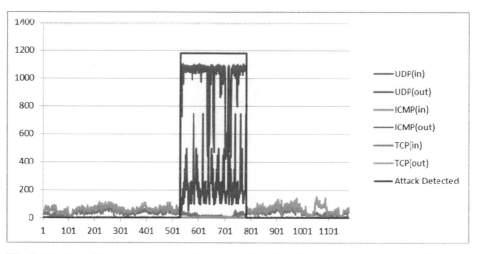

Fig. 9. Number of incoming and outgoing over all traffic. Y axis shows the number of packets per second while X axis shows the time in seconds.

8   Conclusion and Future Work

We have investigated the two main characteristics of bandwidth attack namely the traffic rate and protocol proportion. It is clear from the experiments perform on real network that these two characteristics can detect possible UDP based bandwidth attack. The methodologies presented in this paper has low computational overhead in detection of

UDP bandwidth attacks. The detection scheme based on the monitoring of incoming and outgoing traffic ratio along with the proportion of various protocols for the detection of UDP bandwidth attacks. We are also working to enhance the PSBTRA to detect TCP SYN, ICMP Smurf and other bandwidth attack specially those targeting multimedia traffic/service. The future work can be to add a defense mechanism can also be added to defend against such attacks by filtering the malicious traffic.

Acknowledgment. This research is supported by International Doctrinal Fellowship (IDF) No. UTM.J10.00/13.14/1/128(191) of Universiti Teknologi Malaysia and collaboration with Research Management Center (RMC) Universiti Teknologi Malaysia.

References

1. Lipson, H.F.: CERT CC: Tracking and tracing cyber-attacks: Technical challenges and global policy issues. Special Report CMU/SEI-2002-SR-009 (2002)
2. Blumenthal, M.S., Clark, D.D.: Rethinking the Design of the Internet: The End-to-End Argument vs. the Brave New World. ACM Transactions on Internet Technology 1, 70–109 (2001)
3. RFC 793 Transmission Control Protocol, http://www.faqs.org/rfcs/rfc793.html
4. Albert, R., Jeong, H., Barabási, A.: The Internet's Achilles' Heel: Error and attack tolerance of complex networks. Nature 406, 378–382 (2000)
5. Bellovin, S.M.: Security Problems in the TCP/IP Protocol Suite. ACM Computer Communications Review 19, 32–48 (1989)
6. CERT CC CERT Statistics, http://www.cert.org/stats/
7. RFC 791 Internet protocol, http://www.ietf.org/rfc/rfc0791.txt
8. Howard, J.D.: An Analysis of security incidents on the Internet 1989-1995. In: Ph. D dissertation. Carnegie Mellon University, Carnegie Institute of Technology (1998)
9. CERT CC Denial of Service Attacks, http://www.cert.org/tech_tips/denial_of_service.html
10. Orman, H., Streak, P.: The Morris Worm: A Fifteen-Year Perspective. IEEE Security & Privacy Magazine 1, 35–43 (2003)
11. Jelena Mirkovic, J., Peter Reiher, P.: A Taxonomy of DDoS Attacks and DDoS defense Mechanisms. ACM SIGCOMM Computer Communication Review 34, 39–53 (2004)
12. CERT CC CERT Advisory CA-1998-01 Smurf IP Denial-of-Service Attacks, http://www.cert.org/advisories/CA-1998-01.html
13. Dietrich, S., Long, N., Dittrich, D.: Analyzing distributed denial of service attack tools: The shaft case. In: Proceedings of the 14th USENIX Conference on System Administration, pp. 329–339 (2000)
14. Peng, T., Leckie, C., Ramamohanarao, K.: Survey of Network-Based Defense Mechanisms Countering the DoS and DDoS Problems. ACM Computing Surveys 39, 1–42 (2007)
15. CERT CC CERT Advisory CA-1996-01 UDP Port Denial-of-Service Attack, http://www.cert.org/advisories/CA-1996-01.html
16. El-Atawy, A., Al-Shaer, E., Tran, T., Boutaba, R.: Adaptive Early Packet Filtering for Defending Firewalls Against DoS Attacks. In: IEEE Conference on Computer Communications, pp. 2437–2445 (2009)
17. Wang, X., You-lin Xiao, Y.: IP Traceback Based on Deterministic Packet Marking and Logging. In: International Conference on Embedded Computing, pp. 178–182 (2009)

18. Gil, T.M., Poletto, M.: MULTOPS, A data-structure for bandwidth attack detection. In: Proceedings of 10th Usenix Security Symposium, pp. 23–38 (2001)
19. Kulkarni, A.B., Bush, S., Evans, S.: Detecting distributed denial-of- service attacks using Kolmogorov complexity metrics. Technical Report 2001CRD176, GE Research & Development Center (2001)
20. Manikopoulos, C., Papavassiliou, S.: Network intrusion and fault detection: A statistical anomlay approach. IEEE Communications Magazine, 76–82 (2002)
21. Cheng, C.M., Kung, H.T., Tan, K.: Use of spectral analysis in defense against DoS attacks. In: IEEE Global Communications Conference, pp. 2143–2148 (2002)
22. Wang, H., Zhang, D., Shin, K.G.: Detecting SYN flooding attacks. In: IEEE Conference on Computer Communications, vol. 3, pp. 1530–1539 (2002)
23. Blazek, R.B., Kim, H., Rozovskii, B., Tartakovsky, A.: A novel approach to detection of denial-of-service attacks via adaptive sequential and batch-sequential change-point detection methods. In: IEEE Systems, Man and Cybernetics Information Assurance Workshop, vol. 54, pp. 3372–3382 (2006)
24. Limwiwatkul, L., Rungsawangr, A.: Distributed denial of service detection using TCP/IP header and traffic measurement analysis. In: International Symposium Communication Information Technology, pp. 605–610 (2004)
25. Cabrera, J.B.D., Lewis, L., Qin, X., Lee, W., Prasanth, R.K., Ravichandran, B., Mehra, R.K.: Proactive detection of distributed denial of service attacks using MIB traffic variables a feasibility study. In: IFIP/IEEE International Symposium on Integrated Network Management, pp. 609–622 (2001)
26. Noh, S., Lee, C., Choi, K., Jung, G.: Detecting Distributed Denial of Service (DDoS) Attacks Through Inductive Learning. In: Liu, J., Cheung, Y.-m., Yin, H. (eds.) IDEAL 2003. LNCS, vol. 2690, pp. 286–295. Springer, Heidelberg (2003)
27. Xie, Y., Yu, S.: A Large-Scale Hidden Semi-Markov Model for Anomaly Detection on User Browsing Behaviors. IEEE/ACM Transactions on Networking 17, 54–65 (2009)
28. Xie, Y., Yu, S.: Monitoring the Application-Layer DDoS Attacks for Popular Websites. IEEE/ACM Transactions on Networking 17, 15–25 (2009)
29. Ranjan, S., Swaminathan, R., Uysal, M., Nucci, A., Knightly, E.: DDoS-Shield: DDoS-Resilient Scheduling to Counter Application Layer Attacks. IEEE/ACM Transactions on Networking 17, 26–39 (2009)
30. Yen, W., Lee, M.: Defending Application DDoS with Constraint Random Request Attacks. In: Asia-Pacific Conference on Communications, pp. 620–624 (2005)
31. Yu, J., Li, Z., Chen, H., Chen, X.: A Detection and Offense Mechanism to Defend Against Application Layer DDoS Attacks. In: Third International Conference on Networking and Services, pp. 54–54 (2007)
32. Ahn, V., Blum, M., Langford, J.: Telling Humans and Computers Apart Automatically. Communications of the ACM 47, 57–60 (2004)
33. Wireshark,· Go deep, http://www.wireshark.org/
34. KDD Cup 1999 Data (1999), http://kdd.ics.uci.edu/databases/kddcup99/kddcup99.html
35. DARPA Intrusion Detection Evaluation, http://www.ll.mit.edu/mission/communications/ist/corpora/ideval/index.html
36. TFN2K – An Analysis, http://packetstorm.wowhacker.com/distributed/TFN2k_Analysis.htm
37. TCPDUMP/LIBPCAP public repositor, http://www.tcpdump.org

Robust Data Embedding Based Probabilistic Global Search in MDCT Domain

Ei Thin Su

University Of Computer Studies, Yangon, Myanmar
eithinsu.ucsy@gmail.com

Abstract. The rapid growth of the information technology, data hiding in audio is an important role of digital media protection and secret communication. Thus, a technique of robust data embedding in the modified discrete cosine transform domain (MDCT) of cover speech signal is presented to solve the issues of digital audio steganography application. The major contribution of the proposed scheme is introduced Probabilistic Global Search Lausanne Algorithm (PGSL) as the optimization-based problem transformation method, to search the best positions in the first selected frames of MDCT Domain on cover speech samples. The covert data are embedded into the positions of lowest bit error rate value to guarantee perfect inaudibility and enhance imperceptible as well as robustness between cover and stego audio. Speech signals from TIMIT Dataset of 452 Male and Female speakers were served to the host cover audio data. The distortion between cover and stego audio is evaluated with Informal Listening Test and Spectrogram. Results of data hiding using TIMIT clean utterance showed that the distortions in the stego audio is inaudible and imperceptible from the original cover speech even with high payload in the Spectrogram and Informal Listening Test. The proposed system defined to apply the signal manipulation attacks as resampling and noise addition to increase in the robustness of data embedding scheme. Objective measurement of stego audio quality degradation by data embedding was performed by PSNR value.

Keywords: data embedding, MDCT, PGSL Algorithm, digital audio Steganography.

1 Introduction

The advent of digital multimedia with the information technology revolution has made it extremely convenient for users to transfer information. However, to deliver the confidential information over the web, modern technologies have not fully strong till now, so malicious users can easily attack the security and privacy contents. Thus, it is becoming important to prevent privacy and security break. Digital Audio Steganography is a technology being developed, in which secret information is embedded using imperceptible techniques into the host audio to prevent from unauthorized users or attackers. Thus, any third parties can't be noticed the presence of the secret message within the cover audio. Therefore, audio Steganography allows users more privacy and security at the same time. Inaudibility, robustness and capacity are the most important requirements for audio Steganography. Inaudibility: Measures

A. Abd Manaf et al. (Eds.): ICIEIS 2011, Part I, CCIS 251, pp. 290–300, 2011.

perceptual similarity between cover and stego audio at the embedding process. The strength of the audio Steganography lies inaudibility and imperceptibility to be unnoticeable by the human ear. Payload Capacity: Indicates the amount of hidden bits without distortion.

According to the implementation process of audio Steganography, secret data embedding domain can be divided into time domain and transform domain. In time domain schemes, the hidden bits are embedded directly into the time signal samples. From the view of the performance of audio Steganography, the transform domain is considered better than that of the time domain.

Thus, we focus on transform-domain and the transformation technique is done by applying MDCT. In addition, a number of previously proposed data hiding techniques could not meet all of the requirements for audio Steganography. To overcome these issues, a new robust data embedding approach which modifies the mdct transform domain coefficients and secret bits are embedded into the lowest bit error rate value of the modified coefficients and results in both good quality of stego audio from the cover speech in the Spectrogram and Informal Listening Test.

This paper is organized in seven sections. Section 2 introduced related work of the proposed system. We briefly summarize the necessary background theory in Section 3. The proposed data embedding scheme based on PGSL is described in Section 4, which is followed by the expected outcome of this scheme in Section 5 and its test results that are presented in Section 6. The paper is concluded with remarks on the paper's main contribution in Section 7.

2   Related Work

Audio Steganography is an active research area that has been strongly motivated to solve the privacy protection problem of secret communication. The previous methods in the audio Steganography are Low-bit Encoding, Phase coding, Echo data hiding and Spread Spectrum coding. General methods used (lower sensitivity of Human Auditory System) by a little changing of frequency, phase and amplitude of audio sound files have also been proposed.

In *Low-bit encoding*, the secret message is substituted with the least significant bit (LSB) of each sample of the audio cover file. This method is simple and can be used to embed larger messages, but cannot protect the hidden message from small modifications. Thus, it is rarely used in the real commercial applications. *Phase coding* is based on the phase components of sound as imperceptible which the differences between cover and stego audio to the human ear. Message bits are encoded as phase shifts in the phase spectrum of a digital signal. This leads to inaudible encoding. A characteristic feature of Phase coding is the low data transmission rate that the secret message is encoded only in the first segment of the audio signal. An increase in the length of the segment would have a ripple effect by altering the phase relations between the frequency components of the segment, thus making detection easier. Hence, the Phase Coding method is used only when a small amount of data embedded.

In *Echo hiding*, secret message is embedded by introducing an echo into the discrete audio signal. Echo hiding allows for a higher data transmission rate than least significant bit insertion method. *Spread Spectrum coding* method spreads the secret message across the frequency spectrum of the audio signal. It is robust than Phase coding and Low-bit coding but use complex algorithms. In [1], the author proposed A Genetic-Algorithm Based Approach for audio Steganography that have been withstand attacks like noise addition than simple LSB method. In [2], the method of Audio Steganography by Cepstrum Modification is presented, which combines psycho acoustical masking property of HAS with the decorrelation property of speech cepstrum, that achieved high imperceptible embedding and correct data recovery but low payload.

The method of [3] has proposed Increasing Robustness of LSB Audio Steganography Using a Novel Embedding Method. They described that robustness against noise addition or MPEG compression better than standard LSB method. In [4], the author proposed Speech Information Hiding Using Fractional Cosine Transform. They find in their analysis that the 3rd parameter of FRCT presents property of high frequency, then they use low bit embedding method and over zero rate detection method for embedding secret information into speech signal in FRCT domain. They discoveries in their study provide a new thought for application of FRCT in speech information hiding

In [5], the author presented Telephony Speech Enhancement by data hiding to improve intelligibility and perceived quality of telephone speech. Data hiding is based on the perceptual masking principle; the inaudible spectrum components within the telephone bandwidth can be removed without degrading the speech quality, providing a hidden channel to transmit extra information. They showed that robust to quantization errors and channel noises.

In [6], the authors proposed "Robust Information Hiding in Speech Signal Based on Pitch Period Prediction". In this system, first estimates the pitch period of short time speech signal, and then predicts the next period data by the previous one with one parameter. The secret information is embedded into the predict parameter and thus generates the stego speech.

In the present paper, the effectiveness of data embedding into best coefficients of modified discrete cosine transform on the cover speech sample based PGSL algorithm is examined in terms of the robustness with respect to additive white Gaussian noise with a variety of SNR values and resampling. The objective quality degradation by data embedding is evaluated using Spectrogram and Informal Listening Test between cover speech and stego audio.

3   Background Theory

This section describes MDCT domain and detail PGSL (Probabilistic Global Search Lausanne) algorithm of robust data embedding scheme.

3.1   Modified Discrete Cosine Transform

The modified discrete cosine transform (MDCT) is type-IV discrete cosine transform (DCT-IV). The basic DCT is type II. In the present study, MDCT is defined as the data embedding domain, because MDCT has time-domain aliasing cancellation (TDAC) properties and provides better energy compaction than DCT.

Properties of MDCT
MDCT can be directly estimated the capacity of a transformation scheme by its ability to pack input data into as few coefficients as potential. This allow without audible

distortion in the reconstructed audio. It avoids errors between block boundaries. It has the principle TDAC that is to cancel the errors by adding subsequent overlapped IMDCT blocks (inverse modified discrete cosine transform). So it can be done perfect reconstruction. Because of this advantage, we can fulfill imperceptible issues that the differences between the original and stego audio in the proposed data hiding scheme by applying MDCT transform-domain in general. Thus, MDCT is selected as the secret data embedding domain in our proposed data hiding scheme.

3.2   PGSL Algorithm

PGSL (Probabilistic Global Search Lausanne Algorithm) is the global optimization algorithm. It has been developed by Raphael and Smith in 2002. It is applied in the field of structural engineering to solve the optimization problems for bridge diagnosis. It is a direct search algorithm, to find the minimum of user defined objective function by using global sampling [7]. In PGSL, optimal solutions can be defined through focusing search around sets of good solutions. Tests on benchmark problems having multi-parameter non-linear objective functions exposed that PGSL is advanced algorithms and performs better than genetic algorithms. Moreover, PGSL performs better than other approaches even increased the problem size.

In the fields of diagnosis, design and control, PGSL has already established to be worthful for engineering tasks. PGSL helps to solve complicated problems in a high convergence speed. There is no need to a large number of interrelated parameters. It has the advantage of fewer search parameters. PGSL algorithm has been first used to design the interdigital transducer (IDT) structure of the surface acoustic waves (SAW transducer). To aim at a great advance in the transducer characteristics and decreasing in the lead time of the product design. In PGSL Algorithm, a uniform probability density function is accepted for entire search space in the beginning of search. When good solutions are found, increased the probabilities in these regions. Better sets of points are found in the neighborhood of good sets of points. So, search space is more focus on an area of best points then the convergence is achieved.

PGSL algorithm allows four nested cycles: Sampling Cycle, Probability Updating Cycle, Focusing Cycle and Subdomain Cycle.

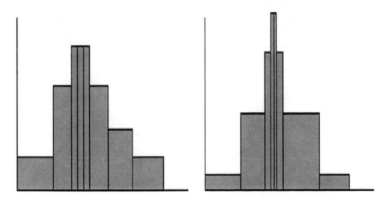

Fig. 1. Evolution of the probability density functions of a variable after several cycles in PGSL algorithm

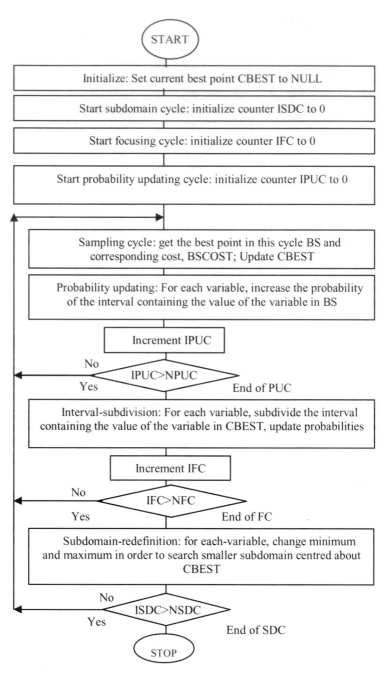

Fig. 2. Flow Chart of PGSL Algorithm

Sampling Cycle: Number of samples is randomly generated according to the current probability density function. Each point is evaluated by user-defined objective function and selected the best point.

Probability Updating Cycle: The sampling cycle is brought up number of probability updating cycle times. After each iteration, the probability density function of each variable is modified using the probability-updating algorithm. This ensures that the sampling frequencies in regions containing good solutions are increased and regions containing bad points are decreased.

Focusing Cycle: Search is focused on the interval containing the best solutions after a number of Probability Updating Cycle, by further subdivision of interval.

Subdomain Cycle: Search space is increasingly narrowed by selecting a subdomain of smaller size center on the best point after each Focusing Cycle.

In the proposed system, the best points of the selected frames are seeked based on the optimized PGSL Algorithm to embed the secret message without distortion as high imperceptibility in the cover and stego audio as well as robustness.

Fig. 1 shows that the evolution of probability density function of a variable after several cycles in PGSL algorithm. In Fig. 2, the flow chart of PGSL algorithm is displayed.

4   Proposed Robust Data Embedding Based on PGSL

This section describes Pre-processing; PGSL based optimal best points searching process and secret data hiding in detail.

4.1   Pre-processing

Firstly define Input as: take 16 bit Clean-host speech from the TIMIT database at the rate of 16,000 per second were selected as the cover audio data. The sampling frequencies were converted to 16 KHz before the embedding stage.

4.2   PGSL Based Optimal Best Points Searching Process

To get the best point for secret data embedding process, firstly input cover speech are applied Framing (non-overlapping frames), Windowing (hanning-window) and Transformation with MDCT. Then, random 5000 bit with binary value 0 and 1 were generated through pseudo random number generator as the secret information. The positions of best coefficients are searched in MCDT domain of the first selected frames by defining the lowest bit error rate value as the best point in the objective function and number of cycle times to search the best position in the main function of the PGSL algorithm.

4.3   Secret Data Hiding Scheme

At the secret data hiding process, covert data is embedded into the best coefficients positions through PGSL algorithm. At first, a pseudo-random function is employed to generate the secret key with binary 0 and 1.

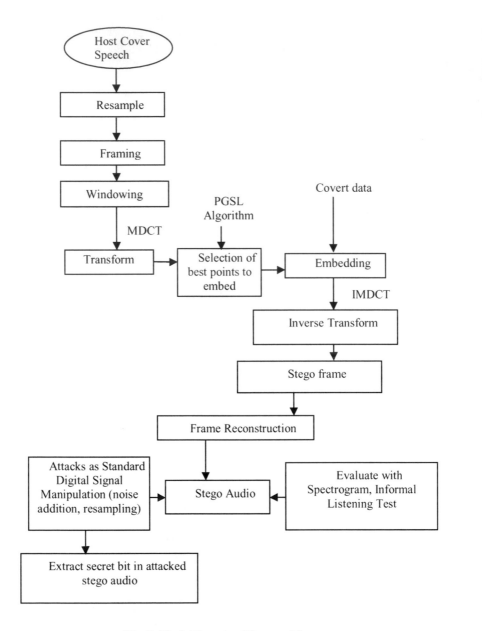

Fig. 3. Block Diagram of Proposed System

In the objective function of PGSL Algorithm, firstly the mdct coefficients in the selected frames of the cover speech are manipulated with the gain factor and added with the secret key. Secondly, the lowest bit error rate positions are searched by subtracting manipulated coefficients from the original coefficients in the objective function of PGSL algorithm. The threshold for the lowest bit error rate (BER) value and require parameter values as the number of cycle times are defined in the main function of PGSL algorithm to search the best position.

After getting the best position through PGSL algorithm, random secret bits are embedded into the best points. Then inverse transformation (IMDCT) and reconstruction is applied to form new audio sequence as stego audio.

At the extraction process, embedded information in each frame is recovered through the best point position and secret key-length used in data hiding process.

The robustness of the proposed system tested with Resampling and noise addition (additive white Gaussian noise) with the overall signal-to-noise-ratio (SNR) was 0 dB, 5 dB, 10 dB and 15 dB were tested. The robustness was evaluated in terms of the bit error rate (BER). No error correction was performed on the embedded data. The results of cover speech and stego audio are shown in Fig. 4, Fig. 5, Fig. 6 and Fig. 7. These figures show that the cover speech and stego audio signals with PSNR above 90.

In Fig. 3, the flow of proposed robust data embedding scheme based on PGSL is displayed.

5   Expected Outcome

Proposed system use clean-host utterances from the TIMIT database, with 16 bit speech samples at the rate of 16 ms is used as the cover audio. High Imperceptibility and inaudibility between original cover speech and stego audio are evaluated with Spectrograms and Informal Listening Tests.

6   Experimental Results

In the experiment using the clean host speech from the TIMIT database include 452 utterances. For the clean host speech with 16 bits per sample at the rate of 16 ms, nonoverlapped frames are used to embed one bit in each of the first selected frames. The quality of evaluated stego audio is tested with Spectrogram and the results are described in Fig. 4, 5, 6 and 7. In these figure shows the Spectrogram of the TIMIT cover speech (original cover audio) and stego (after embedding data which a random 5000 values with binary 0 and 1).

Subjective quality evaluation of the data embedding method has been done by listening to the original cover speech and embedded audio sequences. A total number of all speech at TIMIT database was used as test signals. Clips were 16 KHz speech and represented by 16 bits per sample rate. Duration of each sample was 16 ms.

At all of the test results; the cover host and stego audio are similar and cannot be discriminated and get the PSNR value above 90.

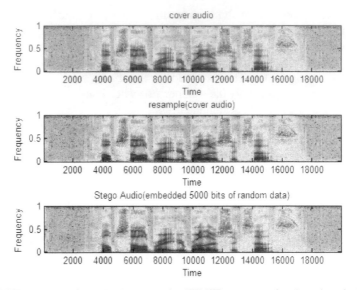

Fig. 4. TIMIT utterance host (top), resample (TIMIT utterance host) and embedded stego (bottom)

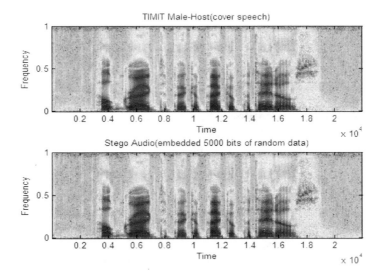

Fig. 5. Spectrogram of TIMIT Host (top) and Stego (bottom)

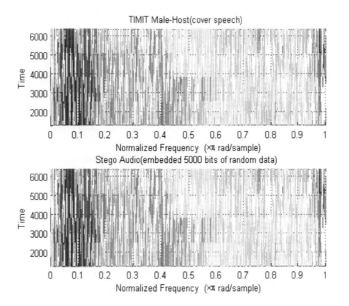

Fig. 6. Spectrogram of TIMIT Male-Host (cover speech) and Stego Audio (embedded random data of 5000 bits with binary value 0 and 1)

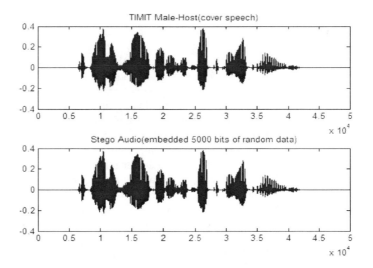

Fig. 7. Original cover speech signal (above) and Stego audio (embedded random data)

7   Conclusion

This paper presented a new technique to improve robustness of the data embedding system using the cover speech. Based on the PGSl algorithm, data embedding in MDCT Domain was evaluated by Spectrogram and Informal Listening Test. The experimental results have shown that the cover speech and stego audio were similar in the Spectrogram Test and inaudible in the Informal Listening Test.

The robustness of data embedding on the subjective quality of audio signals were also investigated by testing the signal manipulation attacks with resampling (up sampling and down sampling) and noise addition of white Gaussian noise (awgn) with the overall signal-to-noise-ratio (SNR) was 0 dB, 5 dB, 10 dB and 15 dB in the stego audio. The quality of secret information was not degraded in the signal manipulation attacks.

The proposed system aim at a great advance in the main characteristics of the audio Steganography, thus the data embedding scheme is done based on two key components: Firstly, the original cover audio is transformed with MDCT and each secret bits are embedded into the secure positions of the best coefficients which have the lowest bit error rate value in the first selected audio samples through PGSL algorithm. Secondly, the presentation of the embedded process verified as high inaudible and imperceptible against distortion of the stego audio from cover speech with PSNR value, Spectrogram and Informal Listening Test. The measurement of perceived audio quality demonstrated to be valuable for secure communication by hiding covert data in the lowest bit error rate positions of the first selected frames on the cover speech.

References

1. Zamani, M., Manaf, A.A., Ahmad, R.B., Zeki, A.M., Abdullah, S.: A Genetic-Algorithm-Based Approach for Audio Steganography. World Academy of Science, Engineering and Technology 54 (2009)
2. Gopalan, K.: Audio Steganography by Cepstrum Modification. In: ICASSP. IEEE (2005)
3. Cvejic, N., Seppanen, T.: Increasing Robustness of LSB Audio Steganography Using a Novel Embedding Method. IEEE
4. Tao, Y., Bao, Y.: Speech Information Hiding Using Fractional Cosine Transform. In: First International Conference on Information Science and Engineering (2009)
5. Chen, S., Leung, H., Ding, H.: Telephony Speech Enhancement by data hiding. IEEE Transactions on Instrumentation and Measurement (February 2007)
6. Chunyan, Y., Sen, B.: Robust Information Hiding in Speech Signal Based on Pitch Period Prediction. In: International Conference on Computational and Information Sciences, pp. 533–536 (2010)
7. Raphael, B., Smith, I.F.C.: A direct stochastic algorithm for global search. Applied Mathematics and Computation 146, 729–758 (2003)

User-Centered Evaluation of Privacy Models for Protecting Personal Medical Information

Suhaila Samsuri[1], Zuraini Ismail[1], and Rabiah Ahmad[2]

[1] Advanced Informatics School, Universiti Teknologi Malaysia
[2] Faculty of Information and Communication Technology,
Universiti Teknikal Malaysia Melaka
umysue@gmail.com, zurainisma@citycampus.utm.my,
rabiah@utem.edu.my

Abstract. Privacy has always been a crucial element in the management of personal medical information. It warrants a comprehensive model during the designing stage of the management system in order to conserve the security of the information. One of the key success factors in protecting the privacy of information is measured by the ability of the users in controlling the flow of the information in the system. This research concentrates on the integrated models of privacy protection for health information environment which can be applied as guidance while designing a secured electronic medical record for health information system (HIS). The system's effectiveness that uses this integrated model is suggested to be evaluated with the user-centred evaluation model (UPEM). This privacy protection model outlined four important components which were based on the findings from the interviews conducted namely legislation, ethic, technology and culture.

Keywords: Privacy, hospital information system, personal medical information.

1   Introduction

A health information system (HIS) has become synonymous with hospital management system ever since it was mentioned by the former US first lady, now the Secretary of State, Hillary Clinton [1]. The ultimate objectives of having this paperless-based information management system are mainly to alleviate the long waiting time for consultation, improve cost reduction as well as promote accuracy of information. Given that one of the core components in HIS is managing patient's medical information, the public are usually unaware that despite the benefits of HIS, the privacy of patient's personal information becomes susceptible to unauthorised parties. According to some researches, the enhancement of technology brought along a risk to privacy, more specifically reference has been made to computerized databases, computer-based record keeping and telemedicine [2].

The determinant of success in the adoption of HIS largely depends on the confidence level of the proprietor of information towards the ability of hospital management in controlling and handling the flow of records in the hospital.

A. Abd Manaf et al. (Eds.): ICIEIS 2011, Part I, CCIS 251, pp. 301–309, 2011.
© Springer-Verlag Berlin Heidelberg 2011

Therefore, it is fundamentally important for hospital management to seriously inculcate privacy preservation into its consideration when deciding to develop HIS for their hospitals, in order for the system to run efficiently and be capable in bringing the intended benefits. One of the key approaches is to provide the user of the system with enough privacy level as a basic requirement of information system at any time and any place [3].

The centre of this study is to discuss the integrated models for protecting Personal Medical Information (PMI) that used to be managed in electronic medical records (EMR) in HIS and the model that can be used to evaluate the privacy of the system. A PMI can be assumed as the most vulnerable information available since it is accessible to many parties such as doctors, nurses, pharmacists or maybe administrators due to its nature. A PMI also is the most important document for patients in order to get the most effective treatment in the hospital. Nevertheless, it could be exposed to the several criminal actions; among them are identity thefts, illegal publication, tempering of insurance policy and health care fraud.

PMI is similar to the definition of Personal Health Information (PHI) by Cavoukian [4] that includes oral or written information about individual; relates to the individual's physical or mental health, identification of the individual, family health history, plan of service for long-term care, DNA information, payment eligibility for health care, individual's substitute's decision-maker and donation of body parts.

The privacy and security of this type of information have been reported to be the prominent concern of the public, patients and providers (e.g. hospitals or health agencies) [5]. Electronic medical record systems contain many assets that are just as valuable to attackers as they are to healthcare providers, as mentioned in one of the researches, if electronic health record systems are not secured (in terms of privacy), patients may get improper healthcare or have life-shattering or embarrassing information exposed due to privacy breaches [6].

It is essential that the information system developers need to observe a comprehensive guidance in designing information management system to be used in HIS which can preserve the security and privacy of PMI [7]. Thus, this paper proposes integration models of privacy protection for health information system which act as a tool of guidance whenever designing a secured electronic medical record for HIS. Visibly, the second part of this paper will explore the previous studies of related field, subsequently followed by the methodologies used in third part. The fourth part of this paper shall discuss the data collection and analysis of the research and finally the conclusion.

2   Literature Review

The information privacy, as expressed by Westin is the control over how information about a person is handled and communicated to others [8] and emphasized by Fried, who stated that "privacy is not simply an absence of information about us in the minds of others, rather it is the 'control' that we have over information about ourselves" [9]. Based on Westin's concept, this research focuses on the theory of 'access control' as promoted by Moor [10] in order to protect individual's information privacy.

In this context, privacy control literally means limiting what personal data is made available to others. In other words, it is how personal data is disclosed and shared with others [11]. There were several studies from well-known researchers that revealed clearly on the effective models proposed for information privacy protection intended to be used in developing secure information system.

The first model was raised by Holvast [12], which in his paper; he mentioned four models of privacy protection suggested by the Electronic Privacy Information Center (EPIC), as follows:

i.   Comprehensive laws: using general law that governs the collection, use and dissemination of personal information by both the public and private sector. An oversight body then ensures compliance.
ii.   Sectoral laws: there are specific laws, governing specific technical applications, or specific regions, such as financial privacy.
iii.   Self-regulation: using a code of conduct or practice established by companies and industries, which engage in self-policing.
iv.   Technology of privacy: using available technology-based systems such as privacy-enhancing technologies that provide several privacy protection mechanisms.

Nonetheless, since the requirement of privacy protection and existing laws and regulations vary between countries, those four models might not be applicable to be applied at once.

The second information privacy protection models were proposed by Fischer-Hübner [13, 14] namely;

i.   Protection by government laws
ii.   Protection by privacy-enhancing technologies
iii.   Self-regulation for fair information practice by codes of conduct promoted by business
iv.   Privacy education of consumers and IT professionals

The Fischer-Hübner's models were much more acceptable by other countries since it referred to any privacy protection laws that were enacted by government. There were three models that seemed similar to what had been proposed by EPIC which included the use of law, technology and self-regulations. Fischer-Hübner had also added another component of education towards privacy protection which was not reflected by EPIC.

The third models were suggested by Peter Swire in his presentation on 'Privacy Today' [15] on ways of protecting privacy that included:

i.   Technology: the adoption of security and privacy mechanism in a system
ii.   Law: the rules and regulations necessary in controlling the information accessibility
iii.   Market: business and commercial organization provide some degree of security and privacy control to protect the customers, but still depends on the organization's requirements
iv.   Individual's choice: it is all up to the customer as an individual to choose any business or commerce that promote best or poor privacy protection.

Other than technology and law, Swire included market mainly because most information privacy cases were directly related to commercial and business dealings. By adding individual's choices as a suggested model, Swire indirectly conformed to the privacy definition by Charles Fried [9] that emphasized on the rights of control by the owner of the information him/her self. All of these proposed models outlined by the previous researches have been the basic platform for this research.

A study must be conducted in ensuring the relevance of the models to be adopted in the development of electronic medical records which are also capable in protecting the privacy of PMI.

3   Methodologies

A preliminary survey was conducted to examine the procedures of PMI management and privacy mechanism embraced by Malaysian HIS hospitals developed by the Malaysian Ministry of Health (MOH). It was a cognitive assessment in validating the feasibility of the research that will lead to the development of a comprehensive privacy protection guideline which suits the Malaysian environment.

There are three main procedures embedded in this study;

i.   Semi-structured interviews that were conducted based on the models and the analysis was then referred to the current Personal Data Protection Act.

ii.   Semi-structured interviews that were selectively conducted with authorized personnel who are highly involved in policy practice and data protection in the government, have hands-on experience in matters related to hospital privacy and data protection policy.

iii. Interviews were also conducted to gauge the practitioners' perspective, whereby the interviewees were chosen due to their knowledge in privacy policy and also their heavy involvement in the development of EMR system throughout Malaysia.

The persons interviewed were selected from nationwide, covering a wide range of responsibilities in the development of hospital information system such as the Information Technology Director and Officer, Electronic Medical Record Officer, doctor and magistrate, as depicted in Table 1.

Table 1. Pilot Study Interviewee

Designation	Number of interview	Organization
Information Technology Director	1	Ministry of Health
Information Technology Officer (*involved in Malaysia Hospital Information System*)	1	Ministry of Health
Electronic Medical Record Officer	1	Government Hospital
Electronic Medical Record Officer	1	Semi-government Hospital
Doctor	1	Government Hospital
Magistrate	1	Malaysian Magistrate Court

Altogether six (6) interviews were conducted between November 2009 and March 2010. Each session took 45 to 50 minutes to complete. The findings from these interviews will be used to compare with the existing privacy protection models and design a new set of models to be used as a guideline in designing a capable electronic medical record system that protects the PMI's privacy.

The models then will be appraised using quantitative studies through a set of questionnaire which will be designed and distributed to respondents whom among are the system's users; administrators, doctors, nurses and other personnel. For this research purpose, the above group of interviewees are selected due to the fact that almost all of them are highly involved with the development or evaluation of HIS.

The effectiveness of the models or systems can then be evaluated using User-centred Privacy Evaluation Model (UPEM) [16]. The three metrics that can be used are as follows;

  i.   User Control over private information: measures the level of identity, location and time of the user while using the system.
  ii.   Expressiveness of Privacy Policies: measures by evaluating the support for mandatory and discretionary rules, context sensitivity and uncertainty handling and conflict resolution.
  iii. Unobtrusiveness of privacy mechanisms: measures the percentage of time the user spends on dealing with privacy alarms, messages and makes decision accordingly.

In a HIS, the system users must be given the authorisation from the authority before granted access to the personal information system as the level of privacy is designed according to need-to-know basis. These users including doctors, nurses and administrative officers are restricted to the information relating to their department only and will not be able to view information belong to other units or department. As they are highly responsible on the management of patient's health records, they are expected to maintain the information privacy and confidentiality.

4   Findings

This research successfully listed a set of important models for information privacy protection based on the preliminary investigation that reasonably suit with the requirements of different countries. The transcripts of the interviews are available in text and the crux of the discussions and points were listed. Unlike the models which were proposed by EPIC, the comprehensive models mentioned below need to be used simultaneously during the early stage of system development to ensure the efficiency of the system. The models proposed are as follows;

Legislation. Legislation or Law is the most decisive factor in protecting an individual's information privacy. As mentioned earlier by the three scholars; Holvast, Fischer-Hübner and Swire, all of them mutually agreed that law (whatever rules enacted by the government that refer to the controlling and the manipulation of personal information) is necessarily significant in assuring individual's right over his/her personal information. As for Malaysia, we already have our Personal Data Protection Act, 2010, as mentioned by a legal expertise,

"Personal health/medical information in Malaysia is categorized under 'sensitive information' in personal data protection act" (Magistrate).

The act is listed seven principles in any act of deliberation and manipulation of an individual's personal information as per the following; general principle, notice & choice principle, disclosure principle, security principle, retention principle, data integrity principle and access principle.

Ethics. Ethics is a term which refers to self-regulation that basically contains several codes of ethics being practiced by a certain organizations or institutions like hospitals. For nations with privacy or data protection law are absent, they can only cling on to their 'codes of ethics' in protecting their individuals or consumers' rights, which also need to be stated in their service policies, as mentioned by EPIC and Fischer-Hübner. The ethical principles are usually conforming to the international standard of services provided in Medical Act or Nurses Act, which cover the policy of individual privacy. As mentioned by one of the officers from Ministry of Health Malaysia,

"Since the personal data protection act has yet been enforced, our employees including doctors, nurses and other staffs are controlled strictly under ethical code of conducts" (Officer 1).

This research has able to list some valuable components included in the ethics that are compulsory for protecting individual or patient's information privacy managed in electronic medical record system; confidentiality code, data protection code and computer use code.

Technology. Technology is also incorporated in the privacy protection ways stipulated by three scholars above. Since the transformation of information management in the hospital into paperless-based system has embarked, the use of privacy mechanism technology is consequently inevitable. One of the interviewees said that,

"We are developing our own health information system to improve security and privacy control over health information management with our own privacy mechanism technologies. Patients will have the chance to access their own personal medical information" (Officer 2).

This model needs to be factored from scratch during the HIS designing stage. Factors that fall under its consideration are; data collection, system design and maintenance, audit & training.

Culture. This is the most crucial model which distinguishes this from other previous studies. Most of the interviewees have cited the culture-based privacy which its practice differ from one country to another. This model replicates with the Moor's perception on privacy which stated, 'the concept of privacy has distinctly cultural aspect which goes beyond the core values. Some cultures may value privacy and some may not' [10]. Western countries should not expect the same privacy practice of their countries as compared to Asian countries, who value the privacy much less than them, as Karat said, 'privacy means different things to different people' [17]. As mentioned by one of the interviewees,

"Malaysia is perhaps not fully ready for the full implementation of privacy according to western concept. We are unique societies where distinction gap in social cultures and values co-exist, unless the modification is done for the privacy concept to suit us" (Officer 2).

It is the instilled culture of the people that determine the extent of privacy preservation of personal information. However, the basic rights of human being still need to be considered and we need to avoid any occurrence of wrong doing in the future. Therefore, some components have been listed for this model; artefacts, shared value and basic assumption.

Based on the findings here and comparison with the other models mentioned by previous studies such as education and training by Fischer-Hübner, market and individual's choices by Swire are subsets in this category. If an organization or institution (i.e. hospital) value privacy as a key factor in their system efficiencies, the management surely will provide the involved employees with sufficient education and training on the secure information privacy management. The exact notion also applies to the market factors and individual's choice. If the government of a particular country (Asian countries especially) considers individual's information as something valuable to be traded of, it is nearly impossible to expect them to safeguard individual's information as what is being practiced in other developed countries. Thus, the proposed model for information privacy protection in this research is resulted from the integration of models suggested by a group of HIS developers and researchers as shown in Figure 1 below;

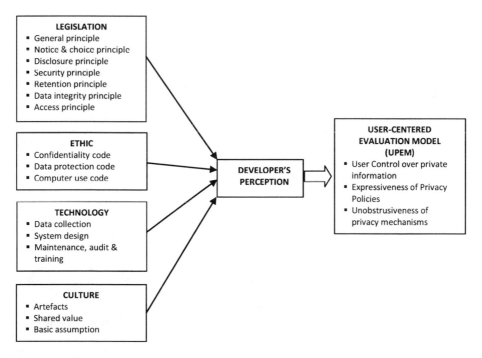

Fig. 1. A proposed model for Personal Information Privacy Protection

5   Conclusion

This model will proceed with assessment of the system by using the UPEM evaluation method as mentioned in the methodology section. It is also can be used to appraise the effectiveness of existing information system in terms of the privacy protection mechanism in place. Over the coming years, this research shall be able to lead the research on owner of information (the person who provides the information which is being managed by another who is a user of a system that is storing and handling the information) perspective and the substantial role of culture element in characterizing the need of society with regards to privacy of information. This parameter is primarily important in determining the type of technology and mechanism of privacy protection which is to be embedded in the information system.

Acknowledgements. Suhaila Samsuri is currently an academic trainee at the International Islamic University Malaysia and pursuing her PhD in Universiti Teknologi Malaysia. This study was funded by the Research University Grant (RUG) from Universiti Teknologi Malaysia. The authors thank to all the interviewees on their cooperation and support in this research.

References

1. Gostin, L.O.: Health Information Privacy. Cornell Law Review (1995),
   http://www.lexisnexis.com
2. Leino-Kilpi, H., Valimaki, M., Dassen, T., Gasull, M., Lemonidou, C., Scott, A., Arndt, M.: Privacy: a review of the literature. International Journal of Nursing Studies 38, 663–671 (2001)
3. Dehghantanha, A., Mahmod, R., Udzir, N.I., Zukarnain, Z.A.: UPEM: User-centered Privacy Evaluation Model in Pervasive Computing Systems. Ubiquitous Computing and Communication Journal (2009),
   http://www.ubicc.org/files/pdf/Paper%20ID%20360%20-%20UPEM_360.pdf (accessed on November 2010)
4. Cavoukian, A.: A Guide to the Personal Health Information Protection Act. Information and Privacy Commissioner of Ontario 46 (2004)
5. Perera, G., Holbrook, A., Thabane, L., Foster, G., Willison, D.J.: Views on health information sharing and privacy from primary care practices using electronic medical records. International Journal of Medical Information 80, 94–101 (2011)
6. Smith, B., Austin, A., Brown, M., King, J., Lankford, J., Meneely, A., Williams, L.: Challenges for protecting the privacy of health information: required certification can leave common vulnerabilities undetected. In: SPIMACS 2010, Chicago, Illinois, USA (2010)
7. Westin, A.: Privacy and Health Information Technology, Information Technology, Health Records and Privacy. Columbia University, Washington D.C., USA (2004)
8. Westin, A.F.: Privacy and freedom. Atheneum, New York (1967)
9. Fried, C.: Privacy, Philosophical Dimensions of Privacy. In: Schoeman, F.D. (ed.), pp. 203–222. Cambridge University Press, New York (1984)
10. Moor, J.H.: Towards a Theory of Privacy in the Information Age. In: CEPE 1997, Computers and Society, pp. 27–32 (1997)

11. Whitley, E.A.: Informational privacy, consent and the "control" of personal data. Information Security Technical Report 14, 154–159 (2009)
12. Holvast, J.: History of Privacy. In: Matyáš, V., Fischer-Hübner, S., Cvrček, D., Švenda, P. (eds.) IFIP WG 9.2, 9.6/11.6, 11.7/FIDIS. IFIP AICT, vol. 298, pp. 13–42. Springer, Heidelberg (2009)
13. Fischer-Hübner, S., Thomas, D.: Privacy and Security at risk in the Global Information Society. In: Loade, B. (ed.) Cybercrime. Routledge, London (2000)
14. Fischer-Hübner, S.: Privacy-Enhancing Technologies (PET), Course Description. Karlstad University Division for Information Technology, Karlstad (2001)
15. Swire, P.: Privacy Today, International Association of Privacy Professionals (2008), http://www.privacyassociation.org (accessed on November 2010)
16. Dehghantanha, A., Mahmod, R.: UPM: User-centered Privacy Model in Pervasive Computing Systems. In: 2009 International Conference on Future Computer and Communication, pp. 65–70 (2009)
17. Karat, J., Karat, C.M., Broodie, C.: Human Computer Interaction viewed from the intersection of privacy, security and trust. In: Sears, A., Jacko, J.A. (eds.) The Human Computer Interaction Handbook: Fundamentals, Evolving Technologies and Emerging Applications, 2nd edn. Lawrence Erlbaum Associates, New York (2008)

The Effect of DCT and DWT Domains on the Robustness of Genetic Watermarking

Abduljabbar Shaamala[1], Shahidan M. Abdullah[2], and Azizah A. Manaf[2]

[1] Faculty of Computer Science and Information Technology, Universiti Teknologi
Malaysia(UTM), Johor, Malaysia
hmsabduljabbar3@live.utm.my
[2] Advanced Informatics School (AIS), Universiti Teknologi Malaysia (UTM),
Kuala Lumpur, Malaysia
{mshahidan,azizah07}@ic.utm.my

Abstract. Watermarking using genetic algorithm for the optimization of the tread-off between the watermarking requirements has attracted the attention of researchers; amongst the watermarking requirements, the robustness is an important one. Watermarking embedded in frequency domain using DWT or DCT can affect the robustness of watermarking, this paper studies the effect of embedding domain on the robustness in genetic watermarking. Results of attacks based on numerical correlation (NC) is analyzed through the paper sections, the DWT results showed more robustness than DCT in watermarking based on GA.

Keywords: watermarking, genetic algorithm. DWT, DCT.

1 Introduction

Since digital multimedia have become progressively advanced in the rapidly growing field of internet application, data securities, including copyright protection and data integrity detection, have become a vast concern. One key for achieving information security is digital watermarking, which embeds hidden information or secret data in the image [1]. This technology works as a suitable tool for identifying the source, creator, owner, distributor, or authorized consumer of a document or image. Watermarking can also be used to detect a document or image is illegally distributed or modified [2].

Watermark techniques can be divided into two groups: Visible and invisible, the visible watermark is used if embedded watermark is intended to be seen by human eyes, For example, a logo inserted into corner of an image. While the invisible watermark is embedded into a host image by sophisticated algorithms and is invisible to the human eyes [3].

Watermarking techniques also can be classified according to its robust as robust, semi-fragile and fragile [3], Robust watermarks are designed to survive intentional (malicious) and unintentional (non-malicious) modifications of the watermarked image [4-6], Semi-fragile watermarks are layout for detecting any unauthorized alteration, and allowing in the same time some image processing operations [7, 8]. On

A. Abd Manaf et al. (Eds.): ICIEIS 2011, Part I, CCIS 251, pp. 310–318, 2011.

the contrary, a watermarking technique that cannot robust against noise or attacks is called fragile technique[3]. Fragile watermarking techniques are concerned with complete integrity verification. Furthermore, watermarking techniques can be classified as blind and non-blind. Blind watermarking [9] techniques don't require access to the original unwatermarked data (image, video, audio, etc.) to recover the watermark. In contrast, non-blind watermarking technique requires the original data [3, 9] needed for extraction of the watermarked. In general, the non-blind scheme is more robust than the blind watermark as it is obvious that the watermark can be extracted easily by knowing the unwatermarked data.

According to the embedding, watermarking techniques divided into two embedding domain, spatial domain and frequency domain [3, 9]. The main concept of spatial domain [10] is to insert a watermark into an image by modifying the gray value of certain pixels in the image [11, 12]. The classical methods are to modify the last significant bits (LSB) of specific pixels of the host image based on the watermark bits [3].For frequency domain, the main concept to insert a watermark into frequency coefficients of the transformed image using the discrete cosine transform (DCT), the discrete wavelet transform (DWT) [13], or other kind of transforms techniques [3, 9].

There are requirements and constraints in design effective watermarking algorithms the three fundamental amongst it are,

- Imperceptibility: should the difference between the watermarked image and the original image not noticeable and visible by human eyes,
- Robustness: is the ability of watermarking to survive and withstand any intentional or unintentional attacks,
- Capacity: is the number of bits embedded into the original image.

The above watermarking requirements are conflicting with each other. If watermark is embedding bits into higher frequency coefficient would change the image as little as possible and achieve the imperceptibility. However, that would reduce the robustness since the watermarked image may experience filtering and the hidden watermark may be vanished. Also if watermark is Embedding bits into lower frequency coefficient would increase the robustness. However, this would sacrifice the imperceptibility [14], [15]. The watermarking problem can be viewed as an optimization problem. Therefor genetic algorithm (GA) can be used for solving such problem [16] [17].

In this paper we present the effectiveness of embedding domain in the robustness of genetic watermarking. Section 2 briefly describes DWT and DCT embedding domain. Then an overview about genetic algorithm (GA) and some related watermark using genetic algorithm are briefly reviewed. In section 3 we disuse some result of previous works and compare attacks results of it in order to identify the robust embedding domain in watermarking using GA.

2   Watermarking in Embedding Domain

2.1   Discrete Cosine Transform (DCT)

Discrete cosine transform (DCT) is a general orthogonal transform for digital image processing and signal processing, with such advantages, as high compression ratio, small bit error rate, good information integration ability and good synthetic effect of calculation complexity. DCT is a widely used mechanism for image transformation and has been adopted by JPEG to compress images; discrete cosine transform (DCT) is a Fourier-related transform similar to the discrete Fourier transform (DFT)[18]. Discrete cosine transform (DCT) turn over the image edge to make the image transformed into the form of even function[19]. It's one of the most common linear transformations in digital signal process technology. The DCT allows an image to be broken up into different frequency bands, making it much easier to embed watermarking information into the middle frequency bands of an image. The middle frequency bands are chosen such that the most visual important parts of the image (low frequencies) is to be avoided without over-exposing it to removal through compression and noise attacks (high frequencies)[20].

In DCT domain, DC component is more suitable to embed watermark than AC component (AC) due to several reasons. Firstly, DC component has larger perceptual capacity. so, after embedding watermark it doesn't cause obvious change for visual quality of original image; secondly, signal processing and noise interference have smaller influence for DC component than AC component[21].

The DCT coefficients for output image $T(u, v)$ are computed according to the input $f(x, y)$ as equation (1). Where f is the input image with size $M \times N$ pixels, M is the row and N is the column of the image, whereas $T(u, v)$ is the DCT matrix.

$$T(u, v) = \alpha_u \alpha_v \sum_{x=0}^{M-1} \sum_{y=0}^{N-1} f(x, y) . \cos\frac{(2x + 1)u\pi}{2M} . \cos\frac{(2y + 1)v\pi}{2N} \qquad (1)$$

Where

$$\alpha_u = \alpha_v = \begin{cases} \sqrt{\dfrac{1}{M}} & u = v = 0 \\ \sqrt{\dfrac{2}{N}} & u \neq v \neq 0 \end{cases}$$

The image recreated by applying inverse DCT according to equation 2.

$$\alpha_u \alpha_v \sum_{x=0}^{M-1} \sum_{y=0}^{N-1} T(u, v) . \cos\frac{(2x + 1)u\pi}{2M} . \cos\frac{(2y + 1)v\pi}{2N} \qquad (2)$$

2.2   Discrete Wavelet Transform (DWT)

The wavelet transformation is a mathematical tool that can examine an image in time and frequency domains, simultaneously [22]. Discrete wavelet transform (DWT) is simple and fast transformation approach that translates an image from spatial domain to frequency domain. The DWT provides a number of powerful image processing algorithms including noise reduction, edge detection, and compression [23]. The transformed image is obtained by repeatedly filtering for the image on a row-by-row and column-by-column basis. An example of decomposing an image by a 2-level wavelet transformation is shown in Fig. 1. Then after applying the 2-level analysis filter bank a four sub-band images will be obtained (LL, LH, HL, and HH),

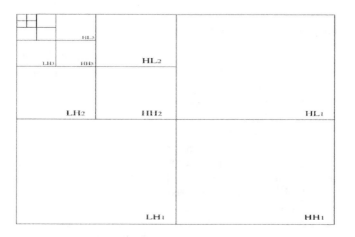

Fig. 1. DWT decompose an image by 2-level

2.3   Advantages of DWT over DCT

According to[24] and [25], there is the DWT advantage over DCT as:

1. No need to divide the input coding into non-overlapping 2-D blocks, it has higher compression ratios avoid blocking artifacts.
2. Allows good localization both in time and spatial frequency domain.
3. Transformation of the whole image introduces inherent scaling.
4. Better identification of which data   is relevant to human perception higher compression ratio.

3   Genetic Algorithms

Genetic Algorithms (GAs) introduced by Holland [24].GA is most widely used amongst the artificial optimization intelligent techniques. A GA is a stochastic searching algorithm based on the mechanisms of natural selection and genetics. GAs has been proven to be very efficient and stable in searching for global optimum solutions.

In general, GAs start with some randomly selected population, called the first generation. Each individual in the population called chromosome and corresponds to a solution in the problem domain. An objective called fitness function is used to evaluate the quality of each chromosome. The next generation will be generated from some chromosomes whose fitness values are high. Reproduction, crossover and mutation are the three basic operators used to repeat many time until a predefined condition is satisfied or the desired number of iteration is reached. According to the applications for optimization, designers need to carefully define the necessary elements for dealing with the GA. Then, the fitness function in addition to the terminating criteria is evaluated with the natural selection, crossover, and mutation operations [25].

3.1   Watermarking Based on GA Related Works

Researchers used GA to optimize the watermarking requirements, Wang et al [26] presented watermarking based Genetic algorithm. They used bit substitution method. Huang et al [27] proposed watermarking method based on GA and DCT domain. They embedded watermark with visually recognizable patterns into image by selection modifying the middle frequency parts of the image. The GA is applied to search for the locations to embed into DCT coefficient block. In addition, Hsiang et al [16] proposed a robust watermarking based on DCT and GA. They tried to design a particle fitness function to solve the tread-off between the three watermarking matrices. On the other hand, they have considered the capacity to be constant. Moreover, Hsiang et al [28] have proposed watermarking based wavelet packet transform (WPT). They have assumed watermarked consists of 0's and 1's all bits of the watermark are embedded into host image. Also, Promcharoen and Rangsanseri [29] presented new approach for watermarking based on DCT. The authors used fuzzy C-mean (FCM) to classify the 8*8 block to texture or non-texture region. They used GA to find out the optimized parameter. As well as, Patra et al [30] proposed the digital watermarking scheme based on singular value decomposition (SVD). The authors used GA to optimize the conflict between quality and robustness. They used Sun et al algorithm for quantization embedding. Furthermore, Li et al [31] proposed watermarking based on DWT domain. They used Arnold transform and GA to improve the performance of watermarking algorithm.

4   Result Analyses

This section studies the effect of watermarking using GA on the embedding domains. Many of researchers have used Lena picture as the host image. They applied some types of attacks on that image after watermark embedding to prove the quality of their works. We chose some pervious works [32] [33] [34] [35] [36] [15] [29] [37] and analyzed their works and study how the attacks were affected by embedded domains. . The normalized correlation (NC) is used as measure of robustness. It calculates the difference between the embedded and extracted watermark defined as:

$$NC = \frac{\sum_{i=1}^{M} \sum_{j=1}^{N} w(i,j)w'(i,j)}{\sqrt{\sum_{i=1}^{M} \sum_{j=1}^{N} w(i,j)} \sqrt{\sum_{i=1}^{M} \sum_{j=1}^{N} w'(i,j)}} \qquad (3)$$

where M and N are the numbers of row and column in the images, respectively. w(i,j) and w'(i,j) are the original and the watermarked image respectively.

Lena picture 516*516 (host image)

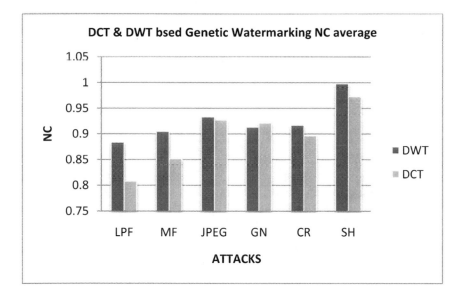

Fig. 2. NC result after attack

The figure shows the attacks effect of on DWT and DCT domains. It shows in image processing operation like low-pass filtering (LPF) and medium filtering (MF) that the DWT domain is better than The DCT domain. Other attacks like JPGE, Cropping (CR) and sharpening (SH) almost have the same results with some advantages of DWT. Gaussian noise (GN) give DCT better result more than DWT.

In the brief, DWT domain is better than the DCT domain for embedding in watermarking based on Genetic algorithm.

5   Conclusions

In this paper, we proposed watermarking based on genetic algorithm and studied the effect of DWT and DCT embedding domain on robustness of watermarking. As the result of the analysis obtained results by using NC measurement. It is clarify the DWT is better than DCT for robustness of watermarking using genetic algorithm. In future work will study the affect of others optimization techniques and watermarking requirements with some testing experiments.

Acknowledgements. This work is part of a project supported by University Technology Malaysia research grant (RUG Tier2 PY/2011/00997).

References

1. Wu, Y.-T., Shih, F.Y.: Digital watermarking based on chaotic map and reference register. Pattern Recognition 40(12), 3753–3763 (2007)
2. Shih, F.Y., Wu, Y.-T.: Information hiding by digital watermarking. In: Pan, J.-S., Huang, H.-C., Jain, L.C. (eds.) Information Hiding and Applications. SCI, vol. 227, pp. 205–223. Springer, Heidelberg (2009)
3. Wang, F.-H., Pan, J.-S., Jain, L.C.: Intelligent Techniques. In: Wang, F.-H., Pan, J.-S., Jain, L.C. (eds.) Innovations in Digital Watermarking Techniques. Studies in Computational Intelligence, vol. 232, pp. 27–44. Springer, Heidelberg (2009)
4. Cox, I.J., et al.: Secure spread spectrum watermarking for multimedia. IEEE Transactions on Image Processing 6(12), 1673–1687 (1997)
5. Lin, P.L.: Oblivious digital watermarking scheme with blob-oriented and modular-arithmetic-based spatial-domain mechanism. Journal of Visual Communication and Image Representation 12(2), 136–151 (2001)
6. Deguillaume, F., Voloshynovskiy, S., Pun, T.: Secure hybrid robust watermarking resistant against tampering and copy attack. Signal Processing 83(10), 2133–2170 (2003)
7. Agreste, S., et al.: An image adaptive, wavelet-based watermarking of digital images. Journal of Computational and Applied Mathematics 210(1-2), 13–21 (2007)
8. Je, S.-k., Seo, Y.-S., Lee, S.-J., Cha, E.-Y.: Self-Organizing Coefficient for Semi-Blind Watermarking. In: Zhou, X., Zhang, Y., Orlowska, M.E. (eds.) APWeb 2003. LNCS, vol. 2642, pp. 275–286. Springer, Heidelberg (2003)
9. Shih, F.: Digital Watermarking and Steganography. In: Fandamentals and Techhniques. CRC Press (2008)
10. Cheung, W.N.: Digital image watermarking in spatial and transform domains. In: Proceedings of TENCON 2000 (2000)
11. Ramkumar, M.: Data Hiding in Multimedia - Theory and Applications. New Jersey Institute of Technology, Newark (2000)
12. Navas, K.A., Sasikumar, M., Sreevidya, S.: A Benchmark for Medical Image Watermarking. In: 14th International Workshop on Systems, Signals and Image Processing, 2007 and 6th EURASIP Conference focused on Speech and Image Processing, Multimedia Communications and Services (2007)
13. Vetterli, M.a.K.: Wavelets and Subband Coding. Signal Processing Series. Prentice Hall (1995)

14. Phadikar, A., Maity, S.P.: Multibit QIM watermarking using M-ary modulation and lifting. In: 2010 International Conference on Signal Processing and Communications, SPCOM (2010)

15. Huang, H.-C., Chu, C.-M., Pan, J.-S.: Genetic Watermarking for Copyright Protection. In: Pan, J.-S., Huang, H.-C., Jain, L.C. (eds.) Information Hiding and Applications. Studies in Computational Intelligence, vol. 227, pp. 1–19. Springer, Heidelberg (2009)

16. Huang, H.-C., Chu, C.-M., Pan, J.-S: The optimized copyright protection system with genetic watermarking. A Fusion of Foundations, Methodologies and Applications 13 (2008)

17. Shih-Hao, W., Yuan-Pei, L.: Wavelet tree quantization for copyright protection watermarking. IEEE Transactions on Image Processing 13(2), 154–165 (2004)

18. Pan, C.-M., Lam, I.-T.: Fingerprint Watermark Embedding by Discrete Cosine Transform for Copyright Ownership Authentication. International Journal of Communications 3(1), 8 (2009)

19. Jiansheng, M., Sukang, L., Xiaomei, T.: A Digital Watermarking Algorithm Based On DCT and DWT. In: International Symposium on Web Information Systems and Applications, WISA 2009 (2009)

20. El-Fegh, I., et al.: Color image watermarking based on the DCT-domain of three RGB color channels. In: Proceedings of the 10th WSEAS International Conference on Evolutionary Computing 2009, pp. 36–39. World Scientific and Engineering Academy and Society (WSEAS), Prague (2009)

21. Eyadat, M., Vasikarla, S.: Performance evaluation of an incorporated DCT block-based watermarking algorithm with human visual system model. Pattern Recognition Letters 26(10), 1405–1411 (2005)

22. Ouhsain, M., Hamza, A.B.: Image watermarking scheme using nonnegative matrix factorization and wavelet transform. Expert Syst. Appl. 36(2), 2123–2129 (2009)

23. Chang, C.-Y., Wang, H.-J., Pan, S.-W.: A robust DWT-based copyright verification scheme with Fuzzy ART. Journal of Systems and Software 82(11), 1906–1915 (2009)

24. Holland, J.H.: Adaptation in Natural and Artifcial Systems. The University of Michigan Press, Ann Arbor (1975)

25. Gen, M., Cheng, R.: Job-Shop Scheduling Problems. In: Genetic Algorithms and Engineering Design 2007, pp. 190–233. John Wiley & Sons, Inc. (2007)

26. Wang, R.-Z., Lin, C.-F., Lin, J.-C.: Image hiding by optimal LSB substitution and genetic algorithm. Pattern Recognition 34(3), 671–683 (2001)

27. Huang, C.-H., Wu, J.-L.: Watermark optimization technique based on genetic algorithms. SPIE (2000)

28. Hsiang-Cheh, H., Yueh-Hong, C., Guan-Yu, L.: DCT-Based Robust Watermarking with Swarm Intelligence Concepts. In: Fifth International Conference on Information Assurance and Security, IAS 2009 (2009)

29. Promcharoen, S., Rangsanseri, Y.: Genetic watermarking based on texture analysis in DCT domain. In: SICE Annual Conference (2008)

30. Patra, J.C., Phua, J.E., Bornand, C.: A novel DCT domain CRT-based watermarking scheme for image authentication surviving JPEG compression. Digital Signal Processing 20(6), 1597–1611 (2010)

31. Li, H.-f., Chang, N., Chen, X.-m.: A study on image digital watermarking based on wavelet transform. The Journal of China Universities of Posts and Telecommunications 17(supplement. 1), 122–126 (2010)

32. Kumaran, T., Thangavel, P.: Watermarking in Contourlet Transform Domain Using Genetic Algorithm. In: Second UKSIM European Symposium on Computer Modeling and Simulation, EMS 2008 (2008)
33. Ning, Z., et al.: An Optimal Wavelet-Based Image Watermarking via Genetic Algorithm. In: Third International Conference on Natural Computation, ICNC 2007 (2007)
34. Yueh-Hong, C., Hsiang-Cheh, H.: Genetic Watermarking Based on Wavelet Packet Transform. In: Ninth International Conference on Hybrid Intelligent Systems, HIS 2009 (2009)
35. Chu, S.-C., et al.: Genetic Watermarking for Zerotree-Based Applications. Circuits, Systems, and Signal Processing 27(2), 171–182 (2008)
36. Lu, Y., Han, J., Kong, J., Yang, Y., Hou, G.: A Novel Color Image Watermarking Method Based on Genetic Algorithm and Hybrid Neural Networks. In: Greco, S., Hata, Y., Hirano, S., Inuiguchi, M., Miyamoto, S., Nguyen, H.S., Słowiński, R., et al. (eds.) RSCTC 2006. LNCS (LNAI), vol. 4259, pp. 806–814. Springer, Heidelberg (2006)
37. Rafigh, M., Moghaddam, M.E.: A Robust Evolutionary Based Digital Image Watermarking Technique in DCT Domain. In: 2010 Seventh International Conference on Computer Graphics, Imaging and Visualization, CGIV (2010)

Frequency Domain Combination for Preserving Data in Space Specified Token with High Security

B. Prasanalakshmi[1], A. Kannammal[2], and R. Sridevi[3]

[1] School of Computer Science and Engineering, Bharathiar University, Coimbatore, India
bplakshmi@ieee.org
[2] Coimbatore Institute of Technology, Coimbatore, India
kannaphd@yahoo.co.in
[3] SCSVMV University, Kanchipuram, India
sridevi.ragu@gmail.com

Abstract. A space specified token may be used in future for the purpose of authentication in all aspects. Digital information to be stored in space specified token should be of minimized size. Such minimization of the digital data is done and stored using watermarking procedure as proposed for secure purpose. For higher security the key to perform watermarking and Encoding/ Decoding is obtained from a Biometric trait as an added feature.

Keywords: Watermarking, Space Specified Token, DWT, Frequency domain.

1 Introduction

Watermark is an invisible mark containing information such as ownership copyright information or protected multimedia data placed on an image that can be detected when the image is compared with the original can neither be removed nor decoded by unauthorised users. It has emerged as a leading technique that could solve the fundamental problem of legal ownership and content authentication for digital data. An invisible and resilient watermark is one that is robust in the face of common image manipulations such as lossy compression, scaling, cropping, filtering, rotation, translation, rescaling, reflection, and brightness contrast adjustment. It is an internal protection mechanism that provides authorization. A large number of images today, that are sent across mobile networks using advanced wireless communication services and through other channels need to be protected with digital watermarks [1].

Digital watermarking algorithms can generally be grouped into two main categories: those performed in the spatial domain and those in the frequency domain. Early techniques embedded the watermark in the least significant bits (LSBs) of image pixels [2]. However this technique and some other proposed improvements [4], [3] has relative low-bit capacity and are not resistant enough to lossy image compression, cropping and other image processing attacks. On the contrary frequency-domain-based techniques are more robust to attacks. In particular Cox et. al. [5] embedded a set of sequences, drawn from a Gaussian distribution, into the perceptually most significant frequency components of an image. In [6] visually

A. Abd Manaf et al. (Eds.): ICIEIS 2011, Part I, CCIS 251, pp. 319–330, 2011.

recognizable patterns were embedded in images, by selectively modifying the middle frequency of the DCTs of the images. Furthermore several methods [6], [7], [8] used the Discrete Wavelet Transform (DWT) to hide data into the frequency domain. In most of the aforementioned techniques the watermark is a random sequence of bits and can only be detected by employing detection theory. In order to bring further improvements in the performance of watermarking algorithms DWT and DCT [9] is made to work together. Two transforms are applied together since this sort of combined transforms could overcome disadvantages of each other, so that effective watermarking approaches could acquire.

1.1   Previous Contributions and Proposed System

Fotopoulos and Skodras [10] decomposed the original image into four bands using the Haar wavelet, and then performed DCT on each of the sub bands; the watermark is embedded into the DCT coefficients of each band. Serkan Emek and Melih Pazarci [11] compared image dependent and additive blind watermarking algorithms that embed a watermark in the DWT-DCT domain by taking the properties of the HVS into account [12]. The image dependent algorithm modulates the watermarking coefficients with original mid-frequency DWT-DCT coefficients [13]. Ali Al-Haj[14] described a combined DWT-DCT digital image watermarking algorithm that embed the watermark in the first and second level of DWT coefficient sets of the host image, followed by the application of DCT on the selected DWT coefficient sets.

In the proposed system watermarking as done by altering the wavelets coefficients of middle frequency coefficient sets of 5-levels DWT transformed host image, followed by the application of the DCT transform on the selected coefficient sets. The proposed method uses all of the HL frequency sub-band in the middle frequency coefficient sets LH_x and HL_x in 5levels DWT transformed image. By this algorithm, coarser level of DWT in terms of imperceptibility and robustness is chosen to apply 4×4 block-based DCT on them, and consequently higher imperceptibility and robustness can be achieved. Also, pre-filtering operation is used before extraction of the watermark, sharpening and Laplacian of Gaussian (LoG) filtering, is used to increase different between information of watermark and hosted image.

The rest of this paper is organized as follows. In section 2, the two transforms and Arnold and its Anti form are introduced briefly. Section 3 describes the embedding algorithm in detail. The extraction algorithm is described in Section 4. Section 5 presents the experimental results to demonstrate the performance of this scheme. The conclusion is drawn in Section 6.

2   Basic Techniques Adopted

2.1   DCT and DWT

Discrete cosine transform (DCT) is widely used in image processing, especially for compression. The procedure adopted for DCT is as below:

1. The image is broken into 8*8 blocks of pixels.
2. Working from left to right, top to bottom, the DCT is applied to each block.
3. Each block is then compressed through quantization.
4. The array of compressed blocks that constitute the image is stored in a drastically reduced amount of space.
5. When desired the image is constructed through decompression, a process that uses the Inverse Discrete Cosine Transform (IDCT).

It is an orthogonal transform, which has a fixed set of (image independent) basis functions, an efficient algorithm for computation, and good energy compaction and correlation reduction properties. Ahmed et. al [17] found that the Karhunen Loeve Transform (KLT) basis function of a first order Markov image closely resemble those of the DCT. They become identical as the correlation between the adjacent pixel approaches to one. The DCT belongs to the family of discrete trigonometric transform, which has 16 members. The 1D DCT of a $1\times N$ vector x (n) is defined as in equation 1 and 2.

$$Y[k] = C[k] \sum_{n=0}^{N-1} x[n] \cos\left[\frac{(2n+1)k\pi}{2N}\right]$$ (1)

where k = 0,1,2,..., N −1 and

$$C[k] = \left| \begin{array}{l} \sqrt{\frac{1}{N}} \; for \; k = 0 \\ \sqrt{\frac{1}{N}} for \; k = 1,2,...,N-1 \end{array} \right|$$ (2)

The original signal vector x(n) can be reconstructed back from the DCT coefficients Y[k] using the Inverse DCT (IDCT) operation and can be defined as in equation 3.

$$x[n] = \sum_{k=0}^{N-1} C[k]Y[k] \cos\left[\frac{(2n+1)k\pi}{2N}\right]$$ (3)

where n = 0,1,2,..., N −1

The Wavelet Series is just a sampled version of CWT and its computation may consume significant amount of time and resources, depending on the resolution required. The Discrete Wavelet Transform (DWT), which is based on sub-band coding, is found to yield a fast computation of Wavelet Transform. It is easy to implement and reduces the computation time and resources required.

The foundations of DWT go back to 1976 when techniques to decompose discrete time signals were devised [5]. Similar work was done in speech signal coding which was named as sub-band coding. In 1983, a technique similar to sub-band coding was developed which was named pyramidal coding. Later many improvements were made to these coding schemes which resulted in efficient multi-resolution analysis schemes.

In CWT, the signals are analyzed using a set of basis functions which relate to each other using simple scaling and translation. In the case of DWT, a time-scale representation of the digital signal is obtained using digital filtering techniques. The signal to be analyzed is passed through filters with different cut-off frequencies at different scales. Fig 1 shows the DWT transformation of a fingerprint sample on five levels.

Fig. 1. DWT transformation on five levels

2.2   Arnold and Anti-Arnold Transform

Usually scrambling transform is used in the pre-treatment stage of the watermark as a way of encryption. Generally, a meaningful watermark image becomes meaningless and disorderly (chaotic) after scrambling transform. Without the scrambling algorithm and the key, the attacker will not re-cover the watermark at all even if it has been extracted from the watermarked image. So the scrambling transform gives a secondary security for the digital products. In addition, after scrambling transform, the spatial relationships of the pixels of a image has been destroyed completely, which makes it evenly distributed in all the space, so the robustness of the algorithm was improved in this way. The processing of the Arnold Scrambling transform can be represented as following equation

$$\begin{pmatrix} x' \\ y' \end{pmatrix} = \begin{pmatrix} 1 & 1 \\ 1 & 2 \end{pmatrix} \begin{pmatrix} x \\ y \end{pmatrix} \ mod \ N \tag{4}$$

Where $x, y \in \{0,1,2, \dots \dots N - 1\}$

Where (x, y) is the coordinate of the pixels in the original space, (x', y') is the coordinate of the pixels after the iterative scrambling computation, N is the size of a square image, also known as the image dimension.

After several rounds of iterative calculations, the image was scrambled. The experimental results and theory analysis prove that it is a one-to-one and period transformation that is when the iterative calculations run to a certain step, the original image can be restored. After analyzing the periodic variation of discrete Arnold transform, Dyson and Falk proposed that for any N>2, the period of Arnold transform meet the conditions of: $T_N < N^2/2$.

From the data on the table 1, we can see that there is no function relationship between the image dimension and the variation of the period, and for some images the period of their transformation are very long and require a large amount of computing time, which is a problem to the watermarking algorithm. Practically, we must choose a certain size of the watermarking image to reduce the computational complexity.

The scrambling level is an important factor to measure the merits of a scrambling algorithm. Also it is known from the period of Arnold scrambling that an image has a variety of scrambling levels after the Arnold scrambling. The best degree of scrambling refers to the number of iterations when the scrambling effect is optimized. The best scrambling effect here means the worst degree of the meaningful image was disordered.

Table 1. The periods of two- dimensional Arnold transformation with different Ns

N	2	3	4	5	6	7	8
Cycle	2	4	3	10	12	8	6
N	32	40	48	50	56	60	64
Cycle	24	30	12	450	24	60	48
N	9	10	11	12	16	24	25
Cycle	12	30	5	12	12	12	50
N	100	120	125	128	256	480	512
Cycle	150	60	250	96	192	120	384

Generally, to solve the anti-Arnold transformation, we must compute matrix's period. The work waste much more resource, especially period with big degree. We use its contra-matrix to solve anti-Arnold transformation, which can save spending, and not need to compute image's period. We can resume the original image, only using anti-Arnold transformation to iterate the same proposition .For the matrix of the Arnold Transformation $A=\begin{bmatrix} 1 & 1 \\ 1 & 2 \end{bmatrix}$, the anti-matrix $A'=\begin{bmatrix} 2 & -1 \\ -1 & 1 \end{bmatrix}$ hence the Anti-transformation is given by equation 5.

$$\begin{pmatrix} x' \\ y' \end{pmatrix} = \begin{pmatrix} 2 & -1 \\ -1 & 1 \end{pmatrix} \begin{pmatrix} x \\ y \end{pmatrix} mod\ N \tag{5}$$

Therefore, the transformation (5) and the Arnold transformation (4) have the same period, so we say (4) is anti-Arnold Transformation. According to above proposition, we can get its anti-Arnold transformation with formula (5). If one image iterates m steps to get scrambled state with Arnold transformation, it can restore its image with the same steps form the scrambled state by anti-Arnold transformation, with no work to compute the image's period.

3   Embedding Algorithm

Transform domain techniques has advantage of special properties of alternate domains to address the limitations of spatial domain and to have additional features. The Host image is made to undergo 5 level DWT watermarking. Embedding the watermarking in the middle level frequency sub-bands HL_x and LH_x gives high degree of imperceptibility and robustness. Consequently, HLx coefficient sets in level five is chosen to make to increase the robustness of our watermark against common watermarking attack, specially adding noise and blurring attacks, at little to no additional impact on image quality. Then, the block base DCT is performed on these selected DWT coefficient sets and embed pseudorandom sequences in middle frequencies. The watermark embedding procedure is explained as below:

Step 1: Perform DWT on the host fingerprint image to decompose it into four non-overlapping multi-resolution coefficient sets: LL_1, HL_1, LH_1 and HH_1.

Step 2: Perform DWT again on two HL_1 and LH_1 coefficient sets to get eight smaller coefficient sets and choose four coefficient sets: HL_{12}, LH_{12}, HL_{22} and LH_{22} as shown in Fig1.

Step 3: Perform DWT again on four coefficient sets: HL_{12}, LH_{12}, HL_{22} and LH_{22} to get sixteen smaller Coefficient sets and choose four coefficient sets: HL_{13}, LH_{13}, HL_{23} and LH_{23} as shown in Fig 1.

Step 4: Divide four coefficient sets: HL_{13}, LH_{13}, HL_{23} and LH_{23} into 4 x 4 blocks.

Step 5: Perform DCT to each block in the chosen coefficient sets (HL_{13}, LH_{13}, HL_{23} and LH_{23}). These coefficients sets are chosen to inquire both of imperceptibility and robustness of algorithms equally.

Step 6: Scramble the Encrypted fingerprint template obtained from [15] with Anti-Arnold algorithm for key times and gain the scrambled watermark   Ws (i , j), key times can be seen as secret key

Step 7: Re-formulate the scramble watermark image into a vector of zeros and ones.

Step 8: Generate two uncorrelated pseudorandom sequences from the key generated from the palm vein [16]. One sequence is used to embed the watermark bit 0 (PN_0) and the other sequence is used to embed the watermark bit 1 (PN_1). Number of elements in each of the two pseudorandom sequences must be equal to the number of mid-band elements of the DCT-transformed, DWT coefficient sets.

Step 9: Embed the two pseudorandom sequences, PN_0 and P N_1, with a gain factor α in the DCT transformed 4x4 blocks of the selected, DWT coefficient sets of the host image. Instead of embedding in all coefficients of the DCT block, it applied only to the mid-band DCT coefficients. If we donate X as the matrix of the mid-band coefficients of the DCT transformed block, then embedding is done as equation 6:

$$X' = \begin{cases} X + \alpha * PN_0 \,, watermark\_bit = 0 \\ X + \alpha * PN_1, watermark\_bit = 1 \end{cases} \tag{6}$$

Step 10: Perform inverse DCT (IDCT) on each block after its mid-band coefficients have been modified to embed the watermark bits as described in the previous step.

Step 11: Perform the inverse DWT (IDWT) on the DWT transformed image, including the modified coefficient sets, to produce the watermarked host image.

4   Extracting Procedure

The Joint DWT-DCT algorithm is a blind watermarking algorithm, and thus the original host image is not required to extract the watermark. Execration algorithm is the same as embedding one, and pre-filtering is used before applying DWT transform to better separate watermark information from host image. The watermark extraction procedure is shown described in details in the following steps.

Step 1: perform combination of two filters as pre-filtering operation. First filter is 3×3 spatial sharpening filter which is defined as equation 7:

$$\begin{pmatrix} 0 & -1 & 0 \\ -1 & 4 & -1 \\ 0 & -1 & 0 \end{pmatrix} \tag{7}$$

This filter enhances contrast of watermarked image. And, second filter is Laplacian of Gaussian filter (LoG). This filter is designed by the equations 8 and 9:

$$h_g (n1, n2) = e^{-\frac{n1^2 + n2^2}{2\sigma^2}} \tag{8}$$

$$h(n1, n2) = \frac{n1^2 + n2^2 - 2\sigma^2}{2\pi\sigma^6 \, \sum_{n1} \sum_{n2} h_g} \tag{9}$$

In these equations 5 and 6 n1 and n2 is the number of rows and columns in filter. The default value for them in h is 5 and 0.6 for σ.

Applying these two filters on watermarked image (that maybe attacked) could cause details of image become more manifest, hence the watermark information which is different from image background become recognizable straightforwardly. Combination of these two filters is helped to concentrate on finding information of watermark by degrading effect of none watermarked part of watermarked image and increasing watermarked part of it.

Step 2: Perform DWT on the pre-filtered watermarked image to decompose it into four non-overlapping multi-resolution coefficient sets: LL_1, HL_1, LH_1 and HH_1.

Step 3: Perform DWT again on two coefficient sets HL_1 and LH_1 to get eight smaller coefficient sets and choose four coefficient sets: HL_{12}, LH_{12}, HL_{22} and LH_{22} as shown in Fig 1.

Step 4: Perform DWT again on four coefficient sets: HL_{12}, LH_{12}, HL_{22} and LH_{22} to get sixteen smaller coefficient sets and choose four coefficient sets: HL_{13}, LH_{13}, HL_{23} and LH_{23} as shown in Fig 1.

Step 5: Divide four coefficient sets: HL_{13}, LH_{13}, HL_{23} and LH_{23} into 4 x 4 blocks.

Step 6: Perform DCT on each block in the chosen coefficient sets (HL_{13}, LH_{13}, HL_{23} and LH_{23}).

Step 7: Regenerate the two pseudorandom sequences (PN_0 and PN_1) using the same key which used in the watermark embedding procedure.

Step 8: For each block in the coefficient sets: HL_{13}, LH_{13}, HL_{23} and LH_{23} calculate the correlation between the mid-band coefficients and the two generated pseudorandom sequences (PN_0 and PN_1). If the correlation with the PN_0 was higher than the correlation with PN_1, then the extracted watermark bit is considered 0, otherwise the extracted watermark is considered 1.

Step 9: The scrambled watermark is reconstructed using the extracted watermark bits.

Step 10: scramble the extracted watermark with Anti-Arnold algorithm with the same key times and gain the scrambled watermark W (i, j), and compute the similarity between the original and extracted watermark.

5   Experimental Results

In this section the results of our study is shown. Several experiments are done to evaluate the effectiveness of the presented watermarking algorithm. In this experiment, a 32×32 binary image is taken as the watermark of face images. By using a row-major algorithm, the scrambled watermark image can be transformed into a binary sequence with a length of 1024. In the proposed method, the four selected 64×64 DWT sub-band is divided into 4×4 blocks giving a total of 1024 blocks. Fig 2 shows some of the original and watermarked images.

With this number of blocks we can embed 1024 bit in our image. The performance of the watermarking methods under consideration is investigated by measuring their imperceptible and robust capabilities for the imperceptible capability, a quantitative index, Peek Signal-to-Noise Ratio (PSNR), is employed to evaluate the difference between an original image O and a watermarked image. For the robust capability, the Mean Absolute Error (MAE) measures the difference between an original watermark W and the corresponding extracted watermark. Fig 3 shows the retriever watermarked face images.

The PSNR and the MAE are, respectively, defined by equation 10 and 11,

$$PSNR(O, \bar{O}) = 10 \log_{10} 255 * 255 \Big/ \frac{\sum_{i=0}^{I-1} \sum_{j=0}^{J-1} \left[\left\| O_{ij} - \bar{O}_{ij} \right\| \right]^2}{I * J} \tag{10}$$

And

$$MAE(W, \widehat{W}) = \frac{\sum_{i=0}^{|S|-1} \|w_i - \widehat{w}_i\|_1}{|W|} \tag{11}$$

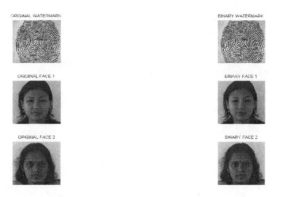

Fig. 2. Original face images and watermark images

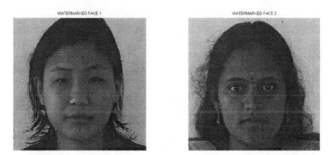

Fig. 3. Watermarked face images

Where $\|.\|_1$, $\|.\|_2$ and $\|.\|$ stands for the L1 norm and L2 norm, and the number of components of a vector, respectively. A larger PSNR indicates that the watermarked image more closely resembles the original image O, meaning that the watermarking method makes the watermark more imperceptible. Generally, if PSNR value is greater than 35dB the watermarked image is within acceptable degradation levels, i.e. the watermarked is almost invisible to human visual system.

A lower MAE reveals that the extracted watermark resembles the original watermark is assessed by comparing with extracted Watermark, where the extracted watermarked image which is further degraded by attacks. If a method has a lower MAE it is more robust. The watermarking performance of proposed method is compared with that of the method of Al-Haj [14] and saeed[17]. To investigate the robustness of these methods, several attacks are simulated to degrade the watermarked images. Besides the quantitative results in terms of the PSNR and the MAE, the experiment also provides visual-comparison results. The presented method requires some parameters with the following values: watermark strength $\alpha = 25$; key times N =12 in Anti-Arnold algorithm.

Table 2 shows the PSNR and MAE values for attack free case. The MAE values compared for each type of attack is as shown in Table 3.

Table 2. Experimental result for attack free case

IMAGE	PSNR	MAE		
		AL-HAJ'S	SAEED'S	PROPOSED
FACE 1	37.82	0.0351932	0.2437861	0.0125489
FACE 2	37.23	0.0878718	0.0312548	0.0245876

Table 3. Experimental Results of Attacked Images

ATTACK	IMAGE	MAE		
		AL-HAJ'S	SAEED'S	PROPOSED
GAUSSIAN LOW-PASS FILTER (SIZE=3, $\sigma = 10$)	FACE 1	0.06123568	0.0144376	0.0985478
	FACE 2	0.10449218	0.03906251	0.02154862
GAUSSIAN LOW-PASS FILTER (SIZE=8, $\sigma = 10$)	FACE 1	0.47432123	0.01213843	0.01152482
	FACE 2	0.42414135	0.02832149	0.01254852
SALT AND PEPPER NOISE ADDITION (5%)	FACE 1	0.06541381	0.01432193	0.00865841
	FACE 2	0.09472563	0.03932514	0.01251414
SALT AND PEPPER NOISE ADDITION (10%)	FACE 1	0.13145131	0.02849175	0.02154712
	FACE 2	0.19284352	0.01491214	0.09187452
CROPPING (10%)	FACE 1	0.03613281	0.01464843	0.009978451
	FACE 2	0.03493152	0.04691254	0.025478639
CROPPING (15%)	FACE 1	0.06312451	0.05178172	0.035874691
	FACE 2	0.06549785	0.07310931	0.058742149
SCALING (50%)	FACE 1	0.21632181	0.23050151	0.199875412
	FACE 2	0.31811871	0.27417338	0.124587963
SCALING (75%)	FACE 1	0.02710305	0.07690776	0.019879625
	FACE 2	0.09155621	0.12835307	0.085745212

6   Conclusion

The basic idea in developing a joint frequency domain model is that the drawback of one method would overcome that of the other. This also obtains much robustness and imperceptibility.

Watermarking is done with embedding the watermark in the special middle frequency coefficient sets of 3-levels DWT transformed of a host image, followed by computing 4×4 block-based DCT on the selected DWT coefficient sets. In extraction procedure, pre-filtering operation, sharpening and Laplacian of Gaussian (LoG) filtering, is used to better detect watermark information from host image. Then, the same procedure as embedding algorithm is applied on pre-filtered attacked image to extract middle frequency coefficients of each DCT block. Afterwards, bits of watermark are extracted by comparing correlation between PN-sequences and these coefficients. Implementation results show that the imperceptibility of the watermarked image is acceptable. Presented method is tested by most of the common image processing attack such as: different size of gaussian filtering as an enhancement attack, adding salt and paper noise, scaling with two common factors: 50% and 75%, cropping, and compression attack. Specially, in case of adding noise and enhancement attack, proposed method show a significant improvement in robustness compare to previous DWT-DCT based method. In as much as, the watermarks can be extracted from the other image processing attack with lower MAE values, proposed method is more robust compare to previous method.

References

[1]   Fei, C., Kundur, D., Kwang, R.H.: Analysis and Design of Watermarking Algorithms for improved Resistance to Compression. IEEE Trans. Image Processing 13, 126–144 (2004)

[2]   van Schyndel, R.G., Tirkel, A.Z., Osborne, C.F.: A digital watermark. In: IEEE Proceedings ICIP, vol. 2, pp. 86–90 (1994)

[3]   Nikolaidis, N., Pitas, I.: Copyright protection of images using robust digital signatures. In: IEEE Int. Conf. Acoustics, Speech Signal Processing, vol. 4, pp. 2168–2171 (May 1996)

[4]   Wolfgang, R., Delp, E.: A watermark for digital image. In: IEEE ICIP, vol. 3, pp. 211–214 (1996)

[5]   Cox, J., Kilian, J., Leighton, F.T., Shamoon, T.: Secure spread spectrum watermarking for multimedia. IEEE Trans. Image Processing 6, 1673–1687 (1997)

[6]   Hsu, C.-T., Wu, J.-L.: DCT-based watermarking for video. IEEE Trans. Consumer Electronics 44, 206–216 (1998)

[7]   Hsieh, M.-S., Tseng, D.-C., Huang, Y.-H.: Hiding Digital Watermarks Using Multiresolution Wavelet Transform. IEEE. Trans. Industrial Electronics 48(5), 875–882 (2001)

[8]   Daren, H., Jiufen, L., Jiwu, H., Hongmei, L.: A DWT-based image watermarking algorithm. In: Proceedings IEEE Int. Conf. Multimedia and Expo., Tokyo, August 22-25 (2001)

[9]   Rao, K., Yip, P.: Discrete Cosine Transform: algorithms, advantages, applications. Academic Press, USA (1990)

[10]   Fotopulos, V., Skodras, A.N.: A Subband DCT Approach to Image Watermarking. In: 10th European Signal Processing Conference 2000 (EUSIPCO 2000), Tampere, Finland (September 2000)

[11]   Emek, S., Pazarci, M.: Additive vs. Image Dependent DWT-DCT Based Watermarking. In: Gunsel, B., Jain, A.K., Tekalp, A.M., Sankur, B. (eds.) MRCS 2006. LNCS, vol. 4105, pp. 98–105. Springer, Heidelberg (2006)

[12]   Emek, S.: DWT-DCT Based Digital Watermarking Techniques for Still Images and Video Signals, PhD's Thesis, Institue of Science, Yıldız Tech. Unv. (January 2006)

[13]   Emek, S., Pazarcı, M.: A Cascade DWT-DCT Based Watermarking Scheme. In: 13th European Signal Processing Conference 2005 (EUSIPCO 2005), Antalya Turkey (September 2005)

[14]   Al-Haj, A.: Combined DWT-DCT Digital Image Watermarking. Journal of Computer Science 3(9), 740–746 (2007)

[15]   Prasanalakshmi, B., Kannammal, A.: Secure Authentication of Space Specified Tokens with Biometric Traits- Face and Fingerprint. IJCSNS International Journal of Computer Science and Network Security 9(7) (July 2009)

[16]   Prasanalakshmi, B., Kannammal, A.: A Secure Cryptosystem from Palm Vein Biometrics. In: ACM Proceedings from ICIS 2009, Korea (November 2009)

[17]   Saeed, Ahmed: Robust Digital Image Watermarking Based on Joint DWT-DCT. International Journal of Digital Content Technology and its Applications 3(2) (June 2009)

A Lightweight and Stable Authentication Method for the Internet Access Control in Smartphones

SeongMin Yoo[1], JinSeung Yoo[2], PyungKoo Park[3], and JaeCheol Ryou[1]

[1] Dept. of Computer Engineering, Chungnam National University
{mingoon,jcryou}@home.cnu.ac.kr
[2] Division of Knowledge Information, KISTI
jsu@kisti.re.kr
[3] Future Network Research Dept. ETRI
parkpk@etri.re.kr

Abstract. Internet users' platform move toward smart mobile devices like smartphones and tablet PCs, so the user authentication and access control for the mobile users are strongly required to support information securities. Mobile devices have weak points like low computing power, limited power, and restricted interfaces compared with the PC. So, these characteristics of mobile devices require light-weight and stable user authentication methods. This paper proposes user authentication LSAM (Lightweight & Stable Authentication Method) applicable to smart mobile devices (representatively Smartphone). LSAM gives a way to identify the users through random matrix displayed on smart mobile devices. Authentication Token used in LSAM is featured with variations on values of the matrix, so it is safe to replay attack and sniffing attack. LSAM does not need additional devices; it is just operated as the interface software on the mobile smartphone. We will show the evaluation criteria of the mainly used hacking techniques like the Challenger Variability, Replay Attack, Brute-force Attack, MITM (Man–In-The-Middle Attack) and measured the degree of defenses of our proposed authentication algorithm to these attacks.

Keywords: Authentication, Smartphone Authentication, Access Control.

1   Introduction

Internet services needed for the securities involve the user authentication. User authentication requires high level of security as important process to supply the information services to the permitted users and requires user convenience to lessen the repulsion to the additional interactions and interfaces. However it is very difficult to support both the security and convenience. For example, commonly used ID and password authentication is easy and simple but it is not safe enough to the internet services needed for the high level of security [1-8]. It is also not convenient for the users to require longer and more complicated password to support the high level of security [9-12].

A. Abd Manaf et al. (Eds.): ICIEIS 2011, Part I, CCIS 251, pp. 331–342, 2011.
© Springer-Verlag Berlin Heidelberg 2011

So, Internet Service Providers determine the appropriate authentication methods to give the applicable level of security and convenience based on what is provided services. Password authentication is suitable for generalized Internet services such as E-mail, blog, BBS (Bulletin Board System), and messenger that require more convenience than security. But high level authentication techniques like OTP (One Time Password) and Certificates are highly required for secured services such as the e-commerce, online banking, government portal, and corporate Intranet access [13,14].

Rapid increase of smartphone penetration has changed the Internet service environment to the mobile internet service that requires security because of portability and private information stored in mobile devices. Smart mobile devices have weak points like low computing power, limited power, and restricted interfaces compared with that of the PC. These characteristics of smart mobiles devices require more light-weight and convenient mechanism than existing authentication. Existing authentication methods operated on the computer box need additional infrastructure which makes it costly to deploy and they are not user-friendly [13,14,15]. These robust user authentications cannot be applicable to smart mobile devices

In this paper, we propose user authentication LSAM (Lightweight & Stable Authentication Method) applicable to smart mobile devices (representatively Smartphones). LSAM gives a way to identify the users through random matrix displayed on smart mobile devices. Authentication Token used in LSAM is featured with variations on values of the matrix, so it is safe for replay attack and sniffing attack. LSAM does not need additional devices; it is just operated as the interface software on the mobile smartphone

This paper is composed of 5 chapters. In Chapter 2, related works we show the surveyed existing user authentication and describe the advantages and disadvantages of each authentication. In Chapter 3, we explain the LSAM authentication methods and define the LSAM authentication protocol. In Chapter 4, we show the evaluation criteria of mainly used hacking techniques and measured the degree of defenses of our proposed authentication algorithm to these attacks. We will conclude this paper in Chapter 5.

2   Related Works

User authentication means a mechanism to identify the users. In this process, the users utilize the password, smart card, finger print etc. as a verification of the identity of users. User authentication can be classified with knowledge-based, object-based, and biometric-based authentication through the verification way [16,17,18].

First, knowledge-based authentication identifies users by using what they know like Password, PIN (Personal Identification Number), and Passphrase. Knowledge-based authentication has strong points such as, it is easy to use and its low cost. Its weak point is that it easily unveils the secret keys [1-8].

Second, object-based authentication identifies users through what they have like the ID card, Credit card, OTP token, and public certificates. These objects are possessed by only authenticated person thus making it secured but these objects have trouble with convenience in carrying it, sometimes it may be costly, needs management, and its risk of being lost.

Third, biometric-based authentication identifies users through their fingerprint, iris, and voiceprint. Biometric-based authentication has benefits that cannot be forged by others, but it also has problems like the cost required to build the system, biometric information cannot be reused when exposed, and it is vulnerable to Replay attack [9,10,11].

Each authentication mechanisms have different pros and cons. Any user authentication cannot satisfy the requirements of both security and convenience.

Password method of the knowledge-based authentication has the advantage that is simply implemented and gives a convenient user interface, but has vulnerability of simple password key like that of dictionary words, simple repeated numbers etc., and of the key-logging attack.

OTP method of the object-based authentication has the advantage of giving the strongest security because only the identified user possesses the H/W token creator that creates a random token. But OTP has trouble with cost, distribution, and management [12-15].

Our proposed LSAM in this paper is an algorithm that creates the random token necessary to the authentication. Randomly created token from the LSAM has dynamic characteristics such as that token key is different with the key at each created time. So, LSAM is more secure than password authentication can be statically characterized. LSAM also gives more convenience than other object-based authentication like that of OTP and PKI because the object is not used.

3   LSAM: A Lightweight and Stable Authentication Method

LSAM is a kind of Challenge & Response authentication method. Challenge & Response authentication method is when the sender gives the challenges that can be replied by specific user to the receiver, and then the receiver relays the answers to the challenge and then back to the sender [22].

Challenge at the LSAM is a $n*m$ matrix created by the server and response value is a user created authentication token using the challenged $n*m$ matrix. Server and users share the Secret Key (K_S) to create the challenge matrix. This is also used to create and verify the authentication token.

3.1   Basic Procedure of LSAM

Authentication procedure of LSAM is composed of 4 phases namely Request, Challenge, Response and Acknowledgement depicted by **Fig. 1**. Each phase is explained as follows.

(1) Request Phase: Request phase is a process that requests the authentication keys from the server by the client. Client sends the Authentication-REQ message having User Identifier (ID) of the user to be authenticated. Receiving this Authentication-REQ message make the server initiate the authentication session.

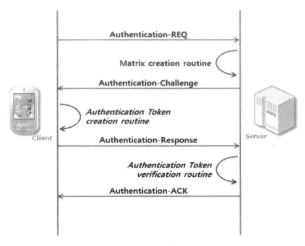

Fig. 1. LSAM Authentication Procedure

(2) Challenge Phase: Challenge Phase is a process to make the Challenge Matrix authenticate the specific user. At the time of receiving the Authentication-REQ message from the client, server creates the Challenge-Matrix (CM) through Matrix creation routine of **Fig. 2**. Matrix creation routine makes the CM in two steps. First step randomly distribute the $n*m$ sized character set on the $n*m$ matrix. Characters of character set are different with other elements. Second step verifies the random matrix whether the authentication token can be made on the random matrix. Section 3.5 will explain this phase in detail.

Fig. 2. Matrix creation routine

Verified CM illustrated above shows the two steps and requested user ID that are temporarily stored in the server. Authentication-Challenge message delivers this information to the client.

(3) Response Phase: Response Phase makes an Authentication-Token (AT) through the received CM. Client (smartphone) display the received CM to the user and create the AT using Token creation routine of **Fig. 3**. Token creation routine has Base-Token (BT) Selection step and Transformation BT to AT step. We will describe the detailed algorithm in section 3.2.

Fig. 3. Token creation routine

This AT value is delivered to the server as Authentication-Response message with user ID.

(4) Acknowledgement Phase: Server will verify the received AT and reply the result of authentications in this phase. When Authentication-Response message is received at the server, it verifies the AT using token verification routine of **Fig. 4**.

Token verification routine has two steps, the re-transformation step and the verification step. Re-transformation step transforms BT from AT then reverse to previous phase 3. Verification step will determine whether the shared key K_S is included in the BT. Section 3.4 will show each step in detail.

Server will give the Authentication-ACK message having the result of token verification to the client and finalize the authentication session.

Fig. 4. Token verification routine

3.2   The Step of Authentication Token Creation

Authentication-Token (AT) of LSAM – response of LSAM Authentication – is created based on the $n*m$ sized Challenge-Matrix (CM) and Secret Key (K_S) of user. K_S is a series of non-duplicated characters from the $n*m$ sized character set and is shared with both user and server.

The creation process of AT has two steps. First, Base-Token (BT) selection step makes an arbitrary character set including the K_S using CM. This step is shown below as follows;

(1) Select an arbitrary character set from the CM.
(2) Select the neighboring (Up, Down, Right, And Left) character centered as previous selected character. But, selected character must not be duplicated with previous selected character sets. We will describe how to select the series of character.
(3) Repeat step 2 until all characters of K_S are included in the selected character sets by order of character in the K_S.

BT is an arbitrary selected character set from the above process. This BT is just a plain character set so this cannot be used as an Authentication Token. If BT is used as an Authentication Token, then BT is exposed to the on-line network channel. BTs are enabled to be easily collected through the sniffing attack. Interference attack for the K_S can transpire [24]. So, BT must be secured from these attacks.

LSAM will transform the BT using substitution algorithm. The value of BT is substituted by coordinates of CM. This transformed BT is used as AT and then delivered to the server.

3.3   Considerations for Token Creation

Base-Token (BT) is a series of characters based on the character set used in the CM, and is a basis of Authentication-Token (AT). BT selection process does not allow the duplicated characters for the BT due to weakness to the brute-force attack. The acceptable BT can be chosen from the CM, and BT is one of the character sets including K_S. If the selection of the duplicated characters from the CM is allowed, attackers can make any possible character set used as BT from the CM. This BT can have unfortunately a train of character set having K_S. Thus authentication can be problem.

So, LSAM restricts that any element of character set of BT must not be duplicated.

3.4   The Step of Authentication Token Verification

The process of the verification to AT is divided with re-transformation to BT from AT and verification of BT.

At the re-transformation step, server transforms the token to AT from BT using CM of user's authentication that is temporarily stored in server during authentication session. AT is composed of the coordinate set of CM and AT is transformed to BT by substituting the corresponding character to the coordinate of CM. BT is re-transformed through this process, then it verifies the BT that is included in order to the User's K_S. Pseudo code shows how to verify the BT as follows.

```
01 : WHILE To the BT's last character
02 :        IF current BT's character != current K_S's character
03 :            IF current BT's character is the last
04 :                Verification fails
05 :            END
06 :            ELSE
07 :                Move to Next BT character
08 :            END
09 :        ELSE
10 :            IF current K_S's character is the last
11 :                Verification success
12 :            END
13 :            ELSE
14 :                Move to Next K_S character
15 :                Move to Next BT character
16 :            END
17 :        END
18 : END
```

Fig. 5. The pseudo code for BT verification

As the above pseudo code shows, this step verifies whether BT has the correct token through and that all characters composed of K_S are included in the character set of BT by composition order of K_S.

3.5   The Step of Challenge Matrix Creation

CM is a challenge for identification of user applied in the authentication token creation process. This process is composed of random matrix creation step and matrix verification step.

At the random matrix creation step, exclusive characters of fixed character set are assigned to the $n*m$ sized matrix. **Fig. 6** gives an example of random matrix having $n = m = 6$, character set = {0-9, A-Z}.

U	S	K	A	5	W
T	1	R	B	4	J
7	2	E	8	F	L
M	D	3	I	0	G
6	O	H	C	Q	P
X	N	V	Y	Z	9

Fig. 6. Case of Challenge Matrix

This random matrix can be discarded. Since duplicated selection from character set on CM is not permitted on the process of BT creation, selected character set would not include character set of user's K_S at the same time.

At the matrix verification step, random matrix is verified whether response to CM can be creatable. **Fig. 7** describes the detail of the verification algorithm. By this algorithm, CM is guaranteed that character set of response can be created including K_S at least once.

4   Security Evaluation

We have considered four evaluation criteria for the safety of security to the LSAM.

LSAM is a one of the Challenge & Response authentication methods. So, we will evaluate the strength of challenger used in token creation to evaluate the degree of response variations in LSAM. We will measure the intensity of Replay attack [24] to evaluate the degree of safeness in authentication token used in the process of Authentication. Lastly, we will measure the degree of defense strength about Brute-force attack [25] and MITM attack [26] to evaluate the safeness of LSAM authentication.

```
01 : Search(row, column)
02 :     IF CM[row][column] == null
03 :        || CM[row][column] == Already passed
04 :        RETURN false
05 :     ELSE
06 :
07 :     IF CM[row][column] == current K_S's character
08 :        IF current K_S's character is the last
09 :           RETURN true
10 :        END
11 :        ELSE
12 :           Move to next K_S character
13 :        END
14 :     END
15 :     ELSE
16 :        IF CM[row][column] == K_S characters that must appear after
17 :           RETURN false
18 :        END
19 :     END
20 :
21 :     IF CALL Search(row-1, column) == true
22 :        RETURN true
23 :     END
24 :     IF CALL Search(row+1, column) == true
25 :        RETURN true
26 :     END
27 :     IF CALL Search(row, column-1) == true
28 :        RETURN true
29 :     END
30 :     IF CALL Search(row, column+1) == true
31 :        RETURN true
32 :     END
33 :     RETURN false
34 : END Search
35 :
36 : IF Search CALL result == false
37 :     CM verification fails
38 : END
39 : ELSE
40 :     CM verification success
41 : END
```

Fig. 7. The pseudo code for CM verification

4.1   Challenger Evaluation

Challenger is an important element to decide the degree of safeness of Challenge & Response authentication. Majority are various challenges and various responses. So, high variation of challenges leads to strong safeness against the password cracking. In case of ID/Password authentication, it is not safe because challenger and response is dependent only on one password.

But, challenger of LSAM is a $n*m$ sized random matrix for the specific user. The probability of creation to the same challenge is shown in the next expression (1).

$$\frac{1}{{}_{n*m}P_{n*m} - c} \tag{1}$$

where, c = a number of matrix that can't create Response Value, CM size = $n*m$

When the size of CM equals to $n*m$, the number of creatable CM reaches to ${}_{n*m}P_{n*m}$. But, all CM cannot lead to a response. So, the number of no-response of CM must be excluded from the total number of CM. That is total number of CM is ${}_{n*m}P_{n*m} - c$.

A constant c of expression (1) is the number of no-response of CM. It is varied with the size of CM and the length of K_S. But the value of c is very small compared with ${}_{n*m}P_{n*m}$.

4.2   Robustness Measure against Replay Attack

Authentication Token is communicated on the network channel during the process of authentication. So, any attacker can collect the theses authentication token and the collected authentication token can be misused in the replay attack.

Password authentication has vulnerability on the Replay attack because the password used as authentication token has fixed and static status. But, the authentication token used at the process of the LSAM Authentication is featured with dynamic. The challenge used at the creation of the authentication token is varied at each authentication times, and authentication token is made using the base token randomly and manually created by user.

Challenge has a limited size, and many authentication token are creatable in one challenge so the probability Replay attack is expressed (2).

$$\frac{{}_{n*m-l_{BT}}P_{n*m-l_{BT}} * \dfrac{{}_{l_{BT}}P_{l_{BT}}}{{}_{l_{Ks}}P_{l_{Ks}} * {}_{l_{BT}-l_{Ks}}P_{l_{BT}-l_{Ks}}}}{{}_{n*m}P_{n*m} - c} \tag{2}$$

where, l_{BT} = a length of BT, l_{Ks} = a length of K_S, , CM size = $n*m$,
c = a number of matrix that can't create Response

Expression (2) shows the number of authenticable CM by the specific AT but this number is small compared to the number of total CMs.

4.3   Robustness Measure against Brute-Force Attack

Brute-force attack technique tries to get the correct answer to any challenge using combinational all response [25]. The reason of only one challenge in the password authentication is vulnerable to the brute-force attack. However, challenge of LSAM Authentication is different at each authentication time making brute-force attack impossible.

We can obtain the number of the brute-force attack trials in expression (3), where brute-force attack that transpired targets to one challenge.

$$\sum_{i=1}^{n*m} {}_{n*m}P_i \qquad (3)$$

where, CM size $= n*m$

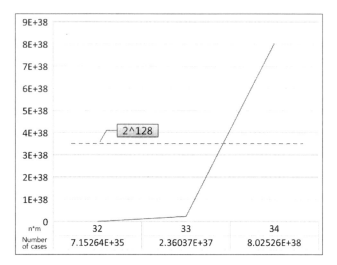

Fig. 8. The number of cases for Brute-force attack

Fig. 8 depicts the computational number of brute-force attack trial where $32 \leq n*m \leq 34$. As shown in **Fig. 8**, brute-force attack should try to break the LSAM authentication at least $1.29*2^{134}$ times where $n*m \leq 34$. This is computationally secure [27].

4.4   Robustness Measure against MITM Attack

MITM attack technique is when the intervened attackers between two network devices relay and attack the two devices [26]. In the case of LSAM authentication, there is a process of filtering based on the K_S of user. This filtering process forces the attacker of MITM not to make a correct challenge with low probability of next expression (4).

$$\frac{c}{_{n*m}P_{n*m}} \tag{4}$$

where, c = a number of matrix that can't create Response Value, CM size = $n*m$

Attacker cannot create the correct CM as the probability of the expression (4). So, user can detect the MITM attack when challenge cannot be created on the given CM.

5   Conclusion

We proposed the new authentication algorithm, LSAM (Lightweight & Stable Authentication Method) applicable to smartphone devices. LSAM gives a way to identify the users through random matrix displayed on smart mobile devices. Authentication Token used in LSAM is featured with variations on values of the matrix, so it is safe on Replay attack and Sniffing attack. LSAM also does not need additional devices; it is just operated as the interface software on the smartphone.

We proposed the evaluation criteria of degree of defenses to the mainly used hacking techniques, Challenger Variability, Replay Attack, Brute-force Attack, and MITM Attack and evaluated security of our LSAM as successful attack rate. As a result of our evaluations, we have shown that the larger the size of CM, the more secure LSAM will be.

Specially, we have proven that LSAM is computationally secure if the size of CM ($n*m$) is larger and equal to 35.

Acknowledgement. This research was supported by Next-Generation Information Computing Development Program through the National Research Foundation of Korea(NRF) funded by the Ministry of Education, Science and Technology (2011-0020516) and the MKE(The Ministry of Knowledge Economy), Korea, under the ITRC(Information Technology Research Center) support program supervised by the NIPA(National IT Industry Promotion Agency) (NIPA-2011-C1090-1131-0005).

References

1. Morris, R., Thompson, K.: Password security: a case history. Commun. of the ACM 22(11), 594–597 (1979)
2. Riddle, B.L., Miron, M.S., Semo, J.A.: Passwords in use in a university timesharing environment. Computers & Security 8(7), 569–579 (1989)
3. Jobusch, D.L., Oldehoeft, A.E.: A survey of password mechanisms: Weaknesses and potential improvements. Compuers & Security 8(7), 587–604 (1989)
4. Feldmeier, D.C., Karn, P.R.: UNIX Password Security - Ten Years Later. In: Brassard, G. (ed.) CRYPTO 1989. LNCS, vol. 435, pp. 44–63. Springer, Heidelberg (1990)
5. Bishop, M., Klein, D.V.: Improving system security via proactive password checking. Computers & Security 14(3), 233–249 (1995)

6. Bunnell, J., Podd, J., Henderson, R., Napier, R., Kennedy-Moffat, J.: Cognitive, associative and conventional passwords: Recall and guessing rates. Computers & Security 16(7), 629–641 (1997)
7. Furnell, S.M., Dowland, P.S., Illingworth, H.M., Reynolds, P.L.: Authentication and supervision: A survey of user attitudes. Computers & Security 19(6), 529–539 (2000)
8. Pond, R., Podd, J., Bunnell, J., Henderson, R.: Word association computer passwords: The effect of formulation techniques on recall and guessing rates. Computers & Security 19(7), 645–656 (2000)
9. Abdullayeva, F., Imamverdiyev, Y., Musayev, V., Wayman, J.: Analysis of security vulnerabilities in Biometric systems. In: PCI 2008 Proc. (September 2008)
10. Uludag, U., Jain, A.K.: Attacks on biometric systems; a case study in fingerprints. In: SPIE-EI 2004 Proc. (June 2004)
11. Broemme, A.: A Risk Analysis Approach for Biometric Authentication Technology. International Journal of Network Security 2(1), 52–63 (2006)
12. Brown, A.S., Bracken, E., Zoccoli, S., Douglas, K.: Generating and Remembering Passwords. Applied Cognitive Psychology 18(6), 641–651 (2004)
13. Yan, J., Blackwell, A., Anderson, R.: Password Memorability and Security; Empirical Results. Security & Pravacy 2(5), 25–31 (2004)
14. Adams, A., Sasse, M.A., Lunt, P.: Making Passwords Secure and Usable. In: Proc. of HCI on People and Comuters, pp. 1–19 (1997)
15. Gutmann, P., Grigg, I.: Security Usability. Security & Privacy 3(4), 56–58 (2005)
16. FFIE Council, "Authentication in an Internet Banking Environment"
17. Weir, C.S., Douglas, G., Carruthers, M., Jack, M.: User perceptions of security, convenience and usability for ebanking authentication tokens. Computers & Security 28(1), 47–62 (2009)
18. Liao, I.E., Lee, C.C., Hwang, M.S.: A password authentication scheme over insecure networks. Journal of Computer and System Sciences 72(4), 727–740 (2006)
19. Joyce, R., Gupta, G.: Identity authentication based on keystroke latencies. Commun. of the ACM 33(2), 168–176 (1990)
20. Kim, H.J.: Biometrics, is it a viable proposition for identity authentication and access control. Computers & Security 14(3), 205–214 (1995)
21. O'Gorman, L.: Comparing Passwords, Tokens, and Biometrics for User Authentication. Proc. of the IEEE 91(12), 2021–2040 (2003)
22. http://en.wikipedia.org/wiki/Challenge-response_authentication
23. Ansari, S., Rajeev, S.G., Chandrashekar, H.S.: Packet sniffing: a brief introduction. IEEE Potentials 21(5), 17–19 (2002)
24. http://en.wikipedia.org/wiki/Replay_attack
25. http://en.wikipedia.org/wiki/Brute-force_attack
26. http://en.wikipedia.org/wiki/Man-in-the-middle_attack
27. Shannon, C.E.: Communication Theory of Secrecy Systems (1949)

Enhanced Email Spam Prevention through Sender Verification Dual Models

Benchaphon Limthanmaphon and Kobkiat Saraubon

Department of Computer and Information Science, Faculty of Applied Science
King Mongkut's University of Technology North Bangkok, Thailand
blt@kmutnb.ac.th, itpart@hotmail.com

Abstract. Spam mails distributed from botnets waste user time and consume resources such as space and network bandwidth. Many works have contribution in spam detection techniques. Mostly, these spam filtering and detection mechanisms are designed to protect the recipients. They do not stop spam spreading out actually. To block the spreading of spam, we design two modules to verify mail sender: Sender Verification (SV) Module and Sender Location Verification (SLV) Module. The first one runs on Mail Submission Agent. It verifies the sender account. The later one runs on Mail Transfer Agent. It verifies spam or ham by considering the sending country location. Since only the mail header is verified in both modules, our approach works well with both text-based spam and other kinds of image spam. Thus, these two separated modules are able to block the spam fast and effectively.

Keywords: spam, spam filtering, anti-spam, spam behavior.

1 Introduction

Over the past few years, the growth of email spam increase dramatically. Internet users may receive lots of mails from both known and unknown sources. These mails are 80% identified as junk or spam mails. Spam mails are unwanted emails that have been sent to a large number of recipients on the Internet for several purposes such as commercial advertisement, phishing or deception, malware distribution, and finally denial of service attacks. Moreover spam consumes several resources: network bandwidth, storage, user time, etc. Thus, tremendous researches purpose mechanisms to detect spam.

Most of the anti-spam techniques have focused on filtering methods based on the content of emails or blacklisting based on IP address. These techniques use various kinds of detection mechanisms running on receiver mailing system. This paper purposes a different approach. Rather than detection, we design two separate modules for preventing spam mail sent out un-solicitously from the sender site. Since malicious imposter emails or botnet spam are a type of email worm that are capable to infect the victim's machine by only double-clicked and further distributed by themselves [6]. To prevent the spreading of botnet spam, we examine the sender mail address before the mail is sent out. Due to the poor security design of the SMTP, email header is easily forged. Botnet takes this ability to hide the origin of the mail

A. Abd Manaf et al. (Eds.): ICIEIS 2011, Part I, CCIS 251, pp. 343–354, 2011.
© Springer-Verlag Berlin Heidelberg 2011

sender. Therefore, it is difficult to track back or prevent the spammer. Most of mail servers thus install the spam detection mechanisms. However, these detection mechanisms are not able to stop the spreading of spam mails. To block the spreading of the spam, we design our work separately in two parts: Sender Verification (SV) on Mail Submission Agent (MSA), and Sender Location Verification (SLV) on Mail Transfer Agent (MTA).

The remainder of the paper is organized as follows. In section 2 we provide the background on email delivery. Our botnet spam prevention system is presented in section 3. In section 4 we brief the related work and discuss our works when compare with others in section 5. Finally, in section 6 we conclude the paper and discuss future work.

2   Background on Email Delivery

In this section we first provide some background on email header followed by the location of IP and MX host. Then we briefly provide the process of mail delivery.

2.1   Email Header

Email header initially contains the address of the recipient, subject and other information. By the time the mail arrives at its destination, its header automatically includes further information like the address of the sender and the time of sending. Thus, it is structured into several fields as follows:

- From: The sender's email address. This field is unchangeable except through changing account settings. Spammers mostly forge this field since they do not want to leave any clue to be traced back. We take this field to affirm the sender in our Sender Verification (SV) module
- To: The recipient's email address
- Date: The local time and date when the mail was sent.
- Received: Tracking information which was generated by the intermediary servers in reverse order and the date when the mail was processed. For example,

```
Received: from telesp.net.br [189.47.130.39] by
ns1.thehost.com with ESMTP (SMTPD32-8.15)
id AAC84A70034; Sat, 09 May 2009 01:32:40 +0700
```

The example shows that the machine ns1.thehost.com received email from telesp.net.br, IP 189.47.130.39. However, the sender's machine name can be faked easily but the sender IP address can be trusted since sender IP spoofing is very difficult to do on botnets and zombie computers.

2.2   Location of IP and MX Hosts

A mail exchange record or MX record specifies MX hosts, which responsible for accepting email messages on behalf of a recipient's domain. Some domains have only one MX host, the others serve a lot. The set of MX records of a domain name specifies how email should be routed. We use sender's MX host to look up the country where it is located in our Sender Location Verification (SLV) module. To find out the country that the IP address belongs to was explained in this work [12].

2.3   Mail Delivery Process

Fig. 1 shows mail submission and delivery process sequence diagram. The delivery process takes several steps described as follows: First, sender creates an email by employing Mail User Agent (MUA). MUA is an application, used to compose and read mail such as Outlook, Eudora, etc. Second, the created mail is submitted to a Mail Submission Agent (MSA) using Simple Mail Transfer Protocol (SMTP). Then, MSA delivers email to Mail Transfer Agent (MTA). Likely, these two agents are parts of mail server. They are the same software with different instances launched with different options. MTA then locates the target host or the receiver address by querying Domain Name System (DNS) service. The DNS server responds with an MX record. After that sender MTA contacts the MX server or receiver MTA, and asks if the host accepts mail for the recipient's username at that domain then sends the mail. Once the receiver MTA accepts the incoming mail, it hands the mail to a Mail Delivery Agent (MDA) for local mail delivery. Finally, email is delivered to receiver mailbox by MDA and can be retrieved by authenticated mail clients.

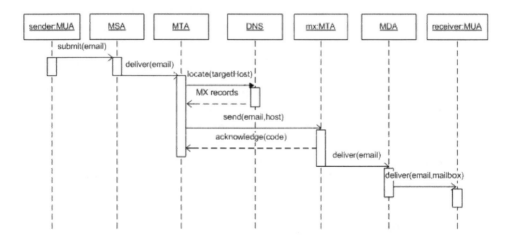

Fig. 1. Mail Delivery Process Sequence Diagram

3   System Architecture

Our spam prevention system is separated in two parts: First, we prevent spam to be transferred to sender MTA by designing the Sender Verification (SV) module. The objective of this part is to verify the existing of the sender. The second part, we design the Sender Location Verification (SLV) module running on receiver MTA. The purpose of this part is to detect whether the delivered mail is spam or not. We analyze sender's email address and compare the location. Location comparison can be used to identify spam mail in our previous work [12] with 96% correctly.

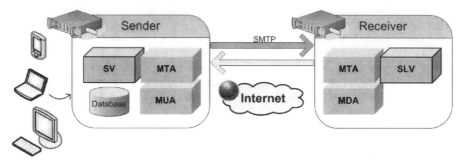

Fig. 2. System Architecture

3.1   Sender Verification (SV) Module

This module is designed to prevent spam to be sent out from the sender's mail server. We consider from the fact that a criminal has to hide his/her identification and left no track. For the spammer, one method that used to masquerade spam as legitimate messages is the use of automatically generated sender name in the "From:" field. Spammer will take the legitimate sender account and send nearly identical messages to numerous recipients at the same time. Thus in this part, the sender is required to affirm that those mails are sent intentionally by legitimate sender. We separate this module in two parts as shown in Fig. 3. First, we examine the existing of sender account, if the sender account does not exist on the server, then we assume that this mail is spam. If the sender account is legitimate, verification is required in the second part. The second part, we examine the sending behavior and sender affirmation is required.

Part I: Examine the Existing of the Sender Account
To examine the existing of the sender account, mail header is extracted after created by using MUA. When the mail is submitted, rather sent it to MTA, MSA will scrutinize the mail header especially the "From : sender@senderdomain" element. Since, this element is easily and often forged, we take the sender name and ask it back to the mail server. Let the mail server queries the sender name from it local account database. If there is no sender name existed, then we conclude that this mail is spam, otherwise, the mail is determined in the second part.

Part II: Examine Sending Behavior and Authentication
In this step, sender authentication and affirmation are required after sending behavior is examined. From the study of botnet spam characteristics and behavior [9, 15, 17], botnet spammers tend to send number of emails faster than average user. Furthermore, they can effectively submit thousands of spam mails in a short duration.

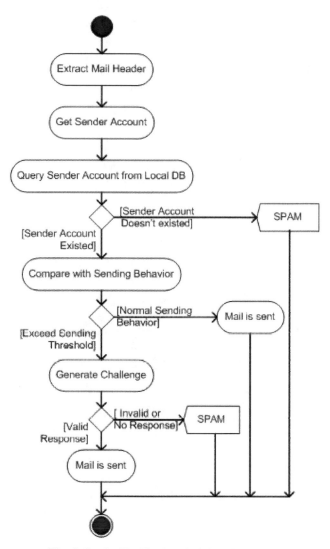

Fig. 3. Sender Verification Activity Diagram

Each bot may send only a few spam emails. However, spam mails are often sent in a highly synchronized fashion as well as exhibit similar sending patterns such as the number of recipients per mail, connection rate or sending frequency and so on. Thus, we consider all of these behavior characteristics. If mail is sent exceed the threshold by comparing with sending behavior, which will be explained later in this section, sender confirmation is required. Challenge-response authentication mechanism is employed to verify sender. This mechanism requires the sender to confirm that he/she wants to send mail. This may burden the legitimate sender. However, if the sending account is used by the spammer, the account owner will be notified and be able to report the administrator.

Sending Behavior. In order to verify whether the mail is sent by the legitimate sender, we construct a set of resilient sending features. These features are formulated based on individual sender behavior or sender preferences. The appropriate sending behavior could be described by collecting some statistic of suitable features. From the fact that, each people has different sending mail activity. For instant, someone always forward mails to heap of his/her friends when he/ she would like to share information or to keep relationship. Someone always send mails to a lot of people in his/her organization because of his/her job duty e.g. for news broadcasting such as the public relation or department administrator. Thus, sending behavior is modeled in three dimensions sending features as shown in Fig 4. When a mail is sent, it is compared with sending behavior. If it exceeded the sending threshold, it is suspected as a spam then sender confirmation is required.

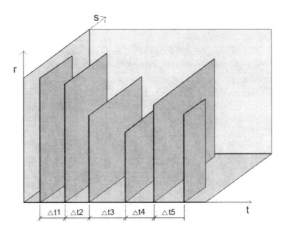

Fig. 4. Three Dimensions Sending Features

To model the sending behavior and sending threshold, several mail features are defined as follows:

r   : Number of recipients
s   : Mail size
m   : Numbers of sending connection
t_i : Sending time i ; where i = 1,2,..m
Δt_i : Sending time interval
μ   : Average sending volume
σ   : Standard deviation

The sending threshold Q is constructed as

$$Q = \sum_{i=1}^{m-1} \frac{s_i r_i}{\Delta t_i} \pm \sigma \qquad (1)$$

where
$$\Delta t_i = t_{i+1} - t_i \ ;$$

$$\mu = \frac{1}{m}\sum_{i=1}^{m}(s_i r_i) \ ; \text{and}$$

$$\sigma = \sqrt{\frac{1}{m-1}\sum_{i=1}^{m-1}(s_i r_i - \mu)^2}$$

The mail is extracted and the following mail features: number of recipients, mail size and sending time interval are taken to compare with the sending threshold. We add the standard deviation in the comparison process for resilient propose. Moreover, we keep the sending threshold in various values (Q1 – Q7) by our experiment that users have different sending mail activities in each day. We decided to keep sending threshold for one week (Q1-Q7). Figure 5 shows the different sending threshold. If mail sending feature differs from these thresholds, it is suspected to be a spam then further authentication is required.

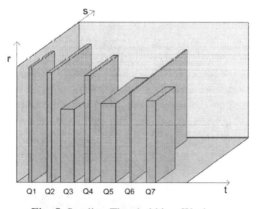

Fig. 5. Sending Threshold in a Week

Challenge/Response Authentication. To adjudicate the suspected mail, we finalized the SV module with the requirement of sender authentication. Based on assumption that spammers are known to quickly adapt their mail to circumvent all available filters, further verification mechanism is needed. Challenge-response authentication mechanism is selected to do this work. This authentication mechanism has some benefits such as the sender does not submit his/ her password so the password will safe from eavesdropping. Another benefit is that this mechanism resists the replay attack since the challenge is randomly generate, the response is unable to reuse.

The Challenge-Response Mechanism is Explained as Following Steps:

1: The Mail Submission Agent (MSA) generates a random number x, called a nonce, and returns this nonce to the sender, known as the challenge.

Denotes as:

$$\text{MSA} \xrightarrow{x} \text{Sender}$$

2: The sender's response is the result of computing a function on the random number and a hash of his/her password $f(x,h(Pass))$

$$SRes = f(x,h(Pass))$$

Denotes as:

$$\text{Sender} \xrightarrow{S\,Res} \text{MSA}$$

3: The mail server stores the hash function of each user's password. When the response arrives, the mail server compares the incoming value to that it calculates. If the quantities match, the sender is authenticated then the mail is sent. If no response or it is not match, the mail is judged as a spam.

Experimental Result

When SV module is deployed on three mail servers within 15 days, we found that 537,284 mails are sent out from 1,413 senders from 157 web sites. Our SV module is able to detect and block 97,853 spam mails, which is about 18.21% of overall sending mails. The result shows that it works effectively.

3.2   Sender Location Verification (SLV) Module

We design this module to cover the sender servers which do not provide Sender Verification (SV) module or any other spam sending filters. Moreover, this module is able to prevent the spam mail that sent from the machine that became a zombie. Therefore, SLV is designed to run on receiver MTA as shown in Fig. 6.

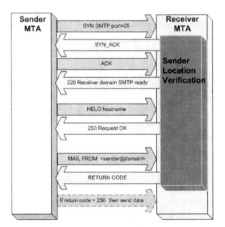

Fig. 6. SMTP with SLV

When the receiver MTA received an email from sender MTA, it will extract the mail header and compare the countries locations between sender IP address and sender MX host. If the countries locations are different, then it will compare the countries locations between sender IP address and sender domain. As proved in [12], if the countries locations are different, we conclude that it is a spam. Receiver MTA will send the code to close transmission channel. Hence, only the mail header is transferred, not the mail body. This helps to reduce network load as well as save disk space.

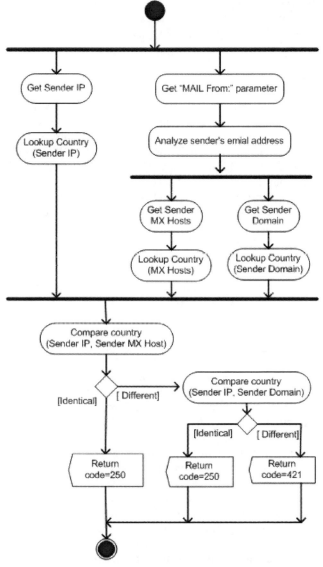

Fig. 7. SLV Sender Location Comparison Activity Diagram

As shown in Fig. 7, return code "421" means "service not available, closing transmission channel". Otherwise, it will return "250" that means "requested mail action okay and completed". Only the non-spam mail will be sent further.

Experimental Result
In 15 days, the receiver MTA got 105,975 mails which attempted to send to 1,413 user target mailboxes. SLV module is able to detect and block 90,420 spam mails, which is about 85.32% of overall receiving mails.

4   Related Work

Nowadays spam mails are widely dispatched for either commercial advertising, computer systems agitation, or launching security attack. There are many defense mechanisms have been designed to deal with these threats. Some works apply machine learning techniques such as Rule-based [1], Bayesian [5], and Neural Network [13] to detect or filter the incoming emails. Chiu et al. proposed an alliance-based anti-spam approach [1]. Several servers participate in the alliance and share the spam rules with each other. The rule exchanges produce the good detect results but suffer from the processing time. Tak and Tapaswi presented an approach of spam filtering based on some queries on the knowledge base [13]. Artificial neural network method is used to detect the spam mails based on their behavior. Their works give the good result. However, the limitation of the memory space and time consumable are the existed problems.

Blacklist is also another common technique that has been used for non-machine learning filtering system. The early work of blacklisting and the standards for email do not prevent the sender from lying about his/her identity at the protocol level [3] or in the mail header [10]. However, Leiba and Fenton [8] proposed a mechanism for domain validation by using digital signature to curtail spoofing and stop phishing. DomainKeys Identified Mail (DKIM) is designed to be used at the domain level. Domain owner is able to control over the use of addresses in the domain. Signer or sending domain is allowed to define its name against improper use while the verifier or receiving domain is able to determine that email came from the domain it claims to.

Some works attempt to prevent spam by analyzing spam behavior [9, 17] and monitoring outgoing path [2, 11, 14]. Duan et al. [2] developed SPOT, a spam zombie detection system by monitoring outgoing message. SPOT is designed based on a statistical method named sequential probability ratio test. Sanchez et al. [11] extracted the Received: header fields of spam emails. They found that almost all the header fields can be faked except the ones inserted by the last mail transfer agent such as Return-Path: and Delivered-To: These information are used to trace the spam delivery paths. Wang et al. [14] proposed a method to detect botnet based on analysis of mail flow, which improve filtering mechanism on gateway firewall layer. This model is able to distinguish legitimate mail and spam upon receiving at MTA. As the same as our work, it does not need to accept the whole mail content or mail body. This mechanism enhances the speed of mail filtering and reduces network delay. Xu et al. [16] investigated and identified spammers by their resource usage patterns. Two groups of resources are usually used by the spammer including: the email address acquirers or harvesters, and the spam servers.

Other works [4, 7] purposed mechanisms to block malicious mail from future inflecting to other systems. Kartaltepe and Xu [7] purposed a blocking mechanism for malicious impostor emails called CAMEL. This mechanism consists of profiler for specifying legitimate users and Reverse Turing Test (RTT) system for discrimination between human being's request and bot program. Klangpraphant and Bhattarakosol [4] proposed EMAS, an e-mail authentication system to protect all spam at the original mail generator. Authentication agent is designed to create a cookie at the sender system whereas the faithful sender agent can used the created cookie to identify the sending mails. However, there are still some costs of cookie created.

5   Discussion

Our work design two parts spam prevention. First part, the SV module is designed to prevent spam mail to be sent out. To assure the existing of the sender, mail header is extracted and verified by Mail Submission Agent. This technique enhances the speed of mail filtering since it does not need to determine the mail content or body like other machine learning techniques. The spam is not able to spread. This reduces network load. Moreover, this technique assists administrators in automatically identified the compromised machines in their networks.

For the second part, SLV module is designed to support the case that the sender does not have any spam detection mechanism or does not install our SV module. It is able to block the spam that sent from the zombie machines. SLV module will work on the receiver MTA. It will detect the spam by comparing the locations as described earlier. Only the mail header is examined. Therefore, when the mail is concluded as a spam, the connection channel is closed. The spam mail body will not be sent any further. This technique will reduce network load and be able to detect spam faster than other techniques. The spam mail body is blocked to be transferred. This detection technique also saves cost in terms of time, disk space, and network bandwidth. Innocent receivers' mail boxes will not be violated.

Lastly, we expect that the SV module and SLV module will be installed on MSA and MTA respectively to enhance spam filtering efficiency.

6   Conclusion

Our work was inspired by a problem with a large number of botnet spam, we have encountered. We designed two separated modules. The first one, Sender Verification Module is constructed on Mail Submission Agent for preventing spam to be sent out from the sender's mail server. The other one, Sender Location Verification Module is designed to run on receiver MTA. These two modules are proved to be the effective spam prevention systems as described in section 3.

Future work, we may try to reduce human intervention in authentication process.

References

1. Chiu, Y.F., Chen, C.M., Jeng, B., Lin, H.C.: An Alliance-based Anti-Spam Approach. In: Third International Conference on Natural Computation (ICNC 2007). IEEE (2007)
2. Duan, Z., Chen, P., Sanchez, F., Dong, Y., Stephenson, M., Barker, J.: Detecting Spam Zombies by Monitoring Outgoing Messages. In: Proceedings IEEE INFOCOM (April 2009)
3. Klensin, J. (ed.): Simple Mail Transfer Protocol, Internet Engineering Task Force, RFC 2821 (April 2001)
4. Klangpraphant, P., Bhattarakosol, P.: E-Mail Authentication System: A Spam Filtering for Smart Senders. In: Proceedings of the 2nd International Conference on Interaction Sciences: Information Technology, Culture and Human (ICIS 2009). ACM, New York (2009)
5. Kosmopoulos, A., Paliouras, G., Androutsopoulos, I.: Adaptive Spam Filtering Using Only Naive Bayes Text Classifiers. In: Email and Anti-Spam (CEAS 2008), CA, USA (August 2008)
6. Kartaltepe, E., Xu, S.: On Automatically Detecting Malicious Imposter Emails. In: Proceedings of the 2005 International Workshop for Applied PKI, IWAP 2005 (2005)
7. Kartaltepe, E., Xu, S.: Towards Blocking Outgoing Malicious Imposter Emails. In: Proceedings of the 2006 International Symposium on World of Wireless, Mobile and Multimedia Networks (WOWMOM 2006). IEEE Computer Society, Washington, DC, USA (2006)
8. Leib, B., Fenton, J.: DomainKeys Identified Mail (DKIM): Using Digital Signatures for Domain Verification. In: Fourth Conference on Email and Anti-Spam, Mountain View, California, USA, August 2-3 (2007)
9. Puniškis, D., Laurutis, R.: Behavior Statistic based Neural Net Anti-spam Filters. Electronics and Electrical Engineering T170 6(78) (2007) ISSN 1392 – 1215
10. Resnick, P. (ed.): Internet Message Format, Internet Engineering Task Force, RFC 2822 (April 2001)
11. Sanchez, F., Duan, Z., Dong, Y.: Understanding Forgery Properties of Spam Delivery Paths. In: Seventh Annual Collaboration Electronic Message Anti-Abuse and Spam Conference (CEAS 2010), Redmond, Washington, July 13-14 (2010)
12. Saraubon, K., Limthanmaphon, B.: Fast Effective Botnet Spam Detection. In: Proceedings of 4th International Conference on Computer Sciences and Convergence Information Technology (ICCIT 2009), November 24-26. IEEE, Seoul (2009)
13. Tak, G.K., Tapaswi, S.: Query Based Approach Towards Spam Attacks using Artificial Neural Network. International Journal of Artificial Intelligence & Applications (IJAIA) 1(4) (October 2010)
14. Wang, C.D., Li, T., Wang, H.B.: Botnet Detection Based on Analysis of Mail Flow. In: Proceedings of BMEI 2009, pp. 1–4 (2009)
15. Wang, M., Li, Z., Xiao, L., Zhang, Y.: Research on Behavior Statistic Based Spam Filter. In: First International Workshop on Education Technology and Computer Science. IEEE (2009)
16. Xu, K.S., Kliger, M., Hero III, A.O.: Identifying Spammers by Their Resource Usage Patterns. In: Seventh Annual Collaboration Electronic Message Anti-Abuse and Spam Conference (CEAS 2010), Redmond, Washington, July 13-14 (2010)
17. Xie, Y., Yu, F., Achan, K., Panigrahy, R., Hulten, G., Osipkov, I.: Spamming Botnets: Signatures and Characteristics. In: Proceedings of the ACM SIGCOMM 2008 Conference on Data communication, Seattle, USA (August 2008)

Extending Use and Misuse Case Diagrams to Capture Multi-channel Information Systems

Sundar Gopalakrishnan, John Krogstie, and Guttorm Sindre

Department of Computer and Information Science
Norwegian University of Science and Technology (NTNU)
Sem Sælands Vei 7-9, 7491 Trondheim, Norway
{sundar,krogstie,guttors}@idi.ntnu.no

Abstract. Use case diagrams is a popular early stage modeling notation for functional requirements, and misuse cases have similarly been explored for security and safety threats and requirements implied by these. One key goal of use case diagrams is simplicity, which make it possible to involve many types of stakeholders. Hence one wants to avoid including too much information in these diagrams. One type of information typically not included relates to the usage context, for instance what kind of equipment to be used to perform the use case. However, for multi-channel information systems, this is often highly relevant, and may in some cases make the diagrams clearer to stakeholders rather than more obscure, as long as the information is presented in a visually intuitive manner. This paper proposes some adapted notations to indicate what equipment is applied in use and misuse case diagrams.

Keywords: Use cases, misuse cases, diagrams, multi-channel, information systems, security.

1   Introduction

Use cases [1] have proven helpful for the elicitation of, communication about and documentation of requirements [2]. Use case diagrams give an overview of the system's functionality, and the textual step-by-step use cases provide the details of what is required of a function .

A core goal for use case diagrams has been simplicity, to make diagrams easy to understand. Normally, the type of equipment to be used for interacting with the information system during the use case has not been considered important enough for inclusion in use case diagrams, although it can be included in some textual templates, for instance in the *Technology and data variations list* in Cockburn's template [3], or in the *Special requirements* section in the RUP template [4]. This may be a good choice in many cases. As stated by Moody [5] in presenting 9 principles for visual notations, symbol deficit, i.e., a concept in the modeling language which has no corresponding graphical symbol, and therefore has to be communicated exclusively by

A. Abd Manaf et al. (Eds.): ICIEIS 2011, Part I, CCIS 251, pp. 355–369, 2011.

textual means, is not necessarily a problem. It could also be a deliberate choice in a trade-off between the principle of semiotic clarity–by which each concept should ideally have a corresponding symbol–and the principle of graphical economy, by which one should avoid too many different symbols.

What to show in the diagram, and what to show only by textual means, therefore becomes a question of priority. Often it will make sense to show only the most important information in the diagram, to give the reader an overview, and to present more details in text. In many information systems, it is not particularly important to document at an early stage what equipment will be used–often it would be some standard desktop PC, and if not, it might also be considered a premature design decision to specify the type of equipment in a use or misuse case, which should rather focus on the requirements level.

However, many modern information systems are increasingly multi-channel [6], meaning that users may want or need to access them through a wide range of equipment or platforms, depending on the user's preference or usage context. For such multi-channel information systems, the capture of equipment requirements might be relevant already at an early stage. Some IT products or services must be possible to use on a wide range of equipment to have sufficient business potential. In other situations, there might be requirements that certain types of equipment are used, e.g., the employee must light portable equipment because he has to carry it while climbing an electrical power mast to do repair work. In yet other situations, there might be requirements that certain types of equipment may not be used – for instance due to security issues. Misuse case diagrams [7] already employ a visual variable (inverting use case nodes to black) to distinguish between use and misuse, a trick which was found to be intuitive and work well with stakeholders in a study by Alexander [8]. Hence, it could also be interesting to investigate whether similar notational extensions could be useful for capturing mobile and multi-channel aspects of information systems, too. In previous research we have looked at mobile aspects (location) in UML activity diagrams [9], in this paper we instead look at multi-channel aspects (equipment types) for use case diagrams. We have the following research questions for this paper:

RQ1: Is it feasible to include multi-channel aspects such as equipment types to be used in use case diagrams, and if so, how can this best be visualized?

RQ2: Can the capture of equipment types also be feasibly combined with the capture of other features that one might want to add to use case diagrams, e.g., security threats (misuse case diagrams), or the location of actions, which is also relevant in mobile information systems.

The rest of the paper is structured as follows: Section 2 discusses background and related work, section 3 discusses what concepts we might want to include in diagrams and textual templates. Section 4 then discusses possible diagram notations. Section 5 provides an analytical evaluation of notation possibilities, whereupon section 6 makes a final discussion and conclusion to the paper.

2   Background and Related Work

In previous work [9-12] we have discussed how to capture location in UML activity diagrams, using various visual variables. All in all we have looked at a wide range of notational opportunities, whereupon many of these have been evaluated analytically [12], and some also experimentally [9-10]. The outcome of the experiments was that color did better than both pattern-fills and UML notes. The analytical evaluation indicated that in addition to colors and pattern-fills, intuitive icons for various locations could also be promising, as well as using pools for locations.

The notation alternatives discussed were inspired by work of Bertin [14], suggesting both planar variables like vertical and horizontal placement, and retinal variables like size, shape, orientation, color, brightness, and texture. Moreover, textual annotation can be used in diagrams instead of or in addition to purely diagrammatic means. An overview of these alternatives and how they might applied to use case nodes is given in Figure 1. In addition to line type, it would also be possible to use line color, thickness, or brightness – but these amount structurally to the same, and are quite poor because differences will be visually subtle and therefore hard to distinguish.

Moody's 9 principles [5] for evaluating visual notations are as follows: semiotic clarity (SC), perceptual discriminability (PD), semantic transparency (ST), complexity management (CM), cognitive integration, visual expressiveness (VE), dual coding, graphical economy (GE), and cognitive fit. These principles have already been applied by Moody and van Hillegersberg for evaluating the entire UML notation in [13]. The difference between that work and ours, is that we are not considering the entire UML, only one diagram type within UML. On the other hand, we are not evaluating that diagram type as-is, but rather trying to apply Moody's principles to inform adaptations of the diagram notation. The six principles with two letter abbreviations in parentheses were used in the analytical evaluation [12] when adapting activity diagrams to capture location, and would be relevant to consider again when adapting use case diagrams. The remaining three principles were discarded because they were not so relevant for our purposes, for the detailed arguments for discarding them, see [12].

Of other related work Sheng and Bentallah [14] have proposed an extension to UML called ContextUML, just with the purpose of modeling multi-channel systems. However, the focus is more on underlying concepts for context-aware services, not so much on visual notations, and not at all on use case diagrams. Prezerakos et al. [15] follow up on ContextUML by adapting it, but again with a focus on underlying concepts and expressing these in existing notations such as UML class diagrams, not proposing any adaptation of use case notation, parts of this approach is further used in Broll et al. [16]. Simons and Wirtz [17] also propose an approach for modeling context in mobile information systems, focusing on underlying concepts and defining a UML profile for these concepts, using class diagrams but no use case diagrams. All in all, it can be seen that the focus is mostly on underlying concepts rather than notations, and to the extent that visual notations are used, these are most typically class diagrams or similar representations including objects, not use case diagrams.

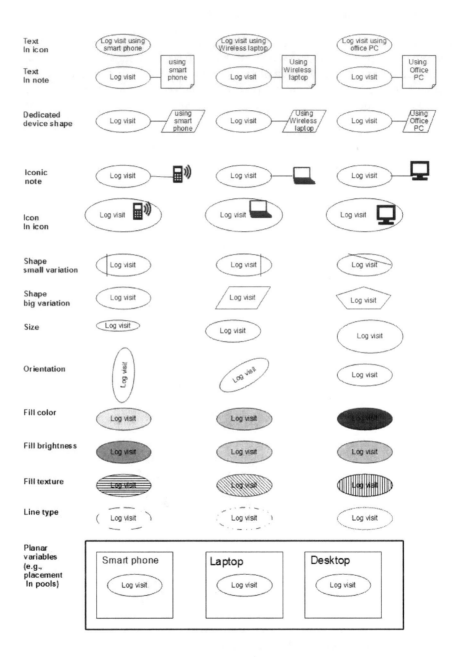

Fig. 1. Possible visual options for showing devices in use cases. In case of b/w printing, the row "Fill color" features nodes that are yellow, blue, and red (left-right).

3   What Concepts to Express?

There is a lot of different information that could be captured for the equipment in question:

- The device, on various levels from the generic (e.g., "smart phone") to specific brands and model numbers, although the more detailed, the more likely to be a premature design decision
- The interaction-type, from generic, being used with two, one, or zero hands (audio-interface) to more specific (touch-screen with stylus)
- The network, if relevant, again from the generic ("intranet" / "internet", "wired" / "wireless") down to specific vendors and service levels
- The relevant software platform, e.g. operating system or web browser used on the device

A diagram would obviously be overloaded if including nodes, symbols or textual annotations for all these three and more. Hence, as a first try we will try to capture in use case diagrams the equipment in a quite generic way, without being too specific about which of the above bullet points are supported. Also it should be noted that this should not have to be captured in all cases, but only where it is actually a requirement that the user should (or should not) be able to perform an activity using certain equipment – or where it poses an additional security challenge if a mis-user has gained access to certain equipment.

Also it can be noted that in some cases the requirement will be that one certain type of equipment shall be used, or that two specific types of equipment can be used. In other cases, the user should have large flexibility and freedom in what equipment to use, for instance "any smart phone with a global market share larger than 5%", or any web connected equipment, whether it be a PC, PDA, smart phone.

4   Visualizing Equipment Types in use Case Diagrams

In line with the research questions RQ1 and RQ2 we can envision several challenges when it comes to designing a suitable notation, from the simplest to the more difficult:

- Simplest: extending use case diagrams only to visualize equipment types, and assuming only one defined equipment type per use case
- More difficult: possibly capturing several equipment types for each use case
- Even more difficult: equipment types not being the only wanted extension to the use case notation, instead needing to combine this with other extensions, like misuse cases and the location of use and misuse cases

These challenges will be dealt with in following subsections.

4.1   Simple Challenge: One Extension, One Equipment Type Per Use Case

This challenge might seem too simple to be of practical interest, but is a good starting point for the discussion, which the harder challenges can then build upon. Figure 1 outlines a number of possible ways to meet the challenge, i.e., various ways use case diagram notation can be adapted to enable the capture of one equipment type per use case. Although there is a huge number of alternatives, with respect to their effect on diagram structure, they can be distinguished into three groups:

- Notations that only make changes within the use case nodes, including the alternatives in Fig.1 called "text in icon", "icon in icon", "shape...", size, orientation, as well as fills inside the node and changes to the line type.
- Notations that introduce a new node in the diagram for the device type beside the use case node, including the alternatives "text in note", "dedicated device shape", and "iconic node".
- Notations that embed the use case node in some bounded area, i.e., the planar alternative at the bottom.

So, it should not be necessary to show examples of all the alternatives, as some major pros and cons can be illustrated by only showing one representative example of each category. Figure 2 shows an example from the first category, using color. Figure 3 shows an example from the second category, using iconic nodes. Finally, Figure 4 shows an example from the third category, using planar variables.

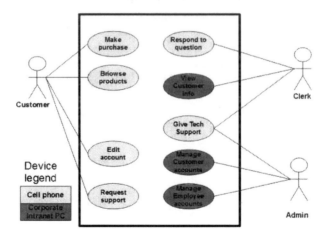

Fig. 2. Showing devices by color (bright: yellow, dark: magenta)

As we can see, the first category (changes inside the node, Fig. 2) have an advantage over the second (new node, Fig. 3) in that it does not have to introduce new nodes, and therefore not new links either. The new links cause a lot of crossing lines, thus cluttering up the picture and making it harder to read. It should be noted, though, that this can be fixed in various ways. One solution could be to place all actors on the left side of the diagram and all equipment icons on the right side. Otherwise, in a modeling tool, one could have options to suppress the visual presentation of equipment unless specifically asked for, and then maybe suppress or tone down the actor links instead. The third alternative, using planar placement in pools (Fig. 4) to indicate what device is used, looks better than the second, but may cause other problems. The traditional usage of a bounding box in use case diagrams has been for the system boundary, while the usage here is quite different and therefore maybe confusing. Moreover, while we have only two different equipment types to distinguish here, a practical case may have many more, requiring a huge number of pools, which make a lot of restrictions on how use case nodes can be placed, thus creating longer or crossing lines and poorer readability (cf. one crossing line in Fig. 4 which was not present in Fig. 2, this effect would be aggravated in bigger examples with more use cases and more bounding boxes).

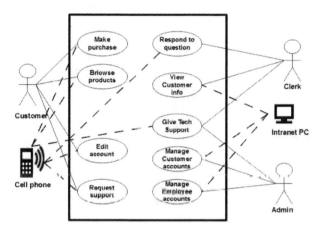

Fig. 3. Showing devices by iconic nodes

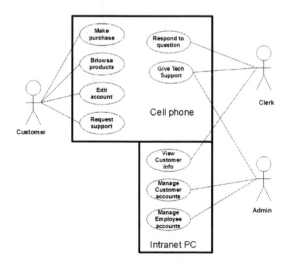

Fig. 4. Showing devices by placement in boxes

From these three simple examples it might therefore seem that color or other approaches that keep the modifications solely on / inside the use case node, might have an edge on other approaches. Not creating any new nodes or bounding boxes, they avoid causing longer or crossing lines, which can be seen as positive according to Moody's principle of complexity management (i.e., avoiding diagrams getting too complex to be easily readable). However, there is also huge variation when it comes to pros and cons within each group. For instance, color is somewhat better than grey-tones or pattern-fills because one can distinguish reliably between a couple more alternatives with color. However, if we have a lot of different equipment types to distinguish between, colors will gradually come so close that users have trouble, and e.g. the "icon in icon" approach might be better. The alternatives using size or orientation are obviously poor. Although they have the same advantages as color in avoiding to create new nodes or lines, they are very counter-intuitive. Size would naturally be taken to mean complexity (a bigger use case) or importance, not a good visual distinction for the type of device. Orientation might similarly mean direction, increase, decrease, not easily device. Besides, it is hard to distinguish reliably between many different angles of orientation. The line type alternative has poor perceptual discriminability (hard to quickly see the difference between many different line types), and the same applies to the "shape, small variation". The "shape, big variation", on the other hand, has the disadvantage of breaking radically with normal use case diagram notation, i.e., people who already know this notation have become accustomed to oval use case nodes, and if these suddenly appear in many wildly different shapes, this will be confusing. The alternative that just uses added text (first row in Fig. 1) may be appealing for making the smallest possible change to mainstream use case modeling. It does however have the disadvantage of creating longer text labels, and close inspection (i.e., reading each label) is required to see which use case is to be performed by which type of equipment, thus not so good according to Moody's criterion for "perceptual discriminability". For the alternatives that do introduce new nodes, the iconic nodes have an advantage of being intuitively understandable, which is good according to Moody's criterion for semantic transparency, and for being easily visually distinguished, which is good for the perceptual discriminability criterion.

So far we have only looked at the simple challenge of one equipment type per use case, now we will turn to more complex situations.

4.2   Several Equipment Types for Each Use Case

The examples of Figures 2-4 are of course ridiculously simple. In a more realistic example, users would be allowed to use several different types of equipment for the same use case. Often this could be according to own preference. E.g., a task can be performed either by desktop or laptop computer, PDA, smart phone, ordinary mobile phone, or ordinary wired phone. In general this could range from two specific equipment types being possible, to almost "any equipment". In other situations, the user might have to use several types of equipment in the same use case, an example would be internet banking using both a one-time password token (or alternatively, getting a one-time password through one's cell phone) and a PC to approve a transaction.

There would be several possible ways to deal with this in the notation alternatives in Figure 1. In general one can distinguish between three approaches to handling multiple equipment types with various visual variables: (i) increased intra-node complexity, i.e., hiding the multiplicity of equipment types inside nodes that are already in the diagram, (ii) increased inter-node complexity, i.e., handling multiple equipment types by introducing extra nodes and/or extra links in the diagram, (iii) increased term or symbol-space, possibly organized in a generalization hierarchy. Figure 5 illustrates these alternatives for the more promising of the notations from Figure 1 (i.e., excluding the hopeless ones, like size and orientation, plus some ok ones which were still clearly bettered by others, e.g., grey-tones or patterns because color is slightly more appealing). Alternative (i) is to the left in each row, alternative (ii) in the middle, and alternative (iii) to the right. Notice that the "text in note" alternative (ii) is the normal approach in current diagram practice (since there is no special symbol for equipment), often also connecting the two specialized use cases mentioning the equipment through a generalization relationship to a more generic "Log visit". So, this will again create more links, although they are not seen in this small illustrative figure.

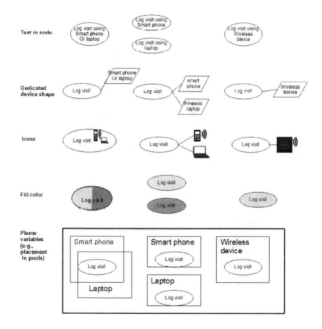

Fig. 5. Showing two devices for each use case

The problem with the left side alternatives, of course, is how much can be crammed into one single use case node (or dedicated device node for the second row). The two first rows need longer texts inside nodes – and even longer if there were more device types. The icons inside the node in the third row are already small, and would be even smaller if there were more equipment types needed. Two colors inside the same node might work, but will quickly break down with higher numbers. Also, the attempt at intersecting bounding boxes for the planar version will very quickly break down with more than two device types. The alternatives on the right side share the advantage of those on the left in not creating more nodes and links. However, the challenge for the two upper textual alternatives is that there must be a plausible term covering the union of the wanted equipment types (and nothing else), maybe "wireless device" might do, but it could also happen that there are other wireless devices that are not wanted for these use cases. For the icon version, we need to create a higher number of icons (since we also need icons for various combinations of equipment types), and possibly less intuitive icons since the underlying concepts will be more abstract. For color, similarly, we are forced to use more colors, quickly reaching a limit to what can reliably be distinguished. Many design guidelines suggest limiting the number of colors in a display to four, with a limit to seven colors. According to the opponent process theory [18], there are six elementary colors, and these colors are arranged perceptually as opponent pair's long three axes: black-white, red-green, and yellow-blue. If using colors to mark semantics of the language concepts, one should not use more than 5-6 different colors in a given view [19].

Potential challenges with both the left side and right side alternatives mean that the middle option of increasing the inter-node complexity might still be an interesting alternative. True, this will create more links in the diagram, and thus probably increase the number of long or crossing lines which are harder to read. However, it does not necessarily increase the number of nodes, since the nodes for the various types of equipment would be there anyway (e.g., for other use cases needing only that type of equipment), and the middle alternative is semantically clearer, needing fewer colors which are then easier to remember, or fewer icons which can therefore be more concrete and intuitive. The planar alternative, however, does not seem to be good in any version if several equipment types have to be captured for each use case. The intersection approach to the left quickly breaks down. The one in the middle would mean replication of use case nodes and placing these in various bounding boxes, hence nodes that reflect essentially the same use case would have to be placed far apart in the diagram, which is harder to comprehend. Alternative (iii) to the lower right in Figure 5 would mean to designate special pools for combinations of several types of equipment, this would again be quite counter-intuitive and thus bad according to the principle of semantic transparency.

4.3   Capturing Both Equipment Types, Misuse and Location

So far we have discussed situations where equipment types have been the only extension to the use case notation. Additional challenges result if this is to be combined with some other extension to the diagram notation. If combining with misuse cases, it must be taken into account that they already use nodes filled with black, so that e.g. color fills will not work very well. If combining with capturing location, whatever visual variable used for location cannot at the same time be used for equipment types, too. E.g., if color-fills were used for location, one cannot use color-fills for equipment, but possibly icons or pattern-fills could be used together with color-fills.

Challenges with misuse cases are illustrated by Figure 6. With color, one could still follow the inversion approach and color the text inside the node instead, so the text in the leftmost black node in Figure 6 is yellow. However, it will be hard to distinguish between yellow text, white text, green text, etc., than between entire nodes filled with the same colors. Hence, this will be poor for Moody's principle of perceptual discriminability. A possible way to work around this is shown for other nodes in the lower row Figure 6, i.e., instead of filling the entire misuse case node with black, a thick black boundary is used, but leaving sufficient space for color-fill inside (or for greytone or pattern, if using this). This gives better perceptual discriminability than just colored text, but is still somewhat poorer than the similar fills were for ordinary use cases, as there is less space left for coloring, and maybe even more importantly, less space left for labeling the misuse case, so that the text needs to be small. The figure also shows possibilities for combining icons with misuse cases, again a thick black rim is one possibility, another is to invert the icon, too, so that it can be shown on a black background, as long as we restrict ourselves to pure black/white icons.

Fig. 6. Equipment with use case nodes (upper) and misuse case nodes (lower), in case of b/w printing, the three leftmost nodes are black and yellow (the very rightmost with yellow letters)

Combining the capture of equipment types with the capture of e.g. location, the question becomes: What visual variable to use for location, and what to use for equipment types? Some possible opportunities: (a) combine color-fills and pattern fills. The nice thing about this is that we would be able to show both equipment and location without creating any extra nodes or links in the diagram. However, there is trouble capturing several locations and equipment types for each use case, which would easily lead to a combinatorial explosion of colors and patterns, which could not possibly be embedded into one node, and would cause a huge number of nodes if choosing the replication approach. (b) use color for location and separate nodes ("iconic note") for equipment, or the other way around. Which one is preferable might depend on the number of different locations to be distinguished vs. the number of different equipment types. In most use case diagrams there would be a fairly limited number of locations in terms of places (e.g., office, client's home, or moving between these), so location might be good for coloring, while equipment types might be better for icons if there are more of these. Besides, equipment might be more concrete and intuitively visualizable than places. (c) using icons for both, for instance in-node icons for the equipment and separate node icons for the locations.

5 Analytical Evaluation of Notation Alternatives

In the following we perform an analytical evaluation of various notation alternatives, using six of the principles from Moody [5] plus some extra ones. The principles taken from Moody are:

- Semiotic clarity (SC): whether the notation has a symbol for every concept
- Perceptual discriminability (PD): whether it is easy to distinguish the symbols for various concepts
- Semantic transparency (ST): whether symbols intuitively reflect their underlying concepts
- Complexity management (CM): whether the notation handles complexity well, i.e. providing abstraction mechanisms and avoiding unnecessary complications
- Visual expressiveness (VE): whether the notation uses as many visual variables as possible, here to be interpreted as if it increases the number of visual variables used since we are only considering an adaptation of an existing notation
- Graphical economy (GE): whether the notation avoids introducing too many different symbols

The additional criteria introduced for the purpose of this specific paper are:

- Multiple devices (MD): how well the notation handles situations where each use case may allow for several different device types, as discussed in 4.2
- Misuse case combination (MC): how well the notation will also work in combination with misuse cases, as discussed in 4.3

The evaluation is shown in Table 1, with scores positive (+), negative (−), and neutral (blank). As can be seen in the rightmost "Sum" column, three alternatives come out as approximately equal, namely "iconic note", "icon in icon", and "fill color". These all have an advantage (+) for having a symbolic distinction for equipment type (semiotic clarity), while the two upper textual alternatives do not offer any separate symbol, and dedicated shape offers a symbol for all kinds of equipment types, which must then be annotated textually, but not to distinguish different equipment types. The three best alternatives also share a + for perceptual discriminability because they are all easy to see quickly, while text requires closer inspection. Dedicated shape is a bit better than the two "text..." alternatives here, because at least you see quickly that the node in question does contain information about equipment type. For semantic transparency, only the two "icon..." alternatives have the advantage of being visually intuitive, while the others only relate to the equipment types in an abstract manner, and the usage of planar variables may even be counter-intuitive, thus getting a minus score. For complexity management, the "icon in icon" and color alternatives have advantages for not creating new nodes, so has the "text in node" alternative, but this at least creates longer label texts. The others create new nodes, or at least force sub-optimal placement of nodes (planar), thus getting a minus. For visual expressiveness, color is the only one introducing a visual variable not previously applied in use case diagrams, while the text, shapes / icons, and bounding boxes are already found there, thus not increasing the expressiveness. On the other hand, for graphical economy, the text and planar alternatives have the advantage, not creating any new symbols. Color or "icon in icon" only barely creates new symbols as e.g. a yellow and blue oval or an oval with a cell phone inside vs. an oval with a laptop inside are still felt to be more or less the same symbol, i.e. both being ovals only with slight varieties. The alternatives introducing new shapes or separate icons much more clearly increase the number of symbols in the notation, thus getting a minus.

For the added criterion concerning the capture of multiple devices for each use case, color was seen to have problems, as there is a clear limit to how many colors can be squeezed into the same use case oval. The same applies to the icon in icon approach. Although a good tool with zooming capabilities would partly overcome this, there would still then be the problem of having to spend a lot of time zooming, thus slowing down the work. Finally, combination with misuse cases also created some challenges for color fills, and also for "icon in icon" (although slightly less challenges, maybe, since icons can be inverted, too), while approaches using text or separate nodes do not have any additional problems with misuse cases, thus getting a plus here.

Table 1. Evaluation of notations

Show device by	SC	PD	ST	CM	VE	GE	MD	MC	Sum
Text in node	-	-			-	+		+	-1
Text in note	-	-		-	-	+	+	+	-1
Dedicated shape				-	-	-	+	+	-1
Iconic note	+	+	+	-	-	-	+	+	+2
Icon in icon	+	+	+	+	-		-		+2
Fill colour	+	+		+	+		-	-	+2
Planar		+	-	-	-	+	-	+	-1

Hence, the evaluation has turned out three alternatives that seem equally good ("iconic note", "icon in icon", and "fill color"). However, equal scores in the table does not necessarily mean that they are equally good, as the scores above are summed up assuming that all the evaluation criteria have the same weight. In case some evaluation criteria are deemed more important, this would change the outcome – for instance, if semantic transparency is given double weight, this would turn the scales in favor of the icon approaches, because of their visual intuitiveness. What is not evaluated in the table, is possible combinations to capture both equipment type and location, as this would have become a quite extensive table with a near combinatorial explosion of possibilities.

6   Discussion and Conclusions

Returning to our research questions, some tentative answers can be provided based on the above outline of notation alternatives and subsequent evaluation.

RQ1: *Is it feasible to include multi-channel aspects such as equipment types to be used in use case diagrams, and if so, how can this best be visualized?* Yes, equipment types can easily be included in use case diagrams also in other ways than the state-of-the-art UML approach of mentioning the equipment type directly in the use case name. The alternatives "iconic note", "icon in icon", and "fill color" seem to be particularly promising. If a large number of devices have to be registered for each use case, "iconic note" may be the best, since the others had some problems in this respect.

RQ2: *Can the capture of equipment types also be feasibly combined with the capture of other features that one might want to add to use case diagrams, e.g., security threats (misuse case diagrams), or the location of actions, which is also relevant in mobile information systems.* Yes, these can be combined, but there were some challenges that had to be worked around, for instance if wanting to use color fills or icons inside use case ovals.

The paper did not come far enough to evaluate which combination of two visual variables might be the best for capturing both location and equipment type. This therefore has to be a topic for further research. Another shortcoming is that so far, the alternatives have only been compared analytically. Although some experiments were performed for similar notational tricks with UML activity diagrams [9-10], one cannot be sure that these experiment results will be directly transferrable to use case diagrams. Hence, further empirical work is needed to assess whether the analytical differences from Table 1 will also be reflected in user performance with and preference for the various alternative notations. Such experiments could also provide insight into possible weighting of the various criteria, which have so far been assumed to be equal. Further investigations should also include the development of tool support for the adapted notations, since experiments will hardly reflect state-of-the-art ways of working if only considering pen and paper tasks with the diagram notations in question. An important point about tool support is also that with a flexible tool, the users do not necessarily have to commit themselves fully to one particular notational choice. Instead they can opt to hide some information, such as equipment types, to see a better overview picture of the use cases, then to display the equipment types when this is of particular interest. With advanced tool support the user might even have an optional choice of many different display possibilities, i.e., selecting at any time whether equipment types should be captured by color, icons, textual labels, or something else - or maybe even combining several of these at the same time (e.g., using both color and textual labels), as redundancy might enhance understanding and reduce the risk of misreading the diagram.

References

1. Jacobson, I., et al.: Object-Oriented Software Engineering: A Use Case Driven Approach. Addison-Wesley, Boston (1992)
2. Weidenhaupt, K., et al.: Scenario Usage in System Development: A Report on Current Practice. IEEE Software 15(2), 34–45 (1998)
3. Cockburn, A.: Writing Effective Use Cases. Addison-Wesley, Boston (2001)
4. Kruchten, P.: The Rational Unified Process - an Introduction. Addison-Wesley, Boston (2000)
5. Moody, D.L.: The "Physics" of Notations: Toward a Scientific Basis for Constructing Visual Notations in Software Engineering. IEEE Transactions on Software Engineering 35, 756–779 (2009)

6. Marchetti, C., Pernici, B., Plebani, P.: A quality model for e-Service based multi-channel adaptive information systems. In: Proceedings of Fourth International Conference on Web Information Systems Engineering Workshops (2003)
7. Sindre, G., Opdahl, A.L.: Eliciting Security Requirements with Misuse Cases. Requirements Engineering 10(1), 34–44 (2005)
8. Alexander, I.F.: Initial Industrial Experience of Misuse Cases in Trade-Off Analysis. In: 10th Anniversary IEEE Joint International Requirements Engineering Conference (RE 2002). IEEE, Essen (2002)
9. Gopalakrishnan, S., Krogstie, J., Sindre, G.: Adapting UML Activity Diagrams for Mobile Work Process Modelling: Experimental Comparison of Two Notation Alternatives. In: van Bommel, P., Hoppenbrouwers, S., Overbeek, S., Proper, E., Barjis, J. (eds.) PoEM 2010. LNBIP, vol. 68, pp. 145–161. Springer, Heidelberg (2010)
10. Gopalakrishnan, S., Krogstie, J., Sindre, G.: Adapted UML Activity Diagrams for Mobile Work Processes: Experimental Comparison of Colour and Pattern Fills. In: Halpin, T., Nurcan, S., Krogstie, J., Soffer, P., Proper, E., Schmidt, R., Bider, I. (eds.) BPMDS 2011 and EMMSAD 2011. LNBIP, vol. 81, pp. 314–331. Springer, Heidelberg (2011)
11. Gopalakrishnan, S., Krogstie, J., Sindre, G.: Capturing Location in Process Models: Comparing Small Adaptations of Mainstream Notation. International Journal of Information System Modeling and Design (forthcoming, 2011)
12. Gopalakrishnan, S., Sindre, G.: Diagram Notations for Mobile Work Processes. In: Johannesson, P., Opdahl, A.L. (eds.) The 4th IFIP WG8.1 Working Conference on the Practice of Enterprise Modelling (PoEM 2011). LNBIP, Springer, Heidelberg (2011)
13. Moody, D., van Hillegersberg, J.: Evaluating the Visual Syntax of UML: An Analysis of the Cognitive Effectiveness of the UML Family of Diagrams. In: Gašević, D., Lämmel, R., Van Wyk, E. (eds.) SLE 2008. LNCS, vol. 5452, pp. 16–34. Springer, Heidelberg (2009)
14. Sheng, Q.Z., Benatallah, B.: ContextUML: a UML-based modeling language for model-driven development of context-aware Web services. In: International Conference on Mobile Business, ICMB 2005 (2005)
15. Prezerakos, G.N., Tselikas, N.D., Cortese, G.: Model-driven Composition of Context-aware Web Services Using ContextUML and Aspects. In: International Conference on Web Services, ICWS 2007 (2007)
16. Broll, G., et al.: Modeling Context Information for Realizing Simple Mobile Services. In: 16th IST Mobile and Wireless Communications Summit (2007)
17. Simons, C., Wirtz, G.: Modeling context in mobile distributed systems with the UML. Journal of Visual Languages & Computing 18(4), 420–439 (2007)
18. Ware, C.: Information Visualization. Morgan Kaufmann, Waltham (2000)
19. Shneiderman, B.: Designing the User Interface: Strategies for Effective Human-Computer Interaction. Addison Wesley, Reading (1992)

A Systematic Management Method of ISO Information Security Standards for Information Security Engineering Environments

Ahmad Iqbal Hakim Suhaimi, Takashi Manji, Yuichi Goto, and Jingde Cheng

Department of Information and Computer Sciences
Saitama University, Saitama, 338-8570, Japan
{iqbal,takashi,gotoh,cheng}@aise.ics.saitama-u.ac.jp

Abstract. An ideal secure information system is not only to keep enough security strength of all components of a target system, but also to ensure all tasks in software life cycle process are done appropriately. Under the consideration, information security engineering environments that integrate various tools to support the tasks are proposed. On the other hand, it is difficult to define generally accepted security strength and its evaluation criteria. ISO information security standards, which regulate various information security related contents are expected, can be used as criteria for the purpose, and should be provided as databases to be used from the tools. However, because standards are always changed and their contents are different from each others, it is difficult to design and manage the databases. This paper proposes a systematic management for information security engineering environments that ensure safety in software life cycle based on the standards.

Keywords: Information security engineering environments, ISO information security standards, Systematic management method.

1 Introduction

An ideal secure information system is not only to keep enough security strength of all components of a target system, but also to ensure all tasks in the software life cycle process are done correctly, appropriately, and securely. Designers, developers, managers, maintainers, and abrogators of target systems that require high security requirements need continuous supports for their tasks to protect the system from continuous attacks by assailants. Because the whole security of any target system is only as good and strong as the weakest link in the system, continuous support only can be provided by a standard. Therefore, some common standards shared by all designers, developers, managers, maintainers, and abrogators of target systems are necessary to all tasks in engineering the systems in order to ensure the strength of the whole security of target systems. At present, the most established and widely accepted common standards are ISO information security standards.

A. Abd Manaf et al. (Eds.): ICIEIS 2011, Part I, CCIS 251, pp. 370–384, 2011.

Moreover, continuous supports should be provided through the whole life cycle of the systems in an integrated way, not in separate tools. For that purpose, information security engineering environments that integrate various tools based on ISO information security standards are proposed to give continuous support for the tasks above [6]. Therefore, the standards should be managed in the environments.

Although the standards should be managed in the environments, these standards are managed ad hoc and there is not yet any management method proposed for the standards in the environments.

This paper presents a systematic management method for ISO information security standards in information security engineering environments, which provide an useful way on how to manage all of the standards in a unified way in order to use these standards easily and effectively in the environments.

2 Information Security Engineering Environments and ISO Information Security Standards

An intrinsic difficulty in ensuring security of information systems is that crackers are active persons who can get knowledge every day and then continuously attack target systems with new techniques. Therefore, from viewpoint of security, it is important to continuously design, develop, manage, maintain, and abrogate security facilities of information systems with high security requirements. Information security engineering environments are engineering environments that integrate various tools to provide comprehensive facilities to designers, developers, managers, maintainers, and abrogaters of information systems such that they can use the tools and facilities to ensure the whole security of the target system anytime continuously [5].

The continuous supports only can be provided by a standard [6]. Because the whole security of any target system is only as good and strong as the weakest link in the system, some common standards are necessary to all tasks in engineering the system in order to ensure the strength of the whole security of target systems. At present, the most established and widely accepted common standards are ISO information security standards. Under the environments' concept, all tasks from design to abolition of information systems are performed based on the standards at whole time.

ISO information security standards are published under Sub Committee 27 (SC 27) in International Organization for Standardization (ISO) [9]. SC 27 is specifically responsible for the standards covering IT security techniques. The standards define various contents related to information security. Certain standards are used as guideline to acquire security certifications and to create security related documents [11]. At present, there are 96 standards are being published in various languages and versions under SC 27 and they are available in PDF and booklet form.

The standards are also underlying all tasks defined in software life cycle process for design, development, management, maintenance, and abolition of secure information systems [7]. This is because the standards rule various methods and criteria that can be used for engineering the tasks. The tasks, from design to abolition of target systems, are carried out based on the standards.

In the environments, the standards are used not only by users, but also used by various integrated tools supporting the users [6]. Users refer to the standards as dictionaries and examples when developing security facilities or creating related documents. Users retrieve terms and explanations defined in the standards when developing security facilities. Users also retrieve existing related documents defined during the development and maintenance of various security facilities based on the standards such as specifications, diagrams, source code, and so on, as examples when creating new, and correcting or editing existing documents. Tools retrieve the standards electronically when supporting users in developing security facilities, creating and editing related documents or security specifications, and so on.

Unfortunately, because of the standards are distributed in form of booklet and PDF, it is difficult to use them with the tools. For booklet form, needed part cannot be retrieved by keyword. While in PDF form, needed part cannot be searched efficiently by using structure of the standards. As a result, the standards cannot be used efficiently.

Therefore, the standards should be managed in a systematic way. The systematic management only can be achieved if the standards are managed as databases. Users and tools in the environments also can retrieve the standards easily by using databases. Moreover, a database system that manages the databases of the standards is necessary to provide infrastructure for integration of all tools as a core component of the environments.

3   Requirement Analysis for Management Method

3.1   Management of ISO Information Security Standards and Issues

Management of ISO information security standards in the environments is operation which to construct and manage the databases for the standards.

In the environments, users store, update, delete, and retrieve data of the standards and their related documents to/from the databases. From viewpoint of usage of the standards, we classified data that should be managed in the environment into four type: ISO information security standards, meta-data of the standards, related documents, and personal data.

Users should manage the data in the environments under appropriate authorization. We classified the authorization of operations depends on the combination of the data. Under data storage authorization, users can store the standards, meta-data of the standards, and their related document. Under data update authorization, users can update meta-data of the standards and their related documents. Under one's permission, any user can delete their personal data. Any user can retrieve any data of the standards and their related documents except personal data defined by other users.

However, there are some issues in managing the standards in the environments. It is difficult to manage the standards as databases in the environments because of the standards' features, and a standard's feature is different from others.

It is difficult to manage multiple versions of the standards. On normal databases, new data usually replace the old one when it was altered. However, it is prohibited to do so for databases that manage standards in the environments. In the environments, the old standards are not discarded even there are new standards available. Therefore, the old versions of the standards should be managed while adding the new ones. However, there is no clear state on how to manage multiple versions of the standards.

Moreover, it is not easy to design databases to manage the standards according to two factors. First, structure of the standards is different. Standards are huge documents that consist of many chapters, and the composition of these chapters is different from others. Moreover, although there are some similarity in certain parts among the standards, the contents of a standard are obviously different each other. Second, even though certain parts of the standards are similar to others, usage of the standards are vary and different. Design of a database depends on the usage of the standards, and therefore, design of a database for a certain standard is different from the databases for other standards. As a result, designing a database for each standard requires a lot of effort.

Therefore, the management of the standards in the environments must be based on a systematic way.

3.2   Requirements Analysis

To manage the standards systematically, we have to consider differences among the standards from viewpoints of life cycle, usage, and composition of the standards.

We defined requirements for systematic management method of ISO information security standards for the environments.

R1: The method should provide its users how to correspond to each event when an event occurs in life cycle of ISO information security standards.

There are four events occur in life cycle of the standards, therefore management method for each event can be considered. The four events are standards are published, revised, renamed, and withdrawn. The standards are published when following happens: the standards are published on ISO main site and there are no previous versions of the standards. The standards are revised when following happens: the contents of the standards are updated, revised, reduced, the structure of the standards is changed, and the description method of sentences in the standards is changed. The standards are renamed when name and number of the standards are changed. However, the content or structure of the standards remains the same. There are no particular changes being made on the standards. The standards are withdrawn when ISO main site indicates the status of the standards is withdrawn. For each event, relationship and differences between versions of the standards must be managed and maintained in the environments. Therefore, the method should show users how to correspond to four events occur in life cycle of the standards.

R2: The method should provide its users with database construction method in a unified way.

Design of a database depends on its usage. Therefore, if the usages are similar, the design of the databases is considerably same and can be classified based on it. We have analyzed usage of the standards by reading through the *Introduction* and *Scope* of all 96 standards. As a result, usages of the standards are basically mechanisms reference, requirements check, best practices reference, and case data reference. Usages of a standard consist of the combination of more than one usage. Based on the combination, the standards can be classified into five groups. Group 1 includes standards whose usages are mechanisms reference, requirements check, and case data reference. Group 2 includes standards whose usages are mechanisms reference and requirements check. Group 3 includes standards whose usages are requirements check and case data check. Group 4 includes standards whose usages are best practices reference and requirements check. Group 5 includes standards whose usages are best practices reference, requirements check, and case data reference. Table 1 shows those groups. As there are five combination of usage of the standards, five ways of database construction method can be considered.

R3: The method should provide its users how to manage common part and non-common part of ISO information security standards separately.

ISO information security standards structure is usually composed from common and non-common part. We have analyzed structure of all 96 standards by checking contents page of all standards. We defined the common part of the standards that are chapters which are same in all 96 standards such as *introduction, scope, reference, term, symbol, structure, appendix*, and *bibliography* of the standards. *Introduction* explains outline or overview of the standard. *Scope* defines scope of the standard. *Reference* explains references to other standard. *Term* define words, abbreviations and definitions used in the standard. *Symbol* defines symbols and their definitions used in the standard. *Structure* gives explanation on the structure of the standard. *Appendix* shows appendixes of the standard. *Bibliography* shows bibliography of the standard. We defined chapters other than above as non-common part of the standard which is mainly the main content of the standard. As the database construction also depends on the structure of the standards, common and non-common part of the standards can managed separately. Therefore, the method should provide its users how to divide common part and non-common part of the standards and how to manage them separately.

Table 1. List of the standards belong to each group

Group	ISO information security standards, ISO/IEC
1	7064:2003, 9797-1:2011, 9797-2:2011, 9798-1:2010, 9798-2:2008, 9798-2:2008/Cor 1:2010, 9798-3:1998, 9798-3:1998/Cor 1:2009, 9798-3:1998/Cor 1:2010, 9798-4:1999, 9798-4:1999/Cor 1:2009, 9798-5:2009, 9798-6:2010, 9798-6:2005/Cor 1:2009, 10116:2006, 10116:2006/Cor 1:2008, 10118-1:2000, 10118-2:2010, 10118-3:2004, 10118-3:2004/Amd 1:2006, 10118-4:1998, 13888-1:2009, 13888-2:2010, 13888-3:2009, TR 14516:2002, 14888-1:2008, 14888-2:2008, 14888-3:2006, 14888-3:2006/Amd 1:2010, 14888-3:2006/Cor 1:2007, 14888-3:2006/Cor 2:2009, TR 15446:2009, 15945:2002, 18014-1:2008, 18014-2:2009, 18014-3:2009, 18032:2005, 18033-1:2005, 18033-1:2005/Amd 1:2011, 18033-2:2006, 18033-3:2010, 18033-4:2005, 18033-4:2005/Amd 1:2009, 18043:2006, TR 18044:2004, 18045:2008, 19772:2009, 19790:2006, 19790:2006/Cor 1:2008, 19792:2009, 21827:2008, 24759:2008, 24762:2008, 27001:2005, 27004:2009, 27005:2011, 27006:2007, 27011:2008, 27031:2011, 27033-1:2009, 27033-3:2010
2	9796-2:2010, 9796-3:2006, 11770-1:2010, 11770-2:2008, 11770-2:2008/Cor 1:2009, 11770-3:2008, 11770-3:2008/Cor 1:2009, 11770-4:2006, 11770-4:2006/Cor 1:2009, 11889-1:2009, 11889-2:2009, 11889-3:2009, 11889-4:2009, 18031:2005, 18031:2005/Cor 1:2009, TR 19791:2010, 24745:2011, 24761:2009, 27000:2009, 27003:2010
3	15408-1:2009, 15408-2:2008, 15408-3:2008
4	TR 15443-1:2005, TR 15443-2:2005, TR 15443-3:2007, 18028-2:2006, 18028-3:2005, 18028-4:2005, 18028-5:2006, 27002:2005
5	15816:2002, 15946-1:2008, 15946-1:2008/Cor 1:2009, 15946-5:2009

4   A Systematic Management Method

4.1   Database System for the Systematic Management Method

A systematic management method for ISO information security standards in information security engineering environments is a method that summarizes steps and ways on how to create databases and store the standards into the databases in a unified way in order to use these standards easily and effectively in the environments. The method includes designing, constructing, maintaining the databases.

A database system for the method is a meta database system that manages more than one database of ISO information security standards. Fig. 1 shows the relationships between databases managed in the database system.

ISO Meta DB manages data of all ISO information security standards' metadata such as standards' name, number, version and language. Common DB manages data of standards' common part such as *introduction, scope, terms, figures, symbols, tables, structure, annex,* and *bibliography* of the standards for all versions, and languages. Usage DB manages data of standards' usage. Criteria DB manage data of non-common part of the standards which are the main contents of the standards for each standard, language, and version. Case DB manages data of related documents created based on data of the standards from criteria DB.

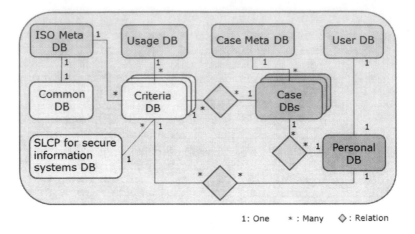

1: One   * : Many   ◇ : Relation

Fig. 1. Relationship between databases in the database system

Therefore, there are multiple databases for both Criteria DB and Case DB. Case meta DB manages meta-data of related documents such as documents' name, language, referred ISO information security standard's name, number, language, version, date created, and so on. Personal DB is constructed for each user, and manages personal data defined by each user. SLCP for secure information system DB manages data of Software Life Cycle Process for secure information system [7], and relationship with ISO information security standards.

In the method, common part of the standards is managed in one common database for all standards, versions and languages. Non-common part of the standards is managed in one database for one standard, version, and language. Based on the analysis, we have designed and constructed a common database to manage data of common part of all ISO information security standards. Users only have to construct a database for non-common part of the standards, and store the data to both common database and non-common database separately.

Because the ISO information security standards' description are different each other, data of the standards are represented in Extensible Markup Language (XML) format in all databases. Generally, standards such as ISO information security standards' structures are established well-structured. However, the description is half-structured, and different for each standard. Well-structured are best expressed in relational format while the half-structured are best expressed in XML format [10]. XML is the most suitable data model to manage the half-structured descriptions because of its flexibility. Therefore, we manage the well-structured in relational format, and the half-structured in XML format.

We constructed the database system by using DB2 Express-C Database Management System [3]. DB2 Express-C is a hybrid database management system which can manage well-structured relation data and half-structured XML data [2]. DB2 Express-C also provides a function called "pureXML" which can manage XML document natively [4]. Furthermore, DB2 Express-C is also bilingual as it understands both SQL statements and XQuery statements [12].

4.2   Procedure

Management of ISO information security standards in the environments is a method on how to design, construct, and maintain databases to manage the standards.

The procedures of the method consist of four phases. The phases are as follows: analyze structure of the standard, design a database schema for non-common part of the standard, prepare data of the standard, and store the data into the database. The procedure of the method is shown in Fig. 2.

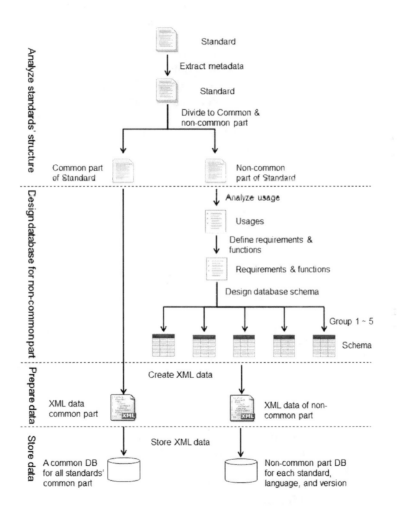

Fig. 2. ISO Information Security Standards' management procedure

At first phase, users analyze structure of a target standard to extract the meta-data of the standard and divide the standard into common and non-common part. The meta-data which are the number, name, version, language and published date of the standard can be extracted from the standard's cover page.

At second phase, users design a database schema for non-common part of the standards. First, users analyze usage of the standard, give requirement analysis and define function of a database to manage non-common part of the standard, and design a database schema to manage non-common part of the standard. When designing the database schema to store non-common part of the standards, users design the database schema depending on usage of the standards. For standards whose usage is mechanism reference, users enumerate all mechanisms defined in the standards, and define relations between the mechanisms. For standards whose usage is requirements check, users enumerate all requirements defined in the standards, and define relation between the requirements. For standards whose usage is best practice reference, users enumerate all best practices defined in the standards, and define relation between the best practices. For standards whose usage is case data reference, users enumerate case data based on the standards, and define relation between the case data. All procedures above are different for each group. Users follow the procedures depending on which group that the standard belongs. Table 2 shows the tasks required for Group 1 to 5. Then, after procedures of each group are done, users design tables to manage each extracted data, and define relations between tables based on the relations defined in each group above.

Table 2. Task for each group

Task	1	2	3	4	5
Enumerate mechanisms defined in the standard.	√	√	-	-	-
Define relations between the mechanisms.	√	√	-	-	-
Enumerate requirements defined in the standard.	√	√	√	√	√
Define relations between the requirements.	√	√	√	√	√
Enumerate best practices defined in the standard.	-	-	-	√	√
Define relations between the best practices.	-	-	-	√	√
Enumerate case data based on the standard.	√	-	√	-	√
Define relations between the case data.	√	-	√	-	√

At third phase, users prepare data of the standard to store into the databases. Users prepare the data based on following conditions. First, users state the name, number, language, and version of the standard for every data. Second, users create only one standard, part, language, and version for one data. Third, users state number of the standard's chapter, clause or item.

At final phase, users store the data of standards' common part into a common database, and data of standards' non-common part into a non-common database.

We have created a guideline for the method in English and Japanese. The guideline can help users to perform the method in order to manage the standards in the environments. The guideline gives basic guide to analyze usage of the standards, help users to prepare XML data and execute SQL/XQuery statement. Detail of the method can be achieved from the guideline [1].

5   Usage of the Method

This section explains how we perform the method step by step to manage ISO information security standards in the environments. We show how we manage the standards when it was published, revised, renamed, and withdrawn.

As an example of new published standards, we store a standard form each group. The standards are ISO/IEC 27003, ISO/IEC 27001, ISO/IEC 15408, ISO/IEC 27002, and ISO/IEC 15946 from Group 1 to 5, respectively. Firstly, we analyze structure of the standards to extract their meta-data which are the number, name, version, language and published date of the standards from the standards' cover. The meta-data of each standard is shown in Table 3.

Table 3. Meta-data of the standard

Number	Name	Ver.	Lang.	Pub. date
ISO/IEC 27003	Information Security Management System Implementation Guidance	1	en	2010/02/01
ISO/IEC 27001	Information Security Management System – Requirement	1	en	2005/10/15
ISO/IEC 15408	Evaluation Criteria for IT Security	2	en	2005/10/07
ISO/IEC 27002	Code of Practice for Information Security Management	1	en	2005/06/15
ISO/IEC 15946	Cryptographic Techniques Based on Elliptic Curved	2	en	2008/04/15

Then, we divide the standards into common and non-common part based on the content page of the standards. Common part and non-common part for each standard are as below.

ISO/IEC 27003

- Common part: *Introduction, Scope, Terms, References, Structure, Annex, Bibliography*
- Non-common part: *Obtaining management approval for initiating an ISMS project, Defining ISMS scope, boundaries and ISMS policy, Conducting information security requirements analysis, Conducting risk assessment and planning risk treatment, Designing the ISMS*

ISO/IEC 27001

- Common part: *Introduction, Scope, Terms, References, Annex, Bibliography*
- Non-common part: *Information security management system, Management responsibility, Internal ISMS audits, ISMS improvement*

ISO/IEC 15408

- Common part: *Introduction, Scope, Terms, References, Annex, Bibliography*
- Non-common part: *Class FAU: Security audit, Class FCO: Communication, Class FCS: Cryptographic support, Class FDP: User data protection, Class FIA: Identification and authentication, Class FMT: Security management, Class FPR: Privacy, Class FPT: Protection of the TSF, Class FRU: Resource utilisation, Class FTA: TOE access, Class FTP: Trusted path/channels, Class APE: Protection Profile evaluation, Class ASE: Security Target evaluation, Evaluation assurance levels, Assurance classes, families, and components, Class ACM: Configuration management, Class ADO: Delivery and operation, Class ADV: Development, Class AGD: Guidance documents, Class ALC: Life cycle support, Class ATE: Tests, Class AVA: Vulnerability assessment*

ISO/IEC 27002

- Common part: *Introduction, Scope, Terms, Structure*
- Non-common part: *Risk Assessment and Treatment, Security Policy, Organization of Information Security, Asset Management, Human Resources Security, Physical Security, Communications and Ops Management, Access Control, Information Systems Acquisition, Development, Maintenance, Information Security Incident management, Business Continuity, Compliance*

ISO/IEC 15946

- Common part: *Introduction, Scope, Terms, Symbols, Annex, Bibliography*
- Non-common part: *Conventions of elliptic curves, Conversion functions, Elliptic curve domain parameters and public key, Notation and conversion functions, Framework for elliptic curve generation, Constructing Elliptic Curves by Complex Multiplication, Constructing Elliptic Curves by Lifting*

From above, it can be clearly seen that non-common part of the standards is different each other. Moreover, the usage of the non-common part is also different. Therefore, it should be managed separately.

Next, we design database schema for each standard because non-common part above is managed in separate databases for each standard. For ISO/IEC 27003, first we enumerate mechanisms and define relations between them. Then we enumerate requirements and define relations between them. After that, we enumerate case data and define relations between them. For ISO/IEC 27001, first we enumerate mechanisms and define relations between them. Then we enumerate requirements and define relations between them. For ISO/IEC 15408, first we enumerate requirements and define relations between them. After that, we enumerate case data and define relations between them. For ISO/IEC 27002, first we enumerate requirements and define relations between them. Then, we enumerate best practices and define relations between them. For ISO/IEC 15946, first we enumerate requirements and define relations between them. Then, we

Table 4. Stored Standards

DB Name	Standard	Data
ISOALL	All below	Common part of all standards below
I27003E1	ISO/IEC 27003	Non-common part of ISO/IEC 27003 English version 1
I27001E1	ISO/IEC 27001	Non-common part of ISO/IEC 27001 English version 1
I15408E2	ISO/IEC 15408	Non-common part of ISO/IEC 15408 English version 2
I27002E1	ISO/IEC 27002	Non-common part of ISO/IEC 27002 English version 1
I15946E2	ISO/IEC 15946	Non-common part of ISO/IEC 15946 English version 2

Table 5. Revised Standard

Old_no.	Old_name	Lang.	Ver.	New_no.	New_name	Lang.	Ver.	Revised date
15408	Evaluation	En	2	15408	Evaluation	En	3	2009/12/15

enumerate best practices and define relations between them. After that, we enumerate case data and defined relations between them. Based on the relations, we design database schema for each standard.

Then, we prepare XML data for both common and non-common part of each standard. Then, we store data of common part for all five standards into a common database, and store data of non-common part to each non-common database that we have designed for each standard. Data stored in each database are show in Table 4.

From above, databases for non-common part of the standards in each group can be constructed by following each group database schema design tasks, and data of the standards can be stored to the databases. Therefore, databases for other standard in the same group can be constructed in the same way.

For revised standards, we store revised version of ISO/IEC 15408. We have stored version 2 of the standard earlier. Next, we store version 3 of the standard. First, we update the meta-data old version of the standard from 'on go' to 'revised' state. Then, we store data of old standard's number, name, version, language, and revised standard's number, name, language, revision date of the old standard to define relation between old and newer standards as shown in Table 5. Next, extract meta-data of the newer standard an store it into ISO Meta DB, and we set at this point the newer standard's status is 'on go'. Then, we analyze structure of the newer standard, design the database schema according

Table 6. Renamed Standard

Old_no.	Old_name	New_no	New_name	Renamed_date
17799	Code of prac.	27002	Code of prac.	2005/06/15

Table 7. Withdrawn Standard

Withdrawn_no.	Withdrawn_name	Lang.	Ver.	Withdrawn_date
15946	Cryptopgraphic tech..	en	1	2011/01/11

```
XQUERY                                          XQUERY
for $term in db2-fn:xmlcolumn("TERM.TERM")/term for $term in db2-fn:xmlcolumn("TERM.TERM")/term
where $term/@iso_number="ISO/IEC 15408-1:2005" where $term/@iso_number="ISO/IEC 15408-1:2009"
return $term                                    return $term
```

```
<term>                                          <term>
 assets                                          assets
</term>                                         </term>
<definition>                                    <definition>
 information or resources to be protected by the entities that the owner of the TOE presumably places
</definition>                                   </definition>
</term>                                         </term>
```

Fig. 3. Differences check between versions

to task of the standard's group, and prepare the data. Then, we prepare and store the data same as procedures for new published standards.

For renamed standards, we store ISO/IEC 17799 that is the previous name of ISO/IEC 27002. First, we update the meta-data old version of the standard from 'on go' to 'renamed' state. Then, we store data of old standard's number, name, version, language, and renamed standard's number, name, language, rename date to define relation between old and newer standard as shown in Table 6. Next, we store meta-data of the renamed standard into ISO Meta DB, and at this point the newer standard's status is set as 'on go'. As there are no particular change

```
SELECT X.* FROM XMLTABLE ('db2-fn:xmlcolumn("TASK.TASK")/term'
              COLUMNS
              task        VARCHAR(100)              PATH 'task/task_name',
              standards   VARCHAR(500)              PATH 'ISO') AS X
```

TASK	STANDARDS
Infrastructure Management	ISO/IEC 13335, ISO/IEC 27001, SO/IEC 27002, ISO/IEC 27006
Human Resource Management	ISO/IEC 13335, ISO/IEC 27001, ISO/IEC 27002, ISO/IEC 27006
Quality Management	ISO/IEC 13335, ISO/IEC 27001, ISO/IEC 27002, ISO/IEC 27006
Risk Management	ISO/IEC 15408
Information Management	ISO/IEC 11770
Software Requirements Analysis	ISO/IEC 11770, ISO/IEC 19790
Software Architectural Design	ISO/IEC 15408, ISO/IEC 15446, ISO/IEC 15816, ISO/IEC 15945,...
Software Detailed Design	ISO/IEC 7064, ISO/IEC 9796, ISO/IEC 9798, ISO/IEC 10118, ISO..
Software Implementation	ISO/IEC 9797, ISO/IEC 10116, ISO/IEC 10118, ISO/IEC 15946, I..
Software Qualification Testing	ISO/IEC 15408, ISO/IEC 15443, ISO/IEC 18045, ISO/IEC 19790,...
Software Integration	-
Software Construction	-
Software Installation	ISO/IEC 13335, ISO/IEC 27001, ISO/IEC 27002, ISO/IEC 27006
Software Operation	ISO/IEC 13335, ISO/IEC 18043, ISO/IEC 27001, ISO/IEC 27002,...
Software Maintenance	ISO/IEC 7064, ISO/IEC 9796, ISO/IEC 9797, ISO/IEC 9798, ISO/I..
Software Disposal	-
Software Documentation Management	ISO/IEC 15408, ISO/IEC 27001, ISO/IEC 27002, ISO/IEC 27006
Software Quality Assurance	ISO/IEC 21827
Software Verification	ISO/IEC 15408, ISO/IEC 15443, ISO/IEC 18045, ISO/IEC 19790,...
Software Validation	ISO/IEC 15408, ISO/IEC 15443, ISO/IEC 18045, ISO/IEC 19790,...
Software Configuration Management	-
Software Review	ISO/IEC 15408, ISO/IEC 15443, ISO/IEC 18045, ISO/IEC 19790,...
Software Problem Resolution	-
Recovery	ISO/IEC 24762
Environment Management	ISO/IEC 11770, ISO/IEC 13335, ISO/IEC 14516, ISO/IEC 27001,...

Fig. 4. Relationships check between task and standards

made to the standards except the number and the published date, we copy the whole database of the old standard.

For withdrawn standards, we considered ISO/IEC 15946 that we have store earlier is withdrawn. First, we update the meta-data of the standard from 'on go' to 'withdrawn' state. Then, we store data of withdrawn standard's number, name, version, language, and withdrawn date as shown in Table 7.

Next, we show some examples that users can use the standards effectively that only can be achieved by managing the standards as databases in systematic way. Fig. 3 shows how users can check difference between term defined in ISO/IEC 15408 for version 2005 and 2009. From the figure, it can be clearly seen that the definition for assets is different in both versions.

Users also can check relationships between tasks of software life cycle process for secure information and ISO information security standards as shown in Fig. 4. From the figure, users can refer to the appropriate standards when performing one of the tasks.

6   Concluding Remarks

We have proposed a systematic management method of ISO information security standards for information security engineering environments, and presented a database system to manage the standards that is an indispensable tool to perform the method. We also have showed how to perform the method for each event in life cycle of the standards. Designers, developers, managers, maintainers, and abrogators of security facilities can manage data of the standards systematically by using the method.

Users can manage ISO information security standards in all kinds of information security engineering environments that have to deal and manage the standards. Therefore, not only users, but also tools in such environments can use the standards easily and effectively.

As future works, we will implement the database system with tools to support users to perform the method. Moreover, other remaining standards should be stored and the proposed method will be evaluated based on it.

References

1. Advanced Information Systems Engineering Laboratory, Department of Information and Computer Sciences, Saitama University: A Systematic Management Method for ISO Information Security Standards,
   http://www.aise.ics.saitama-u.ac.jp/isee/
2. Beyer, K., Cochrane, R., Hvizdos, M., Josifovski, V., Kleewein, J., Lapis, G., Lohman, G., Lyle, R., Nicola, M., Ozcan, F., Pirahesh, H., Seemann, N., Singh, A., Truong, T., Van der Linden, R.C., Vickery, B., Zhang, C., Zhang, G.: DB2 Goes Hybrid: Integrating Native XML and XQuery with Relational Data and SQL. IBM Systems Journal 45, 271–298 (2006)
3. Chen, W., John, C., Naomi, N., Rakesh, R., Manoj, K.S.: DB2 Express-c: The Developer Handbook for Xml, Php, C/c++, Java, and .net. Vervante (2006)

4. Chen, W., Sammartino, A., Goutev, D., Hendricks, F., Komi, I., Wei, M., Ahuja, R., Nicola, M.: DB2 9 pureXML Guide. IBM Corp. (2007)
5. Cheng, J., Goto, Y., Horie, D., Miura, J., Kasahara, T., Iqbal, A.: Development of ISEE: An Information Security Engineering Environment. In: Proceedings of the 7th IEEE International Symposium on Parallel and Distributed Processing with Applications (ISPA 2009), pp. 505–510. IEEE Computer Society Press, Chengdu (2009)
6. Cheng, J., Goto, Y., Morimoto, S., Horie, D.: A Security Engineering Environment Based on ISO/IEC Standards: Providing Standard, Formal, and Consistent Supports for Design, Development, Operation, and Maintenance of Secure Information Systems. In: Proceedings of the 2nd International Conference on Information Security and Assurance (ISA 2008), pp. 350–354. IEEE Computer Society Press, Busan (2008)
7. Horie, D., Kasahara, T., Goto, Y., Cheng, J.: A New Model of Software Life Cycle Processes for Consistent Design, Development, Management, and Maintenance of Secure Information Systems. In: Proceedings of the 8th IEEE/ACIS International Conference on Computer and Information Science (ICIS 2009), pp. 897–902. IEEE Computer Society, Shanghai (2009)
8. Horie, D., Morimoto, S., Azimah, N., Goto, Y., Cheng, J.: ISEDS: An Information Security Engineering Database System Based on ISO Standards. In: Proceedings of the 3rd International Conference on Availability, Reliability and Security (ARES 2008), pp. 1219–1225. IEEE Computer Society, Barcelona (2008)
9. International Organization for Standardization, ISO Standards, http://www.iso.org/iso/home.htm
10. Iqbal, A., Horie, D., Goto, Y., Cheng, J.: A Database System for Effective Utilization of ISO/IEC 27002. In: Proceedings of the 4th International Conference on Frontier of Computer Science and Technology (FCST 2009), pp. 607–612. IEEE Computer Society, Shanghai (2009)
11. Krause, L.: Information Technology – Security Techniques and Standardization. Journal Standards & Interfaces - Special Issue: German National Research 17, 63–67 (1995)
12. Nicola, M., Kiefer, T.: Generating SQL/XML Query and Update Statements. In: Proceeding of the 18th ACM Conference on Information and Knowledge Management (CIKM 2009), pp. 1187–1196. ACM, New York (2009)

Assessing the Factors Influencing Information Technology Investment Decisions: A Survey of Sampled Public Sector Organizations in Tanzania

Obadiah Machupa[1] , Elias Otaigo[2], Daniel Koloseni[3], and Faith Shimba[4]

[1] National Enviromental Management Council
Dar es Salaam, Tanzania
omachupa@yahoo.com
[2,3,4] Department of Information Technology,
Faculty of Computing, Information System and Mathematics
The Institute of Finance Management, Shabaan Robert Street,
Dar es Salaam, Tanzania
{otaigo,koloseni,shimba}@ifm.ac.tz

Abstract. The rationale of this study was to respond to the popular belief that public sector organizations are less efficient and less effective regardless of being equipped with IT investments. The general purpose was to assess the factors which influence decisions on IT investments. While questionnaires were used to collect data from 21 sampled organizations, 'judgmental sampling' method was used in determining the sample size and the 'stated preference' method was used to evaluate the findings. The results of analysis showed that there are some degree of influence from both Business cases and IT business value. On the other hand, alignment was found to have no influence at all. Hence, the study recommends adopting or enhancing use of business cases, IT evaluation for alignment as well as IT governance for business value in public sectors to justify significant capital expenditures.

Keywords: IT investment decisions, IT Business value, Public sector, IT investment, Tanzania.

1 Introduction

Today's business environment is characterized by organizational dependence on information and communication technology (ICT). Most of the offices in private and public sectors are equipped with the information technology (IT), in particular, computers. For example, the ICT Policy for Basic Education cites that almost every office at the headquarters of the ministry of education and vocational training (MoEVT) is equipped with computer, printer and Internet access [1]. The primary objective of an IT investment is to create business value through efficiency and effectiveness gains [2].

There are various factors which affect the business value impact of ITinvestment. Which are reliance on IT business case, alignment of IT and business objectives as the

A. Abd Manaf et al. (Eds.): ICIEIS 2011, Part I, CCIS 251, pp. 385–399, 2011.
© Springer-Verlag Berlin Heidelberg 2011

factors that should drive IT investment decisions if at all the value from IT investment is to be realized [2,3,4].Tanzania Government, similar to other governments, recognizes the importance of strategic IT investment decisions in national development and has been at the forefront in putting in place the policy statements and frameworks to enhance IT choices, particularly in the public sector organizations. For example, the establishment of Ministry of Communication, Science and Technology (in February,2008) with emphasis on ICT matters and the mandatory introduction of the post of Chief Information Officer (CIO) in all government ministries (in early 2008),investment in undersea deployment of fibre optic cable and the construction of the nation broadband backbone are recently remarkable intentions of the government toward fruitful IT investments[5].

However, evidence showed that in public sector organization, IT is not well aligned with business strategy, as prerequisite to realize IT business value [6, 7].

[2] points out that, ad-hoc IT investment decisions as the source of misalignment and argues that IT investment decision processes should be de-politicized as much as possible, priorities be explicitly stated in the organizational plan and decision making process be visible and based on the business needs. Not by chance were the public sector organizations chosen to be surveyed, but, it was by knowledge accrued through experience of the researchers which also was supported by Heeks on the necessity of aligning IT objectives with business objectives as a factor to create business value from IT investments[6].

2   Conceptual Research Model

This study is based on the three identified factors:

IT business cases, IT-Business alignment and IT business value; which are among the pre-requisites for realization of the benefits from IT investment decisions. The extent of influence for each of the factors was assessed using some respective dimensions as follows: IT business case dimensions - Justification for financial analysis, business analysis and IT management analysis (see figure 1).

Alignment between IT and Business strategies: Justification for management perception, IT-governance and IT-maturity level.
Business value from IT: Justification for customer satisfaction, efficiency/effectiveness gain, information access, data storage/ processing and data sharing.

There exists a popular belief of in-efficiency and in-effectiveness in the public sector organizations regardless of such organizations being equipped with IT facilities. This belief may be driven by the aforementioned problems. The National ICT Policy [7] also declares that ICT environment is still faced with management challenges including lack of visionary leadership, though; there are indications that various government ministries, departments and agencies (MDAs) in Tanzania have made significant progress in deploying ICT in their working places.

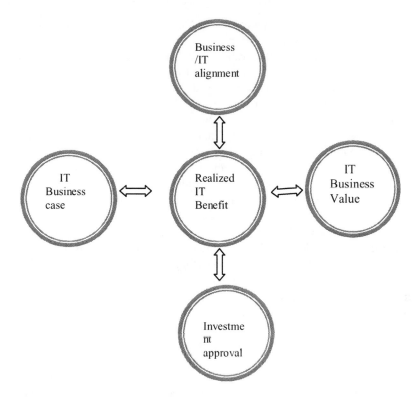

Fig. 1. Research Model (The Model has not been empirically derived, but is based on the researcher's observations)

3   Literature Review

Failure is prone on IT investments. Studies show that over 50% of all IT projects fails [3]. Business case, as the concept of alignment between IT and business and the perception on IT business value are recipes for either success or failure. The discrepancy between the desired and the actual outcomes of IT investment decisions making highlights a possible gap between what is offered in theory and what is used by practitioners. Gaining an understanding of the underlying issues associated with this gap is important, as its existence raises such questions about the efficiency and effectiveness of services delivered by public sector organizations.

3.1   IT Business Case

An IT business case is used to describe a problem and hence outlines a proposal for how the problem will be addressed. The logic of the IT business case is that, whenever resources such as money or effort are consumed, they should be in support of the business (organization) goals. IT business case is therefore a tool that supports planning and decision making and tells the decision makers about why is the IT investment needed, how will the effort solve the problems facing the organization, how does the solution address the problem, what is the recommended IT investment solution, what will happen to the organization (business), when and where will the solutions be deployed, etc. Both real and fictional heroes often have trusted companions that steer them from danger and that a good IT business case is the trusted scout of IT investment decision making as it points out promising opportunities, resolving conflicting arguments, flushes out bad reasoning, exposes inappropriate political plays, shores up claims and simplifies analysis [3]. Further, Dekkers argues that IT business case is an establishment go/no go moment before the start of the project and that it typically consists of business needs, cost-benefit analysis, and risks assessment, vision, business context, project objectives and project plan [8].

More specifically, flawed usage of IT business case justification as major cause

of more than 50% failures in IT investment [3]. They points cost benefit analysis, rationale, evidence and support as major factors to consider during investment decisions. However, Curley adds that the whole process of evaluating IT investments should be depoliticized to reduce the rate IT investments failure [2].

Different studies show that business value from IT investment has been in debate for number of years, but little is documented about the factors which influence IT investment decisions particularly in the public sector organizations [2,3]. Most literature documents economic factors such as profitability and return on investment as the factors that influence IT investment decision. However, those factors can easily be realized in the private sector organizations and not in public sector organizations whose business is service delivery to public.

3.2   Alignment of IT and Business objectives

Alignment of IT and business is reached when IT is embedded in the core operations and core strategies of the organization. It is the process of ensuring that IT services are designed to support goals, mission and vision of the organization.

'IT by itself has no intrinsic value, but its value is when coupled (aligned) with business processes in the organization '[2]. Additionally, IT does not, of itself, deliver business value, instead, points out that the value comes only from changes in work practices and reforms of business processes [4]. Indication for IT/business alignment is that business processes relies upon a robust IT infrastructure and applications, and IT in turn, often supports the business processes in such a way that absence of IT services dramatically affects business processes of the organization.

In order for the business organization to achieve IT business value, it should have the business organization objectives and the IT organization objectives [9]. Dekkers shows that often aligning the goals and objectives of IT organization to those of business organization is a challenge in most organizations [8]. The situation is more serious in the public sector organizations because of bureaucracies, monopoly of service as well as political influence. While addressing the issue of strategic alignment of IT with Business, Curley shows that the business strategy relies upon a robust IT infrastructure and applications, and IT in turn, often supports the business strategy [2].Further, he argues that most problems and constraints are found in the context of business system, and identifies to include organizational process, organizational behavior, future trends on the market place, future available software systems, just to mention the few.

To establish if IT objectives are in line with business vision, concept of alignment is used. Dekkers shows that alignment is when internal arrangement (structure, processes, skills) is in line with external position of the organization (product, market, service) [8].Similarly, an organization can consistently succeeds only when all of its parts are in a strong cause and effect (alignment) relationship and that alignment should be the foremost on the minds of executives decision makers when faced with choices on IT investments [3].Silvius, concludes that the alignment between business strategy and IT investments is still a prominent area of concern [10]. Where Heeks shows that the non alignment problem of business and IT objectives is more dominant in the public sector organizations and thus identifies such non alignment as the impedance to the realization of IT business value[6].

Thus, IT/Business alignment is no longer a 'nice-to-have'; instead, it is a 'must-to-have' since it drives bottom line benefits. This again lays the ground to assess alignment of business with IT opportunities as another factor which influences IT investment decision making.

3.3   IT Business Value

There are number of studies that address the issue of IT business value in the public sector organizations. Heeks compares public sector and private sector organizations to 'old-fashion' and 'modern-fashion' offices respectively when looks on the business value from IT in those organizations [6]. In similarly, Sawe in his paper on the ICT and the Public Sector states that 'Public sector is increasingly seen as the main engine to bridge the digital divide at country level… and can start acting as model users of ICT and be catalysts for others to follow'[11].

IT can do little of value to business but its strategic use can result in creation of IT business value. It is not computers that make the difference, but what people do with them [12]. Curley shows that IT business value includes automation effects (which refer to efficiency perspective), informational effects (which refers to capacity to collect, store, process and disseminate information) and transformational effects (which refers to IT's ability to facilitate and support process innovation or re-engineering) [2].

While addressing analysis of information systems project, Heeks concludes that many projects start without the business value being clearly articulated [6]. As a result, it is difficult to determine whether they are a success from business perspectives. Since business value is the end result of IT investments; there are many factors that affect the value throughout the implementation process. Barbara identifies cooperation among various divisions, departments, and employees within the organization and the technical aspect of implementation as two components in the chain of events towards creation of business value [13].

4   Research Approach

The survey study was used to collect data from the public sector organizations. Each organization was served with one questionnaire that targeted decision makers (Executives, Chief Information Officers (CIO), Chief Technology Officers (CTO) or IT Managers) as all of them involve in IT investment decisions .Data were collected from 21 organizations which were sampled as follows using judgmental sampling method: 13 were government ministries (out of 26 available ministries –this is 50%) and 8 were government departments/ agencies. It is believed that since each government department/agency should follow under a parent ministry then the sample of 8 department/agencies reflects a true picture of the independent autonomous bodies under the 26 parent ministries (this is 30.8%). Data analysis was done using stated preference method.

A three point Likert scale was used throughout the questionnaire. The scale comprises high (H), medium (M), and low (L) to indicate extent of influences for each of the three factors surveyed. The survey questionnaire was hand-delivered, one to each organization, and then collected back by the researchers. Data were coded as H, M and L to denote high, medium and low perceptions respectively. During data analysis H was considered as 'Strongly Agree' while M was considered as 'Agree' and L as 'Not Agree'. In turn, both H and M were considered to indicate positive attitude hence lumped together by calculating their central tendency (Arithmetic Mean) as the 'Overall Agree' score. L was considered to indicate negative attitude and therefore remains as it was recorded. The 'Overall Agree Score' [calculated as (H+M)/2] was considered as the final finding and then compared with 'Not Agree Score' (calculated as L/1 or simply L).

Factors influencing IT investment decisions were assessed using the following dimensions:

- **Reliance on IT business cases**: This was justified by responses on questions testing financial analysis (specifically for cost and benefits), business analysis (specifically for current/future situations) and IT management analysis (specifically for risks).
- **Extent of Business /IT alignment**: This was justified by responses on questions testing IT governance structure (specifically Alignment committee), IT maturity level (specifically Use of variety of software) and Management perception (specifically implementation of IT strategy).
- **Perception of IT business value**. This was justified by responses on questions testing customer satisfaction, efficiency/ effectiveness gains, information access/storage/processing and sharing.

5   Results

This section presents findings and analysis of data for three factors identified to influence IT investment decisions in the public sector organizations.

The factors are: IT business case, alignment between IT and business and business value of IT. These factors were identified in the literature review.

As this survey was intended for decision makers, table 1 presents the roles (positions) of people who responded to this survey. The question to test this statistics was purposely set in order to verify whether the responses to this survey are from the intended group (decision makers).

Table 1. The Roles of respondents

Respondents		Response	Percentage
Decision Makers	Executives (CEO/EO)	5	
	CIO/CTO/ IT Managers	12	80.9
Others	e.g. IT end users, etc	4	19.1
Total		21	100

Both, Executives (Chief Executive Officers-CEOs/Executive Officers-EOs) and Chief Information Officers (CIOs)/Chief Technology Officers (CTOs)/IT Managers play a role in IT investment decision making. Thus the statistics presented in table 1 show that 80.9% (17 out of 21) of respondents were the decision makers. This suggests that the outcomes of the research were from the targeted group of respondents.

5.1   IT Business Case Influence As Implied by the Variables

Table 2 shows distribution of responses for variables of the factor IT business case. Four variables were considered as identified in [3,12]. The variables are: Analysis of current situation, Analysis of future situation, Cost and Benefits analysis and Risk management analysis.

Table 2. Influence of IT business case as implied by the variables

Variables	Total responses	Distribution of responses		
		H	M	L
Current situation analysis	21	10	8	3
Future situation analysis	21	12	6	3
Cost and Benefits analysis	21	7	7	7
Risk management analysis	21	5	9	7
	84	34	30	20

Key: H= High perception, M= Medium perception, L=Low perception

The study found that there is degree of dispersion among results of the variables. However, an analysis of the responses for the variable cost and benefit analysis are distributed, this suggests that the variable influence is neutral as its scores are distributed equally among H, M and L. The cost and benefit analysis seems to be a non conclusive variable though very likely might imply that the variable (cost and benefit analysis) is not considered important during IT investment decisions in the sampled organizations.

The variable, risk management analysis, whose high rating is in column M, is considered to have an influence on IT investment decisions, equally important as those with high ratings in column H .For analysis purpose, the three groups of score (High, Medium. and Low) were then reduced to two, namely, Average (Arithmetic Mean) perception of IT business case reliance and average of no perception of IT business case reliance. Analysis by using proportion/percentage method was carried out as follows in table 3.

Table 3. Influence and non-influence levels for IT business case reliance

H+M+L	H	M	L	H+M	μ1 = (H+M)/2	μ2 = L/1
84	34	30	20	64	32	20

Where μ is a Greek letter representing Average or Arithmetic Mean.
μ1 = Influence for IT business case reliance
μ2 = No influence perceived for IT business case reliance.
We observed that the overall results for IT business case are that: 62% of respondents perceive reliance on IT business case while 38% did not perceive IT business case reliance.

5.2   IT Alignment Influence

Alignment between IT and business (IT/business alignment) is reached when IT is embedded in the core operations and core strategies of the organization. An indication for alignment between IT and business (in short, IT/business alignment) is that business processes relies upon a robust IT infrastructure and applications, and IT in turn, supports the business processes in such a way that absence of IT services drastically affects business processes of the organization.

Table 4 shows the distribution of responses for variables of the factor, IT/business alignment. Three variables were considered in the research as identified in [2, 3, and 9].

- **IT governance:** Typical parameter verified is influence of IT Alignment Committee, also known as IT Selection Committee.
- **Management perception**: Typical parameter verified is implementation of IT strategy, a long term plan of action which explains how IT should be utilized.
- **IT maturity**: Typical parameter verified is usage of different software, as indicator of dependency on IT services and applications in the workplace.

Table 4. Influence of IT/business alignment as implied by the variables

Variables	Total responses	Distribution of responses		
		H	M	L
IT governance (e.g. influence of IT committee)	21	4	6	11
Management perception (e.g. implementation of IT strategy)	21	5	8	8
IT maturity (e.g. Usage of different software)	21	3	10	8
Total	63	12	24	27

(H= High perception, M= Medium perception, L=Low perception)

Table 4 shows that there is degree of distribution of results among the variables. However, by looking the responses for first two variables (IT governance and Management perception), the variables seem to have low influence since they are highly rated in the column L. The reasons for such ratings might be that there are no IT Alignment Committees in the sampled organizations and also that there are no IT strategy. In this regard, the variable, IT maturity, whose high rating is in column M , is considered to have influence on IT investment decisions equally equal to if it were in H column. This result for IT maturity indicates a perceived use of different IT software. However, this is a bit contrary because the other two parameters (IT selection committee and IT strategy), which would form the basis for rational software choices, are rated with negative attitude, meaning that the influences of the two variables are not perceived. Thus, IT maturity indicated by high rating in column M might be because of the so known as 'IT prestige' and not because of the business needs or IT strategy implementation. IT prestige simply imply the use of IT because of social admiration/respect and not because of business needs.

The three groups of score (H, M. and L) were then reduced to two, namely, Average perception of IT/business alignment and Average of no perception. As already explained, the Average perception is calculated as $[(H+M)/2]$ while the No perception is (L/1) or just L. Analysis by using proportion/percentage method was carried out as follows in table 5.

Table 5. Influence and non-influence levels for IT/business alignment

H+	H	M	L	H+M	$\mu3 = (H+M)/2$	$\mu4 = L/1$
63	12	24	27	36	18	27

Where μ = average or arithmetic mean.
$\mu3$ = Influence of IT/business
$\mu4$ = No influence perceived.

The overall results for alignment between IT and business shows that 40% of respondents perceive influence of alignment while 60% do not perceive alignment influence for IT investment decisions in the sampled organizations.

5.3   IT Business Value

IT business value (also known as business value from IT) refers to the impact of IT on organization performance. This impact includes the following: automation impact which refers to improvements in speed, quality, productivity, efficiency, effectiveness and alike, informational impact which refers to capacity to collect, store, process and disseminate information and transformational impact refers to IT ability to facilitate and support process innovation or re-engineering.

Table 6 shows distribution of responses for variables of the factor IT business value. Five variables were considered in this research as identified in [2,6].

The variables are: Easy access to information, Storage and processing of information, Data sharing, Efficiency and effectiveness and satisfaction of IT users. As it can be seen in Table 6 below, there is degree of dispersion among results of the variables. However, an analysis of the responses distribution for the variable easy access to information reveals that the variable influence is neutral as its scores are distributed equally among H, M and L.

The easy accessibility therefore seems to be a non conclusive variable though very likely might implies that the easy accessibility is not considered as an issue during IT investment decisions in the sampled organizations as it is not perceived as an influencing issue.

Table 6. IT business value influence as implied by the variables

Variables	Total responses	Distribution of responses		
		H	M	L
Easy access to information	21	7	7	7
Storage and processing	21	8	6	7
Data sharing	21	10	9	2
Efficiency / effectiveness	21	7	6	8
Satisfaction	21	8	4	9
Total	105	40	32	33

(H= High perception, M= Medium perception, L=Low perception

Looking the responses for the variable, efficiency/effectiveness and the variable satisfaction, the two variables seem to have low influence since they are highly rated in the column L. This implies that there is no efficiency/effectiveness perceived and as a result, there is no satisfaction perceived. This finding is obvious because it is the efficiency/effective that leads into satisfaction, so if the latter is missing, obviously the former must not exist.

The three groups for comparisons were then reduced from three (H, M. and L) to two, namely, average perception of IT business value ((H+M)/2) and average of no perception of IT business value (L/1) or just L.

An analysis by using proportion/percentage method was carried out and is shown in table 7.

Table 7. Influence and non-influence levels for IT business value

H+M+L	H	M	L	H+M	$\mu5 = (H+M)/2$	$\mu6 = L/1$
105	40	32	33	72	36	33

Where μ = Average or Arithmetic Mean.
$\mu5$ = IT Business value influence
$\mu6$ = No influence perceived for IT business value.

Observation shows that the overall results for IT business value is that 52% of respondents perceive IT business value while 48% do not.

5.4   Comparison of Business Case, Alignment and IT Business Value

Comparison for all three factors is given table 8.

Table 8. Findings for all the three factors

Factor	H+M+L	H	M	L	H+M	μp	=	μN = L/1
A	84	34	30	20	64	32		20
B	63	12	24	27	36	18		27
C	105	40	32	33	72	36		33

Where

A = IT business case

B = Alignment between IT and business

C = IT business value

μ = Greek letter representing Average or Arithmetic Mean.

μp = Average perception perceived.

μN = No influence perceived.

Findings in table 8 were plotted and the resulting graph is shown in figure 2.

There exists an influence of IT business case on IT investment decisions. However, this research is inconclusive as to whether the sampled organizations do use IT business case, because, if it were so, the variable 'cost and benefit analysis' (Table

2) would have not been inconclusive (neutral). The report considers that the perceived IT business case might be caused by experience from the current business situation as well as the desired future situation.

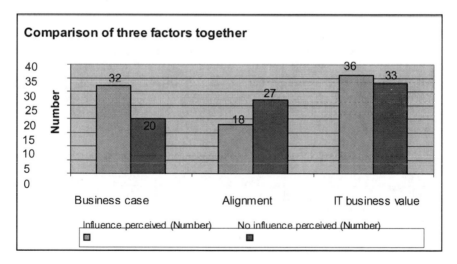

Fig. 2. Graph showing the comparison of the three factors

From figure 2, the following general observations are deduced by observing the three factors: There is no alignment perceived between IT and business objectives.

This concurs with the findings of Table 4 which shows absence of IT selection committee and IT strategy), which would form the basis for alignment. The general implication is that IT objectives are not correctly positioned to achieve business objectives. There exists perception of IT business value but at low magnitude. This is suggested by the small gap that exists between perception and non perception graphs.

5.5   Extent of Ad-Hoc Decisions

The absence of alignment between IT and business objectives as well as the minimal IT value perception observed implies presence of ad-hoc decisions in the sampled organizations. Table 9 shows responses for a question intended to capture the extent of making ad-hoc decisions pertaining to IT investments in the sampled organizations. The reasons to include question that verifies extent of ad-hoc decisions, is the fact that in real world ad-hoc decisions are difficult to avoid completely because, in a changing business environment the future is not certain. Thus ad-hoc decisions can only be kept to minimum but cannot be eliminated completely in practice.

Table 9. Ad-hoc decisions as implied by the variables

Nature of influence	Total			
	Respondents	H	M	L
Urgent requests for IT	21	8	6	7
Availability of funds	21	13	5	3
External factors such as new technology, IT vendors, etc.	21	3	8	10

Key: H=High perception, M=Medium perception, L=Low perception

All of the above decisions were identified as ad-hoc decisions during literature review because they are neither based on IT business case nor based on neither alignment nor IT business value perception. From table 9, it is interesting to note that the variable, external factors, does not influence IT investment decision since its rating is high in the column L. On the other hand, the variable, availability of funds exhibit high influence followed by the variable, urgent requests, because both are rated high in column H.

Table 10. Ad-hoc decisions (Perception & perception findings)

Variab	H+M+L	H	M	L	H+M	μH =	μL =
UR	21	8	6	7	14	7	7
AF	21	13	5	3	·18	9	3
EF	21	3	8	10	11	5.5	10

Where: UR=Urgent requests for IT
AF=Availability of funds
EF=External factors such as new technology, etc.
μ = Represents Average or Arithmetic Mean.
μH = Average perception perceived. , μL = No influence perceived.

It can be noted from table10 that the variable, Urgent requests for IT, is inconclusive since it has equal distribution of scores between μH and μL. However, this finding might imply no influence of the variable. In similar way, availability of funds seems to influence more the decisions while external factors such as IT pioneers seem to have no influence. We found that, the influence of ad-hoc is noted to exist at a rate of 52% while that of no ad-hoc decisions is 48%. The small arithmetic gaps between the two percentages (the difference between 52% and 48%) might be caused by reliance on IT business case.

6   Discussions of Findings

The study recorded an effective response rate of 75% with 80.9% of the respondents belong to the decision makers group. This implies that this paper presents data collected from the targeted group.

6.1   Influence of the IT Business Case

Figure 1 shows perception of IT business case at a rate of 62%. On the other hand, table 2 shows inconclusive (neutral) results for the variable 'cost and benefits analysis' whose responses are equal in all columns (H=7, M=7 and L=7). The cost and benefit analysis is a key indicator of the business case, so if the former (business case) is formally used and practiced, it (cost and benefit indicator) would not have such inconclusive pattern of data. The implication of such contradiction between the overall percentage and the results for cost and benefit analysis indictor may signifies that there was exaggeration in responding the questions pertaining to business case, and hence makes the percentage statistics to require further analysis. However, the general interpretation is that the result shows existence of some level of influence from business case, but the quality of the influence cannot be statistically concluded until further studies.

6.2   Perception of Alignment

Results in Table 4 shows that there is no influence of IT committee and as well as no influence of IT strategy (since in both columns of IT committee and IT strategy, high statistics is found in column L, to signify no influence).The implication of these findings is that there exist problems in IT planning in such a way that no alignment is found. This is an expected and obvious results because in the absence of quality business case no alignment can be found [3].

6.3   Influence of IT Business Value

The responses (Table 6-7) show that 52% perceives degree of IT business value. However, Table 6 indicates that there is no efficiency/effectiveness and there is no satisfaction (since in both columns of 'efficiency/effectiveness' and 'satisfaction', high statistics is found in column L, to signify no influence). Again, efficiency/effectiveness and user satisfaction are key indicators of the business value from IT, so if the former (efficiency/effectiveness and user satisfaction) would have been existing in the sampled organizations, the two would not had such inconclusive pattern of data. The implication of such contradiction between the overall percentage and the results for efficiency/effectiveness and satisfaction may signifies that there was again some exaggeration in responding to the questions pertaining to IT business value , and hence makes the percentage statistics to require further analysis. However, the general interpretation is that the result shows existence of some level of influence from IT business value, but the quality of the influence cannot be statistically concluded until further studies.

7   Conclusions

Based on the analysis of the findings the researcher draws the following conclusions:

Business Case: To the extent, there is some degree of influence from business case though; percentage of influence observed cannot be concluded until further studies. What can be readily concluded is that cost and benefit analysis is not practiced for IT investment decisions in the sampled organizations. Only current work situation and desired future situation (Table 2) seem to be considered and therefore contribute to the observed degree of influence for a business case.

Alignment between IT and business: No evidence of alignment was found.

This conquers with the findings of table 4 which show absence of IT Alignment Committee as well as absence of IT strategy. Normally, it is the job of the business case team to discover and communicate the strongest possible and value alignment related to the investment being analyzed [3]. So since use of business case was found to be undetermined, obviously no alignment can be achieved. The absence of alignment committee, IT strategy and business case team, just to mention few, clearly are recipes for the alignment failure.

IT business value: To the extent, there is some degree of influence from IT business value though; percentage of influence observed cannot be concluded until further studies. What can be readily observed is that there is neither efficiency/effectiveness nor satisfaction perceived.

8   Recommendations

Formal use of Business Case: The use of business case should become increasingly common in public sector organizations to justify significant capital expenditures. This should not only incorporate a financial return on investment (ROI) such as formal cost, benefit and risks analysis, but also includes social and political ROI. This research highly commends use of IT business case as a management confidence–building path towards value promising investment decisions so as to get lid of ad-hoc decisions whose chances to deliver business value is narrow.

IT investments evaluation for 'Alignment': Integration of IT with business performance is a major importance. This integration is what this report is referring to as 'IT-Business Alignment'. How IT is being used and how well is it being used should be strategically evaluated periodically. This is because IT investment evaluation is in itself a learning experience by which an organization can learn how well it used its funds as well as how well IT may be better employed in its processes (alignment). A feedback process may be put in place in the hope that better decisions are made next time around.

Enhancing IT governance for promising Business Value from IT: The strategic use of IT requires an active participation, open and flexible organizational structure, and as importantly, a certain level of harmony with organizational culture. With Chief Information Officers (CIOs)/Chief Technology Officers (CTOs)/IT Managers in place, yet it is recommended to either adopt or enhance IT Selection Committees in the public sector organizations so as to consistently improve IT planning processes which will lead into investment decisions that promise delivery of IT business value.

References

1. URT, "ICT Policy for Basic Education (Draft)" M. o. Education. Tanzania Gorvenment (2007)
2. Curley, M.: Managing Information Technology (IT) for Business Value: Practical Strategies for IT Managers, 3rd edn. Intel Publishing (2005)
3. Keen, J.K., Digrius, B.: Making Technology Investment Profitable: ROI Roadmap to Better IT Business Case (2003)
4. Turban, E., Mclean, E., Wetherbe, J.: Information technology for Management: Making Connections for Strategic Advantage, 2nd edn. (2003)
5. Dhliwayo, J.: Developing a fiber optic backbone for Africa, vol. 2011 (2009)
6. Heeks, R.: Reinventing Government in the Information Age: International Practice in IT-enabled public sector reform. TJ International Ltd. (2001)
7. URT "National ICT Policy" M. o. S. a. Technology. Tanzania Government Printers (2003)
8. Dekkers, H.: IT business case: the role of IT Architecture. Masters (2004)
9. Applegate, L.M., Austin, R.D., Mcfarlan, F.W.: Corporate Information Strategy and Management: The Challenges of Managing in a Network Economy, 6th edn. (2003)
10. Silvius, A.J.G.: Business IT alignment in Theory and Practice. In: Emerald Insight, p. 211 (2007)
11. Sawe, D.: ICT and the Public Sector: Paper presented during workshop on draft for National ICT policy, Royal Palm Hotel 2008 (May 25, 2002)
12. Remenyi, D., Money, A., Smith, M.: The effective measurement and management of IT costs and benefits, 2nd edn. MPG Books ltd. (2003)
13. Barbara, E.: An Integrated Framework for Contextual Factors affecting IT Implementation. IEEE Explore 2008 (2006)

Exploring Homomorphic Encryption in Wireless Sensor Networks

Bhumika Patel[1] and Devesh Jinwala[2]

[1] Department of Computer Engineering,
C. K. Pithawalla College of Engineering & Technology,
Surat, Gujarat, India
bhumikapatel24@gmail.com
[2] Department of Computer Engineering,
Sardar Vallabhbhai National Institute of Technology,
Surat, Gujarat, India
dcjinwala@acm.org

Abstract. The communication paradigm in the Wireless Sensor Networks (WSNs) relies on in network processing i.e. on-the-fly pre-processing of the data sensed by the sensors, on its way to the base station. However, the fallout of in-network processing is that the multihop communication used in WSNs has to be data-centric, unlike the route-centric communication used in conventional networks. This requires that the intermediate nodes have access to the data that jeopardizes the stringent end-to-end security requirements of typical security-critical applications. An approach that promises the combination of end-to-end security and in-network aggregation is Concealed Data Aggregation. In this paper, we discuss our attempts at investigating the feasibility of applying the provably secure homomorphic encryption schemes to the WSNs, within the constraints permissible and without sacrificing any security. Based on our empirical evaluation centered around defined performance metrics, we demonstrate that it is feasible to employ the proposed approach for WSNs.

Keywords: Wireless Sensor Networks, In network Processing, Data Aggregation, Secure Data Aggregation, Privacy Homomorphism.

1   Introduction

WSNs are composed of hundreds or thousands of inexpensive, low-powered sensing devices (often known as sensor nodes or motes) with limited memory, power, computational and communication resources. These sensor nodes together form a communication network, which offers potentially low-cost solutions to an array of problems in military and civilian applications for tracking and monitoring purpose [1][2][3].

Due to the dense deployment of sensor nodes in the target region, the data sensed by neighboring sensors is often redundant and highly correlated. This large amount of data transmitted is usually enormous for the base station to process [4]. On the other

A. Abd Manaf et al. (Eds.): ICIEIS 2011, Part I, CCIS 251, pp. 400–408, 2011.
© Springer-Verlag Berlin Heidelberg 2011

hand, since the sensor nodes are resource starved, it is also inefficient for all the sensors to transmit the data directly to the base station [5].Thus one of the guiding factors in designing the sensor network protocols is to reduce the overall number of packets communicated to the base station [6].

One of the panaceas to reduce the communication costs is to use the data aggregation based *in-network* processing. This essentially means that while the data are being forwarded to the base station (BS), the intermediate nodes employ some form of *on-the-fly pre-processing* on the incoming packets, thus reducing the number of packets to be communicated to the base station. Instead of sending each sensor node's data directly to the base station, an aggregator node collects the data from its neighboring nodes and applies aggregation function and sends the aggregated data to the base station over a multihop path [3]. Such multihop communication requires that the intermediate sensor nodes *inspect* the actual data values, without merely relying on the packet header, to further decide the course of communication of the packet. However, when coupled with the security mechanisms like encryption and authentication, this means that the overall overhead associated is very high due to multiple rounds of the security related operations. In addition, for the security critical applications that require end-to-end security, the link layer encryption-decryption operations pose a security threat.

In the conventional networks, as a panacea to multiple rounds of link layer encryption/decryption, an approach that combines the End-To-End (ETE) security together with in-network aggregation has been employed. Such approach does not require the data to be decrypted at intermediate aggregator nodes once encrypted allowing aggregation operations to be performed on the *encrypted data*. Such encryption is called *Homomorphic Encryption OR Concealed Data Aggregation (CDA)* [3] [6] [7].

In this paper, we attempt the feasibility of applying the provably homomorphic encryption scheme based on symmetric key to the WSNs, as asymmetric schemes could not be as fast as symmetric ones [8]. We specifically explore whether it is possible to do so within the permissible resource constraints and without relaxing any security. In this paper we have empirically evaluated overhead associated with the homomorphic encryption scheme proposed in [9] .Using performance metrics, we demonstrate that it is feasible to employ the proposed approach for WSNs.

The rest of the paper is organized as follows: In section 2, we discuss the relevant background for secure data aggregation in WSNs. In section 3, we describe the design of our approach with implementation methodology. In section 4, we show the experimental setup used to empirically evaluate the algorithms and analyze those results. We conclude our work with the probable further explorations in section 5.

2   Theoretical Background and the Related Work

2.1   Data Aggregation

As mentioned earlier, the main objective of data aggregation is to reduce the overall overhead due to redundant communication [10]. Various data aggregation protocols, based on either flat, tree OR cluster based network architecture have been proposed [3] [4] [10]. Typically, the data aggregation operations are carried out by a node designated as the data aggregator node. Hence, the security of this node is critical because compromise of a single node can jeopardize the overall semantics of the entire protocol.

2.2   Secure Data Aggregation

For security critical applications data are transmitted in encrypted form. Typical in-network data aggregation operation requires plain data to perform aggregation-achieving *hop-by-hop* security (secure data aggregation using plain sensor data [3]). In order to achieve *end-to-end* security it is necessary that aggregation computation must be performed on encrypted data i.e. without decrypting it on intermediate aggregator nodes (secure data aggregation using encrypted data [3]). Such data aggregation is known as Concealed Data Aggregation (CDA). However, the downside of CDA is that it is applicable with a limited set of aggregation functions, such as *sum* and *average* [3]. In the next section, we discuss several such issues associated with the CDA.

2.3   Privacy Homomorphism (PH)

The basis for CDA is cryptographic methods that provide the privacy homomorphism (PH) property, proposed first in 1978 that relies on an encryption transformation such that direct computation on encrypted data can be performed [7] [11]. Formally, an encryption algorithm E ( ) is homomorphic, if for given $E(x)$ and $E(y)$, one can obtain $E(x \circ y)$ without decrypting x, y for some operation $\circ$ where $E(x)$ and $E(y)$ denotes encrypted values of x and y respectively [7].

2.4   Related Work

An extensive overview of secure data aggregation schemes together with security properties achieved is given in [3],[12]. The authors in [8] summarize the homomorphic encryption schemes based on asymmetric key as well as symmetric key cryptography. Privacy homomorphism schemes are basically divided into two types: a) partially homomorphic [6][13] and b) fully homomorphic[14]. Fully homormophic encryption schemes is proposed very recently by [14] that supports evaluations of arbitrary depth circuits.

   However, many existing public key cryptography based privacy homomorphic functions are not feasible for resource limited sensor nodes [3] [8]. Therefore, we restrict ourselves here to the experimentations with the secure data aggregation scheme using symmetric key cryptography only.

   The idea of additive and multiplicative homomorphic encryption in the range of integer, was originally proposed by Sander and Tschudin, where they proposed homomorphic encryption for software protection, protecting mobile agents and mobile code against malicious hosts [15] [16] [17]. Based on that, the authors in [9] proposed homomorphic encryption in the range of integer and real as well.

We here attempt at exploring whether the approach proposed in [9] i.e. the privacy homomorphism for integer and real can be applied feasibly in the resource constrained Wireless Sensor Networks or not. Our experimental evaluations amicable demonstrate that it is possible to do so.

3   Design and Implementation Methodology

3.1   Proposed Approach

As mentioned earlier we explored the homomorphic encryption methods given in [9] for checking their principle suitability to WSNs. We have evaluated aggregation operations, addition and multiplication in the range of integer and addition in the range of real for the given homomorphic encryption methods.

To check practicability to WSNs we are comparing the proposed approach with the additively homomorphic encryption scheme proposed by Castelluccia, Mykletun, Tsudik in [6].

3.2   Methodology of Implementation

We have implemented homomorphic encryption methods for Mica2 motes in TinyOS [18]. Incorporating our homomorphic encryption methods in TinyOS requires changes in certain modules and interfaces in TinySec [5], a generic security package available with TinyOS. Even though we are advocating for end-to-end security, we are testing our proposed scheme for two motes making changes in TinySec.

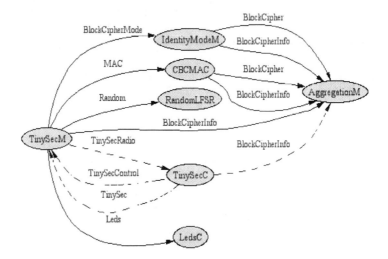

Fig. 1. Part of component graph of our application for HES

3.2.1 Component Graph

Every application in TinyOS is the collection of modules, configurations and interfaces. A typical component graph of an application shows the interconnection between these components. Figure 1 shows part of a component graph of our application. The module AggregationM provides encryption and decryption operation of our homomorphic encryption cipher. The operations related to aggregation of encrypted data are being implemented by TinySec interface provided by module TinySecM.

4   Performance Results and Analysis

We evaluate our schemes based on different metrics viz. memory usage, energy consumption and CPU cycles. In this subsection, we show our experimental results for these schemes based on above-mentioned metrics. Based on these results, we compare the proposed scheme with the existing one to check feasibility of our scheme in WSNs. The notations used for showing empirical results for different approaches are as follows: The additively homomorphic encryption scheme proposed by Castelluccia, Mykletun, Tsudik in [6] as CMT, additively and multiplicatively homomorphic encryption scheme in the range of integer [9] as SHES and MHES, respectively and additively homomorphic encryption scheme in the range of real [9] as RHES. Even though we are presenting results for homomorphic encryption scheme in the range of real, we are comparing CMT, SHES and MHES only because all these approaches follow homomorphic encryption in the range of integer.

4.1   Storage Requirements

We have simulated our implementation for mica2 platform in TOSSIM [19]. The compilation results of our implementation shows memory (RAM and ROM) usage as given in table 1. Figure 2 shows percentage increase in ROM consumption, which is 3.54 for SHES and 3.79 for MHES and percentage decrease in RAM consumption, which is 1.04 for SHES and 1.27 for MHES over CMT. This overhead in ROM consumption is mainly due to random function involved in homomorphic encryption method. RHES involves more overhead for handling real data types.

Table 1. ROM and RAM consumption

Method	ROM usage (bytes)	% increase over CMT	RAM usage (bytes)	% decrease over CMT
CMT	14786	-	868	-
SHES	15310	3.54%	859	1.04%
MHES	15346	3.79%	857	1.27%
RHES	16042	-	859	-

4.2   CPU Cycle Usage

We use Avrora [20] for finding out the CPU cycle requirement of our implementation. Figure 3, shows CPU cycles required for different operations involved in HES i.e. encryption, decryption and aggregation. From figure 4, we can see that SHES requires 9.44% and MHES requires 9.08% decrease in CPU cycle consumption compared to CMT. RHES requires 51159 CPU cycles to perform the same operations.

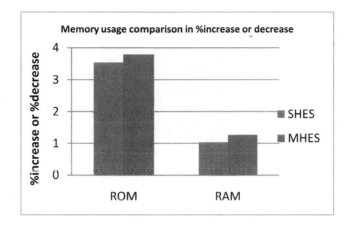

Fig. 2. Memory usage comparison in % increase for ROM and % decrease for RAM

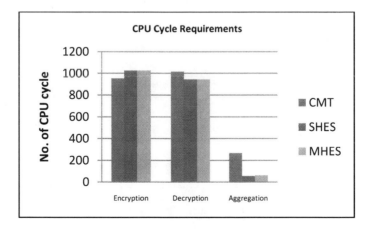

Fig. 3. CPU cycle requirements for different operations

4.3   Energy Requirements

We use Avrora [20] for finding out the energy requirements. We do not require extra overhead in packet size. Hence, no overhead incurred for transmitting extra information. Energy overhead incurred is for execution of encryption, decryption and aggregation related operations. As we have done simulation for two motes we are considering energy consumption at both motes.

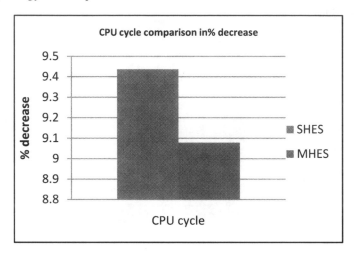

Fig. 4. CPU cycle comparison in % decrease

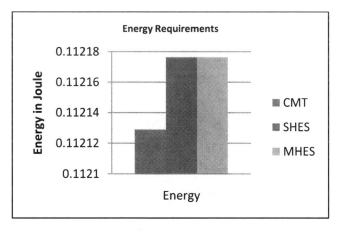

Fig. 5. Energy Requirement

Figure 5 shows energy requirements for all approaches. Figure 6 shows energy requirement in % increase for SHES and MHES over CMT. It is clear from our results that SHES incurs just 0.042203% while MHES incurs just 0.042171 % overhead in energy, which is very less than 1%.

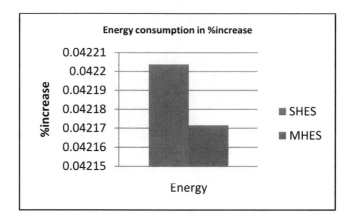

Fig. 6. % increase in energy consumption

From our experimental results, we can clearly say that entailing some overhead in ROM consumption and energy required, our proposed approach provides significant benefit in CPU cycle usage. Therefore, it is feasible to apply such homomorphic encryption scheme to WSNs.

5   Conclusion and Future Work

In this paper, we explored the feasibility of applying a homomorphic encryption scheme, for the operations addition and multiplication in the range of integer and for addition in the range of real, based on symmetric key cryptography in WSNs. We have measured the performance characteristics of the schemes based on different metrics viz. memory usage, CPU cycles and energy consumption. The satisfactory results clearly demonstrate that it is feasible to employ such scheme for WSNs. This work can further be extended to endow with specific network topology e.g. flat or hierarchical to have real composition for WSNs.

References

1. Akyildiz, I.F., Su, W., Sankarasubramaniam, Y., Cayirci, E.: A survey on sensor networks. IEEE Communications Magazine 40(8), 102–114 (2002)
2. Yick, J., Mukherjee, B., Ghosal, D.: Wireless sensor network survey. Computer Networks 52(12), 2229–2230 (2008)
3. Ozdemir, S., Xiao, Y.: Secure data aggregation in wireless sensor networks: A comprehensive overview. Computer Networks 53(12), 2022–2037 (2009)
4. Rajagopalan, R., Varshney, P.K.: Data aggregation techniques in sensor networks: a survey. IEEE Communications Surveys & Tutorials 8(4), 48–63 (2006)
5. Karlof, C., Sastry, N., Wagner, D.: Tinysec: A link layer security architecture for wireless sensor networks. In: Proc. Second ACM Conference on Embedded Networked Sensor Systems, pp. 162–175 (November 2004)

6. Castelluccia, C., Mykletun, E., Tsudik, G.: Efficient aggregation of encrypted data in wireless sensor networks. In: Proc. Second Annual International Conference on Mobile and Ubiquitous Systems: Networking and Services, pp. 109–117 (2005)

7. Peter, S., Piotrowski, K., Langendoerfer, P.: On concealed data aggregation for wireless sensor networks. In: Proc. Fourth IEEE Consumer Communications and Networking Conference, pp. 192–196 (2007)

8. Fontaine, C., Galand, F.: A survey of Homomorphic encryption for Nonspecialists. EURASIP Journal on Information Security, articleno-15, 15:1–15:15 (2007)

9. Guangli, X., Xinmeng, C., Ping, Z., Jie, M.: A method of Homomorphic encryption. Wuhan University Journal of Natural Sciences 11(1), 181–184 (2006)

10. Fasolo, E., Rossi, M., Widmer, J., Zorzi, M.: In-network aggregation techniques for wireless sensor networks: a survey. IEEE Wireless Communications 14(2), 70–87 (2007)

11. Rivest, R.L., Adleman, L., Dertouzos, M.L.: On data banks and privacy homomorphisms. In: Foundations of Secure Computation, pp. 169–177. Academic Press (1978)

12. Alzaid, H., Foo, E., Nieto, J.G.: Secure data aggregation in wireless sensor network: a survey. In: Proc. of the Sixth Australasian Conference on Information Security (AISC 2008), vol. 81, pp. 93–105 (2008)

13. Domingo-Ferrer, J.: A Provably Secure Additive and Multiplicative Privacy Homomorphism. In: Information Security Conference, pp. 471–483 (2002)

14. Gentry, C.: Computing arbitrary functions of encrypted data. Commun. ACM 53(3), 97–105 (2010)

15. Sander, T., Tschudin, C.: On Software Protection via Function Hiding. In: Aucsmith, D. (ed.) IH 1998. LNCS, vol. 1525, pp. 111–123. Springer, Heidelberg (1998)

16. Sander, T., Tschudin, C.F.: Protecting mobile agents against malicious hosts. In: Vigna, G. (ed.) Mobile Agents and Security. LNCS, vol. 1419, pp. 44–60. Springer, Heidelberg (1998)

17. Sander, T., Tschudin, C.: Towards mobile cryptography. In: Proc. of the IEEE Symposium on Security and Privacy, pp. 215–224. IEEE computer society press (1998)

18. Hill, J., Szewczyk, R., Woo, A., Hollar, S., Culler, D., Pister, K.: System Architecture Directions for Networked Sensors. SIGPLAN Not. 35(11), 93–104 (2000)

19. Levis, P., Lee, N.: TOSSIM: A Simulator for TinyOS Networks (September 17, 2003), http://today.cs.berkeley.edu/tos/tinyos-1.x/doc/nido.pdf

20. Titzer, B.L., Lee, D., Palsberg, J.: Avrora: Scalable sensor network simulation with precise timing. In: Proc. 4th International Symposium on Information Processing In Sensor Networks (IPSN), articleno-67 (2005)

An Observation of Cryptographic Properties of 256 One-Dimensional Cellular Automata Rules

Norziana Jamil[1,2], Ramlan Mahmood[2], Muhammad Reza Z'aba[3],
Zuriati Ahmad Zukarnaen[2], and Nur Izura Udzir[2]

[1] College of Information Technology, Universiti Tenaga Nasional, KM7, Jalan IKRAM-
UNITEN,
43000 Kajang, Selangor, Malaysia
[2] Faculty of Computer Science and Information Technology, Universiti Putra Malaysia,
43600 Serdang, Selangor, Malaysia
[3] MIMOS Berhad, Technology Park Malaysia, Bukit Jalil,
57000 Kuala Lumpur, Malaysia
Norziana@uniten.edu.my,
{ramlan,zuriati,izura}@fsktm.upm.edu.my,
muhdreza@gmail.com

Abstract. The robustness of a cryptographic system substantially depends on its underlying elements. Boolean functions are the most frequently used elements in various cryptographic systems, be it block ciphers, stream ciphers and hash functions. However, constructing Boolean functions satisfying all fundamental cryptographic properties are not trivial. We study the cryptographic properties of Boolean functions of biological system namely one-dimensional Cellular Automata (CA) and show that some of its Boolean functions satisfy all mentioned properties on levels very close to optimal and therefore can be recommended as cryptographically strong Boolean function.

Keywords: Boolean functions, cryptographic properties, propagation criteria, correlation immunity, balanced functions, non-linearity, high algebraic degree.

1   Introduction

In cryptography, there are fundamental principles introduced by Shannon [4]: confusion and diffusion. The former aims at concealing any algebraic structure in the cryptographic system while the latter aims at propagating the influence of a single (minor) modification of the input data over the output data. Both principles can be quantified by some properties of the Boolean functions describing the underlying system. Boolean functions are very important underlying elements for numerous cryptographic systems namely block ciphers, stream ciphers and hash functions. Boolean functions for cryptographic purposes have to satisfy a primary cryptographic criterion, namely balance: a balanced Boolean function is a function that cannot be approximated by a constant function [18]. A part from that, other few fundamental cryptographic properties that a Boolean function has to satisfy are high algebraic

A. Abd Manaf et al. (Eds.): ICIEIS 2011, Part I, CCIS 251, pp. 409–420, 2011.

degree, avalanche [1], nonlinearity [10] and correlation immunity [15] with an objective that linear cryptanalysis [12] and differential cryptanalysis [7] cannot succeed faster than brute force attack.

In most of the cases in cryptography, the avalanche criterion was called the propagation criterion in [3]. Historically, Feistel was the first one who coined the term 'avalanche' and noted its importance in the design of a block cipher [8]. Coppersmith [5], a member of the team who designed the Data Encryption Standard (DES), stated that avalanche properties were employed in selecting the S-boxes used in the cipher to withstand various attacks including differential [7] and linear attack [10]. The desired avalanche effect in cryptography is called Strict Avalanche Criterion (SAC) [1]. SAC is the same as the avalanche criterion of degree one. We say that a cryptographic Boolean function satisfies the SAC if changing a single bit in input message resulting in every output bit to change with a probability of half. Satisfying this criterion is an indication of the randomness of the output bits and the resistance of the cryptographic systems over certain statistical attacks such as key clustering attacks [16]. High degree of avalanche increases the effect of message diffusion, whereas a high nonlinearity generally has an impact on the resistance over differential attacks. Siegenthaler [15] who introduced correlation immunity shows that this property is important to protect the cryptographic systems against linear and correlation attacks. Balanced Boolean functions that are correlation immune are called resilient [12]. A resilient Boolean function is a strong function for cryptographic purposes, however, constructing resilient Boolean functions having all security properties remains an open problem. It was shown in literatures, for eg. [17], that there are functions which achieve perfect diffusion and perfect confusion but they are not balanced.

We are interested to study the cryptographic properties of Cellular Automata (CA), a relatively new development in modern science. CA consists of simple automaton propagations based on its rules over finite time. CA rules are represented in Boolean functions, and the brief description of CA rules is discussed in the following section. Moreover, the motivation is increased with the claim made by Wolfram [13], the founder of 1-dimensional CA, who showed that a few CA rules such as rule 30, can be used as a basis for cryptographic purposes. Since then, rule 30 for example, has gained many attractions (see for e.g: [2],[6]) for its chaotic behavior, i.e. it does not repeat with any short period or show any obvious structure, and useful in pseudorandom number generator. Therefore we are interested to investigate all the non linear CA rules since we believe that the output that we managed to get from our experiments will benefit those who are working on cryptographic primitives. The advantage of CA itself is that it can be easily implemented in simple parallel hardware and can guarantee cryptographically good algorithm at a very nice cost [2].

In this paper, balanced CA Boolean functions are first identified, and then the cryptographic properties of the identified balanced functions are computed. We also show that some of the CA functions satisfy all mentioned properties on levels very close to optimal by comparing them with functions used in cryptographic hash functions such as MD-5, and therefore can be recommended as cryptographically strong Boolean function.

This paper is organized as follows: in Section 2, we discuss some preliminaries about CA followed by the relevant background about Boolean functions cryptographic properties in Section 3. Section 4 describes the observations on the cryptographic properties of CA Boolean functions. Some comparisons with Boolean functions used in MD5, SHA-1 and RIPEMD hash functions are carried out in Section 5 and the concluding remarks are made in Section 6.

2   Background

2.1   CA Preliminaries

The simplest CA is a 1-dimensional linearly connected array of 3 cells, usually referred to as a 3-neighborhood CA cells. Each of the cells in the array takes a discrete state s of 0 or 1. A transition function f is used to determine the next state configuration c whereby the value of the ith cell state s_i is updated in parallel using this function in discrete time step t. The next state of a cell at $t+1$ is influenced by its own state and the states of its left and right neighbors at time t. The state configuration c that is specified by a transition function f can be seen as

$$s_i(t+1) = f\{s_{i-1}(t), s_i(t), s_{i+1}(t)\}$$

where $s_{i-1}(t)$ is the state of the left neighbor, $s_i(t)$ as the state for center self (or ith cell) and $s_{i+1}(t)$ as a state for the right neighbor of the ith cell at time t. For a 2-state of 3-neighborhood CA, there are $2^3=8$ possible state configurations c. If the configuration of the ith cell is expressed in the form of a truth table, then the decimal equivalent of its sequence output is referred to as 'rule' R_i. So for a 2-state 1-dimensional 3-neighborhood CA there is a total of $2^8=256$ CA local rules [20]. In our paper, we investigate all the 256 CA local rules.

2.2   Boolean Function

We consider functions from V_n to GF(2) where V_n is the vector space of n tuples of elements from GF(2). A Boolean function is described as a function f on V_n that maps a set of Boolean domain to its corresponding Boolean range. It takes the form of $f:\{0,1\}n \rightarrow \{0,1\}$ where n is a non-negative integer called the arity of the function. If $n=0$, then the Boolean function f will be a constant element for the Boolean range. For other cases, f describes a progression to get into a particular Boolean output by considering some Boolean inputs going through some set and logical calculations. The set operation includes intersection, union and complement while logical operation includes AND, OR and NOT. In other words, we can also say a Boolean function f is a mapping from n binary inputs to one binary output such that, $f(x) : Z^n \rightarrow Z_2$, where $x = x_1, x_2, x_3, \ldots, x_n$ and $f(x) \in B_n$ where B_n represents the set of all 2^{2^n} Boolean functions of n variables.

Definition 1: A Boolean function is said to be linear if the function satisfies
$f(x+y) = f(x) + f(y)$.

Definition 2: A Boolean function is said to be non linear if the function combines more than one set and logic operation.

In a case where $n=2$: this implies $f:\{0,1\}^2 \to \{0,1\}$. This is equivalent to $f: \{00, 01, 10, 11\} \to \{0,1\}$. Thus there are $2^2=4$ linear Boolean functions out of $2^4=16$ Boolean functions with 2 variables. The rest are non-linear ones.

In cryptography, Boolean functions are the underlying elements of cryptographic systems, be it encryption cipher or hash functions. For this purpose, the Boolean functions must have nonlinearity, i.e. at the sufficiently high distance from any affine function. An affine function is just a linear function plus a translation that follows if $R^m \to R^n$ is affine, then there is an $m \times n$ matrix M and a vector b in R^n such that

$$A(x) = M(x) + b$$

This implies $f(x) = m(x) + b$.

The distance between Boolean functions and a set of affine functions is linearly related to the nonlinearity of Boolean functions. To construct a highly non-linear Boolean function is a challenge in cryptography, but in this study we show that it is interesting to start 'constructing' them somewhere.

3   Cryptographic Properties of Boolean Functions

As discussed in the previous section, the robustness of a cryptographic primitive substantially depends on its underlying elements. Boolean functions are the most frequently used elements in a cryptographic primitive and it is very important to determine the cryptographically strong properties which Boolean functions should have. Among the cryptographic properties that Boolean functions must adhere to are balance, propagation criteria, correlation immunity, nonlinearity and high algebraic degree. In this paper, we measure all mentioned properties on the CA Boolean functions. Some important notions are used throughout this section and they are defined accordingly as follows:

Definition 3: The Hamming weight of a Boolean function is the number of 1s in a function binary truth table.
$$Hw(f) = \Sigma_x f(x)$$
Definition 4: The Hamming distance between two functions f_1, $f_2 \in B_n$ is the Hamming weight of the XOR sum of the two functions by referring to the binary truth table of the two functions.
$$Hd(f_1 f_2) = Hw (f_1 \otimes f_2)$$

Definition 5: The correlation between two functions f_1 and f_2 is the approximation of the two functions from each other. It can be measured by
$$Corr (f_1 f_2) = 1 - \frac{Hd (f_1 f_2)}{2^n - 1}$$

Definition 6: A function $f(x)$ is an affine function if it is a linear function or the complement of the linear function.

For example, the following ordering of affine Boolean functions of the 3-variables Boolean function as in Table 1 is obtained:

Table 1. The truth table of 3-variables affine functions

Boolean function	000	001	010	011	100	101	110	111
1	1	1	1	1	1	1	1	1
x0	0	1	0	1	0	1	0	1
x1	0	0	1	1	0	0	1	1
x1+x0	0	1	1	0	0	1	1	0
x2	0	0	0	0	1	1	1	1
x2+ x0	0	1	0	1	1	0	1	0
x2+ x1	0	0	1	1	1	1	0	0
x2+ x1+x0	0	1	1	0	1	0	0	1

The complement of this set of affine Boolean functions is just a translation of 1 to 0, and vice versa. Therefore the complement will produce the same table as that of Table 1 with the conversion of 1 to 0, 0 to 1.

3.1   Propagation Criterion

Feistel [8] was the first one who proposed a propagation criterion needed for all cryptographic functions called avalanche effect. It says that for a function f to produce the avalanche effect is when an average of one half of the output bits is changed whenever a single input bit is flipped. However still in the same year 1979, Kam and Davida [9] introduced the completeness condition which says that each of the output bits depends on all the input bits. It says that a function has a good completeness effect when for each output bit i and each input bit j there exist two inputs which differ only in bit j but whose outputs differ in bit i. Webster and Tavares [1] introduced a notion of Strict Avalanche Criterion (SAC) by combining both avalanche effect and completeness. It says that a function f is said to satisfy the SAC when each of the output bits are changed with a probability of half whenever a single input bits is flipped. That means the desired probability value for SAC test is ½. In this paper, we benchmark the avalanche characteristics of CA Boolean functions against this value.

3.2   Balance

An n-variable Boolean function f is said to be balanced if the Hamming weight, Hw of a function's binary truth table is equal to 2^{n-1}. This is defined as the following:

Definition 9: A function $f(x)$ is said to be balanced when half of the values in the binary truth table is 1s, i.e: $Hw(f) = 2^{n-1}$.

3.3   Nonlinearity

The nonlinearity of a Boolean function f is defined as the Hamming distance Hd of f from the set of n-variable affine functions. A function $f(x)$ is said to be of great nonlinearity if the distance to any affine function l is the minimum possible, $N_f = \min\{Hd(f, l)\}$. The nonlinearity of an affine function is zero, and the nonlinearity of balanced Boolean functions must be below the upper bound,

$$N_f \leq \begin{cases} 2^{n-1} - 2^{1/2\ n-1} - 2 & \text{for even variable} \\ \lfloor 2^{n-1} - 2^{1/2n-1} \rfloor & \text{for odd variable} \end{cases}$$

3.4   High Algebraic Degree

Cryptographic Boolean functions are used in a cryptosystem such as block ciphers and hash functions to achieve diffusion. The cryptosystem is a weak system if the functions have low algebraic degree. To measure the degree of a function, we can represent it first in its Algebraic Normal Form (ANF). The ANF of a Boolean function is the XOR sum of some selected input bits. The algebraic degree of a Boolean function corresponds to the highest degree of a term in the function's ANF. The highest degree that a Boolean function can achieve is n-1, where n is the function's number of variable.

3.5   Correlation Immunity

A correlation immune function can be stated as follows:

Let f is called *kth-order correlation immune function* if $\langle \xi, \varsigma \rangle = 0$ for every ς where ς is the sequence of a linear function $\varphi(x) = \langle \sigma, x \rangle$ on V_n constrained by $1 \leq Hw\ (\sigma) \leq k$. $\langle \xi, \varsigma \rangle = 0$, if and only if $f(x) \oplus \varphi(x)$ is balanced for each linear function $\varphi(x) = \langle \sigma, x \rangle$ on V_n where $1 \leq Hw\ (\sigma) \leq k$.

4   Observations on Cryptographic Properties of CA Functions

There are five cryptographic properties that are measured for CA rules, namely balance, algebraic degree, nonlinearity, propagation degree and correlation immunity. We first measure the balance properties for all the non-linear CA rules and we identified that only the following rules are balanced. There are 52 balanced rules which are:

Rules 23, 27, 29, 30, 39, 43, 45, 46, 53, 54, 57, 58, 71, 75, 77, 78, 83, 86, 92, 99,105, 106, 108, 113, 114, 116, 120, 139, 141, 142, 147, 149, 150, 154, 156, 163, 172, 178, 180, 184, 197, 198, 201, 202, 209, 210, 212, 216, 225, 226, 228 and 232.

Next, we only focus on these rules since balance is the basic fundamental property for cryptographic Boolean functions. For these rules, we measure its nonlinearity and we found that only two rules that have low nonlinearity, '0'. The two rules are rules 105 and 150. These rules also give low algebraic degree, which is '1'. The other rules give highest algebraic degree, which is '2' for 3-variables Boolean function.

As discussed earlier, we want to observe which Boolean functions (rules) with propagation criterion of degree 1, $PC(1)$. Boolean functions with PC of order m means that m input bits are necessary to complement to cause every output bit to change with a probability of half. There are a few results generated from the observation of propagation degree. Rules 23, 43, 77, 78, 113, 142, 178, 212 and 232 have propagation criterion of degree 2. Cryptographically weak rules are rules 30, 45, 54, 57, 75, 86, 99, 105, 106, 108, 120, 147, 149, 150, 154, 156, 180, 198, 201, 210 and 225. Rules which exhibit propagation criterion of degree 1 are rules 27, 29, 39, 46, 53, 58, 71, 83, 92, 114, 116, 139, 141, 163, 172, 184, 197, 202, 209, 216, 226 and 228. For 3-variables Boolean functions, the desired order of correlation immunity is n-1. However none of the CA rules are correlation immune, or in other words all the CA rules have correlation immunity of order 0. The summary of the cryptographic properties of CA rules are described in App. A.

5   Comparison with Boolean Functions of MD-5, SHA-1 and RIPEMD Hash functions

We want to compare the CA rules that achieve good degree of cryptographic properties with MD-5 and SHA-1 Boolean functions. The summary of cryptographic properties of MD-5, SHA-1and RIPEMD hash functions is described below.

Table 2. Cryptographic properties of MD-5, SHA-1 and RIPEMD hash functions Boolean functions

Boolean Functions	Balance	Nonlinearity	Algebraic degree	Propagation criterion of order m	Correlation immunity of order k
F= (x∧y)∨(~x∧z)		2	2	1	0
G= (x∧z)∨(y∧~z)		2	2	1	0
H= x⊗y⊗z		0	0	0	0
I= y⊗(x∨~z)		0	0	0	0
J=(x∧y)∨(x∧z)∨(y∧z)		2	2	2	0
K=x⊗(y∨~z)		2	2	0	0

The functions F is used in MD-5, SHA-1and RIPEMD, G is used in MD-5 and RIPEMD, H is used in MD-5, SHA-1 and RIPEMD, I is used in MD-5, J is used in SHA-1 and K is used in RIPEMD. It is clearly seen that one of the functions used, function H in these three hash functions is a linear function. Only two functions give propagation criterion of order 1 and all functions are not correlation immune.

The analysis shows that some of the CA rules give better cryptographic properties than that used in MD-5, SHA-1 and RIPEMD, described in the following table.

Table 3. Cryptographically good CA functions

Rule	Balance	Nonlinearity	Algebraic degree	Propagation criterion of order m	Correlation immunity of order k
27	✓	2	2	1	0
30	✓	2	2	1	0
40	✓	2	2	1	0
47	✓	2	2	1	0
54	✓	2	2	1	0
59	✓	2	2	1	0
72	✓	2	2	1	0
84	✓	2	2	1	0
93	✓	2	2	1	0
115	✓	2	2	1	0
117	✓	2	2	1	0
140	✓	2	2	1	0
142	✓	2	2	1	0
164	✓	2	2	1	0
173	✓	2	2	1	0
178	✓	2	2	1	0
185	✓	2	2	1	0
198	✓	2	2	1	0
203	✓	2	2	1	0
210	✓	2	2	1	0
217	✓	2	2	1	0
227	✓	2	2	1	0
229	✓	2	2	1	0

We can see that it is a potential to use CA rules in a cryptosystem because some of the CA rules exhibit good cryptographic properties that certainly will increase the robustness of a cryptosystem. Since it is very difficult to have a resilient Boolean function, therefore the correlation property of these CA rules will be studied further. We would like to investigate the correlation immunity of non-uniform CA rules or in other words, when two or more CA rules are used together as one operation.

6   Conclusion

In this paper, we have studied the 3-variable one dimensional non-linear CA rules represented by their Boolean functions against some cryptographically important properties of Boolean functions namely balance, nonlinearity, algebraic degree, propagation criterion of order m and correlation immunity. There are 23 balanced CA rules that achieve high nonlinearity, high algebraic degree and propagation criterion of order 1. From the observation, we also see that they are not correlation immune. However, this is also the case for Boolean functions used in MD-5, SHA-1 and RIPEMD hash functions. Therefore we conclude that the cryptographic properties of these 23 balanced CA rules achieve on levels very close to optimal and therefore can be recommended as cryptographically strong Boolean functions.

Acknowledgments. This work in under purview of a project funded by Malaysia Ministry of Higher Education under FRGS phase II 2010/11.

References

1. Webster, A.F., Tavares, S.: On the Design of S-boxes. In: Williams, H.C. (ed.) CRYPTO 1985. LNCS, vol. 218, pp. 523–534. Springer, Heidelberg (1986)
2. Popovici, A., Popovici, D.: A generalization of the cellular automata rule-30 cryptoscheme. In: Symbolic and Numeric Algorithms for Scientific Computing, pp. 25-29 (September 2005)
3. Preneel, B., Van Leekwijck, W., Van Linden, L., Govaerts, R., Vandewalle, J.: Propagation Characteristics of Boolean Functions. In: Damgård, I.B. (ed.) EUROCRYPT 1990. LNCS, vol. 473, pp. 161–173. Springer, Heidelberg (1991)
4. Shannon, C.E.: Communication theory of secrecy systems. Bell System Technical Journal 28, 656–715 (1949)
5. Coppersmith, D., Knudsen, L.R., Mitchell, C.J.: Key recovery and forgery attacks on the macDES MAC algorithm. In: Bellare, M. (ed.) CRYPTO 2000. LNCS, vol. 1880, pp. 184–196. Springer, Heidelberg (2000)
6. Gage, D., Laub, E., McGarry, B.: Cellular automata: is rule 30 random? (2005) (preprint)
7. Biham, E., Shamir, A.: Differential Cryptanalysis of DES-Like Cryptosystems. In: Menezes, A., Vanstone, S.A. (eds.) CRYPTO 1990. LNCS, vol. 537, pp. 2–21. Springer, Heidelberg (1991)
8. Feistel, H.: Cryptography and computer privacy. Scientific American 228(5), 747–753 (1979)
9. Kam, J.B., Davida, G.I.: Structured Design of Substitution-Permutation Encryption Networks. IEEE Transactions on Computers C-28(10), 747–753 (1979)
10. Matsui, M.: Linear Cryptanalysis Method for DES Cipher. In: Helleseth, T. (ed.) EUROCRYPT 1993. LNCS, vol. 765, pp. 386–397. Springer, Heidelberg (1994)
11. Rothaus, O.S.: On bent functions. Journal of Combinatorial Theory (A) 20, 300–305 (1976)
12. Camion, P., Carlet, C., Charpin, P., Sendrier, N.: On Correlation-Immune Functions. In: Feigenbaum, J. (ed.) CRYPTO 1991. LNCS, vol. 576, pp. 86–100. Springer, Heidelberg (1992)

13. Wolfram, S.: A new kind of science. Stephen Wolfram LLC, Illinois (2002)
14. Wolfram, S.: Universality and complexity in cellular automata. Physica D 10, 1–35 (1984)
15. Siegenthaler, T.: Correlation-immunity of non-linear combining functions for cryptographic applications. IEEE Trans. On Information Theory IT-30(5), 776–780 (1984)
16. Diffie, W., Hellman, M.E.: Privacy and authentication: An introduction to cryptography. Proceedings of IEEE 67(3), 397–427 (1979)
17. Meier, W., Staffelbach, O.: Fast correlation attack on certain stream ciphers. Journal of Cryptology, 159–176 (1989)
18. Millan, W.L., Clark, A., Dawson, E.: Boolean Function Design Using Hill Climbing Methods. In: Pieprzyk, J.P., Safavi-Naini, R., Seberry, J. (eds.) ACISP 1999. LNCS, vol. 1587, pp. 1–11. Springer, Heidelberg (1999)

Appendix A

Table 4. A summary of cryptographic properties of balanced CA rules

Rule	Boolean Functions	Nonlinearity	High algebraic degree	Propagation criterion or order m	Correlation immunity of order c
23	$p \otimes ((p \otimes (\sim q)) \vee (q \otimes r))$	2	2	2	0
27	$p \otimes ((p \otimes (\sim q)) \vee r)$	2	2	1	0
29	$p \otimes ((p \otimes (\sim r)) \vee q)$	2	2	1	0
30	$p \otimes (q \vee r)$	2	2	0	0
39	$((p \otimes (\sim q)) \vee r) \otimes q$	2	2	1	0
43	$p \otimes ((p \otimes r) | (p \otimes (\sim q)))$	2	2	2	0
45	$p \otimes (q \vee (\sim r))$	2	2	0	0
46	$(p \wedge q) \otimes (q \vee r)$	2	2	1	0
53	$(p \vee (q \otimes (\sim r))) \otimes q$	2	2	1	0
54	$(p \vee r) \otimes q$	2	2	0	0
57	$(p \vee (\sim r)) \otimes q$	2	2	0	0
58	$(p \vee (q \otimes r)) \otimes q$	2	2	1	0
71	$((p \otimes (\sim r)) \vee q) \otimes r$	2	2	1	0
75	$p \otimes ((\sim q) \vee r)$	2	2	0	0

Table 4. *(Continued)*

77	p⊗ ((p⊗q) ∨ (p⊗ (~r)))	2	2	2	0
78	p⊗((p⊗q)∨r)	2	2	2	0
83	(p∨ (q⊗ (~r))) ⊗r	2	2	1	0
86	(p∨q) ⊗r	2	2	0	0
92	(p∨(q⊗r)) ⊗r	2	2	1	0
99	((~p)∨r) ⊗q	2	2	0	0
105	p⊗ q ⊗ (~r)	0	1	0	0
106	(p∧q)⊗r	2	2	0	0
108	(p∧ r) ⊗q	2	2	0	0
113	p⊗ (~((p⊗q) ∨ (p⊗r)))	2	2	2	0
114	((p⊗q) ∨ r⊗q	2	2	1	0
116	(p∨q) ⊗ (q∧r)	2	2	1	0
120	P ⊗ (q∧r)	2	2	0	0
139	~((p∨q) ⊗ (q∧r))	2	2	1	0
141	p⊗ ((p ⊗q) ∨ (~r))	2	2	1	0
142	p⊗((p⊗q)∨(p⊗r))	2	2	2	0
147	(p∧r) ⊗ (~q)	2	2	0	0
149	(p∧q) ⊗ (~r)	2	2	0	0
150	p⊗q⊗r	0	1	0	0
154	p ⊗ (p∧q) ⊗r	2	2	0	0
156	P ⊗ (p∧r) ⊗q	2	2	0	0
163	((~p) ∨ (q⊗r)) ⊗q	2	2	1	0
172	(p∧(q ⊗ r)) ⊗q	2	2	1	0
178	((p⊗q)∨(p⊗r))⊗q	2	2	2	0
180	p ⊗ q ⊗ (q∧r)	2	2	0	0

Table 4. *(Continued)*

184	P ⊗ (p∧q) ⊗ (q∧r)	2	2	1	0
197	(~(p∨(q ⊗r))) ⊗q	2	2	1	0
198	(p∧r)⊗q⊗r	2	2	0	0
201	(~(p∨r)) ⊗q	2	2	0	0
202	(p∧(q⊗r))⊗r	2	2	1	0
209	~((p∧q) ⊗ (q∨r))	2	2	1	0
210	p⊗(q∧r)⊗r	2	2	0	0
212	((p ⊗ q)∨ (p ⊗ r)) ⊗r	2	2	2	0
216	p ⊗ ((p ⊗ q)∧r)	2	2	1	0
225	p ⊗ (~(q∨r))	2	2	0	0
226	(p∧q)⊗(q∧r)⊗r	2	2	1	0
228	((p ⊗ q) ∧ r) ⊗ q	2	2	1	0
232	(p∧q) ∨ ((p∨q) ∧r)	2	2	2	0

Digital Images Encryption in Frequency Domain Based on DCT and One Dimensional Cellular Automata

Ahmad Pahlavan Tafti and Safoura Janosepah

Islamic Azad University, Majlesi Branch, Isfahan, Iran
Ahmad.pahlavantafti@poug.org

Abstract. We are living in an age where security of digital information like digital images is becoming more important in many aspects and the tranmission of digital images is increasing over the internal and international computer networks. The protection of digital images from unauthorized access is the main purpose of this paper.

This paper introduced an approach to encrypt a digital image in frequency domain through DCT (Discrete Cosine Transform) and one dimenssional cellular automata. It is based on encryption of some quantified DCT coefficient in high frequencies. We applied our proposed model on one hundred numbers of JPEG grayscale images of size 800 × 800. The experimental results have indicated the robustness of our algorithm.

Keywords: Digital Images Encryption, Frequency Domain Encryption, Cellular Automata.

1 Introduction

Nowadays, digital information are playing a great role in human living and digital images are widely used in many aspects like medicine, transportation and protection. Having a good security model for digital images transmission is very important. The encryption algorithm which have developed for text data are not suitable for multimedia data [1].

Multimedia encryption has become the subject of very exhausive research as its potential to transfer of information more securely. There are two main ways for digital images encryption. These are spatial domain and frequncy domain [2]. Spatial domain encryption is very simple where the frequency encryption is more complicated and reliable [3]. There are two level for digital images encryption; high-level and low-level. In the high-level encryption the content of the digital image is completely disordered and the original image is invisible. In low-level encryption, the content of the digital image is underestandable and visible [4].

In this paper we focused on the frequncy domain and high-level encryption methods. Our proposed model is based on DCT (Discrete Cosine Transform) and one dimenssional cellular automata. We encrypt quantified DCT coefficients in higher frequencies because the details of a digital image are situated in the higher

A. Abd Manaf et al. (Eds.): ICIEIS 2011, Part I, CCIS 251, pp. 421–427, 2011.

frequencies, while the human eyes are most sensitive to lower frequencies than to higher frequencies.

The rest of this paper is arranged as follows. In section 2 we describe one dimenssional cellular automata and their rules. Section 3 introduces the concepts of DCT. Section 4 describes the system design and section 5 focuses on experimental results. Conclusions presents in section 6 .

2   One Dimenssional Cellular Automata Concepts

The history of cellular automata dates back to the 1940s with Stanislaw Marcin Ulam. This polish mathematician was interested in the evolution of graphic constructions generated by simple rules [5]. The base of his construction was a two-dimensional space divided into "cells", a sort of grid. Each of these cells could have two states: ON or OFF [6].

Cellular automata is a discrete dynamic model in space and time [6]. All of the cells arrange in the regular form and have a finite number of states. The states are updated with a local rule. Figure 1 shows a simple two state and one dimensional cellular automata with one line of cells. A specific cell can be either be on (value = 1= red) or off (value = 0= green). The closest cells to cell X are those to immediate left and right, moving along the lines connecting the nodes. The state of X at the time $t + 1$ will be determined by the states of the cells within its neighborhood at the time t. [7].

Fig. 1. One Dimensional Cellular Automata with One Neighborhood for Cell X

We can set a local rule for each cellular automata. For example, we can estimate the value of cell X in time $t+1$ with the following rule [8]:

$Cell[X]_{t+1} = Cell[X-1]_t (OR) Cell[X+1]_t$

Assume that the input sequence is 01110 and we want to use the above rule for our cellular automata, then the output sequence will be 11111. Table.1. shows the output of this cellular automata.

Table 1. An Example of Cellular Automata and Its Rule

Cell Number	0	1	2	3	4
Input Sequence (time t)	0	1	1	1	0
Cellular Automata Rule	$Cell[X]_{t+1} = Cell[X-1]_t (OR) Cell[X+1]_t$				
Output Sequence (time t+1)	1	1	1	1	1

We use one dimensional cellulra atomata with XOR local rule to create a secret key which we want to embed this key into the frequency domain of a digital image. the input sequence in our prosed model is the array list of the high frequency coefficients in a selected block of the original image.

3   DCT

A discrete cosine transform (DCT) expresses a sequence of finitely many data points in terms of a sum of cosine functions oscillating at different frequencies. DCTs are important to numerous applications in science and engineering, from lossy compression of audio (e.g. MP3) and images (e.g. JPEG), where small high-frequency components can be discarded, to spectral methods for the numerical solution of partial differential equations [9] .

The general equation for two dimensional (Image Size: N×M) DCT is defined as follow:

$$F(u,v) = \left(\frac{2}{N}\right)^{\frac{1}{2}} \left(\frac{2}{M}\right)^{\frac{1}{2}} \sum_{i=0}^{N-1} \sum_{j=0}^{M-1} \Lambda(i).\Lambda(j).cos\left[\frac{\pi.u}{2.N}(2i+1)\right] cos\left[\frac{\pi.v}{2.M}(2j+1)\right].f(i,j)$$

In JPEG image compression, each component array in the input image is first partitioned into 8×8 blocks of data. A signal transformation unit computes the DCT of each 8×8 block in order to map the signal reversibly into a representation that is better suited for compression. The object of the transformation is to reconfigure the information in the signal to capture the redundancies and to present the information in a "machine friendly" form that is convenient for disregarding the perceptually least relevant content. The DCT captures the spatial redundancy and packs the signal energy into a few DCT coefficients. The coefficient with zero frequency in both dimensions is called the direct current (DC) coefficient, and the remaining 63 coefficients are called alternating current (AC) coefficients [3]. The lossless compression as illustrated in Figure 2.

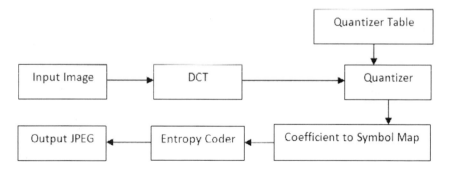

Fig. 2. DCT Diagram For JPEG Compression

As we mentioned in the introduction of this paper, spatial domain encryption is very simple where the frequency encryption is more complicated and reliable [3]. Therefore, we use the frequency encryption in our proposed model. We use DCT to encrypt the original image into the frequency domain and not to the spatial domain.

The DCT is similar to the discrete Fourier transform and transforms a digital image from the spatial domain to the frequency domain [9].

In our proposed system, the DCT is used to frequency transformation of a digital image and the cellular automata is used to create a secret key which we want to put them into the frequency domain of an image.

4   Proposed Algorithm

The main idea of our proposed algorithm is high-level encryption of the digital images in the frequency domain. We decompose the original image into the 8×8 blocks and transform these blocks from spatial domain in frequency domain by the DCT. Then we take the DC coefficient in the set of higher frequencies of the image blocks. These values are encrypted by one dimensional cellular automata with the XOR local rule.

We encrypt quantified DCT coefficients in higher frequencies because the details of a digital image are situated in the higher frequencies, while the human eyes are most sensitive to lower frequencies than to higher frequencies.

Figure 3, shows the block diagram of the proposed system for the digital images encryption.

Here, DCT is used to frequency transformation of a digital image and the cellular automata is used to create a secret key based on high frequencies DCT coefficients. The cell 1 of our proposed cellular automata consists the high frequencies coefficients of the first 8×8 block of the original image, cell 2 consists the high frequencies coefficients of the second 8×8 block of the original image and so on. Then we applied the XOR local rule on these values.

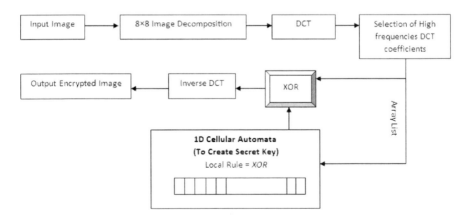

Fig. 3. Proposed System Model for Digital Image Encryption

The encryption algorithm in the frequency domain of the original grayscale image will be as follows:

Encryption Algorithm

Input: .JPEG grayscale image to apply encryption in the frequency domain.
Output: .JPEG grayscale image file.

Step 1: ImageHeight = Height of the Original Image.
Step 2: ImageWidth= Width of the Original Image.
Step 3: Blocck_Rows_Number = ImageHeight / 8
Step 4: Block_Columns_Number= ImageWidth / 8
Step 5: Do (For All Blocks)
a) Get BLOCK
b) DCT (BLOCK)
c) Select High Frequency Coefficients
d) Insert Coefficients into the Array List of Coefficients
e) Insert Coefficients into the one dimensional Cellular Automata
f) Encrypt All Cells of the Cellular Automata with XOR Local Rule
g) Encrypt All Array List and the Out Put of the Cellular Automata With XOR
Step 6: Performs the disordered algorithm on the result block
Step 7: Reconstruction the Image.

5   Experimental Results

In order to evaluate the performance and robustness of our proposed system, we have built a system using MATLAB R2009 and JAVA 3E and perform several tests on a sample dataset. Figure 4 is a grayscale .JPEG image which is related to a lung of a man (Size 800×800) and figure 5 is the encrypted imaged resulted by the proposed system. Figure 6 is a grayscale .JPEG image of a lovely child (Size 800×800). Figure 7 shows the encrypted of this image by this system.

Another experiment which considered is the diffusion of our secret key which is craeted by the one dimenssional cellular automata. Diffusion means that the output bits of the system should depend on the input bits in a very complex way. In a secret key with good diffusion, if one bit of the input text is changed, then the secret key should change completely [10].

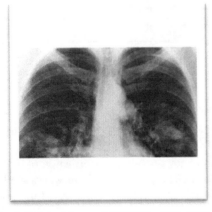   

Fig. 4. Original Image (.JPEG Size 800×800)   **Fig. 6.** Original Image (.JPEG Size 800×800)

Fig. 5. Encrypted Image of Fig 4 (.JPEG Size 800×800)

Fig. 7. Encrypted Image of Fig 6 (.JPEG Size 800×800)

Figure 8 shows the diffusion chart of our proposed system to generating the secret key. According to this chart, we can claim that we generate the robust secret key.

In the proposed algorithm, the image is highly encrypted since the encryption is done by encrypting the basic frequncies and the operation is done not by encrypting all the bytes in the original images. Note that the image size will not increase in our proposed encryption system.

In Table 2, we compare our proposed algorithm with other schemes from the open works in frequency encryption of an image.

Table 2. Comparing our algorithm with others

Proposed System	Encryption Algorithm	Which Items are encrypted?	Size of the encrypted image
Lala Krikor & Sami Baba, 2009	Stream Cipher	Pseudo-Random bit sequence.	It is difference from the original image.
Pommer & Uhl, 2003	Advanced Encryption Standard	Subband decomposition structure.	It is not difference from the original image.
Drogenbroeck & Benedett, 2002	Triple DES and IDEA	Bits that indicate the sign and magnitude of the non-zero DCT coefficients.	It is difference from the original image.
Our Algorithm	Cellular Automata	The higher frequencies of the image blocks which embed in one dimensional cellular automata.	It is not difference from the original image.

6   Conclusions

The proposed algorithm has been applied successfully for digital images encryption. We present a frequncy domain and high-level encryption method based on the one dimenssional cellular automata and DCT. The cellular automata is used to generate a robust secret key and the DCT is used to frequency domain transformation of a digital image. The experimental results indicate that our proposed algorithm works well and the encrypted images are not clear visually and our secret key is generated in a robust manner.

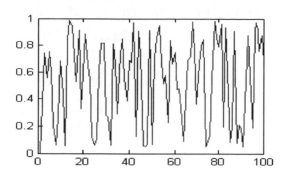

Fig. 8. The diffusion chart of the secret key which is generated by the proposed cellular automata

References

1. Puech, W., Rodrigues, J.: Crypto-Compression of Medical Images by Selective Encryption of DCT. In: 13th European Signal Processing Conference, Turkey (2005)
2. Schneier, B.: Applied Cryptography. John Wiley (1996)
3. Bovik, A.: The Essential Guide to Image Processing. Academic Press is an imprint of Elsevier (2009)
4. Van Droogenbroeck, M., Benedett, R.. Techniques for a Selective Encryption of Uncompressed and Comperessed Images. In: Proceeding of Advanced Concepts for Intelligent Vision Systems, Belgium (2002)
5. http://wikipedia.org
6. Shatten, A.: Cellular Automata. Institute of General Chemistry Vienna University of Technology, Austria (1997)
7. Lafe, O.: Data Compression and Encryption Using Cellular Automata Transforms. Artif. Intell. 10(6), 581–591 (1997)
8. Urias, J.: Cryptography Primitive Based on A Cellular Automata. An Interdisciplinary Journal of Nonlinear Science (1998)
9. Narasimha, M.J., Peterson, A.M.: On the computation of the discrete cosine transform. IEEE Trans. Commun. 26(6), 934–936 (1978)
10. Washington, C.: Introduction to Cryptography with Coding Theory, 2 edn. Pearson Prentice Hall (2006)

Community Trust Stores for Peer-to-Peer e-Commerce Applications

Ahmad H. Fauzi and Hamish Taylor

School of Mathematical and Computer Sciences
Heriot-Watt University,
Edinburgh, United Kingdom
{ahf4,h.taylor}@hw.ac.uk

Abstract. E-commerce applications have evolved from web-based selling via the Internet to selling in a P2P manner. P2P can enhance e-commerce applications to create lower cost systems compared to conventional client-server systems. However, P2P e-commerce applications will only be acceptable to users if they can provide robust, secure and equitable services to the peers involved during commercial transactions. In this paper, we propose use of a P2P shared store for trust information to support community based e-commerce applications. Nowadays, it can be economical and cheap to implement either in the cloud or in a distributed manner over the platforms of participating peers. Usage of a cheap and secure community store for trust data provides an effective alternative to conventional trusted third party support services for e-commerce transactions.

Keywords: P2P, secure, cloud computing, trading forum, inexpensive.

1 Introduction

Peer-to-peer (P2P) offers decentralization, reduced cost of ownership and scalability compared to the client-server model. It organises service delivery around mutual provision of common services among peer computers, not communal service provision via dedicated shared providers. To achieve this, control has to be more decentralized which can make for greater complexity in the design of the P2P software architecture than for client-server systems.

The aim of this paper is to propose and justify the use of a secure community store for trust data which is collaboratively controlled by a group of peers. It can be used for e-commerce applications that involve groups of like minded people who congregate virtually to trade with each other. Such trading forums can be expected to be structured by a number of commonly agreed rules and to have memberships to help ensure that trading conforms to these rules. Trading within these forums might be in the form of sales, auctions or swap sessions depending on their common purposes. Items for trading might be second hand goods, hobby items like stamps, spare tickets or electronic resources like music recordings, movie clips or e-books.

A. Abd Manaf et al. (Eds.): ICIEIS 2011, Part I, CCIS 251, pp. 428–442, 2011.

In such a context, a community repository stores trust related information needed by trading forums such as lists of membership, trading contracts among peers, reputation reports on transactions and public key certificates used to verify the identity of peers. All other non-trust related data such as proposed deals, offers and general communication is passed through the P2P system's messaging service.

Since the store is controlled by a group of peers, it is not considered as a third party. Instead it is the trust support base of the peers themselves. The store is used to support various levels of trust that are related to the dissemination of the identity, status and reputation of a peer in relation to his e-commerce trading. The advent of widespread third party hosting of computer user's data and software on the Internet has reduced to low levels the cost of hosting a community store which holds modest amounts of trust data, is infrequently accessed and has low performance requirements. Cloud computing service providers can securely and cheaply host software that supports such a remotely accessible data repository sitting over a moderate sized storage space. Alternatively, the community store can be hosted in a distributed fashion across the platforms of participating peers under certain assumptions about their availability.

Community trust stores (CTS) are needed to foster trust among peers so that peers can mitigate perceived risks in trading with each other. They need to be available for access whenever trading might take place. Since their function is to store trust information, that data needs to be credible. That can be achieved through supporting joint updates by all concerned parties where the data purports to express the shared knowledge or intent of these parties. However, where the store stores personal opinions, they can be added by a single forum member after verifying his identity as the author of that opinion. Using a community trust store addresses the problem of secure access to trust data among peers. It is also able to tackle the problem of different peers being online at different times. The trust store is not accessed all that frequently but should be available when access is required to it.

The rest of the paper is organized as follows: Section 2 discusses problems and the motivation for a P2P community trust store. Section 3 explains the proposed model for P2P e-commerce and community trust stores. Section 4 outlines the strategy, criteria, roles, benefits, downsides, and architecture of the community store's storage mechanisms. Section 5 describes an example scenario of the P2P trading. Section 6 discusses related P2P research. A summary and conclusion follow in Section 7.

2   Problem Statement and Motivation

Updates of communally agreed trust data to the community store can be limited to joint operations by the concerned parties to ensure that stored data accurately expresses their shared belief or will. Contracts between contracting parties can be limited to being added only by a joint operation of both parties. Membership additions can be constrained to being limited to joint operations of all their

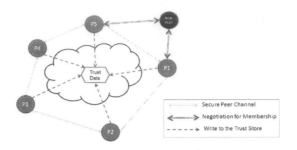

Fig. 1. The Proposed Framework for P2P e-Commerce and Customer Trust Stores

required sponsors. Identity certificates can be limited to being added jointly by all their signatories who are forum members and so on. Other trust data like deal evaluations by one trader of another trader's deal with him are not collective verdicts but personal opinions so they can be added individually so long as the member's identity is suitably verified by his digital signature.

However, there still remains an open issue of how best to combat various forms of unethical collusion in such non-hierarchical communities. For example multiple peers may gang up together to create fictitious trading contracts which are favorably evaluated in bogus reputation reports by the colluding parties. Or they may conspire together in sufficient numbers to succeed in voting for the exclusion of a bona fide member on trumped up grounds. However, these are not problems especial to online trading. They are general problems for all forms of community trading.

3   Proposed Model for P2P e-Commerce and Community Trust Stores

Peer-to-peer computing benefits e-commerce applications since it is cheaper to implement compared to conventional client-server e-commerce applications. The overall proposed framework using P2P and cloud computing technologies in e-commerce applications is depicted in Figure 1. P2P is used as the whole network infrastructure and cloud computing as a subnetwork infrastructure for supporting the CTS. Details of this framework are discussed in following subsections.

An online community trust store can support various types of trading including direct selling, auctions (open-cry or sealed bid), barter trade and lowest offers for solicited services among others. The type of trading determines how goods, cash and services are exchanged with each other. Important issues concern how well contracts are made binding between the trading parties and how well contracts protect the interests of both parties fairly and securely. In direct selling of second hand goods, a peer would typically expect to inspect the item before going ahead with buying it. However for never previously used services offered by a vendor, peers cannot assess the quality of a service before it is rendered and have to rely on feedback or testimonials from other peers that have used that service from that vendor before. For example, in relation to a cleaning service offered by a vendor, other peers would expect to be able to consider feedback from peers that have used that vendor's service before agreeing to hire that cleaner. Different types of trade will have their own distinct requirements and challenges.

3.1   Using P2P for e-Commerce Applications

The proposed model for P2P e-commerce model takes several criteria into consideration:

- Accessibility: Although two peers may not be online at the same time, trust information from each peer should be easily accessed by the other peer on demand.
- Reliability: The trust store system should provide required trust data upon request.
- Tamper proof: Only authorized and involved parties can update and modify trust data.
- Auditable: An audit trail is maintained for all transactions with the trust store.
- Trustable: These properties make the store a trustable source for information provided by authorized parties.
- Confidentiality: Only authorized peers can access confidential information.

The proposed P2P e-commerce trading model starts with at least three peers that have an initial trusted mutual understanding to trade amongst each other. In order to realise this framework, the peers need to 1) store identity certificates of recognised peers; 2) record trading contracts of proposed deals; 3) store transactions stating agreed outcomes of proposed deals; 4) record reputation reports about peer deals; and 5) store membership status of peers. All of the above information are stored in the CTS.

3.2   Using Cloud Computing for the Community Trust Store

The general idea of a CTS is based on the use of shared memory space among the peers. One option to achieve this is to require peers to contribute their file space and hours of online time in return for continued membership of the P2P community. A peer that fails to comply can be threatened with having its membership revoked. Another option is to adopt a cloud computing approach by storing trust data in the cloud. When the trust data is in the cloud, it is not necessary for some peers to be online so that the trust store can be immediately accessed. The cloud space can either be very cheap or free commercially supported storage or voluntarily contributed unused space on networked machines controlled by some participants in the trading community.

A secure CTS using cloud computing network technology is proposed as the more desirable way of implementing the model since it provides the most available way of accessing the latest version of trust related trading and reputation information. It offers:

- Accessibility, the store is the hub for various data operations in e-commerce applications. When using the store, member credentials based on the identity they present in the digital world can be checked. Identity will be established using public key certificates.
- Cheapness, by using each other's resources or cheap computing in the cloud, P2P stores should be able to support an inexpensive system compared to conventional client-server systems.
- Scalability, a cloud implementation of the shared trust store would limit how many peers can use it at the same time. However, that usage will not be frequent or intensive. It is rather more likely that the social dynamics of a very large community will cause it to split into sub-communities with their own community trust stores before the community size grows to the point of saturating usage of a single trust store. Storage requirements will grow linearly with peer numbers.
- Availability, a cloud implementation of the store could be expected to be available 24/7. However, a P2P implementation of the store over the storage space of peers would be dependent on enough peers remaining online at the same time to host the required data. In such cases the community might have to limit trading to communal sessions where a high enough participation rate could be guaranteed so that relevant trust data would be immediately available.

Cloud computing involves applications being delivered as services over the Internet where the hardware in the cloud provides those services [16]. Cloud computing consists of infrastructure, platform, storage, application and services. It allows the application to run in the cloud instead of being run locally on a dedicated machine. However there is always a security risk involved when running an application or storing data in the cloud. As it involves data transactions in and out of the cloud, the possibility of data tampering and loss is a significant risk. There will be issues of trusting the cloud and the reliability of the application hosted in the cloud. A reasonable strategy has to be planned to ensure accessibility of the store within the cloud. However, use of cloud computing technology means that data can be synchronized and updated without having to have cooperating peers online at the same time.

The downside of a using a CTS is its shared nature. Its operation may not be fully reliable and extra assurance would be needed as to whether a third party hosting the cloud is to be trusted. It will have issues of availability when network connectivity is disrupted due to attacks or interruptions of connections or peers disconnect from the peer network. We will discuss later on the elimination of the third party roles to validate and verify a peer. Other issues and weaknesses of using a CTS are trust and safety issues with the store itself.

4   Strategy and Criteria for the Community Trust Store

There are several characteristics for the CTS which need to be manifested in order to manage P2P trading efficiently. The store has to keep relatively small

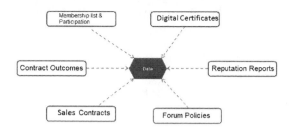

Fig. 2. Data Stored in the P2P Community Trust Store

items of data. Maintaining a small size item in the store will not impose much of space burden as long as the number of such items is not large. It will also ensure that they are easy to replicate or back up and recover quickly. The CTS should always be available when needed but is only likely to be infrequently accessed. The items that will be kept in the CTS are list of current, former and expelled members; digital certificates of members; trade contracts and agreed outcomes; reputation reports of present and past members; trading forum rules and policies; and member's participation data.

As depicted in Figure 2, these items are related to each other. For example, an operation to update the membership list must be signed by the private keys of the minimum number of members required by trading forum policies in order to update the list. Sales contracts are written with feedback signed by the persons involved in the transaction in a hierarchical format so that we can trace back the feedback to specific past transactions. The reputation reports of peers are based on data gathered from transaction feedbacks. Forum policies will be agreed by members in accordance with their collective decision making procedures.

The integrity of content in the store is protected using the private keys of peers. They collectively or individually sign each item they want to store and place it in the trusted community store. There is no general necessity for peers to encrypt the content that they want to write to the store. However there will be exceptions for types of selling such as sealed bid auctions where a bidder needs to encrypt their sealed bid using the auctioneer's public key to stop other peers from discovering their bid. The replication strategy is another way to protect the CTS content. When the content is backed up multiply, the possibility of losing the content is lower.

The decentralized nature of a peer-to-peer system leads to security vulnerabilities in peer-to-peer applications. In order to ensure the store is secure, a security management strategy has to be put in place. It will use preventative measures to reduce the risk of attack and would be expected to include a recovery plan if a security breach is detected. Only peers that are members of the P2P community should be allowed to write data to the store. So, unauthorized peers should have no chance to add anything to the community trust store. Although members are allowed to write new data, they should only be able to append to existing data and only able to edit their own feedback.

A recovery strategy can be used if the store is compromised. If a storage host is compromised such as data being tampered with or becoming inaccessible, the CTS could restore the missing or invalid data from data backups that are stored among member peers. This will ensure that the data is up-to-date and available. Providing a recovery strategy for the P2P system supports fault tolerance and resistance against denial of service attacks. Peers can access the latest data from the CTS each time they are online. That is the reason the size of files in the store should be small in order for quick data backup, replication, updating and recovery. The overall size of the stored data can be constrained by archiving or maybe deleting old records beyond suitable time to live periods. Security strategies that should be implemented include:

- Using public key infrastructure to ensure messages and files exchanged between peers and the CTS are tamper proof
- Regular backup of CTS contents; replication and backup of the CTS contents into other clouds or into distributed storage solutions with the agreement of the peer community
- Validation of P2P software by the peers to avoid malware in the software
- Enforcing punishment for peers that breach security and privacy of others
- Protecting the trust content of the CTS using cryptographic methods that are strong yet efficient in term of performance
- Recording and tracking of trust content being accessed, updated and modified by peers in the CTS

These security strategies will be implemented jointly in accordance with trading forum policies. These address the following risks, weaknesses and threats :

- Security of the application (application level): How can we be sure the application is safe to use? Does it contain malicious code or Trojan horses? How confident are we to install and use the peer application? These are important issues in developing a trusted application. Peers must have adequate assurance it is safe to use the application if using it entails security risks. The software application should use established techniques like signed code and digital watermarks so that it can to be verified and endorsed by the peers. If the source code is made publicly available, compilation of the application can be made by the peer themselves. Apart from peer's endorsement, the endorsement by well known or reliable third parties can be implemented as well to eliminate sceptical doubts related to security of the application. Although publishing the source code publicly ensures transparency of the code in terms of proving there are no malicious code in it, it is acknowledged that this also gives opportunities to attackers to study the code and finds its vulnerabilities.
- Security of communication (network level): These are issues of message confidentiality, peer's identities and ensuring peers are communicating with the person whom the person claims. It deals with ensuring confidentiality and integrity of communication. By using public and private keys as ways to communicate with each other, peers and the CTS should be able to prevent

tampering and modification of trust data. The CTS can identify itself with its own public and private key pairs by signing its sources and messages to peers. By communicating directly with the CTS, peers also eliminate the risk of relying on other peers to obtain trust data thus minimizing the chances of modification of data through the man-in-the-middle attacks, spoofing and masquerading. This issue also includes access to the CTS, which can be blocked by denial of service attacks. Peers will not be able to get the trust data stored in the CTS if the content cannot be delivered due to network failures caused by attackers.

– Security of the environment (user level): In order to create a secure environment, there are issues related to trust among peers, bandwidth limitations, protection against threats, safe backup, recovery and bootstrapping and policies governing peers membership. The peers have to ensure their own machines are secure and safe from malicious code. Peers that are unable to comply with the trading community security policy can be removed from the membership list.

Where the CTS is supported by a third party cloud storage service, we assume that a reputable service provider should be able to ensure a secure environment for the CTS. However, with a proper backup and recovery strategy as proposed, it seems reasonable to expect that the availability of the trust data can be ensured with minimal threat and guarantee with reasonable service downtime. Regular backup of the trust data to different cloud or distributed P2P storage facilities should be able to provide additional assurance that the data in the CTS is safe, recoverable and secure.

5   Scenario of Trading in Proposed P2P e-Commerce Model

Various trading scenarios can be supported by P2P e-commerce. However one of especial interest is low valued good sales in community markets. The proposed P2P trading model suits such low valued good sales. Low valued goods sales often happen in venues like flea markets, garage sales, car boot sales, Sunday markets and charity sales. Characteristics of such trading are low price items; second hand or used items; cash sales for on the spot delivery; no refunds and slim chance of legal redress; buy as seen with no provenance or warranty; prior inspection of goods for sale; and price of item being negotiable.

This type of sale attracts a wide audience as the items are seen as cheap, value for money and potentially a good bargain. However, its characteristics also encourage fraud, fencing, misrepresentation and breach of intellectual property rights (IPR). Nevertheless, it is a popular method of buying and selling worldwide. This type of trading in envisaged as a viable application area for P2P e-commerce. When such trading is done online, it has its own limitations. For example, items which are advertised online are usually described initially using text and pictures via a chosen platform. The description based on text

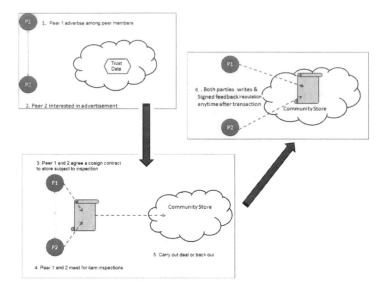

Fig. 3. Sample Scenario in the Proposed P2P Community Trading Model

and pictures can sometimes mislead buyers. Inspection of items is still needed. Buyers will expect to be able to inspect the item and decide if they want to accept the 'as is' condition of the item. Only if the buyer is satisfied with the inspection, will payment be made. Else, the deal is off and the seller will have to find another potential buyer.

The proposed type of scenario for P2P trading involves agreement to buy and then inspection before completing the sale of the advertised goods. Referring to Figure 3, assume that there are two existing peer members, P1 and P2. P1 is selling a second hand text book and posts an advertisement through the P2P messaging service with his digital signature. P2 sees the advertisement and informs P1 he is interested in buying the book. P1 sends a contract to P2 to buy the book as described for a certain price subject to quality inspection arranged with P1. P1 accepts the proposal or negotiates a revised proposal and then both parties sign the contract, agree where and when to meet, and submit the contract to the CTS. Upon meeting P1, P2 inspects the book in order to decide whether it meets the terms of his contract to buy it and P1 assures himself that P2 has the money to pay for it. Whether the transaction goes through or not, P1 and P2 are expected to exchange reputation reports in the P2P trading community by updating the CTS jointly and report on the outcome of their meeting.

The reputation report could be a positive or negative comment related to the transaction. For a specific reputation report on a transaction, only the trading peers will be allowed to contribute reputation reports if they have previously committed a joint contract to the CTS. In the future, other peers that wish to perform trades with P1, can gather feedback on P1 via the CTS and use it to help them to decide whether to initiate a trading transaction with P1.

Some back of the envelope calculations can be used to estimate the use of bandwidth and the data footprint of a CTS being used in P2P e-commerce trading. Trade contracts, reputation reports and contract outcomes will have a size of around 1000 bytes each. PGP digital certificates might average 10000 bytes in size. A transaction might involve access to something like 40 reputation reports, 20 certificates, 10 contracts and 10 contract outcomes on the CTS. It will upload 1 contract, 2 reputation reports and 1 outcome. So it will involve the downloading of 260 Kbytes of data and the uploading of less than 5 Kbytes.

If the trading community comprises 1000 members and each performs 5 transactions per week, 260 Mbytes will be uploaded and less than 5 Mbytes downloaded per week. If the store holds 1 years worth of transactions then it will hold 260 contracts and outcomes, 520 reputation reports and 1000 certificates. This will occupy approximately 11 Mbytes. Together with ancillary data like testimonials, forum policies, logs and so on lets say a total of 20 Mbytes. Even if these are underestimates by 10 times, it is clear that data traffic to and from the CTS and the size of the communal trust database are modest in scale. Hence the CTS should be easy to support in a typical cloud computing environment.

6   Related Work

In this section, we review cloud formations; P2P storage systems; identity and reputation issues; Web of Trust and Public Key Infrastructure.

6.1   Cloud Formations to Support a CTS

Cloud services can be obtained in several ways. One way is by using an existing commercial cloud service such as offered by Amazon Elastic Compute Cloud (EC2)[1], Windows Azure[2] and Google Apps[3]. These providers offer to run code from users on their cloud facilities. They also guarantee security of data stored or applications run within their cloud. However, all three charge money to provide cloud services to customers.

Other than that, a cloud can be formed using existing machines in an organisation such as with in an ad hoc cloud computing approach [1]. This approach uses computing resources harvested from machines within an existing enterprise. For example a P2P trading forum exclusively for staff and student of a university could use available unused computing resources from the university's computing facilities or labs.

6.2   P2P Store

In P2P research, several P2P storage systems have been proposed such as PAST [2], PeerStore [3], Wuala[4] and OceanStore [4].

---

[1] http://aws.amazon.com/ec2/
[2] http://www.microsoft.com/windowsazure/
[3] http://www.google.com/apps/
[4] http://www.wuala.com

PAST storage is formed over peers that are connected with each other over the Internet. Each peer can initiate and route client requests to update or retrieve files. Peers are also able to contribute storage to the PAST system. The files on peers can be replicated on multiple peers to increase their availability. The CTS only needs to store a modest amount of data but it needs to be able to update and to access all data quickly. PAST is rather more suitable for backup of data than supporting CTS contents. PAST is a non-incentives based system which does not reward peers that contribute storage to other peers. PAST nodes and users can use smartcards to authenticate entities and assure the integrity and confidentiality of data. The client can encrypt the content of file using their smartcard before inserting the file into PAST.

The relevant contribution of PeerStore related to peer-to-peer backup systems is its safekeeping and fair contribution scheme. Peers regularly challenge each other to verify their partners are still storing the blocks entrusted to them by asking them to prove they are still storing all block replicas. A partner that fails to answer a challenge is punished by discarding information that the peer has stored on the challenging peers. However, punishing a peer that fails to answer a single challenge might lead to peers experiencing technical failure or downtime losing their backup. On the other hand, a more lenient strategy might encourage free riding among the participating peers. Although PeerStore's intention is to improve high long-term availability instead of short-term availability, the strategy could result in possibly long waiting times for a restore operation to take place. Another problem is that there is no way to decide whether a partner is temporarily off-line or has permanently left the network. A further challenge for Peerstore is that a peer has to look for and find a sufficient and suitable number of partners that can store their data otherwise it will be unable to guarantee the backup of its data. The task of finding suitable partnering peers might also take time.

In Wuala, users can trade local machine storage for online storage. If a user gives up a certain amount of storage space on his computer, he will be given a certain amount of space in the Wuala online storage on the condition that peers have to be online at least 4 hours per day (17%). The amount of online space given is calculated based on the online time. For example, if a user donates 100GB of space, the given online space will be a multiple of the online time percentage and the space contributed. If the online time is 50%, then the online storage will be 50GB. Wuala supports access permissions and client side encryption but could only be used as a community trust store if it was augmented by reliable mechanisms to constrain collective updates to community data by sets of authorised parties. Wuala supports data replication in order to improve data availability where much of its storage facility is offline most of the time. However, it doesn't support incremental encryption which slows down access to recently updated files. For this reason Wuala is more suitable for personal data backup than serving as the host for a CTS.

OceanStore is a global-scale decentralized storage system where many computers collaborate and communicate across the Internet [4]. It uses the Tapestry [5] overlay network which enables it to overcome problems of fault tolerance. The infrastructure is comprised of untrusted servers. However, data is protected through redundancy and cryptographic techniques. It also intended for data to be in a nomadic state where it is not tied to one physical location and is passed freely among hosting machines. An incremental cryptographic technique is used in OceanStore. It avoids the hassle of data decryption, updating and re-encryption. Incremental cryptography makes it possible to quickly update an encrypted document, rather than have to re-compute it from scratch [6]. Only users with the right encryption keys are able to decrypt and read the data. Read and write access of users are managed through the access control list of the OceanStore system. In OceanStore, each data object has a globally unique identifier (GUID). When an object is written into the system, replications of it are created and saved in different locations. These replicas are called floating replicas, because they can be transferred from one location to another. There are two forms of object in OceanStore, the active form and an archival form. Archival forms are spread over many servers and in a stable state where no further updates are necessary. The active or current form of object can be updated. Objects are modified via updates (versioning system) and data is not overwritten. This guarantees faster synchronization among the peers because there is no necessity to overwrite the whole object which would take much longer. A versioning system also allows a more efficient recovery process by only focusing on the update rather than recovering the whole data. It has to search and verify the latest version of data before initiating any necessary recovery process.

OceanStore is a better distributed storage solution for a community trust store than Wuala because of its use of incremental encryption even though it does not address incentives for users to contribute storage space. It would also need to be augmented with mechanisms to enforce trading forum rules and to support shared updates on commonly agreed data.

6.3   Reputation Issues

In general, reputation is the opinion of the public towards a person, a group of people, an organization or a resource. It is the memory and summary of behaviour from previous transactions [7]. Reputation can be used to set expectations when considering future transactions. In the context of peer-to-peer applications, reputation represents the opinion of nodes in the system towards their peers and resource providers [8]. It also allows peers to build trust and confidence which can lead them to make a decision. By harnessing feedback from peers, a reputation based system can help other peers to decide who should be trusted, can encourage trustworthy behaviour and can deter dishonest participants [9]. Without a credible reputation service, dishonest peers will erode the foundations of collaborative applications and generate peer mistrust and application failure [10]. Recent research has shown the significant extent to which a reputation system facilitates fraud avoidance and supports better buyer satisfaction [11], [12], [13], [14]. Here we discuss three relevant reputation issues which are multi dimension feedback, defending peer reputation and peers without previous transactions.

Multi Dimension Feedback. The feedback from peers can be positive, negative or neutral after a transaction. Positive feedback can easily be kept by the parties involved as they will want to use them in promoting their own reputation. Many reputation systems only handle positive reputation reports [9]. Some couple privileges to accumulated good reputation, for example reputation earned from exchange of gaming items or auctioning [15]. However, in trading users are also interested in knowing about the negative reputation of another trader. Negative reputation is a potent indicator to avoid or be cautious about dealing with a particular trader.

We propose using the CTS to store reputation reports on peers. Then, if anyone wants to check on a peer's reputation, such information can be reliably obtained from the CTS. The peer that gives feedback on another peer can store the feedback from his transaction in the CTS and sign it with his digital signature to ensure that the feedback is tamper proof. Dissemination of the reputation report from the CTS across the peer's community provides an alternative source of data if reputation records at the CTS become inaccessible and its signature prevents modification by the assessed peers. It also provides a backup of a peer's reputation.

Reputation based on feedback can implement an expiry date or duration of validity if CTS storage space is tight. Only the more recent transactions of other peers would be kept and any feedback more than that limit would be removed or archived to conserve space. Each feedback will also be logged to keep track of the last transaction, validity and modification. The reputation system will hold two main types of records - reputation reports about individual trades and testimonials about a trader's general trustworthiness to trade with. Apart from direct feedback from peers, transaction logs can serve as a third factor for peers to use to judge a peer's tradeworthiness. Logs contain a summary of specific transactions, its timeline and the outcome of the trading. Peers with little recent transaction history or high non-completion rates or with long average transaction durations may be peers to be wary of when doing business. In order to have a reasonably informative assessment of reputation data, we propose using a multi dimensional reputation system. It covers transaction ratings by other peers using several standard criteria based on Likert scales and free text comments as well as general recommendations by others (testimonials). Standardized ratings using multi dimensional scales can be aggregated and averaged to produce overall reputation values. Together with individual text comments and testimonials they can be used to judge or evaluate whether to deal with a peer.

Defending Peer Reputation. Apart from having an accessible and accurate reputation system, the content of the reputation data needs to be protected and guarded against any threat of unauthorized modification either from the peer itself or by others. As the reputation data is stored in the CTS, it should be invulnerable from being tampered by any peers as long as the information and CTS are well managed. Each feedback will be signed by peers that give the feedback and time stamped by the CTS. If we can match and synchronize the time stamp of peers signing with the time the feedback was created, we should be able to verify whether the feedback is likely to have come from the person that gives the feedback.

Peers should also be given the chance to defend themselves against unfair feedback. As the feedback can be hierarchically added and tracked, peer can give comments on feedback received about them. It is important to have check and balance features to be fair to both trading parties. They can even defend themselves with proof by referring to the trading contract or other reputation reports if they think the feedback is incorrect or misleading to others.

Peers Without Previous Transactions. Since we are aiming to have a CTS for local trading, we assume some peers might know a new peer in-person and based on this knowledge, they can recommend or become the point of reference for the peers by issuing testimonials.

7   Conclusion

We have presented a framework for community trust stores to support P2P e-commerce applications. It uses trading forum membership to control access to the community trust store. We have addressed the problems of trust in P2P e-commerce and proposed a solution that ensures the availability of the store using cloud computing services. The proposed use of cloud computing to host commu-nity trusted store (CTS) is able to service P2P user needs and requirements. The CTS is hardened and secured to ensure the trustworthiness of its content to the P2P trading community. Access to the trust content in the CTS by the peers is recorded and logged. A reputation system and jointly signed trading contracts with trading outcomes provide the trading records of peers. The use of tamper proof evidence and endorsement methods in the CTS which are checkable and guaranteed to nurture trust in the contents of the CTS. They also help to build the trust among peers that use P2P e-commerce applications based on use of a CTS. We are developing a prototype of this type of application based on using CTS stored in an Azure cloud. We will use it to validate our approach.

References

1. Kirby, G.N.C., Dearle, A., Macdonald, A., Fernandes, A.: An Approach to Ad hoc Cloud Computing. Computing Research Repository, abs/1002.4738 (2010)
2. Druschel, P., Rowstron, A.: PAST: A Large-Scale, Persistent Peer-to-Peer Stor-age Utility. In: Proceedings of the Eighth Workshop on Hot Topics in Operating Systems (HOTOS 2001), p. 75. IEEE Computer Society, Washington, DC, USA (2001)
3. Landers, M., Zhang, H., Tan, K.L.: Peerstore: Better Performance by Relaxing in Peer-to-peer Backup. In: Proceedings of the Fourth International Conference on Peer-to-Peer Computing, pp. 72–79. IEEE Computer Society, Washington, DC, USA (2004)

 4. Kubiatowicz, J., Bindel, D., Chen, Y., Czerwinski, S., Eaton, P., Geels, D., Gummadi, R., Rhea, S., Weatherspoon, H., Weimer, W., Wells, C., Zhao, B.: Oceanstore: An Architecture for Global-scale Persistent Storage. SIGPLAN Not. 35, 190–201 (2000)
 5. Zhao, B.Y., Kubiatowicz, J.D., Joseph, A.D.: Tapestry: An Infrastructure for Fault-tolerant Wide-area Location and Routing. Technical report, Berkeley, CA, USA (2001)
 6. Bellare, M., Goldreich, O., Goldwasser, S.: Incremental Cryptography: The Case of Hashing and Signing. In: Desmedt, Y.G. (ed.) CRYPTO 1994. LNCS, vol. 839, pp. 216–233. Springer, Heidelberg (1994)
 7. Oram, A.: Peer-to-Peer, Harnessing the Power of Disruptive Technologies. O'Reilly Media (2001)
 8. Hoffman, K., Zage, D., Nita-Rotaru, C.: A Survey of Attack and Defense Techniques for Reputation Systems. ACM Computing Surveys 42, 1–31 (2009)
 9. Resnick, P., Kuwabara, K., Zeckhauser, R., Friedman, E.: Reputation Systems. ACM Communications 43, 45–48 (2000)
10. Akerlof, G.A.: The Market for 'Lemons': Quality Uncertainty and the Market Mechanism. The Quarterly Journal of Economics 84, 488–500 (1970)
11. Houser, D., Wooders, J.: Reputation in Auctions: Theory, and Evidence from eBay. Journal of Economics & Management Strategy 15, 353–369 (2006)
12. Resnick, P., Zeckhauser, R., Swanson, J., Lockwood, K.: The Value of Reputation on eBay: A Controlled Experiment. Experimental Economics 9, 79–101 (2006)
13. Xiong, L., Liu, L.: A Reputation-based Trust Model for Peer-to-peer E-commerce Communities. In: Proceedings of the 4th ACM Conference on Electronic Commerce, pp. 228–229. ACM, New York (2003)
14. Lin, K.J., Lu, H., Yu, T., Tai, C.E.: A Reputation and Trust Management Broker Framework for Web Applications. In: Proceedings of the IEEE International Conference on e-Technology, e-Commerce and e-Service, pp. 262–269. IEEE Computer Society, Washington, DC, USA (2005)
15. Resnick, P., Zeckhauser, R.: Trust Among Strangers in Internet Transactions: Empirical Analysis of eBay's Reputation System. In: The Baye, M.R. (ed.) The Economics of the Internet and E-Commerce. Advances in Applied Microeconomics, vol. 11, pp. 127–157. Elsevier Science (2002)
16. Armbrust, M., Fox, A., Griffith, R., Joseph, A.D., Katz, R., Konwinski, A., Lee, G., Patterson, D., Rabkin, A., Stoica, I., Zaharia, M.: A View of Cloud Computing. ACM Communication 53, 50–58 (2010)

Temporal Partitioning Algorithm for Dynamically Reconfigurable Computing Systems

Ramzi Ayadi, Bouaoui Ouni, and Abdellatif Mtibaa

Laboratory of Electronic and Microelectronic,
Faculty of science at Monastir, Monastir 5000, Tunisia
ramzi_ayadi@yahoo.fr, bouraoui.ouni@fsm.rnu.tn,
abdellatif.mtibaa@enim.rnu.tn

Abstract. In reconfigurable computing systems, dynamically reconfigurable FPGA are evolving rapidly, due to their flexibility and high performance. The communication cost is one of important factors in dynamically reconfigurable FPGA. This paper proposes a new temporal partitioning algorithm for the dynamically reconfigurable FPGA to reduce communication cost between partitions. To experimentally verify the proposed temporal partitioning algorithm, we apply two benchmarks. They include discrete cosine transform (DCT) 4×4 and DCT 16×16.

Keywords: Temporal partitioning, Reconfigurable Computing Systems, FPGA.

1 Introduction

The temporal partitioning problem [1][2][3] can be seen as a graph-based problem. A program or application can be modelled by a data flow graph. Then, the temporal partitioning divides the input graph into temporal partitions that are configured one after the one on the reconfigurable device. Each partition called also a stage or a micro-cycle and all the micro-cycles form one user cycle. The first temporal partition receives input data, performs computations and stores intermediate data into on-board memory. The device is then reconfigured for the next segment, which computes results based on the intermediate data, from the previous partitions. Figure 1 shows a part of a design that has been partitioned into four partitions. Assuming that a node requires a CLB (Configurable Logic Bloc) and each arc has a 1-byte width, and assuming also a device with a size of 4 CLB and a memory with 3 bytes available for communication. The partitioning, shown in Figure 1.a, needs five CLBs and five bytes while that shown in Figure 1.b uses only three CLBs and three byte. Therefore, the partitioning, shown in Figure 1.a, is undesirable.

In the literature, often the network flow algorithm has been used to reduce the communication cost across temporal partitions. The first network flow algorithms has been used in [4][5] [6] and improved in [7]. The method is a recursive bipartition approach that successively partitions a set of remaining nodes in two sets, one of which is a final partition, whereas a further partition step must be applied on the second one. The following description shows the initial network algorithm as presented in [4][5].

A. Abd Manaf et al. (Eds.): ICIEIS 2011, Part I, CCIS 251, pp. 443–452, 2011.
© Springer-Verlag Berlin Heidelberg 2011

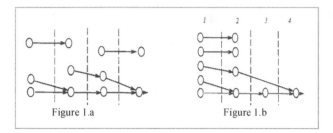

Fig. 1. Temporal partitioning

```
Begin
1. Construct graph G' from graph G by net modelling
2. pick a pair of node s and t in G' as source and sink
3. Find a min cut C in G'. let X be the sub-graph reachable from
s through
augmenting path, and X' be the rest
4. if ( lr • w(X) • ur) then stops and return C as solution
5. if (w(X) <•Lr ) then
collapse all nodes in X to S
pick a node v in X', and collapse v to s
go to step 3
6. if (w(X) >ur) then
collapse all nodes in X' to t
pick a node v in X, and collapse v to t
go to step 3
End
```

Where: w(X) is the total area of all nodes in X; Lr = (1-ε) Rmax , Rmax is the area of the device; ur =(1-ε) Rmax; ε=0,05, S is the source node, t is the sink node. Let us consider the graph G of figure 2.a, after following the net modelling steps, such as presented in [4][5], the new graph G' of figure 2.b is obtained.

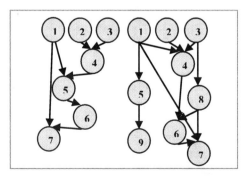

Fig. 2. a: Graph G   **Fig. 2.** b: graph G'

Let us assume 200 CLBs be the area of the device, 100 CLBs be the area of the multiplier,   50 CLBs be the area of the adder, the comparator and the multiplexer. And let us assume a memory with 50 bytes available for communication and each edge has a 32-bit width. We applied the network flow algorithm on the graph of figure 2.a. the   result is shown in figure 3, the network flow algorithm puts nodes T2, T3, T4 in partition P1, nodes T1, T5, T6 in partition P2 and node T7 in partition P3.

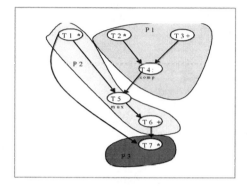

Fig. 3. Temporal partitioning

The network flow may minimize the communication cost. However, the model is constructed by inserting a great amount of nodes and edges in the original graph. The resulting graph may grow too big. In the worst case, the number of nodes in the new graph can be twice the number of the nodes in the original graph. The number of additional edges also grows dramatically and become difficult to handle. Further, the network flow algorithm, is a heuristic algorithm, in fact there is no a mathematical model behind him. Others approaches have used the list scheduling algorithm to minimize the communication cost [8]. The main idea of this method consists in placing all nodes of the graph according its priorities on a list. The first partition is built by removing nodes from the list to the partition until the size of the target area is reached. Then, a new partition is built and the process is repeated until all nodes are placed in partition. The main limitation of this technique is the assignment of nodes, which is based on the control step number (result of ASAP and/or ALAP scheduling) of each node, rather than the interconnectivity between nodes. That's why; in this technique each partition generally includes several parallel tasks. So, if the exchanged data between partitions is important, the memory constraint becomes difficult to reach before building several partitions. In [9] authors combine the integer linear programming and the network flow techniques to minimize the communication cost. The algorithm puts each node in the appropriate partition in order to decrease the transfer of data required between partitions while handling the whole latency of the design. The general problem of this approach is its high execution time. In fact, the size of the computation model which grows very fast and, therefore, the algorithm can only be applied to small examples. In [10] author uses levelling node method to determine the communication cost. However, for each end of stage the method is not a min cut just only a levelling cut.

2   Data Flow Graph

A Data Flow Graph DFG is a directed acyclic graph $G = (V, E)$ where V is a set of nodes $|V| = n$ and E is a set of edges. A directed edge $e_{i,j} \in E$ represents the dependence between nodes (T_i, T_j). For each edge $e_{i,j}$ there is a weight $\alpha_{i,j}$ that represents the communication cost between node T_i and node T_j. We assume that each node has an equivalent hardware implementation, which occupies an area on the chip. Therefore, the nodes as well as the edges in a DFG have some characteristics such as area, latency and width that are derived from the hardware resources used later to implement nodes.

2.1   Node and Edge Parameters

Given a node $T_i \in V$ and $e_{i,j} \in E$.

- a_i denotes the area of T_i

- The latency L_i is the time needed to execute T_i

- For a given edge $e_{i,j}$ which defines a data dependency between T_i and T_j , we define the weight $\alpha_{i,j}$ of $e_{i,j}$ as the amount of data transferred from T_i to T_j.

3   Temporal Partitioning

A temporal partitioning P of the graph $G = (V, E)$, is its division into some disjoints partitions such that: $P = \{P_1...P_k\}$

A temporal partitioning is feasible in accordance to a reconfigurable device H with area $A(H)$ and pins $T(H)$ (number of programmable input/outputs (I/Os) per device); if:

- $\forall P_i \in P$, we have $\sum_{Ti \in P_i} a_i \leq A(H)$

- $\forall P_k \in P$, $e_{i,j} \in E$, we have

$$\frac{1}{2}\left(\sum_{(e_{i,j} \cap P_k) \neq \phi \, and \, (e_{i,j} - P_k) \neq \phi} \alpha_{i,j} \right) \leq T(H)$$

We extend the ordering relation $\leq$ to P as follow: $P_i \leq P_j \Leftrightarrow e_{i,j} \in E$ with $T_i \in P_i$ and $T_j \in P_j$, either $T_i \leq T_j$ or $\leq$ is not defined for T_i and T_j. The partition P is ordered $\Leftrightarrow$ an ordering relation $\leq$ exists for P. An ordered partitioning   is characterized by the fact that for a pair of partitions, one should be always implemented after the other with respect to any scheduling relation.

4   Proposed Algorithm

Our algorithm aims to solve the following problem: Given a DFG $G = (V, E)$ and a set of constraints: *Find the way of graph partitioning in optimal number of temporal partitions such as the communication cost having the lowest value while respecting all constraints.*

Our algorithm is composed by two main steps. The first step aims to find an initial partitioning P_{in} of the graph. This step gives the optimal solution in term of communication cost. Next, if the area constraint is satisfied after the first step then we adopts the initial partitioning, else we go to the second step. Hence, the second step aims to find the final partitioning P of the graph while satisfying the area constrain. If the second step can not find a feasible scheduling then we relax the number of partition by one and the algorithm goes to the first step. And, we restart to find a feasible solution in the new number partitions.

4.1   First Step: Initial Partitioning

Given a data flow graph $G = (V, E)$, we define:

- The weighted adjacency matrix W as follow :

$$W_{i,j} = \alpha_{i,j} ; W_{i,i} = 0$$

- The degree matrix D   as follow :

$$Dii = \sum_{j=1}^{n} W_{i,j} \quad ; D_{i,j} = 0$$

- The Laplacian of G as follow:

$$L = D - W$$

The matrix L satisfies the following property:

$$X'LX = X'DX - X'WX = \sum_{i=1}^{n} D_i x_i^2 - \sum_{i=1}^{n}\sum_{j=1}^{n} W_{i,j} x_i x_j$$

$$= \frac{1}{2}\sum_{i=1}^{n}(D_i + D_i)x_i^2 - \sum_{i=1}^{n}\sum_{j=1}^{n} W_{i,j} x_i x_j$$

$$= \frac{1}{2}\left(\sum_{i=1}^{n} D_i x_i^2 - 2\sum_{i=1}^{n}\sum_{j=1}^{n} W_{i,j} x_i x_j + \sum_{j=1}^{n} D_j x_j^2\right)$$

$$= \frac{1}{2}\sum_{i=1}^{n}\sum_{j=1}^{n} W_{i,j}(x_i - x_j)^2$$

How Minimizing the Communication Cost

Our main goal is how finding the way of partitioning the graph such as the communication cost has lowest value. This section shows how achieving a good solution to such graph partitioning problems.

Given a temporal partitioning of $G = (E, V)$ into k disjoint partitions $P = \{P_1, P_2...P_k\}$; the communication cost, *Com_Cost* (P_m), of partition P_m has been defined in [11] as follow:

$$\text{Com\_Cost } (P_m) = \frac{1}{2}\left(\frac{\sum\limits_{T_i \in P_m \,:\, T_j \in |P_m|} W_{i,j}}{|P_m|}\right) \tag{1}$$

This implies that:

$$\text{T\_Com\_Cost} = \sum\nolimits_{m=1}^{K} Com\_Cost(Pm) = \frac{|V|}{2}\sum\nolimits_{i=1}^{K}\frac{\sum\limits_{Ti \in Pm:Tje|\overline{P}|} Wij}{|Pm|\overline{Pm}|} \tag{2}$$

Where: T_Com_Cost is the total communication cost. $|P_m|$ is the number of nodes inside partition P_m. $|\overline{P}_m|$ be the number of nodes outside the partition P_m. Hence, we have $|P_m| + |\overline{P}_m| = |V| = n$.

given an indicator vector X_m defined as follow:

$X_m(i) = [X_m(1), X_m(2), \ldots \ldots, X_m(n)]'$, where m = 1, 2,...., k and i = 1,2,...n are defined as:

$$X_m(i) = \frac{1}{\sqrt{|P_m|}} \quad \text{if } T_i \in P_m \text{; 0 otherwise}$$

We have:

$$\text{T\_Com\_Cost} = \sum_{m=1}^{K} X_m' L X_m \tag{3}$$

We introduce a matrix Xp (n×k) that contains the k indicator vectors as columns.
We can check that:
$$X_m' L X_m = (X_p' L X_p)_{m,m} \tag{4}$$
Overall, we can achieve:

$$\text{T\_Com\_Cost} = \sum_{m=1}^{K} X_m' L X_m = \sum_{m=1}^{k} (X_p' L X_p)_{m,m} \tag{5}$$
$$= trace(X_p' L X_p)_{m,m}$$

Therefore, using equation 5, the problem of communication cost minimization can be expressed as:

*Minimize (**T_Com_Cost**) => Minimize (**trace** ($X_p' L X_p$)   (6) The standard form of a trace minimization problem can be solved by choosing Xp as the matrix that contains the first k eigenvectors corresponding to the k smallest eigenvalues of matrix L as columns*

Lemma 1. Given a (n×n) matrix **Mp** as follow:

$M_{i,j} = 1/ |P_m|$ if T_i and $T_j \in P_m$; 0 otherwise

We have: $X_p' L X_p = M_p$

Proof:

The ij^{th} of $X_p X_p'$ is $\sum_{m=1}^{k} X_m(i) X_m(j)$. The term $X_m(i) X_m(j)$ will be non-zero if and only if both T_i and T_j, are in P_m, hence the sum is $1/\left|P_m\right|$ when T_i and T_j are in the same partition; 0 otherwise

The above descriptions are summarized by the following steps, form step 1 to step 7

1) Compute the minimum number of partitions K= Min_Part =
$\lceil Area(G) / Area(H) \rceil$

2) Compute the laplacian matrix L(G) of G

3) Compute k lowest eigenvalues of L(G)

4) Construct the (n x k) matrix X_p that have the K eignvectors as columns.

5) Compute Z = X_p X^t_p

6) Construct the (n x n) matrix M_p = $M_{i,j}$ from Z. $M_{i,j}$ = 1 if $Z_{i,j}$ ≥1/n, 0 otherwise.

7) Generate the initial partitioning from matrix M_p

8) If the area constraint is satisfied then final partitioning = initial partitioning; else go to step 2 (we mean by go to step 2: go to final partitioning step)

4.2   Second Step: Final Partitioning

In this step, we start from the initial partitioning P_{in} given by the first step and the set of partitions $P_i \in P_{in}$, where $A(P_i) > A(H)$. Our technique balances nodes from partition Pi to P_j or inversely until the satisfaction of the area constraint. The balance of nodes is based on the force $F(T_i, P_i \rightarrow P_j)$ associated with partition P_i on a node T_i to be scheduled into partition P_j and on the force $F(T_i, P_j \rightarrow P_i)$ associated with partition P_j on a node T_i to be scheduled into partition P_i. For instance let us assume that $P_i < P_j$; $P_i, P_j \in P_{in}$ .These forces are calculated as follow:

$$F(T_i, P_i \rightarrow P_j) = \delta_1(T_i) * OF(T_i)$$

$\delta_1(T_i) = 0$, if there is a node $T_j \in P_i$ and T_j is an output of T_i, otherwise $\delta(T_i) = 1$.

$OF(T_i) = (\dfrac{Nu(T_i)}{Nu(T_i)+1})$, Given a nodes T_i, $T_j \in P_i$; $Nu(T_i) = \sum_{Tj \in Pi} \beta_{i,j} T_j$; $\beta_{i,j} = 1$ if T_j is an input of T_i, 0 otherwise

$$F(T_i, P_j \rightarrow P_i) = \delta_2(T_i) * InF(T_i)$$

$\delta_2(T_i) = 0$, if there is a node $T_j \in P_i$ and T_j is an input of T_i, otherwise $\delta(T_i) = 1$.

$InF(T_i) = (\dfrac{Nq(T_i)}{Nq(T_i)+1})$, Given a nodes T_i, $T_j \in P_j$; $Nq(T_i) = \sum_{Tj \in Pj} \phi_{ij} T_j$; $\phi_{ij} = 1$ if T_j is

an output of T_i, 0 otherwise

In general, due to the scheduling of one node, other node schedules will also be affected.   At each iteration, the force of every node being scheduled in every possible partition is computed. Then, the distribution graph is updated and the process repeats until no more nodes remain to be scheduled.

5   Experiments

In our experiences, we used four approaches, list scheduling [2], initial network flow [11], improved network flow [13] and the proposed approach. In our experiences, we evaluated the performance of each approach in term of whole latency. The figure 4 shows the Color Layout Descriptor "CLD" is a low-level visual descriptor that can be extracted from images or video frames. The process of the CLD extraction consists of four stages: Image partitioning, selection of a single representative color for each block, DCT transformation and non linear quantization and Zig-Zag scanning.

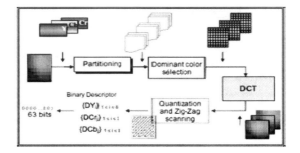

Fig. 4. Block diagram of the CLD extraction

Since DCT is the most computationally intensive part of the CLD algorithm, it has been chosen to be implemented in hardware, and the rest of subtasks (partitioning, color selection, quantization, zig-zag scanning and Huffman encoding) were chosen for software implementation. The model proposed by [14] is based on 16 vector products. Thus, the entire DCT is a collection of 16 tasks, where each task is a vector product as presented in Figure 5.

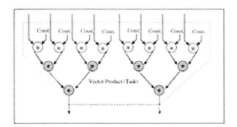

Fig. 5. Vector products

There are two kinds of tasks in the task graph.'' T1'' and ''T2'', whose structure is similar to vector product, but whose bit widths differ. Table 1 gives the characteristic of 4x4 DCT, 16x16 DCT task graphs.

Table 1. Benchmark characteristics

DFGs	Nodes	Edges	Area (CLBs)
DCT 4X4	224	256	8045
DCT 16X16	1929	2304	13919

The table 2 gives the different solutions provided by the list scheduling, the initial network flow technique, the enhance network flow and the proposed algorithm. Firstly, our algorithm has always the lowest number of partitions. In fact, as configuration time of currently dynamically reconfigurable hardware is too large. Thus, the configuration overhead will be a problem because the configuration time mainly occupies the time required to switch a partition to another partition. Therefore, since our algorithm has the lowest number of partitions, it has the lowest latency. Results show an average improvement of 20,5% in tem of design latency. Secondly, the table 2 shows that our partitioning algorithm minimizes communication overhead between partitions for dynamically reconfigurable hardware. The results show an average improvement of 28, 87%, 13, 18%, and 6, 31% for actual applications, compared with three conventional algorithms.

Table 2. Design results

Graph	4X4 DCT Task graph						
Algorithms	Proposed algorithm	List scheduling	Initial Network flow	improved Network flow	Improvement Versus List scheduling	Improvement Versus Initial Network flow	Improvement Versus improved Network flow
Number of Partitions	7	9	9	9			
T.C cost	570	744	634	589	23,38%	10,09%	3,22%
M.C cost	110	105	83	81			
Whole latency	5,770 ns + 7* $C_T \cong 7^* C_T$	4770 ns+ 9* $C_T \cong 9^* C_T$	4395n + 9* $C_T \cong 9^* C_T$	4570 n 9* $C_T \cong 9^* C_T$	22%	22%	22%
Run time	0,2 sec	0,12 sec	0,12 sec	0,12 sec			
Graph	16X16 DCT Task graph						
Number of Partitions	11	15	15	15			
T.C cost	2023	3106	2378	2193	34,86%	14,92%	7,75%
M.C cost	365	297	265	228			
Whole latency	8420 ns + 11* $C_T \cong 11^* C_T$	6610 ns+ 15* $C_T \cong 15^* C_T$	6420ns+15* $C_T \cong 15^* C_T$	7730+15* $C_T \cong 15^* C_T$	26%	26%	26%
Run time	2 sec	1,55 sec	1,55 sec	1,55 sec			
Average improvement in communication cost					28,87%	13, 18%	6, 31%
Average improvement in latency					20,5%	20,5%	20,5%

As conclusion our algorithm has a good trade-off between computation and communication. Hence, our algorithm can be qualified to be a good temporal partitioning candidate. In fact, an optimal partitioning algorithm needs to balance computation required for each partition and reduce communication required between partitions so that mapped applications can be executed faster on dynamically reconfigurable hardware.

6   Conclusion

In this paper, we have proposed a new partitioning algorithm. It based on mathematics formulations. Moreover, the proposed algorithm takes few Central Processing Unit (CPU) time. This algorithm optimizes communication cost between partitions design and the reconfiguration overhead. In addition, to show our algorithm effectiveness, the algorithm is experimented on benchmark circuits such as DCT task graphs. The studied evaluation cases show that the proposed algorithm provides very significant results in terms communication cost and latency versus other well known algorithms used in the temporal partitioning field.

References

1. Bobda: Introduction to Reconfigurable Computing Architectures, Algorithms, and Applications. Springer Publishers, Heidelberg (2007)
2. Cardoso, J.M.P.: On Combining Temporal Partitioning and Sharing of Functional Units in Compilation for Reconfigurable Architectures. IEEE Trans. Computers 52(10) (2003)
3. Jiang, Y.-C., Lai, Y.-T.: Temporal partitioning data flow graphs for dynamically reconfigurable computing. IEEE Transactions on Very Large Scale Integration (VLSI) Systems 15(12) (December 2007)
4. Liu, H., Wong, D.F.: Network flow based circuit partitioning for time-multiplexed FPGAs. In: Proc. IEEE/ACM Int. Conf. Comput.- Aided Des., pp. 497–504 (1998)
5. Liu, H., Wong, D.F.: Network flow based multi-way partitioning with area and pin constraints. IEEE Trans. on Computer Aided Design of Integrated Circuits and Systems 17(1) (January 1998)
6. Mak, W.-K., Young, E.F.Y.: Temporal logic replication for dynamically reconfigurable FPGA partitioning. IEEE Trans. Computer-Aided Design 22(7), 952–959 (2003)
7. Jiang, Y.-C., Wang, J.-F.: Temporal Partitioning Data Flow Graphs for Dynamically Reconfigurable Computing. IEEE Trans. on Very Large Scale Integration Systems 15(12) (December 2007)
8. Ouni, B., Mtibaa, A., Bourennane, E.-B.: Scheduling Approach for Run Time Reconfigured Systems. International Journal of Computer Sciences and Engineering Systems 4 (2009)
9. Trimberger, S.: Scheduling designs into a time-multiplexed FPGA. In: Proc. ACM Int. Symp. Field Program, Gate Arrays, pp. 153–160 (1998)
10. Liu, H., Wong, D.F.: A graph theoretic algorithm for schedule compression in Time-Multiplexed FPGA partitioning. In: Pro. IEEE/ACM Int. Conf. CAD, November 7-11, pp. 400–405 (1999)
11. Biswal, P., Lee, J.R., Rao, S.: Eigenvalue bounds, spectral partitioning, and metrical deformations via flows. In: Proceedings of the 2008 49th Annual IEEE Symposium on Foundations of Computer Science, pp. 751–760 (2008)
12. Kaul, K., Vermuri, R.: Integrate Block Processing and Design Space Exploration in Temporal Partitioning for RTR Architecture. In: Rolim, J.D.P. (ed.) IPPS-WS 1999 and SPDP-WS 1999. LNCS, vol. 1586, pp. 606–615. Springer, Heidelberg (1999)

Formalised Symbolic Reasonings
for Music Applications

Somnuk Phon-Amnuaisuk[1] and Choo-Yee Ting[2]

[1] Music Informatics Research Group,
Universiti Tunku Abdul Rahman, Petaling Jaya, Malaysia
[2] Multimedia University, Cyberjaya, Malaysia
somnuk@utar.edu.my, cyting@mmu.edu.my

Abstract. Symbolic music computing has been around since early AI-music activities. Although interest in this area has declined in the past decades, recently, attempts to create a standard representation for music applications over the internet such as MusicXML and IEEE P1599 have revitalised interests in symbolic music computing. The ability to discuss music using traditional terms musicians would use in their conversation is useful. A knowledge base system that performs inferences in the same abstraction level as a human does would be able to display a clear and clean reasoning process to the human counterpart. This is very useful, particularly from the perspective of knowledge exploitation and knowledge maintenance. In this report, formalised symbolic reasoning of interval spellings and chord spellings are presented. We have shown a formal implementation of symbolic music reasoning using the Z notation. Unambiguous interval spellings and chord spellings are implemented.

Keywords: Symbolic music computing, Formal method, Interval spelling, Chord spelling.

1 Introduction

In order to benefit from the development of music theory over the past centuries, computer scientists should use the same musical properties in their inference process (in their computer programs). Performing inferences at the granularity of vocabulary used in music theory is known as *symbolic computing*. Symbolic computation is not a new idea, as the approach had once dominated the field of artificial intelligence in the 1970s.

Palisca [11] points out that music theory is concerned with the description of the structure of music. By the structure of music, Palisca means *melody, rhythm, counterpoint, harmony* and *form* which includs the consideration of *pitches, intervals, tonal systems, etc.* at a more fundamental level. How should these properties be represented in computers?

There is a wide range of music computing activities, ranging from sound synthesis, music editing tools, music analysis, etc. The common grain size of music knowledge representation is at pitch and time levels. Most works simplify

A. Abd Manaf et al. (Eds.): ICIEIS 2011, Part I, CCIS 251, pp. 453–465, 2011.

pitch representation using *midi note numbers* e.g., C4 is represented as 60. This is convenient since MIDI is a popular standard. However, due to the fact that MIDI has been designed as a communication protocol among digital music instruments, the representation is not ideal for many reasoning tasks. Representing pitch as midi note is, actually, ambiguous. Should the note number 63 be read as D♯4 or E♭4? In this paper, the basic inference processes of interval spellings and chord spellings are discussed. Interval and chord spellings are basic skills for a musician and may seem too trivial to be discussed. However, if music theory is to be exploited symbolically in the inference process, the knowledge representation must use the same vocabulary to facilitate music analysts in the analysis tasks. The following two intervals:, for examples, C4-E♭4 and C4-D♯4 must be spelt as *minor-third* and *augmented-second* respectively. Although E♭ and D♯ are of the same pitch on the piano, theoretically speaking, they are not the same note. The representation of an interval data type for reasoning using computers must distinguish them. Most implementation, however, would not be able to distinguish between them as, in both cases, the two pitches are equally 3 semitones apart on the piano.

To the best of our knowledge, this issue has not been documented and formally discussed. In this paper, we present a formal specification of an interval data type and define some useful operators applicable to pitch and chord data types (e.g., interval spelling, transposition, chord spelling, etc). The presentation is organised into the following sections: 1. Introduction; 2. Literature review; 3. Formal Specifications; and 4. Conclusion.

2   Literature Review

There are many discussions about music representation for computing using computers. Two important issues when formalising a representation are (i) the expressiveness of the representation and (ii) the reasoning efficiency that the representation could offer. In other words, the main concerns are for the expressiveness of the musical properties the representation signifies and how efficient these properties could be synthesised (exploited) to generate new knowledge. It is generally accepted that there is no perfect representation for computing using computers. The representation choice is always dependent on the applications [9]. From the literature, music representation has been experimented in two main streams: *symbolic* and *sub-symbolic* approaches. In this paper, the discussion focuses on the symbolic representation approach.

2.1   Representing Music Symbolically

Musical Instrument Digital Interface (MIDI) is one of the most successful representation paradigms for symbolic music. In MIDI, music is represented at the abstraction levels of instrument, pitch, time and some limited sets of performance instructions (e.g., dynamic and pitch bending). MIDI does not support any extension of those events. For example, MIDI does not facilitate a grouping of simultaneous notes into new data types such as *melody line, chord, etc.* However, this should not be viewed as a drawback of MIDI, rather a design choice of MIDI. That is, it is not the purpose of MIDI to facilitate those requirements.

Many researchers have investigated music representation in the 1980s. The development in this period has blossomed into various focused areas such as musical data input-output purposes (e.g., *DARMS, Common Music, MUSTRAN, SCORE, MusixTex*; see [15]); sound synthesis purposes (e.g., Max Mathews' *Music N* family, *GROOVE*, Buxton's *SSSP*) and automatic composition generating purposes (e.g. *MUSICOMP*, Koenig's *Project I, Project II*, Barry Truax's *POD*).

The development of symbolic music has undoubtedly benefited from the music industry. Commercial packages such as Cakewalk Sonar, Cubase, Finale, Sibelius, etc [1]. have contributed to the research in symbolic music representation. These packages have different internal representations although they appear to perform the same functions. The sharing of music across these packages are through standard MIDI. The popularity of the Internet has created a need for music-sharing over the internet. Recent MusicXML [7,14] and IEEE P1599 [1] are two of the standards that have attempted to provide a unified representation for symbolic music based on XML.

2.2   Basic Operations

Symbolic music representations have been investigated by many researchers [2,6,8,9,13,20,3,10] From the literature, there are some basic operations that have been developed by researches for symbolic computations. Examples of these operations are $add(X, Y)$ and $sub(X, Y)$ (refer to add and subtract operations, where X and Y are each of types *Pitch, Interval* or of types *Time* and *Duration*) [21].

Basic Types

$$\text{Degree} : \{\hat{1}, \hat{2}, \hat{3}, \hat{4}, \hat{5}, \hat{6}, \hat{7}\}$$
$$\text{Accidental} : \{\natural, \sharp, \flat, \times, \flat\flat\}$$
$$\text{Octave} : \{1..8\}$$
$$\text{Pitch} : \langle \text{Degree, Accidental, Octave} \rangle$$
$$\text{Interval} : \mathbb{N} \text{ (natural numbers)}$$
$$\text{Duration} : \mathbb{N}$$
$$\text{Time} : \mathbb{N}$$

Basic Operations Related to Time

Time dimension is the landmark of note events. Basic arithmetic on the time is an essential requirement.

---

[1] See http://www.cakewalk.com; www.steinberg.net; www.finalemusic.com; www.sebelius.com

$$add_{dd} : \text{Duration} \times \text{Duration} \to \text{Duration}$$
$$add_{td} : \text{Time} \times \text{Duration} \to \text{Time}$$
$$sub_{tt} : \text{Time} \times \text{Time} \to \text{Duration}$$
$$sub_{dd} : \text{Duration} \times \text{Duration} \to \text{Duration}$$

Basic Operation Related to Pitches

Pitch comparison is the basic operation of a pitch class, to compare the height between pitches (e.g., C4 is higher than C3). Basic comparisons are greater than; less than; equal to; greater than or equal to; less than or equal to.

$$eq_{pp} : \text{Pitch} \times \text{Pitch} \to \text{Boolean}$$
$$gt_{pp} : \text{Pitch} \times \text{Pitch} \to \text{Boolean}$$
$$sub_{pp} : \text{Pitch} \times \text{Pitch} \to \text{Interval}$$
$$sub_{pi} : \text{Pitch} \times \text{Interval} \mapsto \text{Pitch}$$
$$add_{pi} : \text{Pitch} \times \text{Interval} \mapsto \text{Pitch}$$

The above basic operations on pitch and time facilitate many useful inference procedures. Interval spelling and transposition are the two basic operations in which many other operations could be built from, such as, scale and chord constructions. However, by leaving the *interval* as a natural number, there is still ambiguity in the exact spelling of the interval. In this paper, we show a formal specification of the *interval* data type and their associated *operations* that would resolve the mentioned ambiguity.

3   Formal Specifications

In this section, the formal specifications for *interval spelling* and *chord spelling* operations are described. To avoid confusion when referring to musical symbols in our discussion, the symbols used here are described below.

- Pitch symbols: The middle C (on a piano) is named C4. C5 denotes a pitch an octave higher and C3 denotes a pitch an octave lower from the middle C. Accidentals are put in front of the octave numbers (e.g. C♯4, D♭4).
- Scale degrees: Each pitch in a major scale is represented as a number with a hat on top: $\hat{1}, \hat{2}, \hat{3}, \hat{4}, \hat{5}, \hat{6}, \hat{7}$. The representation of a minor scale is relative to its major scale. Hence, the harmonic minor scale has the following scale degrees: $\hat{1}, \hat{2}, \flat\hat{3}, \hat{4}, \hat{5}, \flat\hat{6}, \hat{7}$.

3.1   Interval Spellings

Here, interval spellings refer to the interval spellings in a conventional music theory fashion (e.g., perfect fifth, minor seventh, etc.). Please take note that the same technique could be used for other variations of interval spelling such as jazz music. The specification is described using the standard Z specifications.

Defined Data Types

Deg, IntQ and IntN are user-defined data types. They represent *scale degree, interval quality* and *interval name* respectively. Note that the surface shape of this representation is immaterial, as what they signify is the crux. The scale degree could be represented as ĉ, d̂, ê and so on. Here, 1̂, 2̂, 3̂ are chosen since they are supposed to be a normalised scale degree (the names are independent of the key signature).

> *Degree* ::= 1̂ | 2̂ | 3̂ | 4̂ | 5̂ | 6̂ | 7̂
> *IntQ*   ::= *major* | *minor* | *augmented* | *diminished*
> | *perfect*
> *IntN*   ::= *unison* | *second* | *third* | *fourth* | *fifth*
> | *sixth* | *seventh* | *octave*

Defined Relations

Two relations *degreeIntMap* (see Table 1) and *chromaticIntMap* (see Table 2) are defined. The *degreeIntMap* may be seen as a fact base providing the mappings between two scale degrees (from two pitches) to interval name

> i.e., (*Degree* × *Degree*) ↔ *IntN*

The *chromaticIntMap* on the other hand, provides the mappings from the interval in semitones and interval name to a correct interval spelling

> i.e., ($\mathbb{Z}$ × *IntN*) ↔ (*IntQ* × *IntN*).

Interval Name Spelling

Interval spelling is a fundamental operation. Other complex operations, such as transposition, figure-bass spelling and chord spelling, could be constructed from interval spellings. It should be pointed out that the exact spelling of an interval by name gives a more concise property rather than the spelling of an interval by the number of semitones.

The schema *SpellInterval$_{pp}$* below shows the spelling of the interval name from two given pitches. In the schema below, *var?* denotes an input variable, *var!* denotes an output variable, $\mathbb{P}$ denotes a power set operator, *dom* denotes *domain of* and *ran* denotes *range of*. The function *sub$_{pp}$*(*Pitch1, Pitch2*) returns the distance between two pitches measured in semitone. The infix operator ◁ in

> {(*d1?, d2?*)} ◁ *degreeIntMap*)

filters *degreeIntMap* by restricting the domain to only {(*d1?, d2?*)}.

Table 1. Relations *degreeIntMap* : (*Degree* × *Degree*) ↔ *IntN*

degreeIntMap : (*Degree* × *Degree*) ↔ *IntN*
degreeIntMap = {(1, 1) ↦ *unison*, (2, 2) ↦ *unison*, (3, 3) ↦ *unison*,   (4, 4) ↦ *unison*, (5, 5) ↦ *unison*, (6, 6) ↦ *unison*, (7, 7) ↦ *unison*,   (1, 2) ↦ *second*, (2, 3) ↦ *second*, (3, 4) ↦ *second*, (4, 5) ↦ *second*,   (5, 6) ↦ *second*, (6, 7) ↦ *second*, (7, 1) ↦ *second*, (1, 3) ↦ *third*,   (2, 4) ↦ *third*, (3, 5) ↦ *third*, (4, 6) ↦ *third*, (5, 7) ↦ *third*,   (6, 1) ↦ *third*, (7, 2) ↦ *third*, (1, 4) ↦ *fourth*, (2, 5) ↦ *fourth*,   (3, 6) ↦ *fourth*, (4, 7) ↦ *fourth*, (5, 1) ↦ *fourth*, (6, 2) ↦ *fourth*,   (7, 3) ↦ *fourth*, (1, 5) ↦ *fifth*, (2, 6) ↦ *fifth*, (3, 7) ↦ *fifth*,   (4, 1) ↦ *fifth*, (5, 2) ↦ *fifth*, (6, 3) ↦ *fifth*, (7, 4) ↦ *fifth*,   (1, 6) ↦ *sixth*, (2, 7) ↦ *sixth*, (3, 1) ↦ *sixth*, (4, 2) ↦ *sixth*,   (5, 3) ↦ *sixth*, (6, 4) ↦ *sixth*, (7, 5) ↦ *sixth*, (1, 7) ↦ *seventh*,   (2, 1) ↦ *seventh*, (3, 2) ↦ *seventh*, (4, 3) ↦ *seventh*, (5, 4) ↦ *seventh*,   (6, 5) ↦ *seventh*, (7, 6) ↦ *seventh*, (1, 1) ↦ *octave*, (2, 2) ↦ *octave*,   (3, 3) ↦ *octave*, (4, 4) ↦ *octave*, (5, 5) ↦ *octave*, (6, 6) ↦ *octave*,   (7, 7) ↦ *octave*}

Table 2. Relations *chromaticIntMap* : ($\mathbb{Z}$ × *IntN*) ↔ (*IntQ* × *IntN*)

chromaticIntMap : ($\mathbb{Z}$ × *IntN*) ↔ (*IntQ* × *IntN*)
chromaticIntMap = {   (−1, *unison*) ↦ (*diminished, unison*), (0, *unison*) ↦ (*perfect, unison*),   (1, *unison*) ↦ (*augmented, unison*), (0, *second*) ↦ (*diminished, second*),   (1, *second*) ↦ (*minor, second*), (2, *second*) ↦ (*major, second*),   (3, *second*) ↦ (*augmented, second*), (2, *third*) ↦ (*diminished, third*),   (3, *third*) ↦ (*minor, third*), (4, *third*) ↦ (*major, third*),   (5, *third*) ↦ (*augmented, third*), (4, *fourth*) ↦ (*diminished, fourth*),   (5, *fourth*) ↦ (*perfect, fourth*), (6, *fourth*) ↦ (*augmented, fourth*),   (6, *fifth*) ↦ (*diminished, fifth*), (7, *fifth*) ↦ (*perfect, fifth*),   (8, *fifth*) ↦ (*augmented, fifth*), (7, *sixth*) ↦ (*diminished, sixth*), ...   (8, *sixth*) ↦ (*minor, sixth*), (9, *sixth*) ↦ (*major, sixth*),   (10, *sixth*) ↦ (*augmented, sixth*), (9, *seventh*) ↦ (*diminished, seventh*),   (10, *seventh*) ↦ (*minor, seventh*), (11, *seventh*) ↦ (*major, seventh*),   (12, *seventh*) ↦ (*augmented, seventh*), (11, *octave*) ↦ (*diminished, octave*),   (12, *octave*) ↦ (*perfect, octave*), (13, *octave*) ↦ (*augmented, octave*),   (12, *second*) ↦ (*diminished, second*), (13, *second*) ↦ (*minor, second*),   (14, *second*) ↦ (*major, second*), (15, *second*) ↦ (*augmented, second*),   (14, *third*) ↦ (*diminished, third*), (15, *third*) ↦ (*minor, third*),   (16, *third*) ↦ (*major, third*), (17, *third*) ↦ (*augmented, third*),   (16, *fourth*) ↦ (*diminished, fourth*), ...}

SpellInterval$_{pp}$
―――――――――――――――――――――――――――

$d1?, d2? : Degree$
$a1?, o1?, a2?, o2? : \mathbb{N}$
$spelling! : (IntQ \times IntN)$
$semitones : \mathbb{Z}$
$temp : IntN$

―――――――――――――――――――――――――――

$semitone = sub_{pp}(\langle d1?, a1?, o1?\rangle, \langle d2?, a2?, o2?\rangle)$
$temp \in \mathrm{ran}(\{(d1?, d2?)\} \lhd degreeIntMap)$
$spelling! = \{(semitone, temp)\} \lhd chromaticIntMap$

―――――――――――――――――――――――――――

The above schema illustrates the way to obtain the exact spelling from two given pitches using symbolic computations. Other variations such as interval spellings from four-part writings, transposing pitch and key could be carried out without ambiguity in enharmonic readings. For example, the key transposition must maintain the correct pitch spelling in the new key e.g., F♯4 in the key of C major should read C♯5 (not D♭5) in the key of G major after the transposition up a perfect fifth from the key of C major.

$$SpellInterval_{pp} : \text{Pitch} \times \text{Pitch} \to \text{IntQ} \times \text{IntN}$$
$$SpellInterval_{satb} : \langle \text{S,A,T,B}\rangle \to \text{seq (IntQ} \times \text{IntN)}$$
$$transpose_{pi} : \text{Pitch} \times \text{IntQ} \times \text{IntN} \to \text{Pitch}$$
$$transpose_{ki} : \text{Key} \times \text{IntQ} \times \text{IntN} \to \text{Key}$$

3.2   Chord Spelling

In this section, we illustrate how to symbolically perform classical chord spellings. Again, although the example is given with a classical genre, the same principle can be applied to chord the spellings in jazz music and pop music. Examples of chord naming in classical theory are shown in Table 3 and Figure 1.

Fig. 1. Chord spellings in tonal music

Table 3. Chord-naming conventions in major and natural minor modes: the left most column shows the set of degree scales, the center shows the chord names and the right most column shows chord symbols.

Scale degree	Chord name	Symbol
Major mode		
$\{\hat{1}, \hat{3}, \hat{5}\}$	Tonic	I
$\{\hat{2}, \hat{4}, \hat{6}\}$	Supertonic	ii
$\{\hat{3}, \hat{5}, \hat{7}\}$	Mediant	iii
$\{\hat{4}, \hat{6}, \hat{1}\}$	Subdominant	IV
$\{\hat{5}, \hat{7}, \hat{2}\}$	Dominant	V
$\{\hat{6}, \hat{1}, \hat{3}\}$	Submediant	vi
$\{\hat{7}, \hat{2}, \hat{4}\}$	Leading	vii^o
$\{\hat{5}, \hat{7}, \hat{2}, \hat{4}\}$	Dominant seventh	V_7
Minor mode		
$\{\hat{1}, \flat\hat{3}, \hat{5}\}$	Tonic	i
$\{\hat{2}, \hat{4}, \flat\hat{6}\}$	Supertonic	ii^o
$\{\flat\hat{3}, \hat{5}, \flat 7\}$	Mediant	III
$\{\hat{4}, \flat\hat{6}, \hat{1}\}$	Subdominant	iv
$\{\hat{5}, \flat\hat{7}, \hat{2}\}$	Dominant	v
$\{\flat\hat{6}, \hat{1}, \hat{3}\}$	Submediant	VI
$\{\flat\hat{7}, \hat{2}, \hat{4}\}$	Leading	VII
$\{\hat{5}, \hat{7}, \hat{2}, \hat{4}\}$	Dominant seventh	V_7

The spelling of a chord is merely a name given to a set of musical properties which are usually described from a collection of pitches. Different chords are seen to carry different functions (in a functional harmony perspective, the chord built from the first note of the scale is always called *tonic*). There are many chord notation styles. Scan through some music theory textbooks and you will find various convention [5,12,17,19]. Here, we follow the chord-naming style using both upper case and lower case Roman Alphabets and numerical symbols as presented in [5]. In this style, the following properties could be unambiguously described: chord quality (major, minor, augmented, diminished, half-diminished, seventh); chord inversion (whether the chord is in the root position, the first inversion or the second inversion); added notes (extra added note such as 2, 4, 6), etc. For example, common perfect cadence progression patterns could be expressed as $I - V - I$ and $i - ii_b - V_7 - i$.

Defined Data Types

Let us demonstrate the chord spelling used in a four part writing task. In part writing, harmony (i.e., chord) describes a collection of pitches (which is a set), triads are sets of three pitch chords, and seventh chords are set of four pitch chords. Also, in this style, information about chord inversion, doubling and omission of pitches are useful. Although the chord naming convention using roman alphabets does not capture doubling and omissions, the information is maintained in the representation [2].

Here, *ChdN, ChdT, Inv, Dlb* are users' defined data types. They represent *chord name, chord type, inversion type* and *doubling* respectively.

$$
\begin{aligned}
ChdN &::= tonic \mid supertonic \mid mediant \mid subdominant \\
&\quad \mid dominant \mid submediant \mid leading \\
ChdT &::= major \mid minor \mid augmented \mid diminished \mid seventh \\
Inv &::= rootPosition \mid 1^{st}Inversion \mid 2^{nd}Inversion \\
Dlb &::= null \mid root \mid third \mid fifth \\
7^{th} &::= null \mid dimished7^{th} \mid minor7^{th} \mid major7^{th}
\end{aligned}
$$

Defined Relations

Relations *chordNameMap* and *chordTypeMap* are defined below. The *chordNameMap* relation is the mapping between normalised scale degrees to functional names of chords. The *chordTypeMap* relation is the mapping between a set of $(IntQ \times IntN)$ to a sequence of $ChdT \times Inv \times Dlb \times 7^{th}$. In the example below, due to limited space, only examples of mappings of all possible chords in root position are presented for the *chordTypeMap* relation (see Table 4).

Chord Spellings

The schema *SpellChord*$_{satb}$ below takes a sequence of four pitches $\langle soprano, alto, tenor, bass \rangle$. The chord spelling is obtained by retrieving a name from the *chordNameMap* relation and other details from the *chordTypeMap*

SpellChord$_{satb}$

$fourPart?$: seq *Pitch*
$root$: *Degree*
$name$: *ChdN*
$seqInterval$: seq$(IntQ \times IntN)$
$spelling!$: $(ChdN \times ChdT \times Inv \times Dlb \times 7^{th})$

$seqInterval = SpellInterval_{satb}(fourPart?)$
$root = getRoot(seqInterval, fourPart?)$
$name = \{root\} \lhd chordNameMap$
$type = seqInterval \lhd chordTypeMap$
$spelling! = \bigcup\{name, type\}$

3.3 Bridging the Gap

Upon examining any standard music theory book, one would see many jargons which are the actual terms musician uses in describing music. Actually, those are just subsets of what are actually used apart from non-standard terms such as *fat sound, muddy sound*, etc. Figure 2 illustrates various music concepts that are hierarchically constructed from basic building blocks of pitch and time.

---
[2] In this paper, pitch omission is not included in the example.

Table 4. The relation $chordNameMap$: $Degree \leftrightarrow ChdN$ and the relation $chordTypeMap$: $seq(IntQ \times IntN) \leftrightarrow (ChdT \times Inv \times Dlb \times 7^{th})$

$chordNameMap$: $Degree \leftrightarrow ChdN$

$chordNamneMap = \{\hat{1} \mapsto tonic, \hat{2} \mapsto supertonic,$
$\hat{3} \mapsto mediant, \hat{4} \mapsto subdominant, \hat{5} \mapsto dominant,$
$\hat{6} \mapsto submediant, \hat{7} \mapsto leading\}$

$chordTypeMap$: $seq(IntQ \times IntN) \leftrightarrow$
$(ChdT \times Inv \times Dlb \times 7^{th})$

$chordMap = \{$
$\langle(major, third), (perfect, fifth), (perfect, octave)\rangle$
$\mapsto (major, rootPosition, root, null),$
$\langle(major, third), (perfect, fifth), (perfect, fifth)\rangle$
$\mapsto (major, rootPosition, fifth, null),$
$\langle(major, third), (major, third), (perfect, fifth)\rangle$
$\mapsto (major, rootPosition, third, null),$
$\langle(major, third), (augmented, fifth), (perfect, octave)\rangle$
$\mapsto (augmented, rootPosition, root, null),$
$\langle(major, third), (augmented, fifth), (augmented, fifth)\rangle$
$\mapsto (augmented, rootPosition, fifth, null),$
$\langle(major, third), (major, third), (augmented, fifth)\rangle$
$\mapsto (augmented, rootPosition, third, null),$
$\langle(minor, third), (perfect, fifth), (perfect, octave)\rangle$
$\mapsto (minor, rootPosition, root, null),$
$\langle(minor, third), (perfect, fifth), (perfect, fifth)\rangle$
$\mapsto (minor, rootPosition, fifth, null),$
$\langle(minor, third), (minor, third), (perfect, fifth)\rangle$
$\mapsto (minor, rootPosition, third, null),$
....
$\langle(minor, third), (diminished, fifth), (perfect, octave)\rangle$
$\mapsto (diminished, rootPosition, root, null),$
$\langle(minor, third), (diminished, fifth), (diminished, fifth)\rangle$
$\mapsto (diminished, rootPosition, fifth, null),$
$\langle(minor, third), (minor, third), (diminished, fifth)\rangle$
$\mapsto (diminished, rootPosition, third, null),$
....
$\langle(minor, third), (minor, sixth), (minor, sixth)\rangle$
$\mapsto (major, 1^{st}\text{Inversion,root,null}),$
$\langle(minor, third), (minor, third), (minor, sixth)\rangle$
$\mapsto (major, 1^{st}\text{Inversion,fifth,null}),$
$\langle(major, third), (major, sixth), (perfect, octave)\rangle$
$\mapsto (major, 1^{st}\text{Inversion,third,null}),$
$\langle(major, third), (minor, sixth), (minor, sixth)\rangle$
$\mapsto (augmented, 1^{st}\text{Inversion,root,null}),$
$\langle(major, third), (major, third), (minor, sixth)\rangle$
$\mapsto (augmented, 1^{st}\text{Inversion,fifth,null}),$
$\langle(major, third), (minor, sixth), (perfect, octave)\rangle$
$\mapsto (augmented, 1^{st}\text{Inversion,third,null}),$
....
$\}$

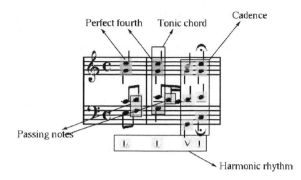

Fig. 2. Music concepts are hierarchically structured from basic building blocks of pitch and time. This construction could give rise to various concepts such as consonance and dissonance intevals, melodic and harmonic progressions, texture and formal structure, etc.

To create music applications that support sophisticated inference capabilities such as music education package that teaches and evaluates students' part-writing skills, resorting the symbolic inference in the style described in this paper is unavoidable. We believe this is an exciting area where many fruitful applications in music education, entertainment and edutainment are waiting for to be explored.

4   Conclusion

Attempts to standardise music representation using XML in MusicXML [14] and IEEE P1599 [1] have revitalised the interest in symbolic music computing in recent years. Symbolic computation is appealing since inner reasoning processes and knowledge contents could be examined. By abstracting knowledge contents to the level of terms common to music theorists, symbolic computations could emulate the reasoning process experts employ.

In the past, most of the implementations of symbolic music computing were ad hoc, partly from the fact that there was no standard for symbolic music representation and also from the fact that there was no established method for software development. As a result, most previous works were isolated and could not find mutual synergy. The developers could not expand the code and could not benefit from others' implementation. The cost of code maintenance and bug fix were also very expensive. To overcome those challenges, the formal specification methodology is adopted in this report. Here, two fundamental symbolic reasonings on *interval spellings* and *chord spelling* are formally illustrated and would serve as a good platform for other complex reasoning processes to extend from.

In this report, symbolic computing of two basic musicianship skills; interval spellings and chord spellings are illustrated using the Z notation [16]. In our approach, the interval and chord spellings could be unambiguously computed, allowing music to be discussed in the way it is done by music literates. Further musical knowledge could be built and extended from the proposed primitives e.g., voice leading theory, tonal theory, etc. We believe this approach could offer mutual synergy to industrial parties involved in music delivery, retrieval, and music education.

References

1. Baggi, D.L.: An IEEE Standard for Symbolic Music. IEEE Computer 38(11), 100–102 (2005)
2. Bel, B.: Symbolic and Sonic Representations of Sound-object Structures. In: Balaban, M., Ebcioglu, K., Laske, O. (eds.) Understanding Music with AI: Perspectives on Music Cognition, ch. 4, pp. 65–109. The AAAI Press/The MIT Press (1992)
3. Bellini, P., Nesi, P., Zoia, G.: Symbolic Music Representation in MPEG. IEEE Multimedia 12(4), 42–49 (2005)
4. Brown, G.J., Cooke, M.: Computational Auditory Scene Analysis. Computer Speech and Language 8, 297–336 (1994)
5. Butterworth, A.: Stylistic Harmony. Oxford University Press (1994)
6. Courtot, F.: Logical Representation and Induction for Computer Assisted Composition. In: Balaban, M., Ebcioglu, Laske, O. (eds.) Understanding Music with AI: Perspectives on Music Cognition, ch. 7, pp. 157–181. The AAAI Press/The MIT Press (1992)
7. Good, M.: MusicXML for Notations and Analysis. In: Hewlett, W.B., Selfridge-Field, E. (eds.) The Virtual Score Representation, Retrieval, Restoration, pp. 113–124. The MIT Press (2001)
8. Harris, M., Wiggins, G., Smaill, A.: Representing Music Symbolically. In: Camurri, A., Canepa, C. (eds.) Proceedings of the IX Colloquio di Informatica Musicale. Also Research Paper 562, Department of Artificial Intelligence, University of Edinburgh (1991)
9. Huron, D.: Design Principles in Computer-based Music Representation. In: Marsden, A., Pople, A. (eds.) Computer Representations and Model in Music, pp. 5–40. Academic Press (1992)
10. Knopke, I.: The Perlhumdrum and Perllilypond Toolkits for Symbolic Music Information Retrieval. In: Proceedings of the International Symposium on Music Information Retrieval, pp. 147–152 (2008)
11. Palisca, C.V.: Theory. In: Sadie, S. (ed.) The New Grove Dictionary of Music and Musicians, vol. 25, pp. 359–385. Macmillan Publishers Ltd., London (1980)
12. Piston, W.: Harmony: Revised and expanded by Mark Devoto. Victor Gollancz Ltd. (1982)
13. Pope, S.T.: The SmOKe Music Representation, Description Language, and Interchange Format. In: Proceedings of International Computer Music Conference (ICMC 1992), pp. 106–109. The Computer Music Association (1992)
14. Recordare: Music XML, http://www.recordare.com/ (last access 2011)
15. Selfridge-Field, E.: Beyond MIDI. The MIT Press (1997)
16. Sheppard, D.: An Introduction to Formal Specification with Z and VDM. McGraw-Hill (1995)
17. Schoenberg, A.: Theory of Harmony (translated by R. R. Carter). Faber and Faber Ltd. (1990)

18. Taupin, D.: MusixTex: Using Tex to Write Polyphonic or Instrumental Music. In: Proceedings of the 1993 TUGboat Annual Meeting, vol. 14(3) (1993), http://www.tug.org/TUGboat/Articles/tb14-3/tb40musictex.pdf
19. Taylor, E.: The AB guide to music theory. The Associated Board of the Royal Schools of Music (publishing) Ltd. (1989)
20. West, R., Howell, P., Cross, I.: Musical Structure and Knowledge Representation. In: Howell, P., West, R., Cross, I. (eds.) Representing Musical Structure, ch. 1, pp. 1–30. Academic Press (1991)
21. Wiggins, G., Harris, M., Smaill, A.: Representing Music for Analysis and Composition. In: Proceedings of the International Joint Conferences on Artificial Intelligence, IJCAI 1989 (1989)

Algorithm for Solving the Model of Multistage Hollow Fiber Membrane Systems and the Identification of Model Parameters

Zhanat Umarova

South-Kazakhstan State University, Shymkent, Kazakhstan
Zhanat-u@mail.ru

Abstract. The given work presents numerical algorithm to solve the model of multi-level hollow-fiber membrane systems and suggests finite-difference scheme for three configurations of the flow: co-flow, counter flow and cross flow. The suggested algorithm is easily programmed and efficient. Identification of parameters of mathematical model of gas separation process has been carried out as well. It is necessary to compare mathematical description with real technological process. With this aim quantative information in the form of model parameters has been introduced and block-scheme of parameters identification of mathematical model of gas separation has been composed.

Keywords: Algorithm, membrane technologies, mathematical model, permeator, flow configuration, counter flow configuration, cross flow configuration.

1 Introduction

In these latter days interest to the development of new constructions of bioenergy installation for processing organic wastes in the terms of anaerobic fermentation to produce gaseous fuel and organic fertilizers in the process of methane fermentation is growing.

Membrane technologies, having a range of advantages allow to extract the fixed component from gas mixture qualitatively, using membrane absorption in counterflow mode between liquid and gas phases of separated membranes in membrane contactor. Furthermore membrane methods are mainly cheaper and ecologically pure.

At present membrane separation is one of the most intensively developing branches of gas separation technology.

While choosing separation process to solve issues, it is necessary to take into account the impact of possible factors, employment of which is available not in all particular situations, therefore one cannot disregard specific criteria, the substantiated choice of the process should meet. It is also necessary to remember two general criteria, used for all separation processes: separation should be realized technically and economically [1].

The technical criterion should support achieving of two main requirements, necessary degree of extraction and quality (purity) of the product. To implement the given requirements sometimes combination of several separation processes is necessary.

A. Abd Manaf et al. (Eds.): ICIEIS 2011, Part I, CCIS 251, pp. 466–476, 2011.

Economic efficiency of the process depends on the cost of the extracted products, which in its turn is defined by the raw material composition.   Decrease of initial concentration of the target product in general leads to net product cost increase.

2 Statement of the Problem

Let's define flow component, passing through the membrane. Gas molecules are sorbed in the membrane, then diffused in it, then adsorbed with liquid on the other side. Or on the contrary. In general view the gradient of chemical potential acts as driving force.

We use Fick's law realization assumption for membrane:

$$j_{im}(x) = \frac{D_{im}}{h_m}(c_{im1}(x) - c_{im2}(x)) \tag{1}$$

Here: j_{im} - flow of i-component from gas phase through membrane, mole/m^3; D_{im} - diffusion coefficient of i-component in the membrane, from assumption they are constant, m^2/s; h_m - membrane thickness, m; c_{im1}, c_{im2} - boundary concentration of the component in the membrane near gas and liquid phase correspondingly, mole/m^3.

The given article presents numerical method, which is possible for modeling multi-component multi-level membrane systems of hollow fiber. The given algorithm is iterative approximation, based on finite differential Gauss-Seidel method and can calculate penetration in co-flow, cross flow and counter-flow mode. The algorithm is easily programmed, efficient and can cope with complementary nonlinearity, such as variable permeability or pressure fall. Computational cost and convergence are defined for several stages of multi level issues of penetration. Results, received by modeling, have been checked experimentally for gas mixture similar to biogas, consisting of methane, carbon dioxide and oxygen.

To begin with, it is necessary to define conservation of gas component   in one-dimensional delivery port and penetration channel. Here to calculate gas amount standard temperature and pressure are employed. To conserve each component, they are considered separately. In assumption that partial volume of gas component i is changed because of its local transmembrane flow, conservation equation can be expressed as following:

$$\frac{dF_i}{dl} = -Q_i' \tag{2}$$

$$\frac{dP_i}{dl} = Q_i' \tag{3}$$

where F and P – flows of volume in the delivery port and penetration channel correspondingly, l - axial coordinate of the membrane and Q – local transmembrane flow. In hollow fiber of gas permeator, local transmembrane flow is usually modeled solving solution-diffusion equation

$$Q_i' = Q_i'' s\pi d = \Pi_i(x_i p_F - y_i p_P)s\pi d \qquad (4)$$

Here s – general quantity of fibers, d – diameter of effective layer, Π - is permeability, p - absolute pressure, x and y are volume particles in delivery port and penetration channel correspondingly. As perfect gas is being considered, volume particles are equal molar fractions. Permeability depends on the range of process parameters, such as temperature, pressure or flow adherence with other gas components and can be included into presented model, if required correlations are known:

$$\Pi_i = f(T, p_F, p_P, x_0, x_1, ..., y_0, y_1, ...) \qquad (5)$$

Conservation equations for i component, defined by equations (2) and (3) – together with conservation equations component of another gas is expressed with the help of the following expressions:

$$x_i = \frac{F_i}{\sum_{i=1}^{k} F_i} \qquad (6)$$

$$y_i = \frac{P_i}{\sum_{i=1}^{k} P_i} \qquad (7)$$

In the configuration of cross flow there is no permeated flow along the membrane and concentration in permeated channel is set as:

$$y_i = \frac{Q_i}{\sum_{i=1}^{k} Q_i} \qquad (8)$$

The considered system consists of 2κ non-linear differential equations, where k – number of gas components. The system can also contain complementary equations, influencing on modeling result and changing process parameters. For example, fall of high pressure in laminar flow along the distance (in the direction) l can be expressed

$$\Delta p_F = \frac{\sum_{i=1}^{k} F_i \eta 128 \Delta l p_{STP} T_F}{s\pi D^4 p_F T_{STP}} \qquad (9)$$

where η - dynamic viscosity of gas, and D - inner diameter of fiber. The given equation presents Hagen-Poiseuille law in the form, appropriate for systems, using volume flows. Dynamic viscosity influences on pressure fall and, as a result, permeability of gas components also depends on concentration of gas components. This introduces complementary factor of adhesion, taken into account in the given numerical experiment.

Equations (2) and (3) can be interpreted as one-dimensional Poisson equations which are differential equations in partial derivatives of elliptic type. Solution of differential equations in partial derivatives of elliptic type can be checked by various methods. The method, suggested in this work, has been received from iterative finite-difference Gausse-Seidel method. Finite-difference discretization for three configurations of flow: co-flow, cross flow and counter-flow for unique i component and field, consisting of discrete points, is shown in Fig.1.

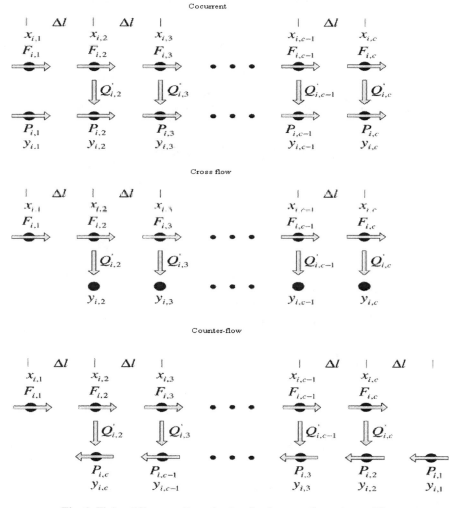

Fig. 1. Finite-difference discretization for three configurations of flow

Points with index $j = 1$ are employed to stipulate boundary conditions of Dirichlet type and do not participate in transmembrane flow [2].

Gradients of volume flow are approximated, employing the first order of finite-difference scheme, directed contrary to the flow:

$$\frac{dF_{ij}}{dl} = \frac{F_{ij} - F_{ij-1}}{\Delta l} \tag{10}$$

$$\frac{dP_{ij}}{dl} = \frac{P_{ij} - P_{ij-1}}{\Delta l} \tag{11}$$

Consequently, equations (1) and (2) can be transformed to calculate evaluation of volume momentary discharge for definite gas components i in discrete point j.

Corresponding equations for co-flow

$$F_{ij}^{n+1/2} = F_{ij-1}^{n} - \Delta l \Pi_{ij}^{n} (x_{ij}^{n} p_{Fj}^{n} - y_{ij}^{n} p_{Pj}^{n}) s \pi d \tag{12}$$

$$P_{ij}^{n+1/2} = P_{ij-1}^{n} + \Delta l \Pi_{ij}^{n} (x_{ij}^{n} p_{Fj}^{n} - y_{ij}^{n} p_{Pj}^{n}) s \pi d \tag{13}$$

Equilibrium of volume flow through membrane will be expressed in the following way:

$$Q_{ij}^{n+1/2} = \Delta l \Pi_{ij}^{n} (x_{ij}^{n} p_{Fj}^{n} - y_{ij}^{n} p_{Pj}^{n}) s \pi d \tag{14}$$

As for counter flow scheme equations:

$$F_{ij}^{n+1/2} = F_{ij-1}^{n} - \Delta l \Pi_{ij}^{n} (x_{ij}^{n} p_{Fj}^{n} - y_{i,c-j+2}^{n} p_{Pc-j+2}^{n}) s \pi d \tag{15}$$

$$P_{ij}^{n+1/2} = P_{ij-1}^{n} + \Delta l \Pi_{ij}^{n} (x_{i,c-j+2}^{n} p_{Pc-j+2}^{n} - y_{ij}^{n} p_{Pj}^{n}) s \pi d \tag{16}$$

In these equations x new constant n has been introduced. Constant n stands for the condition of variables before iterative step, n +(1/2) stands for variable on the half step and (n+ 1), stands for variables after iteration finishes. Full step of iteration for delivery port and penetration channel is expressed by the following extrapolations

$$F_{ij}^{n+1} = F_{ij-1}^{n} + \omega(F_{ij}^{n+1/2} - F_{ij}^{n}) \tag{17}$$

$$P_{ij}^{n+1} = P_{ij-1}^{n} + \omega(P_{ij}^{n+1/2} - P_{ij}^{n}) \tag{18}$$

and in penetrating channel for cross flow configuration

$$Q_{ij}^{n+1} = Q_{ij-1}^{n} + \omega(Q_{ij}^{n+1/2} - Q_{ij}^{n}) \tag{19}$$

where ω – relaxation coefficient.

Solution process is relatively simple. Variables of the flow have been improved in such a way that they can be employed in calculations in following points. Frequent repeating is always carried out in the direction of flow, shown in Fig.1. Flow delivery has been calculated from left to right without regard to employed configuration. Permeated flow in co- current configuration has been calculated from left to right. Permeated flow in configuration of cross flow can be calculated in both directions. After extrapolation flows of volume for each discrete point have been finished, concentrations have been calculated for following iterative step, using equations (6) and (7) or (8). In this relation, other dependent variables as pressure or variable, permeability have been calculated. For example, pressure profile in delivery port can be received from correlation

$$p_{Fj} = p_{Fj-1} - \frac{\sum_{i=1}^{k} F_{ij} \eta_j 128 \Delta l p_{STP} T_{Fj-1}}{s \pi D^4 T_{STP} p_{Fj-1}} \tag{20}$$

The program continues iteration unless condition for each gas component and each discrete point is realized:

$$\left| F_{ij}^{n+1/2} - F_{ij}^{n} \right| \le \delta \tag{21}$$

where δ – convergence criteria. In above mentioned equation, at the beginning iterative step of partial momentary discharge of delivery has been calculated from partial flow of delivery volume, calculated with half step. If for each discrete point absolute evaluation of this difference is less δ or equal δ, the solution is assumed to be convergent. Evaluation δ should be chosen with care; extremely high evaluation will lead to spurious results, extremely low evaluation will lead to very high number of iteration. As a rule, we choose δ in such a way as it is, at least, below thousand of the smallest component flow of volume in the model, that is if the least flow of delivery volume gas component were $1 \text{m}^3/\text{s}$, rational evaluation for δ could be $0.001 \text{m}^3/\text{s}$ [3].

The first iterative step in the solution procedure requires some primary values of gas concentrations and for delivery and penetrating side of the membrane. They can be set for each of discrete points with the help of approximate original assumptions:

$$x_{ij} = x_{i1} \tag{22}$$

$$y_{ij} = \frac{x_{ij} \Pi_i}{\sum_{i=1}^{k} x_{ij} \Pi_i} \tag{23}$$

If pressure fall calculation is required, evaluation clarification for pressure can be provided for each of discrete points. To clarify evaluation it is sufficient to distribute delivery and penetration of pressure along membrane:

$$p_{Fj} = p_{F1} \tag{24}$$

$$p_{Pj} = p_{P1} \tag{25}$$

Solution procedure is illustrated in Fig.2.

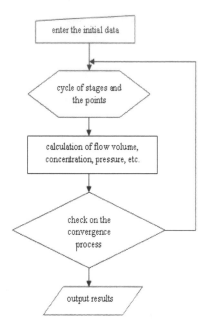

Fig. 2. Solution procedure

Equations, shown above, provide simplified interpretation of the flow in gas permeator. First of all, let's assume that flow in permeator is exactly one-dimensional. Secondly, let's assume that there is no diffusion or dispersion of gas components in direction, parallel to the membrane. Furthermore, we disregard polar concentration at right angle to the membrane. In some theoretical researches it is assumed that there are definite evaluations of selectivity and permeability, higher of which concentration polarization phenomenon in hollow fibers becomes essential.   As a rule, concentration polarization should be taken into account for membranes with high permeability and for separation of gas vapour mixtures.   For example, stationary layer, combined with mass transfer coefficients can be used to model concentration polarization effects for each of discrete points in the presented model. In this case, high-selective system should be researched experimentally to check results defined by the model.

As a rule, behaviour of gas penetration in real processes inflects from simple solution of propagation equations [4]. The given algorithm is able to calculate penetration processes, where permeability is a function of other parameters of the process.

In the given algorithm, reasonable choice of parameters of both solving programs: relaxation coefficient ω and convergence criteria (feature) δ are necessary for successful solution of equations. Mainly, equations system should be low disperse that is ω should be less than 1. Higher evaluations, generally, lead to lower computing time. However, fuzzy systems, such as rigid systems or systems with variable permeability require evaluation decrease and great number of repeating to approximate to converging solution. For simple systems with some components and average selectivity, relaxation factors – usually between 0.4 and 0.9. For systems with high rigidity, caused by selectivity, quick seeping, components can make a solution inconstant. For such issues, restriction of relaxation factor down to 0.05 is necessary to get converging solution.

Let's notice that convergence is achieved during several seconds for simple accounting units of the system. In general, counter flow configuration is needed in lower factors of relaxation and is more expensive in computational relation than co-flow configuration. Calculation of rapidly penetrating components requires further restriction of relaxation factor and longer computing time. For instance, to achieve convergence about 6-7 minutes are necessary for rigid system with two counter flow states and recycling of dissolved substance with gas components.

In regard to multi-level systems, it has been noticed that computing time in significant degree is under the influence of processing flows, more precisely than the systems with relatively great processing flows, which converge slowly. The algorithm in the state is calculated easily identical with complicated systems within reasonable time. Calculation requires some efforts, as solution is in significant degree under the influence of a number of factors, such as boundary conditions and system state. Computing time can be minimized by relaxation factor optimization.

3 Results

To compare mathematical description with real technological process it is necessary to introduce numerical information into the model in the form of model parameters, responding to the given process. The procedure of defining unknown quantities, included into structural mathematical model bears a name of parameters identification [5].

Solution of inverse problem of parametric identification using complementary conditions as experimental data defines unknown parameters, included into mathematical description.

To determine unknown equations coefficients of mathematical description of the process of adsorptive fractionation of gas mixture let's consider inverse problem.

Let's assume inverse problem of parametric identification in operator form. Let us assume that σ – sought quantity, considered as an element of some normalized space Y; y – process state variable, satisfying condition $y \in Y$, and which is function from $x=[x_1,...,x_n]^T \in \Omega$, ($\Omega$ – field of space variables). Consequently, mathematical model of the considered process in general can be shown by the correlation $y = \Lambda(x, \sigma)$. Λ –operator, which we fix, induced by accepted model of the process $\Lambda{:}Y{\rightarrow}Y$; f – known input quantities, considered as elements of normalized space F. Elements of normalized space are connected with process state variables by means of operator $B : f = By$.

The problem consists in finding such σ, leading disparity functional

$$J(\sigma) = \frac{1}{2}\left\| \Lambda\sigma - f \right\|_F^2 \tag{26}$$

to minimum, at exactly fixed input quantities $\Lambda = BY$ and f. At that as f values of process state variable are accepted in several points of the field Ω. These points can be either fixed or change their position with the passage of time.

Let's make a slip in speaking, that such method of solution of inverse problem of parametric identification cannot be employed directly due to the fact that the problem (5) is usually unstable (inverse operator Λ^{-1} is unrestrained) and instead of accurate data Λ and f in practice only some approximations to them Λ_h and f_g are known [3].

Problems of primary data can be inaccurate, as approximate quantitative description of known parameters and availability of random and systematic errors takes a place.   Errors take a place while measuring f. Also, transition to approximate primary data is due to the fact that for numerical solution (5) corresponding computational algorithm is built, where operator Λ is usually approximated by several finite-difference operator and function f is changed finite-dimensional analogues.

Taking into account the made remarks, identification problem can be traced to the definition $\{\Lambda_h, f_g\}$, in total of some approximation $\sigma_{h\delta}$, to the sought solution, which   at converging   errors in problem of operator and right part to zero would provide better approximation in some sense to exact solution of the problem (5). The process of parametric identification is schematically shown in Fig.1. Comparison of f_g and results of solving direct problem $\Lambda_h \sigma$ for fixed approximation to variate σ allows drawing a conclusion about correctness of «setting» of mathematical model under numerical values σ that is about quantative adequacy with physical process.

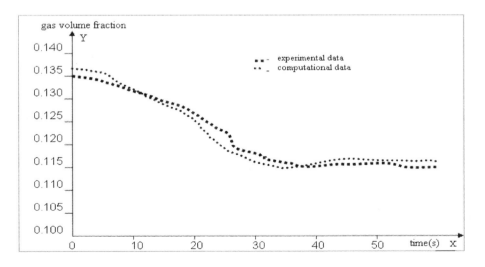

Fig. 3. Calculation of mathematical model accuracy

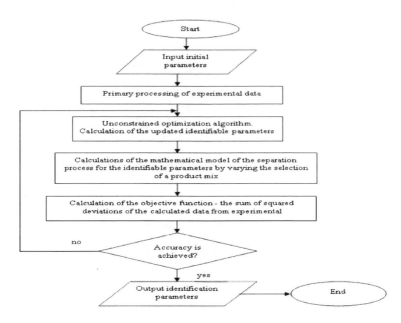

Fig. 4. Block-scheme of identification of mathematical model parameters of gas separation

4   Conclusions

The model proves very good agreement with the experimental results for single stage system. The nonlinearity of the flow in membrane module together with its dynamic response seems to be modeled correctly. The experimental and computational results can be actually found within the measurement error of the analyzer (2% of the measurement span). The generic model is able to simulate the dynamics of the gas permeation systems with multiple stages and recycles as well as for arbitrary number of gas components.

The model can be used for the design and scaling of the gas permeation systems since the model converges to static solution for the times approaching infinity. As applied to adsorption separation process of gas mixture computation model will contain a range of preliminary stages:

1) Formal characterization of experimental data.
2) Formal characterization of minimized criterion.
3) Identification of indefinite parameters.

The final stage of development of mathematical models is to test the adequacy of the experimental numerical data.

To evaluate accuracy of calculation data it is reasonable to use experimental data, differing from those which have been used on the stage of parametric identification [5].

References

1. Dytnersky, Y.I., Brykov, V.P., Kagramanov, G.G.: Membrane separation of gases, Moscow (2001) – Дытнерский, Ю.И., Брыков, В.П., Каграманов, Г.Г.: Мембранная сепарация газовых смесей, Москва (2001)
2. Baker, R.W.: Membranes for vapor/gas separation. Wiley (2001)
3. Nunes, S.P., Peinemann, K.-V.: Membrane Technology in the Chemical Industry. Wiley-VCH, Weinheim (2001)
4. Baker, R.W.: Membrane Technology and Applications. Wiley (2001)
5. Kafarov, V.V.: Methods of Cybernetics in Chemistry and Chemical Technology, Moscow (1988) – Кафаров, В.В.: Методы кибернетики в химии и химической технологии, Москва (1998)
6. Paul, D.R., Yampolskii, Y.: Polymeric Gas Separation Membranes. CRC Press, Boca Raton (1994)
7. Koros, W. J.: Model for permeation of mixed gases and vapors in glassy polymers. Journal of Polymer Science (2003)
8. Robeson, L.M.: Correlation of separation factor versus permeability for polymeric membranes. Journal of Membrane Science 62 (1991)
9. Baker, R.W.: Future directions of membrane gas separation technology. Industrial Engineering and Chemical Research 41 (2002)
10. Ekiner, O.M., Vassilatos, G.: Polyaramide hollow fibers for hydrogen/methane separation - spinning and properties. Journal of Membrane Science 53 (1990)
11. Nikolaev, N.I.: Diffusion in membranes, Moscow (1980) – Николаев, Н.И.: Диффузия в мембранах, Москва (1980)
12. Kumar, R.: Vacuum Swing Adsorbtion Process for Oxygen Production, A Historical Perspective. In: Separation Science and Technology, Calcutta (1996)
13. Kesting, R.E.: Syntetie Polimeric membranes. Mc. Craw-Hill, New York (1971)
14. Chalykh, A.E.: Diffusion in polymer systems, Moscow (1987) – Чалых, А.Е.: Диффузия в полимерных системах, Москва (1987)

Synthetic Experiment in Evaluating the Usability Factor of the Requirement Change Propagation Process Model

Noraini Ibrahim[1], W.M. Nasir W. Kadir[2], Shahliza Abd Halim[3],
Safaai Deris[4], and Maslina A. Aziz[5]

[1-4] Faculty of Computer Science and Information System, Universiti Teknologi Malaysia
Skudai 81310, Johor, Malaysia
[5] Faculty of Computer and Mathematical Sciences, Universiti Teknologi MARA
Shah Alam 40450 Selangor, Malaysia
{noraini_ib,wnasir,shahliza,safaai}@utm.my,
maslina@tmsk.uitm.edu.my

Abstract. The proposed requirement change propagation *(ReChaP)* approach promotes significant supports in simplifying the tedious tasks of requirement change propagation to other software artefacts during software evolution. One of the ReChaP's pillars is the process model, which provides systematic guidelines to simplify the phenomenally time consuming and expensive efforts of the requirement change propagation process. This paper specifically reports on the preliminary results and the observation analysis for the conducted synthetic experiment in academic settings. The experiment's goal is to evaluate the usability quality factor of the process model in terms of five main criteria; efficiency, effectiveness, learnability, satisfaction and usefulness. Our initial findings observe that the proposed ReChaP process model is soundly demonstrated as sufficiently usable, practical enough, and meantime has ideally achieved reasonable percentages for the five comprehensive criteria of the measured usability factor.

Keywords: Synthetic Environment Experiment, Usability Quality Factor, Requirement Change Propagation, Process Model.

1 Introduction

As software evolves, the changing software artefacts will cause the implementation process to be changed and evolved accordingly as well. For that reason, a respective software engineer needs to be able to determine the transformation and thus adjusts the processes to fit his desired aims. The software evolution is based on time-space constraints, where it depends on certain situations such as adding, deleting, and modifying activities that have happened. As a result, the process framework for evolvable software is complex and must be adaptable to represent the situational-problems. Thus, it is very essential to define not only processes that will work, yet it is more important to have a simplified but very specific process that can be conveniently customised to meet the target of all individuals in the organisation team or project.

A. Abd Manaf et al. (Eds.): ICIEIS 2011, Part I, CCIS 251, pp. 477–491, 2011.
© Springer-Verlag Berlin Heidelberg 2011

Apart from that, defining the process model will provide a framework that can be further studied for any enhancement after certain assessment to improve the requirement change performance so as to support software evolution[6]. The clear guidance is very important in order to bring clearer pictures towards the realistic change propagation phenomenon in software evolution. Essentially, the useful process models can lead to a better understanding of the realistic process during requirement change propagation, resulting from abstract theory to real practices. Simply put, the processes could provide easily well-understood guidelines for software engineers to assist them in propagating changes from requirement into software, especially during the development of evolvable software.

In this study, the process models are adopted using a well-accepted Software Process Engineering Meta-Model (SPEM) v2.0 by OMG [2]. The proposed process models provide the detail implementation specification for the ReChaP approach, which represent the specific activities and the details steps in performing the requirement change propagation process. Basically, the activities and steps are designed in detail, particularly from initial stage of requirement, analysis, design and evolution stage of software life-cycles. The defined processes capture the three main components namely activities, roles (actors) and work products (software artefacts) that are generally related in the development and evolution of a software system. The details on implementation specifications for each of the stages can be found from the previous study [3, 4].

The remainder of this paper is organised as follows. Section 2 elaborates on the contextual background for the synthetic environment experiment. Next, Section 3.1 briefly explains further on the metrics to be measured; the usability quality factor and five main criteria; efficiency, effectiveness, learnability, satisfaction and usefulness. Accordingly, Section 3 presents the experimental design details. Section 3.1 describes on the experiment procedures, followed by brief information regarding the environment settings in the laboratory in Section 3.2. In the following Section3.3, discussion will be made on the experimental subjects and their related demographic data. In Section 4, the descriptive preliminary results and the statistical analysis results are presented. Finally, Section 5 concludes the whole findings of this paper and presents the future plans for the next steps in this research.

2   Synthetic Environment Experiment Context

A synthetic experimentation is a classical scientific method that can be used to evaluate empirical studies in the software engineering research and practices [8, 9]. According to [11], synthetic experiment is defined as:

> *"A replicated experiment is conducted in a smaller artificial environment, but in a realistic settings compared to the real projects."*

The basic purpose of synthetic experiment is to analyse any influences towards observation of the result by replicating or reproducing the simpler version in the laboratory [10]. Additionally, the related information regarding the procedures and experiment methods in designing the experiment has been discussed in details previously [5]. In the context of this study, the synthetic experiment is applied as an explanatory research method to look intensively the generic scientific foundation for the process model in the proposed ReChaP approach. Thus, this method is also expected to better understand the real implementation and causal relationships on the phenomenon of requirement change propagation process. In specific, the experiment results interpretation will be made towards the exploratory and explanatory ˜studies by highlighting the experimentation context and design procedures, the quantitative analysis results, the reflection on the measured five criteria that are discussed in the subsequent section 2.1.

2.1 Usability Quality Factor and Criteria

In specific, *"usability"* quality factor is defined as [1]:

"The capability of the software to be understood, learned, used and liked by the user, when used under specified conditions"

Five main criteria are chosen to analyse the usability factor, as illustrated and briefly explained in Fig.1. These criteria are chosen based on Quality in Use Integrated Measurement (QUIM) enhancement model corresponding from several different standards (e.g., ISO 9241, ISO/IEC 9126, IEEE Std.610.12) for usability measurement [7].

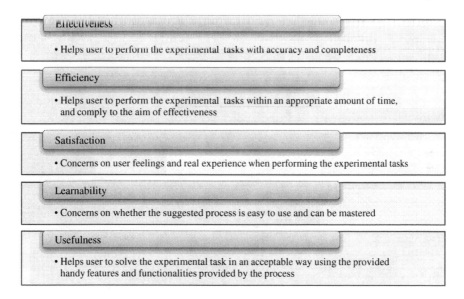

Fig. 1. The five criteria for usability factor

3 Demographic Data

Twenty-three subjects have participated in the experiment. All subjects were undergraduate students enrolled for Requirement Engineering coursework for 2010/2011 session and post-graduate students majoring in SE. Subjects were carefully selected and expected to have minimal understanding on SE theories and principles.

Additionally, subjects must be exposed to the object oriented development techniques (i.e. Unified Modelling Language-UML). This requirement is very important to keep abreast their motivation to participate in the experiment until its completion.

Table 1. Demographic data on subjects' background and experience

Characteristics	Range	Frequency (N=23)	Frequency Distribution
Experience Background			
1. Previous job.	Programmer/ Software Developer	4	17.4%
	Software Engineer /System Analyst	1	4.3%
	Project Leader / Project manager	0	0.0%
	Configuration engineer	0	0.0%
	Quality engineer	0	0.0%
	Other	19	82.6%
2. Experience in Software Engineering Practice.	None	2	8.7%
	Little	13	56.5%
	Average	6	26.1%
	Substantial	2	8.7%
	Professional	0	0.0%
3. Experience in software development.	None	0	0
	Little	9	39.1%
	Average	11	47.8%
	Substantial	3	13.0%
	Professional	0	0
4. Experience in Object-Oriented design using UML modelling.	None	0	0
	Little	4	17.4%
	Average	15	65.2%
	Substantial	4	17.4%
	Professional	0	0.0%
5. Experience in software change management/ maintenance/ evolution.	None	3	13.0%
	Little	14	60.9%
	Average	6	6.0%
	Substantial	0	0.0%
	Professional	0	0.0%
6. Experience in performing requirement change propagation.	None	8	34.8%
	Little	12	52.2%
	Average	2	8.7%
	Substantial	1	4.3%
	Professional	0	0.0%
7. Related software artefacts type involved in performing change request.	Source code	16	69.6%
	Design	16	69.6%
	Requirements	15	65.2%
	Test cases	9	39.1%
	Documentation	13	56.5%
	Other	0	0.0%
8. Participant motivation	Not	0	0.0%
	Poorly	0	0.0%
	Fairly	9	39.1%
	Well	10	43.5%
	Highly	4	17.4%

Table 1. (*continued*)

9. Participation reasons	To gain practical experience in user testing of the SE research project	22	95.7%
	To apply related SE theories and knowledge from coursework	16	69.6%
	Others	0	0.0%
10. Understanding Library System case study application; its environment and functionality.	Not	0	0.0%
	Poorly	1	4.3%
	Fairly	15	65.2%
	Well	7	30.4%
	Highly	0	0.0%

Tab.1 shows the summary of demographic data on subjects' background and experience. The related demographic data on the experimental subjects in terms of their working background, previous experience in SE practices, motivation level in participations, as well as their exposure knowledge and familiarity with the Library System case study, were recorded and further analysed.

In overall, from 23 subjects, only 1 person was a software engineer or system analyst, 4 subjects have been worked as programmer or software developer, and 19 subjects are recorded as others job (industrial trainer and academicians). It can be seen that, almost 82.6% subjects have others job, which is the highest range of subjects' working background, followed by 17.4% of programmer/software developer and finally 4.3% of software engineer/system analyst. For this characteristic of previous job, subjects are allowed to select more than one choice, therefore, the total distribution may add up to more than 100%. The working experience information reflected to the findings on their experiences in SE practises as shown in no.2 characteristics in Tab.1.

It is observed that there is no subject or 0% have admitted that they have professional experience in SE practices in specific. The highest frequency distribution is 56.5% or 13 subjects chose little experience, followed by 26.1% or 6 subjects for average experience, and finally 8.7% or 2 subjects for both none and substantial experience. This information might due to the factor that more than 80% subjects are identified as full-time students that are not yet completing their studies currently.

However, in terms of software development characteristics, the observed findings shown that only 3 subjects disclosed themselves have a quite substantial experience, compared to other 11 subjects with average experience and 9 subjects have little experience in developing software. In contrast, there is no subjects admitted that they have either none or specific professional experience in software development projects. The highest percentage is 47.8% which represents the average experience range, followed by 39.1% for little experience range, then 13.0% for substantial experience range, finally 0% for both none and professional experience ranges. These findings may results from the perspective of subjects' working background experience as software developer and software engineer, as well as subjects' exposure to develop small-scale of industrial-strength applications in performing the assignments during for the coursework for full-time students.

Meantime, as for forth characteristics, it is found that no subjects chose either none or professional specifically in object-oriented design. However, more than half or 15 subjects have average experience, while 4 subjects chose for each little and substantial experience in using UML modelling. The highest distribution of subjects' experience in object-oriented design is 65.2% for average experience range, followed by 17.4% for both little and substantial experience ranges, and, finally 0% for each of none and professional experience ranges. This findings are very much important to conclude whether previous experience in involving with object-oriented design (i.e. UML modelling), is correlated and influencing the causal relationships with the usability factor criteria to be measured later.

From the observation of the fifth characteristics; it is studied that no subjects disclosed themselves have substantial or professional experience for involvement in managing change, but in contrast, more than half or 14 subjects have little experience. Another 3 subjects admitted that they have no particular experience in managing change, while the balance 6 among 23 subjects admitted that they have approximately an average experience range in managing change. The highest percentage is 60.9% which represents the little experience range, followed by 26.1% for average experience range, then 13.0% for no experience range, finally 0% for both substantial and professional experience ranges.

Subsequently for the sixth characteristic, it is shown that there is no subjects or minimum 0% distribution have admitted that they have professional experience in requirement change propagation in specific, but in contrast 8 subjects or approximately 34.8% admitted that they have no former experience. Only 1 subject or 4.3% chose substantial experience range personally, and, another 2 subjects or 8.7% chose average experience. While the balance of 12 from 23 subjects or the highest range is 52.2%, have approximately a little practice in performing requirement change propagation.

Next, the seventh characteristic in Tab.1 depicts further the frequency and the distribution of subjects' prior experience with involved software artefacts while performing change request. From the listed six types of software artefacts (source code, design, requirements, test cases, documentation, others), it is observed that the design artefact is the most artefact that being used in performing the initiated change request. About 69.6% subjects involved in design artefacts, followed by 65.2% subject utilized requirement artefacts, 56.5% subjects experienced with documentation artefacts, and, finally 39.1% subjects experienced with test cases artefacts. In this given questionnaire, subjects are allowed to choose more than one related software artefacts, which results to greater than 100% of total frequency distribution for this aspect of involved software artefacts.

Then, the eighth characteristic in Tab.1 depicts the subjects' motivation towards participation on the synthetic experimentation. From the given debriefing questionnaires, it is observed that the highest frequency distribution value is almost 43.5% or 10 subjects with well-motivated, followed by 39.1% or 9 subject with fairly motivated, and the lowest distribution of 17.4% or 4 subjects are highly motivated. Additionally, there is 0% of the subjects is not or poorly motivated in joining this experimentation. The findings are essential to ensure the selection effect of internal validity is carefully controlled in conducting this synthetic experiment, and the analysis interpreted for this information is fairly concluded.

The finding results of subject's motivation can be reflected to their reasons to participate in the experiment, as shown in the ninth characteristic in Tab.1. Almost 95.7% or 22 subjects are interested to gain practical experience in user testing of the SE research project. In addition to that reason, 16 from 23 subjects or approximately 69.6% subject are also agree that the significance reason in participating is to apply the related SE theories and knowledge from their coursework.

Apart from that, subjects' knowledge about the Library system domain as a case study is also being concerned to observe subjects' exposure and their familiarity on the sample system that being under investigation in performing the required experimental tasks. From the last characteristic in Tab.1, it is found that almost 65.2 % or 15 subjects are fairly familiar to the Library System domain, and 7 of them or 30.4% subjects are very well understand and exposed to the domain environment, while only 1 subject or 4.3% admitted that he or she has poor understanding on Library System.

4   Result Analysis and Quantitative Interpretation

This section descriptively presents the preliminary results and the observation analysis on the conducted synthetic environment experiment in evaluating the usability quality factor of the proposed ReChaP process model in terms of five main criteria; efficiency, effectiveness, learnability, satisfaction and usefulness.

4.1   Results on Effectiveness Criteria

In overall, it is observed that, two tasks namely Task 2 and 3 achieved 100% effectiveness score as compared to 98% for both Task 1 and 4, as illustrated in the following Fig.2. These findings may resulting due to the factor of subjects' previous working background, prior knowledge and experience in the specific phases in software development life-cycle, as reported previously in the Tab.1 demographic data.

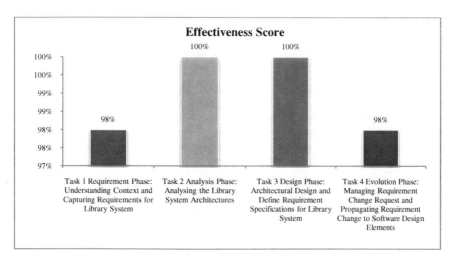

Fig. 2. Overall effectiveness score for 4 tasks

In details, Task 1 is performed during requirement phase, whereby the subjects are instructed to understand the case study context and to capture requirements for Library Systems. From the observation, it is found that only 1 subject is not able to complete all the required. This finding may resulting from the subjects' learning effect in early phase of experimentation, in utilizing the proposed requirement templates definition to classify the collected requirement statements (general: formal/informal requirements) into four types of requirement (functional, performance, constraints, specific quality) as suggested in ReChaP product model element.

The effectiveness criteria for Task 2 are achieving 100% score. All 23 subjects are effectively completed the activity in analysing the related packages for the Library System case study. In this experimentation, subjects are expected to be able to identify at least six important packages, such as: borrow/loan, return/checkout, reserve, renew, search, and register.

Subsequently, the activities designed in Task 3 during design phase have achieved 100% score of effectiveness criteria. All 23 subjects were able to design basic architectural diagrams for Library System such as class and state diagrams. It is also observed that, all subjects have successfully defined the related requirements specifications for the Library System using the support from the ReChaP prototype tool.

However, in Task 4, the overall of 98% effectiveness score has been achieved. All 23 subjects have successfully completed the proposed activities especially in analysing the initiated requirement change requests, performing simple change of modifying a numbers of requirement change as well as validating the changed requirements. In contrast, it is detected that 1 subject is failed to wholly investigate and implement the complex change requests of adding and deleting requirements, even though this step is been supported using the ReChaP prototype tool.

4.2 Results on Efficiency Criteria

Subjects are required to record their time starts and time ends, before and after they have completely performed all the tasks. The efficiency ratings for each task are divided into five scales of time duration i) Too slow : more than 30 minutes, ii) Slow : 20 till 29 minutes, iii) Medium : 11 till 19 minutes, iv) Fast : 6 till 10 minutes, and v) Fast Enough : 1 till 5 minutes. The sets of time duration are been determined by estimating overall time spent by all subjects. Apart from that, other additional factors on subjects' previous working background as well as prior experience in overall SE practices that been discussed in Tab.1, are also being considered while setting up the time duration for the five scales of efficiency.

Firstly, for Task 1, the highest distribution of 10 subjects or 43.5% are efficiently spent the given time in medium range in order to complete the designed activities during this Task 1. Approximately, 5 subjects or 21.7% spent their time efficiently in slow and fast ranges. It is followed by the lowest of 3 subjects or 13.0% that are detected to spend their time more than 30 minutes. Additionally, it is observed that, there is no subject that is fast enough to completely perform the activities during Task 1 within 1 to 5 minutes duration.

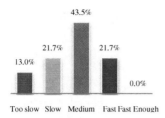

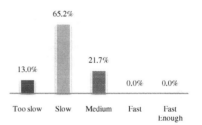

Fig. 3. Distribution of efficiency criteria for Task 1

Fig. 4. Distribution of efficiency criteria for Task 2

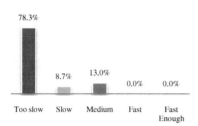

Fig. 5. Distribution of efficiency criteria for Task 3

Fig. 6. Distribution of efficiency criteria for Task 4

As for Task 2, the first highest is 65.2% or almost 15 subjects are capable to analyse packages for Library System case study in fast range time. The efficiency levels for the rest 8 subjects or 34.8% are between 1 to 5minutes, which is fast enough in completing the required activity in Task 2. In contrast, there is no one among 23 subjects were found in the group ranges of too slow, slow and medium time duration.

Subsequently, as for the following Task 3, there is no one of 23 subjects were able to complete the tasks in fast or fast enough range. On the other hand, almost 78.3% or 18 subjects in the group were found in the too slow range to efficiently complete designed four activities. For slow range, it is observed that less 8.7% or 2 subjects were able to perform within 20 to 29 minutes time duration. The balance 3 subjects or 13.0% were moderately able to perform Task 3 in medium time duration.

Finally for Task 4, the highest frequency of 15 subjects or 65.2% distribution of efficiency criteria were fall under slow range group, followed by 5 subjects or 21.7% in medium range, and the lowest 3 subjects or 13.0% were identified in too slow range group. On the other hand, there is none of 23 subjects were observed to be able in completing the required five main activities during evolution phase for less than ten minutes.

The summaries for overall frequency distribution for Task 1 till Task 4 are portrayed in Fig.3 till Fig.6. The variation on the findings of the subjects' efficiency in time duration for completing the four required tasks, might happened due to the subject learning curve that is slowly improving in getting themselves familiar with the system under investigation (i.e. Library System), as well as to adapt with the prototype tool environment and the detailed activities/steps in each phases based on ReChaP process models.

4.3   Results on Satisfaction Criteria

The satisfaction is evaluated by checking subjects' personal feeling and their real experience using the ReChaP prototype tool during completing the required experimental tasks according to the proposed process model, as presented in Tab. 2.

Table 2. Result of Satisfaction Score

Criteria	Scales	Frequency (N=23)	Distribution
1. Allows easier way to perform specific changes on requirements (i.e. addition, deletion and modification).	Strongly disagree	0	0.0%
	Disagree	0	0.0%
	Undecided	0	0.0%
	Agree	13	56.5%
	Strongly agree	10	43.5%
2. Allows easier way to propagate changes from requirement to class and state diagrams.	Strongly disagree	0	0.0%
	Disagree	0	0.0%
	Undecided	0	0.0%
	Agree	15	65.2%
	Strongly agree	8	34.8%
3. In overall, the given process models and its description, provide fairly useful guidelines in managing and propagating requirement change into software design elements.	Strongly disagree	0	0.0%
	Disagree	0	0.0%
	Undecided	0	0.0%
	Agree	18	78.3%
	Strongly agree	5	21.7%
4. In overall, ReChaP approach can fairly simplify the requirement change propagation process to support software evolution.	Strongly disagree	0	0.0%
	Disagree	0	0.0%
	Undecided	0	0.0%
	Agree	16	69.6%
	Strongly agree	7	30.4%

For first satisfaction criteria, it is found that almost all subjects are satisfied, with the highest frequency of 13 subjects or 56.5% choose agree, and followed by the balance 10 subjects or 43.5% choose strongly agree. Alternatively, there is no subjects disagree or unsatisfied with the first satisfaction criteria.

As for second satisfaction criteria, it is studied that no subject were not satisfied with this second satisfaction' criteria. In contrast, approximately the highest 65.2% frequency distribution or 15 subjects were fairly satisfied, and the rest of 8 subjects or 34.8% were strongly agreed that they are satisfied.

Subsequently, for third satisfaction criteria, it is observed that, almost all 23 subjects are satisfied, with the highest frequency of 18 subjects or 78.3% choose agree, the rest of 5 subjects or 21.7% choose strongly agree. On the other hand, there is no subjects disagree or unsatisfied with the third satisfaction criteria.

Finally, almost all subjects were satisfied with this fourth satisfaction' criteria, with approximately the highest 69.6% frequency distribution or 16 subjects were fairly satisfied, and the balance of 7 subjects or 30.4% were strongly agreed that they are satisfied.

4.4 Results on Learnability Criteria

The learnability is evaluated by checking whether the subjects agreed that the proposed process is easy to use and can be mastered, during completing the required experimental tasks while using the ReChaP prototype tool. Basically, three associated questions were intended to measure the learnability criteria from subjects' perceptions, as depicted in Tab.3.

Table 3. Results for learnability criteria

Criteria	Scales	Frequency (N=23)	Distribution
1. It is easy to use the ReChaP approach.	Strongly disagree	0	0.0%
	Disagree	0	0.0%
	Undecided	0	0.0%
	Agree	16	69.6%
	Strongly agree	7	30.4%
2. It is easy to learn to use and the ReChaP approach can be mastered.	Strongly disagree	0	0.0%
	Disagree	0	0.0%
	Undecided	1	4.3%
	Agree	19	82.6%
	Strongly agree	3	13.0%
3. The given process models provide understandable guidelines and detailed steps to perform the requirement change activities.	Strongly disagree	0	0.0%
	Disagree	0	0.0%
	Undecided	2	8.7%
	Agree	18	78.3%
	Strongly agree	3	13.0%

First, the learnability criterion is evaluated from the subjects' perspective whether the proposed ReChaP process model is easy to use in general. From the observation, almost all subjects were seems agree with the easiness in using ReChaP process model, with the highest 16 subjects or more than 69.6% were agree, and the balance of 7 subjects or 30.4% were strongly agree with the first learnability criteria. Among 23 subjects, in general, no perceptions from subject that the proposed ReChaP process model was hard and difficult to use.

The second learnability criterion is more specific compared to the first one. In this second criterion of learnability, subjects' perceptions on the learning easiness to use and master the process model is evaluated. Of 23 subjects, the highest distribution is 19 subjects or 82.6% were fairly agree, followed by 3 subjects or 13% were strongly agree, and only 1 subject or 4.3% chose undecided. In contrast, in overall, none of the subjects were disagree in terms of the second criterion of learnability.

Lastly, the third criterion of learnability is evaluated from subjects' perspective whether the given process model have provide some kind of understandable guidelines and the detailed steps particularly in performing the requirement change activities. It is observed that the top distribution frequency is 78.3%, which represents 18 among 23 subjects that were reasonably agreed in this third learnability criterion. The second highest distribution is 13% or 3 subjects that were strongly agreed, and finally 8.7% or 2 subjects were undetermined to decide in this third learnability criterion. It is also studied that, no subjects were found against to this third learnability criteria.

4.5   Descriptive Results on Usefulness Criteria

This subsection reports on the descriptive results for the usefulness criteria. The usefulness is verified by checking whether the subjects agreed that the proposed ReChaP process model helps to solve the required experimental tasks in an acceptable way, using the handy features and functionalities provided by the prototype tool. Basically, six related questions were designed to evaluate the usefulness criteria from subjects' perceptions, as described in Tab.4.

Table 4. Result of Usefulness Score

Criteria	Scales	Frequency (N=23)	Distribution
1. Allows for easier selection to classify types of requirements.	Strongly disagree	0	0.0%
	Disagree	0	0.0%
	Undecided	0	0.0%
	Agree	16	69.6%
	Strongly agree	7	30.4%
2. Allows for easier way to define the requirement specifications.	Strongly disagree	0	0.0%
	Disagree	0	0.0%
	Undecided	0	0.0%
	Agree	15	65.2%
	Strongly agree	8	34.8%
3. Allows for easier way to choose input statement for requirement specifications (i.e. by fill-in the "< >" placeholders).	Strongly disagree	0	0.0%
	Disagree	0	0.0%
	Undecided	0	0.0%
	Agree	19	82.6%
	Strongly agree	4	17.4%
4. Allows for easier way to express the requirement in consistent manner.	Strongly disagree	0	0.0%
	Disagree	0	0.0%
	Undecided	0	0.0%
	Agree	15	65.2%
	Strongly agree	8	34.8%
5. Allows for easier way to create software design model (class and state diagrams) based on provided metamodels.	Strongly disagree	0	0.0%
	Disagree	0	0.0%
	Undecided	0	0.0%
	Agree	14	60.9%
	Strongly agree	9	39.1%
6. The given process models allow me for easier way to highlight the related artefacts that are being manipulated in each stages.	Strongly disagree	0	0.0%
	Disagree	0	0.0%
	Undecided	0	0.0%
	Agree	21	91.3%
	Strongly agree	2	8.7%

The first usefulness criteria is regarding to ReChaP process model and prototype tool support in terms of easier selection in classifying the four types of requirement, namely; functional, performance, constraint and specific quality. In general, from the statistics in Tab.4, it is concluded that, all 23 subjects were agree with the first usefulness criteria. The highest frequency distribution is approximately 69.6% or 16 subjects were strongly agree, followed by 30.4% or 7 subject that were fairly agree with this criteria. None of 23 subjects were be in opposition to this first usefulness criteria. These results may reflect subjects' viewpoint that, with support from process and automation tool, these two elements in ReChaP approach has relatively provides simpler way in decision-making process to classify requirement types.

Next criteria in evaluating usefulness is by looking further on subjects' agreement whether the process and supporting from prototype have provide more easy way in defining the identified requirement specifications for Library Systems. From the observation, no one from total 23 subjects was in opposition to this second criterion of usefulness. In contrast, all subjects were found agreed, with the top frequency distribution is approximately 65.2% or 15 subjects were fairly agree and followed by 34.8% or almost 8 subject were strongly agree with the second usefulness criteria of the proposed process model and prototype tool supports, in providing more flexible way in defining requirement specifications.

Another criteria is to judge subjects' opinion on the usefulness of ReChaP process and prototype tool support to choose the suitable input statement for required requirement specification, and just fill in the value of specific information for each selected "<   >" palettes/placeholders. Of 23 subjects, almost 19 subjects or approximately 82.6% were the highest distributions that agreed and followed by 4 subjects or around 17.4% distributions were found totally agree to this criteria. No subjects were found in opposition to this criterion.

The forth usefulness criteria is to see subjects' agreement whether they have found that the proposed process with the supports from prototype tool, have provide easier way in consistently expressing the requirement specification. It is studied that the highest frequency distribution is around 65.2% or 15 subjects were fairly agree, followed by 34.8% or approximately 8 subject were found totally agree to this criteria. No subjects were found in opposition to this criterion. It can be conclude that all subjects were almost agree that the elements in the ReChaP approach, especially the prototype tool were very much handy and helpful especially for novice system users, in order to express the requirement specifications in a consistent manner and standardised way based on the pre-defined templates.

Subsequently, the fifth criteria in evaluating subjects' viewpoint for usefulness is judged whether the ReChaP prototype tool and the proposed process model provide more easy way in creating the software design model such class diagram and state diagram artefacts. The top distribution of approximately 60.9% or around 14 subjects were agreed, while the balance 9 subjects or 39.1% were totally agrees to this fifth usefulness criterion.

The last criteria in evaluating the subjects' opinion on usefulness is by looking into overall perspective, whether the proposed process models have assist the subjects in identifying the manipulated software artefacts throughout the whole process in each stages from requirement, analysis, design and evolution. The highest distribution, almost 21 subjects or 91.3% were fairly agreed, and the rest 2 subjects or around 8.7% distribution were found totally agrees with this sixth usefulness criterion. Also, none of 23 subjects are found against with this criterion.

5 Summary

This research performed an exploratory study to investigate whether the proposed ReChaP approach can fairly resilient (support) the software evolution by simplifying process of requirement change propagation to the software design elements. In specific, the focal goal of this paper is to report on the preliminary results and our early analysis findings for the conducted synthetic environment experimentation in evaluating the second pillars of ReChaP approach, namely the proposed process model. The evaluation on usability quality factor of ReChaP process model is comprehensively performed in terms of five major criteria: efficiency, effectiveness, learnability, satisfaction and usefulness.

The synthetic experimentation is conducted in a laboratory testing with academic settings, which the selected experimental subjects are the carefully chosen students from SE department in the faculty. Subjects are motivated in participating the experimentation to gain practical experience involving the user testing in the SE research project that is applicable to their course theories Subjects are guided to perform the required four main experimental tasks that being designed based on the proposed ReChaP process models, ranging from requirement, analysis, design and evolution phases.

In overall, it is observed that the ReChaP process model is sufficiently usable and practical enough to support software development team in providing the methodical process flow in propagating requirement change into software design artefacts (i.e. class diagram and state diagram). In specific, by looking further at the five usability criteria, it is also remarked that the early results of descriptive statistics proved that proposed process model have achieved reasonable percentages for all five criteria of usability quality factor as mentioned in Section 4.

Acknowledgments. This research is partially funded by the **Research University Grant** from the *Universiti Teknologi Malaysia (UTM)* under *Cost Center No. Q.J130000.7128.02J91* and *Ministry of Higher Education (MOHE), Malaysia*. The authors would like to express their deepest gratitude to *UTM* and *MOHE* for their financial support. In particular, the authors wish to thank the students of *SCJ2253 Requirement Engineering* coursework within S*oftware Engineering Department* in *UTM* who taking time out of their busy day during the semester to participate in the synthetic experiment. The authors would also like to acknowledge the respective individuals and members of **ERETSEL-***Embedded Real-Time and Software Engineering Lab* (www.kpnet.fsksm.utm.my/eretsel) for the informative discussions, supportive suggestions and invaluable feedbacks during the time that this research was being conducted. All related documents such as Debriefing Questionnaire, Experimental Tasks and Post-Experiment Questionnaire are available upon request to the authors.

References

1. ISO 9126-1, Software engineering – Product quality – Part 1: Quality model. International Organization for Standardization (2001)
2. (OMG), O.M.G., Software & Systems Process Engineering Meta-Model Specification (SPEM) Version 2.0 (April 2008)
3. Ibrahim, N., Kadir, W.M.N.W., Deris, S.: Simplifying Change Propagation for Volatile Requirement. In: Kadir, W.M.N.W., Mohamad, R. (eds.) Advances in Software Engineering: Research & Practice, RMC UTM, Skudai Johor (2008)
4. Ibrahim, N., Kadir, W.M.N.W., Deris, S.: Propagating Requirement Change into Software Designs to Resilient Software Evolution. In: The 16th IEEE Asia Pacific Software Engineering Conference (APSEC 2009), Penang, Malaysia (2009)
5. Ibrahim, N., Kadir, W.M.N.W., Deris, S.: An Experimental Design Method For Evaluating Usability Factor Of ReChaP Process Model. International Journal of Innovative Computing (IJIC) 1(1) (2011)
6. Lehman, M.M.: Software Evolution. In: Encyclopedia of Software Engineering, vol. 2, pp. 1507–1513 (2002)
7. Seffah, A., et al.: Usability measurement and metrics: A consolidated model. Software Quality Journal 14(2), 159–178 (2006)
8. Sjoberg, D.I.K., et al.: A Survey of Controlled Experiments in Software Engineering. IEEE Transactions on Software Engineering 31(9), 733–753 (2005)
9. Wohlin, C., et al.: Experimentation in Software Engineering An Introduction. Kluwer Academic Publishers, Boston (2000)
10. Zelkowitz, M.V.: An update to experimental models for validating computer technology. Journal of Systems and Software 82(3), 373–376 (2009)
11. Zelkowitz, M.V., Wallace, D.R.: Experimental Models for Validating Technology. Computer, 23–31 (1998)

In the Relation of Workflow and Trust Characteristics, and Requirements in Service Workflows

Wattana Viriyasitavat[1,2] and Andrew Martin[1]

[1] Department of Computer Science, University of Oxford, Oxford, UK
wattana.viriyasitavat@hertford.ox.ac.uk, andrew.martin@comlab.ox.ac.uk
[2] Business Information Technology Division, Department of Statistics,
Faculty of Commerce and Accountancy, Chulalongkorn University, Thailand
wattana.v@acc.chula.ac.th

Abstract. Service-based interactions have become common over the past few years. Nowadays, their applications are visible in several forms including e-commerce, Virtual Organizations, Grid, and Cloud Computing. Proliferation of services leads to the creation of new value-added services composed of several sub-services in a pre-specified manner, known as service workflows. One important challenge is how to ensure security from the viewpoints of both workflow owners and participating services; each of which possesses its own requirements. Although there are a number of proposals regarding this, the comprehensive trust and security requirements are still immature. The intuition to develop a solution generic to service workflows is that workflow and trust characteristics must be incorporated. This article studies on the relationship of workflow characteristics with respect to trust, and then trust and security requirements for service collaborations are synthesized.

1 Introduction

In the era of service, the 'everything as a service' (EaaS) concept enables dynamic resource provisions to be seen and delivered as a service. The advanced technologies such as Service-oriented Architecture (SOA) enable many service-oriented applications to provide beyond simple file sharing or resource access, but rather ubiquitous service provisions. Nowadays, they appear in several forms such as within an organization where services are used as a building block to streamline business processes and its concept is realized in many Enterprise Resource Planning (ERP) solutions; in e-commerce where the interaction is mostly visible occurring between service providers and customers; and in decentralized collaborative environments such as Grids, Virtual Organizations (VO), and Cloud Computing [7], where services become a fundamental element to facilitate collaborations. Proliferation of services has enabled the creation of new value-added services composed of several sub-services in a pre-specified manner, known as service workflows. Nowadays, there are three roles of service workflows in practice (Figure 1 [37]).

A. Abd Manaf et al. (Eds.): ICIEIS 2011, Part I, CCIS 251, pp. 492–506, 2011.

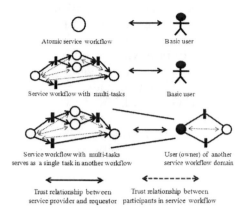

Fig. 1. Three styles of service workflow in practice

1. The first interaction describes the simplest form of a service workflow comprised of one atomic service responsible for a single task.
2. The second interaction illustrates a service workflow in a composite sense where sub-services are coordinated to provide a new value-added service to its consumers. Service consumers only perceive that they interact with only one service offered by a service provider.
3. The last interaction describes the hierarchy concept of sub-workflows, being seen as one service to fulfill a task of another workflow. This increases scalability by permitting a workflow to be hierarchically composed of multiple sub-workflows from different distributed autonomous domains.

The well-known security problem is the involvement of dynamicity and heterogeneity behind service provisions from different autonomous domains. Each of which might possess different security requirement as to determine trustworthiness of others. We demand for well-defined and flexible mechanisms where trust is a high-level abstraction, platform-independent solution that fits into this context. Its original purpose is to enhance security as a complement to the conventional ones including authentication, authorization, confidentiality, access control, etc., which are considered insufficient to cover various application domains in today environments [30]. Especially in the service workflow area, trust manifests itself improving security which can be found in many proposals [27,17,18,14,24]. However, one of the limitations is that they treat security and trust at the inter-domain level, while specifying trust and security requirements to other peer services inside a workflow (inter-service) becomes an important challenge. This is due to the workflow characteristics that make simple security requirements unable to address the actual needs. For instance, in the temporal constraint (refer to R8 in section 4), the transient characteristic of a workflow (refer to C1 introduced in the next section) often requires short-term trust relationship. One service with a requirement stating that other services must possess a valid certificate might need the precise indication of the certificate expiration to be short, or long, corresponding to the need of short- or long-term trust relationship, respectively.

Although trust and security in service workflows has been studied for a past decade, comprehensive trust and security requirements elicited from workflow and trust characteristics is not yet well understood. In this article, we extend the compilation and relationship of workflow characteristics with respect to trust in [38] and synthesize trust and security requirements based on those characteristics. The goal is to provide the information, enabling workflow creators and participating services to appropriately well-aware of security and trust implications in this context.

The remaining of this article is organized as follows. Section 2 provides basic background of service workflows and trust. Then, the associated characteristics of trust and service workflows are comprehensively discussed. In section 4, requirements for trust and security in service workflow collaboration are presented with the suppor tof practical patterns in section 5. Finally, we conclude the article with some future directions.

2 A Quick Glace on Trust and Service Workflow

In the past, workflows would be realized if they could be extended to capture business activities. Advance technologies enable the workflow applicability to go beyond business processes. Its current use is to facilitate inter-organizational and people day-to-day interoperations. In a more complex sense, a service workflow composed of several sub-services in a pre-defined order is used to carry out more sophisticated functions. In other words, completing a specific task usually requires integral results from several services. Workflow Management Systems (WFMSs) ([33,25]) have been introduced to manage this complexity including service composition during workflow formation, service execution during workflow enactment, and workflow interoperation. Many current WFMSs ([9,5]) are extended to support more dynamicity by coordinating disparate autonomous services that may be made available at distributed domains [29].

From the context of use, one of major characteristic (there are also a number of workflow characteristics depending on their functionalities and what context they reside discussed in the next section) of service workflows is that they can be static or dynamic. Firstly, we say a service workflow is static if the process description and structure are invariant, or slightly variant, over time [20]. One example is found in production lines of an automotive industry [16]. The workflow tasks of car manufacturing are split up and assigned to a number of subcontractors exchanging information and material according to a predefined plan. Other existence of the static characteristic can be found in many e-science workflows developed under the myGrid [35] project. During executions, the workflow enactment engine acting as a centralized WFMS exploits a well-defined workflow description to enforce types and order of services invocation and execution.

Table 1. Relationship between Workflow and Trust Characteristics

Workflow Characteristics	Related Trust Properties and Characteristics
Transient (C1) vs Persistent (C2)	Temporary (T1) and Long-term (T2) Trust Relationship*
Static (C3) vs Dynamic (C4)	Hard-security-based (T3) and Soft-security-based (T4) Trust*
Formation (C5) and Enactment (C6)	Hard-security-based (T3) and Soft-security-based (T4) Trust*
Global (C7) vs Local (C8) Management	Inter-domain (T5) and Inter-service (T6) Workflow Trust
All Types of Service Workflows	Centralized (T7) and Distributed (T8) Trust Characteristics
	Service Delegation (T9) and Trust Transitivity (T10)
	Direct (T11), Indirect (T12), and Non-direct (T13) Trust
	Trust in Singleton (T14) and Composite Services (T15)

* Note that the description is not provided but implicitly discussed along the way in each section.

The dynamic characteristic, on the other hand, is conceivable in the situations where unexpected changes are pervasive and common. The dynamic notion means that changes to a workflow can be made on-the-fly in the midst of workflow execution [6]. Since services are entered, developed, degraded, or terminated, in an un-predetermined manner, these result in constant changes in service workflows. These occurrences cause negative impact on efficiency, consistency, as well as security. Especially in the security aspect, it affects on the development of security policies, the change of security requirements, and trustworthiness of participating services. The example of this is given in an intelligent online travel agent. The structure and services of the workflow may be changed from many uncertainties such as emerging of a new airline company, receiving price reduction, and many more [37].

From the examples above, one requirement for trust is that it is able to address both static and dynamic characteristics. Before delving into the trust and security requirements, it is important to describe workflow characteristics with respect to trust (summarized in Table 1). Note that this relation is not absolute as some characteristics are overlapping. The goal is to provide the relation between trust and workflow characteristics, enabling researchers to be appropriately aware of security and trust implications in service workflows.

3   The Relation of Trust Properties and Workflow Characteristics

Before synthesizing trust and security requirements in service workflows, a comprehensive understanding of workflow characteristics with respect to trust [38] (see Table 1) is needed.

Transient (C1) vs Persistent (C2) Workflow Characteristics

Service workflows can be viewed in two characteristics in terms of usage. First, a workflow is transient (ad hoc or short-lived) if services are collaborated in a short time basis (one or few times usage). In most cases, the workflow will be stopped or aborted once its objectives are accomplished. The workflow in short-lived VOs and ad hoc community communication in network exemplify well the transient characteristic. On the other hand, a workflow is said to be persistent if the workflow involves in repeated processes to complete repeated objectives overtime. This characteristic can be found in a number of business processes in ERP solutions such as the car manufacture described earlier, and a payroll system where a workflow of salary paying is repeatedly executed every month. Therefore, each characteristic requires different implications of trust. A transient workflow frequently interacts with strangers, where trust relationship is temporary (T1), while a persistent workflow usually incorporates with known entities requiring longer term of trust relationship (T2).

Dynamic (C3) and Static Workflow (C4) Characteristics

As mentioned, service workflows can be either static or dynamic. A static workflow can be described as there is no change, or small amount of changes, in its components including structure, sequences of services invocation, services involved, and objectives, once it is initiated. A dynamic workflow on the other hand is dealing with constant changes in its components throughout the lifetime [28]. The important characteristics of dynamic workflows represents a number of challenges [31]:

1. Services usually reside in different administrative domains with different properties, requirements and objectives.
2. Services can be continually discovered, created, aborted, or discarded due to the change of requirements [21], which often dictates concomitant changes to other components in a workflow.
3. Services providing the same functionality are available with different attributes, e.g., Quality of Service, availability, reliability, and reputation.

Conventional (hard) security (T3) has extensively exercised in static workflows [2], usually by restricting accesses to authorized user. However, this seems to be impractical and insufficient (high overhead) to address all necessary trust aspects in the dynamic characteristic. It demands for tailored trust mechanisms, encompassing a number of attributes (e.g., reputation, QoS, recommendation, and other properties), that will allow more flexibility. Since workflow applications can behave in either static or dynamic characteristic, we are facing a new challenge of how to select a suitable approach for managing trust and security. Although trust based on hard- (T3) and soft-security (T4) approaches seem to be appropriate in static and dynamic characteristics respectively, this statement is not absolute.

Workflow Formation (C5) and Enactment (C6)

A workflow can be distinguished into two main stages: formation and enactment. The first stage concerns with activities during workflow planning and designing phrases such as the process definitions, workflow structure, service selection and composition, and analysis techniques [3]. The enactment stage involves the interpretation of these elements during execution. Workflow enactment activities generally include process scheduling, on-the-fly service substitution, and structure reformation. Dissimilarity between two stages leads to different needs of trust and security requirements. Conventional security seems to be matched in the formation stage, where most of the operations are relatively static. Workflow enactment activities, on the other hand, encounter more dynamic and uncertain issues. This incurs additional security requirements that cannot be fulfilled efficiently by the conventional approach. As such, incorporating appropriate trust models is a sound approach to support security and cope with heterogeneity and dynamicity in workflow systems.

Global (C7) and Local (C8) Characteristics of Workflow Management

In global workflow management (orchestration), a single centralized WFMS engine is responsible for managing services, coordinating workflow activities, and enforcing security[15]. Generally, services may participate without knowledge that they are part of the workflow. Security requirements, usually encoded in the form of security policies, are globally enforced to every service involved by the workflow owner.

In more complex settings, WFMSs encounter with several thousands of services, which may be available at distributed sites. This complexity cripples the efficiency as well as security enforcement by using the centralized one. Simplifying the management complexity security requirements is needed to lessen possible catastrophic events and simultaneously stimulate flexibility and efficiency of service interoperation. Localizing workflow management (choreography) into multiple WFMSs becomes attractive by permitting each service(s) ability to isolate from a global enforcement boundary. This leads to autonomous security specifications enabling each service to have its own trust judgment. However, coalitions of these services may cause interoperability problems where each possesses its own format of policies and requirements.

In summary, global and local characteristics regard trust in different ways. Complying with the global requirements results in implicitly being trusted by other services, while in local management reciprocally satisfying local requirements (distributed) is a means to establish trust relationship of other services.

Inter-domain (T5) and Inter-service (T6) Trust Characteristics

In service workflows where a service can be hierarchically composed of several sub-services, two perspectives are determined based on the level of interoperation. Firstly, trust situated among interacting services inside a workflow is called inter-service workflow trust (dash lines in Figure 2), where the scope of trust relationship is confined within the borders of a single trusted domain. Another perspective aims at higher layer emphasizing on the inter-domain level (solid

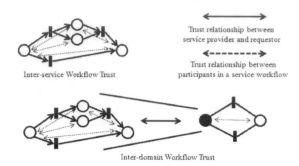

Fig. 2. Internal and External Trust

lines in Figure 2) where trust relationship is established between workflow owners and acquired services. In Figure 2, the left-hand-side workflow, viewed as a
sub-service of the right one, is one domain interacting with another domain on
the right hand side. In our previous work [36], we introduce HENS+ to support
the characteristic of inter-domain workflow trust based on trust being hierarchically propagated throughout the web of interoperation. Complementarily, our
recent work [37] attempts to address the inter-service workflow trust among participating services inside a workflow. Both characteristics are key elements to
facilitate secure interoperation in the inter-domain and inter-service levels.

Centralized (T7) and Distributed (T8) Trust

In this discussion, the major difference between centralized and distributed trust
approaches indicates how a party obtains trust of a target. In the centralized
approach, the most common way to obtain trust of a target is to consult a central trusted third party that has information or relationship of the target in
question and can vouch for its trustability. A party wishing to be part of a workflow in the centralized trust environment is required to be trusted (vouched)
by the third party. Several works in the centralized characteristic are found
in credential-, policy- and reputation-based trust models such as in the use
of digital certificate and the implementation of centralized reputation server.
Currently, a number of works are proposed to support decentralized workflows
([4,23,40]) as to overcome several shortcomings such as flexibility and scalability
problems of the centralized approach. Many researchers attempt to solve these
problems by extending the existing centralized approaches such as the use of
certificate chaining based on Public Key Infrastructure (PKI), "web of trust"
in Pretty Good Privacy (PGP), and distributed reputation systems. Other distributed solutions utilizes a hybrid approach for evaluating "trustworthiness" [29]
by using information from (1) authorized third parties, (2) direct past experience ([32,39]), or (3) indirect opinions from others through referral networks
([12,26]).

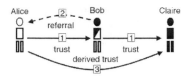

Fig. 3. Trust Transitivity Principle

Service Delegation (T9) and Trust Transitivity (T10)

The notion of delegation is meaningful in the service workflow context, where one service can be hierarchically composed of multiple sub-services and these services might be delegated to other service providers (delegatees). Normally, delegating a service requires constraints to be appended, tightening control on the rights and permissions [11]. This implies that trust is transitive through a set of delegated service providers. The basic idea behind delegation and trust transitivity is that, for example (adjust from [10]), when Alice trusts Bob for a service B, and Bob trusts Claire by delegating some parts of the service B to be executed on behalf of Bob, then Alice can derive a measure of transitive trust in Claire combined with her trust in Bob (Figure 3). These properties are key drivers to leverage dynamicity, scalability, and security of large-scale service workflows, and are efficient to accommodate and coordinate disparate security requirements among participating services.

Direct (T11), Indirect (T12), and Non-direct (T13) Trust Characteristics in Workflow Paths

Considering trust inside a single workflow, interaction along a workflow path can be basically examined in two aspects: direct and indirect [1]. Any interaction occurred between immediate services is considered directed. In this case, there exists trust relationship of the two services possibly being determined by direct experience. Conversely, the indirect interaction occurs between services that are not immediately connected and reflects the different aspect to evaluate trust. For example, in e-scientific workflows [34] the provenance-based technique is used for direct and indirect trust evaluation. Since the existence of some services might affect the willingness of others to participate in a workflow, one may generalize trust relationship of a target service beyond direct and indirect without considering in path connections (non-direct). Based on this, any participating service is able to place trust requirements on other services inside a workflow.

Trust in Singleton (T14) and Composite Service (T15) Workflow. The proliferation of online services nowadays leads to the creation of new value-added services composed of several component services in a pre-specified manner. By considering tasks in a service workflow to be fulfilled by multiple services, the service workflow is considered a form of a new value-added service which is used

Table 2. Relation between trust requirement and trust and workflow characteristics

	C1	C2	C3	C4	C5	C6	C7	C8	T1	T2	T3	T4	T5	T6	T7	T8	T9	T10	T11	T12	T13	T14	T15
R1			✓			✓	✓		✓	✓	✓	✓	✓	✓	✓	✓	✓	✓	✓	✓	✓	✓	✓
R2	✓	✓	✓	✓	✓	✓	✓	✓						✓	✓								
R3	✓	✓	✓	✓	✓	✓	✓	✓	✓	✓	✓	✓											
R4		✓	✓	✓	✓				✓	✓		✓							✓	✓	✓	✓	✓
R5		✓	✓	✓	✓				✓	✓		✓							✓	✓	✓	✓	✓
R6		✓	✓			✓			✓	✓			✓	✓									
R7	✓	✓	✓	✓	✓	✓	✓	✓	✓	✓		✓							✓	✓	✓	✓	
R8	✓	✓									✓	✓											

to support specific purposes. This characteristic incurs a challenging problem of how to evaluate trust in a composite service in compliance with trust from each sub-service. There are existing studies on this issue referred to these articles ([13,8]). However, the problem remains unsettled and becomes more difficult when services are available at different administrative domains; each of which possesses different attributes and requirements.

4   Trust and Security Requirements in Service Workflow Collaborations

This section describes trust and security requirements elicited from trust properties and workflow characteristics. Early security in workflows relies on standard security functions that have long been taken into account while building secure workflow systems, for instance, the implementation of *-based Access Control family, and PKI for confidentiality, integrity. However, existing works regarding security in workflows use a very narrow view by attempting to adapt authorization, access control, confidentiality and integrity methods to the special needs of workflows [22]. These traditional views need to be re-examined. To develop a security solution generic to service workflows, workflow and trust characteristics must be taken into account (see Table 2). It is not a simple task to derive the correct combination that satisfies all needed characteristics. Therefore, it is necessary to define the precise trust and security requirements that will support a shared understanding in securing service workflows.

Interoperability with Local Security Requirements (R1)

In global management(C7), since a centralized WFMS engine is responsible for managing services, security requirements are globally defined and enforced to every service by the workflow owner. In this case, trust isp situated at the domain level between the owner and each service (T5). Moreover, service delegation (T9) that requires transitive trust(T10) to its authorized delegatees also requires the compliance of local security requirements (T14). Furthermore, if the delegated service is in the form of several sub-services, trust in a composite sense (T15) that derives from trust of each individual service is desired. Conversely, in decentralized workflows, no single point of control exists. Security requirements are locally managed (C8), travelling from one to another service [2] (T6), and can exhibit in direct (T11), indirect (T12) or non-direct (T13) characteristics. Access to local resources is typically determined by local security requirements enforced by local security mechanisms.

A variety of security requirements, which may involve in the enforcement of hard (T3) or soft (T4) security, or in centralized (T7) and distributed (T8) trust, makes the integration of independent security policies into global enforcement very challenging, especially when services dynamically join or leave the workflow with free will (C4). As such, it is desirable that security should be maintained locally and the requirements corresponding to the local requirements are specified in a uniform format and advertised among participating services.

Separation of Duty (SoD) (R2)

In either transient (C1) or persistent (C2), and static (C3) or dynamic (C4) workflow characteristics, services with complementary competencies are joined to carry out a sophisticated task. SoD, widely used to circumvent conflict-of-interest situations, ensures that conflicting services cannot be part of a workflow. Typically, a service is assigned to a role where SoD policies are verified based on role assignment. One shortcoming is that this method only allows workflow owners to enforce SoD policies from their own perspectives (C7 and T5), thus preventing participating services from expressing their SoD requirements. To ensure security at this level (C8 and T6), one requirement for trust should allow arbitrary services to impose their SoD requirements to other participating services. Typically, SoD is an essential element in workflow formation (C5) and will be validated when any unexpected change occurs during enactment (C6).

The Association between Tasks and Services (R3)

As noted, several services with complementary capabilities are usually gathered to perform a sophisticated task. On the other hand one capable service is also allowed to execute several tasks in a workflow. For instance, an online patient record service is responsible for acquiring patients' information and providing statistical analysis to the National Health Service. Privacy and confidentiality are two main requirements of the first task, while the latter is concerned more with data accuracy. As a result, the trust level of and properties required for such service is differently determined depending on tasks responsible. This requirement, viewed as a generalized term of R2, can accommodate more security requirements including hard (T3) and soft (T4) characteristics.

Flow- and Task-oriented Property Specification (R4)

In the composite sense (T15) , there are two perspectives for evaluating trust in participating services inside a workflow (T6). Firstly, in flow-oriented executions, one might want to ensure that the services involved in a direct (T11), indirect (T12), or non-direct (T13) of flow possess certain properties (possibly in hard (T3) and soft (T4) characteristics), especially when sensitive information is part of the executions. For example, to protect data privacy, one might require that digitalized patient's records must be transmitted securely, at least by a means of encryption among services involved in the flow. This data should remain secured if it is processed or stored by untrustworthy services, which implies that these services do not have a decryption key. Another perspective focuses on task-oriented executions. The properties of services specific to a particular task must be verified before trusting. This perspective is two-fold: 1) to specify a set of required properties on a single (T14) or a group (T15) of service associated with a particular task, and 2) to specify relative properties of other services that have an influence of trust of the target services in the same task. For example, the insurance claiming task must be approved by two different services, one from an insurance company and another from a contracted hospital. In order to trust a hospital, an insurance service must present to execute that task. This is an exclusive requirement for specifying trust in service workflows.

Both perspectives are necessary to regulate how a workflow is constructed during workflow formation (C5) where most of processes and elements are static (C3), and accommodate dynamicity (C4) of service changes during the enactment stage (C6).

Enforcement of Sequences (R5)

The security of a workflow depends on a sequence of tasks that are related and dependent on one another. This is the special case of the flow-oriented perspective described above. Instead of specifying properties of involved services, this requirement focuses on a sequence of tasks. The dependency of task is important as one particular task might require the results from others to have occurred before, as well as to provide its results to the services involved afterwards [2]. From the view point of the involved services, it is desirable that they are able to specify the properties related to the sequence of tasks and service associated. For example, the task of issuing a cheque for a tax refund can be done after a financial manager and general manager have approved in order.

Flexible Degrees of Restriction (R6)

The absence of the end-to-end visibility of a workflow (either static (C3) or dynamic (C4)), which is often related to the absence of a single overall process ownership (C8), has led workflow research to re-examine and find new ways for workflow cooperation [19]. Varying degrees of visibility enable entities to retain the required levels of privacy, as well as the confidentiality of internal processes. Furthermore, since an involved service can be hierarchically composed of internal delegated sub-services or sub-workflows (T9 and T10), it is sometimes desirable to make them transparent to the upper layer. As such, any change made to a sub-workflow does not transitively interfere to the higher one. This fact gives rise to security difficulties for one service to accurately specify the properties of other services (T6), or sub-services (T6), in a workflow with respect to tasks. In response to this, we demand for flexible mechanisms to express requirements with several degrees of restriction, depending on the degrees of workflow visibility. For example, in higher visibility, one can impose a very strict statement, saying that any service along a path associated with the tasks that require access to a national database must possess a certificate issued by the UK government or, a less restrictive version can be given as all services along a path must have a certificate issued by the UK government.

Protection of Workflow Data (R7)

In all types of service workflows, since data is traversed from one service to another (T6) along a workflow path (implicitly incorporating T11, T12 and T13), it is important to protect the data against security threats, especially when it is highly sensitive. This requirement has been sufficiently accommodated by the protections offered by traditional security functions (T3) and can be enhanced by soft security approach (T4). For example, 'integrity' refers to the prevention of an unauthorized modification; 'authentication' refers to verifying the identity of the services involved in the information; 'authorization' refers to access control enforcement; and 'confidentiality' can be achieved by the use of cryptography. In addition, reputation of services also increases confidence in data protection. These requirements should be addressed as the required properties of any service (T14) that are part of the sensitive data.

Temporal Constraints (R8)

Specifying temporal constraints is an important aspect for security and trust requirement in service workflows. This requirement, usually tied up with temporal information such as temporal credential [temporal credential Fine-grained and History-based Access Control with Trust Management for Autonomic Grid Services], represents fluctuations in trust of a target service(s). As mentioned, a transient workflow frequently interacts with strangers in a short period, where trust relationship is temporary (T1), while a persistent workflow s requires longer term of trust relationship (T2).

5   Practical Patterns

It is useful to look at some practical patterns in real-life workflow examples.

- *Tasks and Services (R3) and Task-oriented Execution (R4)*: In a weather forecast website, only services that belong to the BBC are trusted before providing weather forecast information.
- *Flow-oriented Execution (R4): In order to share information*, a node in a P2P network imposes that the subsequent nodes must possess a reputation score of not less than 0.8.

- *Temporal Constraints (R8)*: A node in a P2P network imposes that the subsequent nodes have shared their information for at least two years.
- *Enforcement of Sequence (R5)*: In e-commerce it is possible to eventually get to a payment service after a booking is made.
- *Protection of Workflow Data (R7)*: A payment services must use SSL for the protection of payment information.
- *Separation of Duty (R2)*: Two services responsible for insurance claiming and approving cannot be the same.

For Interoperability with Local Security Requirements (R1), we require a uniformed representation of the above requirements such that each participating service can interpret the requirements in the same understanding. Flexible Degrees of Restriction (R6) implicitly resides within each requirement based on the degree of restriction.

6   Conclusion

The purpose of this article is to study the relationship between trust properties and workflow characteristics, and the trust and security requirements, which could be tailored to the needs of a particular workflow, are synthesized. Although the focus is put on the requirements for trust and security, it will also be argued this work is useful in specifying of other kinds of requirements for workflow-related systems. A broad range of important trust and workflow characteristics are presented, mainly relevant to enhance security in service workflows. Some strengths and weaknesses of existing works and future research are discussed along the way. The aim is to provide the guideline of security implications in service workflow systems.

References

1. Altunay, M., Brown, D., Byrd, G., Dean, R.: Trust-based Secure Workflow Path Construction. In: Benatallah, B., Casati, F., Traverso, P. (eds.) ICSOC 2005. LNCS, vol. 3826, pp. 382–395. Springer, Heidelberg (2005)
2. Arenas, A.E.: Survey material on trust and security in grids. CoreGRID Project Deliverable D.IA.03 (2005)
3. Botha, R.A., Eloff, J.H.P.: A security interpretation of the workflow reference model. In: von Solms, R., Eloff, J.H.P. (eds.) Proceedings of WG 11.2 and WG 11.1 of IFIP TC11, Information Security – from Small Systems to Management of Infrastructures, Vienna, Austria, vol. 2, pp. 43–50 (September 2, 1998)
4. Das, S., Kochut, K., Miller, J., Sheth, A., Worah, D.: Orbwork: A reliable distributed corba-based workflow enactment system for meteor2 (1996)
5. Dogac, A., Ozsu, T., Kalinichenko, L. (eds.): Workflow Management Systems and Interoperability, 1st edn. Springer-Verlag New York, Inc., Secaucus (2001)
6. Ellis, C., Keddara, K., Rozenberg, G.: Dynamic change within workflow systems. In: Proceedings of Conference on Organizational Computing Systems, COCS 1995, pp. 10–21. ACM, New York (1995)

7. Fox, G., Gannon, D.: Workflow in grid systems. In: Concurrency and Computation: Practice and Experience, pp. 1009–1019 (2006)
8. Hang, C.-W., Singh, M.P.: Trustworthy service selection and composition. ACM Trans. Auton. Adapt. Syst. 6, 1–17 (2011)
9. Hayes, J.G., Peyrovian, E., Sarin, S., Schmidt, M.-T., Swenson, K.D., Weber, R.: Workflow interoperability standards for the internet. IEEE Internet Computing 4, 37–45 (2000)
10. Jøsang, A., Ismail, R., Boyd, C.: A survey of trust and reputation systems for online service provision (2006)
11. Kagal, L., Finin, T., Peng, Y.: A delegation based model for distributed trust (2001)
12. Kamvar, S.D., Schlosser, M.T., Garcia-Molina, H.: The eigentrust algorithm for reputation management in p2p networks. In: Proceedings of the 12th International Conference on World Wide Web, WWW 2003, pp. 640–651. ACM, New York (2003)
13. Kim, Y., Doh, K.-G.: Trust type based semantic web services assessment and selection. In: Proc. 10th Int. Conf. Advanced Communication Technology ICACT 2008, vol. 3, pp. 2048–2053 (2008)
14. Koshutanski, H.: A survey on distributed access control systems for web business processes. I. J. Network Security 9(1), 61–69 (2009)
15. Kuntze, N., Schmidt, A.U., Velikova, Z., Rudolph, C.: Trust in business processes. In: Proceedings of the 9th International Conference for Young Computer Scientists, ICYCS 2008, pp. 1992–1997. IEEE Computer Society, Hunan (2008)
16. Kuntze, N., Schutte, J.: Securing decentralized workflows in ambient environments. In: Proc. IEEE/IFIP Int. Conf. Embedded and Ubiquitous Computing EUC 2008, vol. 2, pp. 361–366 (2008)
17. Lorch, M., Adams, D.B., Kafura, D., Koneni, M.S.R., Rathi, A., Shah, S.: The prima system for privilege management, authorization and enforcement in grid environments. In: Proceedings of the 4th International Workshop on Grid Computing, GRID 2003, p. 109. IEEE Computer Society, Washington, DC, USA (2003)
18. Lu, Y., Zhang, L., Sun, J.: Types for task-based access control in workflow systems. IET Software 2(5), 461–473 (2008)
19. Lynch, C.A.: When documents deceive: trust and provenance as new factors for information retrieval in a tangled web. J. Am. Soc. Inf. Sci. Technol. 52, 12–17 (2001)
20. Marinescu, D.C.: A grid workflow management architecture. GGF White Paper (2002)
21. Moodahi, I., Gudes, E., Lavee, O., Meisels, A.: A Secure Workflow Model Based on Distributed Constrained Role and Task Assignment for the Internet. In: López, J., Qing, S., Okamoto, E. (eds.) ICICS 2004. LNCS, vol. 3269, pp. 171–186. Springer, Heidelberg (2004)
22. Moreau, L., Chapman, S., Schreiber, A., Hempel, R., Varga, L., Cortes, U., Willmott, S.: Provenance-based trust for grid computing position paper (2004)
23. Muth, P., Wodtke, D., Weinenfels, J., Dittrich, A.K., Weikum, G.: From centralized workflow specification to distributed workflow execution. Journal of Intelligent Information Systems 10, 159–184 (1998)
24. Naqvi, S., Coregrid, T.: A study of languages for the specification of grid security policies 1. Technical Report TR0037 (2006)
25. Pagani, D.S., Pareschi, R.: Generalized process structure grammars gpsg for flexible representations of work. In: Conference on Computer Supported Cooperative Work, pp. 180–189 (1996)

26. Page, L., Brin, S., Motwani, R., Winograd, T.: The pagerank citation ranking: Bringing order to the web (1998)
27. Pearlman, L., Welch, V., Foster, I., Kesselman, C., Tuecke, S.: A community authorization service for group collaboration. In: Proceedings of the 3rd International Workshop on Policies for Distributed Systems and Networks (POLICY 2002), p. 50. IEEE Computer Society, Washington, DC, USA (2002)
28. Qiu, Z.M., Wong, Y.S.: Dynamic workflow change in pdm systems. Comput. Ind. 58, 453–463 (2007)
29. Rajbhandari, S., Rana, O.F., Wootten, I.: A fuzzy model for calculating workflow trust using provenance data. In: Proceedings of the 15th ACM Mardi Gras Conference: From Lightweight Mash-ups to Lambda Grids: Understanding the Spectrum of Distributed Computing Requirements, Applications, Tools, Infrastructures, Interoperability, and the Incremental Adoption of Key Capabilities, MG 2008, pp. 10:1–10:8. ACM, New York (2008)
30. Ramchurn, S., Sierra, C., Godo, L., Jennings, N.R.: A computational trust model for multi-agent interactions based on confidence and reputation. In: 6th International Workshop of Deception, Fraud and Trust in Agent Societies, pp. 69–75 (2003)
31. Ramchurn, S.D., Huynh, D., Jennings, N.R.: Trust in multi-agent systems. The Knowledge Engineering Review 19 (2004)
32. Sabater, J., Sierra, C.: Regret: A reputation model for gregarious societies (2000)
33. Sarin, S.K.: Object-oriented workflow technology in inconcert. In: COMPCON, pp. 446–450 (1996)
34. Simmhan, Y.L., Plale, B., Gannon, D.: A survey of data provenance in e-science. Sigmod Record 34, 31–36 (2005)
35. Stevens, R.D., Robinson, A.J., Goble, C.A.: myGrid: personalised bioinformatics on the information grid. Bioinformatics 19(suppl. 1) (2003)
36. Viriyasitavat, W.: Modeling delegation in requirements-driven trust framework. In: Proc. World Conf. Services - I, pp. 522–529 (2009)
37. Viriyasitavat, W., Martin, A.: Formal trust specification in service workflows. In: Proceedings of the 2010 IEEE/IFIP International Conference on Embedded and Ubiquitous Computing, EUC 2010, pp. 703–710. IEEE Computer Society, Washington, DC, USA (2010)
38. Viriyasitavat, W., Martin, A.: Towards the relationship of trust properties and workflow characteristics. To be published in the 7th Asian Internet Engineering Conference (AINTEC) (2011)
39. Witkowski, M., Artikis, A., Pitt, J.: Experiments in building experiential trust in a society of objective-trust based agents. In: Autonomous Agents & Multiagent Systems/International Conference on Autonomous Agents, pp. 111–132 (2000)
40. Wodtke, D., Weikum, G.: A formal foundation for distributed workflow execution based on state charts. In: International Conference on Database Theory, pp. 230–246 (1997)

An Efficient Approach to Machine Control Sound Generation for Interfacing Real and Virtual Environments

Yoo Rhee Oh[1], Hong Kook Kim[2], and Seung Ho Choi[3,*]

[1] Software Research Laboratory, Electronics and Telecommunications Research Institute (ETRI), Daejeon 305-700, Korea
[2] School of Information and Communications, Gwangju Institute of Science and Technology (GIST), Gwangju 500-712, Korea
[3] Department of Electronic and Information Engineering, Seoul National University of Science and Technology, Seoul 139-743, Korea
shchoi@seoultech.ac.kr

Abstract. This paper presents the motivations and methods to generate the machine control sound for the virtual environments. The factors of machine control sound are investigated to handle the sound efficiently in the virtual systems and some of the controllable factors are implemented. First, we propose a new sound file format to find or generate the proper sound with the sound factors in the virtual systems that cause various kind of events and sounds. Then, we apply the proposed sound generating technique to the virtual system for a reality model, especially focused on the MP player.

Keywords: machine control sound, virtual environment, MP player.

1 Introduction

Virtual reality (VR) systems can give a profound impression to the user by combining five senses of human [1]. Among them, the sight and the hearing are principal modals rather than others such as tasting, touching, and smelling. Moreover, the efficient sound in the VR system boosts a more realistic effect on the VR system, which is resulted by the rising effect between the sense of the sight and the hearing [2][3]. In fact, the user feels a lack of the sense of the real in the virtual system if the sounds are not sensitive to the circumstance even though the system provides 3-D images. Assuming that the user pushes a button of the virtual realistic model, the control sound when the user pushes the button strongly has to be played more loudly than the one when the user touches the button weakly. Therefore, this implies that we need to support different sounds to the user according to the user's action on the VR system.

One of the best ways to do such a thing is to break down more and more the primitive sound-controllable circumstance. It, however, is very difficult to collect

---

* Corresponding author.

A. Abd Manaf et al. (Eds.): ICIEIS 2011, Part I, CCIS 251, pp. 507–516, 2011.
© Springer-Verlag Berlin Heidelberg 2011

the sounds appropriate for every possible situation that occurs in the interaction with the realistic model. The reasons are as follows. First, as the circumstances of the VR system are complex, the sound system is required to play out the various sounds adjusted to each complex circumstance. Therefore, it is a very troublesome and inefficient work to collect all possible sounds of the VR system. Second, it wastes the memory of the sound system to save a lot of sound files. Third, the sound file system should search out the appropriate sound file to the circumstance of the VR system momentarily since the VR system needs to play out the suitable sound in the real-time with little delay. However, the file system cannot investigate the suitable sound to the circumstance if the sound file doesn't have any information about the circumstance.

We propose a new method to solve these problems, which is divided into two steps: the preprocessing step and the sound generation step. The preprocessing step is a process for preparing the sounds of the VR system. First, we define the possible circumstances as event types, for example, push the power-on button of the virtual realistic model, drop the model on the floor of the VR system, and etc, and then we determine the default values of each event type and classify several circumstances by an event type. After that, we collect the appropriate sound (default sound) to the default values of each event type. The sound generation step is a process to play out the suitable sound. The sound system investigates the appropriate sound to the circumstance when the system gets some information about the situation of the user's interaction with the virtual realistic model on the VR system. If the suitable sound exists, the sound system plays out the corresponding sound. Otherwise, the sound system transforms the default sound file into the proper sound and then plays out the transformed sound.

The proposed sound generating method cannot be implemented using existing sound file formats since the existing sound files don't have any information of the situation where the sound recorded and thus the sound system cannot determine whether the sounds are suitable to the user's action with the virtual realistic model on the VR system. To solve this problem, this paper proposes a new sound file format that contains some information on the characteristic of the sound and defines some sound factors for the machine control sound to simplify the information about the situation.

The organization of this paper is as the follows. In Section 2, a new sound file format is proposed to find and generate the suitable sound easily. Thereafter, we present some sound factors for machine control sound in the VR systems in Section 3. Next, we propose the sound generating method with the controllable sound factors classified sound factors in Section 4, and the proposed sound system is applied to a VR system in Section 5. Finally, we conclude our findings in Section 6.

2   Proposed Sound File Format

As mentioned in Section 1, the sound system should find and play out the appropriate sound corresponding to the circumstance of the user's action on the VR system to generate the machine control sound efficiently. To support this function on the sound system, the sound file must have some information about the circumstance of the VR system, but any existing sound file format doesn't contain such information. Therefore, this paper proposes a new sound file format by adding some information about the system's circumstance to the existing and popular sound file format, the Microsoft's WAVE file format [4][5]. The existing sound file format is based on a new sound file format to maintain the sound generating procedure (especially the 'play' module).

The Microsoft's WAVE file format is selected as a basic sound file format to be modified. This is because the WAVE sound file format is popular and widely used in many applications. In addition, it supports the multi-channel and high bit-resolution [6]. Thus, the sound generating system should support the multi-channel sound for the VR system since nowadays the multi-channel speaker system, especially 5.1 channel speaker system, is used in the many system to give a spatial sense to the system's user.

The basic form of the Microsoft's WAVE file format consists of the 'RIFF' chunk descriptor, the 'fmt' sub-chunk, and the 'data' sub-chunk. First, The 'RIFF' chunk descriptor contains the chunk id field ('RIFF') and the sound file size field that indicates the file size except the chunk id field, and this field, and the file format field ('WAVE'). Second, the 'fmt' sub-chunk holds the information about the sound format such as an audio format, the number of channels, the sampling rate, the bits per a sample, and etc. Finally, the 'data' sub-chunk includes the chunk id field ('data'), the chunk size field that indicates the size of the sound data, and the actual sound data. Figure 1 shows the Microsoft's WAVE sound file format.

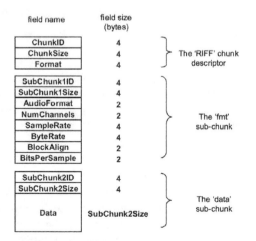

Fig. 1. A Microsoft canonical wave file format

We define a new sound file format by inserting the 'inf' sub-chunk between the 'fmt' sub-chunk and the 'data' sub-chunk of the Microsoft's WAVE file format as shown in Figure 2. The 'inf' sub-chunk contains the sub-chunk id field ('inf'), the sub-chunk size field that indicates the size of the following field, and the sound factors field that includes some information about the circumstance of the user's action with the virtual realistic model on the VR system. We will give a detailed description about the sound factors for the machine control sound on the VR system in Section 3.

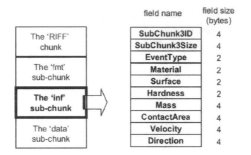

field name   field size (bytes)

The 'RIFF' chunk		
The 'fmt' sub-chunk		
The 'inf' sub-chunk		
The 'data' sub-chunk		

SubChunk3ID	4
SubChunk3Size	4
EventType	2
Material	2
Surface	2
Hardness	2
Mass	4
ContactArea	4
Velocity	4
Direction	4

Fig. 2. The proposed sound file format

3   Sound Factors for the Machine Control Sound

In this section, we define the sound factors for the machine control sound on the VR system as the event type, material, surface, hardness, mass, contact area, intensity, and direction to play out the machine control sound effectively in order to the user's interaction with the virtual realistic model on the VR system. In this paper, the intermediate value is chosen as the default value of each sound factor since it is difficult to collect the sound with the smallest values of the sound factors. Now, the detailed explanation of each sound factor is given in the following subsections.

3.1   Event type

The event type defines the circumstance that the user of the VR system handles the machine such as an MP player, a PDA, and etc. Actually, there exist infinitely many circumstances using the virtual realistic model on the VR systems, but this paper classifies the machine control sounds into three categories to manage the machine control sounds efficiently.

First, the sounds are divided according to the function of the virtual realistic model. Second, the sounds are distinguished by the circumstance that the user of the VR system handles the main body of the reality model. Third, the sounds are classified according to the circumstance in which the user controls the additionally connected objects to the body of the reality model.

The value of the event type is an integer between 0 and 255. The value between 0 and 99 is a sound by a function of the reality model. On the other hand, the value between 100 and 199 is a sound by a control of the reality model's body, and the value of the remaining range is a sound by using an additionally connected object to the virtual realistic model. Table 1 shows an example of the event type for a virtual realistic model.

Table 1. An example of the event type for a realistic model

	Event type	Integer value
By function	Power on	0
	Power Off	1
	Play	2
By control	Drop	100
	Rub	101
	Scratch	102
With earphone	Graze	200
	Drop	201
	Connect	202

3.2 Material

The material indicates what the realistic model has formed by [7]. It is one of the important sound factors since the different sound is generated according to the materials that enclose the two objects when two objects are rubbed. Assume that the realistic model is dropped to the floor of the VR system. The clear sound should be played out if the model and the floor of the system are covered by the metal. However, the muddy sound should be generated if the model and the floor are surrounded by the plastic.

The value of the material is an integer between 0 and 255, and we choose the default value as the metal (integer value 0). Table 2 gives an example of the definition of the material.

Table 2. An example of the material of the realistic model

Material	Metal	Plastic	Wood	Glass
Integer value	0	1	2	3

3.3 Surface

The surface denotes a condition of the realistic model's surface. Assuming that the user of the VR system rubs the realistic model with the hand, the rough surface makes a more noise compared to the fair one.

The value of the surface is an integer between 0 and 255. The minimum and maximum values indicate the most fair surface and the most rough one, respectively. The default value is chosen as 127.

3.4 Hardness

The hardness denotes the degree of the solidness of the VR system's surface [8]. Assuming that the user drops the realistic model on the floor of the VR system, the rubber floor absorbs more sound compared to the wood floor.

The value of the hardness is an integer between 0 and 255. The maximum value indicates the hardest surface and the default value is chosen as 127.

3.5   Mass

The mass indicates the size of the realistic model. Assuming that the user drops the realistic model on the floor of the VR system, the frictional sound is generated more loudly as the size of the model is bigger. This is because the force to the floor is proportional to the weight of the realistic model and the weight increases as the size of the model grows.

The value of the mass is an integer between 0 and 65535. The minimum value indicates the biggest model and the default value is set as 32768.

3.6   Contact Area

The contact area indicates the size of the frictional area between the realistic model and another object or the realistic model and the user of the VR system. Assuming that the user drops the realistic model on the floor of the VR system, the frictional sound by a wide contact area differs from the sound by a narrow contact area [9].

The value of the contact area is an integer type between 0 and 65535. The minimum value indicates the largest contact area and the default value is chosen as 32768.

3.7   Intensity

The intensity denotes the degree of the strength that the user of VR system operates the realistic model. Assuming that the user pushes the button of the realistic model, the sound is played out louder as the user pushes the button more powerfully.

The value of the intensity is an integer between 0 and 65535. The minimum value indicates the strongest power and the default value is set as 32768.

3.8   Direction

The direction indicates the location that the machine control sound occurs on the VR system. If the user handles the realistic model with the right hand, the sound should be played out more loudly through the right channel of a speaker system. If the user drops the realistic model on the left side, the left sound should be generated louder.

The direction factor offers the spatial sense to the user of the VR system. The sounds are controlled by the sound field control when the VR system uses two speakers, and the sounds are handled by the speaker control module when the VR system uses a 5.1 channel speaker system.

The value of the direction has a 3-dimensional vector, and each element of the vector has an integer between 0 and 255 and the default value of each element is chosen as 0.

4   Proposed Machine Control Sound Processing Method

The sound generating system should transform the default sound of the event type and play out the transformed sound if the system has no appropriate sound file corresponding to the circumstance of the VR system. The controllable factors are investigated among the machine control sound factors which were introduced in Section 3. As a result, the intensity factor and the contact area are determined as easily controllable sound factors. In this section, we propose a machine control sound processing method by transforming the default sound into the suitable sound corresponding to the user's action with the virtual realistic model on the VR system, especially with the controllable sound factors such as intensity and the contact area.

The intensity factor means the strength with which the user handles the virtual realistic model on the VR system. Therefore, the sound should be played out proportionally louder as the intensity factor is larger. Therefore, the volume envelope of the sound plays an important role in the processing of the machine control sound with the intensity factor. Hence, we propose a sound processing

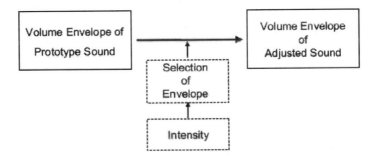

Fig. 3. A flow chart of the machine control sound processing with the intensity factor

method with the intensity factor by transforming the volume envelope of the sound in the time-domain. Figure 3 shows a flow chart of the machine control sound processing with the intensity factor.

First, the prototype sound is determined with the event type that indicates the circumstance of the user's action on the VR system. Second, a part of the prototype sound to be transformed should be selected before the volume envelope of the sound is transformed with the intensity factor. In fact, the intensity factor has an effect on a part of a sound file rather than the entire of that since the sound file contains the sound before controlling the machine, during controlling the machine, and after the event. Finally, the selected part of the prototype sound is transformed into an appropriate sound by multiplying the volume envelope of the sound with the intensity normalized by 32768, where 32768 indicates the default value of the intensity.

The contact area indicates the frictional area in which the user of the VR system handles the virtual realistic model. The change of the contact area influences on the spectrum of the sound. Therefore, we propose a method to process the machine control sound with the contact area factor by transforming the spectrum of the sound. Figure 4 shows a flow chart of the machine control sound processing with the contact area factor. First, as a preprocessing step, the characteristics of the sound spectrum for the contact areas of 10%, 50%, and 100% are obtained by analyzing the sound. And then, the sound generating system has the characteristic of the sound spectrum as an equalizer for each contact area. Second, the prototype sound is determined with the event type that indicates the circumstance of the user's action on the VR system. Finally, the sound is transformed with the equalizer corresponding to the contact area. Figure 5 shows the procedure of the sound control processing with the controllable sound factors, the intensity and the contact area. The sound is processed sequentially with the intensity and the contact area.

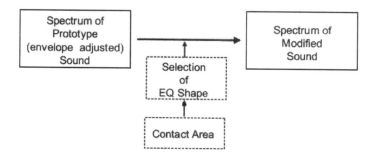

Fig. 4. A flow chart of the machine control sound processing with the contact area factor

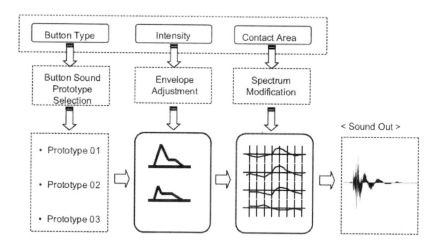

Fig. 5. A overall flow chart of the sound control with factors

5   Application of the Sound Control Processing Method on the VR System

We implemented each machine control sound processing method into a VR system using a virtual realistic model such as an MP player, PDA, and etc.

As a preprocessing step, we collected the sounds with the default values of the material, surface, hardness, mass, contact area, intensity, and direction for each event type and then stored each sound data with the proposed sound file format in a sound file system.

The sound generating system investigated whether the values of the sound factors obtained from the VR system agreed with the default values when the sound generating system got the sound factors corresponding to the circumstance of the user's action on the VR system. If all sound factors agreed with the default values, the sound generating system played out the default sound corresponding to the event type. Otherwise, the sound generating system transformed the default sound into the suitable sound by adjusting the default sound with the sound factors obtained from the VR system.

The sound file system could easily find the default sound corresponding to the values of sound factors by using the proposed sound file format. The sound file system just read the 'inf' sub-chunk and compared the input values of sound factors with the default ones. Moreover the sound generating system excluded the 'inf' sub-chunk from the sound file and used the existing sound playing method such as winmm.lib library, waveOutOpen, waveOutWrite function, and etc, to play a sound with the the proposed sound file format.

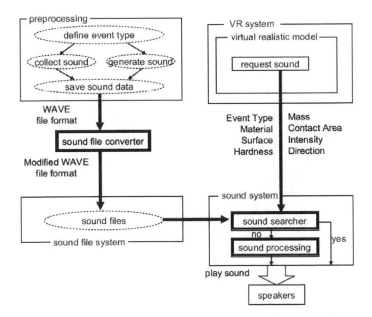

Fig. 6. An application of the sound system on the VR system

The sound generating system had the following merits on the VR system. First, the sound generating system was cost-effective on the system memory since the system just saved the default sound files. Second, the sound generating system could easily investigate whether the suitable sound existed or not by reading the 'inf' sub-chunk in the sound files. Third, the system offered the user-based sound using the sound factors.

On the contrary, the sound system had the following weak points in the VR system. First, the sounds should be well classified into the suitable sound factors. Second, the circumstance that was not defined in the event type could occur. Third, the sound system should get an exact information about the circumstance from the VR system. Fourth, the sound generating process might have a delay.

Figure 6 shows an interaction between the sound system and the VR system.

6   Conclusion

This paper proposed a new sound file format by modifying the Microsoft's WAVE file format to offer the efficient machine control sound in the VR system. In addition, we suggested the method to produce the machine control sound with the controllable sound factors, intensity and contact area. Finally, we applied the technique to play the machine control sound using the proposed sound file format on the VR system. This was an efficient way to implement the user-based VR system since the system offered the suitable sound to the circumstance of the system.

Acknowledgments. This work was supported in part by the basic research project through a grant provided by GIST in 2011.

References

1. Allport, G.: Three Dimensional Navigation Using the Five Senses. In: Proc. of the IEEE Colloquium on Real World Visualization - Virtual World - Virtual Reality, pp. 1–3 (1991)
2. Grohn, M., Lokki, T., Takala, T.: Comparison of Auditory, Visual, and Audio-Visual Navigation in a 3D Space. In: Proc. 9th International Conference on Auditory Display, pp. 200–203. Boston Univ. (2003)
3. Larsson, P., Västfjäll, D., Kleiner, M.: Do we really live in a silent world? The (mis)use of audio in virtual environments. In: Applied Virtual Reality in Engineering and Construction, Goteborg, Sweden (2001)
4. IBM Corporation and Microsoft Corporation: Multimedia Programming Interface and Data Specifications 1.0 (1991)
5. Microsoft Corporation: New Multimedia Data Types and Data Techniques (1994)
6. Microsoft Corporation: Multiple Channel Audio Data and WAVE Files (2001)
7. Avanzini, F., Rocchesso, D.: Controlling Material Properties in Physical Models of Sounding Obejcts. In: Proc. Int. Computer Music Conf., La Habanna (2001)
8. Avanzini, F., Rocchesso, D.: Modeling Collision Sounds: Non-linear Contact Force. In: Proc. COST-G6 Conf. Digital Audio Effects, Limerict, pp. 61–66 (2001)
9. Avanzini, F., Rath, M., Rocchesso, D.: Physically-based audio rendering of contact. In: Proc. 2002 IEEE International Conference, vol. 2, pp. 445–448 (2002)

Multiple Levels of Abstraction Modelling for Service-Oriented Distributed Embedded Real-Time Software Design

Muhammad Waqar Aziz, Radziah Mohamad, and Dayang N.A. Jawawi

Department of Software Engineering,
Faculty of Computer Science and Information Systems
Universiti Teknologi Malaysia
Skudai, 81310, Johor, Malaysia
wamuhammad2@live.utm.my,
{radziahm,dayang}@utm.my

Abstract. The increasing use and reliance on Distributed Embedded Real-Time Systems (DERTS) demand the enhancement of their capabilities. This along with the unique characteristics of DERTS, such as resource constraints, make the design and development more complex. State-of-the-art software development methods like Service-Oriented Computing (SOC) and Model-Driven Development can be used to cope with these complexities. However, both of the methods require the system to be designed at a higher level of abstraction and the details are provided at lower levels. Such design models for DERTS with different levels of abstractions are still currently unavailable. This paper presents four basic design models representing different levels of abstraction, to be used in Service-Oriented DERTS design. The proposed models were applied in the Home Automation domain for verification purposes. This level-by-level modelling does not only simplify the design process, but can also be used as part of a Service-Oriented modelling framework for DERTS. Furthermore, these design models can support service composition during Service-Oriented DERTS development. The service composition modelling would be beneficial for CASE tools development in supporting designers working at different levels of abstraction.

Keywords: Distributed Embedded Real-Time Systems, Software Design, Levels of Abstraction, Service Orientation, Modelling.

1 Introduction

Embedded Real-Time System can be defined as a system consisting of hardware and software components to provide a particular functionality within the allocated time. Besides the hardware and software integration, other factors such as reduced time-to-market and cost, resource constraints, and the shift towards software-intensiveness, increase the design and development complexities. The development complexity of DERTS can be handled at design phase by increasing

A. Abd Manaf et al. (Eds.): ICIEIS 2011, Part I, CCIS 251, pp. 517–528, 2011.
© Springer-Verlag Berlin Heidelberg 2011

the level of abstractions [1]. The use of development models can be helpful in reducing these complexities during system design [2]. Furthermore, Model-Based Design is considered a suitable approach for embedded system development [3]. The design of embedded systems starts with the development of a high-level system model [4].

A common and effective method in engineering for designing complex systems is the use of abstraction [3]. Therefore, it is helpful to specify complex embedded real-time system at higher levels of abstraction. This is in accordance to the Model-Driven Engineering (MDE) process, in which the levels of abstraction should be defined along with the other things [5]. In MDE, the whole or part of an application is generated through models. The notion of MDE is based on defining a system at an abstract level and then refining the abstract system model by gradually including more details. It has been experimentally proven that MDE techniques and development covers more requirements of DERTS development [2].

DERTS require agile, flexible and reusable design; which can be provided by SOC, beside providing other advantages. SOC provides suitable abstraction to cope with the complexity of large systems [6]. Service-Oriented paradigm is based on the concept of self-contained loosely-coupled functional component i.e. service, which interacts with other services through well-defined interfaces [7]. In past, SOC has been used for DERTS development, e.g., to make embedded software design more efficient [8], for device integration and as an infrastructure for distributed embedded devices [9][10], to model devices as services and integrate them with enterprise software [11] etc. Thus, the unique characteristics of DERTS like resource constraints can be handled by the advantages provided by SOC. However, in order to support Service-Oriented development, the architecture must be described at a high level of abstraction [12]. Thus, along with other models showing the details of the design according to different levels of abstraction, this paper presents a high-level design model for Service-Oriented DERTS development that also supports MDE concepts.

During Service-Oriented DERTS development, after the services are identified the proposed design models are useful to specify the system design with different levels of details and to support service composition. Part of the design phase for Service-Oriented DERTS development is shown in Fig. 1. In these models, new modelling constructs were not invented; instead specialized stereotyped elements and the existing UML notations were used. The proposed models were verified through their application in the Home Automation domain. The next section explains the methodology used to develop the models. The basics of service modelling and the concepts we considered while proposing the design models are presented in Section 3. Section 4 presents the details of the models according to different levels of abstraction. The results of applying these models on a Smart Home along with the relevant discussion are presented in Section 5. Section 6 presents the related work and the paper is concluded in Section 7.

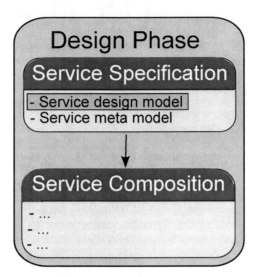

Fig. 1. Service Oriented DERTS design

2   Methodology

This section explains the methodology used in order to derive the models. Our work is based on the design models representing different levels of abstraction, presented in [13] for composition of design patterns. The idea that service and service composition can be thought identical to pattern and pattern composition, allowed us to apply the pattern design models [13] in our work. Furthermore, we extended these models [13] by introducing a device-level model to represent the embedded devices in the design. The important concepts from the Hierarchical Object-Oriented Design (HOOD)[14] models were also incorporated to utilise the hierarchy, connectivity and traceability mechanisms provided by the HOOD models. The detail of how these concepts were utilized is provided in the next section.

3   Service Modelling

In order to fully understand the role of service in Service-Oriented DERTS development, the service and service composition must be modelled. A service model shows the internal details of a service, while the service composition model shows how several services are integrated together. Precise service composition modelling is also needed for the CASE tools development that could support designers for working at different levels of abstraction. Service is used as a building block at a high level of abstraction without showing its details. The details of a service are revealed at the lower levels of abstraction.

The models presented in this paper provide support for the visualization of services at various levels of granularity and details. This visualization can be used as a way of capturing service composition. The proposed models make use of two important concepts from the HOOD [14] design models:

- *Hierarchy*: In HOOD, each object may contain other objects. This concept was not directly followed, but was used in the sense that at higher level of abstraction, the details were contained (hidden) inside the objects. In our models a coarse-grained view of the design was provided as a composition of the services while abstracting their details at a high level. The details were revealed at the lower abstraction levels.

- *Connectivity and traceability* : In HOOD, the interfaces of an object are connected with internal objects. This connectivity is used to trace the interfaces of coarse-grained objects to internal objects and allows the HOOD models to be used at different levels of abstraction. In our models, following a similar approach, services are connected with each other through interfaces. These service interfaces were connected with the internal elements of the service as was shown at the lower abstraction levels, thus providing the traceability support between interfaces to service internal elements.

4   Service-Oriented Design Models

In addition to the internal details of a service and their integration models, as mentioned in the previous section, two other models are also needed to provide granular information about the service. These models are Device-Level model to represent all the devices providing/using any service and Service-Level model to represent the provided services. As a result, we have the following four design models that can help in service composition.

1. Device-Level model
2. Service-Level model
3. Interface-Level model
4. Service-detail model

4.1   Device-Level Model

Device-Level Model is a high level structural view of the system which represents the system as a set of collaborating devices. All the devices, which are either providing or using any service, and their interaction is represented in this model. Each service provider is represented by a type and a name. The name of the provider is used to represent the provider instance name. UML Packages were used to represent a service provider. In order to differentiate them, the UML extension mechanism was used i.e. packages were stereotyped using the type (*device* or *external provider*). The UML extension mechanism can be used to stereotype a package-to-package relationship as a *Uses* relationship between service providers. A device-level model using UML syntax is shown in Fig. 2.

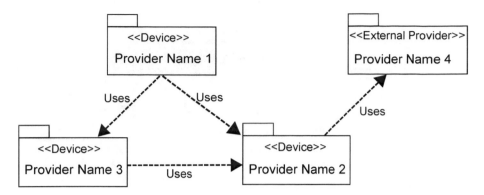

Fig. 2. Device Level Model

4.2   Service-Level Model

Service-Level Model adds more details to Device-Level Model by representing the services provided by each device. This level expresses the system as a composition of services. In other words, it tells which service of one device is using which service of the other device. Thus, it shows the design in terms of services, their providers and the dependencies between them. There are some devices which do not provide any service but they use the services provided by others. These devices are represented as services and designated as *DeviceService*. Each service is represented by a service name and a type. The name of the service would be given by the designer and is used to represent the service instance. A service can have any one of the following types:

<service> ::= <Simple> | <Composite> | <Basic> | <Helping> | <Orchestrator> | <Fundamental>

The *Provides* relationship was used between a provider and the service it provides, while the *Represented* relationship was used between a device and its representation in terms of service i.e. DeviceService. At this level, the *Uses* relationship was still used between two services. However, this relationship was further refined in the later stages to become associations between the interfaces of two services. Since a service is an autonomous unit of functionality it can be considered as a component, therefore services were represented by a UML components as shown in Fig. 3. By using the UML extension mechanism, the components were stereotyped to represent the *type* of a service.

4.3   Interface-Level Model

This model is the refinement of the Service-Level Model which shows the service interfaces and defines the relationship between service interfaces. Service interface is described in terms of Inputs, Outputs, Pre-Conditions and Effects

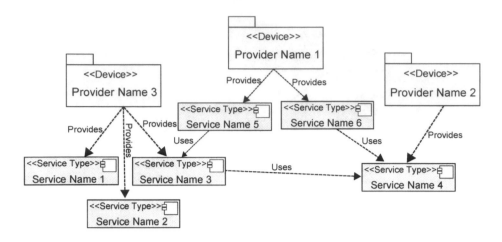

Fig. 3. Service Level Model

(IOPE) of the service. IOPEs represents the inputs and outputs of service internal operations. One class can implement one or more service operations. An operation is represented by a name along with its class name, while a class is represented by its name. The *Uses* relationship of the Service-Level Model is now refined in terms of the relationships between service interfaces. This relationship provides the behavioural description by displaying the interaction between the services. The direction of the arrow in the relationship shows the *required* or *provided* nature of the interface. The UML interface notation (Circle) was used for representing the interfaces as shown in Fig. 4.

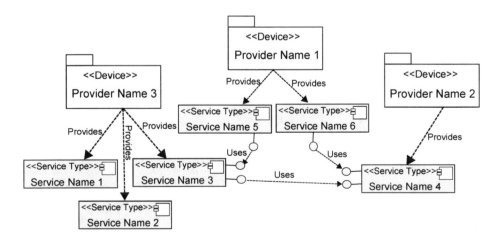

Fig. 4. Interface-Level Model

4.4   Service-Detail Model

The Service-Detail Model takes the design details to another level. At this lowest-level of design, the internal details of the service and the connectivity between the elements of the interface and the internal elements of the service were revealed. Service-Detail Model identifies the internal details of a service in terms of a set of interrelated classes. The relationship between the service internal operations inside classes and the interface is identified. This model identifies the classes that implement service interface. In other words, this model can be used to trace the interface back to the elements of service. UML Class diagram was used to represent service internal design in terms of classes as shown in Fig. 5.

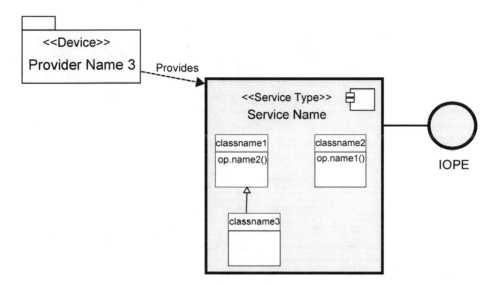

Fig. 5. Service-Detail Model

5   Example - Smart Home

A Smart Home case study was used in order to check the applicability of the proposed models at various levels of abstraction. In the case study, the home appliances provide their functionalities as services. The devices used in the Smart Home case study and the services they offer are presented in Fig. 6.

The Smart Home case study was modelled using the proposed models at all levels of abstraction starting from the top most, the Device-Level. The Device-Level model of the Smart Home case study, shown in Fig. 7, represents all the devices present in the case study. A provider instance name and a type i.e. *device* was assigned to each service provider, except 'Retail Store' whose type is *external provider*. The *Uses* relationship was used between service providers.

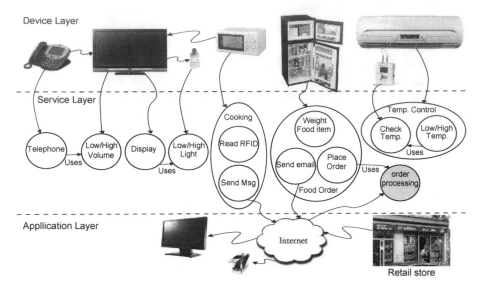

Fig. 6. Service offered in Smart Home

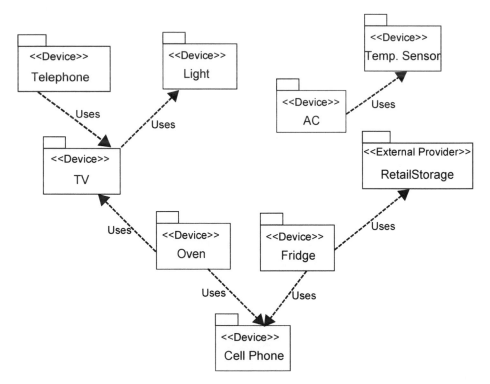

Fig. 7. Device-Level model of Smart Home

In the Service-Level Model, the services provided by the devices were shown along with the relationships between them. The *DeviceServices* were also represented at this level. Each service has an instance name and a type. Fig. 8 displays an excerpt from the case study showing the interaction between three devices, the services they offer and the relationship between them. Note that the device 'Telephone' was represented as *DeviceService*, as it did not provide its own services but used the service of the 'TV'.

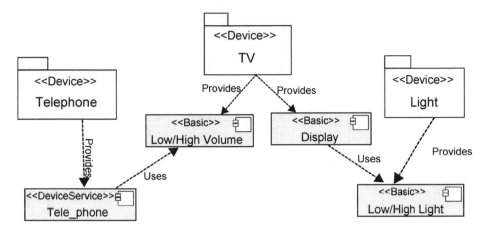

Fig. 8. Service-Level Model example

The Interface-Level Model is the refinement of the Service-Level Model in the sense that it adds the interfaces to the services displayed in the Servie-Level Model. An Interface-Level Model of two devices in the Smart Home is shown in Fig. 9, along with the services they offered and their interfaces.

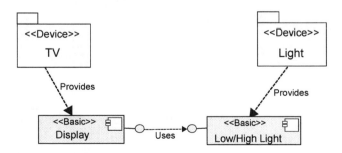

Fig. 9. Interface-Level Model example

The Service-Detail Model shows the internal details of a service. The service internal classes, operations and the relationship between them are shown in this model. An example of a Service-Detail Model is the *Low/High Light* service provided by the 'Light' device, as shown in Fig. 10.

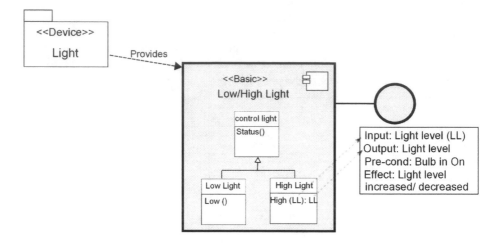

Fig. 10. Example of Service-Detail Model

The details of different levels of abstraction proposed in this paper along with their usefulness towards service composition is shown in Table 1. At a high-level, only the interaction between the devices was shown; then at the next level the services they provided were depicted. The next level showed the interaction between services and finally the services details were shown at the lowest level. This hierarchical feature allows to build a design with the main building blocks only, without exposing the internal details. Furthermore, specifying the design in these different levels of abstraction allows one to select the right design model with required details while abstracting the unnecessary things, thus making the overall design process simple. For example, in case of Smart Home, those interested in knowing about how devices are interacting should view Device-Level model. The internal design, expressed in lower-level models, can be accessed when needed.

Table 1. Usefulness of Proposed Levels of Abstraction towards Service Composition

Levels	Details	Usefulness towards Service Composition	
		What	How
Device-Level	Device Interaction	Providers are involved	Service Providers interact
Service-Level	Services Provided	Services are provided	Services interact
Interface-Level	Service Interaction	Service interface	Interfaces match
Service Detail	Service Internal classes	Internal Classes	Interface is traced

6   Related Work and Discussion

The use of level of abstraction in software design is not a new idea. However, to the best of our knowledge, there is no directly related work with the level of abstraction in Service-Oriented DERTS design. As mentioned previously, the idea used in this paper is based on design models for composition of design patterns [13], but many differences exists between them. First, these design models are used to visualize patterns and pattern composition instead of service and service composition. Secondly, the semantic of the presented models is different in both cases, for example, the pattern-level model represents the system as a composition of design patterns [13] whereas the service-level model in this paper represents only the services provided by devices while the service composition is modelled by interface-level model. Lastly, there is no concept of provider in pattern design models [13] which is provided in this paper in Device-Level model.

The concept of abstraction is also used for modelling real-time and embedded systems [3], which emphasizes to use the level of abstraction for specifying real-time and embedded systems. Both vertical and horizontal type of abstraction are discussed. However, the work is focused on selecting the right abstractions for a modelling language for real-time and embedded systems. Vertical and horizontal abstraction types are also discussed in [2], but the focus of the paper is on highlighting the benefits of MDE for real-time and embedded systems. The concept of level of abstraction is heavily exploited in [5] for defining MDE process.

7   Conclusion

The development complexities of Distributed Embedded Real-Time Systems can be reduced by using the benefits provided by Service Orientation and MDE. By representing a complex system at a higher level of abstraction the design process can be simplified. This paper presents multiple design models that can be used during Service-Oriented DERTS development. Starting with a High-Level Design Model, a DERTS system was represented as a set of interacting devices. In the next level i.e. Service-Level model, all the services provided by the devices were highlighted. The Interface-Level Model showed the interfaces of the provided services. Finally, the realization of the interfaces in terms of classes and operations inside the service was illustrated in Service-Detail Model. This level-by-level modelling can help in simplifying the design of DERTS. This was proven by the application of the proposed models in a Smart Home case study.

Acknowledgments. We would like to thank Universiti Teknologi Malaysia for sponsoring the research through the grant with vote number 00J37 and for providing the facilities and support for the research.

References

1. Marco, A.W., Edison, F., Dalimir, O., Carlos, E.P., Franz, R.: A Case Study to Evaluate Pros/Cons of Aspect- and Object-Oriented Paradigms to Model Distributed Embedded Real-Time Systems. In: Proceedings of the 2008 5th International Workshop on Model-based Methodologies for Pervasive and Embedded Software, pp. 44–54. IEEE Computer Society (2008)
2. Terrier, F., Gerard, S.: MDE Benefits for Distributed, Real Time and Embedded Systems. Management 225, 15–24 (2006)
3. Gérard, S., Espinoza, H., Terrier, F., Selic, B.: Modeling Languages for Real-Time and Embedded Systems. In: Giese, H., Karsai, G., Lee, E., Rumpe, B., Schätz, B. (eds.) Model-Based Engineering of Embedded Real-Time Systems. LNCS, vol. 6100, pp. 129–154. Springer, Heidelberg (2010)
4. Lisane, B., Leandro, B., Luigi, C., Flavio, W., Carlos, E.P., Ricardo, R.: Comparing high-level modeling approaches for embedded system design. In: Proceedings of the 2005 Asia and South Pacific Design Automation Conference, pp. 986–989. ACM, Shanghai (2005)
5. Fondement, F., Silaghi, R.: Defining model driven engineering processes. In: Third International Workshop in Software Model Engineering (WiSME), pp. 1–11 (2004)
6. Brogi, A., Corfini, S., Fuentes, T.: A Two-Tiered Approach to Enabling Enhanced Service Discovery in Embedded Peer-to-Peer Systems. In: Baresi, L., Chi, C.-H., Suzuki, J. (eds.) ICSOC-ServiceWave 2009. LNCS, vol. 5900, pp. 68–82. Springer, Heidelberg (2009)
7. Thomas, E.: Service-Oriented Architecture: Concepts, Technology, and Design. Prentice Hall PTR, NJ (2005)
8. Barisic, D., Krogmann, M., Stromberg, G., Schramm, P.: Making Embedded Software Development More Efficient with SOA. In: 21st International Conference on Advanced Information Networking and Applications Workshops (AINAW 2007), pp. 941–946. IEEE (2007)
9. Cannata, A., Gerosa, M., Taisch, M.: A Technology Roadmap on SOA for smart embedded devices: Towards intelligent systems in manufacturing. In: IEEE International Conference on Industrial Engineering and Engineering Management, (IEEM 2008) (2008)
10. Cannata, A., Gerosa, M., Taisch, M.: SOCRADES: A framework for developing intelligent systems in manufacturing. In: IEEE International Conference on Industrial Engineering and Engineering Management, IEEM 2008 (2008)
11. de Deugd, S., Carroll, R., Kelly, K.E., Millett, B., Ricker, J.: SODA: Service Oriented Device Architecture. In: Pervasive Computing 5(3), 94–96 (2006)
12. Tao, Z., Shi, Y., Sheng, C., Xiangyang, J.: A Modeling Framework for Service-Oriented Architecture. In: Sixth International Conference on Quality Software, QSIC 2006 (2006)
13. Yacoub, S.M., Ammar, H.H.: Pattern-Oriented Analysis and Design: Composing patterns to design software systems. Addison-Wesley (2004)
14. Rosen, J.P.: HOOD: An industrial approach for software design. Hood technical group (1997)

Projects Feasibility Assessment Model Based on Competencies in Organization

Tomasz Kajdanowicz and Kazimierz Fraczkowski

Wroclaw University of Technology, Wroclaw, Poland,
Faculty of Computer Science and Management
{tomasz.kajdanowicz,kazimierz.fraczkowski}@pwr.wroc.pl

Abstract. A proposal for modelling the human resource planning among projects is presented in the paper. The situation when a set of projects is expected to be accomplished in the organization is considered. The presented model provides the answer whether within available human resources with given competencies it is possible to accomplish a set of projects. Moreover the model is able to propose optimized staffing solution given objective function,e.g. maximizing the increase of competencies of the staff. Modelling is based on quantitative description of tasks and employees. The paper presents a case study of model utilization. The preliminary studies on the proposed model allow to conclude that the it reflects the nature of staffing process well.

Keywords: staff scheduling, multiple criteria analysis, project planning, competence scheduling model.

1 Introduction

The resource-constrained staff scheduling in projects continues to be an active area of research[2,3]. Recently this study gathered growing interest from researchers and practitioners trying to provide better models and solution methods. In general such class of problems involves finding a feasible staff schedule, optimizing objective functions that describes desired outcome[9].

The problem becomes more difficult, when the scheduling problem is based on additional constraints like competencies required to fulfil the tasks. Staff scheduling in such a situation requires additional information about competencies of employees [2,5].

Competence, defined according to [11], is of fundamental importance to every company and institution to cope with new markets and new requirements from the customers and clients. It is important to have an understanding of the fact that the knowledge of each worker and a common knowledge for the whole company are of greatest importance to reach the strategic goals and to carry out the strategic plans. Therefore, there have been proposed various approaches to employees' competence development, e.g. [1], as well as its modelling, e.g. [6,10,11].

A. Abd Manaf et al. (Eds.): ICIEIS 2011, Part I, CCIS 251, pp. 529–536, 2011.
© Springer-Verlag Berlin Heidelberg 2011

Companies often are in situation when they need to develop a set of projects at the same time. Obviously, the organization has limited resources and needs to answer the question if within available resources is able to realize whole set of those projects. Moreover projects are given with exact competencies required and the staff scheduling problem needs to address such requirements. Additionally, while preparing the staff schedule, it is usually required to optimize some objective function, e.g. minimizing the execution time, maximizing the increase of competencies of the staff, maximizing the economic outcome, etc.

Problem of resource-constrained staff scheduling is considered in the paper. In the Section 2 a model describing the problem is presented. A short case study presenting the model is provided in the Section 3. Some remarks on the possible computational realization of the model are gathered in Section 4 and finally, the paper is concluded in Section 5.

2   The Model for Projects Feasibility Assessment in the Organization

The general aim of presented model is to answer the question if within available human resources with given competencies it is possible to realize a set of given constrained projects. Moreover, the model should be able to propose the scheduling solution maximizing the increase of competencies of the staff.

2.1   Problem Formulation

The staff assignment problem is considered given a fixed time interval composed of T periods indexed as $t = 1, \ldots, T$ (period t lasts from time $t - 1$ until t). Each of projects $i = 1, \ldots, n$ being staffed are decomposed into a set of interdependent tasks $k = 1, \ldots, K$ and each project itself consist at least of one task (therefore $K \geq n$). Tasks are assigned to particular project by $c_{ik} \in \{0, 1\}$ indicators, where 1 denotes that project ith consist of kth task and 0 otherwise. Moreover single task k may belong only to one project. According to ordering dependencies between tasks each kth task is characterized by the earliest possible start time $\rho_k \in \{1, \ldots, T\}$ and the latest finish time $\delta_k \in \{1, \ldots, T\}$. It is assumed that ρ_k and δ_k are obtained from critical path analysis and therefore the duration of each kth task is known at $t = 0$.

Assuming that during all periods $t \in [0, T]$ the set of employees remains fixed, they may be indexed by $j = 1, \ldots, m$. It means that during the whole time no changes in the staff are considered. Each employee is characterized by a set of competencies $r = 1, \ldots, R$ that describes different fields of expertise, knowledge or skills. Each rth competence possessed by jth employee at given time period t is quantitatively indicated by real number z_{jrt} called competency expertise. According to phenomena of knowledge depreciation that states the nature of human beings, the value of z_{jrt} may change over time. By learning the value of z_{jrt} grows and such process in enterprises is usually considered when employee

j works for task requiring rth competence. In other words, when an employee j does not work in certain task requiring particular competency r, his competence expertise z_{jrt} decreases. The initial values of z_{jr1} are given. By the competence expertise it is understood the employee ability to solve alone a situational and targeted task. Moreover, it is emphasized that theoretical knowledge is not always necessary to solve a task and, what is more, a practical experience and derived from that practical knowledge must always be there to address the task. Here it is not considered the phenomenon of collective knowledge or collective skills, therefore the project description needs to be provided with no community competence expertise indicators.

Each task requiring given competence r may be done by employee j with certain efficiency c_{jrt}. This is relative indicator of the share of work done by jth employee on task requiring rth competence in one period in comparison with employee with the highest possible competency expertise at time t=0. For the convenience and the model clarity it is assumed that the level of competency expertise is directly correlated with efficiency. (Therefore it will be treated equivalently).

Each task k is characterized by work time performed with given competency d_{kr} and denotes the time required by an employee to realize the task in situation when the employee has the highest possible competency expertise. According to previously mentioned critical path analysis it is assumed that all work times for all tasks are known in advance.

It is obvious that each employee has a limited work capacity. Therefore, the jth employee capacity in period t is indicated by $a_{jt} \in [0, 1]$. Moreover due to technical and organizational constraints effective work time in task k and in given competence r may be limited to b_{kr} value, known in advance.

In order to provide the solution for scheduling and proper staff assignment to task requiring particular competences $x_{kjrt} \in [0, 1]$ decision variable is introduced and is interpreted as the time the employee j works in task k in competence r in period t. This constitutes the 4-dimensional array of working times.

For the purpose of reflecting the process of competence expertise grow and decay it is assumed that if an employee j worked during x time in competence r his competence expertise grows by $\alpha_r \times x$ and α_r is a constant related to competence r. Moreover, knowledge depreciation in competence r is reflected by forgetting factor β_r. Under such assumptions the z_{jrt} might be obtained from Eq. 1.

$$z_{jrt} = z_{jr1} - \beta_r(t-1) + \alpha_r \sum_{k=1}^{K} \sum_{s=1}^{t-1} x_{kjrs} \qquad (1)$$

where: z_{jr1} is the competence expertise on the beginning of planning horizon, $\beta_r(t-1)$ reflects knowledge depreciation, and $\alpha_r \sum_{k=1}^{K} \sum_{s=1}^{t-1} x_{kjrs}$ is the competence expertise grow.

2.2   Objective Function

The problem of answering the question if within available resources it is possible to realize a set of projects and if so, what is the best scheduling for that optimizing given criterion, may be represented in terms of work time arrays $x = (x_{kjrt})$ by the objective function in Eq. 2.

$$g(x) = \sum_{r=1}^{R} \sum_{j=1}^{m} (z_{jr(T+1)} - z_{jr1}) \tag{2}$$

The function from Eq. 2 represents the benefits in competence expertise obtained by whole staff in the planning horizon T. The considered problem is now to find a solution $g(x)$ that is maximal.

There exist some constraints in the problem. First of them is the fact that in one period t employee j can not work more than his capacity, according to Eq. 3.

$$\sum_{k=1}^{K} \sum_{r=1}^{R} x_{kjrt} \leq a_{jt} \tag{3}$$

Additionally, the required overall work time d_{kr} for each competence r in each task k must be allocated with proper amount of work time provided by employees, namely see Eq. 4.

$$\sum_{\rho=1}^{\delta_k} \sum_{j=1}^{m} x_{kjrt} = d_{kr} \tag{4}$$

As there exist the technical and organizational constraints, the effective work time in task k and in competence r must be limited to b_{kr}, see Eq. 5.

$$\sum_{j=1}^{m} x_{kjrt} \leq b_{kr} \tag{5}$$

Finally, it is required that all tasks are performed in planned time (between start and due time). It is fulfilled by constraint in Eq. 6.

$$(t - \rho_k)x_{kjrt} \geq 0 \text{ and } (\delta_k - t)x_{kjrt} \geq 0 \tag{6}$$

3   Case Study

Let consider the staff scheduling problem on the very simple and basic example in the hypothetical organization. As presented in Tab. 1, the company is facing the situation when needs to answer the question if it is able to handle two projects, 1 and 2, $n = 2$. The projects consist together of five tasks ($K = 5$). There is one task, number 1, that requires three distinct competencies: 1, 2 and 3; two tasks requires two competencies (tasks 2 and 3) and the rest only one competence.

There are only three distinct competencies (R=3). Each competence in each task needs to be provided within defined time constraints. e.g. the competence 1 in task 1 is ready to be started in period 1 and should be finished till the beginning of period 3. Similarly the required work effort d is presented in next column. The organizational and technological limitation to the work done in each task in each competence is given in the last column (b).

Initially company has knowledge about the project, about its organizational and technological limitations and about initial level of competence expertise for its employees. It can be observed in the Tab. 2 till the column t=0. With such a data the search process for staff scheduling problem starts. It can be performed by various multi-objective optimization methods, e.g. [3,4,8]. For the purpose of this case study it has been chosen the method that tries to allocate as much work effort as possible to the first employee and the rest to the second. What is important, the whole model usually should optimize some objective function, e.g. like in Eq. 2. If the optimization result with any solution it means that the set of project given as an input may be realized by the company within given resources.

As presented in Tab. 3 and Tab. 4 employees have some work effort assigned. The calculation of work effort for each of periods is based on the derivation from the Tab. 1 and Tab. 2. For the first employee it is assigned 0.625 in the task 1 and competence 1 as the overall work limit b holds for that task and competence (is limited to 0.5). The initial competence expertise of first employee for competence 1 equals to 0.8 - she needs to spend 0.625 work effort to fulfil the limit. As the employee still have spare work effort, it has assigned 0.375 in task 4 and competence 2. It does not fulfil whole task and moreover does not cross the work limit. Therefore, the second employee (Tab. 4) has assigned the rest of effort for this task. The value is calculated with respect to initial competence expertise of the second employee. According to projects description (Tab. 1), no other tasks can be started at current period ($t = 1$) and no other work effort can be planned for the period. Therefore the next time period may be planned. However, prior to planning, it is required to update the competence expertise for both employees. The Eq. 1 is employed and the column t=1 filled in Tab. 2. The planning process is repeated as described above for all periods till the end of the projects. In the case study it was assumed that $\forall r$ $\beta_r = 0.05$ and $\alpha_r = 0.3$. Moreover the work capacity for all periods for each of employees was set to 1.

4   Discussion

As it can be observed, the proposed solution for staff scheduling is static. The decision about whole schedule is taken at t=0. Therefore it is required that all tasks and their durations should be known in advance. Moreover the model assumes that available amount of resources (staff) stays constant during T. No changes (new employees, leaves) in staff are considered.

In overall, the presented problem has a continuous multi-objectives optimization nature. The search space consists of the work time arrays x for given set

Table 1. The set of projects to be staffed

Project (i)	Task (k)	Competence (r)	Start time (ρ)	End time (δ)	Work effort (d)	Work limit (b)
1	1	1	1	3	1	0.5
		2	2	3	0.1	0.6
		3	2	3	0.2	0.2
	2	1	3	4	0.1	0.1
		2	4	5	0.05	0.8
	3	1	4	6	1	0.6
		3	5	6	1.9	0.7
2	4	2	1	3	0.6	0.5
	5	2	2	3	0.5	0.6

Table 2. The description of employee competence expertise in the project

Employee (j)	Competence (r)	Competence expertise (z)					
		t=0	t=1	t=2	t=3	t=4	t=5
1	1	0.8	0.937	1.047	0.997	1.247	1.197
	2	0.6	0.662	0.682	0.797	0.747	0.697
	3	0.9	0.850	0.871	1.097	1.047	1.297
2	1	0.2	0.150	0.100	0.350	0.301	0.251
	2	0.7	0.768	0.931	0.897	0.848	0.798
	3	0.8	0.750	0.700	0.997	0.947	1.167

Table 3. The planned work effort for employee 1

Project (i)	Task (k)	Competence (r)	Employee work effort (x)					
			t=1	t=2	t=3	t=4	t=5	t=6
1	1	1	0.625	0.533				
		2						
		3		0.235				
	2	1						
		2						
	3	1				1		
		3					1	
2	4	2	0.375					
	5	2		0.232				

of projects. Under assumptions presented in [7], such kind of problem might be approximated and reduced to multi-objective linear program, that maximizes the objective function. The solution might be obtained by application of multi-objective meta-heuristics such as genetic algorithms or ant colony optimization techniques.

Table 4. The planned work effort for employee 2

Project (i)	Task (k)	Competence (r)	Employee work effort (x)					
			t=1	t=2	t=3	t=4	t=5	t=6
1	1	1						
		2		0.13				
		3						
	2	1			1			
		2				0.056		
	3	1				0.003		
		3					0.899	
2	4	2	0.393	0.130				
	5	2		0.451				

5 Conclusions

A model for competence-oriented staff scheduling problem was proposed in the paper. It has the ability to assess whether the given set of projects with defined competence requirements is able to be realized by organization. The model is able to result with proposal of staffing schedule. It is obtained by optimization of given objective function, such as competence increase maximization of the whole staff. A case study of the model utilization was presented in the paper. The preliminary studies on the proposed model allow to conclude, that it reflects the nature of staffing process well.

Further studies and experiments will concern the staff scheduling problem across many distinct projects with real world data. Moreover, the impact on the solution and computation time will be studied with various types of computational solutions for the problem.

Acknowledgement. This work was supported by The Polish Ministry of Science and Higher Education the research project, 2011-12 and Fellowship o-financed by European Union within European Social Fund.

References

1. Armbruster, D., Gel, E.S., Murakami, J.: Bucket brigades with worker learning. European Journal of Operational Research 176, 264–274 (2007)
2. Alba, E., Chicano, F.: Software project management with GAs. Information Sciences 177, 2380–2401 (2007)
3. Coello, C., Lamont, G., Van Veldhuizen, D.: Evolutionary algorithms for solving multi-objective problems. Springer, Heidelberg (2007)
4. Dasgupta, P., Chakrabarti, P., DeSarkar, S.: Multiobjective heuristic search: an introduction to intelligent search methods for Multicriteria Optimization. Vieweg (1999)
5. Eiselt, H.A., Marianov, V.: Employee positioning and workload allocation. Computers and Operations Research 35, 513–524 (2008)

6. Fraczkowski, K.: Model of mapping activities and competence in ICT projects. Annales UMCS Informatica AI 4, 86–103 (2006)
7. Gutjahr, W.J., Katzensteiner, S., Reiter, P., Stummer, C., Denk, M.: Competence-driven project portfolio selection, scheduling and staff assignment. Central European Journal of Operations Research 16, 281–306 (2008)
8. Jones, D.F., Mirrazavi, S.K., Tamiz, M.: Multi-objective meta-heuristics: An overview of the current state-of-the-art. European Journal of Operational Research 137, 1–9 (2002)
9. Kolisch, R., Hartmann, S.: Experimental investigation of heuristics for resource-constrained project scheduling: an update. European Journal of Operational Research 174, 23–37 (2006)
10. Mansfield, R.S.: Building competency models: approaches for HR professionals. Human Resource Management 35, 7–18 (1996)
11. Shippmann, J.S., Ash, R.A., Battista, M., Carr, L., Eyde, L.D., Hesketh, B., Kehoe, J., Pearlman, K., Sanchez, J.I.: The practice of competency modeling. Personnel Psychology 53, 703–740 (2000)

Development of a Dynamic and Intelligent Software Quality Model

Jamaiah Yahaya[1], Aziz Deraman[1,3], Siti Sakira Kamaruddin[2], and Ruzita Ahmad[2]

[1] Faculty of Information Science and Technology,
National University of Malaysia (UKM), 43600 Bangi, Selangor, Malaysia
[2] School of Computing, College of Arts and Sciences,
Northern University of Malaysia (UUM), 06010 Sintok
Kedah, Malaysia
[3] Vice Cancellor Office, University of Malaysia, Terengganu (UMT),
21030 Kuala Terengganu
Terengganu, Malaysia
jhy@ftsm.ukm.my, a.d@umt.edu.my, Sakira@uum.edu.my,
rita_azura@yahoo.com

Abstract. Previous research has identified factors and attributes for static quality model. This research aims to construct a dynamic and intelligent software quality model for effective software product assessment. Previous model of software quality and known as PQF model consists of two main quality attributes: the behavioural and the human aspect. These two components of quality produce a balance model between technical requirement and human factor. The proposed dynamic intelligent model of PQF (i-PQF) should capable to identify and recommend to the environment if there is any new attribute to be included in the model. This is done by integrating artificial intelligence technique and methods to produce a complete algorithm for assessing software product using intelligent model. It will be tested using a prototype. The new model is useful for organization in assessment of software products as well as to integrate in future researches as a quality benchmark.

Keywords: Intelligent Software Quality Model, Software Assessment, Dynamic Quality Factors.

1 Introduction

Softwares have become an important part of our day to day life and in today's competitive world, the quality of software product is of great concern to the researchers as well as developers. It requires continuous improvement to retain survival of a software company either in private or public sector. Software quality assurance affects both immediate profitability and long-term retention of customer goodwill. In January 2002, Bill Gates demanded Microsoft to think of quality of their products and to produce fewer defects in its products [3]. He realized the importance and emergence of this new definition of quality. He sent e-mail to all employees reminding them the necessities and higher priorities of trustworthy computing [4].

A. Abd Manaf et al. (Eds.): ICIEIS 2011, Part I, CCIS 251, pp. 537–550, 2011.

The past decade has seen rapid development and diffusion of software and ICT related technologies not only in Malaysia but also worldwide. In Malaysia, statistic produced by Malaysia Super Corridor (MSC) (2011) states that 77% from 2520 operational MSC status companies are functioning on software development and information technology, and 8% are working on shared services and outsourcing, 11% are running on creative multimedia, while 4% are functioning on higher learning institutions (see Fig. 1). It shows that software development industry has a significant contribution and impact to the development and success of the MSC. Thus, an appropriate attention is necessary to monitor the quality of software product delivered by these companies as well as other non-MSC companies, organizations and public sectors.

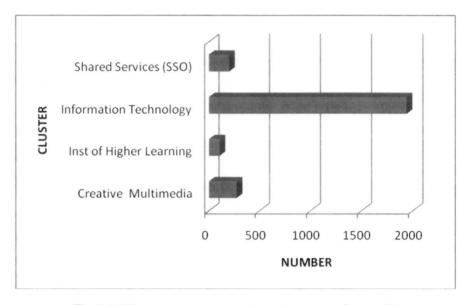

Fig. 1. MSC status companies by technologies cluster. Source: [5]

This paper is organized as follows. In section 2, the discussion focuses on the traditional software quality models. Section 3 discusses the Pragmatic Quality Factor (PQF) which is the basic and static quality assessment model used in this research. Section 4 presents the new dynamic and intelligent software quality model (i-PQF) follows by the research approach and techniques and methods for intelligent and dynamic quality model. Section 7 presents the development of i-PQF and section 8 concludes this paper.

2   Traditional Software Quality Models

International Organization for Standardization (or ISO) defines software as "all or part of the programs, procedures, rules, and associated documentation of information processing system". Software product is defined as "the set of computer programs, procedures, and possibly associated documentation and data designated for delivery to a user" [16]. The term product from the view of software engineer covers the programs, documents, and data. While from the view of user's product is the resulted information that somehow makes the user's world better.

General expressions of how quality is realized in software dealing with "fitness for use" and "conformance to requirements". The term "fitness of use" usually means characteristics such as usability, maintainability, and reusability. On the other hand, "conformance to requirements" means that software has value to the users [6]. ISO defines quality as "the totality of features and characteristics of a product or services that bear on its ability to satisfy stated or implied needs" [16],[7]. IEEE defines software quality as – a software feature or characteristic used to assess the quality of a system or component [8]. Software quality is also defined as the fitness for use of the software product and to conform to software requirements and to provide useful services [17]. Later, software quality is defined as "conformance to explicitly stated functional and performance requirements, explicitly documented development standards, and implicit characteristics that are expected of all professionally developed software" [9].

In many organizations, software is considered as one of the main assets with which the organization can enhance its competitive global positioning in current global economic era. To remain competitive, software firms must deliver high quality products on time and within budget. Software Engineering Institute's Capability Maturity Model (CMM) (cited in Slunghter, Harter and Krishnan [10]) reported the following quote from a software manager: "I'd rather have it wrong than have it late. We can always fix it later". Thus, many complaints have been reported regarding quality of the software. These complaints claimed that software quality was not improving but rather deteriorated steadily and worsening. Therefore, users reported and claimed that software was being delivered with bugs that needed to be fixed and dissatisfied with the product [2],[1].

Denning [2] argued that "software quality is more likely to be attained by giving much greater emphasis to customer satisfaction. Program correctness is essential but is not sufficient to earn the assessment that the software is of quality and is dependable". Software quality and evaluation not only deal with technical aspects but also in dimensions of economic (managers' viewpoint), social (users' viewpoint) and as well as technical (developers' viewpoint) [11].

Dromey [14] stated that an ultimate theory of software quality was like "the chimera of the ancient Greeks, is a mythical beast of hybrid character and fanciful conception. We obliged, however, to strive to make progress, even though we realize that progress often brings a new set of problems". He also suggested that software quality usually referred to high-level attributes like functionality, reliability and maintainability and the important thing to focus was on the priority needs for the software. Dromey stated that priorities vary from product to product and project to project.

Software product quality can be evaluated via three categories of evaluations: internal measures, external measures and quality in use measures [12]. Internal measuring is the evaluation based on internal attributes typically static measures of intermediate products and external measuring is based on external attributes typically measuring the behaviour of the code when executed. While the quality in use measures include the basic set of quality in use characteristic that effect the software. This characteristic includes effectiveness, productivity, safety and satisfaction. This measurement is an on-going research of SQuaRE which is the next generation of ISO 9126 but not fully published and accepted currently. SQuare quality model consists of internal and external measures that include quality in use aspects. It presents similar concept of characteristics and subcharacteristics as in ISO 9126 approach [13].

Our previous study has developed a new enhanced quality model and named as Pragmatic Quality Factor (PQF) [22]. This model has been tested and applied in certification process in several real case studies. It is a static model of quality with fix attributes and measures.

Even though there are several models of quality available from literature, it still believed that quality is a complex concept. Quality is in the eye of the beholder and it means different things to different people and highly context dependent [18] [19]. Therefore, "software quality is nothing more than a recipe. Some like it hot, sweet, salty or greasy" [20]. Thus, there can be no single simple measure of software quality acceptable to everyone. The available software quality models only focus on technical aspects of quality and none of them are considering the user satisfaction and expectation in the measurement. In addition, weight of individual attribute is an important aspect to be included in the research [21].

3   Pragmatic Quality Factor (PQF): A Quality Assessment Model

Our previous research has constructed a new software quality model for effective and practical software assesment that has been tested in several case studies, involving several large organisations in Malaysia [40]. This model is known as Pragmatic Quality Factor or PQF. PQF consists of two main quality attributes: the behavioural and the human aspect. The behavioural attributes concerns with assessing software product to ensure the quality of the software and how it behaves in certain operating environment. They are also known as quality in use. While the impact attributes deal with how the software reacts and impacts to the environment. These two components of quality produce a balance model between technical requirement and human factor. The available software quality model such as the ISO 9126 model does not accommodate the other aspects of software quality requirements [16]. PQF for software assessment model has several interesting features. The features are summarized and shown in Table 1.

As mentioned above, PQF is the quality assessment model that consists of several software quality attributes. Undertaking quality attributes defined in ISO9126 model as the based line of the assessment metrics, we define two sets of attributes, which by means of the behavioural and the impact attributes. The behavioural attributes consist of high level software quality characteristics, which include usability, functionality, maintainability, portability, integrity and reliability. Previous study shows that quality attributes can be classified into different levels and weight [21]. The impact attributes indicate the conformance in user requirements, expectation and perception. Associated with these attributes are the metrics and measurements of the quality. The detail description of PQF can be found in [22].

PQF was applied in software product certification process as a guideline representation for software product assessment and certification. This model is a set of static quality attributes and measures. It is relevant and compatible with the current requirements of software quality assessment and based on empirical study conducted in Malaysia [23]. Even though it provides certain level of flexibility to the organization in the assessment by allowing to choose weight factors but this model unable to improve its components according to current and future requirements [24]. It was identified that quality attributes changes from time to time depending on current requirement.

Table 1. Features and capabilities of the PQF model

Exhibit capability
1. Provides an alternative means to certify software product in a collaborative perspective approach among users, developers and independent assessors. It is considered to provide confidentiality, security and privacy of the software. This approach accelerates the process and eliminates bias during assessment.
2. Provides means to identify quality status of a product using PQF in a practical environment. The quality attributes embedded in PQF is more convincing that meets the additional aspect of quality. The additional aspect of quality deals with human aspects and does not cover in previous software quality models.
3. Provides means to offer flexibility in obtaining certification level with a guided procedure of initializing weight values on quality attributes to meet an organisation's business requirements.

The existing literature of software quality model has consistently highlighted that software quality model act as a static model with some fundamental attributes of software quality. Table 2 shows the summarization of quality attributes in various quality models.

The study reveals that quality attributes need to be updated from time to time to meet current requirements and standard. For example, security and integrity were not included in the previous model such as McCall, Dromey and ISO9126 but were recognized as important and crucial in the current global borderless world. Thus, it is suggested to investigate the potential of flexibility and adaptation to changes of software quality model and attributes based on current and future requirements.

4 New Dynamic and Intelligent Software Quality Model

This new approach in software quality model will be integrating the intelligent technique which will enhanced the existing model of PQF. The dynamic and intelligent aspects of quality can be explored in studying and investigating the development of quality model that capable to notice, learn and adapt the changes in the environment and information needs. The literature study shows that currently the available models do not fulfill the needs of current and future requirements of software quality. It is because the models developed based on static software quality attributes. I-PQF is a new intelligent pragmatic quality factor that can be used as a new model or benchmark in software product assessment. This appearing of a new way to enhance the traditional software quality models which contains an algorithm and artificial intelligence techniques integrated in the model.

Table 2. Quality characteristics present in PQF and previous models

Quality characteristics	McCall (1976)	Boehm (1978)	FURPS (1987)	ISO 9126 (1991)	Dromey (1996)	Systemic (2003)	PQF (2007)
Testability	x	x					
Correctness	x						
Efficiency	x	x	x	x	X	x	x
Understandability		x			X		
Reliability	x	x	x	x	X	x	x
Flexibility	x						
Functionality			x	x	X	x	x
Human engineering		x					
Integrity	x						x
Interoperability	x						
Process Maturity					X		
Maintainability	x	x	x	x	X	x	x
Changeability		x					
Portability	x	x		x	X	x	x
Reusability	x				X		
Usability			x	x		x	x
Performance	x		x				
User Conformity							x

5   Research Approach

This research is implemented in five main phases with the aim is to develop a new intelligent software quality model based on PQF model. The phases are:-

5.1   Theoretical Study

The literature review on the existing research related to software quality and assessment includes the references from journals, books, proceedings and other academic research will be conducted.   The aim of this phase is to investigate the existing mechanism and problems related to software assessment and quality. The detail theoretical aspect of software quality and assessment will be outlined and important features that are expected to contribute in this proposed research will be identified.

5.2 Design of Formal Framework on Intelligent Software Quality

The second phase of this research will be on designing the formal framework on intelligent software quality and assessment. It involves refinement of specific feature of software quality and assessment to be represented using artificial intelligence approach.

5.3 Identify and Propose the AI Technique for Intelligent Software Quality Model (i-PQF)

The third phase of the research is to model the software quality using Artificial Intelligence technique. Several techniques will be studied and the appropriate technique will be chosen to be applied in this model.

5.4 Construction of Intelligent Software Quality Model (i-PQF) and Development of Prototype

The fourth phase of the research is to construct the intelligent software quality prototype. The model and Artificial Intelligence technique discovered in previous phase will be used and integrated to construct a prototype for an intelligent software quality factor.

5.5 Confirmation Study

The proposed model and prototype will be tested and validated in specific software. Feedback from the testing and validation will used to refine the model and prototype.

6 Techniques and Methods for Intelligent and Dynamic Software Quality Model

6.1 Software Quality and Artificial Intelligence (AI)

There are several studies conducted in software engineering particularly in software quality that have included artificial intelligence techniques for several purposes. Some of the identified studies are summarised next.

Khoshgoftaar, Szabo and Guasti [25] studied on exploring the behaviour of neural network in software quality models. Data is collected from components in large commercial software systems and trained them using neural network to observe the relationship between software complexity metrics and software quality metrics.

Lees, Hamza and Irgens [26] investigated the using and applying of case based reasoning (CBR) and quality function deployment (QFD) in software quality assessment. Their aim was to developed a CBR oriented software quality advisor to support the attainment of quality in software development. This was done by reference to quality case histories using software modules from previous designs.

The third study was conducted by Goa, Khoshgoftaar and Wang which dealt with an empirical investigation of filter attribute selection technique for software quality classification [29]. The artificial intelligence technique chosen was feature selection. Feature selection is a process of selecting a subset of relevant features for building learning models. This technique is relevant and appropriate for data preprocessing used in software quality modelling and other data mining problems. This study investigated the performance metrics using multilayer perceptron (MLP) learner with nine different performance metrics.

Colin J. Burgess [28] investigated research in software quality management using artificial intelligence. This research studied the used of artificial intelligence techniques to solve problems in software quality management. It outlined four areas where artificial intelligence techniques have been successfully used. The areas are: 1. The application of genetic algorithms and other search techniques to aid the automatic generation of structural test data. 2. The application of genetic algorithms to the testing of real-time systems. 3. The use of influence diagrams to aid the management of software change. 4. Improving the cost estimation of software projects.

Another research in the areas of software quality and AI was conducted by Martín Agüero et al (2010). This research presented a software quality support tool which was a Java source code evaluator and a code profiler based on computational intelligence techniques. It proposed a new approach to evaluate and identify inaccurate source code usage and transitively the software product itself. The aim of this research was to the software development industry with a new tool to increase software quality[31].

6.2   AI Techniques for Dynamic Software Quality Model

A review on current techniques in artificial intelligence has come up with three suggested techniques or methods for handling dynamic quality model proposed in this research. The techniques being identified are feature selection (FS), artificial neural network (ANN) and case-based reasoning (CBR). Each of this technique will be discussed in the following sections.

- **Feature Selection**

Feature Selection (FS) is a process of selecting a subset of relevant features for building learning models and it used to remove less important features from the training data set. Feature Selection as an important activity in data preprocessing used in software quality modeling and data mining problems that has been extensively studied for many years in data mining and machine learning.

Feature Selection technique has been divided into two categories which are feature ranking technique and feature subset selection technique. Feature ranking technique assesses attributes individually and ranks the attributes according to their individual predictive power. Whilst, feature subset selection technique selects the subset of attributes that collectively have good predictive capability. In feature subset selection technique contains two difference approaches to subset selection which are filter approach and wrapper approach. By using the filter approach, the feature subset is selected independently of the learning method which means ignoring the induction algorithm to assess the merits of features from data. Whilst, wrapper approach is selected using the same learning algorithm that will used for learning on domain represented with the selected feature subset. In this approach, the feature subset selection is done by using the induction algorithm as a black box which means no knowledge of the algorithm is needed. The feature subset selection algorithm conducts a search for a good subset using the induction algorithm itself as a part of the evaluation function [30][32][33][34][35][36].

- **Artificial Neural Network (ANN)**

The artificial neural networks (ANN) are based on the concepts of the human or biological neural networks consisting of neurons, which are interconnected by the processing elements. The ANNs are composed of two main structures namely the nodes and the links. The nodes correspond to the neurons and the links correspond to the links between neurons. The ANN accepts the values of inputs into its input nodes or input layer. These values are multiplied by a set of weights and added together to become inputs to the next set of nodes to the right of the input nodes. This layer of nodes is referred to as the hidden layer. Many ANNs contain multiple hidden layers, each feeding into the next layer. Finally, the values from last hidden layer are fed into an output node, where a mapping or thresholding function is applied and the prediction is made. The ANN is created by presenting the network with inputs from many records whose outcome is already known. By using MultiLayer Perceptron (MLP) as the architecture to learn the data set and used for training the data. While to test the data in software quality models are built by using the different classification algorithm such as Naïve Bayes, K-Nearest Neighbour (KNN), Support Vector Machine (SVM) and Logistic Regression (LR) (see [35] [37][38]).

- **Case-Based Reasoning (CBR)**

Case-Based Reasoning approach is the model which adapting previously stored solutions that have been found to be effective in the solution of earlier problems. The main purpose of Case-Based Reasoning are to ensure the fitness for purpose of a software module, to identify an appropriate set of features which may be used and to describe the performance, metrics and quality characteristics relating to each case. According to the Case-Based Reasoning, the quality attributes will be measured by presenting a list of quality factors and their definition, determined the relationship among the quality factor, established quality factor by using metric performance like Quality Function Deployment (QFD), quantified the quality attributes and calculate the total quality measures for each attributes. Case-Based Reasoning technique have to focus on high dimensionality case reasoning of the data set in the case library to support unexpected reasons from the current cases ([39], [26]).

6.3 AI Methods for Dynamic Software Quality Model

The relevant methods in software quality environment are extremely important to be applied in order to develop an algorithm as a medium to measure and evaluate the software quality factors. In addition, the function of capability in processing the data that provided by the methods chosen always acts as the main part of criteria to become the right methods application in order to fulfill the requirements from the environment. The two methods that are going to discuss here will be : Automatic Hybrid Search (AHS) and Hybrid Feature Selection (HFS). These two methods use wrapper approach in the processing function and both have capabilities in assessing and ranking factors. The wrapper approach is using the same learning algorithm that will be used for learning or classifying the domain represented with the selected feature subset. Furthermore, these methods are relevant and suitable as the appropriateness in term of creating new algorithm as needed in this research. Hence, the weight value of each factors can be calculated and performed in the frequency consistency rate of value in order to make the priority of each factors.

7   The Development of i-PQF : Intelligent and Dynamic Software Quality Model

Feature selection wrapper-based feature ranking technique which is part of feature selection will be considered as the potential AI techniques for this model. It is a process of selecting the relevant features for building learning models and acts as to remove less important features from the training data set. This technique includes the wrapper approach to assess attributes individually and ranks the attributes according to their individual predictive power. Furthermore, this approach uses learning algorithm on domain represented with the selected feature subset.

This technique allows performance to be ranked on the value of each attributes follows by the weights given by the stakeholders. If we compare with another techniques such as ANN and CBR, it seems that these two techniques irrelevant to be used in this new software quality model because both techniques focus on high dimensionality of data.

The mentioned technique will be embedded with selected method to develop algorithm as a medium to measure and evaluate the quality attributes. The identified methods are Automatic Hybrid Search (AHS) and Hybrid Feature Selection (HFS). In this approach, the weight values from the stakeholders can be calculated and performed in the frequency consistency rate of value in order to make the priority of each attributes. The general architecture of this environment is illustrated in figure 2.

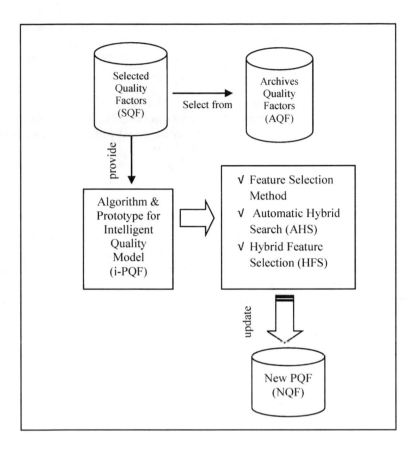

Fig. 2. The General Architecture of i-PQF

The architecture explains that there are two main data needed in this environment for the construction of the intelligent quality model algorithm. The two data are the archives quality factors (AQF) and selected quality factors (SQF). The proposed prototype and algorithms will intelligently produce a new software quality factors (NQF) based on the inputs of SQF. As shown in Fig. 2, the algorithm and prototype will carried out the feature selection wrapper-based feature ranking techniques and automatic hybrid search and hybrid feature selections as the embedded methods. The detail description of the three data involve in this environment is explained in the following:-

- AQF contains all possible software quality factors or attributes such as functionality, maintainability, efficiency, portability, reliability and etc which we can refer from literature.
- SQF represents the selected quality factor that been defined by users from previous data. In this PQF model, users have the opportunities to select the appropriate and relevant quality factors to be applied assessment exercise depending on the organizations requirements. Thus, $SQF \in AQF$.

- NQF represents the new quality factor identified in the environment. NQF is obtained by manipulation of experience and learning capabilities of the system supported by the algorithm and data. In this environment the data will be provided by the SQF.

This research is an on-going research and currently we are at construction phase. With the technique and method identified, an experimental design will be conducted which involves three steps: 1) Input data, 2) data processing and 3) testing. More detail of this implementation will be documented in near future.

8 Conclusions

The proposed dynamic and intelligent software quality model should capable to identify and recommend to the environment if there is any new attribute to be included in the model. Thus, the model will be updated and fulfilled with current and future requirements of assessment. This can be done using artificial intelligence technique and method. The main objective of this research is to develop a dynamic and intelligent software quality model for software assessment. This new model (i-PQF) will provide a complete algorithm and mechanism for assessing software product using intelligent model, which is useful for organization in selection and assessment of software as well as to integrate with other researches and projects as a quality benchmark. This will also too ensure that quality of the software meets the nation's and organisation's requirements and standards in current and for future.

Acknowledgments. The research is funded by the Fundamental Research Grant Scheme, Ministry of Higher Education, Malaysia.

References

1. Whittaker, J.A., Voas, J.M.: 50 Years of Software: Key Principles for Quality. IEEE IT Pro., 28–35 (November/December 2002)
2. Denning, P.J.: What is Software Quality? A Commentary from Communications of ACM (January 1992)
3. Mann, C.C.: Why Software is So Bad? MIT Technology Review 105, 33–38 (2002)
4. Voas, J., Agresti, W.W.: Software Quality From Behavioral Perspective. IT Professional, 46–50 (July/August 2004)
5. MSC: MSC Malaysia Facts and Figures (2011),
   http://www.mscmalaysia.my/topic/12073059402587
6. Tervonen, I.: Support for Quality-Based Design and Inspection. IEEE Software, 44–54 (January 1996)
7. Jenner, M.G.: Software Quality Management and ISO 9001. A Wiley/QED publication, New York (1995)
8. IEEE: IEEE Standard for a Software Quality Metrics Methodology (1993),
   http://ieeexplore.ieee.org/xpl/standards.jsp
9. Galin, D.: Software Quality Assurance: From Theory to Implementation. Pearson Addison Wesley, Harlow (2004)

10. Slaughter, S.A., Harter, D.E., Krishnan, M.S.: Evaluating the Cost of Software Quality. Communications of The ACM 41(8), 67–73 (1998)
11. Buglione, L., Abran, A.: A Quality Factor for Software. In: 3rd International Conference on Quality and Reliability, QUALITA 1999, pp. 335–344 (1999)
12. Suryn, W., Abran, A., Bourque, P., Laporte, C.: Software Product Quality Practices: Quality Measurement and Evaluation Using TL9000 and ISO/IEC9126. In: The 10th International Workshop, Software Technology and Engineering Practice, STEP (2002)
13. Suryn, W., Abran, A., April, A.: ISO/IEC SQuaRE: The Second Generation of Standards for Software Product Quality (2003),
    http://www.lrgl.uqam.ca/publications/pdf/799.pdf
14. Dromey, G.R.: Software Product Quality: Theory, Model and Practice. Software Quality Institute. Griffith University, Brisbane, Technical Report (1998),
    http://www.sqi.gu.edu.au
15. Dekkers, C.A., McQuaid, P.A.: The Dangers of Using Software Metrics to (Mis)Manage. IT Pro., 24–30 (March/April 2002)
16. ISO/IEC 9126: Software Quality Characteristics and Metrics-Part2: External Metrics. Technical Report, ISO/IECJTC1/SC7/WG6 (1996)
17. Schulmeyer, G.G., McManus, J.I.: Handbook of Software Quality Assurance, 3rd edn. Prentice Hall, New Jersey (1998)
18. Voas, J., Laplante, P.: Standards Confusion and Harmonization. Computer 40(7), 94–96 (2007)
19. Kitchenham, B., Pfleeger, S.L.: Software Quality: The Elusive Target. IEEE Software, 12–21 (January 1996)
20. Voas, J.: Software's Secret Sauce: The "-ilities". IEEE Computer, 14–15 (November/December 2004)
21. Yahaya, J.H.: The Development of Software Certification Model Based on Product Quality Approach. UKM PhD thesis (2007)
22. Yahaya, J.H., Deraman, A., Hamdan, A.R.: Software Quality from Behavioural and Human Perspectives. IJCSNS International Journal of Computer Science and Network Security 8(8), 53–63 (2008)
23. Yahaya, J.H., Deraman, A., Hamdan, A.R.: Software Quality and Certification: Perception and Practices in Malaysia. Journal of ICT (JICT) 5, 63–82 (2006)
24. Deraman, A., Yahaya, J.H.: Measuring The Unmeasurable Characteristics of Software Quality Using Pragmatic Quality Factor. In: 2010 3rd IEEE International Conference on Computer Science and Information Technology, Chengdu, China, July 7-10, pp. 197–202 (2010) ISBN:978-1-4244-5539-3
25. Khoshgoftaar, T.M., Szabo, R.M., Guasti, P.J.: Exploring the Behavior of Neural Network Software Quality Models. Software Engineering Journal, 89–95 (May 1995)
26. Lees, Hamza, Irgen: Applying Case-Based Reasoning to System Quality Management (1996),
    http://citeseerx.ist.psu.edu/viewdoc/summary?
    doi=10.1.1.51.7943
27. Briand, L., et al.: Exploring the Relationships Between Design Measures and Software Quality in Object-Oriented Systems. Journal of Systems and Software 51, 245–273 (2000)
28. Burgess, C.J.: Using Artificial Intelligence to Solve Problems in Software Quality Management. In: The 8th International Conference on Software Quality Management (SQM2000), Software Quality Management VIII, SQM 2000, pp. 77–89 (2000) ISBN 1-902505-25-5

29. Gao, K., Khoshgoftaar, T.M., Wang, H.: An Empirical Investigation of Filter Attribute Selection Technique for Software Quality Classification. In: The 2009 IEEE International Conference in Information Reuse and Integration, Las Vegas, Nevada, USA (2009)
30. Goa, K., Khoshgoftaar, T., Napolitano, A.: Exploring Software Quality Classification With a Wrapper-Based Feature Ranking Technique. In: The 21st IEEE International Conference on Tools with Artificial Intelligence (2009)
31. Aguero, M., Madou, F., Esperon, G., Lopez, D.L.: Artificial Intelligence for Quality Improvement. World Academy of Science and Technology 63 (2010)
32. Tadeuchi, Y., Oshima, R., Nishida, K., Yamauchi, K., Omori, T.: Quick Online Feature Selection Method for Regression – A Feature Selection Method Inspired By Human Behavior (2007),
    http://ieeexplore.ieee.org/xpls/abs_all.jsp?arnumber=
    4414117&tag=1
33. Blum, A.L., Langley, P.: Selection of Relevant Features and Examples in Machine Learning. Artificial Intelligence 97, 245–271 (1997)
34. Guyon, I., Elisseeff, A.: An Introduction to Variable and Feature Selection. Journal of Machine Learning Research 3, 1157–1182 (2003)
35. Forman, G.: An Extensive Empirical Study of Feature Selection Metrics for Text Classification. Journal of Machine Learning Research 3, 1289–1305 (2003)
36. Liu, H., Yu, L.: Toward Integrating Feature Selection Algorithm for Classification and Clustering. IEEE Transaction on Knowledge and Data Engineering 17(4), 491–502 (2005)
37. Kumar, R., Rai, S., Trahen, J.L.: Neural Network Techniques for Software Quality Evaluation. In: The Annual Reliability and Maintainability Symposium, pp. 155–161 (1998)
38. Khoshgoftaar, T.M., Szabo, R.M., Guasti, P.J.: Exploring the Behavior of Neural Network Software Quality Models. Software Engineering Journal, 89–95 (May 1995)
39. Kolodner, J.: Case-Based Reasoning. Morgan Kaufmann (1993)
40. Yahaya, J.H., Deraman, A., Hamdan, A.R.: Continuosly Ensuring Quality Through Software Product Certification: A Case Study. In: The International Conference on Information Society (i-Society 2010), London, UK, June 28-30 (2010)

Multi-objective Test Suite Optimization for Event-B Models

Ionuţ Dincă

University of Pitesti, Department of Computer Science
Str. Targu din Vale 1, 110040 Pitesti, Romania
ionut.dinca@upit.ro

Abstract. Event-B is a formalism that is used in modeling and proving the consistency of complex systems. The test suite generation methods have been recently introduced as research theme. In this paper, the multi-objective test suite optimization problem is introduced for Event-B testing. However, there exist many optimization criteria in real-life testing problems. Given that, six specifically multi-objective test suite optimization problems are formulated. Two modern Multi-Objective Evolutionary Algorithms are used for solving them: NSGA-II [6] and SPEA-2 [18]. The experiments have been conducted using five test suites generated from two industrial inspired Event-B models (five different machines).

1 Introduction

Event-B [1] is a formal modeling language for reliable systems specification and verification which was introduced about ten years ago and widely used in industrial projects. The Event-B formalism is supported by a mature tool called *Rodin* (see http://sourceforge.net/projects/rodin-b-sharp) which offers different capabilities such as theorem-proving, composition or model-checking of Event-B models.

Recently, there has been an increasing interest for automatically test suite generation for Event-B models [15,7]. Most approaches generate a large number of test cases for a particular model until a test adequacy criterion is achieved. For example, the ProB tool [13] (available in the Rodin platform) can be used to explore the state space of Event-B models, verify various properties using model-checking and generate test cases along the traversal using certain coverage criteria (e.g. event coverage). This approach has been applied to models from the business application area in [15].

The cost of executing, storing, and maintaining these large test suites can be reduced through *test suite optimization* techniques. The test suite optimization produces a subset of the initial test suite that preserves the original test adequacy criterion by removing the redundant test cases with respect to the considered criterion. However, in real testing problems, there exist multiple test criteria, because a single ideal criterion is simply impossible to be formulated and achieved. Harman argues in his recently paper [9] that single-objective test suite optimization is not useful in practical, because testers typically have many

A. Abd Manaf et al. (Eds.): ICIEIS 2011, Part I, CCIS 251, pp. 551–565, 2011.

different objectives. For example, a frequently optimization problem is to produce a minimal test suite which achieves maximal coverage of the model entities with a minimal execution cost.

This paper introduces for the first time the multi-objective test suite optimization problem for Event-B models. Due to the complexity of this problems (exponentially related to the original test suite size), we chose the Multi-Objective Evolutionary Algorithms for solving them.

The primary contributions of this paper are as follows:

- The paper introduces a multi-objective formulation of test suite optimization problem for Event-B models. Six specifically test suite optimization problems were proposed: minimize the size of the test suite, minimize the number of the executed events, minimize the longest execution path, minimize the execution time, maximize the distribution quality and balance the lengths of the paths while the longest path is minimized. For all this problems, the test adequacy criterion is the event coverage. The mathematical formulations of this problems facilitate the using of multi-objective evolutionary algorithms for solving them.
- In order to increase the confidence, the paper uses two modern Multi-Objective Evolutionary Algorithms for solving the above optimization problems: Non Dominating Sorting Genetic Algorithm (NSGA-II) [6] and Strength Pareto Evolutionary Algorithm 2 (SPEA-2) [18].
- The paper also chose a total of 5 test suites generated from two industrial inspired Event-B models (five different Event-B machines under test) as subjects for the test suite optimization problems.

In the remainder of the paper we describe the Event-B framework (Section 2), introduce the test suite optimization problem for event-B models (Section 3), mathematically define the six different test suite optimization problems (Section 3.1), present the multi-objective evolutionary algorithms (Section 3.2), describe our experiment set up and results (Section 4), and draw the conclusions (Section 5).

2   Event-B and Test Suite Generation

Event-B is a formal method [1] for modeling the states and behavior of a system in order to prove its consistency. The states are modeled by global variables while the behavior is modeled by events. Events transform the system from a state to another state by updating the values of variables. Event-B uses mathematical proof based on set theory and logic to ensure the consistency of modeled system.

The components of an Event-B model are grouped in two categories: *Contexts* and *Machines*. Contexts contain types and constants (the static parts of the system) while Machines contain variables and events (the dynamic parts).

An event has *guards*, *actions* and optionally *parameters*. The guards represent the enabling conditions of the event while actions determine how specific variables change as a result of the event execution. Parameters are local variables whose values can be used for updating the global variables. The general form of an event is

$$\text{Event} \triangleq \textbf{any } p \textbf{ where } G(p, v) \textbf{ then } S(p, v) \textbf{ end},$$

where p is the set of local parameters, v is a set of global variables appearing in the event, G is a predicate over p and v, called the guard and $S(p, v)$ represents a substitution. If the guard of an event is false, the event cannot occur and is called disabled. The substitution S describes how the global variables in the set v are modified. The values of the global variables are constraint by *invariants* which are properties of the system that should be preserved during system execution. The execution of a model starts with a special event which initializes the global variables. At each execution step the set of enabled events (for which the guards are satisfied) is computed and one enabled event is non-deterministically chosen to be executed (all its actions are simultaneously executed).

The Event-B development process is based on *refinement*: a system is modeled as a series of successive refinements, starting with an abstract representation of the system (the details are ignored). Details are added gradually to the abstract model. A refinement step introduces new functionality (new events) or add details of current functionality (a detailed version of an existing event). From a given machine, M_1, a new machine, $M2$, can be built as a refinement of M_1. Therefore this model of development produces refinement chains of Event-B machines.

Our approach for test suite generation. Given an Event-B machine M with $E = \{e_1, e_2, ..., e_m\}$ the set of its events, a test case can be defined as a sequence of events in E that can be executed in the machine M (an execution path). Each test case begins with a special event called *INITIALISATION* which serves to initialize the global variables of the machine before starting the execution of a test case. A test suite is by definition a collection of test cases.

An approach using the explicit model checker ProB was proposed in [15] for test suite generation. It suffers from the classical state space explosion when applied to models with large variable domains. Given that, we chose to implement the algorithm from [12]. It constructs a successive set of finite approximation models for the set of Event-B executable paths up to a length ℓ. The iterative nature of the algorithm fits well with the notion of refinement from the Event-B method. A detailed presentation of this algorithm is out of the scope of this paper. We just say that the algorithm was implemented as a plug-in (for installing instructions see http://wiki.event-b.org/index.php/MBT_plugin) for Rodin platform and was used to generate the subjects for our experiments.

3   Multi-objective Test Suite Optimization for Event-B Models

In this section we introduce the multi-objective test suite minimization problem. We adopt here the definitions from [16]. Generally, a multi-objective optimization problem can be defined as to find a vector of decision variables x, which optimizes a vector of M objective functions $f_i(x), 1 \leq i \leq M$. The objective functions are the mathematical formulations of the optimization criteria. Usually, these functions are conflicting, which means that improvements with respect to one function can only be achieved when impairing the solution quality with respect to another objective function. Solutions that can not be improved with respect to any functions without impairing another one are called *Pareto-optimal solutions*.

Formally, let us assume that, without loss of generality, the goal is to minimize the functions $f_i(x), 1 \leq i \leq M$. A decision vector x is said to *dominate* a decision vector y (we write $x \succ y$) if and only if the following property is satisfied by their objective vectors:

$$f_i(x) \leq f_i(y), \forall i \in \{1, 2, ..., M\} \text{ and } \exists i_0 \in \{1, 2, ..., M\}, f_{i_0}(x) < f_{i_0}(y).$$

The dominance relations states that a solution x is preferable to another solution y if x is at least as good as y in all objectives *and* better with respect to at least one objective. The *Pareto-optimal set* is the set of all decision vectors that are not dominated by any other decision vectors. The corresponding objective vectors are said to from *Pareto frontier*. Therefore, the multi-objective optimization problem can be defined in the following manner:

Given: a vector of decision variables, x, and a set of objective functions, $f_i(x), 1 \leq i \leq M$,

Problem: minimize$\{f_1(x), f_2(x), ..., f_M(x)\}$ by finding the Pareto-optimal set over the feasible set of solutions.

With respect to multi-criteria test suite optimization, the objective functions f_i are the mathematical descriptions of the testing criteria that must be satisfied to provide desired adequate testing of the model. In real industrial testing problems, there exist multiple test criteria, because a single ideal criterion is simply impossible to be achieved. For example, a frequently optimization problem is to produce a minimal test suite which achieves maximal coverage of the model entities with a minimal execution cost. Therefore, this is a *bi-objective minimization* test suite problem.

Formally, multi-objective test suite optimization problem can be defined in the following manner [17]:

Multi-Objective Test Suite Optimization

Given: a test suite TS, a vector of M objective functions $f_i, 1 \leq i \leq M$

Problem: to produce a subset $T \subset TS$, such that T is a Pareto-optimal set with respect to the set of the above objective functions.

In the following, we instantiate this general multi-objective test suite optimization problem with respect to our Event-B models.

Let be an Event-B machine M for which we have generated a test suite TS. Of course, TS satisfies a set of test requirements which are expressed as a level of coverage of the model. In this paper we only consider that the test suite TS achieves the following simple coverage criterion:

Event Coverage Criterion: A test suite $TS = \{t_1, ..., t_m\}$ of m test cases of Event-B model M is said to achieve *event coverage criterion* if and only if for each event e of M there exists a test case $t_i \in TS$ which covers e.

Having the above criterion in mind, we can formulate the following optimization problem:

Test Suite Minimization Problem

Given: A test suite TS generated for a machine M with $E = \{e_1, e_2, ..., e_n\}$ the set of events, and subsets of TS, T_is, one associated with each of the e_is such that any one of the test cases t_j belonging to T_i can be used to cover e_i.

Problem: Find minimal test suite T from TS which covers all e_i.

This problem is NP-complete because it can be reduced to the minimum set-cover problem [5] in the following manner.

We recall that for us a test case $tc \in TS$ is an execution path which consists in a sequence of events from E. Let be $cov(tc) = \{e \in E | tc$ covers $e\}$ the set of events covered by the test case tc. By definition, $cov(tc)$ is a subset of E. Therefore the solution T of the above test suite minimization problem is exactly a minimum set cover for E because

$$\bigcup_{t \in T} cov(t) = E$$

and T is the minimal subset of TS which covers E.

Many solutions have been proposed to solve this test suite minimization problem [4,10,2,14,3]. Due to its exponential complexity, in this paper we use Multi-Objective Evolutionary Algorithms for solving it. For that, we mathematically reformulate it as a constraint be-objective test suite optimization problem (TSO1 problem from the next section).

3.1   Optimization Criteria

Inspired by practical test suite optimization problems from industrial projects [15], we propose here different test suite optimization criteria. In order to solve the optimization problems described in this section using Multi-Objective Evolutionary Algorithms, this criteria are mathematically formulated as 6 different constraint multi-objective optimization problems.

TSO1-Minimizing the size of the test suite. Due to the restrictions of time, obtaining a minimal test suite which achieves maximal level of coverage is of particular interest among testers. Therefore the goal of this problem is to produce a test suite that contains the smallest possible number of test cases that achieve the same coverage (in our case, the event coverage) as the complete test suite. We formulate this problem as a constraint be-objective optimization problem: maximize event coverage (the first objective) by a minimum number of test cases (the second objective) under the constraint that at least a test case has been selected. The problem can be mathematically described in the following manner.

Let be $TS = \{t_1, t_2, ..., t_m\}$ the initial set of m test cases and $E = \{e_1, e_2, ..., e_n\}$ the set of the events to be covered. We recall that $cov(tc)$ is the set of events covered by the test case tc. Given an order between the elements of a set, a subset $T \subset TS$ can be mathematically represented by a binary vector $x = (x_1, x_2, ..., x_m) \in \{0, 1\}^m$ with

$$x_i = \begin{cases} 1, t_i \in T \\ 0, t_i \notin T \end{cases}, 1 \le i \le m.$$

Therefore the constraint bi-objective test suite optimization problem to be solved is the following:

$$\text{Minimize } (f_1(x), f_2(x))$$

Subject to:

$$\sum_{i=1}^{m} x_i \ge 1 \ (T \ne \varnothing)$$

Where:

$$f_1(x) = 1 - \sum_{i=1}^{m} (x_i \cdot \frac{|cov(t_i)|}{n}) \text{ (maximize the coverage)}$$

$$f_2(x) = \frac{\sum_{i=1}^{m} x_i}{m} \text{ (minimize the size of test suite).}$$

A Pareto-optimal solution of the above problem corresponds to a minimal subset of the test suite TS which achieves a maximal level of coverage. More, we can see that $f_1 : \{0, 1\}^m \to [0, 1)$ and $f_2 : \{0, 1\}^m \to (0, 1]$. Therefore we avoid to select the empty set as a solution.

TSO2-Minimizing the number of the executed events. In order to reduce the effort of the testing process, the number of executed events from the whole test suite should be minimized. Therefore we want to obtain test suites which achieve the event coverage criterion with a minimum number of executed events. The first objective function f_1 and the constraint from the problem TSO1 remain valid. Let be $len(tc)$ the length of the test case $tc \in TS$. The second objective function f_2 which can be used to minimize the number of executed events by the subset $T \subset TS$ can be defined as

$$f_2(x) = \frac{1}{\sum_{k=1}^{m} len(t_k)} \sum_{i=1}^{m} (x_i \cdot len(t_i)).$$

TSO3-Minimizing the length of the longest execution path. The longer execution paths are harder to maintain. In this problem we control the lengths of the execution paths by minimizing the length of the longest test case. The mathematical formulation is the following:

$$\text{Minimize } (f_1(x), f_2(x))$$

Where $f_1(x)$ is the same as for TSO1 problem and

$$f_2(x) = \max\{len(t_i)|x_i = 1 \text{ and } 1 \le i \le m\}.$$

The second objective function f_2 is used for minimizing the length of the longest test case.

TSO4-Minimizing the execution time. We measure the execution time for each test case tc from the initial test suite TS. Let us denote by $time(tc)$ the execution time of tc. Then the execution time o a test suite $T \subset TS$ is $\sum_{tc \in T} time(tc)$. In this problem the goal is to minimize the execution time of the test suites. The first objective and the constraint are the same as for TSO1 problem. The second objective function f_2 to be minimized can be defined as

$$f_2(x) = \sum_{i=1}^{m} (x_i \cdot time(t_i)) \text{ (minimize the execution time)}.$$

TSO5-Maximizing the distribution quality. In order to understand the problem proposed here, let us consider a simple example. Let be $T_1 = \{e_1 e_3 e_4, e_1 e_2, e_3 e_2 e_5\}$ and $T_2 = \{e_2 e_2 e_4, e_1 e_2, e_3 e_5\}$ two test suites which cover the set of events $E = \{e_1, e_2, ..., e_5\}$. The events e_1 and e_2 are executed an equal number of times in T_1, while they are not in T_2. We say that T_1 has a better *distribution quality*. Therefore the goal is to obtain test suites with a good distribution of the events. This property is a practical requirement of users.

In the following, we propose an objective function which measures the distribution quality of a given test suite $T \subset TS$. Let be $TS = \{t_1, t_2, ..., t_m\}$ the initial test suite and $E = \{e_1, e_2, ..., e_n\}$ the set of the events. Let be a matrix A which captures the events covered by each test case tc in TS; the number of rows of A equals the number of events to be covered, n, and the number of columns equals the number of test cases in the initial test suite, m. Therefore the entries $(a_{ij})_{1 \leq i \leq n, 1 \leq j \leq m}$ of A are

$$a_{ij} = \begin{cases} k, t_j \text{ covers } e_i \text{ by } k \text{ times} \\ 0, e_i \text{ is not covered by } t_j \end{cases}, 1 \leq i \leq n, 1 \leq j \leq m.$$

Let be $x = (x_1, x_2, ..., x_m) \in \{0, 1\}^m$ the mathematical representation of the test suite $T \subset TS$. We define the matrix $D(x)$ to be

$$D(x) = A \times \begin{pmatrix} x_1 \\ x_2 \\ ... \\ x_m \end{pmatrix}$$

More exactly, $D(x)$ is a vector of n components $d_i(x), 1 \leq i \leq n$. From the definition, the entry $d_i(x) = \sum_{k=1}^{m} (a_{ik} \cdot x_k)$ of D denotes the number of times the event e_i was covered by the test suite T.

Now the mean amount of executions per event in T is exactly

$$m_T(x) = \frac{1}{n} \sum_{i=1}^{n} d_i(x).$$

If the test suite T has a good distribution of the events, we would expect $d_i(x), 1 \leq i \leq n$ values to stay near the mean value $m_T(x)$. Therefore in order to obtain a good distribution of the events we define the objective function to be minimized in the following manner:

$$f(x) = \frac{1}{n} \sum_{i=1}^{n} (d_i(x) - m_T(x))^2.$$

Let us illustrate this definition on our simple example. We consider that $TS = T1 \cup T2 = \{e_1 e_3 e_4, e_1 e_2, e_3 e_2 e_5, e_2 e_2 e_4, e_1 e_2, e_3 e_5\}$. Then, $x_1 = (1, 1, 1, 0, 0, 0)$ and $x_2 = (0, 0, 0, 1, 1, 1)$ are the mathematical descriptions of T_1 and T_2 respectively. Given that, the matrix A will be

$$A = \begin{pmatrix} 1 & 1 & 0 & 0 & 1 & 0 \\ 0 & 1 & 1 & 2 & 1 & 0 \\ 1 & 0 & 1 & 0 & 0 & 1 \\ 1 & 0 & 0 & 1 & 0 & 0 \\ 0 & 0 & 1 & 0 & 0 & 1 \end{pmatrix}$$

and

$$D(x_1) = A \times \begin{pmatrix} 1 \\ 1 \\ 1 \\ 0 \\ 0 \\ 0 \end{pmatrix} = \begin{pmatrix} 2 \\ 2 \\ 2 \\ 1 \\ 1 \end{pmatrix}, \quad D(x_2) = A \times \begin{pmatrix} 0 \\ 0 \\ 0 \\ 1 \\ 1 \\ 1 \end{pmatrix} = \begin{pmatrix} 1 \\ 3 \\ 1 \\ 1 \\ 1 \end{pmatrix}$$

Further calculation shows that $f(x_1) = 0.24$ and $f(x_2) = 0.64$. Therefore the test suite $T1$ has a better distribution of the events.

We formulate this problem as a constraint single-objective optimization problem and search for solutions which minimize $f(x)$ subject to

$$d_i(x) \geq 1, \ 1 \leq i \leq n \text{ (each event is covered at least one time)}.$$

TSO6-Balancing the lengths while minimizing the longest path. Finally, we propose here to balance the lengths of the execution paths while we keep valid the two objectives of **TSO3** problem (achieve event coverage while minimize the length of the longest path). Therefore this problem is a 3-objective test suite optimization problem. We search here for test suites which achieve event coverage by short and balanced execution paths. The third objective function can be mathematically formulated as below.

We remember that $len(tc)$ denotes the length of the test case tc. Let be $T \subset TS$ a test suite and x its mathematical description. First, we define the mean of the lengths as

$$m_T^{len}(x) = \frac{1}{|T|} \sum_{i=1}^{m} (x_i \cdot len(x_i)).$$

If the test suite T contains balanced execution paths, the $len(tc), tc \in T$ values will stay near the mean value $m_T^{len}(x)$. Given that, the third objective function to be minimized can be defined as

$$f_3(x) = \frac{1}{|T|} \sum_{i=1}^{m} (x_i \cdot (len(t_i) - m_T^{len}(x))^2)$$

Table 1. Summarize the six test suite optimization problems

Problem	Type	Constraint	Description
TSO1	be-objective	yes	Minimizing the size of the test suite
TSO2	be-objective	yes	Minimizing the number of the executed events
TSO3	be-objective	no	Minimizing the longest execution path
TSO4	be-objective	yes	Minimizing the execution time
TSO5	single-obj.	yes	Maximizing the distribution quality
TSO6	3-objective.	no	Balancing the lengths + TSO3 problem

We solve all this six test suite optimization problems using multi-objective evolutionary algorithms. In Table 1 we summarize the properties of our problems.

3.2   Multi-objective Evolutionary Algorithms

We chose two modern and widely used Pareto efficient genetic algorithms, NSGA-II and SPEA-2[18].

NSGA-II is a multi-objective genetic algorithm developed by Deb et al [6]. The output of NSGA-II is a set of solutions which are Pareto-optimal solutions. NSGA-II differs from normal genetic algorithms in two main aspects. First, Pareto optimality is used in the process of selection of individuals for the next generation. It performs the non-dominated sorting in each generation in order to preserve the individuals on the current Pareto-frontier into the next generation. For example, solutions on the current Pareto-frontier get assigned dominance level 0. Then, after taking these solutions out, fast-non-dominated sorting calculates the Pareto-frontier of the remaining population; solutions on this second frontier get assigned dominance level of 1, and so on. The dominance level becomes the basis of selection of individual solutions for the next generation.

The second difference concerns the problem of selecting one individual out of a non-dominated pair. In order to achieve a wider Pareto frontier, NSGA-II uses *crowding distance* for make this decision. Crowding distance measures the density of individuals near a particular individual. NSGA-II selects individuals that are far from the others.

A high level outline of the main loop of NSGA-II is presented in the **Algorithm 1**. First, in the line (1) a combined population $R_t = P_t \cup Q_t$ is formed. Then, algorithm assigns (line (2)) dominance level to individuals. Inside the loop (lines (4) to (8)), all the non-dominated frontiers are added to the next generation. The remaining members of the new generation (the population P_{t+1}) are chosen from subsequent non-dominated front in according to the descending order of crowding distance (lines (9,10)). The new population P_{t+1} of size N is used for selection, crossover and mutation to create a new children population Q_{t+1} (*MakeChildrenPopulation* from line (11)). The algorithm uses a binary tournament selection operator, but the selection criterion is based on the crowded-comparison operator $\prec_n$. This operator states that between two solutions from different dominance levels the solution with better level is

---

Algorithm 1. NSGAIIMainLoop

Input: The parent population, P_t
             The children population, Q_t
             The population size, N
Output: The next population, (P_{t+1}, Q_{t+1})
(1) $R_t \leftarrow P_t \cup Q_t$
(2) $\mathcal{F} \leftarrow FastNondominatedSort(R_t)$
(3) $P_{t+1} \leftarrow \varnothing$ and $i \leftarrow 1$
(4)   **repeat**
(5) $CrowdingDistanceAssignment(\mathcal{F}_i)$
(6) $P_{t+1} \leftarrow P_{t+1} \cup \mathcal{F}_i$
(7) $i \leftarrow i + 1$
(8)   **until** $|P_{t+1}| + |\mathcal{F}_i| \leq N$
(9) $Sort(\mathcal{F}_i, \prec_n)$
(10) $P_{t+1} \leftarrow P_{t+1} \cup \mathcal{F}_i[1 : (N - |P_{t+1}|)]$
(11) $Q_{t+1} \leftarrow MakeChildrenPopulation(P_{t+1})$
(12) $t \leftarrow t + 1$

Fig. 1. Outline of the main loop for NSGA-II

preferred. Otherwise, if both solutions belong to the same dominance level, then the solution that is located in a lesser crowded region is preferred.

SPEA-2 uses a regular population and an archive (an external set). The main loop is presented in **Algorithm 2.** We do not provide here a detailed description of this second multi-objective evolutionary algorithm. For a more detailed description the interested reader is referred to [18].

Solution Encodings. When using evolutionary algorithms for solving a multi-objective test suite optimization problem, we must properly encode the possible solutions of the problem. Let be $T \subset TS$ a subset of the initial test suite $TS = \{t_1, t_2, ..., t_m\}$. We use the mathematical representation $x \in \{0, 1\}^m$ of T (see Section 3.1) to encode the possible solutions. Therefore binary encoding is considered to be a natural representation for the possible solutions. The inclusion and exclusion of a test case within a subset of the initial test suite are represented by 1 and 0 respectively in a binary string (*chromosome* string).

4   Experiments

Subjects. We conducted the experiments with a total of 5 test suite subjects of varying sizes and complexity levels. The test suites were generated from two industrial inspired Event-B models: the BepiColombo and SSFPilot models which are publicly available DEPLOY model repository (see `http://deploy-eprints. ecs.soton.ac.uk`). The first 4 machines are different levels of refinements of BepiColombo project and the last machine is the high level of abstraction of SSFPilot model. The sizes of the machines are listed in Table 2.

Algorithm 2. SPEA2MainLoop

Input:	The population size, N
	The archive size, $\overline{N}$
	The maximum number of generations, T
Output:	The nondominated set, A
(Step 1)	**Initialization:** Generate an initial population P_0 and create the empty archive $\overline{P_0} = \varnothing$. Set $t = 0$.
(Step 2)	**Fitness assignment:** Calculate fitness values of individuals in P_t and $\overline{P_t}$.
(Step 3)	**Environmental selection:** Copy all nondominated individuals in P_t and $\overline{P_t}$ to $\overline{P_{t+1}}$. If size of $\overline{P_{t+1}}$ exceeds $\overline{N}$ then reduce $\overline{P_{t+1}}$ by means of the truncation operator; otherwise if size of $\overline{P_{t+1}}$ is less $\overline{N}$ then fill with dominated individuals in P_t and P_t.
(Step 4)	**Termination:** If $t \geq T$ or another stopping condition is satisfied then set A to the set of decision vectors represented by the nondominated individuals in $\overline{P_{t+1}}$. Stop.
(Step 5)	**Mating selection:** Perform binary tournament selection with replacement on $\overline{P_{t+1}}$ in order to fill the mating pool.
(Step 6)	**Mating selection:** Apply recombination and mutation operators to the mating pool and set $\overline{P_{t+1}}$ to the resulting population. Increment generation counter $(t = t + 1)$ and go to (Step 2).

Fig. 2. Outline of the main loop for SPEA-2 [18]

The two models are summarized below:

- *BepiColombo*: This is an abstract model of two communication modules in the embedded software on a space craft. The Event-B model was proposed for formal validation of software parts of BepiColombo mission to Mars. The model has different levels of refinements. In the abstraction, M_0, the main goal of the system is modeled. The details of the system are added through three refinement levels, M_1, M_2 and M_3. The modeling approach starts on the first level with 5 set-type variables and 5 events and ends up with 18 variables and 16 events.
- *SSFPilot*: This is an Event-B model of a pilot for a complex on-board satellite mode-rich system: Attitude and Orbit Control System (AOCS). In [11] the authors present a formal development of an AOCS in Event-B modeling language. They show that refinement in Event B provides the engineers with a scalable formal technique that enables both development of mode-rich systems and proof-based verification of their mode consistency.

Results. The test suite optimization techniques attempt to reduce the test suite cost w.r.t. a given coverage criterion (event coverage in our case). Given that, the percentage reduction will be used as a measure for comparative analysis. To increase the confidence, we compare the results produced by the two algorithms: NSGA-II and SPEA-2.

Table 2. Sizes of five test suite subjects generated from two industrial inspired models (number of events, size of test suites and maximum length of test cases)

Subject	No. of ev.	Size of TS	Max. size of tcs
BepiColombo_M0	5	40	7
BepiColombo_M1	10	170	7
BepiColombo_M2	12	256	7
BepiColombo_M3	16	240	7
SSFPilot_TCTM	13	786	8

Table 3. TSO1. Average reduced sizes for optimized test suite T.

Subject	$f_2(x_{TS})$	NSGA-II		SPEA-2	
		Avg $f_2(x_T)$	Avg%	Avg $f_2(x_T)$	Avg%
BepiColombo_M0	40	1.03	97.42	1.01	97.47
BepiColombo_M1	170	7.59	95.53	8.72	94.87
BepiColombo_M2	256	28.87	88.72	30.98	87.89
BepiColombo_M3	240	26.14	89.10	27.97	88.34
SSFPilot_TCTM	786	228.42	70.93	232.5	70.41

Table 4. TSO2. Average reduced number of executed events for optimized test suite T.

Subject	$f_2(x_{TS})$	NSGA-II		SPEA-2	
		Avg $f_2(x_T)$	Avg%	Avg $f_2(x_T)$	Avg%
BepiColombo_M0	252	8.02	96.8	8.02	96.8
BepiColombo_M1	1300	65.09	94.99	71.93	94.46
BepiColombo_M2	1977	224.42	88.65	236.34	88.04
BepiColombo_M3	1873	204.77	89.06	221.39	88.17
SSFPilot_TCTM	6554	1897.79	71.04	1931.98	70.52

We have used the multi-objective evolutionary algorithm framework jMetal [8] for our experiments. The two algorithms were configured with population size of 100. The archive size of SPEA-2 was set to the same value, 100. The stopping criterion is to reach the maximum number of generation which was set to 100. The both algorithms use the following genetic operators: *the binary tournament selection* operator, *the single point crossover* operator with probability of 0.9 and *the single bit-flip mutation* operator with the mutation rate of $1/m$ where m is the length of the bit-string (i.e. the size of the initial test suite).

For each test suite subject, each optimization problem and each algorithm, 100 independent runs were performed. The results are presented in Tables 3-8. To compare the results, we computed for each problem the specific objective function values for the initial test suite. For example, the column $f_3(x_{TS})$ from the Table 8 indicates the values of the third objective function of the problem TSO6 when computed for the initial test suite TS. Otherwise, in each table,

Table 5. TSO3. Average length of the longest path of optimized test suite T.

Subject	NSGA-II	SPEA-2
BepiColombo_M0	4.69	4.84
BepiColombo_M1	7	7
BepiColombo_M2	7	7
BepiColombo_M3	7	7
SSFPilot_TCTM	8	8

Table 6. TSO4. Average execution time (in seconds) of optimized test suite T.

Subject	$f_2(x_{TS})$	NSGA-II		SPEA-2	
		Avg $f_2(x_T)$	Avg%	Avg $f_2(x_T)$	Avg%
BepiColombo_M0	4.6	0.13	97.07	0.14	96.95
BepiColombo_M1	48.43	1.88	96.11	2.16	95.54
BepiColombo_M2	130.16	12.39	90.48	13.40	89.70
BepiColombo_M3	204.28	20.43	89.99	22.13	89.16
SSFPilot_TCTM	197.80	50.78	74.32	51.38	74.02

Table 7. TSO5. Average distribution quality of optimized test suite T.

Subject	$f(x_{TS})$	NSGA-II		SPEA-2	
		Avg $f(x_T)$	Avg%	Avg $f(x_T)$	Avg%
BepiColombo_M0	520.24	0.16	99.96	0.16	99.96
BepiColombo_M1	8771.4	17.03	99.80	22.45	99.74
BepiColombo_M2	19840.90	238.98	98.79	270.26	98.63
BepiColombo_M3	14432.43	169.14	98.82	191.42	98.67
SSFPilot_TCTM	166187.40	13251.76	92.02	13667.67	91.77

Table 8. TSO6. Average balancing values of the lengths of optimized test suite T.

Subject	$f_3(x_{TS})$	NSGA-II		SPEA-2	
		Avg $f_3(x_T)$	Avg%	Avg $f_3(x_T)$	Avg%
BepiColombo_M0	2.16	0.00	100	0.00	100
BepiColombo_M1	1.81	0.21	88.27	0.22	87.52
BepiColombo_M2	1.57	0.33	78.41	0.34	77.87
BepiColombo_M3	1.62	0.36	77.76	0.37	77.04
SSFPilot_TCTM	2.21	1.15	47.96	1.17	47.05

the average values of specific objective functions of the solutions are indicated. As shown in the tables, the results of the two algorithms are comparable. We obtained high values for the percentage reduction of test suite because of the simplicity of the event coverage criterion.

5   Conclusions

In this paper the multi-objective test suite optimization problem for Event-B testing was introduced. Different optimization criteria were proposed and the resulted problems were solved using two modern multi-objective evolutionary algorithms. For all optimization problems the considered test adequacy criterion was the event coverage. All our optimization problems can be easily formulated in a more general framework: a test suite T must meet a set of n requirements $\{r_1, r_2, ..., r_n\}$ to provide the desired 'adequate' testing of the model. We will consider in the future more complex coverage criteria.

Acknowledgment. This work was supported by the European project DE-PLOY (EC-grant no. 214158).

References

1. Abrial, J.-R.: Modeling in Event-B - system and software engineering. Cambridge University Press (2010)
2. Agrawal, H.: Efficient coverage testing using global dominator graphs. In: Proceedings of the 1999 Workshop on Program Analysis for Software Tools and Engineering, pp. 11–20 (1999)
3. Black, J., Melachrinoudis, E., Kaeli, D.: Bi-criteria models for all-uses test suite reduction. In: Proceedings of the 26th International Conference on Software Engineering (ICSE 2004), Edinburgh, Scotland, United Kingdom, pp. 106–115 (2004)
4. Chvatal, V.: A greedy heuristic for the set-covering problem. Mathematics of Operations Research 4(3) (1979)
5. Cormen, T.H., Stein, C., Rivest, R.L., Leiserson, C.E.: Introduction to algorithms. The MIT Press, Cambridge (2001)
6. Deb, K., Agrawal, S., Pratab, A., Meyarivan, T.: A fast elitist non-dominated sorting genetic algorithm for multi-objective optimization: NSGA-II. In: Deb, K., Rudolph, G., Lutton, E., Merelo, J.J., Schoenauer, M., Schwefel, H.-P., Yao, X. (eds.) PPSN 2000. LNCS, vol. 1917, pp. 849–858. Springer, Heidelberg (2000)
7. Dinca, I., Stefanescu, A., Ipate, F., Lefticaru, R., Tudose, C.: Test Data Generation for Event-B Models Using Genetic Algorithms. In: Zain, J.M., Wan Mohd, W.M.b., El-Qawasmeh, E. (eds.) ICSECS 2011, Part III. CCIS, vol. 181, pp. 76–90. Springer, Heidelberg (2011)
8. Durillo, J.J., Nebro, A.J., Alba, E.: The jMetal framework for multi-objective optimization: Design and architecture. In: CEC 2010, Barcelona, Spain, pp. 4138–4325 (July 2010)
9. Harman, M.: Making the case for MORTO: Multi Objective Regression Test Optimization. In: Proceedings of the 1st International Workshop on Regression Testing (Regression 2011), Berlin, Germany (2011)
10. Harrold, M.J., Gupta, R., Soffa, M.L.: A methodology for controlling the size of a test suite. ACM Transactions on Software Engineering and Methodology 2(3), 270–285 (1993)
11. Iliasov, A., Troubitsyna, E., Laibinis, L., Romanovsky, A., Varpaaniemi, K., Ilic, D., Latvala, T.: Developing Mode-Rich Satellite Software by Refinement in Event B. In: Kowalewski, S., Roveri, M. (eds.) FMICS 2010. LNCS, vol. 6371, pp. 50–66. Springer, Heidelberg (2010)

12. Ipate, F.: Learning finite cover automata from queries. Journal of Computer and System Sciences (in press, 2011), http://doi:10.1016/j.jcss.2011.04.002
13. Leuschel, M., Butler, M.J.: ProB: an automated analysis toolset for the B method. Int. J. Softw. Tools Technol. Transf. 10(2), 185–203 (2008)
14. Marre, M., Bertolino, A.: Using spanning set for coverage testing. IEEE Transactions on Software Engineering 29(11), 974–984 (2003)
15. Wieczorek, S., Kozyura, V., Roth, A., Leuschel, M., Bendisposto, J., Plagge, D., Schieferdecker, I.: Applying Model Checking to Generate Model-Based Integration Tests from Choreography Models. In: Núñez, M., Baker, P., Merayo, M.G. (eds.) TESTCOM 2009. LNCS, vol. 5826, pp. 179–194. Springer, Heidelberg (2009)
16. Yoo, S., Harman, M.: Pareto efficient multi-objective test-case selection. In: Proceedings of International Symposium on Software Testing and Analysis (ISSTA 2007), pp. 140–150. ACM Press (2007)
17. Yoo, S., Harman, M.: Using hybrid algorithm for pareto efficient multi-objective test suite minimisation. Journal of Systems and Software 83(4), 689–701 (2010)
18. Zitzler, E., Laumanss, M., Thiele, L.: SPEA2: Improving the Strength Pareto Evolutionary Algorithm. Tech. Rep., 103 (2001)

Current Practices of Software Cost Estimation Technique in Malaysia Context

Zulkefli Mansor[1], Zarinah Mohd Kasirun[2],
Saadiah Yahya[3], and Noor Habibah Hj Arshad [4]

[1] Faculty of Information Technology Industry
Universiti Selangor, Jalan Timur Tambahan, 45600 Bestari Jaya, Selangor, Malaysia
kefflee@unisel.edu.my
[2] Department of Software Engineering,
Faculty of Computer Science and Information Technology
Universiti Malaya, 50603 Kuala Lumpur, Malaysia
zarinahmk@um.edu.my
[3] Computer Technology and Networking Studies,
Faculty of Computer and Mathematical Sciences,
Universiti Teknologi MARA, 40450 Shah Alam, Selangor, Malaysia
saadiah@tmsk.uitm.edu.my
[4] System Science Studies, Faculty of Computer and Mathematical Sciences,
Universiti Teknologi MARA, 40450 Shah Alam, Selangor, Malaysia
habibah@tmsk.uitm.edu.my

Abstract. Software cost estimation process is frequently debated by software development community for decades. In order to estimate the cost, numerous methods can be used such as an expert judgment, algorithmic model or parametric, top-down approach, price-to-win, bottom-up and many more. Questionnaire and literature survey were carried out in this study. The result from the survey shows that the expert judgment method, which is based on experience and past estimation histories, is commonly use to estimate cost in software development project while the result from the literature shows that COCOMO II provides accurate result because many variables are being considered including the reuse of parameter besides the expert judgment. As a conclusion, expert judgment and algorithmic model are widely used as methods in software cost estimation process and the process was done manually. The integration of these two methods helps in producing accurate result for cost estimation process.

Keywords: Cost Estimation, Expert Judgment, COCOMO II, Software Engineering, Project Management, Software Development Project.

1 Introduction

Cost estimation is a prediction process of defining the required cost in order to get the accurate cost of equipping facility, producing goods or providing services. It is important in managing a project especially for the project manager when proposing a budget for certain project.

A. Abd Manaf et al. (Eds.): ICIEIS 2011, Part I, CCIS 251, pp. 566–574, 2011.
© Springer-Verlag Berlin Heidelberg 2011

The occurrence of common software failure was caused by the poor cost and schedule estimation [1]. That is why accurate cost estimation is needed for software development whether web-based project or application system. For example, current practices of cost estimation for web-based applications process are mostly done manually, causing inaccurate result in cost estimating [18]. Therefore, cost estimation tool is needed to produce an accurate result in estimating the cost for web-based application or any software project development.

An accurate and efficient cost estimation methodology for web-based application is very important for software development as it would assist the management team to estimate the cost. Furthermore, it will ensure the development of cost suits the planned budget and provides a fundamental motivation towards the development of web-based application project.

The objective of this study is to investigate the current practice and identify the suitable estimation method used in software cost estimation process. The discussion of this paper begins with the introduction and followed by the discussion on the literature review. The third section will be the methodology and followed by the discussion on the results. The last section of this paper is the conclusion.

2 Related Works

2.1 Cost Estimation Process

Cost estimation is a prediction process to get close result of required cost. It includes the process of considering the required cost, experiences, time constraints, risks, methods used, schedules, resources and other elements related to the development of a project. Hence, cost estimation is important in managing a project especially to the project manager when proposing budget for certain project. In software development a widely used term is "software project estimation" where its function is to calculate the estimation process. Cost estimation is the determination of quantity and predicting or forecasting within a defined scope of the costs required to construct and equip a facility to manufacture goods or to furnish a service. Included in these costs are assessments and an evaluation of risks and uncertainties.

A cost estimation process considers and determines utilized experience by an expert, calculating and forecasting the future cost of resources, methods and schedule for any project development. It provides input to original baselines and changes the baselines against cost comparisons throughout a project. It is performed at a certain point based on the available information at a certain time. Normally, it includes cost estimation details, a cost estimation summary, basis of estimation which describes the project details, estimation methodologies, type of cost estimation including risk, cost driven, cost adjustment and so on [2],[3].

Estimation is depicted as "black art" because it is a subjective process [4]. One person might take a day to do a task that might only require few hours of another's time. As a result when many people are asked to do the estimation process, they might give different answers and results. But if the work is actually performed, it takes only actual amount of the time and any estimation that did not come close to that actual time is considered inaccurate. To someone who has never involved in estimation process, estimations is just an attempt to predict the required cost and resources. It is important to assume that the project will come in on time in order to have good estimation practices and to improve the accuracy of estimation process. Hence, the project manager can help to create a successful estimation for any software project by applying good techniques and understanding what makes estimation more accurate.

Software project estimation is a form of problem solving and in most cases; the problem that needs to be solved is too complex to be considered in one piece [5]. To solve the problem, it can be decomposed and restructure to a smaller problem. There are software sizing, problem based estimation which is line of code estimation and function point based estimation, process-based estimation, used-case based estimation and reconciling estimations.

The main purpose of doing software estimation is to reduce the amount of the estimated actual cost in software process development. Software estimation is crucial and any cost estimation error can make a difference between profit and loss. Each factor must be well considered and well calculated. Over cost will cause a bad impact to the organization and the developer [6],[16].

In real life, cost estimation process is difficult because it requires the estimator to consider many factors or variables such as hardware costs, travel costs, training costs, man power, environmental, effort, expertise advices and government policies. Effort costs are generally the largest and least predictable development effort. Therefore, most cost estimations estimate the effort cost using man-month (MM) as cost unit. All these factors will affect the overall cost and effort involve in any project that one wants to develop. So, one needs something that can give better result in doing estimation in order to achieve the most accurate result.

2.2 The Importance of Software Cost Estimation

The main idea of applying software cost estimation by an organization is to define why, when and how cost estimation is calculated. The purposes of doing estimation are as follows: i) Planning, Approval and Budgeting: In an organization, senior manager will make the strategic decision based on the accuracy of the estimation. For example, if they want to develop certain project, cost estimation plays an important role to measure whether to proceed, delay or totally stop the project. The cost becomes the most important aspect that needs to be considered. ii) Project Management: Normally, in developing software or any project, the project manager or the team leader needs to do some planning, monitoring and controlling the implementation of certain project and iii) Project Team Understanding: A cost estimation process is normally related to a complete work breakdown structure (WBS). Where else, the project team members will be assigned with particular tasks and will be given within certain duration to do the cost estimation that will avoid any delaying in a project.

Performing estimation is to dictate the output and get the best total cost accuracy. If the cost of software projects is overestimated, then it is difficult to remain competitive in the market place. Therefore, the effect is the developers will have to expend tremendous effort to bring in projects on time and on budget, or there is a cost overrun that has to be paid by the customer or the software company. If the customer incurs the cost, it could result a bad reputation, and that will affect future sales. If the company incurs the cost, it will result in lose of profit, and job or benefits lost. It is also important to remember that both cost and schedule overruns go hand in hand. Schedule overruns can have serious effects on market timing for the customer, and can have a serious effect on the software company's ability to meet other commitments.

2.3 Software Cost Estimation Technique

There are several different techniques that can be applied in software cost estimation whether in web-based application or traditional application [5],[16]. There are eight types of cost estimation techniques namely; Algorithmic Model, Expert Judgment, Estimation by Analogy, Parkinson Ian Estimation, Price To Win, Top-Down Estimation, Bottom-Up Estimation and Machine Learning. Algorithmic Model provides one or more mathematical algorithms which generates cost-estimate software that functions as a major cost driver. Cost drivers are factors that influence the cost of a software project. Four of the most well known algorithmic models are Boehm's COCOMO, COCOMO II, Putnam's SLIM and Albrecht's Function Points. The Constructive Cost Model (COCOMO) is a software cost and schedule estimating method developed by Barry Boehm in 1980s. Then in 1990s, he introduced COCOMO II which is an updated version of COCOMO. It became the most popular model in cost estimation for software development. The model consists of several components or issues such as non-sequential and rapid development process models. It is also inclusive of reuse approaches, reengineering, and application composition and application generation capabilities where Putnam's SLIM and Albrecht's Function Points did not offer in the reuse approaches. COCOMO II is suitable for both small and large project where Putnam's SLIM only focuses on large project. Putnam's SLIM tends to estimate less than the COCOMO II for large size projects. For medium sized projects, both model estimates similarly. For getting an accurate estimation from SLIM or COCOMO II, one has to consistently reconfigure these tools to take into account of all the particular conditions of a project. Albrecht's Function Points is more into sizing technique. So, Albrecht's Function Points normally is just a complementary to COCOMO II and Putnam's SLIM in order to feed the estimation process. COCOMO is reasonably well-matched to custom, build-to-specification software projects; COCOMO II is useful for much wider collection of techniques and technologies. COCOMO II provides an up-to-date support for business software, object-oriented software, and software created via spiral or evolutionary development models, and software developed using commercial off the shelf application composition utilities (Boehm, 1981). COCOMO II includes the *Application Composition* model (for early prototyping efforts) and more detailed *Early Design* and *Post-Architecture* models (for subsequent portions of the lifecycle).

Expert Judgment is a judgment endowed by the subject matter expert in a specific application area, knowledge area, discipline, industry or as appropriate for the activity performed. Expert judgment involves consulting with one or more experts using their experience and knowledge of the proposed project to arrive at the estimate of its cost. This is often used as a complementary method to algorithmic model. An expert judgment is an estimation process made by the estimator based on what he or she had done in previous similar project [7],[8]. They give information based on their memories and experiences. They have found out that expert judgment can be relatively accurate if the estimator has significant recent experience in the software development and planning. By considering this method, it will help cost estimation process to produce accurate results. Estimation by Analogy uses the values of parameters, such as scope, cost, budget, and duration or measures of scale such as size, weight, and complexity from a previous or similar activity as the basis for estimating the same parameter or measure for future activity [16]. This method involves estimating cost of a new project by analogy with one or more completed projects in the same application domain [6]. Parkinson Ian Estimation is based on Parkinson's Law which states that "*work expands to fill the available volume*". This law invoked to calculate the estimated cost to the available resources [9]. Price-To-Win Estimation method is calculated to the price believed necessary to win the job or contract [10]. Even though it may be unethical and cause gross inaccuracies, this method is still widely used today. Top-Down Estimation is a subsidiary technique. "*Once you have established a good overall estimate for the project, you sub-divide it down through the layers of the work breakdown structure, for example, development will be 50% of the total, testing will be 25% etc; then sub-divide development and testing into their components*". With this method, an overall estimated cost for the project is derived from global properties of the software product. The total cost is then split up among the various components. This method is often related in conjunction with other methods mentioned previously. With Bottom-Up Estimating, each component of the software job is separately estimated, and the result is summed to produce an estimated cost of the overall product [11]. Machine Learning involves a computer system that learns how to estimate from a training set of completed projects. Some common examples of this type of approach are neural networks [12],[13],[14],[15],[17].

2.4   Software Size Estimation

Most of the cost models use size of the finished system as an input for cost estimation. The popular size measurement is source lines of code. Two other metrics that are commonly used are function points and object points. In this method, the size of software is difficult to be determined at the early stage. It is important to ensure that the software estimated size that is used in the cost estimation is as accurate as possible. Software Cost estimation model is doing well if it can estimate software development costs within 20% of the actual costs, 70% of the time and within the domain it intended or calibrated [11]. It is important to remember that both the quality of the cost estimation and the quality of the development effort determine the proximity of the final cost and the estimation. This is illustrated in the figure below. The estimating process and development process is dependent and inseparable. The process of meeting the estimation is equally critical to the process of making the estimation.

Concerning the techniques used and cost estimation size discussed in this section; the researcher found that COCOMO II is the best technique that can be used in estimating for web-based application [18]. It is because COCOMO II provides more parameters in order to estimate the cost and produce accurate estimating. Besides, COCOMO II also provides reusability [5], [18]. Since, this study focus on web-based application, reusability concept is suitable where software developer can apply reusability concept in coding, modules and interfaces. The researcher also added expert judgment as an extra technique to estimate cost for web-based application. Based on the five case studies reviewed, experiences gained by expert judgment are very valuable in assisting an estimation process.

3 Methodology

The questionnaire survey was done in order to get the real input based on the current practice of cost estimation from software development community. A set of questionnaire has been developed and distributed to 30 software companies around Kuala Lumpur and Selangor. This is to tabulate responses from information technology background personnel which are identified as project managers and web developers who work closely to cost estimation process in a web development project.

The questionnaires are divided into two parts which are Part A and Part B. In part A, the questions focus on the background and the understanding of current practices of cost estimation process. There are nine questions in this part. The respondents are asked about their position in the company, the cost estimation method that they familiar with and normally used in cost estimation process. Basically, this part concentrates on the current practices in cost estimation process. In part A, there are three metric tables design of which using five (question 2), four (question 3) and three (question 4) point-scales. The rest of the questionnaire is closed-ended questions (question 1, 5,6,7,8 and 9). The second part which is part B concentrates on cost estimation process. There are eight questions in this part. The questions focused on how the cost estimation process was conducted. In part B, all questions are close-ended type.

The following are the sample questions in the questionnaire.

- What is your position in the company?
- Which cost estimation methods do you know?
- Please judge the estimation methods in term of the result accuracy estimation
- Please judge the following estimation methods by the effort necessary for the estimation.
- How many methods do you apply for a single estimation?
- Have you saved the estimated data of recent projects?
- Do you use them for new estimations?
- Generally, at which point of time in the project were you asked for the first binding cost estimation?
- In your opinion, is this the right point of time for a binding estimation?
- How do you estimate the cost?
- What type of software have you developed (made estimation) so far?
- What is type of software you has developed?
- Who is the core person involved in estimation in your company?
- How long that person involves in estimation process?
- What are the methods used by that particular person?
- If you select Algorithmic Model, please choose the model used?
- What is your size measure?

4 Results and Discussion

This section analyses the results on the survey conducted in general. As the paper objective, the authors only discuss in general the techniques used in cost estimation and how the process is done. There are eight project managers and five web developers who responded to this research. This is because people who involved in cost estimation process in an organization are project manager and web developer. As shown in figure 1, the score of 4.75 indicates that the Expert Judgment model achieve the highest average score in this research. It justifies that the project managers have the theoretical and practical knowledge of Expert Judgment in relation to estimation method. It also indicates that the Expert Judgment is the most popular method used. The second highest score shown in figure 2 is 4.375 whereby it is assigned to Price to win method. The third known method with the score of 3.875 is Algorithmic model. The rest of the models have similar scores of two points which explains that these models are the less preferred method in estimation process. As shown in figure 2, the Expert Judgment method is also the most frequent used method in estimation process. The second most frequent used method by the web developer is Price to Win, followed by the Algorithmic Model. All the scores are shown in figure 2.

Based on the survey results, the researcher found out that the current practice in cost estimation was done manually as shown in figure 3 and the most techniques used are expert judgment and parametric model which is COCOMO II as shown in figure 1 and 2.

The study has proved that COCOMO II is the best model to estimate the cost since it has suitable attributed to be considered and calculated. Besides, expert judgment is the most popular technique used to estimate the cost. So, in order to provide good tool for estimation process, COCOMO II is used in providing standard variables that has been defined and expert judgment play important roles in inputting input to the variables provided in COCOMO II. It is because only expert has experiences dealing with previous project.

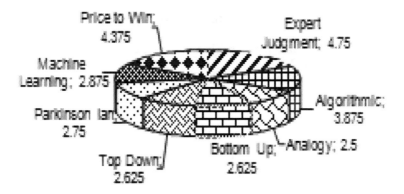

Fig. 1. Estimation Method used by Project Manager

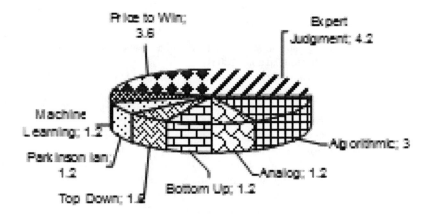

Fig. 2. Estimation Method used by Web Developer

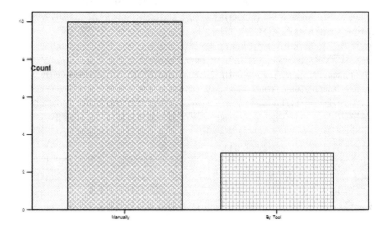

Fig. 3. Method done in estimation

5   Conclusion

In this study, we can conclude that most of software development communities practiced expert judgment and algorithmic model as methods in cost estimation process. This is because when these two methods are integrated, they produce more accurate results as compared with a single method. Therefore, integration of these two techniques is important in order to produce accurate result. However, the estimation process was still done manually. Thus, in the future, an automated tool can be developed to overcome the manual process. Furthermore, price-to win method can be considered as an additional method in cost estimation process.

References

1. Paul, C.: IT Project Estimation: A Practical Guide to the Costing Software. Cambridge University Press, United Kingdom (2003)
2. Pressman, R.S.: Software Engineering: A Practitioner's Approach, 5th edn. McGraw-Hill International Editions (2005)
3. Murugesan, S., Ginige, A.: Web Engineering: Introduction and Perspectives. In: International Conference on Web Engineering, ICWE (2005)
4. Stellman, A., Jennifer, G.: Applied Software Project Management, p. 232. O'reilly, Prentice Hall (2005)
5. Boehm, B.W.: Cost Estimation with COCOMO II, Teaching Material, Center of System and Software Engineering, University of Southern California (2008), http://greenbay.usc.edu/csci577/fall2008/site/coursenotes/ec/charts/ec-11.pdf (retrieved June 10, 2009)
6. Stephen, C.: (2006), http://www.performanceweb.org/CENTERS/PM/media/project-estimating.html (retrieved April 10, 2009)
7. Pressman, R.S.: Software Engineering: A Practitioner's Approach, 4th edn. McGraw-Hill International Editions (2003)
8. Thomsett, R.: Radical Project Management. Gurdon Press, Prentice Hall (2002)
9. Keran, L., Powel, J., Hihn, J.: Validation of Spacecraft Software Cost Estimation Models for Flight and Ground Systems. In: International Society of Parametric Analysts 2002 Conference Proceedings (May 2002)
10. Hihn, J.M., Habib, H.A.: Cost Estimation of Software Intensive Projects: A Survey of Current Practices. In: Proceedings of the Thirteenth IEEE International Conference on Software Engineering, May 13-16 (1991); (Also SSORCE/EEA Report No. 2. August 1990)
11. Parkinson, G.N.: Parkinson's Law and Other S Administration. Houghton-Mifflin (1957)
12. Boehm, B.W.: Software Engineering Economy. Prentice Hall, Upper Saddle River (1972)
13. Zhang, J., Lu, T., Zhao, Y.M.: Study on Top down Estimation Method of Software Project Planning. The Journal of China Universities of Posts and Telecommunication 13(2), 1–111 (2006)
14. Srinivasan, K., Fisher, D.: Machine Learning approaches to estimating software development effort. IEEE Trans. on Software Engineering 21(2), 126–137 (1995)
15. Kumar, E., Krishna, B.A., Satsangi, P.S.: Fuzzy System and Neural Networks in Software Engineering Project Management. Journal of Applied Intelligence 4(1), 31–52 (1994)
16. Shepperd, M.J., Schofield, C., Kitchenham, B.: Estimating Software Project Effort Using Analogies. IEEE Transactions on Software Engineering 23(11), 736–743 (1997)
17. Mittal, A., Prakash, K., Mittal, H.: Software cost estimation using fuzzy logic. ACM SIGSOFT Software Engineering Notes 35(1), 31–52 (2010)
18. Zulkefli, M., Zarinah, M.K., Habibah, A., Saadiah, Y.: E-Cost Estimation Using Expert Judgment and COCOMO II. In: The Proceedings of ITSIM 2010, Kuala Lumpur, Malaysia, June 15-18, vol. 3, pp. 1262–1267 (2010)

XML Based Robust Aspect Composition in Web Service

Eunsun Kim, Hyeongrak Ji, and Byungjeong Lee[*]

School of Computer Science, University of Seoul
90 Cheonnong-dong, Dongdaemun-gu, Seoul, Korea
{eskim1208,risma825}@gmail.com, bjlee@uos.ac.kr

Abstract. Web service technology has been successful in making business applications available through the internet to a large number of users. But because some non-functional attributes such as logging, security, transaction, etc. are scattered in web services, adaptation, composition and reusability of web service are affected. Aspect-Oriented Programming (AOP) helps us solve this problem of web services. Although AOP provides a good way to modularize concerns not designed to collaborate, conflicts may occur when multiple aspects are combined. When multiple aspects are applied to an application at a time, unexpected results can be produced because of aspect interference. Therefore, in this paper we propose a robust aspect composition in web service using XML (Extensible Markup Language). This paper focuses on the representation and composition of aspects at the shared join points.

Keywords: AOP, aspect composition, aspect conflict, XML, Web service.

1 Introduction

Web service technology has been successful in making business applications available through the internet to a large number of users. It not just broadens access to applications but also supports for collaborations between distributed applications. But because some non-functional attributes such as logging, security, transaction, etc. are scattered in web services, adaptation, composition and reusability of web services are affected. Especially, loose-coupled properties between services in Service-Oriented Architecture (SOA) do not guarantee that necessary services always operate normally always. Thus if an error occurs in one service, the error affects other service. Therefore, it is a new challenge to handle errors effectively and not to lead to failure. Aspect-Oriented Programming (AOP) provides a useful way with web services to solve the challenge. AOP is complementary to object-oriented technology. AOP helps us make different concerns independent, such as functional and non-functional requirements of the software system, platform performance and so on, and achieve a better modularization. The concerns are specified as *aspects* in modules and are combined with a base system during a process called *weaving*.

Although AOP provides a good way to modularize concerns not designed to collaborate, conflicts may occur. Two or more aspects behaving correctly when they

---

[*] Corresponding author.

A. Abd Manaf et al. (Eds.): ICIEIS 2011, Part I, CCIS 251, pp. 575–588, 2011.
© Springer-Verlag Berlin Heidelberg 2011

are applied separately may interact in an undesired manner when they are applied together. This is called *aspect interference*[1].

Aspect consists of pointcut and advice. A pointcut selects a set of points in the execution of a program, called join points. An advice consists of the units of execution that are inserted at these join points. Aspect interference occurs when one aspect disables or changes the behavior or applicability (i.e, weaving with the base system) of other aspects. There are different causes for aspect interference [1] :

- At weave-time, the set of join points(pointcut matches) of one aspect can be changed by another aspect.
- At weave-time, aspects that change the static structure of a program(introductions) can cause vague weaving – resulting in different programs – depending on the weaving order [2].
- At run-time, one aspect can modify fields or variables, affecting the behavior of another aspect;
- At run-time, one aspect can change the control-flow of the system, causing a join point of another aspect to never be reached.

The *shared join points* are Join points that are selected by more than one pointcut. Especially, interferences in shared join points occur when multi aspects are weaved. If fixed order of advice execution is not determined by the programmer, the order of advice execution affects the result, and a shared join point can lead to unpredictable and undesired behavior of the woven system. Other studies have already indicated that special attention must be paid to shared join points. Some works studied aspect conflicts or interferences and classified them into conflict types [3, 4]. In order to solve composition problems, an approach was proposed to modularize and compose crosscutting and aspectual concerns at requirement level, while the approach only analyzed conflictions of concerns [5]. Other approach also studied a process driven application based on the Google web service using BPEL engine with aspect-weaving capabilities which can be dynamically adapted with new features and hot-fixed to meet unforeseen post-deployment requirements [6]. However, these approaches did not propose solutions to conflicts at shared join points.

In this paper, we classify aspect types and propose a robust aspect composition in web service using XML (Extensible Markup Language). Our purpose is to manage the conflicting aspect interactions at shared join points.

This paper is organized as follows. Section 2 investigates aspect conflict problems and the related works about our study. In Section 3 we classify into two aspect groups which are conflicting or non-conflicting aspects. When conflicting aspects are combined with other aspects at shared join points, the conflictions should be managed because they may occur. In Section 4 we propose a technique for aspect conflict management and In Section 5 we show a case study. Finally, we draw some conclusions, and suggest directions for future work in Section 6.

2 Related Works

AOP tries to separate crosscutting concerns that are distributed into various components of a system into single modular units, which can be composed with the system during a process of weaving. Unfortunately in practice, the correctness of behaviors of AOP applications is not necessarily guaranteed. This is largely caused by AOP's 'Obliviousness' nature and loss of encapsulation in its applications. Because aspects were not designed to collaborate, conflicts may occur when they are used together. For example it is known that semantic interferences can occur when an aspect for encrypting information in combination with an aspect that finds and removes inappropriate words in text is used [1]. Aspect interference has been classified into four categories [7].

- *Wildcards Pointcut Problem* : the fact that the use of wildcards pointcut leads to accidental join points capture and miss.
- *Conflicts between Aspects* : a situation that order of weaving of a set of aspects is important to ensure the correct behaviors.
- *Circular Dependencies between Aspects* : a situation where the semantic dependencies between aspects form a circle and results in introduction of incorrect behaviors into a system.
- *Conflicts between Concerns* : a situation where a concern needs to change a functionality needed by another concern.

Several works have been quite conducted on the classification of aspects. An analysis of aspect-oriented programs classifies interactions between aspect advice and core methods [8]. Advice may directly interact with a method by augmenting, narrowing, or replacing its execution, or may indirectly interact with a method by using object fields used by the method. A study using data-flow analysis identified spectative, regulatory, and invasive aspects [9]. Spectative aspects only collect information of the application to which they are woven while they do not change the computations of it. A frame for classifying different aspects was presented [3]. The frame describes aspects of many dimensions at the more abstract level. Frame consists of cache, state constraint-synchronization, security, authentication, confidentiality, integrity, and business rules. The frame lays the basis for comparing aspects occurring in different abstract level and domains.

Aspect interference is a practical problem and therefore several techniques were developed to help with detecting aspect interactions. However, few techniques exist to then manage the interactions to remove the conflicts and obtain the desired behavior. Especially, precedence and dependency management is necessary to combine aspects. It may happen that the order in which the weaver applies aspects to the base program determines the behavior of the resulting application. Consider for example two different aspects, caching and authorization. Weaving the caching aspect before the authorization aspect gives rise to semantic interferences. Indeed, when the result of a method has already been cached, that cached value is directly returned before authorization is performed, potentially resulting in security breaches. This is not the case when the authorization aspect is woven first. Also, there are dependencies between aspects. If an aspect on which another aspect is dependent is not woven in the base system, the resulting application does not behave correctly. The most used example is the couple authentication – authorization aspect. Authentication implements the identification of a user while authorization manages access rights with respect to the identified user. These aspects depend on each other to ensure access policy. Nevertheless, these managements do not always guarantee optimal composition [10]. The reasons are the followings.

- We can consider precedence rules between the aspects that are being composed. The advantage is that the precedence is given by the composer of the system without needing to change the composed aspects. However, the disadvantage is that the composition is coarse-grained and limited because it means that one aspect will always take precedence over another aspect, which does not fit all usage scenarios. Moreover, several kinds of interactions are not related to the ordering of the aspects.
- Also, we can consider destructively changing the aspects to make them aware of each other, namely dependency between aspects. This solution makes it possible to have a fine-grained composition but implies that all aspects that participate in the composition are modified. While the aspects are therefore separated from the base code, they are no longer separated from each other and cannot be used in other usage scenarios.

Aspect interactions and aspect interference problems are handled for years. Aspect composition problems were classified into two categories, namely structural conflict and behavior conflict [3]. Aspect conflicts were also classified into three categories that include inherent, accidental, spurious conflicts [4]. This study focused on the problem of managing interactions between aspects that are being composed. It proposed an aspect join point model that focuses on the relations between aspects. It extends existing join point models that focus on the relations of aspects with base program. Some situations were also addressed where developers are prevented from tailoring aspect-oriented semantics in an application-specific manner [11]. The solution of this study is a meta-aspect protocol where parts of the semantics can be redefined. The study makes it possible to define interaction management as semantic redefinitions. As a consequence, aspects may not need to be changed to combine them. Aspect-oriented design patterns were grouped into three categories according to their structure [12]: pointcut, advice, and inter-type declaration patterns. This grouping is particularly useful in determining whether a composition of an aspect-oriented design pattern with another applied pattern needs a change in the pattern. An approach was proposed to modularize and compose such crosscutting, aspectual requirements at requirement level [5]. The approach separates the specification of aspectual requirements, non-aspectual requirements and composition rules in modules representing coherent abstractions, based on well-defined XML templates. However the approach only analyzed and specified concerns. It also handled only confliction analysis of concerns and did not propose concrete solutions.

3   Conflicting Aspect and Non-conflicting Aspect

As shown in Fig.1, web application sends SOAP request based on WSDL of a web service to access the web service and the weaver intercepts the SOAP request and checks if it has join points which can invoke aspects according to the aspect/composition specification file. Then it calls the web service and aspect according to the type of advice specified in the file. Finally, the weaver produces SOAP response and the web server sends it to the web application.

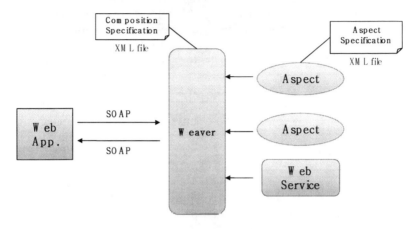

Fig. 1. Weaving process of web service and aspects

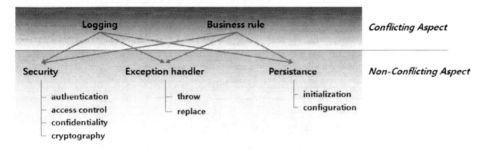

Fig. 2. Aspect classification

In this section, we classify some aspects used in web services. Aspects include cross-cutting as well as frequently used concerns in web environment. In other words, cross-cutting concerns are scattered in base code and common concerns. We also consider that an aspect type can influence on other aspects at weaved time. This does not mean a direct dependency between aspects. Aspects are classified into conflicting aspects and non-conflicting aspects. The conflicting aspects often influence on other aspects when they are combined, where they include logging and business rule aspects. Because these aspects may cause confliction between aspects, they should be managed. Non-conflicting aspects do not affect other aspects largely. They are security, exception handler, persistence and so on. By categorizing aspects, we can not only provide a common frame for classifying aspects, but also make it feasible for deep exploration of general design patterns and weaving specification. We can also prepare the confliction of interferences which may occur between aspects. More detailed information of classification is showed in Fig. 2.

3.1   Conflicting Aspect

- *Logging Aspect*: The logging aspect is the most typical examples of aspects. The log should record all the messages sent and attempts to send a message, even if they are aborted for whatever reason [13]. The goal of logging aspect is to check the activity of the system. Thus, though the contents of the messages are written to the log, they are of no importance to the user, and what matters is only, e.g., the times of the messages sent and the number of lines in the log. The logging aspect is generally used *before* and *after* the execution of an operation. The advice does not alter the control flow of the join point. However, the advice needs the parameters of the join point as input. Furthermore, a logging aspect would have an advice which is applied to many join points. This point may cause conflicts between aspects afterwards. Consider the following example: In case of logging and encryption aspect, both aspects are applied at the same join points when a message is sent in the system and different orders of their application will result in different result of the system [1]. If logging is executed before encryption, the logged message will be the original one. Otherwise, it will be the encrypted message produced by the Encryption aspect. Thus, the logging aspect is a conflicting aspect and influences another aspect.

- *Business Rule Aspect*: Business rule implementation is a necessary part in any enterprise system. This is applied to many aspects to support changes of policy and strategy. It tends to change by new policy, business environment, the regulation over time.

Business rule aspects are tangled with core modules as well as other concerns and bring about duplication. Therefore, the whole module should be modified as business rule specification changes. Business rule can also be extracted as an aspect. A business rule can be a constraint, action enabler, computation or an inference [3,14]. A constraint is a mandatory or suggested restriction on the behavior of the core application. Hence, its advice is an *assertion* that should be executed *before* a join point. An action enabler rule checks conditions at a certain event and applies an action when it finds them. A computation checks a condition and provides an algorithm for calculating the value of a term using typical mathematical operations when the result is true. An inference checks a condition, but establishes the truth of a new fact when it finds the condition true.

When an aspect alters the environment it may have an impact on other composed aspects. For example, a versioning aspect has an impact on the instantiation policy of the aspect *DelaySave* [10]. Indeed, since a document may be represented as several instances of class *Document*, the scope of an instance of *DelaySave* should not be per *Document* object anymore but per a set of *Document* objects which represent a single document. Therefore, a business rule aspect is also a conflicting aspect that influences other aspects.

3.2   Non-conflicting Aspect

- *Security Aspect*: In general, SOA supports loosely-coupled and virtualized services and data-centric networking which provide significant challenges in security. When mission-critical logic functionalities are exposed as Web services, greater security risks are also introduced to the enterprise entities. The system and resources such as services and data need to be protected from threats such as unauthorized access that may be imposed on the system. Usually security can be protected by authentication, access control (authorization), confidentiality, cryptography and so on. Because security as well as logging is spread out in different place, we should extract different security concerns as aspects.

Authentication aspect is related with authorization. Authentication implements the identification of a user while authorization manages access rights with respect to the identified user. Thus it needs to define the priority of many aspects in an aspect type. Confidentiality protects against information being disclosed or revealed to any unauthorized entity by using encryption [10]. The aspect does not alter the routine of the join point. Moreover, the encryption aspect consists of a encryption advice and a decryption advice. Generally the encryption advice inserts after the message is issued, i.e. *after* the join point, while the decryption advice inserts *before* the message is received, i.e. before the join point.

- *Exception Handling Aspect*: Exception handling mechanism was conceived as a way to structure programs that have to cope with erroneous situations. Exception handler is also distributed everywhere. By separating exception handling as aspects, we can enhance attributes such as reliability, maintainability, reusability, and understandability. Especially, we consider that exception handling aspects deal with erroneous situation as well as replace with another web service if a certain web service is not available. When AOP is applied to this mechanism, we can achieve dynamic handling of exception. An exception handling concern is implemented as an abstract aspect and detailed concerns are embodied as concrete aspects.

- *Persistence Aspect*: Some tasks require critical data to be stored for post analysis and executing recovery mechanisms. In web service composition, composition contexts are often invoked to reuse among web services. If the contextual information is not saved, we will have to go through the same process again. Thus, we can extract these tasks into aspects and achieve the optimization of system. Every call to these is weaved with a persistence advice. Whenever a critical function is called, a persistence aspect stores its contextual state information with the help of repository. The persistence aspect works as follows: Once we want to use a service, it first checks whether it is registered in the repository. Otherwise, the persistence aspect saves the contextual information of a service to the repository.

4   Aspect Interaction

In this section, we discuss aspect interactions using XML to avoid conflicts.

4.1   Aspect Management and Composition Using XML

Once a service was developed and distributed, it is difficult to change internal logic of the service. In order to solve this problem, we apply aspects. However, because dealing with aspects is complex, we introduce an intermediary to combine aspects.

XML emphasizes simplicity, generality, and usability over the internet. It is widely used for the representation of arbitrary data structures in web services. In this work we use XML to represent aspects used in web service and composition of aspects. First, we define the aspect specification using XML. Aspect specification schema is represented in Fig. 3. Aspect specification includes several elements which are name, type, concern, pointcut, advice, dependency. The name attribute represents aspect name and type shows whether the aspect is functional or non-functional. The type is functional if web service is unavailable and should be replaced. And the concern attribute involves concerns such as logging, security, exception handler, persistence and so on. The pointcut attribute represents name, expression (execution, call, within,...) and join points of aspect pointcut. The join points are locations where the aspect is weaved and involves methods of an object. The advice element includes point attribute with *before, after,* or *around* values. Each value represents when the aspect is weaved into the base program. The type attribute represents the advice handling which includes *throw, handle* or *replace*. Finally, we can know from dependency attribute whether the aspect is dependent on other aspects. By describing the aspect specification with XML, we can compose aspects with ease. Fig. 4 shows an example of an aspect specification. This aspect replaces an error service with another service which performs the similar function.

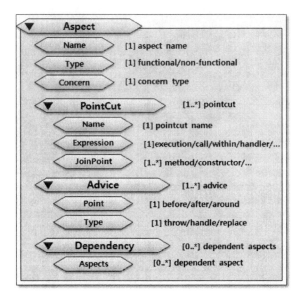

Fig. 3. Aspect specification schema

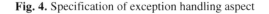

```
<Aspect      name="ExceptionReplace"      type="functional"
  concern="Exception Handling">
  <PointCut      name="ReplaceWS"      expression="handler"
  joinpoint="ExceptionReplace(..)"/>
  <Advice point="around" type="replace"/>
  ...
</Aspect>
```

Fig. 4. Specification of exception handling aspect

We have implemented a framework for service applications that has functions to update message on Twitter home using OpenAPI. This framework handles an exception as an aspect service. Fig. 5 depicts an exception handling process with aspects in the framework. The request interceptor intercepts the request of client and brings the aspect specification for the service from aspect repository. Then request interceptor forwards aspect rule information to service executer. The service broker brings an aspect service for exception handling from service repository and then returns a specification for execution of the aspect service to service executer. The service executer checks whether there are pointcuts applied in advice. It also performs the original service using request message of client. If the exception specified in pointcut is occurred during execution, the service executer should check the type of advice. If the type of advice is "replace" then service engine progresses the search of alternative aspects (services).

Also we should specify composition of aspects. In Fig. 6, The CompositeAspect element consists of name, type, joinpoint, and aspect properties. The type attribute represents whether composition of aspects implements functional or non-functional concern. The joinpoint attribute is locations where a number of aspects are weaved. The aspect property indicates a priority, a name and arguments of this aspect. We consider multiple aspects with the exception for an abstract aspect. The priority attribute means the priority number and name attribute is an aspect name. The args property indicates input parameters of the aspect weaved and the num attribute is the number of parameters. The constraint attribute represents activate / deactivate aspects for successful weaving when aspect should be paused for a moment in the same join point. Therefore we can stably weave multiple aspects at shared join points without modifying the aspect code.

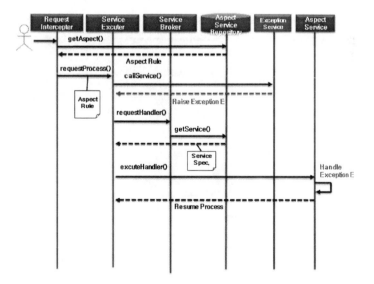

Fig. 5. Exception handler process

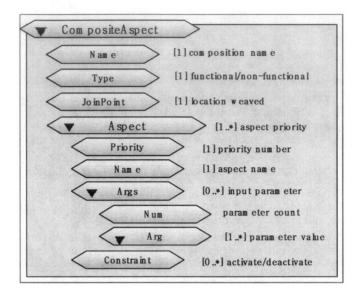

Fig. 6. Aspect composition schema

5　Case Study

Recently web services have broadly been used over internet. In this study, we implemented a prototype of web service application. In this web application the desired web service defined by WSDL is called when client request the atomic service such as weather, news, book and so on. When the application handles the web

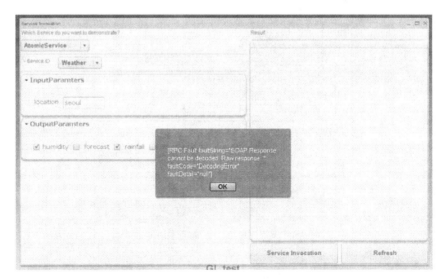

Fig. 7. Error of web service invocation

```
###############################
Request -
Command : commandExecuteAtomicService
Parameter : commandExecuteAtomicService
        AtomicServiceId : 114
        location : seoul
        OutputParams : humidity, rainfall, temperature
Exception !!
Error Occured - doJob
->kr.ac.uos.se.framework.exception.SeRuntimeException: Error Occured - doJob
null
->java.lang.reflect.InvocationTargetException
humidity,temperature,
->kr.ac.uos.se.framework.exception.CSSServiceNotFoundException: humidity,temperature,
```

Fig. 8. Error Message

services, cross-cutting concerns exist throughout a system. Thus we separate the cross-cutting concerns and translate them to aspects as mentioned in the previous section. We show a logging aspect as a conflicting aspect type and an exception handling aspect as a non-conflicting aspect type in this section.

If a user inputs 'seoul' and selects 'humidity', 'rainfall', and 'temperature' information, client program calls a weather service. However, the service does not find the information contained 'rainfall' fact and generates an exception. Fig. 7 and Fig. 8 show the error screen and the console, respectively.

For this problem, we generate an aspect for exception handling. It searches a web service providing information as much as possible. An exception occurring in search will be handled by this aspect. Then client again calls the atomic service for weather and gains the information containing 'humidity' and 'temperature' and no 'rainfall' without error situation (Fig. 9) because there is no web service providing all of 'humidity', 'temperature' and 'rainfall'.

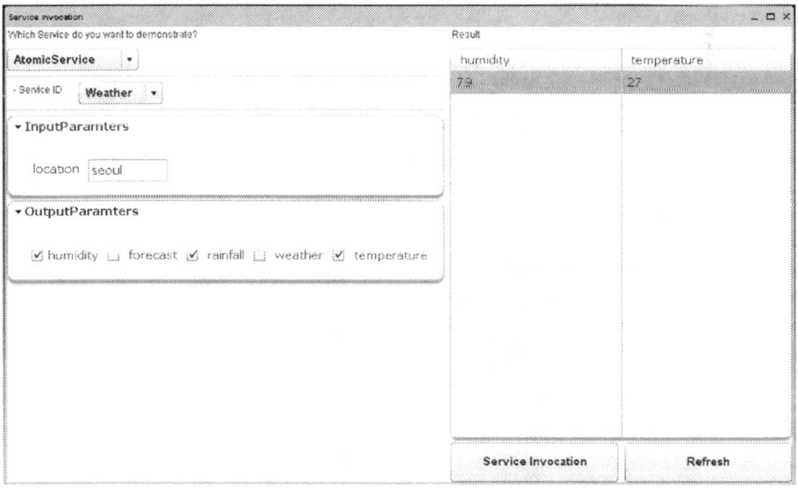

Fig. 9. Web service using exception handler aspect

```
<CompositeAspect name="LoggingException"
  type="functional" joinpoint="ResponseParameter
  MainActionModel.clientRequest">
  <Aspect priority="0" name="Logging">
    <Args num="2">
       <Arg>cmd</Arg>
       <Arg>param</Arg>
    </Args>
  </Aspect>
  <Aspect priority ="1" name="ExceptionWSReplace">
    <Args num="2">
       <Arg>cmd</Arg>
       <Arg>param</Arg>
    </Args>
  </Aspect>
</CompositeAspect>
```

Fig. 10. Composite aspect

```
#############################
Request -
Command : commandExecuteAtomicService
Parameter : commandExecuteAtomicService
        AtomicServiceId : 114
        location : seoul
        OutputParams : humidity, rainfall, temperature
Current Command : commandExecuteAtomicService
Current Command : commandRetrieveAtomicServiceById
class kr.ac.uos.se.framework.db.DBAccessManager :: DataSource instance..... org.apache.tomcat.db
Current Command : commandRetrieveServiceImplementationByAtomicServiceId
### CSSServiceNotFoundException
Current Command : commandRetrieveServiceImplementationByAtomicServiceId
########################
http://www.google.co.kr/ig/api?weather=seoul&
########################
http://weather.yahooapis.com/forecastrss?&u=c&w=1132599&

#############################
Result -
        IsSuccess#@2@#true#@1@#COUNT#@2@#2
        VALUE#@3@#74#@2@#PROVIDER#@3@#google#@2@#KEY#@3@#humidity#@1@#VALUE#@3@#28#@2@#PROVIDER#
```

Fig. 11. Weaving logging and exception handling aspect

We also weave a logging aspect of conflicting aspect type and an exception aspect of non-conflicting aspect type at shared join points. Conflicting aspects may generate interferences between them in the composition. If the advice points of two aspects are 'around' at shared join points, it may cause interference between them. To solve this problem, we specify a composite aspect including two aspects using XML (Fig. 10). By specifying a composite aspect with XML, we can adjust weaving order without modifying aspect codes at run time. We specified the priority of the logging aspect as the first and that of the exception aspect as the second to avoid the conflict.

As shown in Fig. 11, the logging aspect is weaved before exception handling aspect at run time. The messages including 'Current Command:' shows that the logging aspect has been performed. The message 'CSSServiceNotFoundException' indicates that an exception has been occurred. Then, the service 'RetrieveServiceImplementationByAtomicServiceId' has been called to handle the exception by exception handler aspect.

6 Conclusion

AOP helps us make different concerns independent, such as functional and non-functional requirements of software system, platform performance and so on, and achieve a better modularization. However, although AOP provide a good way to modularize concerns not designed to collaborate, conflicts may occur when they are used together. Therefore, in this paper we focused on handling the interference between aspects at shared join points. We classified aspects into conflicting and non-conflicting aspect. Especially when conflicting aspects are applied in composition, interference between aspects may occur. By categorizing the aspects, we can not only provide a common frame for classifying aspects, but also make it feasible for deep exploration of general design patterns and weaving specification. Also we proposed a robust aspect composition in web service using XML. By using XML based specification as an intermediary, we can weave multiple aspects at shared join points without modifying the aspect code in run time. In the future, we will study non-functional concerns when we combine multiple web services.

Acknowledgments. This research was supported by Basic Science Research Program through the National Research Foundation of Korea (NRF) funded by the Ministry of Education, Science and Technology (No. 2010 0025477) and by Center for Intelligent Robotics, 21C Frontier Program.

References

1. Aksit, M., Rensink, A., Staijen, T.: A Graph-Transformation-Based Simulation Approach for Analysing Aspect Interference on Shared Join Points. In: ACM International Conference on Aspect-Oriented Software Development, pp. 39–50 (2009)
2. Havinga, W., Nagy, I., Bergmans, L., Aksit, M.: A Graph-Based Approach to Modeling and Detecting Composition Conflicts Related to Introductions. In: International Conference on Aspect-Oriented Software Development, Vancouver, Canada, New York, pp. 85–95 (2007)
3. Chengwan, H., Zheng, L., Keqing, H.: Towards Trusted Aspect Composition. In: International Conference on Computer and Information Technology Workshop, pp. 643—648 (2008)
4. Bussard, L., Carver, L., Jung, M.: Safe Aspect Composition. In: Workshop on Aspects and Dimensions of Concern at ECOOP 2000, France (2000)
5. Rashid, A., Moreira, A., Araujo, J.: Modularisation and Composition of Aspectual Requirements. In: International Conference on Aspect-Oriented Software Development (2003)
6. Courbis, C., Finkelstein, A.: Weaving Aspects into Web Service Orchestrations. In: IEEE International Conference on Web Services (ICWS 2005), pp. 219–226. IEEE Computer Society, Washington, DC, USA (2005)

7. Tessier, F., Badri, M.: A Model-Based Detection of Conflicts Between Crosscutting Concerns: Towards a Formal Approach. In: International Workshop on Aspect-Oriented Software Development, China (2004)
8. Rinard, M., Salcianu, A., Bugrara, S.: A Classification System and Analysis for Aspect-Oriented Programs. In: ACM SIGSOFT International Symposium on the Foundations of Software Engineering, Newport Beach, CA, USA, pp. 147–158 (2004)
9. Katz, S.: Diagnosis of Harmful Aspects using Regression Verification. In: Foundations of Aspect Languages (FOAL) Workshop (2004)
10. Marot, A., Wuyts, R.: Composing Aspects with Aspects. In: International Conference on Aspect-Oriented Software Development (2010)
11. Dinkelaker, T., Mezini, M., Bockisch, C.: The Art of the Meta-Aspect Protocol. In: ACM International Conference on Aspect-Oriented Software Development, pp. 51–62 (2009)
12. Menkyna, R., Polasek, I., Vranic, V.: Composition and Categorization of Aspect-Oriented Design Patterns. In: International Symposium on Applied Machine Intelligence and Informatics (2010)
13. Emilia, K., Shmuel, K.: User Queries for Specification Refinement Treating Shared Aspect Join Points. In: IEEE International Conference on Software Engineering and Formal Methods, pp. 73–82 (2010)
14. Cibrán, M.A., Hondt, M.D, Jonckers, V.: Aspect-Oriented Programming for Connecting Business Rules. In: International Conference on Business Information Systems (BIS), Colorado Springs, CO, USA (2003)

A Java-Integrated Object Oriented Query Language

Emil Wcisło, Piotr Habela, and Kazimierz Subieta

Polish-Japanese Institute of Information Technology, Warsaw, Poland
emil.wcislo@gmail.com, {habela,subieta}@pjwstk.edu.pl

Abstract. Recently the general-purpose programming languages community has encountered the need for more powerful and more abstract expressions, comparable to query languages. Current proposals, however, still suffer from some aspects of impedance mismatch between programming and query languages. This paper describes a prototype of a Java extension with the user-friendly object-oriented query language SBQL. The resulting functionality is partially inspired by the LINQ language available in the Microsoft .NET framework. The presented solution, although being a prototype, offers a promising performance of query evaluation. We argue that compared to LINQ, several advantages of this can be observed, e.g. with respect to universality, and a less verbose, syntax, familiar to the query language community. Moreover, it offers several unique features including query translation into a native Java code, universal sorting and transitive closure operators, and the support for generic collections. The resulting language is applicable to various data processing problems and provides a starting point for several interesting research areas. The paper presents the language design, Java integration issues, performance considerations and comparison with LINQ.

Keywords: query language, language integrated queries, Java, LINQ, SBQL, SBQL4J.

1 Introduction

Performing queries against data collections and complex data structures is a significant productivity and maintenance issue. Although programming languages allow including complex queries within a program code, the combination suffers from many aspects of mismatch between queries and a host programming language, which significantly reduces the potential gains due to the additional wrapping code and error checking limitations. The LINQ language for the Microsoft .NET platform has removed several aspects of the abovementioned mismatch, achieving a big success. Some shortcomings of that solution are being observed though, including the LINQ's cryptic and non-orthogonal syntax, a relatively weak performance in processing volatile data and the lack of the theoretical foundation for comprehensive and universal query optimization. Nevertheless, the benefits of declarative data processing inside a program code are broadly appreciated. There is a hope that more seamless and elegant approach could also pave a way for providing object-oriented DBMSs with an adequate query language capability, and its standardization, thus replacing the

A. Abd Manaf et al. (Eds.): ICIEIS 2011, Part I, CCIS 251, pp. 589–603, 2011.
© Springer-Verlag Berlin Heidelberg 2011

rather unsuccessful ODMG OQL [1]. Attempts have been made to introduce similar features to Java, assuring strong type checking and host language integration. The approaches vary significantly. Projects like Quaere, JaQUe or QueryDSL work towards expressing queries using standard constructs of Java, but the solutions are problematic due to deep differences between the Java's imperative nature and declarative queries. The resulting syntax is much more complicated than that of LINQ.

Based on the abovementioned assumptions and experiences, we tend to place the primary focus on universality, user-friendliness, minimizing the syntactic sugar, strong type checking, modularity, precise semantics and good performance. The prototype SBQL4J language implementation presented in this paper aims at those objectives so as to match of LINQ and, in some areas, to seek for some advantage over it. The expression part of the resulting language is inspired by SBQL [2], which becomes integrated into Java with no adverse alterations or limitations of its standard features. To achieve this, separating Java and SBQL contexts syntactically has been assumed so that to keep semantics and join points of those languages under control. A simple query example against a table is shown below to illustrate the syntactic solution. The bold font marks the expression beyond the standard Java.

```
Integer[] n = new Integer[] {4, 6, 20, 4, 23, 1, 5, 7};

List<Integer> result = #{ n as i where i > 7 };
```

It is necessary to note the synergy between the expressive power of declarative queries, type checking within the Java environment and the rich set of Java libraries and features. Queries are compiled into a standard Java code and, subsequently, to a Java bytecode, which greatly mitigates the problems with Java version compatibility and reduces the risk of applying this solution in commercial projects.

The rest of the paper is organized as follows. Section 2 briefly presents the SBQL4J semantic foundations. Section 3 outlines the language features and presents some of the operators implemented in the prototype. In Section 4 the solutions for seamless integration with Java are presented. Section 5 presents a critical overview of other approaches to querying Java objects. In Section 6 selected features of the language and comparison with LINQ are highlighted. Section 7 concludes and indicates several areas for further research.

2   Language Foundations and Assumed Programming Model

Expressions of SBQL4J and their integration into Java are based on the Stack Based Architecture (SBA) [2,3] in terms of semantic foundation and the overall vision of query and programming languages interaction. This section summarizes the most essential assumptions of the approach.

Pivotal to SBA is the assumption that query languages can be considered a special kind of programming languages and their design may draw from the experience and architectural solutions of programming languages. Two more SBA rules that assure language simplicity and maximize the usefulness of query results in the context of imperative languages are the following:

- Object relativism – complex objects are perceived as compositions of sub-objects that belong to the same category as the containing object. Subobjects can be processed individually at any level of such composition.
- Internal identification – any programming entity that is to be used independently of others, needs to have its own, internal identifier. This should not be a data from a problem domain to be used explicitly in queries, but rather an internal, automatically assigned identifier which only purposes are to maintain object identity in the computer memory and to assure fast access via the identifier. Internal identifiers allow for building references to any programming entity thus are a key feature e.g. for updating.

Integrating an existing popular query language and a programming language may entail constraints that limit the degree to which those principles can be fulfilled.

2.1 QRES Stack

A Query Result Stack (QRES) is responsible for keeping temporary and final query results. It may not occur explicitly if the language semantics is described through recursive definitions (e.g. fixed point equations in the denotational semantics), however, in the operational semantics it much clarifies implementation and optimization. In the SBQL4J project QRES may not occur in some processing modes due to optimization of performance.

2.2 ENVS Stack and *nested* Function

An Environmental Stack (ENVS) is a data structure representing the program environment in a current control flow point. The idea of ENVS is commonly recognized and it is used in majority of programming languages, including Java. In SBA it consists of sections representing the contexts of current run time environments (a.k.a. activation records). The order of the sections is essential, because in order to bind a name occurring in a code, the stack is searched from its top to its bottom. Each section contains so-called *binders*, which join names with programming entities (usually references to objects). The stack mechanism fulfills the following tasks:

- Binding the names occurring in a query/program code to run time entities;
- Controlling scopes for the names;
- Storing and processing dynamic program entities, such as actual method parameters, return tracks for procedures and methods, auxiliary variables used within some operators (e.g. quantifiers, *for each* iterators), etc.

ENVS has two incarnations: compile time and run time ones. In both cases it behaves similarly, but during static analysis (compilation) it stores and processes the signatures of program entities rather than the entities themselves. If the binding is early (static) and the programming language has the minimal number of first class (i.e. available during run time) features, then the run-time ENVS functions are much reduced (but still it must occur in some form).

The *nested* function is provided to represent the "interior" of an object (but its definition is a bit extended). Given an object reference, it returns binders to internal properties of the object. These binders form a new top ENVS section.

In the SBQL4J project the both incarnations (compile time and run time) of ENVS are implemented. However, in one of the query execution modes it does not occur as its function is implicitly delegated to the native Java environment stack.

3   Query Language Definition

The expression part added to Java is inspired by SBQL abstract query language, though some syntactic features have been adjusted to suit the syntax of the host langauge (Java). The following operators are currently implemented (see [2] for details on their semantics and use) and can be used inside the query part.

- Arithmetic and algebraic: +, -. *, /, %, == , != , >, <, >=, <=, *OR, AND, NOT, instanceof*
- aggregating: *sum, count, avg, min, max*
- set operators: *exists, union, intersect, unique, minus, in,* ',' (comma – structure constructor)
- quantifiers: *all, any*
- non-algebraic operators: '.' (dot – navigation, projection, path expressions), *where, join, order by, close by* (transitive closure – described in the next subsection)
- range operators: [<range>] (i.e.: *collection*[5], *collection*[3..7], *collection*[2..*])
- auxiliary name operators: *as, group as*
- constructor: *new*

3.1   Language Features

The prototype implemented addresses the following goals set during its design:

- Syntax-driven semantics,
- Minimality, orthogonality, relativism, universality, and safety,
- Strong type checking and late binding, early binding applied selectively where possible for performance improvement,
- Uniform handling of primitive and object data within expressions,
- Query results made available as Java types instances,
- Object creation allowed inside queries,
- Neutrality with respect to data persistence.

3.2   Type Checking

Type checking routines verify, for each operator used inside a query, whether its arguments match appropriate signatures. In case an error is detected, a default signature is assigned to that construct so as to proceed with checking and attempt to detect more errors in a single run. Error notification mechanism is integrated with respective routines on the side of the standard Java compiler, so both Java and SBQL-side errors are reported in the same way during compilation.

3.3 Selected Operators Described

To illustrate the approach to language design followed, this section provides a description of four selected operators. All of them are specific to query languages, and according to the SBA terminology are classified as non-algebraic. Operators are mutually orthogonal: in each place where "query" is declared as a part of production, another SBQL4J expression can occur.

3.3.1 Navigation

The operator is evaluated as follows. First, the left-hand side subquery is processed. Next, for each element of its result, a function *nested()* is invoked. That function exposes, in a way dependent to the kind of that subresult structure, the internal environment of the respective subexpression result item and places appropriate name binders onto the ENVS. Next, the right-hand subquery is evaluated against that environment. Its result is added to the final result collection. Two examples of the navigation operator are presented below:

```
department.name
(employee where sname = "Doe").(salary, job)
```

3.3.2 Selection Operator

The operator selects a sub-collection of the left-hand subquery result, for which the right-hand subquery expression returns true. First, the left-hand subquery is evaluated. Next, the function nested() and subsequent evaluation of the right-hand subquery are fired for each element. If the result of the latter is true, the currently processed item of left-hand subquery becomes added to the final result. An example is shown below.

```
employee where salary > 2222
```

3.3.3 Sorting Operator

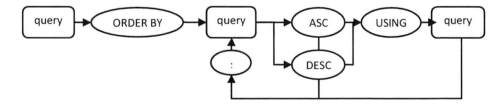

The operator sorts the collection produced by the left-hand side query according to chosen criteria. The function determining the mutual ordering of objects of a particular type can be provided in Java through the java.lang.Comparable interface. Alternatively, a number of different ordering criteria can be specified externally to the object's class definition, through special objects of type java.util.Comparator<T>, where T is the type of objects being sorted. For example, this feature can be used for defining different collations for strings according to particular languages. The implementation of the order by supports both those techniques of specifying ordering. The second subquery, evaluated in the environment of its respective left-hand-side result element (as described for previous operators above) provides the sorting key. Providing asc or desc keyword is optional (ascending direction is considered by default). The using clause allows to specify the abovementioned Comparator object. More than one sorting key can be specified. In this case they are separated with semicolons. Having performed the necessary setup the implementation invokes sorting operation from Java standard library: java.util.Collections.sort(List list, Comparator c). Two examples of the operator use ar provided below:

```
products order by unitPrice
words as w order by w.length(); w using comp
```

3.3.4 Transitive Closure Operator
The operator is evaluated as follows. The left-hand side subquery is evaluated.

Next, for each its element the function *nested()* and the right-hand side subquery are executed. Its result becomes appended to the result of the left-hand side subexpression to be ultimately processed itself by the right-hand side one. Two short examples of the close by operator are shown below:

```
engine close by part
new File("C:\\") close by listFiles()
```

4   Integration with the Programming Language

This section presents the most important technical details of the query language integration with Java. As we can see, the process is very similar to a traditional programming language compilation. In fact, the only difference is the presence of an additional phase of preprocessing. The remaining phases (compilation and execution) are identical between pure Java and SBQL4J. A program involving queries can be compiled with any Java compiler and run against any Java virtual machine compatible with Java 6, hence industrial standard compliance of the solution is maintained.

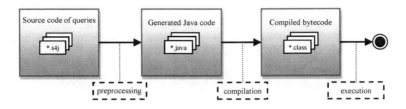

Fig. 1. Construction phases of a program including SBQL4J queries

4.1 Preprocessing Phase

In this phase the source code of queries and the regular Java code is analyzed and syntactic or typing errors are detected. At the first step the code is analyzed by a slightly modified Java compiler. The modification allows to detect the included SBQL4J expressions. For each such a query the type checker is run to validate it. The type checker communicates with the Java compiler, hence it is aware of the names and types coming from the Java context. This means that the preprocessing phase requires accesses not only to the query-augmented Java sources (.s4j files), but also to other sources or libraries needed for regular compilation. The benefit of this solution is the ability to detect both Java and query specific errors early. After the query analysis and type checking procedure complete, the query optimization begins. Two powerful query optimizers: Dead Query Remover [12] and Independent Subquery Optimizer [13] perform query rewriting in order to remove the unnecessary operations and drastically improve performance in many cases. Finally, queries become replaced with standard Java expressions that would perform the query in the execution environment.

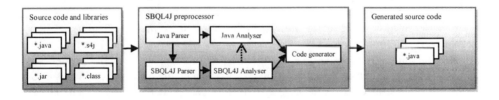

Fig. 2. SBQL4J preprocessing phase

4.2 Compilation Phase

As mentioned above, the SBQL4J compilation phase does not differ from standard Java code compilation. The input to this phase is expressed in pure Java. The code is again parsed and analyzed to produce the code of .class files containing the bytecode to be run with a Java virtual machine.

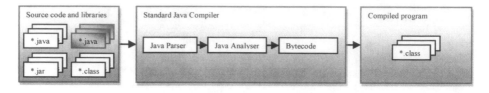

Fig. 3. SBQL4J compilation phase

4.3   Execution Phase

In this phase the program is run and actual data are processed. The Java code behaves differently depending on the mode chosen.

In the INTERPRETER mode, a query is passed in the form of a string. Hence it becomes parsed, and the interpreter is run against its abstract syntax tree. Java objects and classes marked as used in the query are made available to the interpreter. During evaluation they form the lowest section of the ENVS.

When the GENERATED CODE mode is used, a query is translated into a sequence of Java expressions during the analysis phase. Hence further syntactic analysis at runtime is avoided. For each query a Java class dedicated to it is created. Its constructor accepts the Java objects taking part in the query. The class contains the method *executeQuery()* that actually performs the query. The signature of that method varies depending on the type of the query result. This way the type checking is assured for the query results. Several variants of this mode have been implemented so as to explore different options.

- In the SIMPLE mode, the code generated mimics the requests as performed in the interpreter mode. The generated class instantiates objects representing the stacks: ENVS and QRES. The advantage to the interpreter mode is that the query text does not have to be parsed at runtime, hence the execution is faster. Another advantage is reduced memory consumption: the interpreter code is encapsulated in a single method and new stack sections on the side of the Java virtual machine are hence relatively seldom created.
- The NO_QRES mode is similar to SIMPLE. As the name suggest, it eliminates the QRES, using dedicated variables instead. This makes the execution a bit faster and the code generated is more legible. The number of conditional statements and coercions is reduced to the necessary minimum thanks to the stricter type checking and the knowledge of the result multiplicity available after the preprocessing.
- In the NO_STACKS mode further optimizations are incorporated. This mode offers the best performance. It maximizes the usage of Java execution environment in the process of query evaluation. Other modes described above enclose Java objects into special wrappers that adapt them to the SBQL semantics. They deal with the function *nested()* and support name binding against ENVS. In the NO_STACK mode the binding is performed earlier, at the time of code generation. Thanks to it the access to attributes and methods is much faster, providing a ca. 50-times performance improvement compared to the INTERPRETER mode. The code generated is also simpler and hence more legible for the developer.

4.4 Query Execution Performance

Although no systematic benchmarking has been conducted so far, the tests run using LINQ and SBQL4J against [4] sample queries and data, provide some insight into the orders of magnitude of the current performance and the opportunities of improving it. At no surprise, the SBQL4J interpreter mode demonstrated the lowest performance, processing the batch of queries in 2654 ms. In contrast to it, the NO_STACKS generated mode of SBQL4J execution was completed within 260 ms. This is still visibly slower than the result achieved by LINQ on the same task which was 180 ms.

However, we note that the comparison concerns an academic research prototype with only few dedicated query optimization techniques implemented yet, against an industrially significant language being commercially developed for several years. SBQL4J prototype did not yet explored all the potential of query rewriting techniques designed for SBQL [5] or any other kind of optimization (e.g. result buffering). From this point of view, the overall performance results of the prototype can be considered promising.

5 Other Approaches

This section contains short overview of other approaches to integrate queries with existing programming languages: LINQ, JaQUe and Queaic. We briefly characterize their properties and present some critical remarks.

5.1 LINQ

LINQ [6] has been developed by Microsoft Research as an extension to languages of the .NET platform. Its main author is Anders Hejlsberg, the developer of C# and Delphi. The basic functionality of LINQ are queries addressing programming language objects. Its syntax is sugared in the SQL style. An example of a LINQ query is the following:

```
from p in products
select p.ProductName;
```

LINQ consists of about 37 operators, in particular, selections, projections, aggregate functions, grouping and others. It has extensions for querying XML documents and relational databases.

The LINQ operators in many cases represent similar, non-orthogonal functionalities, what can be observed e.g. among: orderBy, OrderByDescending, ThenBy, ThenByDescending, that enable sorting functionality in ascending and descending order. The syntax contains a lot of syntactic sugar, for instance, the above query consists of 8 lexical tokens, while an equivalent query in SBQL

```
products.ProductName
```

consists of 3 tokens only, which seems more legible and easier to maintain. The approach assumed in LINQ makes formulating more complex queries and comprehending them really difficult.

A next problem concerns limited universality. The LINQ developers assumed that an argument of a query must be of an object implementing the interface IEnumberable, while for a query language it is desirable to be capable of addressing any objects, not necessarily collections. A more foundational issue of LINQ is (in contrast to SBQL) the lack of solid theoretical foundations that are essential in order to develop universal query optimizers consistently. Performance remains to be an issue of LINQ. Although LINQ queries are eventually translated to standard operations of the assumed programming language, the performance overhead is still intimidating. According to some performance tests LINQ queries are even 2847 slower [7] in comparison to the optimal code designed without the query language.

There are some proposals from OMG to integrate LINQ with Java. However, this attempt meets political problems: LINQ is owned and patented by Microsoft and the Java standard is under the control of Sun.

5.2 Queare

Queare [9] is another attempt to introduce a query language to Java. Its authors paid attention to express queries using standard Java syntax. An example Queare query is the following:

```
from("n").in(numbers).where(lt("n",5)).select("n");
```

Queare uses static import and enumeration features of Java. Several operators are available: selections, projections, grouping, sorting, etc.

Because the declarative nature of a query language is much different from imperative nature of Java, introducing queries through standard Java syntax is at the cost of important aspects of the query language. Queare does not support strong typing at the compile time, because names used in queries are passed as objects of the *String* type. Hence, they can be resolved (bound) after the values of these objects are known, i.e. during the run time. Such an approach implies several further disadvantages. Because static analysis of queries is impossible, any query optimization methods based on query rewriting are not possible either. Translating a query to the optimal code of the program execution environment is impossible too, because to this end the early analysis of the query is a prerequisite. In our opinion, adapting Java syntax to queries creates more problems than it solves. We do not believe that with the use of such simple tricks one can mitigate the fundamental differences between programming and query languages.

6 Syntax and Expressive Power Advantages

This section is intended to provide further details on SBQL4J by giving several examples that at the same time highlight some important features of the language, often advantageous to other approaches. Data structure used in queries is shown in Fig. 4[1]. It is assumed that a variable Dept is available in the query evaluation context.

---

[1] All attributes in the sample were actually encapsulated as private attribute, but made publically available to read with accessor methods.

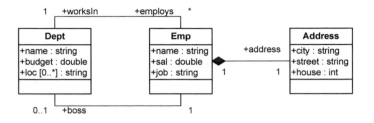

Fig. 4. Class diagram for data structure used in exemplary expressions

6.1 Mimimizing the Syntactic Sugar

One of the primary considerations when designing the language was making the syntax intuitive (though not necessarily resembling popular query language) and keep the syntactic sugar at reasonable minimum. This is visible in the code below, where the number of lexical units has been compared with LINQ. The first query retrieve department objects accompanied with average salaries of their employees.

```
List<Struct> depts = #{ Dept join avg(employs.sal)};
```

This results with expression of 8 lexical units compared to 30 in case of LINQ:

```
var query1 =   from d in Dept
               select new {   dpt = d, avg =
          (from e in d.employs select e.sal).Average() };
```

LINQ enforces the use of internal variables in queries (such as *d* and *e* in the above query). In SBQL4J, similarly to SQL, such variables can be avoided in majority of cases. Moreover, LINQ uses at least three different kinds of auxiliary naming: iteration variables (*d* and *e*), variables used in the lambda notation and structure field labels (*dpt* and *avg*). In SBQL4J there is only one semantic category of auxiliary naming that can be used in all contexts (iteration variables, variables bound by quantifiers, structure field labels, etc.). Unification of the auxiliary naming makes the language conceptually and semantically simpler, more orthogonal and better prepared for query optimization.

The next example involves constructing a tuple of primitive values. For each department it retrieves its name and the sum of employee salaries except for bosses:

```
List<Struct> query7 = #{
      Dept.(name, sum((employs minus boss).sal)) };
```

Again, SBQL4J allows for brief formulation of this expression, resulting in 14 lexical units compared to 38 of LINQ:

```
var query7 = from d in Dept
      select new {
         DeptName = d.dname,
         StaffSalary = (from e in d.employs
```

```
        where e != d.boss
        select e.sal).Sum()        };
```

Another example involves a universal quantifier. The query returns the names of cities where all of the departments have their offices:

```
List<String> query10 = #{
 (unique Dept.loc) as deptcity
 where all (Dept) (deptcity in loc) };
```

This query can be formulated in LINQ in the following way, involving however more lexical units (40 against 18):

```
var query10 =
  from city in Dept.SelectMany(d => d.loc).Distinct()
  where Dept.All(d => d.loc.Contains(city))
  select new { City = city };
```

6.2 Constructing Derived Data in Queries

Wherever the expression result type is not just an object, a primitive value or a collection of one of those kinds, it is necessary to represent that result with an appropriate construct of the Java object model. By default, when a query is constructed as in the examples above, the result is a collection of a generic Struct class provided by the SBQL4J library. Elements of that structure can be retrieved by their index, accordingly to the position of a given field in the query expression, or using a key (label), in case a name has been assigned to it with an auxiliary name operator. This genericity however comes at the cost of a weaker type checking of such a structure content. We may want to avoid it, by providing a dedicated class for such a result structure. It is made possible by allowing object construction inside SBQL4J expressions. In the example below, the data on employees having lower salaries is listed this way.

```
List<Employee> emp = data.getEmps();
List<SalaryData> underpaidEmpData = #{
     (emp where sal < 2222).
     new SalaryData(name, sal, worksIn.name) };
```

6.3 Using Transitive Closure

Although the transitive closure is usually associated with processing recursive data structures stored in a database, its potential area of application is in fact much broader. Sometimes, apparently quite easy tasks cannot be formulated without the transitive closure. In the example below we show the case where calculating a proper bag of numbers requires such an operator. The query is as follows. For each interval $[i, i+100)$, $i = 0, 100, 200, ...$ get the number of employees having the salary within this interval. The maximal salary is unknown when writing the query.

```
List<Struct> res = #{
(0 as i close by ((i+100) where i <= max(Emp.sal))
   as i ) join
  (count(Emp where sal >= i and sal < i+100) as c) };
```

The result is a bag of structures { *i*(*lower_bound*), *c*(*nbr_of_emps*) }. The transitive closure is used to calculate the bag {*i*(0), *i*(100), *i*(200), ... *i*(*maxsal*)}, where *maxsal* is the maximal salary rounded to full hundreds. Note that the number of elements in this bag is initially unknown, hence the use of the transitive closure. Even such a simple query is impossible to express in SQL and LINQ.

6.4 Double Grouping

Consider the following example. For each location give the set of department names that are located at it, the average salary of bosses of these departments and the number of clerks that are (possibly) employed at these locations.

```
List<Struct> res = #{
(unique(Dept.loc) as X).
((Dept where X in loc) group as Xdepts). (
    (Xdepts.name) group as XdeptsNames,
    avg( Xdepts.boss.sal) as XdeptsBossAvgSal,
    count(Xdepts.employs where job - "clerk"))
                                as XdeptsClerks )   };
```

This query formulated in SQL requires two *group by* clauses according to different criteria and each of the grouping should be differently named. Naming of groups is not provided in the SQL syntax, hence straightforward formulation of this query in SQL is impossible. It is an open question if and how the query can be formulated in LINQ.

7 Conclusions and Future Development

Extending a popular general-purpose programming language with query constructs brings important advantages and opens new perspective for programmers and software architects. At the same time it constitutes a significant design challenge regarding the functionality, performance and alignment with an existing language. In this paper the main initial results of a project intended to provide Java with such a functionality have been presented. It is necessary to emphasize that the significant additional expressive power is introduced without impairing existing Java constructs and employs the synergies between those languages. The solution draws on the LINQ experience and, following a similar architecture, shares most of its advantages. At the same time however, being designed on a different background, the solution provides several further advantages.

The resulting language seems to be capable of popularizing the concept of seamless query language integration for object-oriented databases in particular, as well as for other, general applications of programming languages. Its full compatibility with existing Java execution environments reduces the risk of applying it in software development projects, because queries can be replaced with Java codes generated from them and the extension usage can be given up if decided so, without rewriting the existing code. The solution also provides new insight into the SBQL research and development, providing it with several new features and opening a way for its stronger integration with general-purpose programming languages.

The following directions of future research are considered as the next steps.

7.1 Universal API for Database Systems and Other Resources

The existing implementation of SBQL4J allows to query Java objects. Similar functionality can be considered for other data sources (e.g. databases, repositories, XML documents, directory services or search engines). Provided a metamodel of such resources is available, strong type checking could be maintained as in the case of SBQL4J. Two architectural variants of such functionality can be considered:

- Translation of queries into a native expression language of a given resource. In this case the semantics is not altered. Such an approach is exemplified e.g. by [10] where SBQL is translated into SQL. A similar philosophy is assumed by LINQ. However such an approach is not always suitable from the practical point of view as a given resource may require some specific access methods.
- Combination of semantically independent subqueries. SBQL expressions and the native expressions for a given resource kind could be combined in a single query. Based on the syntactic rules and metadata information, those parts of query would be parsed and processed by their respective engines. This can be considered as an idea of extending SBQL with further sub-languages (similarly as Java has been extended with SBQL4J). This is an option offering a higher flexibility but at the same time entailing a significant complexity. However, syntactic integration is merely a single aspect of the overall information system integration [11].

7.2 Ad-hoc Queries and Runtime Type Checking

Currently, SBQL4J queries require compile-time analysis, e.g. to identify the variables from the surrounding Java context that have been used in the queries. Coupling of that process with the Java compiler excludes the analysis of queries created at the runtime. The support for such queries would significantly extend the area of the language applications, so that user-defined or program-generated ad-hoc queries could be performed. The extension requires altering the type checking mechanism to allow its collaboration with run-time type identification mechanisms.

7.3 Query Optimization

The research performed in the context of SBQL resulted in many query optimization techniques (see e.g. [5]). The current implementation of SBQL4J is prepared for development towards that direction: its query analysis and type checking mechanism lays necessary foundation for various techniques based on query rewriting.

7.4 Integrated Development Environment (IDE) for SBQL4J

Providing programming environment aids is essential for the language user-friendliness as well as for productivity. Hence the creation of such an IDE for SBQL4J, based on one of popular such platforms (e.g. Eclipse), as an upgrade of an existing Java source code editor, is one of the priorities of the further development.

References

1. Cattel, R., Barry, D. (eds.): The Object Data Standard: ODMG 3.0. Morgan Kaufmann (2000)
2. Subieta, K., et al.: Stack-Based Approach (SBA) and Stack-Based Query Language (SBQL), http://www.sbql.pl
3. Subieta, K.: Theory and Construction of Object Query Languages. Polish-Japanese Institute of Information Technology Editors (2004) (in Polish)
4. Microsoft Corporation, 101 LINQ samples, http://msdn.microsoft.com/en-us/vcsharp/aa336746.aspx
5. Płodzień, J.: Optimization Methods in Object Query Languages. PhD Thesis (Institute of Computer Science Polish Academy of Sciences) (December 2000)
6. Microsoft Corporation, Official LINQ project homepage,
   http://msdn.microsoft.com/en-us/netframework/aa904594.aspx
7. Soni, R.: LINQ Performance – LINQ to Collection,
   http://www.dotnetscraps.com/dotnetscraps/post/LINQ-Performance-Part-1-LINQ-to-Collection.aspx
8. Triger, K.: JAva integrated QUEry library, http://code.google.com/p/jaque/
9. Norås, A.: Quaere project homepage, http://quaere.codehaus.org/
10. Wiślicki, J.: An object-oriented wrapper to relational databases with query optimisation. PhD Thesis (Technical University of Łódź) (June 2008)
11. Lentner, M.: Integration of data and applications using virtual repositories. PhD Thesis (Polish-Japanese Institute of Information Technology) (June 2008)
12. Płodzień, J., Subieta, K.: Query Optimization Through Removing Dead Subqueries. In: Caplinskas, A., Eder, J. (eds.) ADBIS 2001. LNCS, vol. 2151, pp. 27–40. Springer, Heidelberg (2001)
13. Płodzień, J., Kraken, A.: Object Query Optimization through Detecting Independent Subqueries. Information Systems 25(8), 467–490 (2000)

A Design of Centralized Persistent Computing System

Quazi Mahera Jabeen, Muhammad Anwarul Azim, Yuichi Goto, and Jingde Cheng

Department of Information and Computer Sciences
Saitama University, Saitama, 338-8570, Japan
{mahera,azim,gotoh,cheng}@aise.ics.saitama.u-ac.jp

Abstract. Persistent Computing Systems (PCSs) were proposed as a new generation reactive systems that are dependable and dynamically adaptive. They provide services to their users anytime and anywhere during system maintenance, upgrade, reconfiguration and even during various attacks. PCSs have demand not only for distributed systems but also centralized systems. To implement PCSs, Soft System Bus (SSB) based systems were proposed. Although a design and implementation method of SSB-based systems exists for distributed PCSs, any requirement analysis, design, and implementation method of SSB-based centralized PCSs (SSB-based CPCSs) have not been addressed yet. This paper presents requirement analysis of SSB-based CPCS, proposes its design, and investigates available techniques to realize SSB-based CPCS.

Keywords: Persistent Computing, Soft-System Bus, Centralized Persistent Computing System, Centralized Computing.

1 Introduction

A persistent computing system (PCS) [3] is a reactive system that functions continuously anytime without stopping its reactions even when it is being maintained, upgraded, or reconfigured, it had some trouble, or it is being attacked. PCSs have two key characteristics or fundamental features: (1) persistently continuous functioning, i.e., the systems can function continuously and persistently without stopping its reactions, and (2) dynamically adaptive functioning, i.e., the systems can be dynamically maintained, upgraded, or reconfigured during its continuous functioning and reacting. Here "function" means "provide correct computing service to end-users" and "reaction" means "react to the outside environment".

PCSs can be classified into two types: distributed PCSs and centralized PCSs (CPCSs). A distributed system consists of multiple computers that communicate through a computer network, even spread over large geographical area. Jobs of the system are distributed to the networked computers and the computers interact with each other in order to perform the jobs. A centralized system is a system where all computing and/or tasks are done at a central computer and the processing is also controlled in the central computer. The purpose of distributed PCSs is to provide a mechanism or methodology for design, development, and maintenance of reconfigurable and long-lived reactive systems with the requirements of non-stop service, high reliability, and security. On the other hand, the purpose a CPCS is to

A. Abd Manaf et al. (Eds.): ICIEIS 2011, Part I, CCIS 251, pp. 604–617, 2011.
© Springer-Verlag Berlin Heidelberg 2011

provide services continuously and persistently in a centralized environment. Various small-scale systems provide their services from a centralized infrastructure and they may want to provide their services continuously and persistently.

Cheng proposed SSB-based system [2] to realize PCSs. An implementation method for SSB-based distributed PCSs was proposed and simulated by Selim et.al [7]. However, to realize SSB-based system for CPCSs was not addressed. Moreover, there is no study done for CPCSs regarding requirement analysis, design and implementation. This paper gives requirement analysis of SSB-based CPCSs, proposes a design for SSB-based CPCSs, investigates available techniques to realize the SSB and proposes possible solutions for some existing problems.

The rest of the paper is organized as follows. Section 2 represents an overview of PCSs and SSB-based systems. Section 3 gives requirement analysis of SSB-based CPCSs and investigates available techniques for implementing the SSB. Section 4 has design of an SSB-based CPCS. Section 5 shows the implementation issues and concluding remarks are given in Section 6.

2 Persistent Computing Systems

2.1 Concept of PCS

A reactive system is a computing system that maintains an ongoing interaction with its environment, as opposed to computing some final value on termination [2]. A traditional computing system often has to stop its running and functioning when it needs to be maintained, upgraded, or reconfigured, it has some trouble, or it is attacked. A PCS is a reactive system that functions continuously anytime without stopping its reactions during maintenance, upgrade, reconfiguration of the system and even during it have some trouble or it is attacked. PCSs have two key characteristics or fundamental features:

1. persistently continuous functioning, i.e., the systems can function continuously and persistently without stopping its reactions, and
2. dynamically adaptive functioning, i.e., the systems can be dynamically maintained, upgraded, or reconfigured during its continuous functioning and reacting.

Here "function" means "provide correct computing service to end-users" and "reaction" means "react to the outside environment". If a computing system cannot react at all then it will be called a dead state. The dead state is undesirable in a PCS. So, we can define a PCS as a reactive system which will never be in a dead state such that it can evolve into a new functional state in some (autonomous or controlled) way, or can be recovered into a functional state by some (autonomous or controlled) way.

There are some computing systems can be regarded as PCSs. A good example is the Internet. If we regard the Internet as a huge computing system, then as a whole it is continuously dependable and dynamically adaptive and therefore is a PCS. Another example similar to the Internet is the telecommunication network. Regardless of the methodology and/or paradigm of persistent computing, its aim is to design and develop PCSs with various scales in order to satisfy requirements of continuous availability, reliability and security for applications.

A centralized PCS is small-scale reactive-systems that provide all features of the PCS in a centralized environment. Many organizations provide services in a centralized environment and they may want to provide non-stop services. Many small-scale organizations and applications that are not distributed by nature may want to use centralized system for simplicity, cost effectiveness and easy administration and want their services to be persistent. A CPCS is necessary for that kind of organizations.

2.2 SSB-Based System

An SSB-based system [2] consists of a group of control components (CCs) including self-measuring, self-monitoring, and self-controlling components with general-purpose which are independent of applications, a group of functional components (FCs) to carry out tasks of the application, some data/instruction buffers, and/or some data/instruction buses. The buses are used for connecting all components and buffers such that all data/instructions are sent to target components or buffers only through the buses and there is no direct interaction that does not invoke the buses between any two components and buffers.

Conceptually, an SSB is simply a communication channel with the facilities of data/instruction transmission, preservation and to connect components in a component-based system. It may consist of some data-instruction stations (DISs), which have the facility of data/instruction preservation, connected sequentially by transmission channels, both of which are implemented in software techniques, such that over the channels, data/instructions can flow among DISs, and a component tapped to a DIS can send data/instructions to and receive data/instructions from the DIS. Fig 1 shows the architecture of SSB-based systems,

The most important requirement of SSB is that an SSB must provide the facility of data/instruction preservation such that when a component in a system cannot work well temporarily all data/instructions sent to that component should be preserved in some DISs until that component resumes to get designated data/instructions. Therefore, other components in the system should work continuously without interruption.

From the viewpoint of software architecture, we can consider that SSB and the CCs are the most general and basic elements of SSB-based systems such that any target software application system can be designed by connecting FCs and the CCs with various types of SSB [2]. That means if SSB and CCs can be implemented as a package, then any target software application can provide continuous and persistent services by connecting its FCs with the package.

Under the software development methodology, SSB and the CCs can provide a standard and unified way of component-based development. Developers just need to design and develop FCs of a target application at first and then integrate the FCs and the ready-made CCs with SSB into the target application. Our main concentration is to design and development of CCs and SSB, which we will refer to as "*control part*" from this section.

An SSB may be implemented as a distributed one as well as a centralized one. Selim et.al [7] implemented a prototype of SSBs for large-scale distributed systems. He used peer-to-peer network based middleware as SSBs.

There is no investigation about SSB-based systems for centralized PCS. Moreover, for CPCS, no study done regarding requirement analysis, design and no implementation method exists for CPCS.

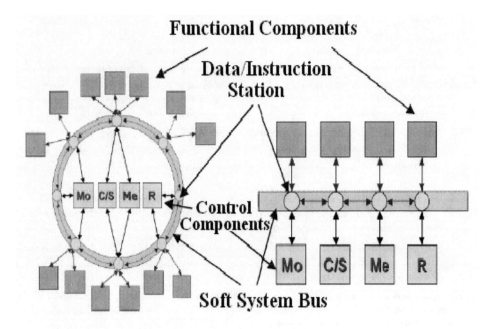

Fig. 1. Circular and linear architecture of SSB-based Systems

3 SSB-Based CPCSs

3.1 Requirement Analysis of SSB-Based CPCSs

Before presenting requirements for SSB-based CPCS, we have following assumptions:

- The hardware and operating system of a CPCS do not fail.
- The computer has enough computing resources, e.g, the amount of main memory, CPU speed, storage etc.

In this section, we will denote the requirements of SSB as 'RS', the requirements of CCs as 'RC' and the requirements of FCs as 'RF'. Though development of FCs is the responsibility of the developers of target application, to receive services from our SSB-based CPCS we have identified the requirements of FCs that must be satisfied by them.

We adopted the requirements for SSB described in [8], and introduce some specified requirements, those are as follows:

RS1. Data Transmission and Communication: The SSB should have the ability to transfer data among components. It should provide inter-process communication method to communicate among components.

RS2. Component Coupling: The SSB has to provide support to the components in a way that the interacting components need not present at the same time. The components can identify themselves by their process IDs only.

RS3. Data Preservation: The SSB should provide the facility of data preservation which means that data can be stored temporarily if the receiver is not able to receive data. If any destination component is not present the SSB should have the ability to preserve data temporarily and deliver data when the destination component becomes active.

RS4. Availability: Since data transmission among components is done by SSB, failure of SSB will interrupt the persistent running of the system. So we should ensure the availability of SSB in such a way that any component can transfer data through SSB anytime.

RS5. Runtime Upgrade and Maintainability: Any component should be able to replace with upgraded/maintained version and to connect to the SSB during runtime without stop running of the whole system.

RS6. Reconfigure-ability: Several components may need to be added in the system at runtime. The SSB should allow those new components to be added to CPCS without interrupting the system.

RS7. Transmission Model: The SSB should allow both one-to-one and one-to-many communication because in the lower level of SSB one-to-one communication is necessary but in the upper levels broadcasting may be needed that uses one-to-many communication.

RS8. Unified Interface: The SSB should provide support to be used in different platforms (for example, operating systems) and provide support to communicate among different type of programs.

RS9. FC and CC Authentication: The SSB should provide an authentication protocol for FCs and CCs so that they can connect with SSB through the authentication process.

RS10. Data Format for Communication: The SSB should provide a fixed data format for FCs so that FCs can communicate with the SSB by sending data/instruction according to the format.

RS11. SSB Security: The SSB should work in a secured way. The design of SSB should not have any flaw that can be exploited by various attacks (for example, SSB buffer overflow). Every connected component, communicate to and from SSB, must have authentic permission. SSB must confirm the protection of individual component space inside memory from being overlapped and leaked.

We defined the requirements for CCs of the SSB-based CPCS as follows:

RC1. Location: Since our proposed design is for centralized systems, CCs should reside in the main memory of a computer.

RC2. Continuous Functioning: Since CCs are the core components, failing of CCs are undesirable. Therefore, for runtime upgrade and maintenance, the CCs should run continuously.

RC3. Monitoring of FCs: The CCs should monitor the behavior of FCs and identify and report about faulty events occurred in the system to the functional components. The CCs perform these tasks based on the system information it received from FCs.

RC4. Monitoring of Control Part: The CCs should also monitor and identify faulty events of the *control part* and report about the faulty events to a special CC whose responsibility is to take necessary actions when any faulty event occurs in the system.

RC5. Access Control: The CCs have to work independently without any unwanted interruption and domination from outside world. So, the operations and information of CCs should be invisible and inaccessible from outside of CPCS, e.g., users, developer and administrator of FCs.

RC6. CC Security: To provide continuous and persistent services, CCs should work in a secured way and should be well protected from various attacks.

To receive services from SSB-based CPCS, FCs should satisfy the following requirements:

RF1. Authentication: To connect with the SSB, the FCs should pass the authentication process provided by the SSB. So, the FCs should support the authentication protocol provided by the SSB.

RF2. Credential: Each FCs should provide its credentials to the SSB by which the system can recognize them and can operate on FCs by their process IDs.

RF3. Communication Method: The FCs should use the same communication method used in the SSB.

RF4. Data Format: The FCs should have a fixed data format to communicate with the SSB that means, the FCs should send data/instructions to the SSB according to the format demanded by the SSB.

RF5. Information Support: The FCs should provide all necessary system information needed by the CCs for the purpose of monitoring FCs (for example-system logs).

3.2 Technique Investigation for SSB

In our design of SSB-based CPCS, one of the main purposes of SSB is to facilitate communication among processes. For centralized systems we are searching for an appropriate Inter Process Communication (IPC) method such that the IPC can satisfy a number of requirements of SSB described in section 3.1. We do not examine all kinds of IPC method, for example some IPCs are not platform independent, some IPC methods are for communicating in network environment and parallel programming environment. We have analyzed some of the IPC methods [1, 5, 9] and found that asynchronous message queue and asynchronous message passing can satisfy most of our requirements. Table 1 shows a list of IPC methods and the requirements satisfied by them.

All IPCs have the ability of data transmission, so the first requirement can be satisfied by all IPCs. Although some IPC provides authentication process for messages, they do not provide authentication process for components. Security is a huge issue. We cannot claim that an IPC have full protection against various security threats. Component coupling and data preservation facility is provided by most of the IPC methods except *synchronous message passing*. In *synchronous message passing* communicating components are halted for acknowledgment, which means they have to wait for each other until message transmission completes. Since *synchronous message passing* provides all other facilities, we cannot use it for the lack of component coupling and data preservation. Although both kind of pipes (*Anonymous pipe* and *Named pipe*) and *shared memory* have component coupling and data preservation ability, they do not provide unified interface. No IPC method can ensure availability of them and cannot provide runtime upgrade and maintainability feature.

Asynchronous message passing (AMP) and *asynchronous message queue (AMQ)* provides most of the facilities. In *AMP*, buffering is required to store messages and components can perform independently. It allows multiple connections at runtime. When new components need to be added in the system, it can communicate in the system by passing messages to other components. In *AMQ* data are stored in a queue until the receiver receives it. Both of *AMP* and *AMQ* can provide one-to-one and one-to-many transmission facility. Both of them provides unified interface. From the table we see that *AMP* and *AMQ* can satisfy most of the requirements of SSB. But *AMP* does not provide channel like SSB. Message queues are most widely used in distributed systems. Several commercial implementation of message queues are also available that works well in distributed systems [4]. But there is no of implementation of message queue exists for centralized systems.

Table 1. IPC methods comparison against requirements of SSB. Requirements that can be satisfied marked with "√" symbol and non-satisfied requirements are marked with "−"symbol in the table.

IPC Methods	Requirements of SSB										
	RS1	RS2	RS3	RS4	RS5	RS6	RS7	RS8	RS9	RS10	RS11
Anonymous Pipe	√	√	√	−	−	−	−	−	−	−	−
Named Pipe	√	√	√	−	−	√	√	−	−	−	−
Shared Memory	√	√	√	−	−	√	√	−	−	−	−
Asynchronous Message Queue	√	√	√	−	−	√	√	√	−	−	−
Synchronous Message Passing	√	−	−	−	−	√	√	√	−	−	−
Asynchronous Message Passing	√	√	√	−	−	√	√	√	−	−	−

From the above discussion, it is clear that none of the available IPC methods can fully satisfy the requirements of SSB for a CPCS. A combination of *AMP* and *AMQ* may be served as SSB but the requirements of availability, runtime upgrade and maintainability, security, components authentication, data format of FCs will still be remain. Since *AMP* is proved as a better IPC, we can use it as the communication method in our SSB-based CPCs.

4   A Design of a SSB-Based CPCS

4.1   Architecture

Fig 2 shows an architecture of SSB-based CPCS. The FCs perform some specific tasks of the target applications and will be implemented by the application developers. The control part consists of SSB and three kinds of CC - the self-monitor component (Mo) to examine and identify faulty or lost events, the Reporter component (Re) to interpret identified faulty or lost events and report about it and the self-actuator component (Ac) to take necessary actions. The control part also has two databases CC Database (CCDB) and Event Database (EDB) to keep information about the tasks of control part.

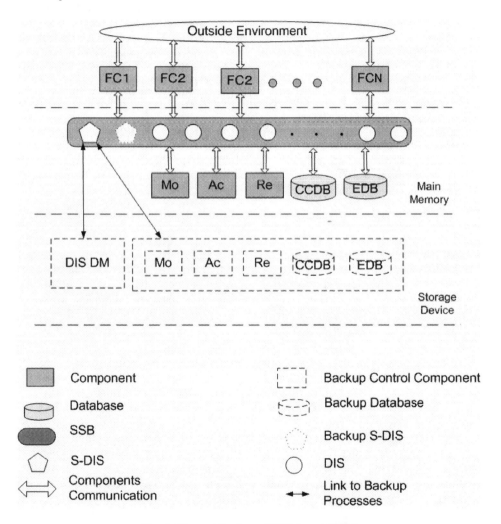

Fig. 2. The architecture of SSB-based CPCS

The SSB consists of a number of DISs for data/instruction preservation. The DISs have buffer to store data/instructions temporarily. Each components of the system (both CCs and FCs) connects with the DISs. Each component has allocation for a DIS. When a component has to communicate with other components it must communicate via its allocated DIS. If any destination component is not active, the DIS stores data/instructions until the destination component becomes active.

As we see from previous section that available techniques cannot provide all facilities of SSB, we introduce a special purpose DIS in SSB to fulfill remaining requirements of SSB, named as 'Super DIS' or in short, S-DIS. The S-DIS has a number of functions. DISs are just temporary data storage to store data/instructions and send them to their destination addresses. The S-DIS is responsible for managing the DISs. It provides access permission to FCs by providing authentication process to FCs and by checking other requirements of FCs. It also provides authentication process to CCs. It allocates DISs for FCs and CCs, maintains routing table to facilitate communication among components and DISs, restores data/processes from backup when needed and maintains detail information of backup items. We named the functions of S-DIS as *Access Permission*, *DIS Allocation*, *Lookup Service*, and *Backup and Restore* which we will describe in this section one by one. The S-DIS also contains two tables to keep related information of its functions named as *Lookup Table* and *Table of Backup Items*.

When any FC wants to join with the SSB-based CPCS, it has to send its credentials, communication method it used to the *Access Permission* of S-DIS. When new FC wants to be a part of the SSB-based CPCS, they have to send request to the *Access Permission* of S-DIS at first. The *Access Permission* operation will then check if that component is an authentic FC. The *Access Permission* also checks if the FC can satisfy other requirements demanded by the SSB-based CPCS. If the FC can satisfy all of the requirements, then the *DIS Allocation* operation allocates DISs for the FCs to communicate with the system via DISs. The *Access Permission* sends access permission notification with its allocated DIS address to the FC. Once an FC has authentication permission, it can communicate with other FCs through its allocated DISs. Therefore whenever that FC wants to communicate with another FCs, it doesn't need to send authentication request to S-DIS and the S-DIS don't have to allocate DIS for that FC each time. The authentication process is also same for CCs.

The *DIS Allocation* also responsible to allocate DISs for CCs also, but in that case CCs do not need to connect with the system through the *Access Permission*. Since SSB-based CPCS is constructed by the combination of CCs and SSB and CCs are permanent components of the system, *DIS Allocation* directly allocates DISs for the CCs. The *Lookup Table* has list of authenticate FCs and CCs with their DIS IDs and DIS addresses, respectively. The *Lookup Service* is responsible for maintaining the *Lookup Table*. It creates entry in the *Lookup Table* whenever any new FC joins in the system, and deletes entry from the table whenever any FC leaves the system. If DIS of an FC or CC failed, the *Lookup Service* will notice that and inform it to the *DIS Allocation* operation. The *DIS Allocation* will then allocate a new DIS for the FC/CC and the *Lookup Service* updates that information to the *Lookup Table*. In this way the availability of DISs to FCs can be ensured.

Suppose that a new FC, say FC1 wants to join in an SSB-based CPCS and wants to communicate with FC2 that has already joined in the system. There are two steps involved. In the first step, FC1 sends request to an S-DIS and it checks if FC1 can satisfy all requirements to join in the system. If FC1 can satisfy the requirements, *Access Permission* then asks *DIS Allocation* to allocate a DIS for FC1. After allocating a DIS for FC1, say DIS1, the *Access Permission* will send notification of access permission to FC1 with its allocated DIS address. In step 2, FC1 sends data/instruction to DIS1 and the name of the destination component where it wants to send data/instruction, in that case FC2. The DIS1 then find out the DIS address of FC2 from the *Lookup Table* of S-DIS. Let the DIS of FC2 is DIS2. DIS1 then sends data/instruction to DIS2 using the routing mechanism provided by the SSB. DIS2 will then transfer data/instruction to FC2. Both of the steps are shown in Fig 3. Using this strategy communication will occur among component-to-component. If CCs wants to communicate with FCs, this will also be done in a similar way.

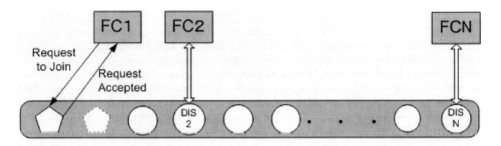

Step 1: FC1 sends request to S-DIS to join SSB-based CPCS

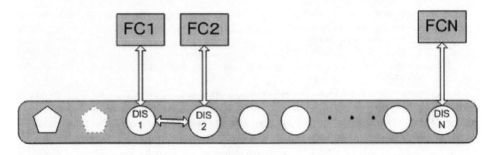

Step 2: FC1 Communicates with FC2 through their allocated DISs

Fig. 3. Two steps of FC1 to communicate with FC2

Since CCs are the core part of any SSB-based systems and required to provide continuous functioning, to ensure that we make backup processes of each of the CCs and the two databases. The backup files are stored in the storage device. The *Backup and Restore* has a link with the backup files and is responsible to restore the backups. We denote the running CCs as "active CCs". Each active CC sends and receives data/instruction through its allocated DIS. They also replicate data to their corresponding backup CCs. The *Backup and Restore* is responsible to recover data or lost events. So when any CC fails or loose some events the *Backup and Restore* can recover those events of lost CC from the backup CC. The *Backup and Restore* sends the lost data or events to active CCs in form of executable files. The *Table of Backup Items* is contains name of backup CCs, their addresses in backup location and other related information. By using this table it will be easily understood that which CC have backup in which location and its related information. Suppose when the self-monitor performs any task, all data/instructions go through its allocated DIS, say DISMo. Each time DISMo receives any data/instruction; it is replicated to the backup self-monitor by the self-monitor component. When active self-monitor loose any event or instruction then it can be recovered by searching the backup address of self-monitor using the *Table of Backup Items* and restoring the least recently backed up data/instruction and continuing to as earlier as required. Plainly, the backup self-monitor will first transfer data/instructions to DISMo and finally from DISMo to the active self-monitor. By following this backup protocol we can ensure continuous functioning of CCs.

One of the main features of PCS is availability. We can clearly see from Table 1 that none of the IPC methods can fulfill the availability SSB. In the distributed implementation of PCS, availability is achieved by two basic techniques. First is, reliable and dynamic peer-to-peer networks of DISs. Second is, replicating (in main memory) the information of one DIS to several other DISs located not essentially in a single geographical area [6]. Obviously, none of the techniques can be adopted in CPCS directly. The SSB fails when all DISs fail. All DISs in an SSB fail at a atime is a very rare case. We can assume that this will not happen.

However, a DIS may fail with its data that are not reached to its destination. To protect lose of data from DISs we keep a *DIS Data Management (DIS DM)* table in storage that contains a list of running processes and their related data for each DISs. Each time any DIS receives data/instruction, they replicates those data/instruction to DIS *DM*. When any DIS fails with any undelivered data/instructions, the *Backup and Restore* notices that and restores the data/instructions. In the operation of *S-DIS*, *DIS DM* and *Backup Processes,* all the files can be implemented as XML file format and the all the data tables can be implemented as stacks.

We keep two S-DISs in our design so that if one S-DIS fails another one takes the responsibility. The running S-DIS is the active S-DIS and the second one is the backup S-DIS. Both of the DISs have the same power to exercise the operations. But the active S-DIS has the authority and responsibility regarding the actions.

One important task of CCs is to monitor the behavior of the entire system (both of FCs and *control part*) to detect and report about faulty events occurred in the system. This task is done as follows: the self-monitor will collect various system information of FCs. As mentioned earlier FCs are required to send their system information to CCs. Since that is a huge information, they are kept in CCDB. The self-monitor then identifies is there any faulty events occurs in the system or not. If it detects such kind of events occurred, it then separates those event information and sends them to the EDB. That means EDB contains only information about faulty events. From EDB the self-reporter interprets those events to human readable format. Since those identified faulty events have occurred in the FCs, self-reporter sends this information to both the self-actuator and to the developer or administrator of the FCs. Since the maintenance of the *control part* are also done by control components, the procedure is as follows:

after monitoring the behavior of *control part* if the self-monitor detects any faulty event it will send that event information to the EDB as stated earlier. Then the self-reporter reads information of events from the EDB and report about events to the developer or administrator of the *control part* only in this case. The self-actuator plays an important role when any faulty event occurs in the system. The self-actuator has some predefined rules such as - name of an event and actions to take. For the faulty events of *control part*, the self-actuator performs necessary actions needed based on the events occur. For the faulty events of FCs, if the event occurs due to any shortcoming of *control part*, then this is the responsibility of self-actuator to take necessary actions. Otherwise, if the event occurs due to faults in FCs then this is the responsibility of developers and/or administrator of FCs to take necessary steps.

5 Implementation Issues

In our SSB-based CPCS design, we proposed *AMP* as communication method among components and SSB. How can we realize the SSB for our CPCS using available techniques is still an issue. One way is, if we can combine techniques used in *AMQ* and *AMP*, which means we have to introduce a new method for SSB by combining those two IPCs that will provide communication channel like *AMQ* and transfer data using *AMP*. DISs may be implemented in SSB by declaring message buffers, but implementation of S-DIS will not be possible using available IPC techniques.

We have shown that we can satisfy the availability of CCs and DISs by replicating their data/processes and restores them by the *Backup and Restore* Operation of S-DIS. But how can we ensure the availability of S-DIS is a big issue. We can assign the S-DIS to the responsibility of backing up itself. The code of *DIS Allocation*, *Lookup Service* and the *Lookup Table* will be backed up to the backup S-DIS. When the active S-DIS fails, from that point of time, the backup S-DIS gets the full authority and continues working without trouble as active S-DIS. The restore operation is not essential for S-DIS. Because, according to architecture, backup S-DIS has full power as active S-DIS except the authority to command. Backup S-DIS automatically gains the authority when the active S-DIS fails.

How SSB provides runtime upgrade and maintainability in such a way that any component is able to replace with a new component without stop running of the whole system is another important issue. Existing techniques cannot provide such facility. We can use self-actuator component to solve this issue. The self-actuator component will keep track of memory data used by each components and which instruction currently being executed. If any component needs to be replaced with a new component in the system, the self-actuator component can update information (memory address, last instruction executed) of the old component to the new component so that the new component can run from the last execution point of the old component.

The authentication protocols to authenticate FCs and CCs are not decided. The formats of data to communicate among FCs, CCs and SSB are not given. To monitor the system behavior how the system information is created are not defined. One possible solution is the use of system log files. For FCs the log files will be created by developer/administrator of FCs for *control part* it will be created by developer/administrator of CCs.

The proposed design is to test first in a simulation environment. For simulation, it is necessary to define the detail design including protocol, data format, replication technique etc. The background, the parameters, and the simulation tool also have to be defined. After identifying these, the architecture must be tested by running simulation. This issue still remained unsolved. With the effort the operation and events in SSB-based CPCS can be ordered in chronological sequence. As a result the discrete-event simulation tool will be helpful.

6 Concluding Remarks

This paper is our first attempt to design Centralized Persistent Computing Systems (CPCSs). In this paper, we presented requirement analysis for Soft System Bus (SSB) based CPCS (SSB-based CPCS), proposed design for SSB-based CPCS, investigated implementation issues. We are now working on the remaining issues to realize CPCS.

This paper is a conceptual work on CPCS. There are a lot of opportunities to work on CPCS in future. At first data format for each components including backup CCs have to be defined. The authentication process for FCs, format of their credential, data format to communicate have to be defined.

One of the major contributions will be the implementation of S-DIS because S-DIS is the most powerful part in the design of SSB-based CPCS. After implementing the S-DIS, it has to placed inside the SSB so that it can work as an inside part of SSB.

Another major contribution will be implementation of self-actuator component as it is responsible to manage faulty events. To implement this component we have to define a list of faulty events that may occur in the system and set of rules defining related actions that should be taken against the events. After solving all of the particular issues, future works includes development of a CPCS and apply the CPCS design to any application domain.

References

1. Bovet, D.P., Cesati, M.: Understanding the Linux Kernel, 3rd edn. O'Reilly Media (2005)
2. Cheng, J.: Connecting Components with Soft System Buses: A New Methodology for Design, Development, and Maintenance of Reconfigurable, Ubiquitous, and Persistent Reactive Systems. In: Proceedings of the 19th IEEE-CS International Conference on Advanced Information Networking and Applications, pp. 667–672. IEEE Computer Society Press, Taipei (2005)
3. Cheng, J.: Persistent Computing Systems as Continuously Available, Reliable, and Secure Systems. In: Proceedings of the 1st International Conference on Availability, Reliability and Security, pp. 631–638. IEEE Computer Society Press, Vienna (2006)
4. IBM: An Introduction to Messaging and Queuing. Document Number: GC33-0805-01 (1995)
5. Matthew, N., Stones, R.: Beginning Linux Programming, 4th edn. John Wiley and Sons (2007)

6. Selim, M.R., Endo, T., Goto, Y., Cheng, J.: Distributed Hash Table Based Design of Soft System Buses. In: Proceedings of the 2nd International Conference on Scalable Information Systems, pp. 78:1–78:4. ICST (Institute for Computer Sciences, Social-Informatics and Telecommunications Engineering), Brussels (2007)
7. Selim, M.R., Goto, Y., Cheng, J.: A Replication Oriented Approach to Event Based Middleware Over Structured Peer-to-Peer Networks. In: Proceedings of the 5th International Workshop on Middleware for Pervasive and Ad-Hoc Computing, pp. 61–66. ACM Press, Newport Beach (2008)
8. Selim, M.R., Endo, T., Goto, Y., Cheng, J.: A Comparative Study Between Soft System Bus and Traditional Middlewares. In: Meersman, R., Tari, Z., Herrero, P. (eds.) OTM 2006 Workshops. LNCS, vol. 4278, pp. 1264–1273. Springer, Heidelberg (2006)
9. Silberschatz, A., Galvin, P.B., Gagne, G.: Operating System Concepts, 7th edn. John Wiley and Sons (2005)

Author Index